Information Services Today

Information Services Today

AN INTRODUCTION

Second Edition

EDITED BY

Sandra Hirsh

ROWMAN & LITTLEFIELD
Lanham • Boulder • New York • London

Published by Rowman & Littlefield
A wholly owned subsidiary of The Rowman & Littlefield Publishing Group, Inc.
4501 Forbes Boulevard, Suite 200, Lanham, Maryland 20706
www.rowman.com

Unit A, Whitacre Mews, 26-34 Stannary Street, London SE11 4AB

British Library Cataloguing in Publication Information Available

Library of Congress Cataloging-in-Publication Data Available

ISBN: 978-1-5381-0299-2 (cloth : alk. paper)
ISBN: 978-1-5381-0300-5 (pbk : alk. paper)
ISBN: 978-1-5381-0301-2 (electronic)

∞™ The paper used in this publication meets the minimum requirements of American National Standard for Information Sciences—Permanence of Paper for Printed Library Materials, ANSI/NISO Z39.48-1992.

Printed in the United States of America

For my husband, Jay, who has brightened every day for more than 25 years, and my daughters, Hayley and Leah.

And in loving memory of my mom and librarian, Gail Schlachter, who was an inspirational role model to me and many library professionals in the field.

Contents

An online supplement is available at
https://rowman.com/Page/hirshsupplement/second_edition

Archived webinars are available at
http://ischool.sjsu.edu/informationservicestoday/webinars

Figures

Tables

Appendixes

Abbreviations

AACU	Association of American Colleges and Universities
AAP	Association of American Publishers
AASL	American Association of School Librarians
ACLU	American Civil Liberties Union
ACRL	Association of College and Research Libraries
ADA	Americans with Disabilities Act
ADA	Archive of Digital Art
ADDIE	Analysis, Design, Development, Implementation, Evaluation
AECT	Association for Educational Communications and Technology
AI	artificial intelligence
AIC	American Institute for Conservation
AIIP	Association of Independent Information Professionals
AILA	American Indian Library Association
ALA	American Library Association
ALIA	Australian Library and Information Association
APALA	Asian/Pacific American Librarians Association
APCs	article processing charges
APIs	application programming interfaces
ARL	Association of Research Libraries
AS/RS	automated storage and retrieval systems
ASIS&T	Association for Information Science & Technology
ATLA	American Theological Library Association
A/V	audiovisual
BCALA	Black Caucus of the American Library Association
BCP	business continuity planning
BCP/DR	business continuity planning and disaster recovery
CALA	Chinese American Librarians Association
CC	Creative Commons
CC BY	Creative Commons Attribution Only
CC0	domain dedication
CCC	Copyright Clearance Center
CCSDS	Consultative Committee for Space Data Systems
CCSS	Common Core State Standards
CDO	Chief Data Officer
CFL	Center for the Future of Libraries
CIO	Chief Information Officer
CIPA	Children's Internet Protection Association
CLIR	Council on Library and Information Resources
CLR	Council on Library Resources

COAR	Confederation of Open Access Repositories
COPPA	Children's Online Privacy Protection Act of 1998
CPL	Chicago Public Library
DAMA	Data Management Association
DCC	Digital Curation Centre
DCMI	Dublin Core Metadata Initiative
DDC	Dewey Decimal Classification
DHS	Department of Homeland Security
DMCA	Digital Millennium Copyright Act
DMP	data management plan
DOAJ	Directory of Open Access Journals
DOJ	Department of Justice
DPN	Digital Preservation Network
DPOE	Digital Preservation Outreach and Education
DRP	disaster recovery planning
EEOC	Equal Employment Opportunity Commission
EFF	Electronic Frontier Foundation
ELA	English Language Arts
EO	executive order
ER&L	Electronic Resources and Libraries (an annual conference)
ETL	extract, transform, load
FACT Act	Fair and Accurate Credit Transactions Act
FCC	Federal Communications Commission
FCRA	Fair Credit Reporting Act
FERPA	Family Educational Rights and Privacy Act
FIPPs	Fair Information Practice Principles
FISA	Foreign Intelligence Surveillance Act
FISMA	Federal Information Security Management Act
FLSA	Fair Labor Standards Act
FRAD	Functional Requirements for Authority Data
FRBR	Functional Requirements for Bibliographic Records
FTC	Federal Trade Commission
FTE	full-time enrollment
FTE	full-time equivalency
GLBT	gay, lesbian, bisexual, transgender
GWLA	Greater Western Library Alliance
HIPAA	Health Insurance Portability and Accountability Act of 1996
HR	human resources
HTML	hypertext markup language
IA	information architecture
ICT	information communication technology
ICOLC	International Coalition of Library Consortia
IDEO	innovation, design engineering, organization
IFLA	International Federation of Library Associations and Institutions
ILL	interlibrary loan
ILS	integrated library system
IMLS	Institute of Museum and Library Services

IoT	internet of things
IP	intellectual property
IPTF	Internet Policy Task Force
IR	institutional repository
ISBD	International Standard Bibliographic Description
ISO	International Standards Organization
ISP	internet service provider
ISTE	International Society of Technology in Education
IT	information technology
JD	Juris Doctor degree
KM	knowledge management
KPI	key performance indicator
LC/LOC	Library of Congress
LCC	Library of Congress Classification
LCSH	Library of Congress Subject Headings
LIS	library and information science
LLAMA	Library Leadership Administration and Management Association
LMS	learning management systems
LOCKSS	lots of copies keep stuff safe
LSA	Library Services Act
LSCA	Library Services and Construction Act
LSP	library services platform
LSSI	Library Systems and Services, Inc.
LSTA	Library Services and Technology Act
MARC	machine-readable cataloging
MLA	Medical Library Association
MLIS	Master of Library and Information Science
MODS	metadata object description schema
MOOC	massive open online course
NASW	National Association of Social Workers
NDIIPP	National Digital Information Infrastructure and Preservation Program
NEDCC	Northeast Document Conservation Center
NGSS	Next Generation Science Standards
NIH	National Institutes of Health
NISO	National Information Standards Organization
NIST	National Institute of Standards and Technology
NN/g	Nielsen Norman Group
NSA	National Security Agency
NSF	National Science Foundation
OAI	Open Archives Initiative
OAIS	Open Archival Information System
OCLC	Online Computer Library Center
OER	open education resources
OLAP	online analytical processing
OMB	Office of Management and Budget
ONIX	ONline Information eXchange
OPAC	online public access catalog

PDA	personal digital assistant
PDA/DDA	patron-driven acquisitions/data-driven acquisitions
PHI	protected health information
PII	personally identifiable information
PIPEDA	Personal Information Protection and Electronic Documents Act of 2000
PLA	Public Library Association
PLN	personal learning network
PPRA	Protection of Pupil Rights Amendment
PREMIS	Preservation Metadata Implementation Strategies
Q&A	question and answer
RA	reader's advisory
RDA	resource description and access
RDF	resource description framework
RDM	research data management
REFORMA	National Association to Promote Library & Information Services to Latinos and the Spanish Speaking
RFP	request for proposal
RLG	Research Libraries Group
ROI	return on investment
RUSA	Reference and User Services Association
SAA	Society of American Archivists
SaaS	software-as-a-service
SCANS	Secretary's Commission on Achieving Necessary Skills
SIP	submission information package
SIS	student information system
SLA	Special Libraries Association
SMS	short message service
STEAM	science, technology, engineering, art, and mathematics
STEEPED	society, technology, education, the environment, politics, economics, and demographics (Center for the Future of Libraries categories)
STEM	science, technology, engineering, and math (disciplines)
SWOT	strengths, weaknesses, opportunities, threats
TVA	Tennessee Valley Authority
URI	uniform resource identifier
USAIN	United States Agriculture Information Network
USER	Understand, Structure, Engage, Reflect
UX	user experience
VIS	virtual information service
VLS	virtual librarian service
WEMI	works, expressions, manifestations, and items (FRBR group 1 entities)
WIPO	World Intellectual Property Organization
WWW	World Wide Web
XML	extensible markup language

Online Materials

Ten archived webcasts aligned with this book that are moderated by editor Sandra Hirsh and feature selected chapter authors are available at ischool.sjsu.edu/informationservicestoday/webinars.

Accompanying this textbook is a comprehensive online supplement that provides readers information about additional readings, online resources, websites and blogs, and more. In addition, the online supplement also provides the following components to extend the text printed in the chapter.

Online supplement link: https://rowman.com/page/hirshsupplement

Foreword

In 1986 Joan Bechtel called for a shift in how librarians viewed themselves and suggested "that we begin to think of libraries as centers for conversation and of ourselves as mediators of and participants in the conversations of the world."[1] Conversations are more than informal banter. Conversations are how we define and interact in the world. These conversations between people, groups, and societies, and indeed with ourselves, are how we define the world. Throughout this new edition of *Information Services Today: An Introduction*, you will see the evidence of these conversations in the form of citations and callouts.

What you have in your hands is a conversation that is both reifying and, in some cases, challenging the shared construction of information services and professionals. The book may have the trappings of a textbook, or feel like some fixed expression, but underneath the artifact is a roiling, intense, and thoughtful dialogue about what it means to be an information professional. The editor has worked hard to craft and direct that conversation, and the authors offer a wealth of expertise to aid the beginner and the longtime practitioner in the field. Now you are invited into the dialogue with the belief that you shall be the architects of the future.

The chapters of this book show implicitly, if not explicitly, that the common and established understandings of the field are evolving. Note how on nearly every page authors put forth definitions that in times past might simply have been assumed. This is not the case only with newer terms to the field such as *design thinking* (chapter 23) or *user experience* (chapter 14) but also with long-held common terms beyond the information field, such as *leadership* (chapter 37), *diversity* (chapter 5), and *intellectual freedom* (chapter 35). This need to constantly put forth definitions is not simply a reflection of the text's introductory character. The meanings and uses of these terms are fundamentally changing throughout the field itself.

Don't let the figures and discussion questions fool you—the concepts of what constitutes an information service and an information professional are moving, evolving, adapting, and transforming. Here is what you have to know about that fact: it is a very good thing. Why is it a good thing? Shouldn't you just wait for it to be settled and buy the third (or twenty-fifth) edition? No. Why? Because it is ultimately an invitation to join the conversation. This is true of those new to the field, and those seeking to come up on the current state of the conversation.

All living and viable professions are in a state of flux. They are in flux because they are constantly adjusting to other fields, new technologies, and new realities. If a field stops adapting, it is irrelevant—there is nothing to talk about.

This book is a point in time in those conversations. The authors assembled here represent some of the leading voices in that conversation—people of authority and experience. However, the next point in time, the next edition, the next conference or service or phase, will not be gifted to you. It will be influenced by you. That is the unstated invitation—or, as I see it, the obligation this text presents to you. If the field is a conversation, you are now part of that conversation.

R. David Lankes
University of South Carolina

NOTE

1. "Conversation, a New Paradigm for Librarianship?" *College and Research Libraries* 47 (3), 219-24.

Preface

The second edition of *Information Services Today: An Introduction* is not your typical introductory text-book. Like the dynamic, ever-changing information field itself, this textbook goes far beyond providing the foundational concepts central to students, instructors, and information professionals; it engages the reader with the key issues, challenges, and opportunities on the horizon. This essential overview of what it means to be a library and information professional has been updated to reflect recent changes brought about by new technology and the increasingly global and diverse nature of information and its users. The text provides a broad overview of the transformation of libraries as information organizations, why these organizations are more important today than ever before, the global and techno-logical influences on how we provide information resources and services, the growing need for information literacy, and the skills and competencies needed to manage today's information organizations.

The new edition features chapter updates to address changes in information services, introducing new topics such as strategic planning, change management, design thinking, advocacy, and data management and analysis, and includes new contributing authors. The book begins with an overview of libraries and their transformation as information and technological hubs within their local and digital communities. It covers the various specializations within the field—emphasizing the exciting yet complex roles and opportunities for information professionals in a variety of information environments. With that foundation in place, it presents the fundamentals of information services, delves into management skills needed by information professionals today, and explores emerging issues related to the rapid development of new technologies. The book addresses how libraries and information centers serve different kinds of communities, highlighting the unique needs of increasingly diverse users and how information organizations and information professionals work to fulfill those needs.

This book provokes discussion, critical thinking, and interaction to facilitate the learning process. The content and supplemental materials—discussion questions, rich sets of online accessible materials, multimedia webcast interviews featuring authors from this book discussing the trends and issues in their respective areas, and chapter presentation slides for use by instructors—give readers the opportunity to develop a deeper understanding of and engagement with the topics. Additionally, this book recognizes the broad range of environments that people with master's of library and information science (MLIS) degrees work in, which include both libraries and other information settings. Thus, this book does not focus exclusively on libraries, but instead encompasses *all* kinds of information organizations.

PURPOSE

This second edition of *Information Services Today: An Introduction* demonstrates the ever-changing landscape of information services today and the need to reevaluate curricula, competency training, and one's personal learning network in order to stay abreast of current trends and issues, and more significantly, remain competent to address the changing user needs that the information community must meet. Specifically, the book:

- provides a thorough introduction, history, and overview of the state of the field,
- gives a broad and global perspective of what it means to be a library and information professional today,

- addresses why information organizations and information and technological literacy are more important today than ever before,
- discusses how technology has influenced the ways that information professionals provide information resources and services in today's digital environment,
- highlights current issues and trends and provides expert insight into emerging challenges, innovations, and opportunities for the future, and,
- identifies career management strategies and leadership opportunities in the information profession.

The book begins with an overview of the current information landscape and what it means to be an information professional today and into the future. Emerging trends in technology and the global information landscape are highlighted with an emphasis on the role of lifelong learning for adapting to and leading change. This forward-thinking perspective is anchored in a historical overview of the transformation of libraries as information and technology hubs within their communities.

AUDIENCE

The book has for four different audiences.

First and foremost, it is aimed at the new student in an information school or a library and information science program who is learning the foundational core of a library and information science (LIS) curriculum. Students will gain a solid foundation of the types of environments information professionals work in, the type of work they do, the influence of technology on how communities access and use information, and the many special issues (e.g., intellectual freedom, copyright, and information privacy) that define the information landscape and will likely have implications for them during their career as an information professional. From the book's first chapter highlighting essential competencies for today's information professional to its concluding chapters on career strategies and leadership, students will gain an insight into the various opportunities—both academic and professional—that are available to them. Students will also benefit from one of the primary themes addressed throughout the book: the value and significance of lifelong learning as an essential component of success in the information profession.

Second, with the continuous expansion and evolution of technological and cultural influence on how information professionals store, access, use, and manage information, the book is also aimed at current information professionals. Given the rapid pace of change and innovation in the information field, information professionals must continuously stay abreast of the current issues and emerging trends. This book serves as both a "refresher course" and introduction to future trends for information professionals committed to their professional development. The authors provide effective strategies for addressing the needs of information users and environments today, while forecasting the issues, challenges, and opportunities on the horizon. An understanding of these issues helps information professionals keep current and their organizations adapt to change in the future. The ongoing and future success of information organizations is reliant on continual professional development and advancing the skill sets of the individuals who work in them; this book addresses that need.

Third, this textbook targets the non-LIS professional by providing a snapshot of the field of library and information science. It defines the information organization and its various functions and highlights the essential roles that information professionals perform in the community, business world, educational system, and even the global environment. In a nutshell, this book provides any reader a glimpse of information organizations and the value they add to the community and contributes to an overall understanding of the complex, technological, and global information environment all must navigate.

Finally, the book is written for instructors at information schools and schools of library and information science. With leading industry and academic experts represented throughout the book, accompanied by discussion questions, examples, and case studies—in addition to the instructor's supplement that includes additional discussion questions, exercises, webcasts, and chapter presentation slides—the book provides instructors of foundational LIS courses a practical guide for their curriculum development and, more importantly, their students' learning.

EXPERTISE

The editor of this collective edition has drawn on her extensive and varied expertise and experience as a library and information science educator, leader, researcher, and professional both in library and other information environments to identify the key themes and topics to be addressed in this textbook, as well as the best experts to address them. She has applied her own library and information science skill set working for more than a decade in leading Silicon Valley companies on user experience and research and development—giving her a firsthand realization of the range of possibilities for information professionals to work in many different environments in a variety of positions. As the director of the School of Information at San José State University, she works with leading professionals and educators from around the world on developing new curricula covering the important topics facing the information profession today. Such topics include, but are not limited to, emerging technologies, changes in information user behavior, data analysis, cybersecurity, information ethics and privacy, change management, design thinking, community engagement, global communities, and more. Each of these topics has been introduced in this book by today's leading experts.

Of tremendous value to this book are its contributing authors. These authors were specifically chosen for their expertise, passion, and commitment—not only to the field of information science but also to the professional development of tomorrow's information leaders. The authors collectively represent some of the largest programs in library and information in the United States (both iSchools and LIS schools), library directors, library consultants, and information professionals from the profession's most valued organizations such as the American Library Association, Educopia Institute, SPARC, Praxair, LYRASIS, and more. These authors were further selected for their global perspectives and engagement with different types of information landscapes. Together, these contributing authors weave their unique expertise and perspectives to address the key themes of the book.

KEY THEMES AND LEARNING OBJECTIVES

Key themes were identified to provide a thorough, yet broad, introduction to the field of library and information science and to address the issues, terminology, and resources that every information professional should know. The key themes for the second edition of *Information Services Today: An Introduction* are consistent with the themes of the first edition, with the addition of a greater focus on diversity and the global information landscape. Working with the authors on the specific scope for each chapter, the editor has crafted a cohesive collection of essential topics and key themes applicable to the work of information professionals today. As a result of reading this book, readers will gain a foundational understanding of:

- the history of libraries and information organizations,
- the diverse and global nature of today's information landscape,
- the emerging trends and issues that will help information professionals remain forward thinking (for their organization as well as their own professional development), and
- the need for information organizations to find new and innovative ways to reach users wherever they are and provide information and resources whenever they need it.

Readers will also understand that:

- information and technology literacy is a growing need in communities (e.g., public, academic, social, government, and organizational) and remains a primary function of information organizations—and of information professionals, and
- information organizations will continue to provide value to their communities—but to thrive, they will need to remain creative, innovative, and technologically advanced.

Readers will be able to:

- address challenges and key issues in the field and for the sustainability and essentialness of the information organization,
- understand the role of assessment in demonstrating value to the communities they serve as well as in advocating on behalf of the organization, its services, funding, and the rights of its users,
- identify new competencies, roles, and opportunities for information professionals, and
- continue learning, exploring, and innovating through a wealth of key resources that are provided.

ORGANIZATION

This second edition of *Information Services Today: An Introduction* is organized into six parts, providing a clear focus on today's key issues and trends.

Part I, "Information Landscapes: Cultural and Technological Influences" presents the historical transformation of the information organization while demonstrating how these organizations remain true to their core mission of serving the diverse needs of their community. Part 1 also highlights the heart of the information organization's existence—the information professionals—and their innate understanding of community. Chapter 1 provides a dynamic foundation to the book by addressing current issues, emerging trends within the information field, and new competencies facing the information professional today. Chapter 2 provides a comprehensive history in which the author highlights the transformation of the library from a repository to an information center that is focused on information literacy and technology rather than books. Chapter 3 traces emerging trends and issues in the profession along multiple dimensions with an emphasis on the value information professionals bring to their communities. This chapter also provides a wealth of resources for information professionals to stay abreast of these trends. Chapter 4 addresses the diverse communities and information needs served by information organizations and provides the reader with tools, strategies, and resources for effectively understanding and working with these communities. Chapter 5 expands upon the discussion of diversity in the community while addressing critical issues for today's times, such as equity of access and social justice.

Part II, "Information Professions: Physical and Virtual Environments" examines the changes in specific information environments, including those that serve students through school and academic libraries, members of the community through public libraries, and clients through special libraries and information centers. A valuable takeaway of part II is the identification of various career options—both within the library setting and outside of it—that utilize the unique skill sets and competencies of today's information professional. Chapters 6 through 9 address both the similarities and uniqueness of the different types of information organizations where information professionals work, including school libraries (chapter 6), academic libraries (chapter 7), public libraries (chapter 8), and special libraries (chapter 9). Each chapter addresses the organization's environment (including the physical or virtual space and the communities it serves), as well as the specific competencies needed for successfully meeting the needs of its users. Chapter 9 also provides an in-depth look at a "day in the life" of a variety of information professionals, providing the reader with a broad overview of the diversity of opportunities in the information professions.

Part III, "Information Services: Engaging, Creating, and Collaborating via Technology" highlights the various roles—both in person and behind the scenes—that guide users through the information-seeking process. The roles information professionals perform in providing information and technology literacy instruction to assist the user are also explored. The concept of user-centered design that takes the user's experience into account is presented, as are the models of the hyperlinked library, creation culture, and makerspaces. Chapter 10 provides an in-depth look at how to manage resources in the digital environment across a multiplicity of roles. Chapter 11 highlights the role of information intermediation and reference services, including how these roles have changed with digital collections, the internet, and mobile applications. Chapter 12 presents the reader with the rapidly evolving technical side of information organizations including automated systems, cataloging and authority control, metadata, and linked data, as well as a thorough look at the evolving role of the integrated library system. Chapter 13 introduces preservation and curation issues with both analog and digital materials with a look at where these complex issues will be headed in the future. Chapter 14 explores user experience with an emphasis on how to design services, programs, and spaces to meet the needs of a variety of users. This chapter also discusses the tools needed to engage users in the process of creating a great user experience. Chapter 15 defines access services, discusses the evolution of the concept, and addresses how an access services department might be organized (e.g., e-Reserves, interlibrary loan, and stacks management), managed, and assessed. Chapter 16 discusses the essential service of providing information and technology literacy instruction in a variety of settings, with special sections on the digital divide, accountability, technological changes, and training and assessment of literacy programming. Chapter 17 focuses on the hyperlinked library and the challenges and opportunities of an "anywhere, anytime" information access model. Part III ends with chapter 18, which introduces the concept of creation culture and makerspaces in information organizations. This chapter highlights not just what kinds of opportunities are available but also how to leverage the desires of patrons and shared resources to engage users.

Part IV, "Managing Information Organizations: Management Skills for the Information Professional," provides an overview of the key management issues and strategies for information organizations. Chapter 19 introduces the strategic planning process with a step-by-step approach. Chapter 20 provides a look at the skills needed for change management, including a selection of case studies to demonstrate just how those skills can be applied in information organizations. Chapter 21 focuses on managing budgets and addresses a range of internal and external factors (e.g., governmental, economical, etc.) that have budgetary implications. Chapter 22 discusses key principles for managing personnel and specifically addresses important considerations related to hiring, onboarding, and both progressive and positive discipline. Chapter 23 moves the discussion to strategies for innovation in the information organization by focusing on design thinking. Chapter 24 discusses collection management and the important role that strategic planning plays in ensuring a technologically rich collection. Chapter 25 continues with the technology theme by exploring management strategies for current and emerging technologies including automating operations and the new generation of technological resources. Chapter 26 brings in the important role of managing data and data analysis, which is essential for evaluating services, planning future initiatives, and demonstrating value. In chapter 27, the focus moves outward to marketing and outreach as well as communication skills. Finally, chapter 28 continues the outward focus by looking at advocacy.

Part V, "Information Issues, Influences and Consequences," explores the profession's ethical code and the ideals of intellectual freedom, including how those principles have been challenged in the past and how they are likely to be the focus of controversy in the future. It also examines some legal issues related to information access, such as copyright and information licensing. Chapter 29 kicks off this section with a chapter devoted to information policy and its evaluation. Chapter 30 addresses the profession's code of ethics that guides information professionals to perform their work and serve their communities while upholding the field's professional values. Chapter 31 focuses on the evolving field of copyright and the Creative Commons. Information licensing follows in chapter 32. Chapter 33 discusses the challenges and opportunities of open access and the role of information professionals in the open-access movement. Chapter 34 provides an overview of information privacy and cybersecurity, while chapter 35 tackles the difficult issue of intellectual freedom and how technology, social change, and the changing publishing landscape affect intellectual freedom. The authors in this section highlight the information professional's responsibility in upholding the user's rights on critical issues and present the unique challenges that information organizations and professionals face in doing so.

The book concludes with part VI, "Information Horizons: Strategies for Building a Dynamic Career as an Information Professional," with the aim of energizing readers as they manage their career in the information profession. Chapter 36 provides specific career management strategies that guide readers—whether they are new to the information field, changing careers, or are current LIS professionals considering a new direction in their careers—to discover how their skill sets match up to a variety of opportunities both within the library field and in other information environments. Chapter 37 addresses the importance of leadership and highlights the various opportunities new and current information professionals can pursue.

SPECIAL FEATURES

Each chapter engages the reader. Textboxes highlight the chapter's key points. "Check This Out" boxes provide links to useful content where the reader can view an example supporting a concept presented in the chapter, check out an important resource mentioned in the chapter, or view a website of interest. Tables and figures enrich understanding.

Discussion questions embedded in each chapter facilitate engagement in the classroom setting—whether physically in a classroom setting or online via discussion boards. These questions are designed to get the reader to think more deeply about the chapter's content and discuss how the concepts may apply to real-life scenarios.

While the book was approached purposively to build upon learning concepts presented earlier in the book, readers can also begin and end where they want to. Each chapter's content is unique and complete to its topic; however, some content will naturally overlap the content of other chapters. When a concept is presented that is addressed in more detail in another section or chapter, a cross-reference to that chapter is provided. This way, learning is adaptable to the reader's or the classroom's unique needs and can begin and end in any sequence.

EXPANDED LEARNING

One of the overlapping themes of this introductory LIS textbook is the value placed on lifelong learning. A key emphasis is that learning should not end with this textbook—nor does it end with the MLIS degree. Successful and satisfying careers in the field of library and information science are based on the commitment to adapt to change, engage with new ideas, and continuously learn. Continuous learning is the only means for meeting the diverse, complex, and changing needs of the global information community.

With that in mind, an online supplement has been compiled for the readers to accompany this book available at https://rowman.com/Page/hirshsupplement/second_edition. This supplement provides the reader with a "library" of supplemental readings, websites, blogs, expanded text, and additional resources that enables readers to extend their learning on each chapter's content while staying current in a rapidly changing field.

The social, technological, and global environments in which information users dwell today create exciting opportunities for the information professional across many institutional and organizational settings. To remain effective and competent in today's information environment, information professionals must not only understand the nature of information *today* but must also remain cognizant that information, and the ways users access, use, and even create information, will dynamically change in the future. That change begins with every new piece of information published (in print or online), every new technology developed, and every piece of new knowledge sought; change is happening every second of every day, 24/7. The success of information professionals in serving their information communities is dependent on their commitment to lifelong learning and professional development.

This second edition of *Information Services Today: An Introduction* encapsulates the knowledge and experiences of industry leaders and rewards every information professional who reads this book with the foundational knowledge and resources necessary to begin—or recharge—their careers as competent, transformative, and forward-thinking information professionals.

Acknowledgments

It is with heartfelt gratitude that I acknowledge the many individuals who assisted in the writing of this book. This was a collaborative effort, and I could never have completed a book project of this size and complexity without the help and support of the following people.

First and foremost, I want to acknowledge the tremendous work that my colleague Elaine Hall, San José State University School of Information's communications consultant and project manager, did on this book. Her outstanding contributions and ideas, organizational skills, professionalism, and attention to detail are evident all throughout the book. Despite her own busy work and family schedule, she worked many weekends and late-night hours with me to ensure that we delivered the project on time and with the quality we both strived for. I am especially grateful that she agreed to work on this book project again—especially since she worked on the first edition of the textbook when she was my research assistant. While others might have said "never again" if they were approached again to work on this ambitious project, Elaine was enthusiastic to tackle the second edition of this book with me and was brimming with excitement for the project and with new ideas for enhancements to the book content and editing process. I can't imagine having a better person to work with me on this project!

I also am very grateful to my research assistants who contributed to this project. Laurel Brenner assisted in the early stages of the book project, particularly by helping with the book proposal, the author's style guide, and the Google project site. Bintal Patel and Stephanie Flood assisted with style-guide editing and index preparation. Mary Vasudeva assisted in editing the second and final chapter drafts, developing visual components for the chapters, ensuring that chapters adhered to the *Chicago Manual of Style*, and supporting the overall project flow so the project could stay on schedule. I also would like to thank San José State University School of Information students Holley Cornetto, Lauren Hall, and Suzanne Maguire, who assisted with creating PowerPoint slides of chapter content to support and enhance the instructional experience.

Thanks also go to Dr. Linda Main, my associate director at the San José State University School of Information. Not only is she wonderful to work with on school business, but she also provided invaluable help early on in this project—helping me to brainstorm topic areas and identify possible contributors, as well as generally serving as a sounding board for the project. I also want to acknowledge the many helpful suggestions and ideas that I received from other SJSU School of Information faculty.

I appreciated working with my acquisitions editor, Charles Harmon, at Rowman & Littlefield. I am grateful that he originally approached me with the idea for this book project and that he was interested in having me update the book for a second edition. Charles is such a pleasure to work with, and I have valued his timely support, publishing expertise, and friendship over the years.

I am also extremely grateful to the many new and returning contributors to this book. I am honored to have worked with so many of the great leaders, scholars, and information professionals in our field today, and I appreciate their willingness to share their expertise, passion, and commitment in writing the second edition of this important foundational text for the library and information science field.

I feel especially lucky to have such a supportive family. First, a huge thank-you to my husband, Jay, for his patience and support while I worked on this book project, particularly as I was frequently working late into the night and on weekends. We had many personal trips and projects that Jay kept moving forward during the writing of this second edition. One of our biggest projects was remodeling our house and redoing all of our landscaping. Jay made sure that these important projects were implemented the way that we wanted—and I am particularly grateful that he did most of the house painting! I also want to thank my daughters, Hayley and Leah, for their love and support while they were working on their university studies.

Finally, I am grateful to my mom, Gail Schlachter, who passed away shortly after the publication of the first edition of this book. My mom was the one who inspired me to enter the exciting field of library and information science. If not for her encouragement and showing me the way, I would never have pursued this rewarding career. Her memory continues to inspire me to this day.

Part I
Information Landscapes
Cultural and Technological Influences

Information professionals must both *zoom in* on the individual user and his or her specific problem situation, cognitive and affective state, and end goals, and then *zoom out* to the level of the group, organization, or community to consider the broader expectations, access and resource constraints, and emerging technologies that will impact current and future information needs.

—Heather O'Brien and Devon Greyson, chapter 4

Libraries and information organizations continue to evolve so they can best meet the needs of their user communities in response to the changing information landscape. From their beginnings, libraries have served as gateways to information and education and have provided opportunities equitably for diverse communities. With an array of programs, services, and materials, they encourage, engage, and promote information literacy and lifelong learning. While information organizations have changed and will continue to do so in exciting and innovative ways, their core mission is stronger than ever, and they are envisioning and embracing a future that combines learning, sharing, and creating knowledge and experiences that meet the needs of their users.

Part I explores the early beginnings of libraries and their growth and development in response to changing user needs and an ever-evolving society. Part I also considers the different ways that information organizations maintain their core values of serving users' diverse information needs while supporting intellectual freedom, equity of access, and social justice. It also highlights the role of technology in driving innovation while reminding the profession of the importance of continuing to adapt, evolve, and stay proactive in the face of continuous social, cultural, and technological change.

1

The Transformative Information Landscape

WHAT IT MEANS TO BE AN INFORMATION PROFESSIONAL TODAY

Sandra Hirsh

The field of library and information science (LIS) is facing one of the most dynamic and transformational periods in history. Societal and cultural trends toward a more participatory culture present both opportunities and challenges for the information organization. Information organizations are responding by adopting a vision for themselves as the technological hub of their communities—meaning they integrate technologies, design creative spaces and instructional tools, and create new opportunities for learning and exploration. Information users are now coming to the information organization—both in person and online—asking for access to information and resources, asking for technologies, and asking to engage with others in creative and collaborative activities. Indeed, providing access to technology is now, and will continue to be, a top priority for information organizations as they "redefine their roles as digital knowledge centers"[1] and community hubs for creativity and connectivity.

The 2017 *NMC Horizon Report—Library Edition*[2] identifies several "big picture themes" that will impact information organizations, their services, and their value over the next five years. These include:

- Information organizations will remain the gatekeepers to information and knowledge.
- New media and technology will become integrated into the organization's strategic planning.
- Information organizations will need to balance their roles between independent inquiry and collaboration.
- Information organizations will need to place greater emphasis on user design and accessibility in order to serve their communities effectively.
- Digital fluency and literacy will become a core responsibility of the information organization.
- Advancing innovative services and operations requires reimagining organizational structures.
- Artificial intelligence and the internet of things (IoT) will impact the utility and reach of information service.[3]

These themes are repeated throughout this textbook, emphasizing the need for information organizations, and the professionals who work in them, to be forward thinking, innovative, and user focused in order to remain relevant and essential to the communities they serve. After completing this chapter, readers should have a better understanding of:

- the global nature of information and information work today,
- the innovative and user-defined information services provided in those environments,
- how information organizations can adapt to emerging trends in the information landscape,
- essential and in-demand competencies for today's information professional, and
- resources for lifelong learning and professional development.

GLOBAL TRENDS IMPACTING INFORMATION SERVICES

In today's information landscape, information professionals must constantly survey the information and technology environment to identify trends that have implications for the information field. Adapting to these changes is part of what makes being an information professional so interesting and exciting.

Defining the Global Information Landscape

The International Federation of Library Associations and Institutions (IFLA)[4] reports that the global information landscape has been impacted by a higher, more universal value (and need) for information literacy skills, a rapid expansion of online education resources, and the "proliferation of hyper-connected mobile devices . . . that will transform the global information economy."[5] Even the nature of the information organization has morphed "beyond the physical space, with online resources, social media, crowdsourcing, and mobile services changing how collections and services are accessed and shared while on the go."[6] Indeed, these online resources are producing new possibilities for learning and exploration as organizations collaborate and hyperlink to connect their resources together—creating access to virtually endless amounts of information. As a result, information organizations around the globe are responding to the opportunities and threats imposed by technological innovations and to the impact these technologies have on the global information landscape for the information user.

Supporting and extending the findings from the IFLA reports, Australian Library and Information Association (ALIA)'s report "Future of the Library and Information Profession: Public Libraries"[7] identified key priorities, many of which apply across all library types. The themes raised in the ALIA report center around advocacy, equality of opportunity, access, technology, budget, and spaces. Each of these are defined further below.

Advocacy: Information professionals need to engage in advocacy for many reasons. One reason is to make sure that funders understand the true value of information organizations. Another reason is to ensure that communities and key stakeholders realize the range of services and programs offered by today's information organizations. For example, today's information organizations manage and provide access to information in all formats (not just books) as well as support information users in knowledge creation and community activities and the opportunity to explore new and emerging technologies (see also chapter 28: "Advocacy"). Whatever the reason, the advocacy message needs to focus on the *value* of information services by defining the "why" more than the "how" in order to meet the community's needs (see also chapter 4: "Diverse Information Needs").

Equality of opportunity: A core foundational principle of the information field is equal access to information for all (see also chapter 30: "Information Ethics"). It is essential for information organizations to adopt a passion and commitment to equity of access, inclusion, and social justice, and continue to apply these principles in their organizations to address the changing needs of their communities (see also chapter 5: "Diversity, Equity of Access, and Social Justice").

Access: Information organizations need to ensure that people can access information when it is convenient for them. By expanding customer service models, for example, ones that offer services 24/7, virtual services, and/or mobile services that go out into the community, information organizations will be able to meet the needs of their communities whenever and wherever they are.

Technology: As technology evolves, so will information organizations' need to advance the tools and technology they provide to information users to access information and to learn and create new knowledge. Thus, information organizations need to provide access to both analog and digital resources, as well as new and emerging technologies (see also chapter 13: "Analog and Digital Curation and Preservation"; chapter 25: "Managing Technology").

Budgets: Information organizations need to juggle many pressures on their budgets. For example, as journal prices rise, information organizations have to reevaluate their budgetary priorities and explore new approaches for meeting the needs of their communities, such as through consortia partnership agreements (see also chapter 21: "Managing Budgets" and chapter 32: "Information Licensing").

Spaces: Information organizations need to develop new types of spaces to meet the changing needs of their communities, particularly to support their communities in exploration, discovery, and learning through collaboration and play (see also chapter 18: "Creation Culture and Makerspaces").

Global Trends: Challenges and Themes

As the information landscape continues to change, information organizations face challenges that they will need to address. The IFLA identifies three overarching and universal themes and challenges that face information organizations around the world:

1. the need to define the role of information organizations;
2. the availability of skills, infrastructure, and funding; and
3. the need for coordination and collaboration.[8]

First, information organizations are defining (and redefining) what their role is within the community. This is challenging to define due to the technological, cultural, environmental, and political influences that constantly force information organizations to redefine their mission and the value of their services.

Second, information organizations are focusing on the skills, infrastructure, and funding they need in order to offer new and evolving services, programs, and technologies. As new technologies are introduced and begin to saturate the community, information organizations need to address important and sometimes challenging questions:

> Information organizations need to build collaborations with other organizations within their community to effectively, creatively, and innovatively provide new technologies and services that meet the community's needs.

- Does the community have the skills to effectively utilize these technologies?
- Does the information organization have the infrastructure to adopt and provide the technology (or service or program needed to engage with the technology) to the community?
- How will the information organization access funding for the integration of the new technology?[9]

Third, information organizations need to coordinate and collaborate in order to thrive in the changing information landscape. Information organizations need to build collaborations with other organizations within their community to effectively, creatively, and innovatively provide new technologies and services that meet the community's needs.

While these are common themes for all information organizations, other trends vary by geographic region and country. Many countries still struggle with the ability to provide access to physical library space or do not have the infrastructure to support access to the virtual information landscape. Funding sources and political environments also place pressure on local libraries across the globe, increasing the need for advocacy and justifying the information organization's value to its community (socially, economically, and academically). IFLA's 2016 Update Report[10] provides additional insight about themes that arose from global discussions and case studies in response to their 2013 report[11] (see textbox 1.1).

TEXTBOX 1.1

Trends Impacting Information Organizations around the World

Africa

- Challenges exist around infrastructure, connectivity, and digital skills.
- Massive open online courses (MOOCs) and open education resources (OERs) are providing widespread learning opportunities.
- Privacy, data protection, and the value of national data policies are being questioned as private data moves into the public domain.

Asia and Oceana

- Information organizations are challenged regarding their importance.
- Mobile technologies are redefining communities.
- Information organizations need to leverage new technologies and partnerships.

Europe

- Information organizations are facing new challenges in copyright, access to digital content, and e-lending.
- There is a trend toward erosion of privacy, which pits control against empowerment.
- Information organizations need to strengthen strategic collaborations.

Latin America and Caribbean

- Information organizations need to overcome connectivity to address social exclusion and inequality.
- Digital developments are having both positive and negative outcomes.
- Information organizations are encountering barriers to library reinvention and development.[12]

INFORMATION SERVICES TODAY

Around the world, information organizations share one primary mission: to serve and transform their communities. In order to transform communities, information organizations must transform their spaces, embracing both the physical and virtual information environments. Information professionals must also adopt new ways of *engaging* their communities effectively and efficiently in these spaces. In fact, the information organization's value and relevance is dependent on its ability to identify and effectively adapt to new technologies, provide access to technology and information, and help users engage with technology and information so as to transform lives and communities.

Adapting to New Technologies

Technology continues to change the way communities interact and use, access, and communicate with information. What is exciting about these changes is what it can mean for the information organization. Information organizations have the opportunity to develop themselves as the technological and information hub of their community. They can do this not only by providing access to the technologies desired by their community but also by adapting their spaces and their services as "hubs" for learning and exploring.

To effectively adapt to today's information users and engage their community, information organizations must develop effective strategic planning initiatives that are forward thinking and adaptive (see also chapter 19: "Strategic Planning"). Information organizations will need to stay ahead of the curve in identifying how users engage with today's technology, while keeping a keen eye on the impact that emerging technologies will have on user behaviors and, therefore, the information organization and its services (see also chapter 3: "Librarianship: A Continuously Evolving Profession"). Such strategies for information organizations may include:

- become the essential, one-stop resource for information and technical literacy instruction,
- provide access to mobile and online learning resources,
- become the gateway to global digital resources,
- integrate as many emerging technologies into services as possible, and
- provide an environment of exploration and play to learn these new technologies.

In addition to strategic planning, information organizations must also engage in change management strategies that help everyone in the organization uphold a mission-forward vision of innovation, creativity, and exploration (see also chapter 20: "Change Management").

Providing Access to Technology and Information

Providing access to basic information and technology must be a high priority for information organizations and is the "most important function" underlying the organization's existing resources.[13] By enabling access to information and technology, information organizations ensure everyone has the ability to participate, learn, and engage—and in doing so, they transform communities. At a fundamental level, access begins with free speech and the freedom to share ideas with others—but it does not end there (see also chapter 35: "Intellectual Freedom"). Jill Bourne states that "when access is paired with the tools and skills for understanding and using" information, agency—the capacity of individuals to act independently and to make their own choices—is built. Consequently, the "pairing of access + agency = a sweet spot for [information organizations]."[14]

TEXTBOX 1.2

Today's Technology Helps Patrons Curate, Create, and Engage with Information

Technology can work to not only engage patrons in the library but also help them curate and create. Examples of creativity in the library environment include:

- Tablets and mobile phones help children learn literacy skills and stimulate their imagination.
- Makerspaces enable people to engage with each other and create new knowledge.
- Coding hack-a-thons teach usable skills.
- Innovation labs provide opportunities to help local entrepreneurs develop their ideas.[15]

By offering free access to both physical and digital collections, developing creative learning spaces for technological exploration, and providing staff who are knowledgeable about new technologies and their various applications, information organizations will transform themselves as technological hubs of their communities.

Influencing How Society Engages with Technology and Information

Information professionals need to integrate information communication technologies (ICTs), design creative and engaging learning spaces, and expand opportunities for learning and exploration.[16] By doing this, they not only respond to the diverse needs and interests of the community, they also "foster personal development for individual community members while simultaneously facilitating organizational innovation[17] (see also chapter 4: "Diverse Information Needs"). Consequently, today's information professionals need the skills to:

- develop initiatives that blend information literacy with social media,
- make library tools available at the point of need for users,
- enable users to interface with information in a natural and personalized manner, and
- allow [users] to design their own learning outcomes.[18]

TEXTBOX 1.3

Dokk1 Provides Access to a World of Information and Entertainment

A key trend in influencing how users interact with the technology and information is the offering of flexible spaces that accommodate independent study and tranquility as well as group collaboration and community engagement. For example, Dokk1 is a large new library and citizens services center in Aarhus, Denmark, that has a mission to "provide free access to a world of information, inspiration, learning and entertainment."[19] Dokk1 provides users with a diverse set of services that transcend those typically offered in a library by including a range of city government services. Additionally, Dokk1 meets the needs of the community by providing flexible spaces for reading, studying, creating, learning, and engaging with others.[20]

THE TRANSFORMATIVE AND GLOBAL INFORMATION PROFESSIONAL

The influence of technology in today's information organization and the need for skilled information professionals is stronger today than ever. LIS career expert Kim Dority states:

> Trying to get a handle on what library technologies LIS professionals need to know can be a challenge, as both the tasks and the tools that librarians are taking on seem to be changing daily. Nevertheless, it's especially important for [information professionals] to be aware of technology skills and knowledge that are in demand, because increasingly these tools will be central to successful career performance.[21]

In addition to the importance of developing key technological competencies, the transformative and global information professional needs to develop a broad range of skills and competencies as identified by several recent studies. These competencies are essential in preparing information professionals for today's information landscape while developing new skills that will position them, and the organizations they work in, well into the future.

Skills and Competencies for Today's Information Professional

In addition to the foundational and technical competencies that are specific to the field of library and information science such as managing, providing access to, and organizing information, information professionals need competencies that prepare them to engage with their communities, advocate for their needs, demonstrate leadership, and collaborate with others. The essential skills and competencies for today's information professional include: soft skills, communication and outreach skills, leadership and management skills, a user-centered mind-set, and technological skills (see textbox 1.4).

TEXTBOX 1.4

Essential Skills and Competencies for Information Professionals

Soft Skills
- Critical thinking
- Independence, time management, multitasking
- Collaboration
- Professional networking

Communication and Outreach
See also chapter 27: "Communication, Marketing, and Outreach Strategies"; and chapter 28: "Advocacy."

- Advocacy
- Communication skills
- Marketing
- Presentation skills

Leadership and Management
See also chapter 19: "Strategic Planning"; chapter 20: "Change Management"; and chapter 21: "Managing Budgets."

- Budgeting and fund-raising
- Change management
- Crisis management
- Leadership
- Project management
- Strategic planning

User-Centered Mind-Set
See also chapter 4: "Diverse Information Needs"; chapter 5: "Diversity, Equity of Access, and Social Justice"; and chapter 11: "Information Intermediation and Reference Services."

- Customer services
- Diversity sensitivity
- Library services and management
- Reference and research

Technological Skills

See also chapter 25: "Managing Technology"; and chapter 26: "Managing Data and Data Analysis in Information Organizations."

- Data analysis
- Technological expertise[22]

New Skills and Competencies Needed for Information Professionals

As technologies change and the information landscape continues to evolve, so will the knowledge, skills, and competencies that information professionals need to meet the needs of their communities. Several of these current and emerging areas are included in this book. To name a few:

Data Analytics is addressed in terms of how analyzing data can help make decisions, demonstrate value, and answer complex questions for information organizations (see also chapter 26: "Managing Data and Data Analysis in Information Organizations").

Creation Culture and Makerspaces is addressed in terms of how information professionals create maker learning communities as well as opportunities that delight, motivate, and inspire communities (see also chapter 18: "Creation Culture and Makerspaces").

User Experience is addressed in terms of presenting a range of techniques that can be applied to understand user needs and wants and to create great experiences for information users (see also chapter 14: "User Experience").

Privacy and Cybersecurity is addressed in terms of threats to personal data from online activities, the role of government in improving cybersecurity, and basic measures information professionals can take to help ensure information privacy and security (see also chapter 34: "Information Privacy and Cybersecurity").

Open Access is addressed in the terms of providing free, immediate availability of scholarly articles on the open internet (see also chapter 33: "Open Access").

Design Thinking is addressed in terms of the problem-centered, iterative process for finding problems and creating innovative and user-centered solutions to them (see also chapter 23: "Innovative Library and Information Services: The Design Thinking Process").

These core competencies are now expected of today's information professionals and should be an important part of formal LIS education and lifelong learning endeavors.

LIFELONG LEARNING AND THE INFORMATION PROFESSIONAL

Learning, however, does not end with the MLIS. "This [is] made clear through the innumerable 'what I didn't learn in library school' articles and blog posts as well as the range and number of webinars, online short-courses, post-degree certifications, conference workshops, etc., offered by RUSA and other divisions of ALA as well as state library."[23] The good news is that many students and graduates of LIS programs realize that their skills must remain relevant and they must remain knowledgeable and skilled in the latest technologies.

Information professionals have many opportunities to engage in lifelong learning activities, such as additional degrees, advanced certificate programs, massive online open courses (MOOCs), and open education resources (OERs), etc. However, perhaps the most influential learning activities are those pursued through their personal learning network (PLN): a series of online and in-person connections used to enhance learning, such as through professional groups, social networks, blogs, and microblogging sites, and any other platform where ideas are exchanged. The value in the PLN lies in the activities engaged within it that expand learning and understanding and include:

- interacting and exchanging information and resources,
- accessing mentors (and becoming a mentor!),
- sharing knowledge, experiences, and ideas, and
- collecting and creating an information guide to professional development and lifelong learning.[24]

> By interacting and exchanging ideas through global networks, information professionals gain insight into new and emerging trends, how these trends are impacting different types of organizations, the concerns and issues information organizations are facing as a consequence of these trends, and the exchange of ideas and strategies for effectively adopting and integrating new technologies into their organizations—and therefore, their communities.

PLNs are also the information professional's gateway to active participation in the global information landscape and becoming a global information professional. By interacting and exchanging ideas through global networks, information professionals gain insight into new and emerging trends, how these trends are impacting different types of organizations, the concerns and issues information organizations are facing as a consequence of these trends, and the exchange of ideas and strategies for effectively adopting and integrating new technologies into their organizations—and therefore, their communities. Chapter 3, "Librarianship: A Continuously Evolving Profession," offers several recommendations for resources to add to the information professional's PLN. For a list of online resources for engaging in global learning networks, check out chapters 1, 3, and 36 in the online supplement.

Environmental scanning and trend spotting are also useful approaches for information professionals to continue their learning and to stay abreast of the trends impacting the information profession. One valuable resource is the Center for the Future of Libraries (CFL), which helps information professionals do the following:

- "Identify emerging trends relevant to libraries and the communities they serve.
- Promote futuring and innovation techniques to help librarians and library professionals shape their future.
- Build connections with experts and innovative thinkers to help libraries address emerging issues."[25]

The CFL website focuses on seven key categories: Society, Technology, Education, Environment, Politics (and Government), Economics, and Demographics (STEEPED).[26] Information professionals who stay abreast of how these trends impact (positively and negatively) the information community will become

---

Discussion Questions

Think about your social networks, the sites you visit, and the resources you accessed when considering a career in the field of library and information science. What resources do you already have in place that provide a foundation for building your PLN? What NEW resources do you need to add? And, what actions will you take to ensure your PLN is up to date, relevant to your goals, and providing resources for lifelong learning, engagement, and influence?

tomorrow's leader (see also chapter 37: "Leadership Skills for Today's Global Information Landscape"). Libraries, nonprofit organizations, businesses, and governments alike need information professionals who are knowledgeable about the trends, opportunities, issues, and concerns of the information landscape today (see also chapter 9: "Working in Different Information Environments: Special Libraries and Information Centers"). Furthermore, these information professionals demonstrate an ability to help organizations adapt to change in the future: another essential quality of the information professional!

CONCLUSION

Information professionals have a unique opportunity today to integrate new technologies into their organizations and therefore become community anchors—a place to explore, create, play, learn, discover, collaborate, and share. Information organizations and the professionals that work in them are also the community's advocate and protection, willing to fight for intellectual freedom; diversity, equity and inclusion; privacy and protection; and information and technology literacy. In doing so, the community will identify the organization as a safe harbor and as an essential resource for accessing books and other resources for learning and exploration, interacting with technology and digital resources, and connecting with global resources and communities. It is an exciting time for information organizations. It is an even more exciting time to become an information professional!

NOTES

1. J. McKendrick, *Libraries: At the Epicenter of the Digital Disruption: The Library Guide Benchmark Study on 2013/14 Library Spending Plans* (Information Today, Inc., 2013).
2. New Media Consortium, *NMC Horizon Report, 2017 Library Edition*, https://www.nmc.org/publication/nmc-horizon-report-2017-library-edition/.
3. Ibid.
4. IFLA, *Riding the Waves or Caught in the Tide? Navigating the Evolving Information Environment: Insights from the IFLA Trend Report* (The Hague, Netherlands: IFLA, 2013), http://trends.ifla.org/files/trends/assets/insights-from-the-ifla-trend-report_v3.pdf.
5. A. Bolorizadeh, M. Brannen, R. Gibbs, and T. Mack, "Making Instruction Mobile," *Reference Librarian* 53, no. 4 (2012): 373–83. doi:10.1080/02763877.2012.707488.
6. ARUP, *Future Libraries: Workshops Summary and Emerging Insights* (London: ARUP, 2015), 5.
7. Australian Library and Information Association, *Future of the Library and Information Science Profession: Public Libraries*, 2014, https://www.alia.org.au/sites/default/files/ALIA-Future-of-the-LIS-Profession-04-Public_0.pdf.
8. IFLA, *Riding the Waves or Caught in the Tide?*; Dan Mount, *IFLA Trend Report 2016 Update*, https://trends.ifla.org/files/trends/assets/trend-report-2016-update.pdf.
9. Mount, *IFLA Trend Report Update 2016*.
10. Ibid.
11. IFLA, *Riding the Waves or Caught in the Tide?*
12. Mount, *IFLA Trend Report Update 2016*, 3.
13. B. Mehra, K. Black, and J. Nolt, "What Is the Value of LIS Education? A Qualitative Study of Three Perspectives of Tennessee's Rural Libraries," *Journal of Education for Library and Information Science* 52, no. 4 (2011): 265–78.
14. Jill Bourne, "Finding the Sweet Spot for Libraries in the Digital Age," *Knight Blog*, last modified September 11, 2014, http://www.knightfoundation.org/blogs/knightblog/2014/9/11/finding-sweet-spot-libraries-digital-age/.
15. "New Programs for the Future of Public Libraries," Innovative, February 13, 2017, https://www.iii.com/new-programs-for-the-future-of-public-libraries/; see, for example: Cupertino Library Foundation, "Cupertino Teen Hackathon a Huge Success," http://cupertinolibraryfoundation.org/cupertino-teen-hackathon-a-huge-success/.

16. McKendrick, *Libraries: At the Epicenter of the Digital Disruption*.
17. ARUP, *Future Libraries*, 18.
18. Bolorizadeh et al., "Making Instruction Mobile."
19. Dokk1, "About Dokk1," accessed September 28, 2017, https://dokk1.dk/english/about-dokk1.
20. Ibid.
21. Kim Dority, "Technologies Librarians Need to Know," *LibGig*, June 20, https://www.libgig.com/technol ogies-librarians-need-know/.
22. Eileen Abels, Lynne C. Howarthe, and Linda C. Smith, *Envisioning Our Information Future and How to Educate for It*" (Boston: The *#InfoFuture* Project, 2017), http://slis.simmons.edu/blogs/ourinformationfuture/ files/2017/08/WhitePaper_Abels_Howarth_Smith_Final_Aug28.pdf; John Carlo Bertot, Lindsey C. Sarin, and Johnna Percell, *Re-envisioning the MLIS: Findings, Issues and Considerations* (College Park: University of Maryland Press, 2015), available at: http://mls.umd.edu/wp-content/uploads/2015/08/ReEn visioningFinalReport.pdf; San José State University School of Information, *MLIS Skills at Work: A Snapshot of Job Postings, Spring 2017*, http://ischool.sjsu.edu/sites/default/files/content_pdf/career_trends.pdf.
23. M. Kern, "Continuity and Change, or, Will I Ever Be Prepared for What Comes Next," *Reference and User Services Quarterly* 53, no. 4 (2014): 282–85.
24. Jan Holmquist, "Global Learning Networks," in *Information Services Today: An Introduction*, ed. Sandra Hirsh (Lanham, MD: Rowman & Littlefield, 2014), 379.
25. American Library Association, "Center for the Future of Libraries," 2017, http://www.ala.org/tools/ future.
26. American Library Association, "Trends," http://www.ala.org/tools/future/trends.

2

Libraries, Communities, and Information

TWO CENTURIES OF EXPERIENCE

Christine Pawley

Chapter 2, "Libraries, Communities, and Information: Two Centuries of Experience," connects the reader to the origin and evolution of the library while also telling the story of how these organizations have become the technologically advanced, forward-looking organizations in which users now take center stage. Dr. Christine Pawley is in a unique position as an award-winning book author and former director of the Center for the History of Print and Digital Culture at the University of Wisconsin–Madison to offer a keen understanding of the historic and contemporary factors essential to the development of the information field and provide a critical perspective on how these institutions and systems contribute to the global knowledge infrastructure in the twenty-first century.

Pawley opens the chapter by highlighting the first century of the public library, where foundational structures and competencies in cataloging, classification, and reference services were developed. She elaborates on the development of the library as a publicly funded agency and the eventual incorporation of libraries into universities and schools. Through this development, many standards and principles were developed by organizations such as the American Library Association. More recently, she notes, school, academic, and special libraries also became technologically advanced, now reaching their patrons beyond the library's physical walls.

Pawley concludes with a summary of the current state of libraries and information services, noting that libraries have become increasingly connected to each other, sharing content, collaborating on programs, and engaging in what is now identified as the global knowledge infrastructure. This chapter provides an important framework for thinking about the library and information field—how information organizations and the profession have evolved over time and where the field is heading.

★　★　★

Today's global knowledge infrastructure links individuals to information agencies and services all over the world, with libraries as an essential component. The term "infrastructure" is often used to refer to large physical systems, like electric power and the internet, that we expect to be *reliable*, *standardized*, and *widely available*. The knowledge infrastructure has many interlocking components.

Some are tangible, like buildings, books, equipment, and wiring. Some are intangible and include legal, financial, administrative, epistemological, and ethical systems.[1] This chapter explores how libraries have developed as a component of the knowledge infrastructure over the past two hundred years. After completing this chapter, readers should have an understanding of how evolving and increasingly complex (but often messy) technical, intellectual, legal, financial, administrative, and social systems emerged and meshed into the institutions recognized as information organizations today. This chapter also addresses how these institutions and systems contribute to the global knowledge infrastructure in the twenty-first century.

For the first one hundred years of their history, public libraries led in developing the major elements of knowledge infrastructure, including:

- intellectual systems such as cataloging, classification, materials selection, and reference work,
- spatial systems that directed the flow of materials, patrons, and librarians, both within the library's walls, and beyond them through outreach programs,
- legal systems that enabled communities to tax themselves and administer libraries as a public service, and
- educational systems that prepared librarians to work using standard principles and technologies.

In the second half of the twentieth century, school, academic, and special libraries also became technologically advanced, and libraries developed into forward-looking organizations in which users took a central place. By the beginning of the twenty-first century, the ubiquitous adoption of electronic systems enabled libraries more than ever to reach patrons beyond their physical walls. At the same time, many libraries find that patrons continue to value their spaces as a vital part of their local communities.

PART 1: NINETEENTH-CENTURY BEGINNINGS

In 1800, the Reverend William Bentley (1759–1819) of Salem, Massachusetts, embodied the republican ideal of an informed citizen.[2] Fluent in twenty languages and knowledgeable about local and global affairs, his personal library of four thousand volumes was one of the largest in the country—he was a kind of walking encyclopedia. Although he relied on books and newspapers for information, these sources were expensive and thinly distributed, so Bentley also relied on a network of personal contacts—men and women from all walks of life—in his efforts to become knowledgeable on all topics. However, in the coming decades, changes in print technology and a rapid expansion of publishing and literacy would make generalists like Bentley obsolete as Americans sought knowledge in texts rather than individuals and as these texts numbered far more than any single person could own or even read.

America Transforms in the Nineteenth Century

In Bentley's day, America was largely rural, reliant on free white labor in the North and enslaved black labor in the South. The patchy school system favored boys, while colleges largely existed to educate the all-male clergy. Affluent white men dominated the young republic. They believed its success depended on the participation of well-informed citizens—free, white, property-owning men with the education and ability to elect the best representatives. By the end of the century, America was an industrial giant, its population swollen by immigrants from Europe and Asia. Native American resistance to white settlement had been crushed and many Native groups banished to remote reservations. After the devastating Civil War (1861–1865), slavery was outlawed, but the political and economic subjugation of African Americans continued. Citizens were normalized as white and of European descent; it would be the 1940s and 1950s before Asians were permitted citizenship, and the 1960s and 1970s before African Americans could fully exercise their constitutional right to vote.

In the industrial north, capitalism created a burgeoning middle class of clerical and professional workers, but during the Gilded Age (1870s–1880s) an enormous gulf opened between the very rich and the working class. Nearly 40 percent of Americans inhabited cities where poor people lived and worked in unhealthy and dangerous conditions. To combat the stark inequality, between 1890 and 1920 (the Progressive Era) federal, state, and municipal governments began to regulate aspects such as child labor, public health, and transportation. Women could not vote, but white girls and boys enjoyed free schooling, and colleges sprang up for men and women. Rising literacy and industrialization combined with technological changes had produced an explosion in publications, from newspapers and other ephemera to solid reference tomes. Cheaper prices brought print to a wider audience; its distribution facilitated by railroads and an increasingly effective postal service. Fiction was especially popular, but some cultural authorities worried about the effects of its unmediated radical and even immoral ideas on an impressionable population. Modern libraries began in this century of rapid change, sponsored by the developing middle class, and became part of an emerging national knowledge infrastructure.

Academic Libraries Develop Slowly

Although schools and colleges proliferated during the nineteenth century, academic libraries contributed little to higher education's expansion, reflecting a reliance on textbook memorization rather than original research. South Carolina College constructed the first purpose-built academic library in 1840, and Harvard acquired its first purpose-built library in 1841 (although its library dated back to the seventeenth century). At that time, only thirty colleges had holdings of at least a thousand volumes.[3] Fifty years later, in 1932, a survey of college libraries revealed that, at more than two hundred four-year liberal arts colleges, over half the book collections contained fewer than thirty thousand volumes, and only thirty-three institutions contained more than sixty thousand.[4] Not until after the mid-twentieth century were most academic libraries transformed from underused storehouses into dynamic learning spaces. Instead, the nineteenth-century library movement drew inspiration from the free public libraries that emerged mid-century out of an earlier mix of social and school district libraries.

Early "Public" Libraries

In Bentley's time, "public" libraries were those not owned by private individuals and included social, circulating, and school-district libraries as well as college libraries. Books were expensive, so in the Colonial era some townspeople formed clubs to share them, based on subscription or shared purchase.[5] Such social libraries became common in New England and Mid-Atlantic states before spreading west with Yankee settlers, and by 1850, there were more than one thousand, though services and collections were limited, and most existed only briefly.[6] They usually catered to the white social elite, but groups of African Americans also founded reading rooms, libraries, and literary societies where people gathered to share texts. For black readers as well as white, reading was an exercise for the good of the community, rather than primarily for individual self-improvement.[7] Circulating libraries were also common, renting out books (mostly novels) to whoever could afford to pay. By 1820, more than half of their collections consisted of fiction, which made them suspect in the eyes of those who ran their nonprofit counterparts.[8]

Public Funding for Free Libraries

School district libraries began in New York State in 1835, where libraries for general use could be funded through taxes.[9] In 1849, New Hampshire allowed municipalities to levy taxes for a free community library, followed by Massachusetts in 1851. The 1854 opening of the Boston Public Library boosted free public library development elsewhere, and by 1875 all New England states had passed enabling laws that provided a legal and financial infrastructure for free libraries.[10] Other states passed similar laws, and gradually the free public library idea took hold, as establishing a local library became one of the ways in which pioneering communities put down roots and proclaimed their value.[11] For inspiration, public libraries drew on what some were calling the library "faith" or "spirit," believing that reading could transform individuals and society for the better and that free public libraries promoted democratic progress.[12] As tax-supported institutions though, they, like the circulating libraries, depended on popular appeal. Despite some

> " For inspiration, public libraries drew on what some were calling the library 'faith' or 'spirit,' believing that reading could transform individuals and society for the better, and that free public libraries promoted democratic progress. "

leading librarians' disapproval, many catered to local demand and heavily stocked their shelves with fiction.[13] Public libraries had quickly learned to be responsive to their communities.

Women's Clubs Found New Libraries

Some free public libraries emerged out of older social libraries, but often it was a local women's group that established a new public library.[14] Like social libraries, the new libraries often had restricted opening hours and outdated collections occupying cramped and inadequate quarters, usually rented. By the end of the century, cities were replacing these makeshift spaces with architect-designed libraries, some on a grand scale. Echoing halls and high-vaulted ceilings provided a suitable setting, some thought, for practicing the library faith. But not all agreed. The Chicago Public Library's first director, William Frederick Poole, complained that such buildings wasted space and presented a fire hazard.[15] Competing for funds were "branch" libraries—small-scale subsidiaries situated in neighborhoods. The Boston Public Library opened its first branch in 1871 and by 1875 had five more. Some branches started as "delivery stations" located in stores where readers could order books for pickup.[16] In 1909, the new Chicago Public Library director, Henry Legler, made branch libraries a priority, seeing them as a way to make libraries "accessible to the entire community."[17] In response to the demand from neighborhoods with large immigrant populations, the Chicago Public Library's branch libraries also provided books in seventeen languages, helping to internationalize the knowledge infrastructure.[18] Urban libraries established the model of providing a downtown central or "main" library with branches in local neighborhoods, which would become accepted organizational infrastructure in the twentieth century.

Carnegie Philanthropy Boosts Standardization

Rural communities lagged in providing purpose-built libraries, but between 1886 and 1917, the Carnegie Corporation systematically funded 1,689 public and academic library buildings in the United States. Disparaging monumental libraries as wasteful, its secretary, James Bertram, devised sample plans and suggested functional design features, such as an open plan and low bookcases, that drew inspiration from department stores and factories. These plans helped standardize patrons' library experiences, as well as librarians' work.[19] Midwestern and Western states benefited most, but in cities and villages across America, the public library, providing free access to books and information, along with quiet, clean, well-lit, and heated space for reading (a luxury for those living in cramped and noisy accommodations) became a familiar institution. Often packed with readers and enjoying widespread support, many had become a cornerstone of their communities.

Libraries as Spaces for Self-Improvement and Social Harmony

Although library leaders might appeal loftily to the library faith, at the local level, librarians and patrons understood public libraries as spaces for the fostering of what historian Wayne Wiegand calls "social harmony" through demonstrating acceptable behaviors and providing "collections and services" that offered citizens "models for successful living, solving problems, and achieving an orderly life at the same time that they mediated in peaceful ways a set of ever-shifting cultural values."[20] Over time, these functions continued to evolve, as Americans broadened their understanding of "community" and "citizenship" to include people often ignored—or worse, discriminated against—during the previous era.

Librarians Create a Profession

The year 1876 marked several milestones in the development of librarianship. In that year, leading librarians formed the American Library Association (ALA) and founded the *Library Journal*, librarianship's first regular publication.[21] Librarians began to think of themselves as colleagues in a wider professional system and proposed standard service principles. A central figure was Melvil Dewey (1851–1931), creator of the Dewey Decimal Classification system, founding member of ALA, and first editor of *Library Journal*. These principles were systematically transmitted to the next generation through library education, which began in 1887 with formal classes at Columbia College under Dewey's direction and as apprenticeship schemes in large public libraries. No federal funding for libraries yet existed, but following Dewey's example in New York State, some states were establishing library commissions or state libraries to provide advice to local communities.

> **Did You Know?**
>
> The ALA's motto, coined by Melvil Dewey and adopted in 1879, was "the best reading for the largest number at the least cost," and helped librarians see themselves as mediators of wholesome literature.

PART 2: TWENTIETH CENTURY–EARLY TWENTY-FIRST CENTURY: GROWTH AND DEVELOPMENT

By 1900, the building blocks of the library profession were in place, and topics that would preoccupy librarians for much of the new century were already matters of professional concern. Developments in communication technology, such as the telegraph and telephone, and increased speed of print production and distribution were influencing how librarians did their work and what services they could offer. The twentieth century saw many changes in these technologies, but many of the systems that eventually harnessed them were evident in the early 1900s.

New Technologies Lead to Information Overload

Information overload was already a concern. In 1924, William S. Learned noted a "phenomenal improvement in speed and accuracy of communication," and complained that even the "trained student" found examining an unfamiliar topic "almost prohibitive" in terms of time.[22] His suggested solution was a "central intelligence service" that would provide not only "'polite' literature," but also information for commercial and vocational fields.[23] Essential elements already existed in such public libraries as that of Cleveland, Ohio: open shelves, adult education, children's and youth services, and branches and delivery stations in schools and neighborhoods. Other specialized services included the Business

Library at Newark, New Jersey, the Teachers' Library in Indianapolis, and technology departments in cities like Detroit and Pittsburgh.[24] At the same time, corporations and government agencies were also beginning to set up specialized information services. In the early 1900s, for example, Wisconsin's Charles McCarthy set up the first Legislative Reference Library as a state agency, an idea that spread to other states and prompted Congress to establish the Legislative Reference Service in 1914.[25]

Libraries Develop Creative Solutions to Serve New User Groups

Public libraries were reaching out to new user groups. Some library commissions sent out traveling libraries—boxes of books deposited in homes, stores, and post offices, some in foreign languages— to reach readers in remote areas. The first horse-drawn bookmobiles were in operation in the early 1900s, and quickly became motorized as vehicles and road systems developed.[26] Public libraries had generally excluded children under the age of twelve, but in the 1880s and 1890s, Caroline Hewins and Anne Carroll Moore led a new field in which librarians managed specially designed children's rooms and services such as storytelling. Librarians became cultural authorities in the rapidly growing area of children's publishing.[27] Librarians also worked enthusiastically to "assimilate" European immigrants. Large urban libraries routinely collected books in foreign languages; by 1913, 10 percent of the New York Public Library's holdings were printed in twenty-five foreign languages.[28] Even in the sparsely populated West, librarians provided foreign-language materials to reach diverse audiences.[29]

But African Americans, Native Americans, and Asian immigrants were still poorly served. In Chicago, it was 1931 before the largely African American South Side acquired the George Cleveland Hall branch, led by the Chicago Public Library's first black library director, Vivian G. Harsh.[30] In the 1940s, about 44 percent of whites living in thirteen Southern states had access to free library service, but the percentage for black Americans was less than half that, and the services themselves were generally much inferior.[31]

Expanded Financial and Legal Infrastructure

Dependent on local taxes, many public libraries struggled for funding and reached a crisis with the onset of the Great Depression in 1929. The advent of the New Deal persuaded ALA that federal funding was the answer because many libraries benefited from the 1935 creation of the Works Progress Administration (WPA).[32] In Kentucky, "pack horse librarians" distributed books in remote mountain areas.[33] In New York City, workers ran open-air reading spaces and bookmobile services, and in Philadelphia, workers contributed five million cards to a union catalog project.[34] Following World War II (1941–1945), ALA repeatedly tried to persuade Congress to allocate federal funds to state public library initiatives. Finally, in 1956, the Library Services Act (LSA) funded books, salaries, and equipment (but not buildings or land) in mostly rural communities. In the following five years, over two hundred new bookmobiles served rural schools as well as the general public.[35] But the stock of library buildings was aging. In 1964, the LSA was renewed as the Library Services and Construction Act (LSCA) and renewed again in 1996 as the Library Services and Technology Act (LSTA), reflecting a shift to buildings and then to bytes. Federal e-rate (or Universal Service) legislation also passed in 1996, setting a discounted rate for network connections to libraries and schools.[36] In 1995, the Bill and Melinda Gates Foundation helped provide computers to public libraries in disadvantaged areas and extended the program in 1997 to all state-library certified public libraries that served low-income communities.[37]

Libraries Develop Collaborative Units

At the state or county level, libraries combined to form large collaborative units, such as multicounty library systems, to increase efficiencies and save money. However, in the late 1970s, a new threat to local funding escalated: a tax revolt that originally emerged out of Southern white resistance to desegregation and spread to the rest of the United States.[38] In Fresno County, California, for example, LSCA money bought a bookmobile to serve mostly Mexican American farmworkers in the San Joaquin Valley, but with the passage of a tax-cutting proposition in 1978, "La Biblioteca Ambulante" suffered successive budget cuts. In 1989, Owen Smith, one of only two remaining part-time assistants who also worked half-time with the Corrections Department, commented, "What I see in the jail is . . . the result of migrants not being able to acquire the information they need to learn English, to learn to read, and to cope with the system adequately. A lot of library work can be done for what it costs to keep someone in jail for a year."[39]

Libraries Promote Intellectual Freedom

Librarians gradually moved away from prescriptively steering patrons toward "wholesome" reading and instead promoted an embrace of intellectual freedom (see also chapter 35: "Intellectual Freedom"). During World War I, librarians had actively censored collections, as anti-German sentiment resulted in the outright suppression of German-language reading materials.[40] During the 1930s, however, they had begun to oppose censorship, passing the first version of the Library Bill of Rights in 1939, and in the postwar period they resisted McCarthyism. In the mid-1960s, ALA opened its Office of Intellectual Freedom, with the aim of helping librarians and others withstand censorship, while educating the public about the right to read.[41] But some librarians practiced passive censorship, and issues of intellectual freedom continued to present others with professional moral dilemmas as their support for intellectual freedom clashed with local demands for restrictions, especially on books for children.[42] Librarians also debated whether their role should be primarily consumerist (give them what they want) or educative (give them what they need). In the 1970s, libraries learned to acknowledge the importance of the "library in the life of the user" rather than the "user in the life of the library."[43]

Libraries Embrace Multicultural Values

Passage of the LSCA fit well with President Lyndon Johnson's Great Society initiative, which, with the Civil Rights movement of the 1950s and 1960s, encouraged a fundamental shift toward embracing multicultural values in libraries. Children's services led the way. In the 1930s, Charlemae Hill Rollins, an African American children's librarian, had issued a call for children's books that reflected black children in a positive light.[44] In the 1960s and 1970s, African Americans in the South fought successfully to desegregate public libraries.[45] In the 1970s and 1980s, public librarians serving adults as well as children began to learn the language of diversity (see also chapter 4: "Diverse Information Needs" and chapter 5: "Diversity, Equality of Access, and Social Justice"), although not all agreed that it was valuable.[46]

Reenvisioning School and Academic Libraries

In the postwar period, thousands of small school districts consolidated, and in the larger multigrade schools, school libraries became the norm (see also chapter 6: "Literacy and Media Centers: School Libraries"). With passage of the GI Bill, which made college affordable to millions of veterans, and the increase in research activity, colleges and universities vastly expanded their programs and facilities, including their libraries (see also chapter 7: "Learning and Research Institutions: Academic Libraries"). New teaching methods reflected the emphasis on research, as federal funds for science, engineering, and technology flowed onto campuses during the 1960s and early 1970s. Academic libraries adopted user-friendly policies, like open stacks, unrestricted circulation, and group meeting spaces. Although the financial situation worsened from the late 1970s on, libraries maintained their newly valued status on campus, becoming showcases to attract students (and their parents) in an era of increasing inter-institutional competition.

Education for Librarianship Is Transformed

Colleges and universities became the sole providers of education for librarianship, and between 1961 and 1976, twenty-three new schools were founded. However, between 1978 and 1991, fifteen schools closed.[47] In the 1970s, library schools began to incorporate the term "information" into their titles, and more schools followed in the 1980s, adopting the phrase "library and information science" (or "studies," LIS). By the mid-1990s, some LIS schools were beginning to drop the "L word" and to form the iSchool movement.[48]

Libraries Become Early Adopters of New Information Technologies

Academic libraries quickly adopted new information technologies; in 1967, for example, a group formed Ohio College Library Center (OCLC, now the Online Computer Library Center).[49] OCLC developed into a worldwide cooperative cataloging and bibliographic utility that emblemized a growing dependence on interlibrary collaboration in the second half of the twentieth century. Flat or declining budgets combined with rising costs meant that research libraries could not succeed without adaptation, for example, by forming groups like the HathiTrust, a consortium of research libraries. Founded in 2008, this consortium now provides access to digitized content of over thirteen million volumes through collaboration that allows libraries to benefit from each other's collections and from economies of scale.[50]

> **Check This Out**
>
> HathiTrust, founded in 2008, now provides access to digitized content of over thirteen million volumes through collaboration that allows libraries to benefit from each other's collections and from economies of scale. *Visit:* https://www.hathitrust.org/.

As libraries depended increasingly on electronic formats for their collections, librarians became experts in data management and licensing systems. Outraged at soaring access prices, especially for scientific journals, librarians promoted open access, for example, through SPARC (Scholarly Publishing and Academic Resources Coalition).[51] In the early twenty-first century, libraries facilitated mobile use of information through first wired and then wireless access to electronic resources but still invested heavily in space for physical texts and their readers (see also chapter 33: "Open Access").

The Library without Walls

In the 1990s, public libraries started offering web-based information services accessible to patrons in remote locations. This trend intensified in the 2000s, as libraries adopted mobile and cloud technologies. But appreciation of and investment in libraries as community spaces persists, as innovations such as makerspaces have taken their place beside longer-standing services to walk-in patrons (see also chapter 18: "Creation Culture and Makerspaces"). Cities large and small continued to build libraries. In Chicago, the city constructed a new downtown library

> " Appreciation of and investment in libraries as community spaces persists, as innovations such as makerspaces have taken their place beside longer-standing services to walk-in patrons. "

in 1991 and saw its investment rewarded in higher circulation as well as higher in-library use. The Chicago Public Library also built new branches.

A New Role for Libraries: Information Literacy

As academic library collections shifted emphasis to electronic resources and the internet became more accessible to students, academic libraries led the way in establishing a new subfield of librarianship: information literacy (see also chapter 16: "Teaching Users: Information and Technology Instruction").

Public librarians, too, accepted the need for information literacy among the general population, and some states began to identify information literacy as a key competency for all K–12 students. Librarians frequently appealed for justification to values for citizen empowerment and democracy. In 2000, the Association of College and Research Libraries (ACRL) Information Literacy Competency Standards for Higher Education (see online supplement), for example, included the goal of creating "a more informed citizenry." Far from setting up the long-dead William Bentley as an ideal, they were referring to skills of critical evaluation, efficient access, and understanding ethical aspects of information use.[52] Informed citizenship seemed as important in the early twenty-first century as was the case in the early nineteenth and twentieth centuries.

> " Public librarians, too, accepted the need for information literacy among the general population, and some states began to identify information literacy as a key competency for all K–12 students. "

CONCLUSION

Through digital technologies, libraries have become increasingly connected to each other and to their far-flung patrons and now contribute to a knowledge infrastructure with global reach. Libraries also find that patrons continue to prize their spaces as a vital contribution to the public life of their local communities. Despite these significant roles, information organizations continue to have to justify both their existence and their operating principles, to balance competing needs, and above all to be knowledgeable about changing technological, social and cultural, economic, and environmental conditions. As always, a key to their institutional success is an information profession composed of individuals who are skilled, knowledgeable, flexible, and ethical, and who can effectively demonstrate the institution's value to funders, voters, and other community stakeholders.

NOTES

1. Paul N. Edwards, *A Vast Machine: Computer Models, Climate Data, and the Politics of Global Warming* (Cambridge, MA: MIT Press, 2010), xvi; 8–9. See also "Knowledge Structures: Intellectual Frameworks and Research Challenges," http://knowledgeinfrastructures.org/.

2. Richard D. Brown, "William Bentley and the Ideal of Universal Information in the Enlightened Republic," in *Knowledge Is Power: The Diffusion of Information in Early America, 1700–1865* (New York: Oxford University Press, 1989), 197–217.

3. Dean Groszins and Leon Jackson, "Colleges and Print Culture," in *An Extensive Republic: Print, Culture, and Society in the New Nation*, ed. Robert A. Gross and Mary Kelley (Chapel Hill: University of North Carolina Press, 2010), 322.

4. Neil Radford, *The Carnegie Corporation and the Development of American Academic Libraries, 1928–1941* (Chicago: American Library Association, 1984), 14.

5. David S. Shields, "Eighteenth-Century Literary Culture," in *The Colonial Book in the Atlantic World*, ed. Hugh Amory and David D. Hall (Chapel Hill: University of North Carolina Press, 2007), 474–75.

6. Jesse Shera, *Foundations of the Public Library: The Origins of the Public Library Movement in New England, 1629–1855* (Chicago: University of Chicago Press, 1949), 69; Kenneth E. Carpenter, "Libraries," in *An Extensive Republic: Print, Culture, and Society in the New Nation*, ed. Robert A. Gross and Mary Kelley (Chapel Hill: University of North Carolina Press, 2010), 279.

7. Elizabeth McHenry, "'An Association of Kindred Spirits': Black Readers and Their Reading Rooms," in *Institutions of Reading: The Social Life of Libraries in the United States*, ed. Thomas Augst and Kenneth Carpenter (Amherst: University of Massachusetts Press, 2007), 107.

8. Carpenter, "Libraries," 278.

9. Haynes McMullen, *American Libraries before 1876* (Westport, CT: Greenwood, 2000), 124–25.

10. Sidney Ditzion, *Arsenals of a Democratic Culture: A Social History of the Public Library Movement in New England and the Middle States from 1850 to1900* (Chicago: American Library Association, 1947), 30, http://archive.org/stream/arsenalsofademoc006465mbp/arsenalsofademoc006465mbp_djvu.txt.

11. For an account of the public library's role in one such community, see Christine Pawley, *Reading on the Middle Border: The Culture of Print in Late Nineteenth-Century Osage, Iowa* (Amherst: University of Massachusetts Press, 2001), esp. 61–116.

12. Douglas Raber, *Librarianship and Legitimacy: The Ideology of the Public Library Inquiry* (Westport, CT: Greenwood Press, 1997), 39, 67.

13. Wayne A. Wiegand, *Main Street Public Library: Community Places and Reading Spaces in the Rural Heartland, 1876–1956* (Iowa City: University of Iowa Press, 2011), 148.

14. Paula D. Watson, "Founding Mothers: The Contribution of Women's Organizations to Public Library Development in the United States," *Library Quarterly* 64, no. 3 (1994): 233–69, http://www.jstor.org/stable/4308944.

15. William. F. Poole, "Progress of Library Architecture," *Library Journal* 7, no. 134 (1882): 1908–9.

16. Walter Muir Whitehill, *Boston Public Library: A Centennial History* (Cambridge, MA: Harvard University Press, 1956), 195.

17. Chicago Public Library, *38th Annual Report* (1909–1910): 17.

18. Chicago Public Library, *42nd Annual Report* (1913–1914): 23, 27–28.

19. Abigail Van Slyck, *Free to All: Carnegie Libraries and American Culture, 1890–1920* (Chicago: University of Chicago Press, 1995), 34–40.

20. Wiegand, *Main Street Public Library*, 186. See also his *Part of Our Lives: A People's History of the American Public Library* (New York: Oxford University Press, 2015), 265.

21. American Library Association, http://www.ala.org/; *Library Journal* (online version only): http://lj.library journal.com/.

22. William S. Learned, *The American Public Library and the Diffusion of Knowledge* (New York: Harcourt, Brace and Co., 1924), 8, 12, https://archive.org/details/americanpublicli007473mbp.

23. Ibid., 12.

24. Ibid., see especially chapter 2, "The Tax-Supported Public Library as an Agency for the Systematic Diffusion of Knowledge among Adults," 26–56.

25. Paul D. Healey, "Go and Tell the World: Charles R. McCarthy and the Evolution of the Legislative Reference Movement, 1901–1917," *Law Library Journal* 99, no. 1 (2007): 36, http://www.aallnet.org/main-menu/Publications/llj/LLJ-Archives/Vol-99/pub_llj_v99n01/2007-02.pdf.

26. Christine Pawley, *Reading Places: Literacy, Democracy, and the Public Library in Cold War America* (Amherst: University of Massachusetts Press, 2010), 68–72.

27. Anne Lundin, "Anne Carroll Moore: 'I Have Spun Out a Long Thread,'" in *Reclaiming the American Library Past: Writing the Women In*, ed. Suzanne Hildenbrand (Norwood, NJ: Ablex, 1996), 187–204.

28. Dee Garrison, *Apostles of Culture: The Public Librarian and American Society, 1876–1920* (Madison: University of Wisconsin Press, 2003), 217.

29. Joanne E. Passet, *Cultural Crusaders: Women Librarians in the American West, 1900–1917* (Albuquerque: University of New Mexico Press, 1994), 154.

30. Laura Burt, "Vivian Harsh, Adult Education, and the Library's Role as Community Center," *Libraries & the Cultural Record* 44, no. 2 (2009): 234–55.

31. Eliza Atkins Gleason, *The Southern Negro and the Public Library: A Study of the Government and Administration of Public Library Service to Negroes in the South* (Chicago: University of Chicago Press, 1941).

32. "The New Deal," *United States History*, last modified August 9, 2014, http://www.u-s-history.com/pages/h1851.html.

33. Donald C. Boyd, "The Book Women of Kentucky: The WPA Pack Horse Library Project, 1935–1943," *Libraries and the Cultural Record* 42, no. 2 (2007): 111–28.

34. Martha H. Swain, "A New Deal in Libraries: Federal Relief Work and Library Service, 1933–43," *Libraries & Culture* 30, no. 3 (Summer 1995): 268–70.

35. Pawley, *Reading Places*, 259–60.

36. "Universal Service," *Federal Communications Commission*, last updated September 30, 2014, https://www.fcc.gov/general/universal-service.

37. John Carlo Bertot, Charles R. McClure, and Joe Ryan, "Impact of External Technology Funding Programs for Public Libraries: A Study of LSTA, E-rate, Gates, and others," *Public Libraries* 41, no. 3 (May/June 2002): 166–71.

38. Kevin M. Kruse, *White Flight: Atlanta and the Making of Modern Conservatism* (Princeton, NJ: Princeton University Press, 2007).

39. Rachael Naismith, "Library Service to Migrant Farm Workers," *Library Journal* 114, no. 4 (1989): 54.

40. Wayne A. Wiegand, *An Active Instrument for Propaganda: The American Public Library during World War I* (New York: Greenwood, 1989).

41. Louise S. Robbins, *Censorship and the American Library: The American Library Association's Response to Threats to Intellectual Freedom, 1939–1969* (Westport, CT: Greenwood, 1996), esp. chapters 3 and 4.

42. Emily Knox, "The Challengers of West Bend: The Library as a Community Institution," in *Libraries and the Reading Public in Twentieth Century America*, ed. Christine Pawley and Louise S. Robbins (Madison: University of Wisconsin Press, 2013).

43. Douglas L. Zweizig, "Predicting Amount of Library Use: An Empirical Study of the Public Library in the Life of the Adult Public" (PhD diss., Syracuse University, 1973).

44. Charlemae Hill Rollins, *We Build Together: A Reader's Guide to Negro Life and Literature for Elementary and High School Use* (Chicago: National Council for Teachers of English, 1941).

45. Cheryl Knott, *Not Free, Not for All: Public Libraries in the Age of Jim Crow* (Amherst: University of Massachusetts Press, 2015).

46. See, for example, Julia Stephens, "English Spoken Here," *American Libraries* 38, no. 10 (November 2007): 41, 43–44.

47. Margaret F. Stieg, *Change and Challenge in Library and Information Science Education* (Chicago: American Library Association, 1991), 28–29.

48. For information about the iSchools organization, see "iSchools: Leading and Promoting the Information Field," http://ischools.org/; for a historical overview of the development of education for librarianship, see Christine Pawley, "'Missionaries of the Book,' or 'Central Intelligence' Agents: The Contest for Library Education in Twentieth-Century America," *Libraries: Culture, History and Society* 1, no. 1 (2017): 72–96.

49. See https://www.oclc.org/en/home.html.
50. John P. Wilkin, "Meanings of the Library Today," in *The Meaning of the Library: A Cultural History*, ed. Alice Crawford (Princeton, NJ: Princeton University Press, 2015), 244–49.
51. Scholarly Publishing and Academic Resources Coalition, https://sparcopen.org/.
52. Association of College and Research Libraries (ACRL), "Information Literacy Competency Standards for Higher Education," last modified July 12, 2014, http://www.ala.org/acrl/standards/informationliteracy competency.

3

Librarianship

A CONTINUOUSLY EVOLVING PROFESSION

Stephen Abram

Chapter 3, "Librarianship: A Continuously Evolving Profession," highlights the many trends that impact information professionals today and emphasizes how information professionals must continuously adapt to change. As head of Lighthouse Consulting and with his background in leadership in special library organizations, Stephen Abram provides needed insight for information organizations as they adapt and evolve in response to the evolutionary trends of the late twentieth and early twenty-first centuries.

Some changes, notes Abram, are easy to see, such as new technology, while other changes, such as social behaviors that impact information organizations, are harder to identify. A key challenge for information organizations today is that they serve a hybrid world where some people prefer the old ways and others race forward to new modes of behavior. Cooperation on a sustainable and scalable basis is another significant challenge emphasized by Abram.

Key professional competencies addressed by Abram include leadership, strategic planning, an understanding of the economic context, and the ability to embrace change. Abram not only concludes chapter 3 with an emphasis on the importance of lifelong learning but also provides the reader a wealth of essential resources, such as lists of LIS reports, statistical datasets for information organizations, and recommended readings. These resources are further extended in the online supplement.

★   ★   ★

Throughout history, libraries and other types of information organizations have continuously adapted to changing environments and technology—with collections evolving from scrolls to the codex, card catalogs to online catalogs, print indexes to full-text databases, and in-person reference support to virtual reference services. Add in huge interventions starting from the fringes (e.g., the internet, e-mail, social media, etc.), and you see adaptation and evolution on a very large international scale. As societies have grappled with the pressing issues of their time and place, information organizations have wrestled with those same challenges (e.g., should information organizations be places where racial segregation is practiced?). Information organizations today continue to adapt and evolve, not just as reflections of the changes in society but also as thought leaders in their communities and as places of research that drive those changes (see also chapter 2: "Libraries, Communities, and Information: Two Centuries of Experience").

This chapter explores the evolutionary trends of information organizations and information professionals in the late twentieth and early twenty-first centuries. After completing this chapter, the reader should have an understanding of how information professionals must continuously adapt to change—not only for survival but also to thrive as agents of change.

A "change agent" is anyone who helps an organization or community transform by improving business and learning processes and personal and professional interactions (see also chapter 20: "Change Management"). These changes expand beyond e-books and the web by representing a fundamental challenge to the underpinnings of the profession's values and the basic business models and missions of information organizations.

While technology gets most of the attention when change is discussed, the main thrust of change in information communities is human behavior. Some changes are easy to see, such as new technology, while other changes, such as social behaviors that impact information organizations (e.g., web-savvy users who demand virtual access to resources), are harder to identify. Despite its complexity, change is important to the history of information organizations. As a wise person once said, dinosaurs did not die out because of climate change; they died out because they failed to adapt. A key challenge for information organizations is that they serve a hybrid world where some people prefer the old ways and others race forward to new modes of behavior. Libraries must have a foothold in all camps to succeed.

CHANGE AND ADAPTATION IN THE INFORMATION PROFESSION

The history of the information profession is characterized by the need to adapt to change. People who act as catalysts for change have five basic philosophies or skills: they have a clear vision, are patient yet persistent, ask tough questions, are knowledgeable and lead by example, and maintain strong relationships built on trust.[1] Historically, change was easier to adapt to, since changes took place over a longer period, and society and technology did not transform as rapidly as they do today. For example, it took centuries for the book format, global literacy, and universal education to spread widely, and, indeed, more modern technologies such as television and the telephone took many decades to widely penetrate the market. Such is not the case today, with technological changes moving across the globe in mere years. And with each technological change, human behavior also changes—changes that can no longer be defined by generation.

> Information professionals used to have time to respond and evolve, but the information revolution is just that—a revolution where things change rapidly. This ever-evolving environment requires a stronger set of competencies and leadership skills to steer the institution and its staff.

Information professionals used to have time to respond and evolve, but the information revolution is just that—a revolution where things change rapidly. This ever-evolving environment requires a stronger set of competencies and leadership skills to steer the institution and its staff. Bureaucratic processes, which have traditionally comprised best practices in the public sector to protect the public purse, have become the enemy of nimbleness, which is needed in this environment. Especially for those who work in the public sector, there is a need for cultural change within the information organization. Proactivity instead of reactivity is one place to start. Information professionals need to do more than just see the changes currently happening; they need to get out in front of them—forecasting what is to come and proactively moving ahead to adapt to these changes.

There are dynamic tensions in the information field between conservative approaches to change and a more aggressive approach. Balancing these tensions and having the ability to identify trends and adapt to change are rare and important attributes of leaders in the information profession (see also chapter 37: "Leadership Skills for Today's Global Information Landscape"). Some of the critical and difficult questions that the profession's leaders struggle with every day include:

- What trends are "real," and which ones are fads?
- Which trends are relevant to information organizations and worth an investment of time and effort to explore?
- Which trends are more important than others, and how do information professionals set priorities?
- What strategies can be used to bring staff, management, and communities along the curve of innovation, especially when the future opportunities and threats are clear to some but not to others?

There are definite benefits to spotting trends early. As an example, those who saw the internet, mobile devices, or smartphones as opportunities early in their transformation were better prepared to respond to these trends. Similarly, the profession's innovators who jumped in with both feet to the Second Life 3-D immersive environment or QR codes gained experience that helped them evaluate future gamification, geo-location, near-field communication (such as iBeacons for mobile phones), and 3-D learning environments. Today, for example, information professionals experiment with drones, Apple iBeacons,[2] and gamification with augmented and virtual reality, visualization tools, and linked data. Each will follow its own arc; some will reach mass adoption, and some will be evolutionary distractions. Learning happens every step of the way, and the learning curve is usually too steep to start late.

The right strategy is to explore opportunities and take risks in a careful and controlled way through betas, pilots, experiments, and trials. One strategy is to work in partnership with vendors as they research and experiment. Another is to work through associations, collaboratives, and consortia to share the expense, effort, and risk with others. Information professionals can also pilot new ideas with small groups of targeted end users to get feedback on their ideas and innovations.

THE VALUE OF THE INFORMATION PROFESSIONAL

Two things help professionals choose to evolve: a focus on the core values that never change, and knowledge regarding the distinct value they deliver better than anyone else in their community.

Information professionals are fundamentally about transforming lives. Information professionals who focus on information transactions, such as circulating books and DVDs or answering in-person reference questions, are missing the opportunity to communicate the true contributions they provide to their communities. Information organizations should not define themselves solely based on their collections and services (e.g., web search engines, e-books, podcasts). Instead, the focus should be on the impact of information professionals on people's lives. As such, the role of information professionals continues to evolve beyond the physical setting to one where they are positioned as drivers of change. Information professionals must continue to serve as advocates on important issues, such as the right to read, academic and intellectual freedom, digital rights and copyright, and censorship (see also chapter 28: "Advocacy").

> The role of information professionals continues to evolve beyond the physical setting to one where they are positioned as drivers of change. Information professionals must continue to serve as advocates on important issues, such as the right to read, academic and intellectual freedom, digital rights and copyright, and censorship.

Stephen Abram

DRIVERS OF EVOLUTION

To what extent are information organizations aligned with user expectations, trends, and best practices? What must change to better position the information organization to face the challenges of the next ten to fifteen years and to ensure that the organization continues to be a relevant and meaningful community institution? These are critical questions to consider in ensuring that the information profession continues to evolve and thrive in the future (see also chapter 4: "Diverse Information Needs").

One way to critically assess the organization's capacity to anticipate and respond to a changing world is through strategic planning (see also chapter 19: "Strategic Planning"). Strategic planning is about abandoning outdated practices and embracing change. A strategic plan needs to chart a bold new direction for the organization that is consistent with the changing needs of users (and, perhaps more importantly, nonusers) so it will be a useful tool for predicting and managing future service delivery.

A key component for planning for change is to review the economic context. There are macroeconomic trends that are big, global trends that affect information organizations, such as recessions, depressions, and stock market changes. There are microeconomic trends that are local, municipal, state, or national trends that affect information organizations closer to home, such as natural disasters, political changes in state and local government, and immigration/demographic changes. There are also economic changes on the organizational level, such as changes in executive leadership, mergers and acquisitions, or fiscal revenue or sales success. Regardless of their origin, each trend requires a thoughtful response. As is discussed later in the chapter, information professionals need to position the information organization effectively as having an important impact on the parent organization's decision making and not just be viewed as a cost center. Forecasting the economic context of the organization or community will deliver insights regarding the strategic direction that the organization's decision makers need to consider.

> " A strategic plan needs to chart a bold new direction for the organization that is consistent with the changing needs of users (and, perhaps more importantly, nonusers) so it will be a useful tool for predicting and managing future service delivery. "

Looking at the big picture, major changes to the information profession are already taking place. The functions and roles of information organizations are changing with the surge of information and technologies. These organizations are no longer simply "warehouses" for print material that is borrowed by residents for off-site use—if they ever really were. Increasingly, these organizations are information, program, and cultural centers supporting a wide range of community, business, or research activities and objectives. The way people are using information is also shifting, with physical access plateauing and remote access increasing. The function and design of information organizations are evolving in response to these changing roles and demographic shifts, emerging technologies, and increasing consumer expectations for what they want out of the organization's service portfolio.[3]

Looking specifically at the significant trends affecting information professionals and organizations today, these changes are grouped into three areas as demonstrated in table 3.1.

Lifestyle and societal trends have significant implications for ways that information organizations need to evolve. For example, changes in family structures and dynamics (the rise of nontraditional family structures, the declining predominance of two-working-parent households, a rise in commuter lifestyles, increased urbanization, and shared households) have implications for information organizations in terms of hours of operation, asynchronous (virtual) programming, and the delivery of programs and services both within and outside their physical location.[4] (See appendix 3.1: "Lifestyle and Societal Trends" for a more comprehensive explanation of these trends.)

Table 3.1. Significant Trends Affecting the Information Profession.

Lifestyle and Society Trends	Technology Trends	Facility and Service Trends

Accessibility
Digital Divide
Discretionary Time Deficit
Desired Use of Leisure Time
Environmental ("Green")
  Concerns
Family Structure and
  Dynamics
Health and Wellness
Immigration
Information Literacy
Labor Trends
Partnership and Collaboration
"Smart" Device Expectations
Web-Savvy Users
	Online Learning
	Wireless Expectations
	Digital Download Kiosks
	Mobile Device Arena
	Live-Streaming
	E-Book Readership
	User-Created Content
	"Cloud" Computing
	Computer Training Space
	3-D Printers
	Virtual Libraries
		Libraries Are Destinations
		Multiservice
		Community Engagement
		Makerspaces
		Little Free Libraries
		Customer-First Focus

Technology trends are constantly and rapidly developing, making them hard to predict. One key trend, the growth of online learning and open education resources (OER), has created issues that, to date, have largely affected academic libraries (see also chapter 7: "Learning and Research Institutions: Academic Libraries"). However, e-learning is starting to influence services in public libraries too. For example, in the United States, the Los Angeles Public Library (LAPL)[5] system offers a fully accredited online high school with full credits, diplomas, and graduations. LAPL provides a wonderful resource that offers users access to e-learning programs for adults and high school students and makes a huge difference at the individual level of impact (see appendix 3.2: "Technology Trends" for a more comprehensive explanation of these trends).

Facility and service trends point to an information organization that is much more integrated into the affairs of the community. The makerspace movement (see also chapter 18: "Creation Culture and Makerspaces") is a good example of trends in this category, with information organizations providing spaces for users to collaborate, learn hands-on skills, and create and produce something such as music, videos, jewelry, games, robotics, and electronics (see appendix 3.3: "Facility and Service Trends" for a more comprehensive explanation of these trends).

FORECAST: EMERGING TRENDS AND ISSUES

The future trends and issues mentioned above will require information professionals to remain forward thinking—both for their organizations as well as their professional development. How will information professionals evolve and adapt in the coming years?

In his report, *Confronting the Future*, Roger Levien addresses the major issues facing information organizations and provides a framework for envisioning the future (see figure 3.1). Levien introduces four "dimensions," each of which consists of a continuum of choices that lie between two extremes.[6]

While the framework was specifically designed for public libraries, these dimensions can also be applied to other information organizations (see also chapter 6: "Literacy and Media Centers: School Libraries," chapter 7: "Learning and Research Institutions: Academic Libraries," and chapter 9: "Working in Different Information Environments: Special Libraries and Information Centers"). To meet the challenges they will face in the future, information organizations must make strategic

4 Dimensions for Envisioning the

Future of Information Organizations

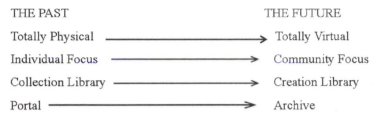

THE PAST | THE FUTURE
Totally Physical ⟶ Totally Virtual
Individual Focus ⟶ Community Focus
Collection Library ⟶ Creation Library
Portal ⟶ Archive

Figure 3.1 Four Dimensions for Envisioning the Future of Information Organizations. *Adapted from Roger Levien, "Confronting the Future: Strategic Visions for the 21st Century Public Library,"* American Library Association Policy Brief, *no. 4 (2011).*

choices concerning their place on each of the four dimensions identified by Levien. These four dimensions are described below.

Dimension 1: Physical to Virtual

This dimension relates to the form of the information organization as a facility and to the format of its collection. On one end of this spectrum is a purely physical organization; however, this sort of organization is no longer considered realistic. On the other end is the virtual organization—a space on the web that hosts all of the organization's services and collections and is accessible to users through the organization's web presence anywhere over the internet. On this spectrum, most modern libraries are somewhere in the middle, still offering a physical building and collection, while increasingly providing virtual features, such as e-books and online services.

Dimension 2: Individual Focus to Community Focus

This second dimension relates to the type of service provided by the information organization and the point of focus for its users. The extremes, in this case, are individual-focused organizations and community-focused organizations. Organizations that focus on the individual seek to accommodate each user independently with quiet study space, privacy, comfort, and minimal distractions. In this scenario, the primary relationship is between the information professional and the individual user. Those organizations that focus on the community look to provide space for community interaction and group work. These organizations, often identified as "community centers," invest considerable resources in a broad range of services, events, and programs that engage the community. They also often contain archives of local records, artifacts, memoirs, and memorabilia.

Dimension 3: Collection to Creation

This third dimension relates to how information organizations interact with and engage their users. On one end of the spectrum is the collection-focused organization, where users come to enjoy and experience the materials in the organization's collection. This organization is a repository of intellectual and recreational information available for the user to explore. The other extreme is an organization where, instead of simply exploring the works of others, users are encouraged to see the organization as a creative space where equipment and facilities are provided to produce their own creative products.

Librarianship

Dimension 4: Portal to Archive

This fourth dimension of Levien's report relates to the ownership of the collection. In the portal model, the materials available to users are not the property of the information organization. Instead, the information organization acts as a facilitator between the user and resources that are available through other organizations. On the other end of the spectrum is an archive model, where the information organization's role is to possess documentary materials in a range of genres and mediums. In the archive model, the information organization has an important role in assembling and disseminating local information (and not simply historical information). This information organization is a living community resource that tells the community's story—past, present, and future.

> Planning and implementing successful strategies that span and engage the digitally literate and nonliterate, technology aware and technology phobic, and cover diverse kids, teens, and adults are big challenges.

Today's information leaders are not just managing organizations stacked with books and reference materials, but something far more complex and complicated. Leaders must now manage a hybrid organization with a market of users who display infinite levels of diversity (see also chapter 5: "Diversity, Equity of Access, and Social Justice"). Planning and implementing successful strategies that span and engage the digitally literate and nonliterate, technology aware and technology phobic, and cover diverse kids, teens, and adults are big challenges.

Discussion Questions

Using Levien's typology, where is the library on these continuums today? In your view, where should the library be in ten to fifteen years? How can a strategic plan assist information professionals in repositioning themselves on these continuums?

SUSTAINABILITY OF TWENTY-FIRST-CENTURY INFORMATION ORGANIZATIONS

Some challenges regarding the value and sustainability of information organizations remain—especially in terms of taking risks and influencing decision makers, building cooperative relationships, and ensuring adequate funding. While some information professionals can adapt and evolve to meet the challenges of a changing environment, too many information professionals still shy away from risk, avoid confrontation, and lack strong ties to decision makers. Information professionals must develop the leadership capabilities necessary to thrive in this dynamically changing environment, while encouraging staff to embrace change and fighting the need for too much control in an increasingly ambiguous future (see also chapter 37: "Leadership Skills for Today's Global Information Landscape"). Information professionals also need to develop effective soft-management skills

> Information professionals must develop the leadership capabilities necessary to thrive in this dynamically changing environment, while encouraging staff to embrace change and fighting the need for too much control in an increasingly ambiguous future.

(e.g., vision, influence, presentation skills, professional networking, change and risk management strategies, strategic budgeting, and marketing) to improve their influence and positioning.

Stephen Abram

Another significant challenge is cooperation on a sustainable and scalable basis. Information organizations had a huge vision when the Online Computer Learning Center (OCLC) was created in the 1970s. This not-for-profit collaborative redefined the cataloging and metadata space and is a key part of such services as Amazon and Google Books. However, since then, no other entities have been created and continued on such a global scale to effectively address the challenges of scalability, content creation, systems, apps, websites, and more. For example, initiatives such HathiTrust,[7] Digital Public Library of America,[8] and Europeana[9] show promise but still require maturing to achieve full utility. Consortia struggle with issues of scale. To get the best prices through cooperative buying, they must get bigger and more powerful as they bring information organizations to the table as buyers. The technological changes happening in the information field provide opportunities for consortia to become major infrastructure players for the information sector.

Sustainability of information organizations cannot be discussed without mentioning funding (see also chapter 21: "Managing Budgets"). Unfortunately, recent financial trends typically involve reduced funding for information organizations, while expecting the same level of services, or even expanded services. This situation puts information organizations in a difficult position. The solution to this problem is both complicated and complex. Some organizations and jurisdictions have been able to clearly articulate the case for adequate funding, and, as a result, they have thrived, while some have been forced to reduce services or close due to lack of funding. The long-term solution rests in better communication, advocacy, and relationships with decision makers, as well as efforts to drive productivity enhancements and cost efficiencies (see also chapter 27: "Communication, Marketing, and Outreach Strategies"). For example, initiatives, such as the Political Action Committee for libraries in the United States, have been very successful in public library levy votes, as has the Federation of Ontario Public Libraries Open Media Desk social media campaign. While libraries, for example, tend not to be businesses, they must behave in a businesslike fashion (using expected best practices) in today's public funding environment.

Check This Out

Online Computer Learning Center (OCLC). *Visit:* http://www.oclc.org

Discussion Questions

What trends do you consider important that have not been touched on in this chapter or this book? Are they different for different types of libraries (special, academic, public, school)?

ESSENTIAL RESOURCES TO STAY AHEAD OF THE CURVE

So how can information professionals stay ahead of the curve and avoid fighting fires? How should information professionals learn about the future? It is simple really—*read widely*. Information professionals must engage in continuous environmental scanning to be successful and adaptive—and not just every five years as part of a strategic planning process. While it is important that information professionals read professional development content that comes from library and information science literature and sources, it is equally important that information professionals extend their learning by following publications in focused subject fields (such as user experience, copyright law, etc.) and experts in popular culture, technology, education, and other areas that are of interest. Print is rarely the right medium for exploring trends. Blogs, discussion boards, and conferences are where the real action takes place.

What resources, blogs, readings, strategies, and social media should be in the professional's personal learning network (PLN)? While the real transformative trends tend to happen on the fringes, it is useful to read a variety of resources to gain insight regarding how innovators and early adopters are experimenting and pioneering with new methods, technologies, and ideas. Some examples of quality research organizations that cover the information profession are described below, and additional resources are covered in the book's online supplement.

The NMC Horizon Reports: The NMC Horizon Project charts the landscape of emerging technologies for teaching, learning, research, and creative inquiry annually. Their reports cover trends in higher education, K–12 education, technology, museums, and academic libraries.[10]

Pew Research Center's Internet and American Life Reports: The Pew Research Center's Internet and American Life Project examines how U.S. residents use the internet. They also track trends regarding views on the nation's libraries every year in numerous reports. The project's reports are based on nationwide surveys and qualitative research, including data collected from government agencies, technology firms, academia, and other expert venues.[11]

OCLC Research: OCLC Research is an organization that focuses on helping libraries, archives, museums, and other cultural heritage institutions better understand a range of trends. For example, some of the organization's recent research activities focus on metadata management (LinkedData), technology, user behavior, OER, standards, scholarly publishing, digitization, and collection sharing.[12]

Discussion Questions

What resources are you adding to your PLN—personal learning plan? How much time will you devote daily or weekly to scanning the horizon?

Statistics: There are many primary sources for statistics related to libraries and other types of information organizations, offering a rich source of information to explore (see also chapter 3: "Statistical Datasets for Information Organizations" in the online supplement).

CONCLUSION

Today's information professionals are charged with taking the reins of strategy and leading the charge for change. Hallmarks of dynamic information professionals in the twenty-first century include the ability to envision a better future, manage and lead change, and participate with their "tribe" of like-minded colleagues in building a better future—not just for their organizations but also for all information users. Choosing to make an impact is the first step. The resources described in this chapter can help professionals remain in a mode of lifelong learning—another hallmark of a great information professional. Ultimately, for information professionals to remain what they are—vital and essential hubs of their communities—they must continuously adapt and change to effectively address the ongoing changes in the world around them.

APPENDIX 3.1: LIFESTYLE AND SOCIETAL TRENDS

The following list of lifestyle and societal trends is not intended to be exhaustive, but it provides a flavor of some of the more prevalent trends and emerging issues that may impact information organizations. It is essential to keep an eye on social changes, government policy, and political trends, as issues such as health care, school funding, immigration, or national and state/provincial funding of libraries can create additional burdens on libraries to fill the gap or address the opportunities in increased attention on or funding for library programs and service portfolios.

Accessibility: Accessibility is the umbrella term for the ability to serve all users, including those with visual, auditory, learning, or mobility challenges. These issues will be at the forefront of information service delivery for years to come, especially as equitable access to digital resources increases in importance.

Digital Divide: Digital divide refers to differential access to digital resources and services caused by demographic, economic (poverty), geographic, and other issues. It is a complex issue that encompasses physical access, education, affordability, and more. Information users range from those who are the most intensive and capable web users (e.g., creating websites, writing blogs, uploading videos, and producing digital content) to those who are "inactive" participants who may be online but do not participate in social media or interactive content. Digital, semi-digital, and non-digital users will create tensions in equitable organizational strategies.

Discretionary Time Deficit: Trends over the past ten or more years suggest that "lack of time" continues to be a barrier to participation in all "discretionary" activities, including information usage. The growth in leisure time that was forecast in the 1970s has not materialized, and people are increasingly pressed for time.

Desired Use of Leisure Time: While commentators disagree on the extent to which people will have more leisure time in the future, they predict a significant shift in *how* people will use their leisure time.[13] These projections see a relative decline in traditional recreational activities (team sports, stamp and coin collecting, etc.) and a significant increase in social networking, online entertainment, and virtual experiences in free time. Information organizations need strategies that tie their leisure collections beyond books on hobbies and recreational reading into a diversified program package.

Environmental and "Green" Concerns: There is a heightened awareness among the Millennial market for everything "eco-friendly" and "green." This awareness may have significant implications for all aspects of information service delivery, including facility development and design, program development and delivery, materials development and processing, and information dissemination.

Family Structure and Dynamics: Statistical trends indicate a rise in nontraditional family structures (e.g., single parent, divorced parents, multiple-households, same-sex marriage, etc.), the declining predominance of two-working-parent households, a rise in commuter lifestyles, increased urbanization, and shared households. These dynamics have implications for hours of operation, asynchronous (virtual) programming, and the delivery of library programs and services.[14]

Health and Wellness: These concerns will continue to be a top-of-mind issue/concern to society and an increasing focus of government spending in the coming years. North American society has an aging population with corresponding health and aging issues simultaneously with a very large, young Millennial population in their child-rearing years. Information professionals who can provide accessible, high-quality health/wellness resources, or electronic information or links to other health information providers will be well positioned to meet growing demand for this type of information.

Immigration: New immigrants in search of affordable housing will continue to relocate in communities on the periphery of a country's largest cities. Research has shown that immigrants may have different expectations of information organizations, public and social services, and technology. The public library and its partners will have a key role to play in orienting newcomers to the community and the range of services available. Information organizations are working on new immigrant orientation and partnerships with settlement agencies to drive program awareness and cardholder growth.

Information Literacy: Beyond Reading: Information organizations have a long-standing role in providing access to information and ensuring information literacy (i.e., teaching proficiency in finding information and assessing its relevance, authoritativeness, and value). There is no question about the need for information literacy in an unregulated and ever-expanding digital universe. Information organizations need to develop strategies for information fluency including the full range of digital literacies, reading literacies for all ages, and the ability to sift information for quality and usefulness in a too-much-information world (see also chapter 16: "Teaching Users: Information and Technology Instruction").

Labor Trends: Growing employment opportunities tend to be in knowledge industries in North America including health care, technology/computer systems, professional services, and small/

entrepreneurial businesses. Information organizations that can partner with other agencies to provide training and employment services and other collaborations in these areas will increase their profile and relevance in the community.

Partnership and Collaboration: Organizational partnerships are evolving and expanding, and the organization's role in helping users navigate through the plethora of content and information available will continue to be an important one. Information organizations can make sense of multiple levels of government for citizens and residents to access the services their tax dollars pay for.

Private Schools, Alternative and Charter Schools, and Homeschooling: These options appear to be on the rise. The increased appeal for private schools, alternative and charter schools, and homeschooling imposes a challenge for many information organizations as the support systems for homework and learning. Some U.S. states have passed legislation requiring public schools to support home learners. That said, homework help is a growing part of the service portfolio for many information organizations as school library hours are cut or diminished altogether.

Smart Device Expectations: Smart devices go beyond smartphones and include tablets, phablets, and the internet of things. Those under the age of twenty-five are not "passive recipients" of education, media, or technologies; they learn differently and seek and use information differently than previous generations—having grown up in a twenty-first-century web world. The challenge for information organizations will be to engage the mobile user and adopt responsive design strategies.

Web-Savvy Information Users: Information users are increasingly participating in a variety of internet-based activities: browsing, borrowing, retrieving, downloading, and interacting with web content. Most internet users are experienced web users and have been online for more than five years. These experienced users have higher expectations of all types of information organizations. On the other hand, they may dismiss the need for information organizations altogether if they have an unclear view of how information organizations and information professionals can add value and deliver the goods.

Zoomers: The aging of the population is resulting in a new wave of older adults with different expectations, needs, and interests than the previous generation. Traditionally, seniors have been a key niche segment for many information organizations. This generation of retired baby boomers will demand more, placing pressure on information organizations to meet that challenge.

APPENDIX 3.2: TECHNOLOGY TRENDS

With rapid developments in the field of computers and information technology, predicting the future of technology as it affects information services is particularly challenging. Current trends, however, indicate that access to all forms of information and content will become increasingly associated with smaller, more powerful, and more versatile handheld wireless devices (see also chapter 25: "Managing Technology"). Some current and emerging trends and their implications for information organizations follow:

Online Learning: Although MOOCs (massive open online courses) and OER (open education resources) are creating issues that largely affect academic libraries, increasing opportunities are developing for public libraries. In the United States, many library systems have offered 24/7 learning resources that offer users online learning through access to e-learning programs, including Gale Cengage's *Gale Courses* (online adult e-learning) and their accredited online high school that is offered through public libraries. Lynda.com offers technology training in a scalable way. Many users are not trying for full degrees but are ornamenting their résumés with nanodegrees, technology boot camps, online certificates, and other skills-based learning models.

Wireless Expectations: People expect all public areas, including information organizations, to have free Wi-Fi. Worktables with plug-ins for laptops or other mobile devices will be increasingly needed, and group workspaces wired for laptops are in high demand. Some information organizations are lending wireless hotspots. Some organizations are also taking part in beacon mesh networks throughout their communities or taking advantage of whitespace broadband to lower costs and increase diffusion.

Digital Download Kiosks: Kiosks started as e-vending machines that were placed in areas that could not support a full branch or high traffic areas like bus, train, and transit stations. They required power outlets and a connection to the organization's network. Excitingly, beacons, like Apple's iBeacon, serve as small hotspots that allow users to download e-books, audiobooks, videos, music, and games directly to their smartphones and handheld devices or tablets. Some beacons allow for two-way communications and engagement with users as well as data gathering. Others, like LibraryBox, can create a hotspot with content without the need for electricity or internet access.

Mobile Device Arena: The explosion of mobile device usage is replacing the laptop/desktop model and creating a post-PC era where BYOD, or "Bring Your Own Device," is common.

Increasing Demand for Audio and Video Live-Streaming: These growing demands require reliable high-speed access. Users are increasingly downloading and/or transferring video and audio content to their own devices while video has begun to dominate web traffic. Recommendation systems are proliferating as a way that users make choices. Recent video streaming initiatives from Apple, Facebook, and Amazon are changing the world of video delivery along with micro-video services like Periscope and Snapchat.

Voice Response and Control: A proliferation of voice response communication tools like Apple's Siri, Amazon's Alexa, or Microsoft's Cortana are battling it out for keyboard-free interface.

E-Book Readership and Sales: Recent Pew Research indicates a growing influence of e-book readership.[15] This phenomenon of print versus e-book sales seen over the last few years has started to slow and appears to have reached a plateau indicating that there will be a hybrid market for many more years.

Publishers, Information Organizations, and e-Books: There have been some promising pilots concerning evolving relationships between publishers and information organizations, but the challenges of accessing, owning, leasing, and affording "book" content is still a struggle. The Toronto-based start-ups Wattpad and Rakuten Kobo show the emergence of a large self-publishing portfolio in libraries and beyond.

User Contributions to Content: Information users are not only browsing, borrowing, and downloading, but they are increasingly creating and interacting with content available through the web. The information organization as publisher is a trend in some public libraries.

"Cloud" Computing: Cloud computing continues to be a major technology trend that is moving most content and software into the cloud—especially for public institutions in order to reduce costs of technology ownership. This trend places pressure on information organizations to identify cooperative solutions for information systems innovation and integration—forcing many more library systems into consortial organization structures. It will also create opportunities for greater collaboration on content acquisition and deployment.

Hardware Size Shrinking but Space Needs Growing: Although computer hardware is becoming more compact, the total amount of space for a computer workstation is not significantly reduced.

Computer Training Space and Equipment: The information organization's role as a training center for hands-on instruction in the use of computers, application software, and internet-based resources will continue to grow.

Latest Technology Tools: 3-D printing has now reached the consumer market; consumers can now buy 3-D printers at retailers like Staples. This technology is being implemented in many makerspaces in information organizations (see also chapter 18: "Creation Culture and Makerspaces"). The Maker Movement aligns well with North American science, technology, engineering, arts, mathematics (STEAM) education goals.

Privacy: It is becoming a huge issue in some markets and within library and information science that user privacy data needs protecting, and libraries are a key place to receive privacy and computer safety advice.

Information Organizations as Centers for Technology and Innovation: The advent of the "virtual library" and technology, in general, has changed the way in which core information services are being delivered and will continue to have a major impact on future services (see also chapter 10: "Digital Resources: Digital Libraries"). Information organizations are offering more services online (and doing so at an accelerating rate by taking advantage of consortia to negotiate universal access), including virtual/digital reference services, electronic databases, and e-books. Most libraries find the majority of their usage is now virtual, but the type of usage is different. It is evolving.

APPENDIX 3.3: FACILITY AND SERVICE TRENDS

The facility and service trends discussed in this section are closely interrelated to other trends above. They point to an information organization that is actively integrated into the affairs of the community. It is an outward-looking information organization that is heavily invested in all aspects of community life and very closely linked to other community service providers. The key trends can be briefly listed as follows:

Information Organizations Are Destinations: Placemaking refers both to the process and philosophy of planning and creating a public space within a community—with a lot of thought given to cultural tourism, or "cultural capital," and architectural design.

Information Organizations as Multiservice Providers: Information organizations are increasingly forums for community learning and expression, serving as technological, employment, business development, cultural, art, and heritage centers for their communities. Many European public libraries, such as Aarhus DOK1 in Denmark, DOK in Delft, Netherlands, and the Library of Birmingham, UK, have adopted these models. This trend has started in some North American libraries, for example, in Toronto, Chicago, Los Angeles, and Chattanooga.

Information Organizations Fostering Community Engagement: While information organizations have always been disseminators of information, innovative organizations are no longer content with one-way communication. Information organizations strengthen neighborhoods and communities by creating connections and understanding needs, going out into their communities, and fostering collaborative relationships to build relevant and responsive information services (see also chapter 17: "Hyperlinked Libraries").

Information Organizations with Makerspaces: Provided with the space, tools, and encouragement, information organization users can come together in makerspaces to collaborate, learn hands-on skills, and create and produce music, videos, jewelry, games, robotics, electronics—and anything in between.

Information Organizations That Break the Box: Some pilot initiatives are challenging the idea of an information space. These include the Little Free Library movement, information organizations as vending machines in any location for borrowing content, bookmobiles that become book bicycles, book burros, or wireless access from a hybrid traveling car.

Information Organizations with a Customer-First Focus: Today's information organizations are adopting a customer-first focus. For many, this has resulted in:

- improved hours of operation,
- self-checkout technology,
- online booking systems to pay fines, register for programs and computers, renew and reserve items,
- quiet spaces for study and work,

- partnership spaces—theaters, meeting rooms, social work staff, etc.,
- comfortable spaces for socializing,
- light food and beverage services,
- expanded programming and dedicated resources for target groups (e.g., children, teens, seniors, cultural groups, students, etc.),
- helpful, available staff who engage with the user in the information organization ("walk the floor"), and
- information-rich technology and training opportunities.

Not only do these improvements better serve the organization's customers, but they also result in an operationally efficient organization and a functional work environment for staff.

NOTES

1. George Couros, "Characteristics of a Change Agent," *The Principal of Change*, last updated January 26, 2013, http://georgecouros.ca/blog/archives/3615.
2. Apple, Inc., iBeacon, accessed September 6, 2017, https://developer.apple.com/ibeacon/.
3. Association of College and Research Libraries (ACRL), "Academic Library Statistics," 2015, http://www.ala.org/acrl/publications/trends; Association of Research Libraries (ARL), "Statistics and Assessment Surveys (Canada & US)," 2017, https://www.arlstatistics.org/home; Institute of Museum and Library Services (IMLS), "Research Data Collection," 2014, https://www.imls.gov/research-evaluation/data-collection/public-libraries-survey; National Center for Education Statistics (NCES), "Surveys and Programs," 2017, https://nces.ed.gov/; Public Library Association (PLA), "PLDS and PLAmetrics," 2017, http://www.ala.org/pla/resources/publications/plds; Counting Opinions, 2017, http://www.countingopinions.com. In the United States and Canada, Counting Opinions is a private sector consulting service that specializes in library data and satisfaction and effectiveness studies.
4. MarketingCharts, "American Households Are Getting Smaller—and Headed by Older Adults," 2012, http://www.marketingcharts.com/traditional/american-households-are-getting-smaller-and-headed-by-older-adults-24981/.
5. See Los Angeles Public Library, http://www.lapl.org/diploma.
6. Roger Levien, "Confronting the Future: Strategic Visions for the 21st Century Public Library," *American Library Association Policy Brief*, no. 4 (2011), http://www.ala.org/offices/sites/ala.org.offices/files/content/oitp/publications/policybriefs/confronting_the_futu.pdf.
7. HathiTrust Digital Library, 2017, https://www.hathitrust.org/.
8. Digital Public Library of America, 2017, https://dp.la/.
9. Europeana, "Europeana Collections," 2017, http://www.europeana.eu/portal/en.
10. New Media Consortium, "NMC Horizon Project," 2017, https://www.nmc.org/nmc-horizon/.
11. Pew Research American and Life Project, "Libraries," 2017, http://libraries.pewinternet.org/.
12. Online Computer Library Center, "OCLC Research," 2017, http://www.oclc.org/research.html.
13. Mark Aguiar and Erik Hunt, "Measuring Trends in Libraries: The Allocation of Time over Five Decades," *Quarterly Journal of Economics* 122, no. 3 (2007): 969–1006.
14. MarketingCharts, "American Households Are Getting Smaller."
15. Andrew Perrin, "Book Reading 2016," Pew Research Center, December 1, 2016, http://www.pewinternet.org/2016/09/01/book-reading-2016/.

4

Diverse Information Needs

Heather O'Brien and Devon Greyson

Chapter 4, "Diverse Information Needs," redirects the focus of the first three chapters from the trends and history of the information organization to its user. Heather O'Brien and Devon Greyson bring their extensive skills as instructors and researchers to cogently argue that anticipating and meeting the information needs of specific user groups through programs, services, and information systems is key to the success of information organizations. Astutely recognizing the ambiguity in identifying information needs, O'Brien and Greyson note that information needs may be known and specifically addressed by users, or they may be unclear or unacknowledged until identified and met by an information professional.

While expressed information should be taken at face value, other needs may require the information professional to explore and understand the factors that created the need, in order to understand the need itself. To be proactive, information professionals should develop the skills to anticipate the needs of the community they serve based on societal, economic, and technological trends. Information professionals should also work to identify the role that emotion and behavior play within the information need.

Looking carefully at several case studies, O'Brien and Greyson identify diverse information needs and the various individual and contextual factors that shape them, as well as how information professionals identify and meet information needs in their work. Within these case studies, the authors emphasize that meeting these needs is essential for the sustainability of information organizations and services.

★   ★   ★

Information need is a fundamental concept in library and information science (LIS). Human information needs form the basis of many types of information work. Anticipating and meeting the information needs of specific user groups through programs, services, and information systems is key to the success of information organizations, and represents a substantial stream of research and professional work.

Information needs, like information users, are diverse. Consider the following scenarios:

- A sales representative needs to verify an airport code to ensure the successful shipment of goods.
- A recent immigrant, who is learning the language of his new country, seeks housing and employment.

- A physician uses point-of-care tools to improve the speed and accuracy of her diagnosis of a patient's illness.

In each scenario, individuals' motivations and information-seeking strategies differ based on individual (micro-level) characteristics such as cognitive abilities or geographic location; relational factors (meso-level) such as who is available to help fill information needs; higher-level (macro-level) influences such as IT infrastructure and cultural values; and task-specific factors such as the currency of the requested information. All information needs are temporal and may shift and evolve over time and place as people interact with, interpret, and make sense of information.[1] The needs of the new immigrant, for example, will evolve over time as he gains familiarity with the local language and environment. Once he finds initial housing and employment, his information-seeking goals may shift to meeting other needs, such as health care, family support, entertainment, or finding housing and work that is closer to his ideal.

This chapter examines and unpacks the construct *information need*, using a combination of theoretical approaches, a multilevel model, and four case studies. The case studies feature information professionals striving to assess and meet the needs of multiple user populations in a variety of settings, and emphasize how micro-, meso-, and macro-level factors inform information needs. After completing this chapter, the reader should have an understanding of information needs and the various individual and contextual factors that shape them, as well as how information professionals identify and meet information needs in their work.

DEFINING INFORMATION NEEDS

The concept of information need has been understood, defined, and applied in multiple ways. For some, information needs are responses to a *problem situation*. Needs stem from recognizing a problem that is preventing an individual from moving forward. Information seeking is a natural course of action to reduce uncertainty,[2] fill a knowledge gap, or make sense of one's world.[3] The problem-centered view sees information behavior as a process whereby people encounter situations that prompt them to acquire knowledge or skills, seek information, and engage in decision making and sense making as they determine how well the located information meets their need.

This perspective is contested, as it assumes that information seeking is the natural course of action resulting from a need. Yet people who need information may not seek information; rather, they might engage in information avoidance, lack the skills or motivation to seek useful information, or not recognize what others (e.g., librarians, family) perceive to be a need.

Further, not all information acquisitions are needs driven; for example, casual information encounters (e.g., via channel surfing, checking social media) do not have an imperative need for information.[4] The lack of clarity around the basic definition of information further complicates the relationship between needs and seeking. Who determines whether and when an individual or group has a need for information, and (how) do information professionals distinguish needs from what a person wants, demands, or expects?[5] There is a great deal of ambiguity around the definition of information need and the relationship between information needs and other activities such as seeking.

An outcome-oriented definition is that an information need represents "the information that individuals ought to have to do their job effectively, solve a problem satisfactorily, or pursue a hobby or interest happily."[6] This pragmatic definition can be operationalized in professional settings; it acknowledges potential constraints (micro, meso, and macro) to obtaining information and takes into account a variety of tasks and contexts of use. While some might argue that information needs are only needs when perceived by users, the above definition is noncommittal on this point, and others have suggested that there is a state of "incognizance"[7] in which one does not know enough to understand or articulate what their needs are. Information professionals cannot always make decisions about programs, systems, and services based on well-articulated information needs; these may be the tip of the iceberg when it comes to the full information need of the user.

> " To be proactive, information professionals must work to anticipate the needs of communities based on larger societal trends *before* needs are perceived and expressed. "

Information professionals must take seriously, and strive to meet, information needs articulated by their users. Even trivial-seeming requests may help build relationships and lead to more significant queries in the future. However, receiving articulated information requests is rarely sufficient for assessing, understanding, and meeting the information needs of a user group. Also, information professionals must seek to understand the many factors that structure and influence information needs. Further, to be proactive, information professionals must work to anticipate the needs of communities based on larger societal trends *before* needs are perceived and expressed.

THEORETICAL APPROACHES TO INFORMATION NEEDS

In his book *Information Need*,[8] Cole identifies three dominant perspectives within information needs research:

1. Information needs are inferred from behaviors that imply a need for information.
2. Contextual factors give rise to information needs.
3. Information needs are a normative part of the human condition.

Information Needs as Implied by Information Behaviors

Wilson defines the domain of information behavior as "the totality of human behavior in relation to sources and channels of information, including both passive and active information seeking, and information use."[9] Within this framework, information activities range from formulating queries or questions, selecting information sources, and extracting ideas from text and multimedia through reading, skimming, and so on.[10] Information needs not only motivate information activities,[11] but may be analyzed according to the information behaviors they initiate. Information needs themselves are not observable[12] and therefore reside in a "black box"[13] into which one cannot directly see. By examining how people interact with formal (e.g., information databases) or informal (e.g., friends and family) information systems, information professionals can infer needs.

> " While behavior may allow information professionals to predict or typify information needs in their organizations or user communities, it does not necessarily allow information professionals to understand and engage with individuals, in their own contexts, around their complete and current information needs. "

There are two main critiques of this approach. First, it does not account for what people are thinking and feeling, only what they are doing. When people recognize, articulate, and try to fulfill a need, they not only engage in different activities (e.g., consulting others, targeted searching) but also in cognitive processes (e.g., perceiving, interpreting)[14] and affective states (e.g., uncertainty, frustration).[15] As information research has increasingly explored the role of emotions in information behavior, it has become clear that emotion in some situations plays a substantial role in shaping information seeking and use. Second, while behavior may allow information professionals to predict or typify

Heather O'Brien and Devon Greyson

information needs in their organizations or user communities, it does not necessarily allow information professionals to understand and engage with individuals, in their own contexts, around their complete and current information needs. Some needs may remain covert or unexpressed due to stigma or shame around a topic (e.g., personal health issues, members of stigmatized groups).[16] Other times, incognizance, defined as a lack of awareness of a need, serves as a barrier to information seeking, encountering, and use.[17]

Information Needs and Context

Information needs are highly contextual; different social and material contexts give rise to different information needs (see also chapter 5: "Diversity, Equity of Access, and Social Justice"). Therefore, information needs may be approached according to "the user's life world."[18] The life world is made up of various sub-worlds (e.g., home, school); each sub-world contains different reference groups (e.g., peers, teachers) and human and/or technological information systems with which to interact. Information needs arise from situations in the sub-world and from the social roles individuals assume in specific contexts.[19] The importance of context in shaping information needs and human responses to such needs may explain why there is such an abundance of information behavior research that groups populations based on occupation (e.g., lawyers, physicians), demographics (e.g., age, socioeconomic status), and role (e.g., patient, hobbyist).[20] It is likely impossible to arrive at a universal method for assessing and evaluating information needs, but it is manageable to consider a specific setting and the information needs that evolve for the people operating within these settings.

> It is likely impossible to arrive at a universal method for assessing and evaluating information needs, but it is manageable to consider a specific setting and the information needs that evolve for the people operating within these settings.

Understanding the user's context is important not only in human response to information needs but also in the design of information systems. One technique used in systems design is the creation of a persona, or a description of a fictitious user. The persona is a rich story constructed from pertinent information derived from potential and actual users to give the designer a clear picture of whom it is being designed for.[21] Personas need not be constrained to the development of technology applications, but can be adopted in the design of information services and programs. The contextual perspective allows information professionals to consider various factors related to individuals, their circumstances, and their workplaces or communities that precipitate and influence their information needs.

Information Needs and the Human Condition

Lastly, information need as part of the *human condition* is rooted in positive psychology. Maslow's *Theory of Human Motivation*[22] represents needs as a pyramid, with basic needs (i.e., food, shelter, security) grounding the hierarchy. As basic needs are satisfied, people pursue higher-level needs such as love; esteem; and, ultimately, self-actualization. Whether information need is a fundamental human need remains an unresolved question. Nonetheless, there are aspects of Maslow's work that have been adapted in LIS to inform thinking around information needs. Taylor[23] built upon Maslow's position that needs are conscious and unconscious by proposing that people move through stages of recognizing they have

Discussion Question

Why is it so difficult to define information needs?

an information need (visceral), articulating that need in their minds (conscious), and then determining how to turn that need into a question (formalized). Taylor's stages, developed in libraries, form the backbone of the reference interview (see also chapter 11: "Information Intermediation and Reference Services"). It is a key task of information intermediaries (i.e., information professionals) to help people articulate their information needs as queries to obtain an optimal outcome.

A MULTILEVEL FRAMEWORK FOR CONSIDERING INFORMATION NEEDS

This chapter has considered what an information need is, as well as behavioral, contextual, and psychological components thereof. Next, it will explore the information needs of diverse users as encountered in various settings. Information professionals must both *zoom in* on the individual user and his or her specific problem situation, cognitive and affective state, and end goals, and then *zoom out* to the level of the group, organization, or community to consider the broader expectations, access and resource constraints, and emerging technologies that will impact current and future information needs. As such, ecological systems theory[24] is useful for adopting a multilevel view in which information needs are shaped by the following:

> Information professionals must both *zoom in* on the individual user and his or her specific problem situation, cognitive and affective state, and end goals, and then *zoom out* to the level of the group, organization, or community to consider the broader expectations, access and resource constraints, and emerging technologies that will impact current and future information needs.

Individual factors: socioeconomic status, literacy level, cultural background, motivation, interest, social role, prior topical knowledge, and technology proficiency.

Relational factors: the extent of one's social and/or professional network.

Environmental (community or societal) factors: technology infrastructure, norms and values, culturally specific "ways of knowing" and communicating.

Task- and situation-specific factors: factors that influence the purpose for which information is sought and the characteristics of information and resources that are prioritized and valued (e.g., accuracy, timeliness, format).

Temporal factors: how the passage of time influences and changes information needs within an individual and society.

These multiple layers influence a given information need and also interact with each other, creating a dynamic ecological system in which information needs arise, and ideally, are resolved. Figure 4.1 illustrates a simplified ecological systems model adapted for understanding and addressing user information needs.

To connect the theoretical discussion with real-world application, real-life examples of information needs and efforts to meet them are presented below. These case studies[25] represent four information professionals working in the United States and Canada—a public teen services librarian, a systems librarian working in a nonlibrary organization, a special health librarian, and a virtual academic librarian—who vary in terms of years of experience, communities served, geographic location, and type of organization for which they work. Within these concrete examples, it is evident that multiple levels of factors are at work shaping information needs, and that meeting these needs is important for the sustainability of information organizations and services.

Heather O'Brien and Devon Greyson

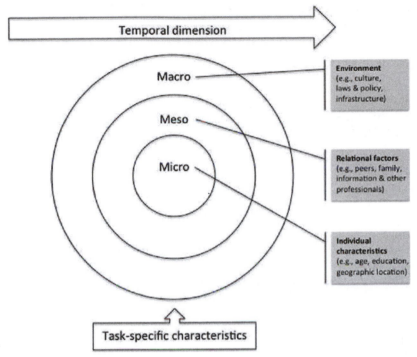

Figure 4.1 Understanding and Addressing Information Needs. *Created by authors.*

Case Study 1: Teens in a Public Library

Aubri Keleman, a public teen services librarian, notes that sometimes teens approach the library for help solving a specific information need (see also chapter 8: "Community Anchors for Lifelong Learning: Public Libraries"). At other times, it is the job of the information professional to get to know local youth and key community members or organizations to assess potential unexpressed needs. Specific to teen populations, she finds that "keeping up on pop culture does help with a certain number of kids," but it is most important to build trust relationships with youth and local youth service providers to stay in touch with the ever-evolving local youth culture. Additionally, teen librarians should bear in mind the interaction between teen development and information needs,[26] including sensitive treatment of personal and potentially stigmatized needs, e.g., sexuality.[27]

> Keeping up on pop culture does help with a certain number of kids, but it is most important to build trust relationships with youth and local youth service providers to stay in touch with the ever-evolving local youth culture.

Aubri describes a successful teen program her library initiated in response to information needs observed within the community:

> [T]here was a certain period of time where the teenagers at one of our rural libraries were in conflict with the police and also were doing things like skipping out on court dates, . . . so it seemed like we needed to talk to kids both about what rights they had, and ways that they could make things go smoother for themselves.

In response to this observed need for information among local youth, the library invited a lawyer in to give a workshop about legal rights and procedures, to clarify and demystify for the teens what to expect from the police, as well as to discuss the consequences of resisting arrest.

The information need, in this case, was influenced by individual characteristics (i.e., a population of rural minors), relational factors (i.e., negative relationships between youth and the law, neutral or positive relationships between youth and the library), and environmental factors (i.e., lack of access to legal information, and possibly a conflict of cultural values and norms). It was timely, as court dates are time sensitive and the community was experiencing an escalation of negative teen-police interactions. The library staff crafted a program aimed at meeting the observed information need. Aubri says that in this case, "I think it was clear from what happened after that, that there was less conflict. And again we had that relationship with the teens, so we could say, you know, 'Are you showing up for your court date? What's going on? Do you have any more questions?'"

While Aubri encourages information professionals to try new programs to meet perceived information needs, she cautions not to be too hung up on every program being a success: "I think it's important that we don't, as professionals, decide that there's an information need, and then become frustrated because people . . . don't feel that information need in their life."

Case Study 2: Systems Librarianship and Serving Students with Print Disabilities

Systems Librarian Tara Robertson works for a government-funded organization with a mandate to format-shift academic materials (e.g., textbooks) for use by students with print disabilities. As she puts it, on an individual level, "we're using technology to solve a user's need." On a higher level, "education can be a really transformative force. Or it can keep people out. So I think we're kind of a bridge."

While students come to Tara via a formal referral process, this does not mean it is always simple to elicit or assess user needs. Some come knowing exactly what they need (e.g., an audiobook of a textbook), but others may not. Tara explains that a personal conversation is required: "[W]ith students, if they don't know what they want I'll ask them about how their print disability impacts their reading or impacts their studying. And that seems to be the right question to ask. At the beginning, I wasn't really sure how to ask it."

Such a conversation allows the information professional not only to discover micro-level factors such as how a student's specific disability affects his/her reading, but also makes space for other factors that might influence the particular need. These include meso-level factors (e.g., students' relationship with their school's disability coordinators), temporal factors (e.g., when they need the materials by), and task-specific factors unique to the material or field of study. Tara also observes macro-level factors that influence student information needs. These include budgetary constraints for postsecondary education and support services, provincial policies encouraging certain types of education over others, and the stigma around having a disability. Understanding these is less likely to come out of a direct conversation with users and more likely to arise from experience with the community.

Tara emphasizes the essential nature of collecting multiple forms of assessment data when designing information systems. Specific methods include: card-sorting exercises with staff and students, "guerilla user testing" with members of the target group (in one case, this involved taking chocolate bars to a high-traffic student area as an incentive to provide website feedback), analytics, and library statistics such as circulation and database usage. While many of these methods are quantitative, Tara also stresses the importance of qualitative information via focus groups, surveys, and one-on-one follow-ups to validate the quantitative statistics:

> [Y]ou can't just look at the data without asking people—because you could see a big drop and go, "Oh, okay, so that's not a useful resource." And it's like, "Oh, someone drove a truck through

Heather O'Brien and Devon Greyson

the front of the library that day, and it was closed." And if you talk to someone they'll tell you that, and it makes the data make sense or contextualizes it.

Tara cautions against relying on library staff perceptions of what is working to meet user needs. In a previous systems job where she was transitioning a library to a new integrated library system (ILS) and website, she recalls, "I had quite a few disagreements with the reference librarians because the way that they thought things were happening, the data suggested the opposite." She stresses the importance of welcoming negative feedback, as it can be useful for helping information organizations improve their ability to meet user needs.

> We rarely get [comments] that say, "Your service sucked," or "It didn't work for me." So that's the piece that we're missing. And I think everyone here is really keen to figure out more, like we get really enthusiastic when we get negative feedback [laughs] because we're like, "Okay! What went wrong? Let's track it!"

While this emphasis on continual assessment of how well a system is meeting user needs is time intensive, Tara reminds us that if what an information service is doing is not helping, "all that time is wasted." Assessment of a service's success meeting user needs is essential for sustainability and funding advocacy within many organizations. Tara's organization reports to the government annually, and she finds that solid assessment results can be a useful advocacy tool for organizational funding and support.

> " Assessment of a service's success meeting user needs is essential for sustainability and funding advocacy within many organizations. "

Case Study 3: Medical Professionals in a Special Library Setting

Diane (pseudonym), a health information specialist for fifteen years, is currently the librarian for 150 staff within a health organization. She supports diverse user needs through the provision of resources, instruction, and referrals, maintenance of a health policy database, and archival records management. Diane's users are professionals with work-related information needs and seeking; therefore, she works within an embedded model of health librarianship.[28]

Diane takes a task-based approach to anticipating and meeting employees' needs, where different organizational units have specific types of needs. Understanding the work performed within the organization is key. She says, "It takes time to get a sense of organization and individual needs. . . . Working on projects, organization communications or strategies, team meetings are all ways in which I gain knowledge of information needs."

Gathering intelligence about information needs is also part of sustaining library services within the organization. Without proactive work on the part of the information professional, employees may not recognize the role of the library in their work. Diane relayed an example of a staff member who thought "you could get everything on the internet for free" but now sees the value of resources the library subscribes to. Building relationships with users means assessing and meeting user needs is an ongoing conversation:

> " Building relationships with users means assessing and meeting user needs is an ongoing conversation. "

> It's about knowing the client and following through with them. For example, after doing a literature search for someone, you might come across further information that you forward along—"I read

this article and thought you would be interested," and "Here's the abstract, let me know if you would like the full text."

One challenge that Diane encounters is how to fulfill information needs given macro-level and temporal constraints. For example, she sees information literacy instruction as a growth area for the library but is challenged to deliver instruction effectively given employees' time limitations and the existing institutional professional development framework. Additionally, working to foster relationships across departments is difficult. Current struggles include educating the information technology (IT) unit about the library's functions and trying to better support organizational records management needs with limited staff. Of determining needs she says, "Sometimes this is simple and straight-forward. Sometimes it involves more of an iterative process to determine the real need. Sometimes it involves providing options. It still involves good reference skills. It involves getting to know client needs."

Yet, trying to meet these needs involves negotiating within the larger macro-level of the organizations' structure, culture, and technological infrastructure (see also chapter 9: "Working in Different Information Environments: Special Libraries and Information Centers").

Case Study 4: Virtual University Students

Students are one of the most studied user populations in LIS. Currently, there is much emphasis on computer-mediated learning and the information needs of online learners (see also chapter 16: "Teaching Users: Information and Technology Instruction"). Samantha Sinanan, manager of Library Instruction and Technical Services with Virtual Librarian Service (VLS), provides library and information services to online universities in the United States (see also chapter 7: "Learning and Research Institutions: Academic Libraries" and chapter 10: "Digital Resources: Digital Libraries").

For Samantha, academic librarians have a very clear role in working with educational institutions to assess and meet students' information needs: We "break down this massive amount of information into digestible chunks" and give students skills they can "carry through their academic program and into their professional lives." Another responsibility is staying abreast of current trends. Recently, for example, she has been looking at tools such as mobile applications and authentication methods that allow for seamless access to library resources and creating library portal pages with a high degree of usability because we need to "be creative and efficient in the ways we reach students" and to choose "instructional supports and strategies" that are relevant to them and meet them where they are.

> Meeting the students where they are emphasizes the technological affordances and constraints of the online environment.

Meeting the students where they are emphasizes the technological affordances and constraints of the online environment. VLS relies on asynchronous communication with students, which has both challenges and benefits:

> We need to work harder at the point of contact to make sure we get it right. But we know that for many of the students in an online environment, the asynchronous mode works for them. Additionally, it allows us to sit down and carefully think about our responses, and we have the opportunity to follow up with the student.

There are also collection management issues in the world of online libraries—embargoes placed on recent content and items not available in electronic format (see also chapter 24: "Managing Collections"). Virtual librarians "don't have a choice" but to be literate and comfortable with IT. Since begin-

Heather O'Brien and Devon Greyson

ning her job five years ago, Samantha has had to "fearlessly embrace technology" and learn the skills to work with new systems, applications, and software.

A major question is how to provide instruction and information in the virtual environment. Samantha asks, "We are designing instructional supports, but are the students using them?" and "How do we deliver information in manageable, understandable chunks without compromising our mission, or oversimplifying [the information]?" The students with whom Samantha interacts have chosen online education because it fits their lives. In typical reference encounters, Samantha looks at micro-level factors (e.g., program of study, student status) and the complexity of the information need being presented. She tries to deliver the right amount of information to students and pitch it at the right level. For example, a nursing student in a Registered Nursing (RN) or Master of Science in Nursing (MSN) program will require a different level of information than a doctoral student in nursing.

Getting a sense of students' information literacy is paramount. Although information literacy "lay[s] the foundation for the student's entire academic experience," Samantha feels that some students are not

> **Discussion Questions**
>
> How might we assess information needs? Why might some approaches work better than others with certain user groups or in particular settings?

conscious of this need, and that these skills are not encouraged in the "age of Google where in many cases you enter a string of words and get back what you want." Also, they tend to focus on immediate needs for tangible information, rather than the building blocks for locating and evaluating it.

At the macro level, VLS serves numerous online universities, each with "[its] own culture" and a diversity of programs. VLS liaises with faculty, program directors, and student success coordinators at the universities, and this collaboration is based on a common goal: "Everybody wants the students to succeed." Part of this collective effort is working toward student retention. This is a concern for the library itself (i.e., when students don't come back, does this mean they were served successfully?), and for the institutions that VLS supports. Samantha says, "We all have our part to play, including the library. . . . We don't want "students lost in cyberspace," frustrated, or "dropping out and fading away."

CONCLUSION

Information need is a "fuzzy" concept yet central to the existence and mission of information organizations. Needs relate to information behaviors, such as seeking, avoidance, and assessment, and are highly context sensitive. Information needs may be known and specifically addressed by users, or they may be unclear or unacknowledged until identified and met by an information professional. Expressed information needs must be taken at face value, but other needs are more effectively met when the information professional attempts to gain an understanding of the factors that create and influence specific needs.

Aubri's case study highlights the importance of being in touch with a user community, through direct observation/interaction and via networks of service providers. Tara's story emphasizes the importance of using data to challenge librarians' perceptions of user needs and how well they are being met, as well as of adopting a mentality of continuous assessment. Diane's message is that the special library must demonstrate value through collaboration and formal and informal means of assessing organizational and individual information needs. Samantha stressed meeting students where they are and fulfilling articulated needs while also working on latent information literacy needs to promote student success and retention.

Information professionals working with different groups and communities encounter diverse user needs. While the specific needs, as well as strategies to meet them, vary greatly depending on the context and user, it is imperative to assess information needs *and* how well we are meeting them. The sustainability of information organizations depends on it.

ACKNOWLEDGMENTS

We appreciate our interviewees: Aubri Keleman, Tara Robertson, Diane, and Samantha Sinanan for sharing their insights and experiences for this chapter.

NOTES

1. Devon Greyson, "Evolution of Information Practices Over Time," *Proceedings of the Association for Information Science and Technology* 53, no. 1 (2016): article 53.
2. Carol C. Kuhlthau, "Inside the Search Process: Information Seeking from the User's Perspective," *Journal of the American Society for Information Science* 42, no. 5 (1991): 261–71, http://ptarpp2.uitm.edu.my/silibus/insidesearch2.pdf.
3. Brenda Dervin, "What Methodology Does to Theory: Sense-Making Methodology as Exemplar," in *Theories of Information Behavior*, ed. Karen E. Fisher, Sandra Erdelez, and Lynne E. F. McKechnie (Medford, NJ: Information Today, 2005), 25–30.
4. David Elsweiler, Max L. Wilson, and Brian K. Lund, "Understanding Casual-Leisure Information Behavior," in *New Directions in Information Behavior*, ed. Amanda Spink and Jannica Heinström (UK: Emerald Group Publishing, 2011).
5. Tom D. Wilson, "On User Studies and Information Needs," *Journal of Documentation* 37, no. 1 (1981): 5.
6. David Nicholas, *Assessing Information Needs: Tools, Techniques and Concepts for the Internet Age* (London: Aslib, 2000), 20.
7. Beth St. Jean, "'I Just Don't Know What I Don't Know!' A Longitudinal Investigation of the Perceived Usefulness of Information to People with Type 2 Diabetes," *Proceedings of the American Society for Information Science and Technology* 49, no. 1 (2012): 1–10.
8. Charles Cole, *Information Need: A Theory Connecting Information Search to Knowledge Formation* (Medford, NJ: Information Today, 2012).
9. Thomas D. Wilson, "Models in Information Behavior Research," *Journal of Documentation* 55, no. 3 (1999): 249–70.
10. Gary Marchionini, *Information Seeking in Electronic Environments* (Cambridge: Cambridge University Press, 1995).
11. Charles Naumer and Karen E. Fisher, "Information Needs," in *Encyclopedia of Library and Information Sciences*, third edition (London: Taylor and Francis, 2009), 2452–58.
12. Nicholas J. Belkin and Alina Vickery, *Interaction in Information Systems: A Review of Research from Document Retrieval to Knowledge-Based Systems* (London: British Library, 1985).
13. Cole, *Information Need*, 65.
14. Robert S. Taylor, "Question-Negotiation and Information Seeking in Libraries," *College & Research Libraries* 29, no. 3 (1968): 178–94, http://crl.acrl.org/content/29/3/178.full.pdf.
15. Kuhlthau, "Inside the Search Process."
16. Jessa Lingel, and Danah Boyd, "'Keep It Secret, Keep It Safe': Information Poverty, Information Norms, and Stigma," *Journal of the American Society for Information Science and Technology* 64, no. 5 (2013): 981–91.
17. Beth St. Jean, "Factors Motivating, Demotivating, or Impeding Information Seeking and Use by People with Type 2 Diabetes: A Call to Work toward Preventing, Identifying, and Addressing Incognizance," *Journal of the American Society for Information Science and Technology* 68, no. 2 (2016): 309–20.
18. Wilson, "On User Studies and Information Needs," 5–6.
19. Ibid., 9.
20. Donald O. Case, *Looking for Information: A Survey of Research on Information Seeking, Needs and Behavior* (Bingely, UK: Emerald Group Publishing, 2012).
21. Lene Nielsen, *Personas—User Focused Design* (New York: Springer, 2012), 1–2.

Heather O'Brien and Devon Greyson

22. Abraham H. Maslow, "A Theory of Human Motivation," *Psychological Review* 50 (1943).
23. Taylor, "Question-Negotiation and Information Seeking in Libraries."
24. Urie Bronfenbrenner, *The Ecology of Human Development: Experiments by Nature and Design* (Cambridge, MA: Harvard University Press, 1979).
25. Aubri Keleman, Tara Robertson, "Diane," and Samantha Sinanan, telephone interviews by Heather O'Brien and Devon Greyson, June 2014.
26. Denise E. Agosto and Sandra Hughes-Hassell, "Toward a Model of the Everyday Life Information Needs of Urban Teenagers, Part 1," *Journal of the American Society for Information Science and Technology* 57, no. 10 (2006): 1394–1403.
27. Jennifer Burek Pierce, "Young Adult Sexual and Reproductive Health Information Needs," in *Youth Information-Seeking Behavior II: Context, Theories, Models, and Issues*, ed. Mary K. Chelton, and Colleen Cool (Lanham, MD: Scarecrow Press, 2007), 63–91.
28. Devon Greyson, Soleil Surette, Liz Dennett, and Trish Chatterley, "'You're Just One of the Group When You're Embedded': Report from a Mixed-Method Investigation of the Research-Embedded Health Librarian Experience," *Journal of the Medical Library Association* 101, no. 4 (2013): 287.

5

Diversity, Equity of Access, and Social Justice

Patty Wong, Miguel Figueroa, and Melissa Cardenas-Dow

Chapter 5, "Diversity, Equity of Access, and Social Justice," introduces diversity as a concept integral to the missions and values of information organizations. Diversity, notes the authors, encompasses several key terms, including equity, inclusion, and multiculturalism. With their background in serving underserved groups, diversity initiatives, and outreach, Patty Wong, Miguel Figueroa, and Melissa Cardenas-Dow are uniquely situated to explore how difference strengthens organizations and communities when those differences are respected and acknowledged. The authors further highlight the fact that as an information organization strives to support learning, engagement, and a sense of community, its efforts should also be aligned toward supporting social justice for all members of the community.

The valuing, celebration, and recognition of differences among members of a given community may still leave issues of equity unanswered. An information organization's engagement with a community requires that it confront such issues. More significantly, how an organization addresses these issues is one of the most important aspects of the work done by the information organization.

It is essential that information professionals understand that people do not experience life through a single lens, but rather through a mix of experiences, perspectives, and understanding. By understanding these unique experiences and perspectives, information organizations and professionals can focus on the unique needs of their community while avoiding what the authors refer to as "group think." It is, therefore, an information professional's responsibility and goal to learn about that community's diversity by becoming more familiar with linguistic preferences, social customs, and cultural norms and to develop strategies to best serve the full community.

★   ★   ★

This chapter starts from the basic belief that difference—and the differences between people and groups—strengthens organizations and communities when those differences are respected and acknowledged. This focus on difference can accelerate innovation within the information organization and advance social justice efforts within the community, both of which should be priorities for information professionals. Research shows that organizations that leverage multiple, diverse perspectives can experience better business performance[1] and have access to alternative ways of thinking and behaving that advance innovation.[2] Even as information organizations examine their internal workings, they exist within complex systems of power wherein certain segments of the community experience privilege while others contend with inequities. As the information organization strives to support learning, engagement, and a sense of community, its efforts should be aligned toward supporting social justice for all members of the community. Information organizations have tremendous opportunities to work with diverse professionals within their organization and diverse populations in their communities. Through these efforts, information organizations can strengthen their work preserving and contributing to the creation of information and ultimately improve the experience of every member of their community.

This chapter introduces diversity as a concept integral to the missions and values of information organizations and information professionals. It provides an overview of what the terms diverse and diversity mean, the characteristics that are commonly addressed by diversity work and diversity efforts, and the relationship of diversity to other tenets of the profession. After completing this chapter, the reader should have an understanding of intercultural communications and collaboration, cultural competencies within the information organization, and how to develop with and from work with diverse communities.

WHAT DO WE MEAN BY DIVERSITY?

Inevitably, conversations about diversity and diverse communities include several key terms—diversity, equity, inclusion, and multiculturalism. Each term is important and represents a specific approach to and activities for addressing differences among groups of people. But truly strategic organizations use a specific term intentionally based on culture, priorities, and aspirations. To help clarify how diversity is used in this chapter—and to benefit future discussions about multiculturalism, diversity, equity, and inclusion—it is important to define them.

Multiculturalism: While less frequently used as a strategic goal or priority, multicultural or multiculturalism remains an important concept in developing services and programs. In 2005, the American Association of Colleges and Universities (AACU) released a series of three reports as part of its "Making Excellence Inclusive" initiative. In one of the reports, *Making Diversity Work on Campus: A Research-Based Perspective*, authors Jeffrey F. Millem, Mitchell Chang, and Anthony L. Antonio provided a simple definition of multiculturalism as "recognition or celebration of different cultures."[3] Month-long cultural celebrations, cross-cultural dialogues, or rotating exhibits of different cultures embody some of the most popular multiculturalism efforts.

Inclusion: Inclusion assumes that an organization or community is composed of many different talents and perspectives, and so inclusion efforts seek to create an environment where those unique skills, perspectives, and experiences are valued. Inclusion efforts reinforce individuals' worth and dignity by creating a strong sense of involvement and belonging.

Equity: Equity has become a key term for organizations in academia and government, especially where issues of compliance might be of concern. Equity assumes the existence of avoidable or remediable differences in the experiences of individuals, often resulting from their inherent or acquired characteristics (racial/ethnic; gender, sexuality, or sexual identity; physical ability or cognitive difference; social or economic status; geographic). The pursuit of equity requires recognizing the different experiences each individual may have and working to upend those avoidable or remediable differences in order to create a more equitable experience.

Diversity: The AACU paper mentioned above includes a useful definition for diversity. "In addition to conceiving of diversity in terms of composition and as an exploration of differences, we would add to the definition an interest in opposing unfair forms of exclusion, prejudice, and discrimination. . . . Indeed, perhaps more importantly for our definition of diversity, we firmly believe that diversity is fundamentally about work—very time-consuming and difficult work."[4] Diversity initiatives focus on groups that have previously been excluded or experienced prejudice or discrimination and adopt active, significant, and intentional efforts to overturn or correct these experiences (see appendix 5.1: "Most Common Characteristics of Diversity"). Similar to equity, diversity requires concerted effort to change long-standing systems to provide a more equal experience for all people.

From the Profession

Over the past several years, the American Library Association (ALA) has placed a significant focus on these issues through a special Task Force (and later Working Group) on Equity, Diversity, and Inclusion. As part of its work, that group offered definitions to provide a more encompassing understanding of these complex terms (see textbox 5.1).[5]

This chapter intentionally uses the terms *diversity* and *diverse* to acknowledge that exclusion, prejudice, and discrimination still exist in communities throughout the world. The use of *diversity* also acknowledges that information organizations and information professionals can actively work to upend these realities.

TEXTBOX 5.1

Definitions for Equity, Diversity, and Inclusion from the *Final Report of the ALA Task Force on Equity, Diversity, and Inclusion*

Equity: Equity is not the same as formal equality. Formal equality implies sameness. Equity, on the other hand, assumes difference and takes difference into account to ensure a fair process and, ultimately, a fair (or equitable) outcome. Equity recognizes that some groups were (and are) disadvantaged in accessing educational and employment opportunities and are, therefore, underrepresented or marginalized in many organizations and institutions. The effects of that exclusion often linger systemically within organizational policies, practices, and procedures. Equity, therefore, means increasing diversity by ameliorating conditions of disadvantaged groups.

Diversity: Diversity can be defined as the sum of the ways that people are both alike and different. Visible diversity is generally those attributes or characteristics that are external. However, diversity goes beyond the external to internal characteristics that we choose to define as "invisible" diversity. Invisible diversity includes those characteristics and attributes that are not readily seen. When we recognize, value, and embrace diversity, we are recognizing, valuing, and embracing the uniqueness of each individual.

Inclusion: Inclusion means an environment in which all individuals are treated fairly and respectfully; are valued for their distinctive skills, experiences, and perspectives; have equal access to resources and opportunities; and can contribute fully to the organization's success.

What Characteristics Do Diversity Efforts Address?

Diversity efforts usually respond to or address the needs of specific groups or cultures within the larger community. These groups form around shared inherent or acquired characteristics of difference (as defined in textbox 5.2). For different people, some of those characteristics may be inherent or acquired, depending on their life circumstances.

TEXTBOX 5.2

Characteristics of Diversity

- Inherent diversities are those characteristics of difference that are material to who we are—gender, race and ethnicity, physical and cognitive ability, age, and sexual orientation and identity.
- Acquired diversities are those characteristics that have changed through our experiences and choices—educational attainment, linguistic ability, immigrant experience, family composition, and relationship status.

What are currently considered the most apparent characteristics for diversity efforts—gender, race and ethnicity, physical and mental ability, age, and sexual orientation—are usually inherent diversities and have evolved as societal and cultural changes have brought to light the unique experiences of people who shared a common characteristic of difference. Efforts focused on gender diversity that sought to address differences in experiences between men and women have expanded to understand the social construct of gender and now may consider gender expression rather than an either/or approach to male and female. Understanding of groups can also change, as has been the case with revisions to organizations' understanding of Hispanic populations or distinctions between Asian populations and Pacific Island populations. The work of diversity changes as awareness of unique experiences and the exclusion, prejudice, or discrimination experienced by groups of people becomes more widely known and acknowledged.

> While considerations for inherent diversities can help to upend exclusion, prejudice, or discrimination, considerations for acquired diversities can help organizations be vigilant of homogeneity and the resulting limits on understanding, development, and innovation.

While considerations for inherent diversities can help to upend exclusion, prejudice, or discrimination, considerations for acquired diversities can help organizations be vigilant of homogeneity and the resulting limits on understanding, development, and innovation. There can and should be acknowledgment of the unique experiences resulting from differences in economic status, educational attainment (e.g., first-generation college experience), family or relationship composition (e.g., single-parent, adoptive or foster, multigenerational families, single, married, partnered), immigrant experience, geography (e.g., rural, urban, suburban), work experience, linguistic abilities, and religious beliefs. By understanding the unique experiences and perspectives resulting from both acquired and inherent differences, organizations can avoid group think and design more inclusive services or programs.

To help broaden understandings of diversity and diversity efforts, many organizations use a "diversity wheel." Figure 5.1 illustrates the multitude of experiences through which people experience

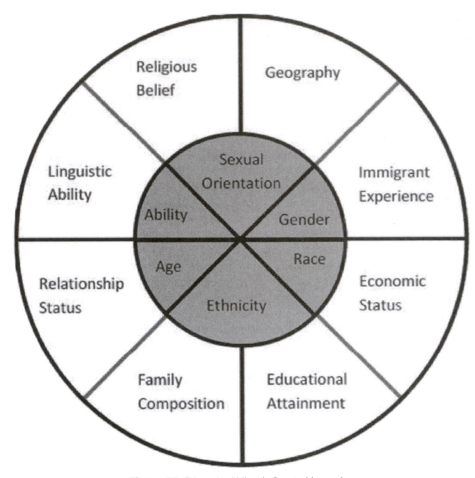

Figure 5.1 Diversity Wheel. *Created by author.*

their lives. The diversity wheel helps illustrate that people do not experience life through a single dimension, but rather through multiple perspectives (e.g., their economic background, their race and ethnicity, their gender identity, and so on), each of which influences their experience.

It is important to remember that diversity work should be responsive to the community being served. As an organization considers its community, it may identify prominent community characteristics and seek to better understand the experiences of those individuals. For example, an information system that covers a large service area might prioritize the differences in experience between rural and urban users. Organizations may also determine that certain characteristics need to be better refined. For example, in a large and diverse Asian or Hispanic population, differences in national origin may be particularly important. Diversity is work; it must be responsive and adaptive—not maintain a static adherence to any set of definitions.

DIVERSITY, EQUITY OF ACCESS, AND INTELLECTUAL FREEDOM

Diversity connects with, complements, and advances two key principles of the information profession—intellectual freedom and equity of access (see also chapter 35: "Intellectual Freedom").

Information professionals' commitment to intellectual freedom compels them to support and protect information users' rights to read, seek information, and speak freely.[6] Understandings of

Patty Wong, Miguel Figueroa, and Melissa Cardenas-Dow

different user needs (see also chapter 4: "Diverse Information Needs") have informed numerous intellectual freedom policies supported by the ALA, including diversity in collection development,[7] universal right to free expression,[8] access to resources and services regardless of gender identity or sexual orientation,[9] services to persons with disabilities,[10] and linguistic pluralism.[11] These policies advise information professionals to not only collect a diverse set of materials but to also develop a diverse set of services to actively provide information to the many different people that need it.

> Diversity connects with, complements, and advances two key principles of the information profession—intellectual freedom and equity of access.

Equity of access builds upon what information organizations have traditionally termed outreach, where organizations develop special programs or projects for under- or unserved—and often diverse—populations (e.g., adult new and nonreaders, the incarcerated, people experiencing poverty or homelessness, the differently abled, racially and ethnically diverse communities, immigrants, the geographically isolated, the elderly, and homebound populations). Many outreach services see great success, but too often depend on special funding or specialists dedicated to the work. Changes in staffing, funding, or priorities can disrupt the services and end the relationship with the particular community. Equitable access encourages a shift from developing special services for specific user groups to sustaining quality services for all user groups at all times by actively and regularly considering the multiple perspectives by which individuals encounter the information organization and its services.[12] Increasingly, equitable access requires engaging with diverse users to better understand their needs, interests, and aspirations for the information organization. Equitable access seeks to recognize the diversity of users and develop information services responsive to their unique experiences. Equitable services and policies are developed through an appraisal of and engagement with the diverse landscape in which information users operate.

> Increasingly, equitable access requires engaging with diverse users to better understand their needs, interests, and aspirations for the information organization.

INTERCULTURAL COMMUNICATION AND COLLABORATION

Among the most important diversity endeavors that information organizations can undertake is the provision of equitable access to information through the inclusion of diverse communities in the design and delivery of programs and services. It is the information professional's responsibility and goal to learn about their community's diversity by becoming more familiar with linguistic preferences, social customs, and cultural norms and to develop strategies to best serve the full community. Professionals can meet individuals where they are and work collaboratively with community representatives to address those needs in an effective and positively impactful way. Including representatives from diverse communities can improve understanding and discussion of cultural values—and there is no better method of learning about a community than through direct participation. Community outreach is also critical, as service development should be accompanied by trusted and respected activities that demonstrate genuine

> Among the most important diversity endeavors information organizations can undertake is the provision of equitable access to information through the inclusion of diverse communities in the design and delivery of programs and services.

interest and engagement and ultimately cultural interchange (see also chapter 27: "Communication, Marketing, and Outreach Strategies").

The complexity of communication and its importance is only heightened when communicating across diverse communities. Effectiveness is much preferred over efficiency (see textbox 5.3). Active listening and awareness of the individual or group dynamic are essential to establish a trusted and reliable dialogue and connection with the audience.

TEXTBOX 5.3

Effective Communication Strategies for Serving Diverse Communities

Leave your ego at the door: Colleagues often have the best ideas, resources, and solutions; the optimal role of information professionals is often one of active listener and facilitator. A healthy appreciation for continual learning and humility offers greater depth to cultural development as an individual and within one's organization.

Check assumptions related to privilege and class: Everyone comes with a set of ideals and lessons intrinsic to his or her environment and experience. Information professionals should remove any presumptions and assumptions that stem from a certain position or societal standing; these factors may influence the information professional's intent and motivation in determining service delivery needs for others.

Filter out the centrist lens: Other, perhaps less traditional, perspectives can be valuable in analysis and operational considerations.

Develop a knowledge base: Increasing one's personal and professional awareness, perception, and understanding of the demographic framework is a hallmark of culturally engaged agencies.

Language

Language is an incredibly important element in cultural competency, especially when working with ethnic diversity. There are many factors involved in one's choice and preference of language—where and how one develops linguistic skills, the social context, and common use of language at home compared to other environments. When learning more about the demographics in a service community, knowledge of the many languages spoken at home, immigration factors, and birthplace can influence communication. Consider, for example, the differences between Castilian Spanish and conversational Spanish or the many dialects of Cantonese and the distinction between Taiwanese and Mandarin. Even within a common language, understanding language preferences of diverse communities can be incredibly important. The uses of terms such as *differently abled* or *disabled* or *Hispanic* or *Latino* may vary across communities.

Distinctions in language apply to both oral and written communication. Word choice and translations of library card registration forms or fliers, room signage, and other public information should be considered carefully and determined with community members' input. Ultimately, there is no substitute for actual knowledge of the community and reliable interpretation with experts from the community.

Social Customs

Familiarity with social customs demonstrates respect and authentic interest in developing services that reflect community values. Customs may include everything from meal preparation to gift giving to taking off one's shoes before entering a facility to offering the oldest member of the group the choicest morsels of the meal before others. Becoming familiar with social customs and being mindful of differences and similarities in customs deepens understanding and appreciation of community diversity. As with language, respecting a culture's ownership of a custom and acknowledging their right to share and define customs, their appropriate use, and their significance is important.

> " Becoming familiar with social customs and being mindful of differences and similarities in customs deepens understanding and appreciation of community diversity. "

Cultural Norms

Activities that may be commonplace for some may be unusual for others. These situations may include behavior related to family communication and hierarchy, discipline, and cultural pride. Diverse communities may maintain cultural practices and norms that are unfamiliar to the larger community. Simultaneously, customs of the larger community may be foreign to diverse communities. For example, the concept of information or educational materials available for borrowing may be new to first- or even second-generation immigrant communities who had no similar experiences in their home country. Current cultural norms may also be a combination of traditional and contemporary practices, influenced and shaped by larger community expectations.

CONTRIBUTING TO A CULTURALLY COMPETENT ORGANIZATION

Developing culturally competent organizations is key to information organizations' diversity efforts. Cultural competence is defined as a set of congruent behaviors, attitudes, and policies that come together and enable a system, agency, or professionals to work effectively in cross-cultural situations.[13] Textbox 5.4 lists five essential elements that should be present at every level of an organization, including policy making, administration, and practice, and should be reflected in the attitudes, structures, policies, and services of the organization.[14]

TEXTBOX 5.4

Five Essential Elements for a Culturally Competent Organization

1. Values diversity,
2. Has the capacity for cultural self-assessment,
3. Is conscious of the dynamics inherent when cultures interact,
4. Has institutionalized cultural knowledge, and
5. Has developed adaptations of service delivery reflecting an understanding of cultural diversity.

Leading Cultural Competency

An organization's leadership provides support and sets expectations for cultural awareness and acumen. Change most often materializes when beginning with a review of organization mission, vision, and values and organizational goals and priorities to reflect a commitment to diversity.

Transformative change can only take place if the organization creates safety and structures to learn through deeper engaged conversations about strengths, values, assumptions and biases, fears, class and privilege, and expectations. The resulting dialogue breaks down barriers to full understanding and stronger personal and professional revelation, leading to organizational cultural competence.

Building an organization that is culturally competent is a progressive, transformative process, requiring consistent systematic engagement and change. It involves taking risks, allowing for learning through failure, commitment, and perseverance.

Diversity Committees and Employee/Community Interest Groups

Moving an organization toward a more diverse and inclusive system requires opportunities for engagement. Information professionals bring their cultural values and experiences into an organization, which can benefit the group and be shared with the community. Bringing people together, both within the organization and across the community, around shared characteristics of difference or across differences, can help strengthen diversity efforts and engage new allies and supporters.

A diversity committee or group should be developed formally with a name and scope that is focused on inclusion as an institutional value. Groups should have goals and objectives that reflect cultural competencies as a system process. It should never be assumed that staff or community members from diverse backgrounds automatically participate in these efforts; allow people to contribute as they deem appropriate (see also chapter 5: "Outreach and Partnership Resources" in the online supplement).

Partnerships

Information professionals have no shortage of community-based and profession-based organizations to reach out to and partner with to improve diversity efforts.

Valuable partners and resources may also exist outside of the information profession in organizations supporting allied professions, such as educators, social workers, medical professionals, and government or nonprofit professionals (see also chapter 5: "Diversity Information Resources" in the online supplement).

TEXTBOX 5.5

Associations That Actively Promote Diversity Services

Several organizations within the information profession actively promote service to diverse communities.

- State libraries and state library associations are particularly key for understanding the local community and environment.
- Ethnic library associations
  - American Indian Library Association (AILA)[15]
  - Asian/Pacific American Librarians Association (APALA)[16]
  - Black Caucus of the American Library Association (BCALA)[17]
  - Chinese American Librarians Association (CALA)[18]
  - The National Association to Promote Library & Information Services to Latinos and the Spanish Speaking (REFORMA)[19]
- The American Library Association, including its policy offices, divisions, and round tables, provides numerous communities focused on diversity efforts.

Talent Management

As with other skills, developing cultural competency requires a talent management plan that includes training and evaluation, performance measures, mentoring and coaching, and structured and informal communication. Organizations can work to identify information or talent gaps in staffing or operations and work to address those through staff trainings, meetings, and sharing opportunities that advance cultural competencies (see also chapter 22: "Managing Personnel").

Recruitment, selection, and retention efforts are particularly important in fostering cultural competency, as individual perspectives and experiences are valued. Leaders can work with human resources departments to develop job descriptions that convey the organization's commitment to diversity and inclusion. Specific recruitment strategies might include the use of supplemental questions that focus on work with diverse communities, prioritization of multilingual and multicultural skills and abilities, the participation of community representatives in the selection process, and promotion of opportunities through diversity advocates and organizations.

Shared Leadership—Boards, Friends, and Volunteers

Cultural competency extends to the shared leadership of an organization, including boards, friends groups, and volunteers. An informed and educated leadership and governance structure is critical to advancing cultural competency (see also chapter 37: "Leadership Skills for Today's Global Information Landscape"). Training opportunities can be shared with an organization's community leadership and support bodies, including volunteers and even elected officials. Engaging leaders in goal setting, planning, and implementation of efforts toward a culturally competent and inclusive organization is incredibly important (see also chapter 19: "Strategic Planning" and chapter 20: "Change Management").

Discussion Question

Cultural competence involves behaviors, attitudes, and policies that allow an organization to work effectively in cross-cultural situations. How might an information organization develop cultural competency reflective of a new culture or population that has been recognized in the community?

INFORMATION ORGANIZATIONS AND COMMUNITY DEVELOPMENT

Information organizations are uniquely positioned to provide a venue and forum to focus on shared opportunities and highlight attention to and broaden understanding about community and diversity.

Information Organizations Support Communities

Through collections, programs, and services, information organizations contribute to the community, and with these contributions have opportunities to serve and support diverse communities while promoting deeper cross-cultural understanding. Many information organizations allocate funding specifically to purchase bilingual and multilingual materials relevant to the community. By including materials in a variety of formats, featuring a diversity of authors and illustrators, and addressing subjects in all areas, information organizations can reflect the diversity of the community. Establishing collection development policies that advocate selection and purchasing of materials that are reflective of the community's diverse needs is important. Community members can contribute to the development of collections by providing input into the selection, arrangement, and promotion of materials (see also chapter 24: "Managing Collections").

Programming that highlights and reflects the community's diverse cultural values is a key step toward a more inclusive organization and community. Programs and services can be community driven and community created through partnerships with community-based organizations. Programming can also advance engagement at a community-wide level through conversations that promote cultural exchange. As a respected institution, an information organization can facilitate important discussions around what might be difficult topics, such as equity, race, social justice, and cultural values. An outward- and community-facing organization provides greater opportunities for progressive institutional change.

Recruitment to community leadership positions, including boards, friends groups, and volunteers, should include considerations of diversity both to advance diversity efforts in the community and as a means to strengthen the organization through the inclusion of multiple perspectives and talents. Outreach, promotion, and partnerships provide additional opportunities to advance diversity efforts. Dedicating staff time and operational funding to maintaining a broad community presence across a range of community members is critical. Additionally, sharing communications through these connections and channels creates true ownership, respect, and involvement across the community.

Communities Support Information Organizations

As communities become more actively engaged in the production of knowledge and information, they can turn to information organizations as not only sources for content but also as repositories for the information and resources they create. By actively engaging in diversity efforts, information organizations can be at the forefront of knowledge and information cocreation with members of the community. Partnerships with diverse communities can result in unique and valuable local cultural history resources, artistic collaborations, or even social or entrepreneurial projects.

Diverse communities can support information organizations' role in preservation and access (see also chapter 13: "Analog and Digital Curation and Preservation"). Involvement from diverse communities can help ensure that information organizations collect and preserve the materials that are most important to documenting a community and its members. Information organizations that fail to engage diverse communities are likely also to fail to preserve their historical records. Diverse communities can work with information organizations to acquire and contextualize unique collections that advance research and guarantee access to materials for future generations.

Finally, information organizations that engage diverse communities remain relevant across their communities. Diverse communities provide efficient systems for the sharing of information. As individuals gather around shared differences, they also share experiences and insights with their peers. The information organization that engages a diverse community ensures that its services, programs, and value are promoted within that community.

INFORMATION ORGANIZATIONS AND SOCIAL JUSTICE

The valuing, celebration, and recognition of differences among members of a given community may still leave issues of equity unanswered. An information organization's engagement with a community requires that it confront such issues. How an information organization addresses these issues, which often manifest as social problems and concerns that the entire community is also working to address, is one of the most important manifestations of diversity and cultural competency work done at institutional levels.

The library and information science profession has a long, but sometimes complicated, history acknowledging and working to take on issues of equity, diversity, and inclusion. The profession's development of spaces and organizations; the systems, tools, and policies for the use and provision of information; and its engagement with individual users, groups, and other organizations—all factor into its commitment to equity, diversity, and inclusion.

The commitment to address disparities in society through efforts focused on equity, diversity, and inclusion is commonly referred to as social justice. The National Association of Social Workers (NASW) defines social justice as "the view that everyone deserves equal economic, political and social rights and opportunities."[20] Work in information organizations, through its emphasis on equitable access and intellectual freedom, often mirrors and supports the work done by social workers in attempting to fill the gaps left by social and political disparities. From programs addressing the reading and technology needs of elderly patrons to services and programs supporting new immigrants in the process of becoming better

> How an information organization addresses these issues, which often manifest as social problems and concerns that the entire community is also working to address, is one of the most important manifestations of diversity and cultural competency work done at institutional levels.

acquainted with their new country, information organizations play vital roles in bridging the gaps community members experience.

Starting with the premise that our social world is made up of structures and systems that all members of society engage in and are engaged by, a social justice framework acknowledges concepts—oppression, power, and privilege—that are important for information professionals to understand.

Oppression

The NASW white paper, "Institutional Racism and the Social Work Profession: A Call to Action," provides a practitioner-focused definition of oppression in society: "People experience oppression when they are deprived of human rights or dignity and are (or feel) powerless to do anything about it."[21] This definition highlights two significant aspects of equity: dignity and rights. The lack or diminishment of either human dignity or human rights increases the state of oppression experienced and decreases the opportunity for equity. Information organizations' support for intellectual freedom and equitable access should center on human dignity and human rights in the development of programs, services, and policies.

Power

One of the most important notions regarding discrepancies of power within society is the idea that "the benefit of access to resources and social rewards and the power to shape the norms and values of society"[22] are connected to society's shared ideas of merit and justice. As discussed above, understanding diversity, equity, and inclusion can help information professionals be more sensitive to segments of the community who may be relegated to lesser status and have fewer means to act upon, participate, and engage with their civic environment. Indeed, NASW writes:

> It is the combination of policies, practices, or procedures embedded in bureaucratic structure that systematically lead to unequal outcomes for groups of people. . . . In this environment disparities are often tolerated as normal rather than investigated and challenged.[23]

Privilege

The idea that some groups of people rightly and deservedly occupy the fringes of society is the same idea that allows the perpetuation of oppression and the practices, policies, and procedures that uphold social inequity. Information organizations and professions, in their commitment to equity, diversity, and inclusion, must be aware of such pervasive mind-sets and make strides to counter them. At the center of these mind-sets is the concept of privilege: the unacknowledged, unrecognized, and unearned ways that bestow access, rights, and benefits to particular groups over others. Peggy McIntosh in her seminal essay, "White Privilege: Unpacking the Invisible Knapsack,"[24] defined racial privilege by describing it and likening it to male privilege, another kind of unacknowledged way of being that affords unearned benefits to a particular group over others.

Privilege is very difficult to see and define. However, it can be described as the opposite or inverse of oppression. McIntosh, in describing her attempts to reflect on her own privilege, wrote, "The pressure to avoid it is great, for in facing it I must give up the myth of meritocracy. If these things are true, this is not such a free country; one's life is not what one makes it; many doors open for certain people through no virtues of their own."[25] Individuals and communities who experience oppressive conditions also experience the lack of privilege.

INFORMATION ORGANIZATIONS ADVANCING SOCIAL JUSTICE

As information organizations are institutions created and sustained through collective and concerted efforts of individual people, the issues of oppression, power, and privilege are present in them. These issues are manifest in the content and organization of collections, the creation and imposition of policies (see also chapter 29: "Information Policy"), the placement and support of locations and buildings, and the engagement and inclusion of members of the community.

Todd Honma notes that the development of library and information services in the United States can be viewed as one that

> speak[s] to a common hegemonic U.S. rhetoric of white ethnic assimilation and meritocratic advancement, both of which have been critiqued extensively by scholars in the social sciences, particularly for their fallacious ideals of an egalitarian U.S. society that ignores ideological and material discriminations based on race.[26]

Today, while an information organization's enduring mission is to foster lifelong learning, it is highly critical that the organization and its personnel be reflective of how it pursues that mission. To pursue a mission of social justice, an information organization must question how its policies, structures, and procedures are supportive of the community and how its collective efforts can be inclusive and aligned against oppression.

Information organizations and information professionals can pursue social justice across their practice. In the composition of collections, professionals can consider the voices and perspectives that are represented and privileged and consider efforts to create more inclusive and authentic collections. In the description and organization of information, professionals can consider the terms and structures used to catalog and organize content. Over the past several decades, information professionals have considered the bias inherent in subject headings and advocated for more inclusive terms. Most recently, library users and professionals raised concerns over the use of "illegal alien" in the LC Subject Heading system.[27] As public spaces, libraries and information organizations have a history entwined with racial segregation—and while some professionals advocated for the desegregation of spaces and services, many others did not. The segregation and inequity of spaces continues into the present in the form of underfunded, understaffed, or under-resourced locations in more diverse service areas. Information professionals have a history of adapting services and programs to address urgent needs and emerging populations, but shifting populations and rapidly evolving community needs make programming and outreach a constant opportunity for information organizations to demonstrate their commitment to social justice.

While many social justice efforts can be initiated by an inward focus on the information professional's practice, increasingly professionals are adopting a method of turning outward to work with communities to identify their priorities for social justice. The information organization, like many other institutions, can no longer assume a role of authority over the communities they serve. In an increasingly networked and connected world, individual members of the community have the technology and power to organize and address specific issues. This shift provides an opportunity for information organizations to turn outward, acknowledge and accept the pressing issues and aspirations of community members, and work collaboratively to address them. This philosophy can be seen in initiatives like the American Library Association's Libraries Transforming Communities, which integrates elements of the Harwood Institute for Public Innovation, or the Aspen Institute's Dialogue on Public Libraries.[28]

It would be nearly impossible to perfectly navigate around the potential marginalization of different members of the community, but information organizations, by being both self-reflective and turning outward, can make significant strides toward a more just society. As information professionals work to address issues of equity, diversity, and inclusion within their organizations and communities, they likely also begin to address the inextricably linked social issues, concerns, and conflicts within their communities.

CONCLUSION

Information organizations and information professionals are well positioned to serve diverse individuals and advance diversity and social justice efforts within their communities. Diversity efforts strengthen the work of information professionals and ultimately improve the position of the information organization in its community. The efforts involved, including understanding a community's characteristics of difference, engaging in intercultural communication and collaboration, developing cultural competency within the organization, and recognizing the opportunities for the information organization to contribute to social justice require time, skill, and attention. The ultimate rewards, however, include greater support for the information organization and information professionals and greater advancement toward the organization's and community's mission and goals.

APPENDIX 5.1: MOST COMMON CHARACTERISTICS OF DIVERSITY

Provided below is a list of the most common characteristics of diversity, with brief descriptions of how these differences are currently conceived and how they might evolve in the future.

Gender

Gender diversity (or gender equality) efforts usually focus on traditional male and female understandings of gender and seek to advance the representation of women in traditionally male-dominated programs or services. As the understanding of gender increases, gender diversity may also expand beyond the common gender norms. Nonbinary gender diversity includes understanding for individuals' gender identity (self-concept), gender expression (outward gender expression), and gender role (place within society's male/female gender assignments). This expanded understanding of gender may also intersect with efforts to address differences in sexuality or sexual orientation.

Race and Ethnicity

In the United States, diversity efforts focused on race and ethnicity have traditionally aligned with the race and ethnicity (e.g., Hispanic or Latino) categories identified in the U.S. Census as standardized by the U.S. Office of Management and Budget (OMB). The current race question in the U.S. Census asks individuals to self-identify using the following terms:

- *White:* A person having origins in any of the original peoples of Europe, the Middle East, or North Africa.
- *Black or African American:* A person having origins in any of the Black racial groups of Africa.
- *American Indian or Alaska Native:* A person having origins in any of the original peoples of North and South America (including Central America) and who maintains tribal affiliation or community attachment.
- *Asian:* A person having origins in any of the original peoples of the Far East, Southeast Asia, or the Indian subcontinent including, for example, Cambodia, China, India, Japan, Korea, Malaysia, Pakistan, the Philippine Islands, Thailand, and Vietnam.
- *Native Hawaiian or other Pacific Islander:* A person having origins in any of the original peoples of Hawaii, Guam, Samoa, or other Pacific Islands.

Individuals are provided the opportunity to report more than one race.

Additionally, the OMB requires agencies to use a minimum of two ethnicities in collecting and reporting data: Hispanic or Latino and Not Hispanic or Latino. *Hispanic or Latino* refers to a person of Cuban, Mexican, Puerto Rican, South or Central American, or other Spanish culture or origin regardless of race. Individuals reporting Hispanic or Latino ethnicity may also report specific categories—Mexican, Mexican American, or Chicano; Puerto Rican; Cuban; another Hispanic, Latino, or Spanish origin; and write-in answers.

As evidence of the evolving understanding of difference and diversity, in preparation for the 2020 U.S. Census, the Census Bureau has tested multiple new formats for race and ethnicity questions, including the option for reporting nationalities within specific categories, new categories for individuals of Middle Eastern or North African ancestry, and even the substitution of the terms "race" and "ethnicity" for the more generic "categories."[29]

Diversity efforts designed to address race and ethnicity usually focus on advancing the representation and participation of non-White individuals in programs and services and in decision-making bodies and organizations.

Physical and Mental Ability

Differences in physical and mental ability vary greatly among individuals, making it difficult to clearly identify all of the characteristics that could be a priority for diversity efforts in this category. The Americans with Disabilities Act (ADA), one of the most comprehensive pieces of civil rights legislation that prohibits discrimination and guarantees equal opportunities for people with disabilities, does not specifically list the impairments or differences that the legislation addresses. Rather, the ADA defines disability as "a physical or mental impairment that substantially limits one or more major life activities, a person who has a history or records of such an impairment, or a person who is perceived by others as having such an impairment."[30]

Many current discussions of difference in physical and mental abilities address visible and invisible differences and permanent and temporary differences. Because of the range of differences, many advocates encourage allowing individuals to express their physical or mental difference as they define it rather than assigning a specific category to a perceived physical or mental difference.

Diversity efforts designed to address physical and mental abilities usually seek opportunities to include, accommodate, or design for persons with different abilities in programs and services. These efforts also seek to ensure the participation and representation of people with different abilities in decision-making bodies and organizations.

Age

The multiple generations represented in today's communities and organizations carry with them different experiences and perspectives. Generational differences may become even more apparent in communities as baby boomers (born 1946–1964) begin to enter retirement and as younger generations, raised in the midst of significant technological change, emerge as independent decision makers and tastemakers. Generational differences can include differences in values, communication styles, work expectations, and political and social beliefs.

In the workplace, diversity efforts focused on age seek to offset age discrimination, which is often experienced by older adults, but also by young and emerging professionals. In organizations and communities, diversity efforts focused on age can help encourage participation and representation from across generational lines.

Sexual Orientation

The unique experiences of lesbian, gay, bisexual, and transgender (LGBT) people form a final—and still emerging—category of diversity that is frequently addressed by organizations. Sexual orientation is based on an individual's attraction to people from the opposite, the same, or both sexes. As mentioned above, gender identity (self-concept), gender expression (outward gender expression), and gender role (place within society's male/female gender assignments) may also be included in this area of difference. Society's changing understanding of sexual orientation and the personal nature of this category make it difficult to fully define the range of identities contained within this category. Relying on an individual's expression or self-definition may provide the greatest understanding.

In the workplace, diversity efforts focused on sexual orientation seek to offset the discrimination faced by LGBT employees and patrons. In organizations and communities, diversity efforts focused on sexual orientation can help encourage participation and representation from across the spectrum of experiences. These efforts may be especially important for older populations, which might be particularly vulnerable to discrimination and exclusion based on sexual orientation; LGBT parents and families, which may face exclusion or prejudice due to perceived nonconformity to the preconceived family composition; and children and young people, where the pressures of dealing with emerging sexuality or self-discovery are compounded by a sense of difference from their peers.

NOTES

1. Cedric Herring, "Does Diversity Pay? Race, Gender and the Business Case for Diversity," *American Sociological Review* 74, no. 2 (April 2009).
2. Ronald S. Burt, "Social Origins of Good Ideas," *American Journal of Sociology* 110, no. 2 (September 2004), http://web.upcomillas.es/personal/rgimeno/doctorado/SOGI.pdf.
3. Jeffrey F. Millem, Mitchell J. Chang, and Anthony Lising Antonio, *Making Diversity Work on Campus: A Research-Based Perspective* (Washington, DC: Association of American Colleges and Universities, 2005), http://www.aacu.org/inclusive_excellence/documents/Milem_et_al.pdf.
4. Ibid.
5. American Library Association, *Final Report of the ALA Task Force on Equity, Diversity, and Inclusion* (Chicago: American Library Association, 2016), http://connect.ala.org/files/TFEDIFinalReport%202016-06-06.pdf.
6. "Intellectual Freedom: Issues and Resources," American Library Association, 2014, http://www.ala.org/advocacy/intfreedom.
7. "Policy B.2.1.11 Diversity in Collection Development," *American Library Association Policy Manual*, ALA Council, 2013, http://www.ala.org/aboutala/governance/policymanual.
8. "Policy B.2.1.12 Universal Right to Free Expression," *American Library Association Policy Manual*, ALA Council, 2013, http://www.ala.org/aboutala/governance/policymanual.

9. "Policy B.2.1.15 Access to Library Resources and Services Regardless of Sex, Gender Identity, Gender Expression, or Sexual Orientation," *American Library Association Policy Manual*, ALA Council, 2013, http://www.ala.org/aboutala/governance/policymanual.

10. "Policy B.2.1.20 Services to Persons with Disabilities," *American Library Association Policy Manual*, ALA Council, 2013, http://www.ala.org/aboutala/governance/policymanual.

11. "Policy B.2.3.1 Linguistic Pluralism," *American Library Association Policy Manual*, ALA Council, 2013, http://www.ala.org/aboutala/governance/policymanual.

12. Satia Marshall Orange and Robin Osborne, "Introduction," in *Outreach to Equity: Innovative Models of Library Policy and Practice* (Chicago: American Library Association, 2004).

13. T. Cross, B. Bazron, K. Dennis, and M. Isaacs, *Toward a Culturally Competent System of Care*, Vol. 1 (Washington, DC: Georgetown University, 1989).

14. Ibid.

15. American Indian Library Association, accessed September 17, 2017, http://ailanet.org/.

16. Asian/Pacific American Library Association, accessed September 17, 2017, http://www.apalaweb.org/.

17. Black Caucus of the American Library Association, 2017, http://bcala.org/.

18. American Library Association, "Chinese American Librarians Association," 2017, http://www.ala.org/aboutala/affiliates/affiliates/cala.

19. REFORMA, (2017), http://www.reforma.org/.

20. "Social Justice," National Association of Social Workers, 2017, http://www.socialworkers.org/pressroom/features/Issue/peace.asp.

21. National Association of Social Workers, "Institutional Racism and the Social Work Profession: A Call to Action," 2007, https://www.socialworkers.org/diversity/InstitutionalRacism.pdf.

22. Ibid.

23. Ibid.

24. Peggy McIntosh, "White Privilege: Unpacking the Invisible Knapsack," *Peace and Freedom Magazine*, July/August, 1989, retrieved from https://nationalseedproject.org/white-privilege-unpacking-the-invisible-knapsack.

25. Ibid.

26. Todd Honma, "Trippin' Over the Color Line: The Invisibility of Race in Library and Information Studies," *InterActions: UCLA Journal of Education and Information Studies* 1, no. 2 (2005), retrieved from https://escholarship.org/uc/item/4nj0w1mphttps://escholarship.org/uc/item/4nj0w1mp.

27. Jasmine Aguilera, "Another Word for 'Illegal Alien' at the Library of Congress: Contentious." *New York Times*, July 22, 2016, retrieved from https://www.nytimes.com/2016/07/23/us/another-word-for-illegal-alien-at-the-library-of-congress-contentious.html.

28. Libraries Transforming Communities, http://www.ala.org/tools/librariestransform/libraries-transforming-communities; The Aspen Institute, Dialogue on Public Libraries, http://www.libraryvision.org/.

29. Kelly Mathews, et al., *2015 National Content Test: Race and Ethnicity Analysis Report*, 2017, https://www.census.gov/programs-surveys/decennial-census/2020-census/planning-management/final-analysis/2015nct-race-ethnicity-analysis.html.

30. United States Department of Justice Civil Rights Division, "Introduction to the ADA," 2014.

Part II

Information Professions
Physical and Virtual Environments

"Libraries have been—and still are—centers of knowledge and resources for tens of thousands of communities. They are the hubs across which networks of learning connect millions of users and all kinds of scholarly activities."

—Andy Havens[1]

Libraries and information organizations have always provided resources and services to support their communities. While that certainly has not changed, what has changed is the adoption of many new and different roles by information professionals to creatively meet those needs. Their roles span the gamut from school librarian in an elementary school to embedded librarian in a college science course, from reference librarian to innovations librarian in a public library, from legal librarian to nonprofit archivist, and from data manager to data analyst. Information organizations of all types are also adapting, renovating, and reimagining just what an information space might look like today—resulting in new opportunities for users to create, learn, and study in learning commons, makerspaces, and even virtually.

Part II explores changes, innovations, and possibilities in specific information environments—from those that serve students to those that serve businesses, from virtual to physical, with the focus always on how to meet the needs of the user and the community. A valuable takeaway of Part II is the identification of various career options—both within the library setting and outside of it—that utilize the unique skill sets and competencies of today's information professional.

NOTE

1. Andy Havens, "From Community to Technology and Back Again," *NextSpace*, no. 20 (January 2013): 4–11, retrieved from http://library.oclc.org/cdm/singleitem/collection/p15003coll11/id/19/rec/5.

6

Literacy and Media Centers

SCHOOL LIBRARIES

Mary Ann Harlan

Chapter 6, "Literacy and Media Centers: School Libraries," provides the reader with an understanding of the responsibilities of the school librarian, the instructional program of the school library, and how the space in a school library supports new instructional models. With over twenty years of school librarian experience, Dr. Mary Ann Harlan adeptly explores the many roles of the school librarian, which include program manager, literacy expert, collaborator working with classroom teachers in curriculum planning and instruction, and mentor providing individual mentoring to the school community.

School libraries are rapidly evolving to meet the literacy and information needs of twenty-first-century students. Teaching students to access, evaluate, and use information and how to become active participants in the global landscape environment is the core responsibility of the school librarian. Knowledge of school library standards from organizations like the American Association of School Librarians (AASL) and understanding of educational standards like The Common Core are essential for today's school librarian. Harlan also addresses the Next Gen Science Standards (NGSS) and how school librarians support and collaborate with science teachers and students to meet these standards.

Harlan further notes the important and relatively new role of the school library as a learning commons where school librarians model lifelong learning and mentor community members in information skills and collaborative and creative learning. The varied roles, competencies, and skills of school librarians are addressed throughout this chapter.

★   ★   ★

School libraries (or media centers) provide fundamental services to primary and secondary schools (K–12). Their function is to serve the learning needs of the school community. While this is an apparently simple and obvious mission in the modern era, it is also complex. As a space, school libraries are learning centers filled with resources and tools that support learning. However, it is the services provided by information professionals, such as instruction and support for students and teachers engaged in inquiry and literacy practices, that are at the heart of the school library.

The mission of a school library is to support the school's work to educate youth, primarily by supporting the core curriculum. However, school libraries embrace more than merely supporting the academic curriculum of the school. In addition to providing resources and tools that teachers and students can use to access and create information while building knowledge within curricular standards, they also support personal learning beyond the classroom. Through instruction, mentoring, and coaching, school librarians encourage inquiry and knowledge building in an environment that offers a flexible space for collaborative learning, personal pursuits, and sharing of knowledge. This chapter identifies the unique role of the school librarian as a teacher, highlights the way they work as managers, and finally introduces the school library as a space. After completing this chapter, the reader should have an understanding of the responsibilities of the school librarian, the instructional program of the school library, and how the space of a library supports new instructional models.

ROLES OF SCHOOL LIBRARIANS

Today's roles for school librarians, based on early twentieth-century models of school librarianship, began to expand in the 1960s to include the role of instruction. In the twenty-first century, school librarian responsibilities range from program manager to literacy expert (e.g., reading, information, digital), to collaborator working with classroom teachers in curriculum planning and instruction, and to mentor providing individual mentoring to the school community. The section below outlines both the sustaining and emergent roles of school librarians.

Teaching and Modeling Information Literacy

The information literacy role of school librarians is the primary function of school librarianship (see also chapter 16: "Teaching Users: Information and Technology Instruction"). Teaching students to access, evaluate, and use information, both within their academic environment and as citizens of a democracy, is at the heart of the school library curriculum.

As curriculum standards for core subject areas emerged to guide instruction, school librarians also developed curricular standards. These learning standards have continued to evolve over time. In 1998, guidelines for school libraries and learning standards were established, providing librarians with an important set of instructional benchmarks regarding information literacy. The American Association of School Librarians (AASL),[1] along with the Association for Educational Communication and Technology (AECT),[2] published *Information Power*[3] a report that describes nine student learning standards (see table 6.1).

These learning standards guided instructional goals in school libraries as students, teachers, and school librarians began to navigate a new era of information abundance. The AASL standards were consistent with the definition of information literacy provided by the American Library Association (ALA) published a year later, defining information literacy as the ability "to recognize when information is needed and have the ability to locate, evaluate, and use effectively the needed information."[4]

In 2007, AASL updated the student learning standards to reflect twenty-first-century trends, publishing *Student Learning Standards for the 21st-Century Learner*.[5] AASL recognized four Student Learning Standards—each encompassing multiple benchmarks. Each standard addresses four types of knowledge needed by students: skills, dispositions, responsibilities, and self. The AASL 21st-Century Student Learning Standards recognize that

- learning requires engaging deeply with information,
- citizens are responsible for being ethical users of information, and
- learning *does not* only occur in a classroom, or the structures of school.

Mary Ann Harlan

Table 6.1. Student Learning Standards.

The student who is information literate . . .   • accesses information efficiently and effectively.   • evaluates information critically and competently.   • uses information accurately and creatively.
The student who is an independent learner is information literate and . . .   • pursues information related to personal interests.   • appreciates literature and other creative expressions of information.   • strives for excellence in information seeking and knowledge generation.
The student who contributes positively to the learning community and to society is information literate and . . .   • recognizes the importance of information to a democratic society.   • practices ethical behavior in regard to information and information technology.   • participates effectively in groups to pursue and generate information.

Source: American Association of School Librarians (AASL) and Association for Educational Communication and Technology (AECT), *Information Literacy Standards for Student Learning* (Chicago: American Library Association, 1998).

The benchmarks provide a road map within the standards of learning goals as students develop information skills. They reflect the importance of inquiry learning, the responsibility of the learner, and information skills. They also acknowledge the need for communication, collaboration, creativity, and critical thinking.[6] The Student Learning Standards have been compared to a document describing their connection to Common Core State Standards (CCSS) used in forty-two states. This demonstrates how the curriculum of the school library supports the curriculum of the school. In fall of 2017, AASL released new learning standards that can be found on the AASL website.[7]

Developing Digital Literacies

Embedded in the AASL student learning standards are references to technology as a tool to access, use, and create information. Thus, the AASL standards highlight another key role of school librarians—to develop students' digital literacy. Digital literacy is defined here as the ability to use technology to learn and to contribute to the global community. Digital literacy assumes that knowing the tool is not enough; it is also important to know how to use the tool as an active member of the digital community and to enhance and transform one's learning.

While AASL twenty-first-century student learning standards are the basis for instruction practices in school libraries, these practices are also informed by standards developed by other organizations, such as the International Society of Technology in Education (ISTE). In 2016, ISTE updated their *Standards for Students*[8] and include seven categories as shown in textbox 6.1.

There are many overlaps between student learning standards published by ISTE and the AASL, such as digital citizenship including the ethical use of information and a focus on knowledge production and

> **TEXTBOX 6.1**
>
> **ISTE's Student Standards**
>
> • Empowered Learners
> • Digital Citizen
> • Knowledge Constructor
> • Innovative Designer
> • Computational Thinker
> • Creative Communicator
> • Global Collaborator

sharing. Both standards help guide school librarian practices that encourage instruction regarding technology literacy. For teachers, the ISTE standards for students can shape the focus on pedagogy. The ISTE standards have an additional component: Standards for Educators.[9] As school librarians are often the education technology experts in their schools, they need to keep current on new and emerging technologies, evolving techniques for embedding technologies in classrooms to transform teaching and learning, and issues related to privacy and safety (see also chapter 3: "Librarianship: A Continuously Evolving Profession"). The ISTE standards for teachers can help school librarians maintain their expertise, as they participate in lifelong learning to stay current in emerging digital practices.

Teaching as Curriculum Generalists

Core subject-area standards have shaped the practice of school librarians, providing opportunities for them to collaborate with classroom teachers in curriculum planning and instruction. One major transition in practice occurred following the introduction of Common Core standards. The Common Core standards are the adopted national curriculum standards for K–12 students in the United States. The Common Core standards for math and English language arts curriculum were introduced in 2009[10] and have since been adopted by forty-two states. The Common Core English Language Arts (ELA) standards[11] are especially significant to the practice of school librarians as they include literacy standards for history/social science, science, and technical subjects and emphasize literacy—be it digital, print, visual, or audio.

Because the Common Core standards emphasize building knowledge through interaction with information, they provide opportunities for school librarians to collaborate with classroom teachers

> Because the Common Core standards emphasize building knowledge through interaction with information, they provide opportunities for school librarians to collaborate with classroom teachers to foster this type of learning.

to foster this type of learning. For example, a Common Core standard for writing emphasizes the need for students to learn to conduct research, including research projects based on focused research questions. School librarians have expertise in identifying a student's information needs; helping students develop research questions and find and evaluate information based on quality, accuracy, and relevance; and determining how to present the answer so that others may benefit and do so in an ethical manner. This new emphasis on the process of responsible research presents opportunities for school librarians to collaborate with classroom teachers to team-teach and model information literacy skills. With this transition to new learning expectations for students under the Common Core, both students and teachers need support and instruction in modern information practices.

Another Common Core standard that has shaped the practice of school librarians in recent years emphasizes the ability to use and analyze complex, real-world texts. Complex texts are the types of texts students encounter in their everyday lives and their classrooms. They include primary source documents, news reports, research papers, journal articles, policy briefs, narrative nonfiction, and informational texts. As literacy experts and collection developers, school librarians provide both the resources necessary for teachers to use complex texts in their classes, as well as professional development for teachers regarding how to help their students analyze and engage a complex text. As they develop the school's collection and plan ways to address this standard in each class, school librarians bring their knowledge regarding how to evaluate a text both for quantitative and qualitative reading levels, how to assess the text's appropriateness for a student, and how the text relates to a subject. School librarians build their collection with complex, real-world texts that extend beyond print items

Mary Ann Harlan

and include audio, visual, and digital texts. As our world becomes increasingly global with diverse perspectives, the capacity to analyze real-world texts has emerged as a key component of citizenship.

Another national standards movement has influenced the practice of school librarians and shifted their role to be more involved in curriculum planning and instruction. The Next Gen Science Standards (NGSS)[12] were developed by a coalition consisting of the National Research Council, the National Science Teachers Association, the American Association for Advancement in of Science, and Achieve. They were introduced in 2011 and promote a national approach to science standards. While the NGSS are not a part of Common Core, they adopt similar approaches to student learning and include an emphasis on student performance rather than content knowledge, student inquiry in building and applying scientific knowledge, and an integrated approach throughout K–12. School librarians can support science teachers and students by facilitating inquiry, making connections in the curriculum, and teaching skills related to demonstrating knowledge.

As curriculum generalists, school librarians have a basic understanding of each of the content area standards and an in-depth awareness of how teachers teach, or implement, content-area standards in their classrooms. This is a key element to being a school librarian.

Program Manager

School librarians are responsible for managing the library. Managing a school library includes circulation (see also chapter 15: "Accessing Information Anywhere and Anytime: Access Services"), collection development (see also chapter 24: "Managing Collections"), management of volunteers, promotion, and marketing of the library (see also chapter 27: "Communication, Marketing, and Outreach Strategies"), and advocacy for how school librarians assist and support student learning (see also chapter 28: "Advocacy"). School librarians develop policies and processes, in collaboration with the school community and with approval by the school board, to uphold the values of information access and user privacy, such as those related to selecting materials and dealing with challenged materials. This includes working with filtering and acceptable-use policies that are both legal and open enough to support student learning (see also chapter 35: "Intellectual Freedom"). It also includes circulation policies. School librarians also maintain and manage a budget that allows the program to grow; this often includes seeking funds and advocating for the program (see also chapter 21: "Managing Budgets"). Managing a budget requires school librarians to be aware of funding categories and opportunities, grants and donations, as well as the day-to-day accounting of their budget. They are responsible for managing a collection, selecting appropriate materials, and organizing the collection for use. They oversee a staff that includes student and parent volunteers, as well as paraprofessional support (see also chapter 22: "Managing Personnel"). As maintenance of the program is the responsibility of the school librarian, they need the capacity to develop a strategic plan within the parent organization (school) in order to ensure relevance and use of the school library by the school community (see also chapter 19: "Strategic Planning").

INSTRUCTIONAL MODELS IN SCHOOL LIBRARIES

As school librarians increasingly focus on instruction, they engage with students through three different schedules of student contact with the library: fixed, flexible, and mixed. Fixed schedules are based on students coming to the library with their class once a week or every two weeks. Fixed schedules lend themselves to direct instruction and programming and have a limitation regarding collaboration. Flexible schedules occur when teachers schedule class time in the library as needed. This model allows for instruction that is embedded in classroom curriculum and relies on collaborative approaches to instruction. Mixed schedules combine fixed and flexible scheduling, with certain times of the day open for classes in need of research and inquiry-instruction. Within the three schedules, there are different instructional models including: direct instruction or programming such as storytime, inquiry-based learning models, and connected learning models. This chapter focuses on inquiry-based learning and connected learning as models of instruction in school libraries.

Inquiry-Based Learning

Over the last several decades, some K–12 teachers and librarians have implemented inquiry learning at their schools. Although policies implemented under the era of No Child Left Behind[13] and Race to the Top (2001–2011)[14] emphasized basic skills needed for success in high-stakes student testing and curtailed widespread implementation of inquiry-based learning, the more recent transition to Common Core standards and its focus on helping students develop real-world skills needed for college and careers has returned the focus of K–12 schools to inquiry-based learning. Inquiry-based learning is defined by the following key components: real-world, relevant questions or problems; questions and investigations that build on student's interests and prior knowledge; connecting school-based learning with out-of-school experiences; and iterative investigation using a variety of resources. This includes experts in the field, primary and secondary sources, investigation in the field, construction and presentation of new knowledge, and reflection. There are several models of inquiry-based learning as outlined in table 6.2.

> As information specialists, school librarians can be at the forefront of implementing opportunities for inquiry learning, with its emphasis on twenty-first-century skills, such as collaboration, communication, creativity, and critical thinking.

The key to inquiry-based learning is student ownership of the learning process, shifting the role of the teaching team to that of coach and model. As information specialists, school librarians can be at the forefront of implementing opportunities for inquiry-based learning, with its emphasis on twenty-first-century skills, such as collaboration, communication, creativity, and critical thinking (also emphasized in the Common Core standards).

Table 6.2. Models of Inquiry-Based Learning.

Model	Description	Example
Problem-based learning	Students investigate and design a solution to a real-world problem, often derived from their community.	Designing a program to address bullying in their school.
Project-based learning	Students engage in a project that solves or addresses real-world concerns.	Designing and producing an alternative energy source for their neighborhood.
Guided inquiry	Students select a topic relevant to their lives and are guided through an in-depth research process.	Students engage in an academic research paper and are guided through the process of developing an essential question, planning a course of action, gathering information from primary and secondary sources, using information to shape and refine their initial question, gathering supporting information, and planning a presentation that is shaped for a specific audience.

Mary Ann Harlan

Connected Learning

Another learning model that can be used by school librarians is Connected Learning.[15] Connected Learning is based on three learning principles and three design principles as highlighted in textbox 6.2.[16] As a framework for learning, school librarians who design learning opportunities using the three design principles of Connected Learning support both inquiry-based learning and the focus of the Common Core standards. For example, production-centered learning relates to Common Core standards associated with the presentation of knowledge and ideas. The principle of openly networked learning allows school librarians to address the ethical use of information in the presentation of knowledge, an important component of the AASL 21st-Century Student Learning Standards. By focusing on a shared purpose in designing learning opportunities, students need to develop the skills necessary to be successful in collaboration, a strand in both CCSS standards and emphasized in the 21st-Century Student Learning Standards. Connected Learning imagines a world in which education is the responsibility of a distributed network—embracing learning as occurring in different contexts throughout one's life.

In designing learning opportunities, school librarians should recognize the principles of learning and how they relate to familiar learning models, such as inquiry-based learning approaches. In emphasizing the interest-powered learning, school librarians recognize and leverage intrinsic motivation. This deepens the inquiry-based learning models of project-based and problem-based learning by allowing students to engage in projects of personal relevance. For example, collaborative groups can focus on community projects that are of deep interest to the participants, while still connecting to core academic content. In recognizing the role of peers in supportive learning, school librarians can encourage connections between learners with similar interests while empowering youth to demonstrate their expertise. School librarians can also identify, support, and encourage the development of academic skills while students are engaged in learning opportunities. By identifying the skills students develop, school librarians help students learn reflective practices that allow for the transference of skills between disciplines.

As curriculum generalists, school librarians bridge the subject areas for a multidisciplinary approach. As information specialists, they instruct and mentor students in inquiry-based and connected learning. This is a unique role within the school.

> **TEXTBOX 6.2**
>
> **Connected Learning and Design Principles**
>
> Learning Principles
>
> - Interest powered
> - Peer supported
> - Academically oriented
>
> Design Principles
>
> - Production centered
> - Openly networked
> - Shared purpose

Promoting Reading and Basic Literacy

The most familiar role for school librarians is reading promotion. As far back as the earliest mention of school libraries in the 1920s, the library was seen as a place for students to obtain personal reading materials. School libraries have long had a role of providing students not only with print materials to support curriculum but also books that students read for pleasure. School librarians model a love of reading through reading-related activities and promoting reading materials. Even in the Information Age, with format changes and the availability of audio or e-books, the focus on reading promotion remains an important role for school librarians.

This historical focus on supporting and promoting reading has evolved into today's role for school librarians, who act as literacy experts. The role of literacy expert is especially significant in the twenty-first century, as literacy is a complex notion that includes the ability to decode, comprehend, and create a variety of types of texts. School librarians teach strategies for predicting, summarizing, and synthesizing multiple texts. They incorporate media literacy into information literacy instruction, encouraging students to analyze and use information in a variety of formats. Furthermore, the emerging emphasis on complex texts has reemphasized the role of the school librarian in developing textual literacy through providing complex texts that engage core curriculum.

> ### Discussion Question
>
> Discuss the mission of the school library. What competencies does the school librarian need to possess to effectively support the library's mission both in the library and in the classroom?

While supporting core curriculum remains a primary mission of the school librarian, school librarians are also responsible for encouraging and modeling reading for pleasure. This means it is incumbent on the school librarian to be aware of interest-based trends of the community served by the library along with trends in genres, popular titles, and award-winning and notable titles in both state and national awards. Such awards include the Newbery[17] and Coretta Scott King awards,[18] Caldecott[19] and Printz[20] awards sponsored by ALA, the National Book Award[21] for youth, and various state reader awards and lists. By staying current, school librarians provide opportunities for students to find stories they like to read.

SCHOOL LIBRARIES AS PLACE FOR SERVICES

School libraries have the potential to be a *third place*. While third place theory deserves more attention than provided in this chapter, the significance to school libraries lies in the idea that there are three spheres of learning: the home sphere, the work or school sphere, and an additional space in a public environment that serves as a community anchor, such as public libraries (see also chapter 8: "Community Anchors for Lifelong Learning: Public Libraries"). School libraries fall firmly in the school space. However, the environment of the school library can also act as third places, encouraging students to engage in individual inquiry, pursue collaborative projects of interests, and enjoy a space where they can connect with community mentors. For instance, school libraries support individual inquiry, individual reading interests, and individual pursuits in ways that classrooms do not necessarily provide. School libraries that engage in connected learning frameworks assist students in making connections based on their interests with mentors and other community members who share that interest, even if that interest is beyond the school's curriculum. In other words, despite the location of school libraries on school campuses, they support a much broader type of learning.

> " The school library as a third place has an additional benefit for students, as it offers a place of refuge—a space where an individual can pursue information needs and interests that they may not be able to explore in other environments due to perceived risk. "

The school library as a third place has an additional benefit for students, as it offers a place of refuge—a space where an individual can pursue information needs and interests that they may not be able to explore in other environments due to perceived risk. School librarians must strive to provide safe, welcoming spaces for students in need of quiet time and space. School libraries that have implemented the learning commons model, which includes space for collaboration, should consider how to also provide space for quiet contemplation, study, and reading. In the section below, the learning commons is explored in more depth.

Mary Ann Harlan

School Libraries as Learning Commons

As inquiry-based learning takes hold in schools, school libraries are beginning to reshape how space and resources are used to serve the learning community. Many are now defined as learning commons, challenging stereotypes of school libraries solely as repositories of materials and places for independent learning.

Learning commons are defined as learning, project, and research spaces. In a single space, they combine elements typically associated with libraries, computer labs, and collaboration areas. Learning commons offer a flexible space that can easily be reconfigured for use as a performance space, for small group collaborative work, or for independent study. Additionally, learning commons are trending toward incorporating elements of makerspaces, particularly media and digital makerspaces, equipped with project-oriented tools, such as cameras, editing hardware and software, and robotics and electronic equipment (see also chapter 18: "Creation Culture and Makerspaces"). The philosophy of a learning commons invites students to construct their understandings and design their work.

School libraries are well suited to serve as school learning commons. They have existing research resources, computers for accessing information, and furniture that encourages collaboration, such as movable tables. School learning commons are improving their spaces by adding tools and resources for learners, such as the addition of design-based software, peripherals necessary to create digital media, and space to collaborate and perform both online and offline. As information professionals begin to understand the potential of makerspaces in school libraries, incorporating hands-on opportunities for design-based learning has become a fundamental component of many learning commons. These design-based learning opportunities include technology

> **Discussion Questions**
>
> How does a learning commons model support and encourage connected learning? How does the learning commons support inquiry-based learning?

mentioned above as well as items such as 3-D printers, robotics peripherals, and programming tools, and may even include something as simple as Legos to encourage spatial design. In this space, there is a responsibility of encouraging learning through access to tools not readily available to all students.

School learning commons offer 24/7 access to learning. Virtual learning commons are more than school websites. While they provide access to databases, online catalogs, links to recommended sources, and tutorials in information skills, they are also providing interactive space. Students and teachers can build and contribute to a learning commons, providing collaborative knowledge-building opportunities, peer expertise, and mentoring. This includes building recommendations for reading, research tools, and school projects. However, it can also act as online space for display of art, writing, and other activities. As they produce work in this online space, students engage in real-world publication and the global community.

Perhaps the most important element of the learning commons that school librarians can provide is modeling lifelong learning and mentoring community members in information skills. As information literacy experts who understand how to use technology to present learning, school librarians are well situated to manage the environment of a learning commons. They act as liaisons to experts in the community, both local and global. Learning commons incorporate the whole school learning community; they do not exist as separate entities based in individual classrooms. School learning commons are the heart of the school, the place where students, teachers, curriculum, and interests come together, but also reach out beyond school walls to participate in inquiry.

CONCLUSION

In the Information Age, school libraries are the hub of learning. School librarians provide instruction, mentoring, resources, tools, and connections to support inquiry both for class curriculum and for informal learning. They are integral to a school community, and the school librarian can impact learning and teaching and infuse information literacy skills into students' experiences while supporting curriculum and content standards. They develop unique relationships with learners and model lifelong learning in spaces that provide a multitude of activities.

NOTES

1. American Association of School Librarians (AASL), http://www.ala.org/aasl/.
2. Association for Educational Communication and Technology (AECT), http://aect.site-ym.com/.
3. American Association of School Librarians (AASL) and Association for Educational Communication and Technology (AECT), *Information Literacy Standards for Student Learning* (Chicago: American Library Association, 1998).
4. American Library Association (ALA), *Standards for the 21st-Century Learner*, http://www.ala.org/aasl/sites/ala.org.aasl/files/content/guidelinesandstandards/learningstandards/AASL_LearningStandards.pdf.
5. International Standards for Technology in Education (ISTE), "Standards for Students," 2017, http://www.iste.org/standards/standards/for-students-2016.
6. Ibid.
7. American Association of School Librarians, "Learning Standards and Program Guidelines," accessed September 7, 2017, http://www.ala.org/aasl/standards.
8. International Standards for Technology in Education (ISTE), "Standards for Students."
9. International Standards for Technology in Education (ISTE), "Standards for Educators," 2018, http://www.iste.org/standards/standards/standards-for-teachers.
10. Common Core State Standards Initiative, "About the Standards," 2018, http://www.corestandards.org/.
11. Common Core State Standards, "English Language Arts Standards," 2018, http://www.corestandards.org/ELA-Literacy/.
12. Next Gen Science Standards, "About the Standards," last modified June 25, 2014, http://www.nextgenscience.org/standards/standards.
13. U.S. Department of Education, "No Child Left Behind," https://www2.ed.gov/nclb/landing.jhtml.
14. U.S. Department of Education, "Race to the Top," https://www2.ed.gov/programs/racetothetop/index.html.
15. Mimi Ito, Kris Gutierrez, Sonia Livingstone, et al. *Connected Learning: An Agenda for Research and Design* (Irvine, CA: Digital Media and Learning Research Hub), http://dmlhub.net/sites/default/files/ConnectedLearning_report.pdf.
16. Ibid.
17. Association for Library Service to Children, "Newbery Awards," accessed September 7, 2017, http://www.ala.org/alsc/awardsgrants/bookmedia/newberymedal/newberymedal.
18. American Library Association, "Coretta Scott King Book Awards," accessed September 7, 2017, http://www.ala.org/emiert/cskbookawards.
19. Association for Library Service to Children, "Caldecott Medal," accessed September 7, 2017, http://www.ala.org/alsc/awardsgrants/bookmedia/caldecottmedal/caldecottmedal.
20. Young Adult Library Services Association, "Printz Award," accessed September 7, 2017, http://www.ala.org/yalsa/printz-award.
21. National Book Foundation, "National Book Award," accessed September 7, 2017, http://www.nationalbook.org/nba2017.html#.WV2mW4jytRY.

7

Learning and Research Institutions

ACADEMIC LIBRARIES

Todd Gilman

Chapter 7, "Learning and Research Institutions: Academic Libraries," explores the diverse roles and respon-
sibilities of academic librarians today, as well as the roles that are emerging. Academic libraries today find
themselves at a crossroads as they repurpose their spaces, staff, and limited funds to accommodate a future
featuring many fewer print volumes and a much different service model. Dr. Todd Gilman brings his expertise
as an academic librarian and editor of Academic Librarianship Today *to explain the varied activities in*
which academic librarians engage their community of learners and researchers, and duties they perform for
students, faculty, and the institution.

Some of the emerging roles for academic librarians include working in instructional technology, meta-
data or research informatics, and scholarly communication. Academic librarians often have a number of other
responsibilities, such as providing information literacy and technology literacy instruction, meeting publishing
and scholarship expectations, and serving on committees in the university and the profession. Many issues
in today's information landscape shape the work of today's academic librarian, such as emerging literacies
that require novel approaches to instruction, research support, economic pressures, and intellectual property
challenges within the digital domain.

Key trends include the changing models for reference service and collection development in academic
libraries, as well as a growing focus on assessment and data-driven approaches to achieving strategic ob-
jectives that have resulted in increased hiring of dedicated assessment librarians or heads of assessment.
Throughout this chapter, Gilman addresses these varied roles, trends, and competencies required of academic
librarians today.

★ ★ ★

Academic librarians perform many of the same duties as school, public, and special librarians: reference, outreach, collection development, collection maintenance, cataloging, archival processing,
digitization of rare and unique materials, preservation, conservation, interlibrary loan and document
delivery, and cultivating relationships with donors. As members of academic communities and employees of academic libraries, however, academic librarians serve different constituencies and perform

different duties than their counterparts in school, public, and special libraries. Librarians in junior colleges, community colleges, and four-year colleges serve undergraduates, faculty, and staff, both on campus and virtually. Librarians in research universities, by contrast, serve graduate students among these constituencies, again both on campus and online. Academic librarians often hold subject master's degrees or doctorates in addition to the MLIS degree. Many enjoy tenure-track faculty status.

The purpose of this chapter is both to elucidate the roles and responsibilities academic librarians assume today and to forecast trends and issues that will require them to continuously and creatively adapt to the inevitably evolving roles that the future of academic libraries will require. After completing this chapter, the reader should have an understanding of the many and varied activities in which academic librarians engage and duties they perform, as well as the challenges they face given the current climate of higher education in North America.

ACADEMIC LIBRARIANS TODAY

Academic librarians work closely with students, faculty, and staff in colleges and universities. Because they serve in a higher education environment, they are typically expected to have more, or more specialized, formal education than other librarians. Job postings for academic library positions frequently require a subject master's degree or a doctorate in addition to, or in some cases instead of, the MLIS, because of the often specialized nature of the duties they must perform. For example, an area studies librarian (sometimes called an "area curator") specializing in the region of Latin America at a research university might be expected to have an advanced degree (preferably a PhD) in history or literature in addition to proficiency in Spanish and, preferably, Portuguese. This is because such a position typically entails collection development work in multiple languages (including Catalan) and research consultations with teaching faculty and graduate students.[1] Jim Neal, 2017/18 ALA president, coined the term "feral professionals" to describe an increasingly visible class of academic library employees who are hired without the MLIS into positions in "systems, human resources, fund-raising, publishing, instructional technology, and facilities management," for example, because they offer valuable education and skills that MLIS holders typically lack[2] (more on this below under "Emerging Roles").

> **Discussion Question**
>
> What are the implications for the academic library workforce and for the condition of the academic library workplace of hiring non-MLIS holders?

Many colleges and universities grant faculty status to their librarians (whether tenure track or nontenure track) since the librarians are expected to demonstrate achievements on a par with teaching faculty, including conducting research that leads to presentations at professional conferences, publication, or both. Librarians with so-called academic appointments, by contrast, often must advance through one or more promotion review cycles before being granted continuing (or permanent) status. These librarians may or may not be required to conduct research and publish; in many such cases, a record of excellent service and evidence of a strong commitment to professional development are sufficient to earn a continuing appointment.

EMERGING ROLES FOR ACADEMIC LIBRARIANS

Many academic librarians today offer expertise in instructional technology, metadata or research informatics, and scholarly communication.

Todd Gilman

Instructional Technologists

Instructional technology enables librarians to create research or subject guides for library resources that support academic courses, topics, or disciplines taught in colleges and universities, and to impart specific research or information literacy skills at a distance. These guides, often known as LibGuides, allow students and faculty to access library resources without having to ask a librarian for assistance.

TEXTBOX 7.1

Examples of Library Guides from Yale University Library

English Language and Literature Research Guide.[3] The library guide includes subject area links related to English literature in addition to reference resources.

British History Guide: At a Glance.[4] This guide focuses on online history resources and connects to related library guides.

European History.[5] This guide focuses on the variety of different resources on European History available both in the library and externally. It also connects to additional, related library guides.

Metadata Librarians and Research Informationists

Two emerging roles for academic librarians focus intensively on data, specifically metadata librarians and research informationists.

Metadata Librarians

Data curation constitutes one of the newest and increasingly important evolving roles for academic librarians, and experts in informatics might help faculty and students with digital humanities data curation or e-science projects.[6] Digital humanities (DH) data curation involves working with text encoding, format and encoding management, technical aspects of data repository systems, data description, digital preservation, and metadata[7] (see also chapter 13: "Analog and Digital Curation and Preservation").

Metadata is essentially "data about data" associated with a specific type of information resource or subject area and is needed to describe digital assets (see also chapter 12: "Metadata, Cataloging, Linked Data, and the Evolving ILS"). Its current vogue represents a seismic shift for the generations of librarians schooled in Machine-Readable Cataloging (MARC), the standard format for all catalog and authority records that contain standardized and encoded descriptions of library resources since the 1960s. Technological innovations, as well as the adoption of Resource Description and Access (RDA),[8] Functional Requirements for Bibliographic Records (FRBR),[9] and non-MARC schemas, have led to the expansion of cataloger roles, which now comprise description of electronic acquisitions and digitized collections, batch loading of records, and institutional repository work. Revealing hidden collections through digital projects has become a high priority for many libraries, and such projects require the expertise of metadata specialists.[10]

> Three external factors motivate advances in catalog and metadata librarianship in academic libraries: financial exigency, competition from free search engines like Google Scholar, and the need to justify cataloger positions that appear to be redundant given automation and vendor-supplied records.

Currently, three external factors motivate advances in catalog and metadata librarianship in academic libraries: financial exigency, competition from free search engines like Google Scholar, and the need to justify cataloger positions that appear to be redundant given automation and vendor-supplied records.[11]

TEXTBOX 7.2

The Future of the Metadata Librarian

Many of these new activities, such as working with linked data or the Semantic Web, or RDA/FRBR, require additional training. According to Myung-Ja Han and Patricia Hswe, the metadata librarian position continues to evolve, and the position of the metadata librarian within the organizational structure of the academic library may be shifting: Will all cataloger roles eventually merge with metadata librarian roles? Han and Hswe opine that the main difference between the two roles is that metadata librarians must master a wider variety of standards, schemas, and emerging technologies than catalogers.[12]

Research Informationist

The research activities of e-science involve what is often referred to as big data (a generic term for a wide variety of large data sets used for research and decision making) and focus on developing new computational tools and infrastructures to support scientific discovery. Funding agencies, such as the National Science Foundation (NSF)[13] and National Institutes of Health (NIH),[14] now require scientists to provide open access to the underlying data gathered as a result of grant-funded research (see also chapter 33: "Open Access"). Since January 2011, proposals submitted to NSF must include a data management plan (see also chapter 26: "Managing Data and Data Analysis in Information Organizations"). In response, some specialized academic librarians, known as research informationists, are helping campus scientists comply with the requirements to create the plans and to archive and share the gathered data. For example, according to Spencer D. C. Keralis et al.:

> The research informationist must demonstrate a wide range of knowledge, including facility with data management, data preservation, funding compliance, and grant writing, in addition to core librarian skills such as expertise in database and web searching, a deep understanding of how information is organized, critical thinking, writing, and speaking before an audience.

> In the libraries at the University of Illinois at Urbana-Champaign, the liaison librarians serve the disciplines most affected by the NSF mandate, and they drive support for data management. The life sciences librarian developed a links web page to give researchers access to information from funding agencies, information about data repositories, and a list of services, including help in developing a data curation profile for research projects using Purdue's Data Curation Profile Toolkit (originally developed in partnership with the UIUC Graduate School of Library and Information Science).[15]

To succeed in this role, the research informationist must demonstrate a wide range of knowledge, including facility with data management, data preservation, funding compliance, and grant writing, in addition to core librarian skills such as expertise in database and web searching, a deep understanding of how information is organized, critical thinking, writing, and speaking before an audience.[16]

Scholarly Communications Librarians

In light of the major technological and economic disruptions to the publishing system, academic librarians have become increasingly committed to transforming the scholarly communication system to better meet the needs of researchers and the academy. Scholarly communications librarians advise faculty on authors' rights and publishing options, advocate for more open and accessible scholarship, and have even taken on the role of publisher themselves.[17] Moreover, many academic librarians conduct research themselves and publish in their field, whether in librarianship or in other disciplines related to their subject expertise.

Libraries and university presses are also helping create a more equitable and efficient publishing system by experimenting with innovative publishing models. Collaboration between libraries and university presses has become increasingly common,[18] especially as university administrative structures change. As of 2016, around 30 percent of campus-based members of the Association of American University Presses (AAUP) now report to libraries, more than double the number five years ago.[19] Collaborations often harness the prestige, disciplinary expertise, and editorial prowess of the press and the libraries' strengths in digital technologies, metadata, and organization of information to create forward-looking, technology-enhanced publications. Libraries are also independently assuming the role of publisher, primarily with open-access journals.[20] Some university presses have become part of the library system.

With the growth of the larger open-access movement, a proposed solution to the high cost of access to research materials whereby authors make the results of their research free to all, the concept of the Institutional Repository (IR) has become compelling to colleges and universities in the past decade. At campuses that have adopted a formal open-access policy, academic librarians now work to set up and populate electronic IRs for faculty and staff publications and data sets. Materials in IRs can have different levels of access: some are available only to the campus community, for example; others, to the larger scholarly community or to anyone with access to a computer. Many of these digital efforts raise new copyright concerns (see also chapter 31: "Copyright and Creative Commons"), so academic libraries now recruit or train specialists who can field faculty and staff questions about which materials can and cannot be shared freely.[21]

> **Discussion Question**
>
> What can academic librarians do to encourage the teaching faculty at their institutions to advocate for open access to scholarly materials?

Because MLIS programs cannot usually provide libraries with advanced skills and expertise needed to fill these and other emerging roles, academic libraries have benefited from hiring non-MLIS-holders who can. Since 2003, the Council on Library and Information Resources (CLIR) Postdoctoral Fellowship Program has attempted to match academic libraries with doctoral-trained individuals who can offer them such advanced expertise as in-depth subject knowledge, cutting-edge pedagogy, data curation, and experience with scholarly communications and digital humanities projects.[22]

RESEARCH AND PUBLICATION

As noted earlier in this chapter, academic librarians also conduct research and publish articles and books on both discipline-specific and LIS subjects. Librarians with tenure track faculty status are typically required to do research to achieve promotion and tenure. Publication expectations of tenure-track librarians might not in all cases be as rigorous as those for teaching faculty, since librarians devote most of their professional time to the performance of primary job responsibilities and typically hold twelve-month appointments. Still, expectations are high, and promotion and tenure will be either granted or denied after five to seven years of service based on a thorough review of all aspects of performance. Librarians with nontenure-track status or administrative appointments (managerial and professional staff with nonfaculty status) are often encouraged to conduct research and publish, but they have other means of demonstrating professional competency, such as excellent service to library users, building collections, and committee work, that allow them to advance through the ranks without research and publication. There is no one-size-fits-all model when it comes to research and publication among academic librarians.

INFORMATION AND TECHNOLOGY LITERACY INSTRUCTION

Accreditation commissions and colleges and universities have acknowledged the importance of developing students' capacity for critical thinking. As a result, many academic librarians who work in public services offer information literacy and technology literacy instruction for undergraduates and graduate students in partnership with teaching faculty. Information literacy instruction typically involves helping students to identify a need for information, locate the needed information, evaluate the quality of the information found, and use it effectively, legally, and ethically.[23] Some academic librarians work diligently with faculty to follow the Association of College and Research Libraries' (ACRL) Information Literacy Competency Standards for Higher Education[24] when they teach students. In 2000, ACRL defined five information literacy standards, which must be met in order for an individual to be considered information literate. Each ACRL standard is subdivided into several performance indicators, and these indicators are further divided into outcomes. The standards outline competencies, skills, and outcomes that students are expected to achieve to be deemed information literate. They suggest that librarians and faculty prepare training sessions together so that they are targeted to the students' and faculty's disciplinary focus. Overall, they stress that librarians and faculty should "work together to develop assessment instruments and strategies in the context of particular disciplines."[25]

TEXTBOX 7.3

ACRL Literacy Standards

- The information literate student determines the nature and extent of the information needed.
- The information literate student accesses needed information effectively and efficiently.
- The information literate student evaluates information and its sources critically and incorporates selected information into his or her knowledge base and value system.
- The information literate student, individually or as a member of a group, uses information effectively to accomplish a specific purpose.
- The information literate student understands many of the economic, legal, and social issues surrounding the use of information and accesses and uses information ethically and legally.[26]

By contrast, ACRL's new Framework for Information Literacy in Higher Education, written in 2015 and approved in 2016, presents six frames, each featuring a *threshold concept* determined to be an integral component of information literacy,[27] rather than focus on standards and performance indicators (see also chapter 16: "Teaching Users: Information and Technology Instruction"). The term *threshold concept* comes from the study of higher education and is used to describe core concepts that, once understood, transform the perception of a given subject.[28] Many librarians will find threshold concepts challenging; they will require a concerted effort to integrate into practice.

A recurring concern arising from the previous ACRL Standards was the linear, check-the-box structure of the model, which many librarians felt diminished the lived experiences of the students.[29] Information literacy development can be unpredictable and not as clear-cut as the 2000 ACRL Standards imply. Models with competency-based structures typically assume that there are right and wrong ways to seek, evaluate, and use information. Detractors argue that such models implicitly characterize learners as passive consumers of information. Such a characterization does not acknowledge the literacy skills that many students already possess. As a result, learners who are judged based on their ability to meet the Standards can feel that their nonacademic information experiences are irrelevant to academic and college life.[30] Advocates of new critical and relational approaches to information literacy (such as the approach presented in the ACRL Framework) instead recommend creating guidelines that embrace, enhance, and challenge an individual's understanding of information.[31]

Other librarians take a more informal approach to instruction, seeking mainly to impress upon students the hazards of relying solely on Google and Wikipedia for college-level research and explaining and demonstrating alternatives, such as librarian-authored research guides, bibliographies, indexes, and other scholarly resources, including academic monographs, essay collections, and peer-reviewed journal articles. Technology literacy instruction typically involves training students in the use of computers (including iPads or other tablets) and a variety of software, from electronic library catalogs and archival finding aids to free and fee-based bibliographic and full-text databases to mobile apps to citation management programs such as RefWorks,[32] Zotero,[33] EndNote,[34] or Mendeley.[35]

Those who teach information literacy and technology literacy often perform these duties in their capacity as library liaisons to academic departments. In the past decade or so, a model of service known as the embedded librarian or, in a purely virtual environment, as the so-called embedded e-brarian, has become popular. Embedded librarians seek to reach students where they are, rather than wait for students to come to them. They might serve as a co-teacher by means of a virtual presence in an online course offered to their institution's students or to students enrolled in a faculty member's massive open online course (MOOC); hold office hours in an academic department, student union, cafeteria, or writing center; or offer brief introductory visits to face-to-face classrooms at the invitation of teaching faculty.[36]

> Embedded librarians seek to reach students where they are, rather than wait for students to come to them.

SERVICE TO THE UNIVERSITY AND PROFESSION

Academic librarians also serve on campus, state, and national committees (see also chapter 37: "Leadership Skills for Today's Global Information Landscape"). If they have faculty status, they may be involved in campus governance, enjoying a place at the table alongside members of the teaching faculty and the central administration. Librarians serving on statewide library or education committees might act as advocates for the implementation of educational standards involving information and technology literacy in state college and university systems (see also chapter 28: "Advocacy"). Librarians serving on committees sponsored by the Association of Research Libraries (ARL) or ACRL develop guidelines and standards for adoption by academic library professionals nationwide. These guidelines and standards address a range of professional concerns including:

- best practices in fair use for academic and research libraries,
- screening and appointment of academic librarians,
- services to undergraduate students,
- interlibrary loan of rare and unique materials,

- preservation, security, and theft in special collections,
- distance learning library services, and
- recommended competencies for special collections professionals.[37]

NEW MODELS FOR REFERENCE SERVICE, TEACHING, AND LEARNING

Academic librarians today face a significantly decreased demand for traditional reference service (see also chapter 11: "Information Intermediation and Reference Services"). The growth of the web has made academic library users more self-sufficient. As a result, many reference desks in colleges and universities have been either eliminated or merged with other service points such as circulation or computing services; others have moved to a tiered model, in which frontline staff might be students or nonprofessional library workers. Members of the frontline staff are trained to answer basic questions and to refer more advanced questions to professional librarians. Related to this development, another model of service emerged about fifteen years ago, often referred to as learning commons, information commons, or digital commons. Based in part on the concept of "one-stop shopping," this is a full-service learning, research, and project space typically combining library resources with a computer lab and moveable and modular furniture in a repurposed space designed to facilitate both individual and group work.[38] Professional librarians working under such service models are able to focus more on high-level research questions, consultations, and outreach to faculty and students. A more cutting-edge and exciting scion of these spaces are the so-called design labs, collaborative making facilities, creativity labs, digital humanities (DH) labs, and other teaching and learning facilities springing up within libraries at the University of Michigan, Carnegie Mellon University, MIT, Barnard College, and Yale (to name just a few examples), which also have a "do-it-yourself" ethos underpinning them.[39]

Though it might be argued that nothing defines academic libraries so much as constant change, specific developments shape current priorities and affect the nature of future academic library work. Steven Bell, Lorcan Dempsey, and Barbara Fister discuss many of these developments in *New Roles for the Road Ahead: Essays Commissioned for ACRL's 75th Anniversary*.[40] Fister points to emerging literacies that require academic librarians to devise novel approaches to instruction and research support, often calling on new skill sets and training. Likewise, economic pressures and intellectual property issues arising in the digital domain, along with consolidation and entrenchment of big for-profit database companies and publishers, now require librarians and paraprofessionals to educate themselves and others about open access and scholarly communication.

New approaches to teaching and learning in colleges and universities are affecting the work of academic libraries. Kelly E. Miller has considered how research librarians seek to become more student-centered than they have been in the past, and offers seven strategies for achieving this goal. Miller's piece points to new skills needed in libraries: pedagogy, outreach, and assessment.[41]

COLLECTION DEVELOPMENT, ACCESS, AND PRESERVATION

The costs for materials for academic libraries have risen so dramatically in recent decades that most libraries cannot keep up and have been forced to introduce drastic cost-cutting measures. While costs for print books rise steadily, particularly challenging are the exorbitant prices of so-called Big Deal electronic serials packages (large bundles of electronic journals) offered by publishers such as Elsevier, Emerald, Sage, Springer, Taylor & Francis, and Wiley in the science, technology, engineering, and mathematics (STEM) fields.[42] To make matters worse, these prices increase each year by a fixed amount (e.g., 5 percent). If libraries back out of a Big Deal, they can lose 60 percent of their access to content while still paying more for individual subscriptions than they were paying before. However, even print journals have high costs associated with them since they must be checked in, bound, stored, and reshelved after patron use.

Many libraries have adopted a policy prioritizing electronic format for journals (sometimes known as an "e-priority policy" for short) and canceling print subscriptions whenever possible to avoid duplication and its attendant costs. Most academic libraries have become comfortable with deaccessioning or moving their print journal collections to off-site storage once they have secured reliable digital surrogates for these materials (see also chapter 24: "Managing Collections").

As another efficiency measure, patron-driven or data-driven acquisitions (PDA/DDA) are also on the rise. Under this acquisitions model, e-book vendors allow libraries to load records into their online catalogs for e-books and e-journals that the library has not yet purchased, enabling discovery by the libraries' patrons. If a patron uses an e-book or journal article beyond a certain agreed-upon threshold (for example, he or she reads a given number of e-book pages or downloads an article), the text is acquired by and charged to the library. In this way, libraries only pay for what their patrons actually use.

Still, the question of long-term electronic preservation remains an issue. Most e-book vendors have not addressed this question adequately, forcing libraries to rely on partial solutions such as the Digital Preservation Network (DPN)[43] and HathiTrust.[44] DPN was established to ensure long-term preservation and access; it uses a federated approach to preservation, storing multiple copies of collections in numerous places. HathiTrust is a large-scale partnership of academic and research libraries offering millions of titles, including content digitized via the Google Books project and the Internet Archive. Even combined, DPN and HathiTrust leave much digital library material vulnerable to permanent loss.[45]

Since separate library systems cannot typically share access to electronic journals or books between them because of copyright and licensing restrictions (e.g., Columbia University cannot share its licensed electronic holdings with Yale), many academic libraries have banded together in recent decades to form consortia in order to share print materials as efficiently and at as low a cost as possible (see also chapter 32: "Information Licensing" and chapter 31: "Copyright and Creative Commons"). Cooperative collection development constitutes a related initiative that many academic libraries are considering as a cost-saving measure. In this model of collection development, partner libraries agree to divide up collecting areas between them (such as African or central Asian materials or small press books) in order to build complementary rather than duplicative collections and share their acquisitions freely with each other.[46]

TEXTBOX 7.4

Examples of Partnership Arrangements

- All the Ivies (Brown, Columbia, Cornell, Dartmouth, Harvard, University of Pennsylvania, Princeton, and Yale) plus MIT, the University of Chicago, Duke, and Johns Hopkins now freely share their materials using a patron-initiated rapid book request and delivery system.[47]
- The Greater Western Library Alliance (GWLA), a consortium of thirty-three research libraries located in the central and western United States, offers interlibrary loan reciprocity between its members (GWLA members also realize cost savings on library materials thanks to cooperative negotiation of discounts and licensing agreements).[48]

ASSESSMENT IN THE ACADEMIC LIBRARY

To continuously demonstrate the library's value to campus stakeholders, academic librarians frequently concern themselves with assessment. Assessment is a process used by libraries to learn about the needs of users in order to improve academic programs, teaching, student learning, and the library's role in the research activities of students and faculty.[49] Many academic libraries now employ a dedicated assessment librarian or head of assessment who oversees the library's assessment activities by collecting, analyzing, and reporting assessment data, and developing a data-driven approach to achieving strategic objectives.

Library assessment uses various quantitative and qualitative research methods including website usability testing, observation, focus groups, interviews, and satisfaction surveys.[50] The most widely adopted library satisfaction survey is LibQUAL+, a service quality survey developed by ARL.[51] Others include ClimateQUAL (a survey designed to understand organizational climate and diversity perceptions of library staff) and MINES for Libraries (a transaction-based survey that collects data on the purpose of use of electronic resources). Ithaka S+R developed the Local Faculty and Student Surveys for Libraries[52] program in response to library managers' expressed interest in the perceptions of their faculty and students. In order to accommodate the unique needs of special collections, the Archival Metrics[53] project sought to promote a culture of assessment among archives by creating standardized user-based evaluation tools and other performance measures. Ideally, assessment plans should be driven by and linked to the larger institution's mission, vision, and values; and all goals and outcomes should be agreed upon, specific, and measurable.[54]

TEXTBOX 7.5

Assessment-Based Library Programs

Programs and services that typically become the focus of assessment efforts include:

- reference
- information and technology literacy
- library collections (especially concerning print versus electronic collections and how well collections meet curricular and research needs)
- scholarly communication programs and services
- library liaison programs
- library design and furnishings
- library technology
- remote and in-house access to library resources
- resources to support distance education
- library value

A major driver of assessment in colleges and universities is accreditation. Accrediting agencies perform two primary duties: quality assurance and institutional improvement. They formulate guidelines for continuous assessment, and they ask colleges to define goals and prove that they are using these goals to seek and respond effectively to feedback. Accrediting bodies typically value information literacy outcomes, so academic librarians are encouraged to identify information literacy language in accreditation documents and use it to integrate information literacy skills into teaching and assessment activities across campus. Generally, academic librarians should monitor their users' understanding of the role of the library in their teaching, learning, and research as well as their users' success in gaining access to needed materials.

CONCLUSION

Academic libraries today find themselves at a crossroads. Most now accept the notion that they must repurpose their spaces, staff, and limited funds to accommodate a future featuring many fewer print volumes and much different service models than they and their campus stakeholders have become accustomed to: a future in which digital resources, flexible spaces with modular furniture, facilities such as design or quantitative reasoning labs, writing and other co-located student service centers, 3-D printers, and espresso book machines have replaced the miles of metal book stacks, the reference and circulation desks, the quiet reading rooms, the jamming photocopiers and noisy microfilm readers of the past. Yet some academic libraries, mainly in an effort to appease an aging yet still powerful faculty on campus, still insist on making only incremental changes; they do so at their peril. Whether we like it or not, the look of future success is clear. Students and, increasingly, faculty, expect libraries to meet them where they are, and the academic libraries that can do this are leading the way. They will be the ones that survive and thrive in today's campus culture, where senior administrators expect to see a measureable return on every dollar invested in their libraries: whether it be through increased gate counts, the number of downloads of e-books or journal articles, or the reputation of the library director among his or her faculty peers.

NOTES

1. Thea Lindquist and Todd Gilman, "Academic/Research Librarians with Subject Doctorates: Data and Trends 1965–2006," *Portal: Libraries and the Academy* 8, no. 1 (2008): 31–52; Todd Gilman and Thea Lindquist, "Academic/Research Librarians with Subject Doctorates: Experiences and Perceptions, 1965–2006," *Portal: Libraries and the Academy* 10, no. 4 (2010): 399–412. Jennifer Ferguson offers the most recent contribution to this discussion by surveying and comparing advanced subject degree requirements with existing dual-degree options in "Additional Degree Required? Advanced Subject Knowledge and Academic Librarianship," *Portal: Libraries and the Academy* 16, no. 4 (2016): 721–36.
2. James G. Neal, "Raised by Wolves: The New Generation of Feral Professionals in the Academic Library," *ACRL Twelfth National Conference* (2005): 302, http://www.ala.org/acrl/sites/ala.org.acrl/files/content/conferences/pdf/neal2-05.pdf.
3. Yale University Library, "English Language and Literature Research Guide," 2017, http://guides.library.yale.edu/english?hs=a.
4. Yale University Library, "British History Guide: At a Glance," 2017, http://guides.library.yale.edu/ushistory?hs=a.
5. Yale University Library, "European History," 2017, http://guides.library.yale.edu/content.php?pid=607882.
6. Joyce L. Ogburn, "The Imperative for Data Curation," *Portal: Libraries and the Academy* 10, no. 2 (2010): 241–46.
7. Arianne Hartsell-Gundy, Laura Braunstein, and Liorah Golomb's recent edited volume, *Digital Humanities in the Library: Challenges and Opportunities for Subject Specialists* (Chicago: Association of College and Research Libraries, 2015), provides a good exploration of what DH means for the work of academic librarians.
8. Eric Miller, "An Introduction to the Research Description Framework," *Bulletin of the American Society for Information Science and Technology* 25, no. 1 (1998): 15–19.
9. IFLA Study Group on the Functional Requirements of Bibliographic Records, *Functional Requirements of Bibliographic Records: Final Report* (München: K. G. Saur, 1998), http://www.ifla.org/VII/s13/frbr/frbr.pdf.
10. Jeanne M. K. Boydston and Joan M. Leysen, "ARL Cataloger Librarian Roles and Responsibilities Now and in the Future," *Cataloging & Classification Quarterly* 52, no. 2 (2014): 233. For a list of funded projects by the Council on Library and Information Resources Hidden Collections initiative, see http://www.clir.org/hiddencollections/awards.
11. Ibid., 241.
12. Myung-Ja Han and Patricia Hswe, "The Evolving Role of the Metadata Librarian," *Library Resources & Technical Services* 54, no. 3 (2010): 129–41.
13. National Science Foundation, accessed September 17, 2017, https://www.nsf.gov/.
14. National Institutes of Health, accessed September 17, 2017, https://www.nih.gov/.

15. Spencer D. C. Keralis, Shannon Stark, Martin Halbert, and William E. Moen, "Research Data Management in Policy and Practice: The DataRes Project," in *Research Data Management: Principles, Practices, and Prospects* (Washington, DC: Council on Library and Information Resources, 2013), 26.

16. Lisa Federer, "The Librarian as Research Informationist: A Case Study," *Journal of the Medical Library Association* 101, no. 4 (2013): 301. The above discussion of the roles of metadata librarian and research informationist draws mainly on Marta Brunner and Jennifer Osorio, "Recruitment, Retention, Diversity, and Professional Development," in Todd Gilman, ed., *Academic Librarianship Today* (Lanham, MD: Rowman & Littlefield, 2017), 145–46.

17. Ronald C. Jantz, "A Vision for the Future: New Roles for Academic Librarians," in Gilman, ed., *Academic Librarianship Today*, 229–30.

18. The Association of American University Presses, "Press and Library Collaboration Study," 2013, http://www.aaupnet.org/images/stories/data/librarypresscollaboration_report_corrected.pdf.

19. Charles Watkinson, "Why Marriage Matters: A North American Perspective on Press/Library Partnerships," *Learned Publishing* 29 (2016): 342–47.

20. See, for example, the 118 libraries listed in Library Publishing Coalition Directory Committee, *2017 Library Publishing Directory* (Atlanta, GA: Library Publishing Coalition, 2017), https://www.librarypublishing.org/sites/librarypublishing.org/files/2017%20Directory.pdf.

21. See an extensive list of U.S. college and university IRs here: "Customers," Digital Commons, https://www.bepress.com/products/digital-commons/why-digital-commons/customers/. For a recent overview of IRs see Brian Owen, "Open Access, Institutional Repositories, E-Science and Data Curation, and Preservation," in Gilman, ed., *Academic Librarianship Today*, 197–210.

22. For more information, see Council on Library and Information Resources, "CLIR Postdoctoral Fellowship Program," last updated 2017, http://www.clir.org/fellowships/postdoc.

23. For a recent overview of this topic, see Carrie Forbes and Peggy Keeran, "Reference, Instruction, and Outreach: Current Methods and Models," in Gilman, ed., *Academic Librarianship Today*, 85–100.

24. Association of College and Research Libraries (ACRL), "Information Literacy Competency Standards for Higher Education," 2000, http://www.ala.org/acrl/standards/informationliteracycompetency.

25. Ibid.

26. Information Literacy Competency Standards for Higher Education," Association of College & Research Libraries, June 25, 2016, retrieved on July 5, 2017, http://www.ala.org/acrl/standards/informationliteracycompetency.

27. Association of College and Research Libraries (ACRL), "Framework for Information Literacy for Higher Education," last updated February 11, 2016, http://www.ala.org/acrl/standards/ilframework.

28. Jan H. F. Meyer and Ray Land, "Threshold Concepts and Troublesome Knowledge (2): Epistemological Considerations and a Conceptual Framework for Teaching and Learning," *Higher Education* 49, no. 3 (2005): 373–88, doi:10.1007/s10734-004-6779-5.

29. Laurie Kutner and Alison Armstrong, "Rethinking Information Literacy in a Globalized World," *Communications in Information Literacy* 6, no. 1 (2012): 25–33.

30. James K. Elmborg, "Critical Information Literacy: Implications for Instructional Practice," *Journal of Academic Librarianship* 32, no. 2 (2006): 192–99, doi:10.1016/j.acalib.2005.12.004.

31. Ibid.

32. Refworks, https://www.refworks.com/.

33. Zotero, https://www.zotero.org/.

34. Endnote, http://endnote.com/.

35. Mendeley, http://www.mendeley.com/.

36. Alice L. Daugherty and Michael F. Russo, eds., *Embedded Librarianship: What Every Academic Librarian Should Know* (Santa Barbara, CA: Libraries Unlimited, 2013). For a recent reconsideration of the role of the library liaison, see Danielle Cooper and Roger C. Schonfeld's Issue Brief, "Rethinking Liaison Programs for the Humanities," *Ithaka S+R*, July 26, 2017, https://doi.org/10.18665/sr.304124.

37. See http://www.arl.org/; http://www.ala.org/acrl/standards.

38. Laurie A. MacWhinnie, "The Information Commons: The Academic Library of the Future," *Portal: Libraries and the Academy* 3, no. 2 (2003): 241–57.

39. See Jennifer Conlin, "The New Frontier: Libraries with No Limits," *Michigan Alumnus*, 2015, last updated 2017, http://alumni.umich.edu/alumnus/the-new-frontier-libraries-with-no-limits/; and University of Michigan Design Labs, https://www.lib.umich.edu/design-labs; Carnegie Mellon University's Integrative Design, Arts & Technology Network's IDeATe@Hunt collaborative making facility, http://ideate.cmu.edu/about-ideate/facilities/; MIT Libraries, "Strategic Plan, 2014–2016," November 6, 2013, https://libraries.mit.edu/wp-content/uploads/2014/01/strategic_plan_2014-2016.pdf; MIT Libraries Space Programming Group, "Guiding Principles for the MIT Libraries Spaces—Working DRAFT," August 18, 2014. A position description in an advertisement for Dean of the Barnard Library and Academic Information Services ("BLAIS") says that "the new Dean will oversee the relocation of the Barnard Library from Lehman Hall (1959) to a new, 128,000 square foot, Skidmore, Owings and Merrill–designed Teaching and Learning Center slated to open in August 2018. This building promises to be the new signature for Barnard's four-acre, Morningside Heights campus and a dynamic hub promoting innovation by students and faculty across departments and disciplines. It will house the Library's core circulating collections and the special collections and archives. In addition, the new space will include: a digital commons with five cutting-edge teaching labs (Movement Lab, Empirical Reasoning Center, Digital Humanities Lab, Creativity Lab and Multimedia Lab); a Computational Science Center; departmental offices for Economics, History, Political Science and Urban Studies; the Barnard Center for Research on Women; and the Athena Center for Leadership Studies; plus conference facilities and a café," Barnard College, "Dean of the Barnard Library and Academic Information Services ('BLAIS')" advertisement, *Chronicle of Higher Education*, 2016, https://chroniclevitae.com/jobs/0000920425-01; and Yale University Library Digital Humanities Lab, http://web.library.yale.edu/dhlab.

40. Nancy Allen, ed., *New Roles for the Road Ahead*: *Essays Commissioned for ACRL's 75th Anniversary* (Chicago: Association of College and Research Libraries, 2015), http://www.ala.org/acrl/sites/ala.org.acrl/files/content/publications/whitepapers/new_roles_75th.pdf.

41. Kelly E. Miller, "Imagine! On the Future of Teaching and Learning and the Academic Research Library," *Portal: Libraries and the Academy* 14, no. 3 (2014): 329–51, http://dx.doi.org/10.1353/pla.2014.0018.

42. Karla L. Strieb and Julia C. Blixrud, "Unwrapping the Bundle: An Examination of Research Libraries and the 'Big Deal,'" *Portal: Libraries and the Academy* 14, no. 4 (2014): 587–615, doi:10.1353/pla.2014.0027.

43. See http://www.dpn.org/.

44. See http://www.hathitrust.org/digital_library.

45. LOCKSS, CLOCKSS, and Portico, three further digital preservation solutions, should be mentioned in this context. See https://www.libraries.rutgers.edu/rul/staff/collection_dev/reports/lockss-clockss-portico.shtml.

46. Association of Research Libraries. "21st-Century Collections: Calibration of Investment and Collaborative Action," last updated 2012, http://www.arl.org/storage/documents/publications/issue-brief-21st-century-collections-2012.pdf.

47. See http://www.borrowdirect.org/.

48. See http://www.gwla.org/.

49. Joseph R. Matthews, *The Evaluation and Measurement of Library Services*, second edition (Westport, CT: Libraries Unlimited, 2017); Peter Hernon, Ellen Altman, and Robert E. Dugan, *Assessing Service Quality: Satisfying the Expectations of Library Customers*, third edition (Chicago: American Library Association, 2015).

50. Quantitative research methods quantify numerical data to allow generalization of the results from a sample to an entire population of interest (e.g., gate counts in a new library space in a given sample). Qualitative methods, by contrast, are used in an effort to understand users at a deeper level (for instance, user experience of orientation and navigation within the new library space).

51. See https://www.libqual.org/home (accessed Jan. 12, 2018).

52. See "Local Faculty and Student Surveys for Libraries," *Ithaka S+R*, 2016, http://www.sr.ithaka.org/work-with-us/surveys.

53. "About Archival Metrics," Archival Metrics, http://www.archivalmetrics.org.

54. The information in this paragraph draws chiefly from Nisa Bakkalbasi, "Assessment and Evaluation, Promotion, and Marketing of Academic Library Services," in Gilman, ed., *Academic Librarianship Today*, 218.

8

Community Anchors for Lifelong Learning

PUBLIC LIBRARIES

Pam Smith

Chapter 8, "Community Anchors for Lifelong Learning: Public Libraries," highlights the characteristics of today's public library, which is focused on providing a welcoming learning space and enticing the community to engage with new ideas and with each other. Noted director of Anythink Libraries and 2017–2018 Public Library Association President Pam Smith discusses how public libraries are evolving from a focus on primarily circulating physical materials to this new focus on engaging with the community in new ways.

Smith identifies three key roles for public libraries today. Public libraries are serving as centers of learning and engagement, stretching the boundaries and reframing the institution with an emphasis on generosity and the removal of barriers to make libraries more user friendly. They are also serving as community anchors, providing a place for people to connect with each other and engage in civic discourse. Finally, they are serving as conveners and connectors, developing relationships with community businesses, artists, and organizations to provide opportunities for the library to expand its services and programs without requiring library staff to bring all the resources and skills to the table. The concepts behind this evolution in libraries, from books to people and from transactions to relationships, model patterns that are occurring in our social and cultural networks as well. Smith also discusses how public library spaces need to model patterns that are occurring in the user's social and cultural network and better align with these changes by creating welcoming, hospitable, and user-friendly spaces.

Information professionals are essential to successful public libraries. As information professionals working in public libraries shift from serving as keepers to guides, they need different competencies. Smith notes how being able to form strong partnerships and relationships, as well as demonstrating empathy and generosity, are required competencies for today's professional in the public library.

★ ★ ★

The role of public libraries is evolving from that of a physical space centered on the book to a place that supports people and their lifelong learning endeavors. This shift has occurred partially because of the availability and access to information on the internet and social media as well as the variety of formats for published material, from books to recorded books to e-books, podcasts, and videos. While books, movies, and music are still core library products, the reliance on the circulation of physical materials is no longer the most critical role of public libraries.

As a result of this shift, public libraries are examining their mission, values, organizational structures, spaces, staffing, collections, programs, and services. In order to remain relevant, public libraries must be more than book warehouses. The value of public libraries begins with collections of materials and extends deep into the heart of the community. Public libraries are cornerstones to the democratic ideal and aspirations of our nation. The stories of innovation and self-reliance, and the ability to dream big, work hard, and build a positive life are often connected with the use of public libraries. After completing this chapter, the reader should have an understanding of the significant role public libraries play in their communities and the changes occurring in libraries as they evolve into centers for learning.

PUBLIC LIBRARIES: HISTORICAL TRANSFORMATIONS

Public libraries in the United States began with Benjamin Franklin's lending library in Philadelphia (see also chapter 2: "Libraries, Communities, and Information: Two Centuries of Experience"). The original notion of creating a community that shared books was both pragmatic and generous. Books in the early years of the United States were expensive, rare, and difficult to acquire. The concept of borrowing books was a unique idea that built upon a sense of trust and community. A community that shared ideas and read similar books provided a platform for civic discourse, critical analysis, and thinking.

As libraries evolved, the idealistic values and purpose of the public library expanded. Librarians from John Cotton Dana[1] to Jesse Shera[2] and Vartan Gregorian[3] have articulated the ideals that bridge the role of the library in the twenty-first century. Modern ideals of the public library include the preservation of information, the protection of the freedom to read, the pursuit of happiness, and the support of intellectual curiosity. The aspirational nature of the public library holds the information professional to high standards.[4] The Public Library Association states that "public libraries open possibility."[5]

> "This philosophical underpinning of the public library as a symbol of democracy, defender of First Amendment rights, and place where one can pursue their hopes and dreams elevates libraries in our culture while placing weighty demands upon the institution."

Public libraries are more than just buildings or icons or ideas—they are a wellspring of possibility. Unlike any other institution, public libraries have a unique and unparalleled ability to bring people and knowledge together. They fill communities with the vitality of learning. The joy of personal growth. The excitement of advancing with the times. Libraries are right there . . . continually opening new passages for anyone who enters. Because public libraries are and always have been where possibility lives.[6]

Vartan Gregorian, president of the New York Public Library from 1981 to 1989, positions the role of the public library as an institution with the highest of aspirational goals:

In our democratic society, the library stands for hope, for learning, for progress, for literacy, for self-improvement and for civic engagement. The library is a symbol of opportunity, citizenship, equality, freedom of speech and freedom of thought, and hence is a symbol for democracy itself.[7]

This philosophical underpinning of the public library as a symbol of democracy, defender of First Amendment rights, and place where one can pursue their hopes and dreams elevates libraries in our culture while placing weighty demands upon the institution. The public library is the ultimate democratic symbol where all are welcome. In a world of cultural divisions, the public space of inclusion becomes even more valuable. Perhaps because the mission is so noble, the ability to evolve, morph, and reinvent the institution is even more critical to the long-standing success of libraries. And the success of public libraries is critical at a time when communities are hungry for cultural support systems.

As the first director of the Denver Public Library at the turn of the twentieth century, John Cotton Dana was ahead of his time; many of his ideas were considered heretical for public libraries. He objected to closed stacks, believing that patrons should be allowed to browse freely throughout the library collection. The focus of public libraries at the time was on acquiring, organizing, and lending materials. This attention to the book required the design of spaces, policies, and systems that maintained their security. The role of the librarian was to ensure a sense of decorum, respect, dignity, and organization within the library. The image of the librarian behind a vast reference desk was an indicator of control. The mystery of the classification systems, the card catalog, the cross-references, and the Library of Congress subject headings created a maze for a typical patron (see also chapter 12: "Metadata, Cataloging, Linked Data, and the Evolving ILS"). Closed stacks were the norm, requiring the patron to request an item by locating the proper call number and title, and providing this information to the library staff. The item was then retrieved while the patron waited for the appropriate material to be delivered. The concept of the reading room instilled the research behavior and quiet protocol that is still associated with libraries today. Public libraries were solemn places reserved for serious study, rigor, and contemplation. Dana sparked a paradigm shift when he introduced radical ideas, including open, accessible stacks, flower arrangements, and light and airy reading rooms.[8] He even promoted the idea of publicly circulating artwork collections in museums and public libraries. His concept of the public library was one of creating a space for happiness and learning, as noted in his quote: "The public library is a center of public happiness first, of public education next."[9]

Public libraries have demonstrated over time that they are adaptive institutions and can readily address community needs—from emergency recovery after floods or hurricanes to gathering places for community conversations addressing local issues. The sheer number of public libraries ensures that people have widespread access to books, computers, and library programs for all ages. Public libraries also help people with internet connectivity. In fact, virtually all (98 percent) public libraries provide free public access to wireless internet.[12] Public libraries in the United States are predominantly funded and governed through local control, and the establishment of a public library in a town center is a powerful sense of pride for a municipality and county governments.

TEXTBOX 8.1

Public Libraries Outnumber Starbucks

In the United States today, there are more public libraries than Starbucks. According to the American Library Association, there were 16,559 U.S. public libraries in 2014.[10] This contrasts with just over 13,000 Starbucks in 2016.[11]

KEY ROLES OF PUBLIC LIBRARIES TODAY

In today's digital environment, the widespread availability of content diminishes the importance of the library as a book-lending institution. Books, music, and movies are readily available and are easily accessed through vendors such as Amazon, Barnes and Noble, and iTunes. However, the public library is much more than a collection of materials. The public library provides a platform for interaction with ideas of all shapes, forms, and cultures. In some ways, the public library is a chameleon, adapting to the varying needs of diverse communities (see also chapter 4: "Diverse Information Needs"). The public library morphs into the catalyst, the platform, and the connector for community engagement and learning. Key roles for the public library today include serving as:

A center of community learning and engagement, providing collections and other services to support the lifelong learning and curiosity of users.

The anchor of the community, providing a place for people to engage and connect with culture, neighbors, ideas, and trends, and providing a place where civic discourse can take place.

A convener and a connector, bringing partners to the table to solve problems and bringing people to share their expertise to mentor and coach in support of people's creativity, innovation, and entrepreneurial interests.

Each of these roles is explored in greater depth below.

Center of Learning and Engagement

In some communities, the public library in the town square is a gathering place, a center for the community, and a place where programs, ideas, and books become the basis for learning. The concept of the library as a learning laboratory creates a platform where learning occurs in multiple ways. Public libraries have an array of tools to support the quest to learn almost anything. One of the assets of public libraries is the support for just-in-time or informal learning for all ages. Informal learning focuses on the natural curiosity of a person who learns at his or her own pace and drives his or her own learning path. That path might start with reading a book or listening to a podcast or having a conversation with a friend that sparks a quest to know more. Informal learning is often situational, on a need-to-know basis. Learning how to use a piece of new technology or plan a travel adventure or solve a personal dilemma are situations in which a person needs to acquire additional information or skills in order to accomplish a goal. The public librarian is adept at meeting people on their own terms, quickly understanding the inquiry and creating connections to a path of learning.

> The public librarian is adept at meeting people on their own terms, quickly understanding the inquiry and creating connections to a path of learning.

The shift from a focus on collections to creating learning experiences is occurring in both museums and public libraries. In museums, the collections, especially donated collections, have traditionally driven the program and services. Historically, the educational program and experience were focused on the collection; the work of the curators and museum educators was focused on providing the history and story of the artifact. Today, museums are concentrating on creating experiences for museumgoers that enhance their visits, resulting in both loyalty and financial support.

In public libraries, the preservation, organization, and control of the collection were historically key goals (see also chapter 13: "Analog and Digital Curation and Preservation"). Today, creating interactions, marketing ideas, and designing learning opportunities—both large and small—are beginning to take shape as key focus areas in public libraries. Creating a sense of wonder and surprise are as important as curating a collection that intellectually engages a community. Public libraries support learning in a range of ways, such as providing transactional services like checking out books and videos and social experiences for people to use library workspaces to think, sit quietly, and reflect. The relative safety and security of the public space in libraries, combined with the idea that all are welcome, positions the public library as the great community space. People enjoy reading a newspaper, having a cup of coffee, writing their novel, or doing their homework in the public space of the library. There is comfort in spending time in the public sphere, and libraries are one of the few public places that are open to all members of the community free of charge.

Van Gogh's Learning Path Demonstrates Informal Learning Potential of Public Libraries

Sometimes the informal learning path takes the form of a desire for mastery of a subject. The artist Vincent van Gogh taught himself how to paint by first reading books on drawing. He started with charcoal and pencil sketches. He moved to Paris and began to work with color, experimenting with still-life painting and producing floral pieces. He began using acquaintances as models. He painted the postman over and over. He learned from other impressionist painters, borrowing from their styles and brushstrokes, and then developed his own distinctive style. His passion for his craft drove him to create his own learning path based on his drive to perfect his technique and expression. Books, observation, collaboration, practice, and failure were some of his learning tools. He was part of a community of artists, learning from other experts and experimenting with new colors and styles.[13]

Learning in public libraries can be like nibbling at a smorgasbord. Public libraries provide a vast array of programs to choose from on topics such as cooking, knitting, jewelry making, craft brewing, painting, or photography. Youth programs encourage children to explore the world of dinosaurs, sports, art, magic, music, and more. The public library is a marketplace of ideas, available for adventure and discovery. Public librarians curate talent from the community in order to connect users with a large breadth of expertise. The skills of the members of the community are becoming as valuable as books (see also chapter 18: "Creation Culture and Makerspaces").

Thinking about public libraries as learning spaces merely stretches the boundaries and reframes the institution. Public library programs are common, but shifting the organization's key mission to support learning and curiosity requires a new paradigm for the work of the public library. Today, there are examples of public libraries that are beginning to provide new models. The most successful institutions are those that take time to reflect and collaborate with their communities to create new systems of thinking for public libraries.

For example, after more than ten years of planning, the town of Aarhus, Denmark, opened a new library called Dokk1.[14] Their design strategy was to plan a new library for people, not books. From the outdoor playscape where children learn about the geography of the world to the large, open flexible spaces for exploration, creation, participation, and excitement, the public library provides a sense of empowerment and involvement, and supports innovation in the community. The team at Dokk1 used the Model Programme[15] as their inspiration, applying a design thinking approach to design the space. The process, as developed by D. Skot-Hansen and colleagues at the Royal School of Library and Information Science in Copenhagen, resulted in providing individual zones for inspiration, learning, meeting, and performance.[16] One of Dokk1's criteria for success is the percentage of community involvement in their programs. Currently, over 80 percent of their programs are engaged with some type of community participation. This ranges from community partners who utilize the library space to provide programming independent of library staff to people who come to the library to use the space as a studio or performance space to organized programs that are coordinated with library staff. This is a key shift from typical library programs where library staff drive the topics, agenda, organization, and coordination of programs.

Discussion Questions

How should librarians be thinking about public libraries in the twenty-first century? How can public librarians support creativity, communication, collaboration, and critical thinking skills?

Community Anchor

Developing relationships and partnerships with community businesses, artists, and organizations is becoming an essential practice. Public libraries in the United States are experimenting with new models that meet the unique needs of their communities. A few examples include:

- Madison Public Library in Madison, Wisconsin, supports creativity through the Bubbler, an initiative that connects the community with artists in residence—poets, painters, sculptors, textile artists, animators, and more.[17] These connections help provide a dynamic learning experience for people who participate in their workshops and performances.
- Richland Library in South Carolina is designing its spaces to facilitate studio experiences, for instance, ballet dancers performing for children and after-hours programs for young adults.[18]
- Los Angeles Public Library's online GED programs provide a path to work and educational success for students who wish to complete their high school diploma.[19]
- Multnomah Public Library welcomes immigrants to attend citizenship classes so they can achieve naturalization status.[20]
- Libraries across the country partner with food bank programs to provide after-school snacks and summer lunches for children.
- Anythink Libraries just outside of Denver, Colorado, centers its work on supporting people and their quest to learn, collaborate, and create.[21] Its spaces are organized for experiences ranging from reading to playing and collaborating to creating. The library experience is participatory, giving customers a greater depth of involvement for them to take ownership of the library and their experience. The library is a place of inspiration and reflection. Books and information support these experiences and serve as learning anchors.

Collaborating with key partners and stakeholders provides opportunities for the public library to expand its services and programs without requiring library staff to bring all the resources and skills to the table. The public library as convener brings newfound respect to the library.

The shift from a library space dedicated to books to a public library primarily focused on supporting the needs of the community and learning requires significant restructuring, training, and allocation of resources. However, in order to restructure, librarians need to align their thinking about their work with a focus on the public library as community space. Table 8.1 outlines some of these changes, starting with the shift from books to people.

> Collaborating with key partners and stakeholders provides opportunities for the public library to expand its services and programs without requiring library staff to bring all the resources and skills to the table. The public library as convener brings newfound respect to the library.

The concepts behind this evolution of public libraries, from books to people and from transactions to relationships, model patterns that are occurring in social and cultural networks as well. The decentralization of power results in institutions that are collaborative, supportive, and participatory (see also chapter 17: "Hyperlinked Libraries").

Convener and Connector: Supporting Creativity, Innovation, and Entrepreneurialism

By supporting the creativity and collaboration of their communities, public libraries are helping people to not only connect with ideas but also with careers, new passions, and each other. This helps support the quality of life for the whole community. Libraries are well positioned as hubs

Table 8.1. Evolution of Public Libraries.

From	To
Books	People
Transactions	Interactions/Relationships
Solo	Collaborative
Formal	Informal
Information	Meaning
Passive	Experiences
Predictable	Surprising
Serious	Play

for creative, innovative, and collaborative engagement (see also chapter 18: "Creation Culture and Makerspaces"). Libraries are places where it can be safe to learn things through play. The range of programming occurring in libraries paired with the cornucopia of ideas found in their collections is brain food for any creative person. Just like an outdoor green market filled with fresh fruits, vegetables, and local goods, a library is a marketplace of ideas, experiences, and opportunities to collaborate with experts. Creativity is about solving problems, making associations by observing patterns and connecting things in new ways. Creativity is about dreaming of what could be instead of being trapped or satisfied by the status quo.

Public libraries are places of opportunity, where ideas or dreams can be tested out. Small business incubation centers supporting start-ups provide workspace, collaboration, mentoring, and business connections. Numerous public libraries have developed business incubation centers and coworking spaces. Philadelphia Free Library has launched the Business Resource and Innovation Center.[22] They support entrepreneurs through spaces, resources, networking and mentorship. Libraries are safe spaces to be creative, try out ideas, and find the support to take risks.

Innovation and entrepreneurialism have been central to the success of the United States. Inventions from the lightbulb to the iPhone have shaped the nation's character. The tinkering model or design thinking process sets the stage for inventing the next idea—big or small. Years ago, children learned how to farm, cook, sew, or fix the family car or bicycle by watching their parents and neighbors, then working on small projects, and gradually developing their own skills. Their hands-on learning was based on watching, testing, and experimenting. This concept is being reintroduced in public libraries.

For example, the Philadelphia Free Library is providing workforce development through education that supports career paths to actual jobs.[23] Not only do they have extensive job training programs and support, they have developed a tie-lending program for job seekers. People can check out a necktie to complete their interview outfit from the collection of forty-eight ties as part of the TakePart initiative. Their Culinary Literacy Center is a commercial-grade kitchen that is both a cooking school and a dining space where people learn about nutrition, healthy cooking, and meal preparation on a budget.

Discussion Question

How can library professionals help communities shift their perceptions of traditional public libraries to allow for innovation?

TWENTY-FIRST-CENTURY SKILLS

Critical skills for success in the twenty-first century are vastly different from typical skills in formal education, where teachers spend time pouring information into students' heads, then testing and moving on to more information. Success in today's world requires the ability to problem-solve, collaborate, and communicate in a myriad of formats (written, verbal, and digital). The four key skills are communication, collaboration, critical thinking, and creativity. Libraries are already positioned well to help strengthen these skills in their patrons, as this combination of skills is a natural outcome of library programs where people learn things together.

One example is through participation in community gardens, where people learn how to manage community projects, till the soil, and utilize the best planting and watering techniques, all while they are getting to know their neighbors. The tagline for Denver Urban Gardens is "growing community one garden at a time."[24] Libraries are beginning to host community gardens as an extension of their regular programs. The community runs the garden, makes the decisions for policies and governance of the garden, researches best practices for gardening, and provides mentoring and informal gardening classes. Gardening requires critical thinking and adaptive problem solving. Designing irrigation systems for small garden plots requires problem solving. Working in a democratically run garden requires good communication and collaboration skills. Becoming part of a community of practice, in this case gardening, is very different from having a garden in one's own yard. Working together as a team creates interdependency and a sense of ownership and responsibility for the greater good.

ORGANIZATIONAL STRUCTURES THAT SUPPORT CENTERS OF LEARNING

Public libraries that are merging new innovative approaches with traditional book-centered services are discovering that creating a community-learning anchor requires new systems, new structures, and new ways of operating. Fresh thinking is needed to reconfigure the library mission as well as its day-to-day management. Cohesive structures that are intentional start with an examination of mission and vision. Or, as Simon Sinek suggests, "Start with 'why?'"[25] As the why of public libraries shifts to supporting the community and people's success and happiness through learning, the public library's structures and organizational systems need reexamining.

Space Design for Learning, Adventure, and Discovery

There is a traditional pattern for library space planners, whether one is building a new public library or renovating an older space (see also chapter 23: "Innovative Library and Information Services: The Design Thinking Process"). It starts with counting things: counting books, desks, chairs, tables, people, and shelving units. The next step is to project growth of the collection over time. The space is then designed around these counted items and projections. In today's evolution of public libraries, collection spaces are shrinking while space for programming and learning is increasing. Learning spaces require flexibility, including flexible furniture, light, and space for supplies. People learn in different ways. Some prefer the solitude of the corner of a room. Some learn better in groups.

Public library spaces that are designed for books are planned for maximum storage capacity and for security of the collection. Rows and rows of shelving at right angles form a maze or confining environment. Books shelved in a classification system are displayed with the spines out, covered with a call number label. Contrast this with a typical bookstore, where the layout is designed for discovery and marketing of books and materials. Books are displayed cover out and organized topically to form a marketplace of discovery. Public libraries are now learning from these retail models to better market their materials, enticing the community to engage with new ideas from popular collections.

Spaces designed for people start with a sense of welcome. Attention to detail in furnishings, color, light, and signage are critical components to creating a space where people want to engage in discovery and an adventure in learning. A sense of style that is cohesive, that elevates and inspires, is essential for public library furniture. Imagine a favorite space, museum, study, or living room. Connections to nature, outdoor views, and natural light summon a sense of well-being and spark thinking and creativity. Creating an ambience that makes people feel welcome, comfortable, and capable is part of creating a learning environment.

> "Creating an ambience that makes people feel welcome, comfortable, and capable is part of creating a learning environment."

Hospitality

In his bestselling book, *Setting the Table: The Transforming Power of Hospitality in Business*, renowned restauranteur Danny Meyers defines hospitality as knowing that someone is on your side.[26] An important element of public libraries is creating an experience that sets people up for success. Hospitality starts with a sense of generosity. Just like the way a space is designed, hospitality is about making people feel welcome, taking time to listen to what is important, and helping people feel safe and understood. This takes both emotional intelligence and empathy. This requires staff who are naturally curious and love being around people. Staff who are happy and optimistic will be the underpinnings of an organization that is known for its hospitality. In order to hire and retain happy staff who are curious and enjoy working in a collaborative environment, public librarians must redefine the ideal staff profile, develop job descriptions, conduct interviews to identify candidates who best match that profile, and then provide training, coaching, and performance evaluations that support the library's values and mission (see also chapter 22: "Managing Personnel"). Librarians typically possess a love of books and have a natural drive to solve problems and puzzles. Relationship building is now a key skill to ensure success in the public library sphere.

Barriers

The customer experience can be frustrating in some public libraries because of barriers based on policies (see also chapter 29: "Information Policy"). Examining the barriers is a first step, followed by reinventing the customer experience and changing policies to make public libraries more user friendly (see also chapter 35: "Intellectual Freedom"). This requires a closer look at the rules, policies, and procedures. Each library must make its own decisions, but elimination of some of the strict regulations can have a huge impact on the customer experience. Of course, overdue fines are one of the barriers that interfere with people being able to use the library. This is especially true in the case of children, who usually do not have the transportation to return books in a timely manner or pay for their fines. A library card can open the world to a child, and having a card with fines hinders the opportunity for reading and learning at the library. Experimenting with extended grace periods or eliminating fines altogether, is a significant step toward eliminating one of the key reasons people abandon their public library. A number of public libraries have recently eliminated some or all fines including Columbus Metropolitan Library and the San Jose Public Library.[27] Anythink libraries eliminated fines in 2009, and this has shifted the work experience of line staff. Instead of having to tell people they cannot check out a book or use a computer until they pay their fines, now staff spend time developing relationships and making connections with customers.

Examining the obstacles to a delightful experience starts with a pair of keen eyes outside of the library building. What message is being sent by the look of the public library, the signs, and the presentation? Does the public library look inviting or forbidding? How are people greeted as they first connect in person, by phone, or via the website? All of these details can be either opportunities for hospitality or moments that create barriers. Creating a cohesive look, feel, and style of service that is consistently deployed in the public library supports the user experience. This translates to processes and policies as well. How challenging is the library card application process? Are there rules in place to encourage or discourage use? (See also chapter 14: "User Experience.")

PROFESSIONAL COMPETENCIES: MORPHING FROM KEEPERS TO GUIDES

No matter what the space is like or what materials or services are offered, the most critical part of every public library is its staff. Library staff are essential to successful public libraries operating as centers for learning. Key competencies and skill sets are shifting and expanding. The role of the librarian as keeper of the books required a person who was meticulous at organization, had an exceptional memory, was a voracious reader, followed policies and rules, and ran a tidy library. Of course, this is an exaggeration in most cases.

Today's public librarian is a person who enjoys building partnerships and relationships. Public library work is more of a calling than a career. Public librarians have relationships with customers that, for example, result in high school students completing their diplomas and provide lifesaving first aid. From the first visit to a public library for story hour to a game of chess with seniors, the library is a home away from home. The public librarian sends that welcoming friendly message of inclusion. Two key skills needed by public librarians are empathy and generosity. Whether a patron needs a smile or someone to listen to a story or a piece of advice, public librarians' work requires a certain amount of emotional intelligence.[28] The work of librarians today is also to facilitate continuous learning and to help the community in solving their unique issues. Associate Professor Michael Stephens with the School of Information at San José University redefines the work of the profession in his statement: "Librarians help people make sense of the world."[29] The role of the librarian is becoming more like a guide, helping people discover their path and explore their interests (see textbox 8.2).

> Today's public librarian is a person who enjoys building partnerships and relationships. Public library work is more of a calling than a career.

This requires an endless quest to understand, be understood, and create a path with people who are seeking a discovery. This discovery may be an address, a career, a business opportunity, a dream, a solution to a major life problem, or an aspiration to find a small moment of happiness by reading a poem, listening to music, talking with a friend, painting a picture, making a meal for friends, or telling one's own story.

TEXTBOX 8.2

Public Librarians as Guides

- They collaborate with communities and customers to define and find the learning goals and path.
- They help people design their trail so they can arrive at their desired destination.
- They help people navigate ambiguity.
- They are like sleuths and trailblazers.
- They are connectors.
- They are problem solvers, experts, and advisors.

- They are credible.
- They transfer knowledge freely.
- They instill self-confidence.
- They are catalysts.
- They are explorers and dreamers.
- They open people's eyes to change.
- They are intuitive and persuasive.
- They are charismatic and entertaining.
- They are confident seekers who are self-directed.
- They are optimistic.
- They connect people with possibility.
- They motivate people to explore lives filled with adventure and discovery.

CONCLUSION

Public libraries today are both the archives of the world's culture and history and the platform for future possibilities. As the world becomes more interconnected and complex, public libraries remain that unique public space that opens doors for all. People of all ages, ethnicity, political ideology, cultures, and religion are respected and treated with dignity. Public libraries are the places where:

- one can listen to people of different faiths and cultures talk about values, challenges, and similarities,
- community members can talk and learn with people from all walks of life and be reminded of shared humanity and shared vulnerability,
- a homeless person can sit at the same table with a millionaire and read the local newspaper,
- a community can gather online or in person to connect with the opportunities of the larger world and forge their own collective future,
- individuals can connect to ideas, opportunities, and mentors to turn their own dreams into successful and happy lives, and
- the history of the world is remembered.

The public library is the anchor in the community that actively practices the basic principles of democracy. Public libraries are hope.

NOTES

1. John Cotton Dana, *A Library Primer* (Chicago: Library Bureau, 1899).
2. Jesse Shera, *Introduction to Library Science: Basic Elements of Library Service* (Santa Barbara, CA: Libraries Unlimited, 1976).
3. "Vartan Gregorian," *Wikipedia*, August 22, 2017, https://en.wikipedia.org/wiki/Vartan_Gregorian.
4. Public Library Association, http://www.ala.org/pla/about.
5. Public Library Association, "Public Libraries Open Possibility," 2017, http://www.ala.org/pla/leadership/advocacy/videos.
6. Ibid.
7. Vartan Gregorian, "Libraries as Acts of Civic Renewal," Kansas City Club, October 17, 2002.
8. Cotton Dana, *A Library Primer*.
9. Ibid.

10. American Library Association, "Number of Libraries in the United States," 2017, http://www.ala.org/tools/libfactsheets/alalibraryfactsheet01.

11. Statista, "Number of Starbucks stores in the United States from 2015 to 2016," accessed September 30, 2017, https://www.statista.com/statistics/218360/number-of-starbucks-stores-in-the-us/.

12. ALA Factsheet 26, http://www.ala.org/tools/libfactsheets/alalibraryfactsheet26.

13. Timothy Standring, *Becoming Van Gogh* (New Haven, CT: Yale University Press, 2012).

14. Dokk1, https://dokk1.dk/english.

15. D. Skot-Hansen et al., "The Four Spaces: A New Model for the Public library," *New Library World* 113, nos. 11–12 (2012): 586–97.

16. Ibid.

17. Madison Public Library Bubbler, http://madisonbubbler.org.

18. Richland Library Studio, https://www.richlandlibrary.com/studio.

19. Los Angeles Public Library Career Online High School, https://www.lapl.org/diploma.

20. Multnomah Public Library, https://multcolib.org/immigrants-and-citizenship.

21. Anythink Libraries, https://www.anythinklibraries.org/thestudio.

22. Philadelphia Free Library Business Resource and Innovation Center, https://libwww.freelibrary.org/programs/bric/.

23. Philadelphia Free Library Career Center, https://libwww.freelibrary.org/programs/jobseekers/index.cfm.

24. "Denver Urban Gardens," *Mile High Mamas* (blog), June 29, 2011, http://www.milehighmamas.com/blog/2011/06/29/denver-urban-gardens-growing-community-one-garden-at-a-time/.

25. Simon Sinek, *Start with Why: How Great Leaders Inspire Everyone to Take Action* (New York: Portfolio/Penguin, 2011).

26. Danny Meyer, *Setting the Table* (New York: Harper Collins, 2006).

27. Jennifer Dixon, "Doing Fine(s)?" *Library Journal*, April 4, 2017, http://lj.libraryjournal.com/2017/04/budgets-funding/doing-fines-fines-fees/#_.

28. Daniel Goleman, *Emotional Intelligence* (New York: Bantam Books, 1995).

29. Michael Stephens, "Library as Classroom: Hyperlinked Learning Experiences for All," Colorado Association of Libraries Annual Conference, October 24, 2015, http://tametheweb.com/speaking-presentations/presentations-ive-given/.

9

Working in Different Information Environments

SPECIAL LIBRARIES AND INFORMATION CENTERS

Crystal S. Megaridis

Chapter 9, "Working in Different Information Environments: Special Libraries and Information Centers,"
explores the wide-ranging opportunities for information professionals to work in many information settings.
In this chapter, Crystal Megaridis, manager of library services at Praxair Inc., a global Fortune 300 company,
brings her expertise to bear on the diverse roles, opportunities, and challenges that are unique to special
libraries and the information professionals who work in them.

Megaridis briefly takes us back to the special library's beginning in 1909 with the first Special Library
Association gathering and then describes the unique and innovative special libraries of today. Special librari-
ans inhabit a variety of work environments from law firms to nonprofit organizations. Some special librarians
work as independent information professionals. Special librarians perform a variety of roles including serving
users specifically interested in the field of focus, create and manage organizational systems, analyze data,
identify competitive advantages, and even demonstrate return on investment.

Regardless of the location or size, Megaridis explains, the special library and information center should be
strategically aligned to serve its parent organization and the community it serves. To offer depth to this discus-
sion, she includes four "Day in the Life" experiences to provide a sampling of the different environments special
librarians and information professionals work within: a corporate organization, a nonprofit organization, a
government organization, and an independent information professional. Collectively the author's overview of
special libraries and the "Day in the Life" scenarios illuminate the varied work of special librarians. She also
identifies the competencies special librarians need to support the unique needs of the communities they serve.

★   ★   ★

The world of special libraries and information centers is vast, varied, and exciting, yet it is often the sector of librarianship that people are least familiar with. Many special libraries and information centers have collections that are unavailable to the general population; therefore, the public often is unaware these information centers even exist.

This chapter describes the many interesting environments where special libraries and information centers are found, as well as the diverse roles, opportunities, and challenges that are unique to special librarians and information professionals. Current practitioners from a variety of unique information centers share their "Day in the Life" experiences to provide a sampling of the different environments special librarians and information professionals work within.

After reading this chapter, the reader should have an understanding of the variety of information centers that constitute this sector of information work, the unique aspects of the special library and information center environment, and the many opportunities and roles that exist for special librarians and information professionals today.

WHAT IS A SPECIAL LIBRARY/INFORMATION CENTER?

The forerunners of today's special libraries and information centers can be traced to legal and medical special collections of the eighteenth and nineteenth centuries. These special collections, as well as membership libraries with scientific and historical collections, were more for educational purposes than supporting any organization's operations.[1] However, during the post–Civil War era, collections of information began to emerge within businesses, such as chemical manufacturers and engineering firms, and workers became responsible for these collections.[2]

As this sector of librarianship developed in the early twentieth century, information professionals working with nontraditional library materials (such as standards, technical reports, and patent files) and newer technologies in these information centers felt the need for a separate support organization beyond the American Library Association (ALA). The fundamental reason these information professionals felt they needed a new association was stated well in 1925 by Richard H. Johnston, librarian, Bureau of Railway Economic Statistics, and president, Special Library Association, 1914–1915: "Special library work, therefore, is the skillful application not of the sources of information but of the information provided by these sources to the needs of the organization."[3] In 1909, at the annual ALA conference, John Cotton Dana founded the Special Libraries Association (SLA).[4] With an initial membership of just forty-five, they represented sixteen separate and distinct interests among them.[5] Today, the Special Libraries Association provides support, educational opportunities, an annual conference, and twenty-six specialized divisions (e.g., Competitive Intelligence, Legal, Pharmaceutical and Health Technology) and nine caucuses (e.g., Archival and Preservation, User Experience) to support their members' needs.

Special Libraries and Information Centers Today

Special libraries and information centers today can be found in a wide variety of parent organizations. They provide resources and services in support of organizations, such as companies, museums, government agencies, and hospitals. Special libraries and information centers are often one of many departments or functions strategically aligned to support the overarching goals of the parent organization.

Each special library and information center is truly unique. Some special libraries and information centers are 100 percent virtual with no physical collection, providing only electronic resources and services to a global, multilingual user group. Other special libraries and information centers are comprised of historical documents or artifacts that must be physically housed in temperature-controlled environments. Most special libraries and information centers fit somewhere on the spectrum in between, offering resources and/or services that best meet the needs of their stakeholders.

Special librarians and information professionals typically

- serve a distinct population of customers or clients with unique requirements,
- provide decision-ready information products,
- create and manage organizational systems for internal knowledge, and
- analyze big data to identify insights and discern competitive advantages.

Figure 9.1 Types of Special Libraries. *Created by author.*

Work Environment

Information professionals working in special libraries and information centers may be collocated in a facility or library, embedded in different departments, or distributed globally. Depending on the organization, there may be a solo information professional, or there may be forty or more information professionals on a team. Regardless of the location or size, the crux of the special library and information center is to be strategically aligned to serve its parent organization. In the special library environment, those who use the resources and services are typically considered customers, clients, or users.

Some special librarians and information professionals operate their own independent service. Their environment may be a home office relying on screen sharing technologies to meet with clients or may be a traveling office meeting at client locations, coffee shops, or even in collaborative workspaces. There may be no physical collection, and the information professional may rely heavily on access to online subscription content for primary and secondary research and information.

Important to these information professionals is the ever-present need to determine whether or not their products and services provide value to the organization.[6] To assess the value, information professionals measure the usage of the products, platforms, and services that they provide. Measuring the usage helps information professionals demonstrate the return on investment (ROI) that organizations get in exchange for their services. Information professionals can then make fact-based decisions on retaining or changing the information products and services they provide.[7] ROI is equally important to the independent information professional, as well as stakeholders of an information center.

Roles, Opportunities, Challenges, and Trends

While all information professionals are involved with acquiring, managing, and sharing information, special librarians also provide decision-ready information. All activities of the information professional

Crystal S. Megaridis

should be in support of the institution's mission. Often, information professionals become experts in very specific areas of information products and research. They also get to know their clientele very well, as they are usually a defined group, such as scientists, attorneys, artists, or donors. The close rapport information professionals develop with their clientele allows them to keep their customer's needs top-of-mind and provide new and relevant information to them on a regular basis.

Roles of the Special Librarian and Information Professional

Often operating as a "business within a business," the special librarian and information professional in an organization needs an entrepreneurial spirit in developing and managing library operations. Information professionals need to carefully evaluate products within the context of their client's needs and negotiate with vendors. Information professionals are frequently involved in research and information analysis of complex questions. Information professionals may spend hours or days fulfilling a single information request. Some are involved with internal knowledge management projects, whereby they design and implement information systems to capture, manage, and retrieve internal knowledge for the organization. Other information professionals design and manage information portals of subscription content. For the solo information professional, bits and pieces of all of these activities may be included in their role. All special librarians and information professionals, whether working as an independent professional or in a large firm, are involved with marketing products and services.

Newer roles that extend beyond the scope of the typical information organization include information professionals who are embedded within teams, such as business development or information technology, with titles including business analyst, knowledge manager, or user experience (UX) designer.[8] These roles provide information work within a team and may not be connected to an information center at all. In some instances, the information professional may be a department head for a team of information professionals; a leader of several departments including the information center; the organization's chief information officer (CIO), who provides vision and leadership to multiple information departments such as information technology (IT); or even the chief data officer (CDO), who is responsible for enterprise-wide governance for information assets.[9]

Opportunities and Challenges

Rapid advancement in technology provides great opportunities for special librarians and information professionals to find new ways to achieve success. Clients, often digital natives in this information age, expect a fast response for information and answers to their questions. Special librarians and information professionals meet those expectations through experimenting with and implementing new technologies.

Currently, some of the most pressing challenges for the special librarian and information professional include information expectations, literacy, globalization, marketing, and copyright. Customers and clients of information centers often lack knowledge about non-internet sources of information that may be vital to their success. Special library and information center customers often need guidance to discern when to use open literature through the internet versus when subscription sources are a must. Likewise, skills for evaluating credible information from questionable sources may need to be developed. The "information on demand" environment has brought new information expectations to the workforce and employee workflow processes. The special librarian and information professional must educate clients, who in some situations value speed of information access over quality of information, as this can jeopardize fact-based decision making in the organization. Therefore, the information professional's ability to successfully teach information skills is key.

Globalization brings interesting challenges of information distribution, export controls, and language barriers. As many people are unaware of special libraries and information centers and their roles, marketing of resources and services is even more critical in these environments than in other library sectors. Understanding and managing copyright compliance often falls to the special librarian and information professional. Adherence to copyright law, as well as agreements with vendor content, must be followed by all employees/members of an organization to avoid legal consequences.

Current Trends

Demographic shifts in the workforce and the exponential growth in data have important implications for special libraries and information centers. In 2015, millennials became the largest generation in the U.S. workforce.[10] With each new generation comes differences in approaches to work, and the millennial generation is no exception. As digital natives, millennials live and work in a world where information is always flowing around them. Expectations for fast answers are high, yet verifying and qualifying information is often not performed, which can be detrimental to decision making. To serve this population well, special librarians and information professionals can build solutions into the daily workflow processes for fast access to credible information sources these information workers need.

As machine technologies have evolved, they now provide analytic abilities to take information from disparate sources, turn it into insights and intelligence, and thereby facilitate better decision making. Predictive and prescriptive analytics are areas that information professionals can facilitate. New on the horizon is cognitive analytics, which offers a deeper level of dynamic information analysis and is another area to which special librarians and information professionals can contribute.[11]

COMPETENCIES FOR THE SPECIAL LIBRARIAN AND INFORMATION PROFESSIONAL

Check This Out

The Special Libraries Association (SLA) has prepared a list of Core Competencies for professionals working in a special library or information center. *Visit*: http://www.sla.org/about-sla/competencies/.

Special librarians and information professionals usually hold a master of library and information science degree (MLIS). The Special Libraries Association (SLA) has prepared a list of core competencies for professionals working in a special library or information center.[12] SLA's core competencies were revised in 2016 and include information and knowledge systems, services, and resources; information and data retrieval, organization and analysis; information ethics; and, enabling competencies, such as critical thinking, adaptability, and relationship building.

Understanding the business with which the information center operates is critical to the success of the information center and its information professionals. Depending on the type of special library or information center, there may be additional desired competencies, such as in the areas of law, science, history, patents, technology, or health care. For example, a law librarian might hold a Juris Doctor (JD) degree. Other information professionals may hold a bachelor's or master's degree in a subject area related to their organization. Strong research and analysis skills are important in many special libraries and information centers, as the information professional is often seeking answers for clients, rather than references to information. For example, chemistry li-

Discussion Question

What skills or competencies do you feel are most essential for success as a special librarian?

Crystal S. Megaridis

brarians may need to be well versed in chemical structure searching; likewise, patent librarians should be well trained in patent database searching and may even be patent agents. The willingness to be flexible to learn and implement new technologies is key to all roles.

Leadership skills are invaluable to the special librarian and information professional. Information professionals need strong negotiation, decision-making, communication, and project management skills so they can engage in successful customer relationship management, vendor management, and marketing. Information professionals also need to function effectively in a variety of team environments, whether that is working within or leading cross-functional teams.

For information professionals working as a solo librarian, an independent information professional, or those leading a team, skills in business operations and management are also valuable.

Support Organizations

In addition to the SLA, there are countless other associations that have emerged to support different types of special libraries and information centers, such as:

- Medical Library Association (MLA),
- American Theological Library Association (ATLA), and
- Association of Independent Information Professionals (AIIP).

The value these associations bring to their members is immeasurable, as no matter the size or type of the information center, there is always the need for support, development, encouragement, and mentorship from a network of similar information professionals.

Table 9.1. Support Organizations.

AALL	American Association of Law Libraries
ACRL	Association of College and Research Libraries
AIIP	Association of Independent Information Professionals
ARLIS	Art Libraries Society
ARMA	Association of Records Management and Administrators
ASIS&T	Association for Information Science & Technology
ATLA	American Theological Library Association
CSLA	Church and Synagogue Library Association
MLA	Medical Library Association
SCIP	Strategic and Competitive Intelligence Professionals

A DAY IN THE LIFE OF INFORMATION PROFESSIONALS IN DIFFERENT ENVIRONMENTS

The following vignettes provide insights from four different information professionals who work in corporate, nonprofit, independent, and government environments. While each is a unique special library, some characteristics of special libraries cross all of these working environments, including strategic alignment, supporting unique clientele, marketing, and relationship building.

Day in the Life in the Corporate Organization: Scott Brown, Cybrarian, Oracle

My official title at Oracle, Inc. (a global software and cloud provider) is Senior Cybrarian. I admit there is a part of me that cringed the first time I heard of the *cybrarian* title. But I have learned that it resonates with my clients and offers a great marketing "hook."

Oracle has one hundred thirty-five thousand employees serving four hundred twenty thousand customers in more than one hundred forty five countries. As a company, it realized revenue of $37 billion in FY16, and its customers include almost all of the top companies globally, literally across every industry. I have worked at Oracle for two and a half years, and I have been a researcher in the technology industry for fifteen years. I still learn something new every day.

My role at Oracle, along with my two colleagues in the Virtual Information Services (VIS) function, splits into two big areas: managing business and technical resources that are available organization-wide, such as EBSCO and Safari Books Online; and providing "high-touch" research and information services to strategic groups and initiatives across the company.

Because we are only three people, we need to make some hard choices about how to spend our time most effectively. So how do we decide who and what is strategic? Primarily, our company strategy and stakeholders determine this. Since we report up through Human Resources, VIS provides support and research services for major workforce initiatives at Oracle. At the same time, we also strive to build relationships with many different groups in the company: sales, marketing, product groups, our engineers, and regional leads across the globe. In the morning, I might find overnight e-mails and internal social media posts from Australia and Singapore, India, and the UK, then from the East Coast of the United States, and into my closer time zones, starting back with Australia in the early evening.

While all of our resources are self-service, we know the value of what we do depends heavily upon building trust and relationships with Oracle employees and our strategic clients. This process often starts with awareness of what we have to offer. We regularly hear: "I didn't know we had access to all of this!"

The key to building our strategic relationships, however, is not simply talking about the great content we have. It is about making sure we deliver content that is relevant to the business at the point of need—which takes time and requires an eye for spotting opportunities. As we listen to the strategic "themes" from across the company and from our key clients, we can deliver research and information that is increasingly relevant and responsive to the company and our clients' needs and current projects.

> **Components of Building Trusted and Lasting Relationships**
>
> - Responsiveness
> - Understanding the client's rapidly-changing environment
> - Putting in the extra effort when it is really needed
> - Providing perspective on the information
> - Learning from the clients

As we demonstrate the value of our information services in this way, we find that clients often come back to us: "You helped me with this; can you help me with this other project?" Responsiveness, a willingness to understand our client's rapidly changing environment, being willing to put in the extra effort when it is needed, providing our perspective on the information, and being willing to learn from our clients—all of these are critical components of building trusted and lasting relationships. By being able to support and give so much to our clients, they become a part of our information network, so when we need to turn to them for support or information, they are there for us as well.

Like many learning and development professionals, the great majority of information professionals working in corporate settings have difficulties concretely illustrating the value and impact of what we do. We know what we do provides value, and our clients know this as well—but how do you measure revenue and ROI of intangibles, such as better information, or a smarter, more skilled, and more informed workforce?

The short answer is—it is very difficult to do. But there are instances where we can directly point to a project, a product, or an initiative, and say that, yes, we had direct business impact. Our research has contributed to new product proposals, clarified new target markets for our products, and enabled more effective ways of ultimately serving our customers better.

I love the impact that my work can have on such a broad scale. I love that I can bring so many of my skills to bear in one position—from creative writing to in-depth research to data visualization and video production. I love connecting with the people I work with. And I love the project-driven nature of the work, where I have the opportunity to learn new skills and pick up new knowledge every day. As a lifelong learner, it is difficult to imagine a more satisfying role.

A Day in the Life in the Nonprofit Organization: Joyce Fedeczko, Managing Librarian and Archivist, International Fertilizer Development Center

I serve as the library manager and archivist for the International Fertilizer Development Center (IFDC), a 501(c)(3) nonprofit public international organization (PIO) headquartered in Muscle Shoals, Alabama. There are about seventy-five staff at the headquarters and over eight hundred employees in the field in Africa, Bangladesh, Myanmar, and other locales. IFDC is led by our president/CEO and governed by a board of directors, many affiliated with international global organizations themselves. IFDC researches fertilizer technology that is then transferred to smallholder farmers around the world. I provide, promote, manage, and evaluate library services and resources in fertilizer chemistry and engineering, agronomy, and economics. Additionally, I help the IFDC staff connect via online communities, such as Yammer and SharePoint.

Moving from for-profit to nonprofit corporate libraries, my fundamental library impact remains to stay on target with the organization's strategies, mission, and values. Wherever I work as a librarian, I do physical plant management of the library space and collection, software resources management, contracts negotiation, public presentations, team building, and leadership work with staff. Also, collaboration with subject specialists from many disciplines, vendor relations, product-use training, reference service, cataloging, creation of subject-specific research guides, data management, and internet and database searching fill my days. I maintain my professional knowledge of current information and e-library science disciplines by attending professional information management meetings, webinars, and conferences. I maintain membership in the Special Libraries Association, serving as the Treasurer for the Food, Agriculture and Nutrition Division, and am a member of the United States Agriculture Information Network (USAIN) to liaise and work with other local and state librarians on behalf of IFDC.

Because IFDC helps smallholder farmers in developing nations grow and sell more food, we have an international staff who travel from Alabama to work in farm fields in foreign nations, especially in sub-Saharan Africa, to support self-sufficient food production. As a solo librarian supporting research, I bring strategic value to the work of our organization by effectively partnering with our library's global clients and our staff of agronomists, soil scientists, economists, and chemical engineers to link information products and services to their research needs, all within the bounds of a very limited budget. IFDC is donor funded, and not every cent used at headquarters goes directly to the farmers in developing nations. Rigorous vetting of resources, being necessary to support those working directly with the farmers, is the norm. To provide high-level information consulting to our global staff, I proactively perform scientific, agricultural, and business information research and analysis to keep our staff up-to-date on international fertilizer issues. Also, I implement specific research upon request, mostly using the internet and some specialized niche databases, such as AgNIC[13] and AGRICOLA[14]—all free resources. Occasionally, I initiate the development of new information products and services, such as finding freeware applications for project management and contracts. I curate and develop agriculture-related content and resources, such as a list of free database resources available only to our foreign-based staff and a taxonomy of fertilizer terms of interest to all of our staff, for use with IFDC's knowledge management system and photos-from-the-field collection.

Our library is open to the public because we house materials from the closed Tennessee Valley Authority (TVA) National Fertilizer Development Center. Besides working in the library and archives, a librarian's labor in a nonprofit may include fund-raising. I also provide research assistance to IFDC's project development unit, and their job is to bring in new public and private funds to support IFDC's global mission.

A Day in the Life as an Independent Information Professional: Jan Knight, Bancroft Information Services

As an independent contractor, I work from a home office so my commute consists of shuffling down the hall to my office. I refer to my services as "providing insight to entrepreneurs from start-ups to grown-ups," and I achieve this by providing what is typically called Secondary (desk) Market Research and writing services. I am a generalist; thus, I could be working on the internet of things, hard cider markets, sustainable fishing, and medical devices all within a week or month. I occasionally enlist a domain expert or a collaborator to help with complementary services or research instead of employees, but I do almost everything myself.

A unique challenge as an independent information professional is that if I do not take time to market my services well, I do not make money! Most of my days include a combination of marketing my services (networking in person or via social media), creating client proposals, initiating or responding to e-mails and phone calls with clients, potential clients, colleagues, collaborators, and vendors, and then back to actually performing the research and writing of deliverables that keep me in business. Here is what I do on a representative day:

8:00 a.m.—8:30 a.m.: As I am not a morning person and work from home, I typically ease into the day by reviewing social media feeds and news highlights, some for personal enjoyment but most to keep up with trends and news on industries I work in. Technology is just one area where I market my services more aggressively, so I follow pertinent Twitter feeds like @TechCoHQ, @wearableguru, and Facebook feeds from sections of business magazines like *Fast Company* and *Entrepreneur*.

8:30 a.m.—11:30 p.m.: I respond to what I see as urgent e-mails, phone calls, or texts. Active client projects take priority; potential client issues come next, and then scheduling meetings, phone conferences, or setting up web meetings and the occasional screen-share session. Most educational or business development webinars I attend seem to occur during this time slot due to my time zone. During this morning block of time, I do try to put in at least two solid hours of research and writing.

11:30 a.m.—2:00 p.m.: During this time, I sneak in a short break for lunch, and I tend to work on miscellaneous tasks like invoicing clients, dealing with banking issues, contacts with vendors, volunteer board activities for my professional association, and some of the ongoing business-related activities.

2:00 p.m.—6:00 p.m.: I am told I am a little unusual in that when left to my own devices and schedule, this is the best time for me to do serious work. Serious work to me is billable work for a client, work where I have to be able to think clearly and strategically and that usually involves searching online databases such as IBISWorld, Profound, LexisNexis, and so on, as well as drilling down into other online sources. Much of my work includes researching markets, competitors, and industries and helps to shape business plans, business development, marketing plans, and similar activities. During

Crystal S. Megaridis

this focused time is when I find I not only perform the research well, but also can usually work on the written customized deliverable. I mostly create reports in Word document format or Excel and occasionally PowerPoint. I also work on projects that I like to refer to as "research-driven writing" projects that can include creating market snapshots, industry snapshots, or whitepapers for clients.

After 6:00 p.m.: When attending a business networking event every week or so, I am out from about 5:30 to 8 p.m. If not, I will admit to often sneaking back into my office after dinner to "just spend an hour catching up on e-mail" or "finishing that presentation." The flexibility of my schedule allows me to focus when I need to, choose to get dressed at noon if necessary, and market myself online at all hours!

A Day in the Life in the Government Organization: Michele Masias, Law Librarian, Justice Libraries, U.S. Department of Justice

I am a law librarian on the library staff at a large federal government agency, the Department of Justice (DOJ). As with any government entity, the work I do directly supports the mission of the DOJ, which entails leading the nation in ensuring protection of all Americans while preserving their constitutional freedoms. A day in the life for me includes several aspects of librarianship, such as reference and research, collections, managing web content, marketing, and more. It is also anything but routine, and it gives me great satisfaction knowing that the work I do makes a difference to our country and significantly impacts people's lives.

An essential part of my daily work is providing reference and research assistance to the attorneys and staff at the DOJ. A typical reference request may be routine and take little time to complete, such as downloading a citation, finding an article, or locating a company incorporation record. It could also mean answering a complex research request such as vetting or finding an expert, answering an in-depth legislative history question, or providing comprehensive information about a company or person, which could take many hours to complete.

Attorneys and staff at the DOJ work long hours, so having information available 24/7 on our Virtual Library and ensuring the site is as welcoming and helpful as walking into a library for assistance is essential. In order to enable our patrons to accomplish simple research tasks on their own, we have developed a robust DOJ Virtual Library. It hosts our catalog, digitized special collections, access to our electronic resources, and a variety of customized research guides such as legislative history, finding and vetting of experts, public records, company information, and more. Although maintaining our Virtual Library is unquestionably a collaborative effort, managing several pages on the Virtual Library is also a necessary task in my role as a government librarian.

The Justice Libraries' print and electronic collections are immense, comprised of one million print/microform items and over a $1 million worth of electronic resources. In order to maintain print and electronic collections, part of my job consists of collection development and maintenance. Working collaboratively across library departments, I routinely assess our libraries' collections and user needs, assist in the selection and de-selection of print and electronic library materials and resources, and participate in the development of collection and workflow procedures and policies. I also work closely with Civil Division staff, providing acquisition assistance that ensures they have the print and electronic resources needed on hand to accomplish their litigation work. Time permitting, I fit in other responsibilities, such as developing and delivering library-related instruction; actively marketing the library, including producing our monthly newsletter; and chairing the Workforce Planning Committee, which is charged with aligning the needs and priorities of the DOJ Libraries staff in a way that addresses current and future workforce needs.

Each element of my position description is directly tied to a DOJ mission outcome, such as accountability for organization results, taxpayer value, and more. One example is tracking reference and research requests, which affords me the opportunity to convey how the information or service I provided contributed to the agency's mission. Another is my support of the acquisition process for the Civil Division, which offers tremendous organizational efficiency by eliminating duplicate or unused resources and saves money for DOJ and taxpayers. Using these methods and more, I am able to demonstrate how my work supports the DOJ mission and at the same time provide our staff with the information needed to articulate the value of our library at any given moment—a critical element to ensuring visibility and viability.

I manage these tasks and more on a daily basis by being adaptable and comfortable with shifting priorities and deadlines. I also use a variety of technologies and tools within Outlook to help keep me organized. Moreover, my quest for knowledge, love of learning, and pride for the work I do on behalf of the Department of Justice keeps me energized and devoted to my job.

CONCLUSION

This chapter covered how each special library and information center is unique and how there are a wide variety of opportunities and paths available. A number of exciting opportunities face this sector of information work, including the use of advanced technologies to make sense of large amounts of information and data, as well as adapting to changes in information workflows within organizations. Special librarians and information professionals have a unique opportunity to contribute to the advancement of the organizations they serve.

NOTES

1. Elin Christianson, "Special Libraries: Putting Knowledge to Work," *Library Trends* 25, no. 1 (1976): 399–416.
2. Edythe Moore, "Corporate Science and Technology Libraries," *Science & Technology Libraries* 8, no. 1 (1988): 51–60, doi:10.1300/J122v08n01_05.
3. R. H. Johnston, "Why Special Libraries?," *Special Libraries* 16, no. 1 (1925): 3–6.
4. Robert V. Williams, "The Documentation and Special Libraries Movements in the United States, 1910–1960," *Journal of the American Society for Information Science* 48, no. 9 (1997): 775.
5. Johnston, "Why Special Libraries?"
6. Tara Murray, "How Much Is a Special Library Worth? Valuing and Communicating Information in an Organizational Context," *Journal of Library Administration* 53, no. 8 (2013): 462–71, doi:10.1080/019308 26.2013.882200.
7. Ebsco, "The ROI of Corporate Libraries and Research Solutions—White Paper," June 28, 2016, https:// help.ebsco.com/interfaces/EBSCO_Guides/General_Product_FAQs/ROI_of_Corporate_Libraries_Re search_Solutions.
8. Tara Murray, "The Forecast for Special Librarians," *Journal of Library Administration* 56, no. 2 (2016): 188–98.
9. Susan Moore, "Build Your Career Path to the Chief Data Officer Role," Gartner, Inc., 2016, http://www .gartner.com/smarterwithgartner/build-your-career-path-to-the-chief-data-officer-role/.
10. Richard Fry, "Millennials Surpass Gen Xers as the Largest Generation in the U.S. Labor Force," Pew Research Center, May 11, 2015, http://www.pewresearch.org/fact-tank/2015/05/11/millennials-surpass -gen-xers-as-the-largest-generation-in-u-s-labor-force/.
11. Fred Maymir-DuCharme, "Cognitive Analytics: A Step toward Tacit Knowledge," *Systemics, Cybernetics and Informatics* 12, no. 4 (2014): 32–38, http://www.iiisci.org/Journal/CV$/sci/pdfs/HA342OE14.pdf.
12. The Special Libraries Association (SLA), "Competencies for Information Professionals," http://www.sla .org/about-sla/competencies/.
13. Agricultural Network Information Collaborative, "Home," http://www.agnic.org/.
14. USDA National Agricultural Library, "Home," http://agricola.nal.usda.gov/.

Part III

Information Services

Engaging, Creating, and Collaborating via Technology

The library as an institution has been fundamental to the success of our democracy. Libraries provide access to the skills and knowledge necessary to fulfill our roles as active citizens. Libraries also function as essential equalizing institutions in our society."

—John Palfrey[1]

A fundamental aim of information services is to help users find and get access to the information that they need—both directly through user-facing reference services and indirectly through the behind-the-scenes creation of metadata. However, these information service roles are changing due to evolutions in technology, the information landscape, and user needs and expectations—and new exciting roles are emerging. Information services today require that information professionals assume a broader range of responsibilities: providing copyright expertise, creating linked data, preserving both digital and analog content across diverse and complex media, and providing access to digital resources, among others. It is an exciting time to be part of an information profession that is continuing to grow and change at a rapid pace!

Part III extends beyond the areas of access to information and the organization of resources and services to provide the reader with tools and resources for engaging, teaching, collaborating, and partnering with the members of the community it serves. In part III, authors provide insight into how information services are increasingly focused on engaging users in participatory ways in the hyperlinked library, helping users create new knowledge through makerspaces, and ensuring that information services are designed to provide outstanding user experiences. It further offers the information professional a journey for examining the skills and competencies needed to provide useful, timely, and relevant information services that are accessible anywhere, anytime, and on any device at their fingertips 24/7.

NOTE

1. John Palfrey, *BiblioTech: Why Libraries Matter More Than Ever in the Age of Google* (New York: Basic Books, 2015).

10

Digital Resources

DIGITAL LIBRARIES

Lisa Gregory and Amy Rudersdorf

Chapter 10, "Digital Resources: Digital Libraries," focuses on the growth of digital resources and how information professionals are providing access to information and meeting user needs through the digital library. Lisa Gregory and Amy Rudersdorf, with their extensive background in data management and digital technology, provide insight into the challenges and benefits of digital resources and the digital library and discuss the tasks and skills required of the digital librarian.

Given the nature of primarily virtual audiences who are often anonymous and geographically disparate, Gregory and Rudersdorf note the importance of using analytics to understand users. Data-driven decision making involves gathering and analyzing information to make informed decisions about which resources to produce, how and for whom to produce them, and how much staffing and funding is needed to provide for their creation. In an attempt to justify increasing expenditures when many believe "everything's online already," information managers are further challenged in managing expectations to support growth.

The authors address crucial competencies for the digital librarian. One of the skills needed is understanding and having the ability to manage three types of digital information: licensed content, content that information professionals create, and content donated by others. Other skills include incorporating linked data; being able to preserve and deliver digital materials; understanding software development; educating for digital literacy; marketing, designing, managing, and creating online content; and understanding intellectual property and copyright, including open access. These competencies and the many roles performed by the digital librarian are explored throughout this chapter.

★   ★   ★

As today's information professionals survey their workplaces, what they see is in some ways a world apart from those who staffed their same offices just a few decades ago. With the advent of networked computing, shared digital resources, and the ubiquity of technology in the lives of many people, the boundaries of information organizations have become fluid and far reaching. Information professionals passionately embrace and adapt to the challenge of understanding and meeting users' needs, which demands rigorous training, personal flexibility, and shifting resources.

The digital library goes by many names, but involves information products and services that are organized, described, delivered, and preserved through technology. The same core tenets of the information professions in past decades undergird the profession today—organizing information for easier retrieval and guiding information seekers to appropriate resources. What differs is the challenges and opportunities afforded by technology, whether in creating resources, managing them, or communicating about them to users. Information organizations are diverse and serve different needs based on their locations, materials, access to resources, and users' needs. However, there are several characteristics and issues that most digital libraries share.

> The digital library goes by many names, but involves information products and services that are organized, described, delivered, and preserved through technology.

This chapter focuses on the day-to-day challenges and benefits that technology has introduced into the information profession. It begins by describing some of the overarching demands common to many digital libraries. Following that, it explores the varying roles of a digital librarian. After completing this chapter, the reader should have an understanding of both the big ideas and specific tasks an information professional will confront and negotiate while managing a digital library, as well as the types of skills a digital librarian must bring to the table to be successful.

MANAGING THE DEMANDS FACING DIGITAL LIBRARIES

Today's digital libraries face a formidable array of challenges, requiring leaders who understand the challenges and know how to address them. To manage expectations means finding ways to understand the digital library's primary virtual audience. It means making hard choices about allocating funds to new ventures while sustaining old ones. It means planning strategically for a changing technological future. It means making sure the digital librarian's skill set is diverse and technology based.

Managing Users' Needs and Expectations

Through its website, electronic resources, and e-mail and chat reference services, information organizations reach users every day who are often anonymous and geographically disparate (see also chapter 11: "Information Intermediation and Reference Services"). Users of today's information organizations are no longer limited to those who come through the door. While on-site services are extremely important,[1] an information organization's most frequent and fervent users may, in fact, live miles away, and may never speak directly to a staff member or touch a physical item.

This situation presents challenges as information professionals try to understand a relatively unknown audience, particularly when it comes to choosing what the information organization offers online and how to deliver virtual services. Both passive (web analytics) and active (surveys and focus groups) methods of gaining user data can provide a lot of information regarding an information organization's audience. However, it can be difficult to fully identify and reach the users who may benefit most from an institution's services and resources. It can also be challenging to describe this audience in terms that appeal to those decision makers who provide an information organization with its funding.

These digital library users, both known and unknown, are part of a technologically demanding public. As of 2016, 88 percent of U.S. adults use the internet.[2] Both the casual information seeker and the most rigorous researcher expect resources and services to be made digitally accessible. When it comes to public libraries, users rank "free access to computers and the internet" as well as "research resources" as important for libraries to offer.[3] In the academic library sphere, the "speed and convenience" of immediate access to resources is highly desirable, and "more digital content of all kinds and

Lisa Gregory and Amy Rudersdorf

formats is almost uniformly seen as better."[4] Increasing mandates to support open-access publishing and mobile content delivery drive academic libraries to find creative and sustainable ways to support more and varied digital content. Government agencies, schools, cultural institutions, and corporations help reinforce this expectation with the delivery of crucial information online.[5] As providers of broadband access, lenders of mobile devices, and hubs for technological training, information organizations strive to meet the needs of the technologically demanding public while maintaining their current services related to analog materials.

Managing Resources

Information professionals wholeheartedly weave e-resources and digital services into their institutions to meet users' needs as efficiently and robustly as possible. Often, new technology expands an information organization's services in exciting ways, whether it is increasing the searchability of journals that were formerly only available in print, or tapping into a new audience by developing a social media strategy.

As institutions add these services, staffing, financial resources, and strategies have to shift to accommodate them. Catalogers incorporate linked data, which makes disparate information sources machine actionable. Infrastructure expands to preserve and deliver digital materials. Administrators decide how to position their institutions in their communities to help make a case for continued funding. In a climate of static budgets or budgets that make only modest gains,[6] it can be challenging to shift money from long-established print priorities to digital resources. While digital libraries are no longer a new concept, many institutions are still in an ongoing transition from discrete and/or grant-funded digital library projects to stable and sustainable digital library programs.[7] Finding trained staff and sustainable financial resources can be a challenge from the largest to smallest libraries.

Managing Information

Information organizations today steward three types of digital information: licensed content, content they create themselves, and content donated by others. In some ways, these three types of digital resources have a lot in common with their print equivalents. For e-books and e-journals, institutions make purchasing agreements and catalog content. Digitized content requires reference support just as its analog counter-

> **Three Types of Digital Information**
>
> - licensed content
> - self-created content
> - content donated by others

parts do. Donations still involve establishing donor relationships and agreements. These similarities belie the many ways information organizations have had to expand or adapt existing resources to manage digital information. As a result, information organizations can end up working with outdated systems that accommodate inventorying and tracking of analog materials while taking on new systems for digital content.[8] The rights and responsibilities attendant to content, whether licensed, created locally, or received as a donation, encompass a wider spectrum than before, within a rapidly evolving landscape full of stakeholders.

In addition, there are practical issues that put an information organization in a mediating position between users and content providers, negotiating new rules for digital surrogates of print items. Information professionals find themselves weighing risks

> Information professionals find themselves weighing risks and rewards when deciding whether or not items in their collections can be made available digitally, considering privacy concerns, copyright law, and the needs of both item creators and users.

and rewards when deciding whether or not items in their collections can be made available digitally, considering privacy concerns, copyright law, and the needs of both item creators and users. From course reserves to historic photographs, information professionals attempt to discover the best way to organize and present the information their users need while respecting legal concerns.

Managing Expectations of Stakeholders

Information professionals working within parent organizations inevitably end up advocating for their services with those who are unfamiliar with libraries, archives, or information management (see also chapter 28: "Advocacy"). Information professionals try to quantify the value of these services in a way that all can understand,[9] in an attempt to justify increasing expenditures when many believe "everything's online already" and that digital is less expensive than analog. Because the growing digital library requires implementing new technology, increasing infrastructure, and ongoing training, those managing digital libraries find they must excel at managing expectations to support this growth. It can be difficult to report on and to explain parallels and discrepancies between physical metrics like foot traffic versus virtual metrics like website page views. How much is a "visit" to a digital library worth? What is the return on investment for a digitized annual report, when the institution can be so far removed from the users? Scoping services to an audience can be difficult when, as mentioned above, that audience could be the entire planet. Managing digital content and maintaining a keen grasp on the needs of stakeholders and staff demand a suite of new skills, which will be discussed below.

Discussion Question

Digital libraries must balance a number of competing priorities with limited funds. List the criteria you would use to target materials for digitization. Examples may include "high use materials," "fragile materials that could be retired from physical handling," etc.

THE DIGITAL LIBRARIAN'S VITAL ROLES

When reading job postings for a digital librarian, data curator, metadata librarian, or scholarly publishing coordinator, one may wonder how one person could be expected to do and know everything outlined in the posting. As far back as 2006, Choi and Rassmussen predicted that "digital professionals will be required to have more breadth and depth of knowledge and skills across the dimensions of traditional library knowledge, technology, and human relations."[10]

Roles of the Digital Librarian

- Describer
- Collector
- Educator
- Copyright Advisor
- Manager
- Negotiator
- Researcher
- Technologist

While some digital librarian skills are unique, many are found in the current information professional tool kit. Responsibilities like project management, collaboration, outreach, education, and resource description are as important to the digital librarian as to others in the field. Along with those abilities, it is especially important that digital librarians remain up-to-date in their knowledge of technological change (see also chapter 3: "Librarianship: A Continuously Evolving Profession"). For example, they need to stay abreast of software development, innovative services other institutions are offering to users, newly developed standards and best practices, and much more. As more content and services move into the online environment, digital librarians must maintain a firm grasp on the complexities of intellectual property and copyright, including Creative Commons, Rightsstatements.org, and other resources supporting the use of born-digital and digitized content (see also chapter 31: "Copyright and Creative Commons").

It is fair to say that the modern librarian's required skill set is varied and long. While computer skills and web knowledge are highly preferred, it might be surprising to see that interpersonal and communication skills are considered even more important[11] (see chapter 27: "Communication, Marketing, and Outreach Strategies"). This will be a common thread through the eight generalized roles of a digital librarian described below.

Describer

Describing objects is one of the oldest and most fundamental roles of a librarian. Organized description allows for discovery, and this is still what allows for efficient information seeking in today's library. For digital librarians, metadata have taken a central role in how libraries do business (see also chapter 12: "Metadata, Cataloging, Linked Data, and the Evolving ILS").

Digital librarians create metadata application profiles and describe archival and special collections materials using a variety of standards and controlled vocabularies. They generate online finding aids or guides to contextualize resources. They aggregate data through protocols for metadata harvesting and, increasingly, through linked open data. With linked open data, computer programs are able to use library vocabularies to logically connect information about the same topic with unique identifiers instead of mining data for similar terms. Linked data is how Google can tell the difference between Venus (painting), Venus (planet), and Venus (tennis player). Catalogers describe content in digital formats and manage the circulation of e-readers, personal hotspots, and similar connective devices. Many catalogers are leading their institution's transition from their MARC-based OPACs to RDA-driven discovery systems.

These types of information professionals may be referred to as metadata librarians or data technologists.

Collector

Digital library collections begin in much the same way as the collections that reside in stacks and archival boxes, although they are stored in digital or institutional repositories, in the cloud and data grids, and on servers and hard drives (see also chapter 24: "Managing Collections" and chapter 25: "Managing Technology"). Their long-term maintenance is equally important and often far more complicated than print counterparts, which in most cases are relatively safe on stable shelves in temperature- and humidity-controlled environments. While digital collections may not be organized by Library of Congress classification number, digital objects are typically assembled logically—often by format (photography collections), topic (Kennedy assassination papers), or even geography (Minnesota Digital Library).

Whether they are working with born-digital data or digitized copies of physical objects, digital librarians must understand how to identify the best means of describing, storing, and providing access to that content today, and evolve those processes to maintain the integrity of the content over time. In effect, collectors must think like digital forecasters, exploring how to preserve and provide ongoing access to digital content into an unknown future.

These types of information professionals may be called digital curators, digital archivists, digital stewards, digital preservationists, or digital librarians.

Educator

The term "library educators" often describes professors teaching in library or information science schools, or reference staff who perform bibliographic instruction (see also chapter 16: "Teaching Users: Information and Technology Instruction"). But for the digital librarian, "education" can mean outreach and marketing. They can be responsible for designing, managing, and creating content for an institution's website, blog, or social media presence. This requires a combination of design or web scripting skills, as well as knowledge of exhibit curation, writing for the web, and social media platforms. As educators, digital librarians must create tools to guide users in navigating the challenges of researching, finding, and using appropriate information resources. It is vital that the digital librarian can guide an audience with varied degrees of digital literacy.

Digital librarians must be willing to maintain the currency of their own knowledge even as they are writing, teaching, and presenting about it. They often must educate decision makers about the work they do and the staffing, technologies, and knowledge required, even before they can advocate for resources to support this work.

Educator is a role that is part of most digital librarians' job responsibilities and is not specific to a single type of digital professional.

Copyright Advisor

A digital librarian needs to have a solid grasp of the copyright status of the items in their collections to assign legally viable, understandable, and actionable copyright statements. They may need to play a leadership role in educating administrators and donors about concepts like fair use, public domain, and orphan works. Equally important is establishing the level of risk their institution is willing to take, preparing themselves to address queries from the public and colleagues. Advocating for greater access to content and educating stakeholders about copyright and fair use are important roles that digital librarians can play to effect positive change for patrons today and into the future.

> Advocating for greater access to content and educating stakeholders about copyright and fair use are important roles that digital librarians can play to effect positive change for patrons today and into the future.

Information professionals responsible for preservation (see also chapter 13: "Analog and Digital Curation and Preservation"), including digital reformatting and the preservation of born-digital objects, need to understand the implications of copy making, one of the many important components of preservation librarianship (check out appendix 10.1: "Case Study—Planning for Distributed Digital Preservation" at the end of this chapter). Through their work in building and sustaining institutional repositories, information professionals guide authors of academic papers through the complexities of peer review and restricted versus open-access publishing (see also chapter 33: "Open Access"). While many larger academic libraries now staff lawyers in their scholarly publishing units, information professionals without legal training may be responsible for some of the tasks listed here. They may be referred to as digital publishing librarians, digital scholarship librarians, or some combination therein. Some roles identified in this section will also be part of the total skill set of any number of information professionals working in digital libraries.

Manager

The role of manager is not unique to digital librarians; however, how and what digital librarians manage is unique. The digital library is technology based, so staff must research and select the technologies that balance user and staff needs with their institution's available resources and policies (see also chapter 25: "Managing Technology"). Writing and managing grants, from preparing reports to ensuring that timelines are met, are often necessary qualities for an information professional working in a digital library world (see also chapter 21: "Managing Budgets" and chapter 22: "Managing Personnel").

Unlike friendly shelves filled with colorful books, the "stuff" that digital librarians manage (or "steward" or "curate") is data accessed from unseen servers. This can cause a disconnect for those who are more familiar with the management of physical objects. When objects have form, stakeholders can more easily conceptualize the expenditures for their long-term care. Because costly requirements for data management may not be readily apparent, it becomes the digital librarian's job to advocate for the resources to meet the challenge of long-term stewardship and access.

An added complexity for the digital library manager is that costly IT-project work is often done in collaboration with other units within the information organization or even geographically dispersed institutions. The skills required for the successful digital library manager in this distributed paradigm are many—financial planner, IT analyst, human resources specialist, fund-raiser, and excellent communicator—and are often not those taught to digital librarians in school. Like many of the other categories listed in this chapter, those who are not in administrative roles may still share some subset of managerial duties.

Actual management titles might include head, coordinator, director, or manager of a data/digital/ virtual unit within an information organization.

Negotiator

Digital librarians learn early on the art of negotiating because many aspects of what they do affect, or are affected by, the work of their colleagues. For example, in some institutions, digital reformatting services is a stand-alone unit that works with resources managed by other departments, namely, archives, special collections, and preservation. Metadata description may be performed by another department—perhaps cataloging or technical services. Yet another department may be responsible for implementing and managing the information technology supporting storage and systems. Selection of materials for inclusion in the digital repository may be done by curators, institutional stakeholders outside of the library, or members of the public. Traversing the needs, personalities, and unique cultures within each of these units requires the digital librarian to be a deft communicator and translator.

In addition, digital librarians often work with vendors to outsource reformatting or metadata production, design and build websites, or purchase repository software. Purchasing negotiations can be as straightforward as choosing the lowest bidder in a request for proposal (RFP) process or as complex as going head-to-head with e-journal bundlers to get the best price for subscriptions. The information professionals responsible for this type of work must research options, competition, and pricing, and understand local needs and resources before entering negotiations with a vendor they likely will work with for a very long time.

Negotiator is a role that is part of most digital librarians' job responsibilities and is not specific to a single professional position.

Researcher

Digital librarians perform research in support of the resources made available to their patrons. For example, the digital librarian's research can provide historical context for online exhibits, ensure long-term access to digital heritage, or offer advice on making faculty authorship open access.

Because so much of the digital librarians' output is freely and publicly accessible, understanding how users want to interact with these resources is integral. Usability and understanding user behavior should be fundamental to the design and production of any online resource (see also chapter 14: "User

Experience"). Usability research can take many forms: one-on-one interviews, focus groups, recorded navigation testing, and use cases and surveys are just some of the ways that usability is researched and tested. Whatever type of usability testing the information professional performs, the resulting data will provide insight and guide decisions for improving online resources.

Decisions about how to scope their work based on large-scale information gathering is a third key aspect of digital librarians' research. Data-driven decision making involves gathering and analyzing information to make informed decisions about which resources to produce, how to produce them and for whom, and how much staffing and funding to provide for their creation. User studies, like those mentioned above, are perfect examples of data-driven decision making. This informed process is a guiding principle behind what digital librarians do and why they do it.

Discussion Questions

This chapter posits the idea that a digital librarian must take on multiple roles. Do you see this as different from the roles of information professionals before the digital age? Do you foresee changes in digital librarianship in the future as technology advances and evolves, and the amount of data increases exponentially?

Technologist

The last skill that is required—and probably the most obvious—is a strong aptitude for and comfort with technology. Not everyone needs to know how to program in Python or do crash recovery on a laptop. At a minimum, a digital librarian working with digital collections, websites, and online exhibit building must be comfortable with HTML and style sheets. Information professionals responsible for building or maintaining digital repositories and creating digital content must have a strong understanding of metadata standards (e.g., Dublin Core, MODS, VRA Core, etc.), structured data (e.g., XML, RDF), and data-sharing protocols (e.g., the Open Archives Initiative Protocol for Metadata Harvesting [OAI-PMH]). Digital curation librarians must have knowledge of a variety of analog and digital media formats (or know where to go to learn about them), their storage and reformatting needs, and the ability to steward and evolve digital preservation administration and technologies.

> Most digital librarians should—at the minimum—have a basic understanding of content management systems, databases, metadata standards, and web technologies.

Digital librarians typically work closely with IT professionals who may or may not have library backgrounds. As alluded to under the "negotiator" section above, communicating with programmers and systems administrators can sometimes be a challenge. Just like information professionals, IT professionals have their domain-specific vocabulary. In fact, the term "library" has a fundamentally different meaning in the programming world (a collection of scripts that can be referred to from the central code, so that the same lines of code do not have to be produced over and over). When building technologies or communicating technical requirements, digital librarians should bring their IT partners into the picture early to help make sure everyone operates with common goals.

The technology skill sets needed by digital librarians are as varied as the technologies that surround us. However, most digital librarians should—at the minimum—have a basic understanding of content management systems, databases, some metadata standards, and web technologies.

Lisa Gregory and Amy Rudersdorf

CONCLUSION

Most information organizations operating in the United States today interact with their audiences in one digital way or another. The challenges faced by information professionals working with digital content require skills apart from the ones needed fifty or even twenty years ago. From this chapter, it should be clear that these skills are many! The good news is that best practices have been established, and that digital librarians do not work alone. Technology affords professionals the opportunity to stay well in touch with others tackling the same problems; indeed, it is crucial for the digital librarian to collaborate, not only to avoid reinventing the wheel but also to strengthen the community's common mandates and ends. Information professionals owe it to their audiences to be transparent about their ethics and their passionate goals for digital information literacy, and to be rigorous in their professional standards so that they can ensure the virtual future lives up to the foundation laid by information professionals of the past.

APPENDIX 10.1: CASE STUDY—PLANNING FOR DISTRIBUTED DIGITAL PRESERVATION

Since 2004, MetaArchive Cooperative has been providing a distributed storage system that allows institutions to preserve their digital content in a way that adheres to accepted best practices. Taking advantage of the LOCKSS (Lots of Copies Keep Stuff Safe)[12] system, the Cooperative leverages the geographically distributed locations of its partners to create a redundant network of servers. Institutions sustain the Cooperative by taking responsibility for a portion of the technology infrastructure. Partners must host a server and, in turn, their content is automatically replicated to seven other servers, one of which is located at the Library of Congress. Content is not overwritten—instead new versions are kept alongside originals in case unintentional changes occur.

One of the core values of the Cooperative is to empower and encourage institutions "to build their own preservation infrastructures and knowledge rather than outsourcing this core service to external vendors."[13] Truly, as an institution accumulates digital materials, the preservation of those materials must become a core service. Following established digital preservation best practices means thoughtful stewardship, detailed planning, and full infrastructure support. Digital files require planning and care to keep them viable: "In the digital area, benign neglect fails, and fails spectacularly."[14] With a service like the MetaArchive Cooperative, individual institutions can take advantage of the knowledge of their cohort. Preservation problems can be addressed by the group, instead of tackled by a single location. The investment of multiple partners can help ensure long-term sustainability. Costs are kept lower when shared.

The Cooperative is a tailor-made example of successful and sustainable collaboration in digital library services. It demonstrates the capacity of institutions to find a digital solution that upholds their responsibility to their users and materials, follows industry best practices, and stewards limited resources in a strategic way.

NOTES

1. Katherine Zickuhr, Lee Rainie, Kristen Purcell, and Maeve Duggan, "Section 2: Public Libraries' Importance and Impact," in *How Americans Value Public Libraries in Their Communities* (Washington, DC: Pew Research Center, December, 2013), http://libraries.pewinternet.org/files/legacy-pdf/PIP_Libraries%20in%20communities.pdf.
2. Pew Research Center, "Internet/Broadband Fact Sheet," January 12, 2017, http://www.pewinternet.org/fact-sheet/internet-broadband/.
3. Zickuhr et al., "Section 2: Public Libraries' Importance and Impact."

4. Lynn S. Connaway and Timothy J. Dickey, "Digital Information Seeker: Report of Findings from Selected OCLC, RIN and JISC User Behaviour Projects," March 2010, http://www.jisc.ac.uk/media/documents/publications/reports/2010/digitalinformationseekerreport.pdf.

5. Larry Johnson, Samantha Adams Becker, V. Estrada, and A. Freeman, *NMC Horizon Report: 2015 Library Edition* (Austin, TX: The New Media Consortium, 2015), http://www.nmc.org/publication/nmc-horizon-report-2015-library-edition/.

6. Lisa Peet, "Gaining Ground Unevenly," *Library Journal*, February 10, 2016, http://lj.libraryjournal.com/2016/02/budgets-funding/gaining-ground-unevenly-budgets-funding/.

7. Blue Ribbon Task Force on Sustainable Digital Preservation and Access, *Sustainable Economics for a Digital Planet: Ensuring Long-Term Access to Digital Information*, 2010, http://blueribbontaskforce.sdsc.edu/.

8. Marshall Breeding, "Forging Ahead through Times of Major Transitions," *Computers in Libraries* 31, no. 10 (December 2011): 26–29.

9. Megan Oakleaf, *The Value of Academic Libraries: A Comprehensive Research Review and Report* (Chicago: Association of College and Research Libraries, 2010), http://www.ala.org/acrl/sites/ala.org.acrl/files/content/issues/value/val_report.pdf; Betsy Kelly, Claire Hamasu and Barbara Jones, "Applying Return on Investment (ROI) in Libraries," *Journal of Library Administration* 52, no. 8 (November, 2012): 656–71, doi:10.1080/01930826.2012.747383.

10. Choi Youngok and Edie Rasmussen, "What Is Needed to Educate Future Digital Librarians: A Study of Current Practice and Staffing Patterns in Academic and Research Libraries," *D-Lib Magazine* 12, no. 9 (2006), http://www.dlib.org/dlib/september06/choi/09choi.html.

11. Michaelis Gerolimos, Afrodite Malliari, and Pavlos Iakovidis, "Skills in the Market: An Analysis of Skills and Qualifications for American Librarians," *Library Review* 64, nos. 1-2 (February 2, 2015): 21–35, doi:10.1108/LR-06-2014-0063.

12. Lots of Copies Keep Stuff Safe, https://www.lockss.org/.

13. Meta Archive, "How DDP Works," https://metaarchive.org/how-ddp-works/.

14. Tyler O. Walters, and Katherine Skinner, "Economics, Sustainability, and the Cooperative Model in Digital Preservation," *Library Hi Tech* 28, no. 2 (June 15, 2010): 259–72, doi:10.1108/07378831011047668.

11

Information Intermediation and Reference Services

Johanna Tunon

Chapter 11, "Information Intermediation and Reference Services," addresses the changing roles of the reference librarian with the advent of the internet and "Reference 2.0" services. Johanna Tunon, an expert in digital instruction and design, identifies changing roles of reference services and information intermediation in the twenty-first century. After noting the role of reference services before the internet, she explores the impact of new technologies on reference services, the changing methods of information intermediation and instruction, and the strategies for addressing the decentralized and distributed roles of today's reference librarians.

Tunon aptly traces the major shifts in reference content from the rise of internet archives and search engines like Google to the creation of digital content, noting that most information users no longer need bricks-and-mortar libraries as their gateway to access information. She identifies new types of more detailed reference questions and the tools that have been developed to respond to these questions. She further highlights new virtual reference tools that have been developed, which extend the reach of traditional reference services and provide a "high-tech and high-touch" approach by offering computer-mediated reference services via e-mail, chat/instant messaging, texting/short message service (SMS), voice chat and cloud-based videoconferencing, synchronous and asynchronous instruction, and more 24/7.

Throughout the chapter, Tunon addresses the competencies of reference librarians. Today's professionals need to prepare for changing user behaviors, help engage patrons with new information tools and resources, and partner with other organizations to maximize both programming and services. Today's reference librarians and information intermediators of all kinds need to be proactive and energetic, creative, innovative, open, and technologically advanced.

★   ★   ★

The advent of the internet and "Reference 2.0" services have changed the role of reference librarians in the last quarter century from passive purveyors of information to information intermediators and facilitators who help patrons access information in a myriad of new ways. This chapter examines the changing roles of reference services and information intermediation in the twenty-first century. After completing this chapter, the reader should have an understanding of:

- the role of reference services before the internet,
- the impact of new technologies on reference services,
- the changing methods of information intermediation, and
- the strategies for addressing the decentralized and distributed roles of today's reference librarians and other information intermediators.

REFERENCE SERVICES BEFORE THE INTERNET

Up until about one hundred fifty years ago, information professionals primarily focused on the acquisition and organization of library holdings. In his 1876 paper, "Personal Relations between Librarians and Readers," Samuel Swett Green[1] introduced the concept of reference services as information intermediation through the process of helping users resolve a particular query, interest, task, or problem.

The pre-internet reference model provided librarian-centric reference services[2] at a reference desk staffed by professional librarians. Reference interviews were conducted to better understand the information needs of users. Reference questions ranged from ready reference questions for discrete facts, data, or information and verification of bibliographic information to directional, procedural, technical, subject, and specialized research questions. Reference librarians were typically supported by a physical reference collection of encyclopedias, dictionaries, atlases, thesauri, handbooks, directories, government documents, print indexes, and more that were housed nearby for ready access. Many of these roles remain essential for serving information users today, such as:

1. recommending, interpreting, and evaluating information resources to help users meet their information needs,
2. providing library instruction and training, and
3. offering readers' advisory services.[3]

While these roles remain the cornerstone of reference service, as reference services adapt to new trends in how information users seek information, so too must the competencies and definitions of reference services be redefined, as is demonstrated in textbox 11.1.

TEXTBOX 11.1

Key Competencies for Reference Services

Key competencies defined by the Reference and User Services Association (RUSA), as adopted in 2008:

- visibility/approachability
- interest
- listening/inquiring
- searching
- follow-up consulting and advising[4]

These guidelines are currently under revision. According to a 2016 report, "What's in a Name? Toward a New Definition of Reference,"[5] the definition of reference services needs to be revisited to reflect current trends in reference services and should include the following competencies:

- instruction
- interpreting user needs
- advocating for one's information institution
- programming
- assessment
- design thinking

THE IMPACT OF NEW TECHNOLOGIES ON REFERENCE SERVICES

The rise of the internet in the 1990s began disrupting reference services as access to information was no longer place bound.[6] Subscriptions to reference resources (e.g., NewsBank[7] and Web of Knowledge[8]) and free electronic reference collections (e.g., ERIC[9] and PubMed[10]) became commonplace, while print reference tools, like *Reader's Guide to Periodical Literature and Books in Print*,[11] became increasingly obsolete. Print reference resources housed in libraries, which took up massive amounts of shelving space, shifted to bundled digital collections like those offered by Credo Reference,[12] Gale Virtual Reference Library,[13] and Oxford Reference.[14] The digitization of millions of print books in massive digital collections, such as Google Books,[15] Internet Archive,[16] and the HathiTrust Digital Library,[17] began to provide 24/7 direct access to scholarly resources that did not require information intermediation.[18] Additionally, the creation of a staggering amount of new digital content over the last two decades has resulted in the rise of online repositories, such as the Digital Public Library of America.[19]

Consequently, most information users no longer need brick-and-mortar libraries as their gateway to access information, and they no longer need information professionals to help mediate their access to information. Search engines (e.g., Google,[20] Bing,[21] Yahoo!,[22] and DuckDuckGo[23]) have provided users with easy access to everything from web-based images and books to maps, videos, and patents. As a result, information that people used to access in libraries, such as the value of a 2006 Camry in the *Kelley Blue Book*[24] or content for a fifth-grader's class project on California missions, can now be easily accessed 24/7 online. The result is a self-service society where people routinely conduct their own unmediated online searches.

> **Check This Out**
>
> RUSA's Guidelines for Implementing and Maintaining Virtual Reference Services. *Visit:* http://www.ala.org/rusa/sites/ala.org.rusa/files/content/resources/guidelines/GuidelinesVirtualReference_2017.pdf.

As access to information became easier through the advent of personal devices, cloud computing, and app technologies, people started asking information professionals new types of reference questions. This has led to the development of new reference tools that assist information professionals in providing value to users by finding answers to complex questions:

Algorithm-based search engines, such as Google and Bing, and computational knowledge engines, such as Wolfram Alpha, allow intelligent searching within documents.[25]

Database search features from vendors such as ProQuest[26] enable searching anywhere in the document.

Discovery tools, from vendors such as EBSCO,[27] Primo from Ex Libris,[28] and WorldCat Discovery Services[29] from OCLC, permit global searching.

Citation index tools, such as Google Scholar's Cited By tool,[30] provide a free and more comprehensive alternative to Web of Knowledge's[31] citation indexes for identifying the impact of articles in specific fields of knowledge and new trends.

Citation management tools such as EndNote[32] and Zotero[33] make it easier to ethically cite information.

Cloud-based translation tools, such as Google Translate,[34] enable information professionals to communicate with patrons who speak different languages with increasing accuracy.

VIRTUAL REFERENCE TOOLS

The advent of the internet also made seamless and multimodal virtual reference tools possible, providing users with multiple points of entry to hubs of information. Virtual reference services, sometimes called digital or mobile reference services, extend the reach of traditional reference services by offering users synchronous and asynchronous computer-mediated reference services via e-mail, chat/instant messaging, texting/short message service (SMS), voice chat and cloud-based videoconferencing, and more. Web-based applications on smartphones and other mobile devices provide users with additional mobility, and the global reach and "anytime, anywhere" point-of-need access of these new tools mean that reference services no longer need to be place bound.[35]

Despite the use of technology in these interactions, virtual reference interviews are not that different from face-to-face transactions, because many of the same reference skills and techniques are used. Textbox 11.2 describes different virtual reference tools that reference librarians can use to support user needs.

TEXTBOX 11.2

Virtual Reference Tools: Opportunities and Challenges

Opportunities

- Synchronous reference options like chat provide more opportunities for information professionals to ask clarifying questions and provide real-time feedback.
- Text messaging provides the option to interact synchronously or asynchronously.
- Virtual librarians using immersive technologies such as Second Life to provide reference services originally showed promise but have not gained wide popularity.
- Other options, like co-browsing with users, have shown more staying power.
- More in-depth research consultations and individualized instruction can be conducted using conference technologies, either free (e.g., Google Hangout, FaceTime, and Skype) or subscription-based (e.g., Collaborate, Elluminate, GoToMeeting, and WebEx) technologies.

Challenges

- Asynchronous tools like e-mail are impersonal and present challenges for the information professional who cannot easily clarify questions for the user because these tools do not provide immediate responses to queries.
- Real-time typed interactions can be cumbersome, and the success of voice chats depends on network connections.

Because many information institutions do not have the staff to offer extended hours of virtual reference services, online cooperative reference services that offer around-the-clock help have become another reference option. The Online Computer Library Center (OCLC)[36] offers QuestionPoint[37] as a 24/7 reference cooperative that includes chat, e-mail, and a reference knowledge base of libraries from around the world. Other information institutions participate in consortia arrangements, such as Florida's statewide Ask a Librarian[38] consortium of public and academic libraries. Challenges arise, however, because staffing of the virtual reference desk is shared among the various participating libraries, which can result in information professionals being asked to answer questions about library systems with which they have no personal experience.

Check This Out

QuestionPoint: OCLC's cooperative virtual reference service. *Visit:* https://www.questionpoint.org/.

Technological advances have also impacted reader's advisory services that information professionals offer in school and public libraries. Information professionals use reader's advisory tools such as NoveList,[39] LibGuides,[40] and Pinterest;[41] these are used to provide local recommendations on topics ranging from Christian fiction and graphic novels to popular crafts and local history. Users may also get reading recommendations from outside services, such as those that are offered by Amazon and GoodReads and social media applications including Facebook and Twitter.

Reference librarians today continue to play an educational role by helping users learn how to locate, navigate, and evaluate information (see also chapter 16: "Teaching Users: Information and Technology Instruction"). Library instruction offered to groups or individuals goes by many names, ranging from library instruction and bibliographic instruction to information literacy and, most recently, transliteracy. Instruction can be conducted for groups and individuals in person or online. NetMeeting, first used to deliver library instruction synchronously in a 1997 experiment, provided instruction for distance students as an alternative to traditional face-to-face instruction.[42] Since then, new tools include streaming media to deliver screencasts, webinars, and webcasts that can be embedded in courses at the point of need. Information professionals offer online synchronous group instruction, but they can also offer instruction for online and individual users regardless of their physical location using tools including Collaborate,[43] WebEx,[44] and GoToTraining.[45] Asynchronous videos and screencasts can be created using tools such as Screencast-O-Matic[46] and Jing,[47] or other online interactive tools like Guide on the Side[48] for point-of-need instruction.

Four different types of online question and answering (Q&A) services have emerged for helping people fulfill their information needs:[49]

Community-based Q&A, such as Yahoo! Answers,[50] allows users to exchange information in a threaded discussion with an asker and one or more answers.[51]

Collaborative Q&A, such as WikiAnswers,[52] uses a system of collaboratively edited questions and answers so that community peers can collaboratively refine the phrasing of questions and answers.

Social Q&A, such as Quora,[53] have e-commerce live chat applications used by members of a personal networking group to ask and answer questions by other members of the same social network.

Expert-based Q&A, such as LibAnswers,[54] offers a hybrid solution with the ability to provide questions and answers or a knowledge database of frequently asked questions as well as e-mail, a web form, and Twitter integration.

Web 2.0 social tools also encourage interaction and sharing through blogs, wikis, and group messaging. Social media tools, including Pinterest, Instagram, Snapchat, Facebook and Twitter, are frequently used for promoting library resources and services and for engaging with personal learning networks. These technological advancements in social tools have had a profound effect on library and information services, contributing to changes in the ways that reference services are delivered and to the development of a new service model called "Reference 2.0."[55] Reference 2.0 uses collaborative social networking tools to provide digital reference services in the twenty-first century.

Reference 2.0 services have made it possible to move beyond the place-bound services offered at the reference desk to a two-way seamless interaction between information users and reference librarians who facilitate information intermediation services. For example, co-browsing of a user and librarian via chat reference expands the reach of reference services. Twitter makes it possible for reference librarians to amplify their social networks by tweeting when they may want expert help with specific questions.[56] Information professionals use other social media, such as blogs, Twitter, Instagram, and Pinterest, to promote reference services and enhance information intermediation.

Since users today have online access to decentralized, distributed, and often free sources for information intermediation services, reference services offered by libraries are competing with a variety of other information intermediation options in this age of Google. However, information professionals have unique expertise and skills that are otherwise not available to users via these other information intermediation options. Specifically, reference librarians provide value-added help to users with specialized research questions, can address patron-driven wants, and provide a "high-tech and high-touch" approach desired by many patrons. This expertise positions them to be knowledge professionals in the age of Google.[61]

CHANGING METHODS OF INFORMATION INTERMEDIATION

The accelerating pace of technological change has increasingly diversified and decentralized the ways that information services are offered.[62] One approach to providing information services in libraries uses a single integrated service point for circulation and reference services staffed primarily by well-trained paraprofessionals. Another approach uses tiered reference services, with paraprofessionals and student workers[63] who answer routine questions (e.g., about holdings, policies, directions to the bathroom) and professional librarians who are contacted for more difficult questions (see also chapter 15: "Accessing Information Anywhere and Anytime: Access Services"). As a result, reference librarians are increasingly reserved for consultations when users need help with more in-depth questions.[64] This gives these information professionals time to offer services such as My Librarian, which provides labor-intensive personalized help for individuals by addressing their information mediation needs.[65] The choice of multimodal approaches for delivering in-person and online reference services depends on the needs of the specific library.[66]

The advent of virtual assistants, such as Apple's SIRI, Amazon's Alexa, Microsoft's Cortana, and Facebook's Jarvis and other chat bots that are providing unmediated answers to questions, exemplify other ways that information is being disseminated (see also chapter 25: "Managing Technology"). Given the growth of these artificial intelligence (AI) applications by Apple, Amazon, Google, and Microsoft and other technological advancements, as well as declines in the number of reference transactions in libraries over the last quarter century, information professionals have engaged in discussions about what the future of reference services will be. The declines in the reported numbers of reference transactions may be due in part because of the development of all of these new online resources and search tools.[67] The Association of Research Libraries (ARL) reported reference transactions decreasing by 69 percent between 1991 and 2012,[68] while the Pew Research Center's *Libraries 2016* report found that reference help in public libraries had decreased by 15 percent between 2012 and 2016.[69] Another reason for the decline in the number of reference transactions is because of the shift to the consultation role by librarians who answer the more in-depth and time-consuming questions such as those related to knowledge creation.[70] To help demonstrate their value, reference librarians have increased their efforts to quantify the relevancy of their information intermediation services and to document the return on investment of reference services being provided[71] (see also chapter 28: "Advocacy").

Changing user needs (see also chapter 4: "Diverse Information Needs"), increasing social media capabilities offered through Reference 2.0, and declining reference usage statistics have put pressure on libraries to reach out to users in new ways. As a result, libraries have focused more on providing outreach services.[72] In fact, outreach—promoting the services and resources offered by information organizations to the broader community of users—has been identified by Tyckoson[73] as the fourth area of responsibility that continues to be handled by today's reference librarians (see also chapter 27: "Communications, Marketing, and Outreach Strategies").

Some new approaches to reference outreach have also been adopted. For example, roving reference, sometimes called roaming reference, uses a retail approach to outreach by providing reference services in high-traffic areas away from the reference desk.[74] This usually takes the form of helping patrons at points of need in the library rather than at a designated stationary location. A similar approach offered by outreach or community librarians serves a comparable role outside the library facility. These reference models have been fueled by the advent of tablets and cell phone technologies. Although these efforts have raised the visibility of information professionals, locating users who may want help can sometimes be challenging.

More targeted outreach efforts also provide visibility for information professionals so they can more easily engage with users. For example, some information professionals have used Pokémon Go[75] to reach out to new visitors in libraries, while others use library events including Harry Potter parties, International Game Day, and Comic-Con events.[76] Other libraries have focused on underserved populations, such as promoting library services to help immigrants, the homeless, seniors, and more.[77]

> **Check This Out**
>
> Examples of Roaming Reference. *Visit:* Librarian on the Loose at the University of Minnesota: https://library.morris.umn.edu/services/librarian-loose and Librarian with a Latte at the University at Albany, SUNY: http://liblogs.albany.edu/librarynews/2013/04/got_questions_got_research_anx.html.

Embedded librarianship offers yet another approach to outreach that uses librarians as information intermediaries as part of a team or community. For example, public librarians can be embedded in local government or community organizations. Academic librarians may have office hours in academic departments or can be embedded in online classes, participate on the curriculum planning committee at the departmental or university level, or be part of the instructional technology team who designs the academic courses[78] (see also chapter 7: "Learning and Research Institutions: Academic Libraries"). Frequently, embedded librarians develop those collaborative relationships organically with faculty and students, patrons, city administrators, and even medical teams doing rounds in a hospital.[79] Whatever the role, embedded librarians help provide relevant information for their team or community.

> Providing course-integrated instruction and research assistance for students ensures that an information professional is available at the point of need in the curriculum.

Perhaps the most successful application of embedded librarianship is when information professionals are fully embedded in team-taught information literacy components of online courses and face-to-face classes.[80] Providing course-integrated instruction and research assistance for students ensures that an information professional is available at the point of need in the curriculum.[81] Librarians who provide face-to-face instruction may also create instructional modules used in flipped classrooms where students can view instructional modules before class; providing instruction asynchronously before class frees students to focus on applying what they learned when they are in the classroom.[82]

One major challenge with embedded librarianship is the issue of scalability to ensure that there are enough information professionals embedded in core classes. For example, embedded librarians may be inserted in as many as thirty or more classes per eight-week period. One solution that institutions like San José State University[83] have utilized is to provide asynchronous information literacy instructional modules that can be easily customizable and embedded into courses.[84] This provides a solution for information professionals to take an active role as information intermediators in online education courses so they can reach online students who might never set foot in a library.

Discussion Question

What should the marketing and outreach roles be for reference librarians?

NEW ROLES FOR INFORMATION MEDIATORS

As information-seeking behaviors become increasingly user driven, virtual, and self-directed, reference librarians have taken on new roles for mediating between users and their access to information. These new responsibilities are illustrated by the array of job titles, as listed in textbox 11.3.[85] These emerging roles frequently entail interdepartmental responsibilities that range from managing learning resource centers in schools and higher education to using learning management systems that provide access to digital resources and reference services.

Learning and knowledge are at the center of this shift away from information professionals simply helping users find information. Brian Kenney has argued that users in the communities being served are looking for ways to do things rather than simply to locate information.[87] R. David Lankes, on the other hand, has framed the issue in terms of a new mission for information professionals in that they are improving society by assisting in the creation of knowledge

> TEXTBOX 11.3
>
> **New Titles for Information Mediators**
>
> - Information services librarian
> - Digital librarian
> - Liaison librarian
> - Online services librarian
> - Distance librarian
> - Emerging technology librarian
> - Innovation catalyst librarian
> - Marketing and outreach librarian
> - Community librarian
> - Immigrant services librarian[86]

by users in library communities.[88] There are four critical but diverse areas where librarians function as information intermediators, as discussed below.[89]

Information Literacy

Information professionals are meeting the new types of diverse and global information needs of users by providing information literacy instruction. School librarians use the American Association of School Librarians' (AASL) Standards for the 21st-Century Learner[90] to support traditional school students and homeschoolers in developing "information skills that will enable them to use technology as an important tool for learning now and in the future"[91] (see also chapter 6: "Literacy and Media Centers: School Libraries"). Similarly, academic libraries address information literacy skills described in the Association of Colleges and Research Libraries' (ACRL) Framework for Information Literacy for Higher Education[92] (see also chapter 7: "Learning and Research Institutions: Academic Libraries"). Meanwhile, public libraries are using a number of approaches to offer classes that address information and technology literacy skills as they teach users new technologies, offer programs on topics like estate planning, and help adults complete high school degrees via the Smart Horizons Career Online High School[93] in Florida (see also chapter 8: "Community Anchors for Lifelong Learning: Public Libraries"). These public libraries are also expanding access to higher education through resources such as the College Depot at the Phoenix Public Library.[94] Homework help and tutoring services are provided for school students and homeschoolers alike, and fun classes for preschool children are being offered on computer coding to support STEM (Science, Technology, Engineering, and Math) initiatives.

Service to Diverse Constituents

Information professionals are serving many different constituent groups. In public libraries, information professionals are helping immigrants with reading literacy and providing classes in English as a second language. They are also providing story hours for children with autism and parenting techniques for addressing their children's reading needs to their parents. Similarly, academic libraries ensure that online learning students receive equivalent levels of library instruction as on-campus students, providing instruction that is timely and ongoing and that helps students learn how to use and cite information ethically for their class assignments.[95] And, finally, school libraries offer homeless children a place to study after school while public libraries are finding ways to provide homeless adults everything from computer access to social services.

Service to Local Businesses and the Community

Information professionals are also helping local businesses and workers in the community. Information professionals offer classes in résumé writing, interview skills, computer skills, and job skills development.[96] Local business people can take classes on how to find grants for a nonprofit or how to navigate the world of business contracts or even can get one-on-one advice on issues ranging from procurement to licensing and local government policies.

Technology Literacy

Finally, information professionals are helping patrons learn how to use new technologies and develop new skills. Libraries are making more of an effort to help seniors learn various technologies like Kindles and iPads, while makerspaces and beta spaces allow users to foster experimentation and scholarship through the sharing of resources and knowledge by using new technologies and building prototypes[97] (see also chapter 17: "Hyperlinked Libraries" and chapter 18: "Creation Culture and Makerspaces").

CASE STUDY

Information Professionals Introduce Innovative Technologies

Librarians like Chad Mairn at St. Petersburg College in Florida are at the vanguard of information professionals who are bringing innovative technologies to libraries and other types of information organizations.[98] He manages the Innovation Lab on the Seminole Campus and offers the Pinellas Comic and Maker Con and a Maker Boot Camp.[99] As an information intermediary who helps patrons with emerging technologies, he stresses that information professionals need to be able to help patrons with everything from simply using 3-D printers to designing items that use 3-D printing.[100]

In the twenty-first century, information professionals need to prepare for changing user behaviors, help patrons with new information tools and resources, and partner with everyone—from people in universities and schools to local organizations and community groups. This means that reference librarians and information intermediators of all kinds need to be creative, innovative, and technologically skilled. Information intermediators need to keep up with new skill sets so they can offer the high-touch/high-tech reference services their users want. Whatever the model used or the type of information organization, it is important to integrate reference services with other parts of the organization to address the needs of users.[101]

> **Discussion Question**
>
> How do you envision reinventing reference services offered in your information organization in terms of service to diverse communities?

CONCLUSION

In the twenty-first century, the definition of information intermediation focuses on cultivating information literacy, creating knowledge, and helping users learn how to do things. Reference librarians are key to achieving this goal and must be forward thinking in serving the needs of their communities. This entails the efforts of information professionals who are open and adept at identifying what is changing. As information professionals, reference librarians understand that they can no longer wait passively for patrons to come to use the library's services. Instead, reference librarians are proactively and energetically promoting the library, as well as the value and significance of the library's services and resources to the community.

At the core, reference services and information intermediators will continue to serve their communities by addressing the fundamental mission of helping users acquire knowledge and satisfy information needs through creativity, innovation, and outreach, while remaining technologically relevant in the twenty-first century.

NOTES

1. Samuel Swett Green, "Personal Relations between Librarians and Readers," *Library Journal* 1, no. 1 (1876): 77–78.
2. David A Tyckoson, "What Is the Best Model of Reference Service?," *Library Trends* 50, no. 2 (2001): 183. See also Dennis B. Miles, "Shall We Get Rid of the Reference Desk?," *Reference and User Services Quarterly* 52, no. 4 (2013): 320.
3. Kay Ann Cassell and Uma Hiremath, eds., *Reference and Information Services: An Introduction*, third edition (Chicago: Neal-Schuman, 2014), 5–8.
4. American Library Association, "Guidelines for Behavioral Performance for Reference and Information Service Providers," 2017, http://www.ala.org/rusa/resources/guidelines/guidelinesbehavioral.
5. Anne Houston, "What's in a Name? Toward a New Definition of Reference," *Reference & User Services Quarterly* 55, no. 3 (Spring 2016): 186–88, https://journals.ala.org/index.php/rusq/article/view File/5927/7512.
6. Jeanie M. Welch, "Who Says We're Not Busy? Library Web Page Usage as a Measure of Public Service Activity," *Reference Services Review* 33, no. 4 (2005): 371.
7. Newsbank, 2017, http://newsbank.com.
8. Web of Knowledge, 2017, http://www.webofknowledge.com.
9. ERIC, http://eric.ed.gov.
10. PubMed, https://www.ncbi.nlm.nih.gov/pubmed/.
11. *Reader's Guide* is published by Wilson and there is a retrospective index for 1890 to 1982; "Books in Print," 2017, http://www.booksinprint.com.

12. CREDO, 2017, http://www.credoreference.com.
13. Gale Virtual Reference Library, http://www.cengage.com/search/showresults.do?N=197+4294904997.
14. Oxford Reference, 2017, http://www.oxfordreference.com.
15. Google Books, http://books.google.com.
16. Internet Archive, http://www.archive.org.
17. HathiTrust, http://www.hathitrust.org.
18. Andrew Weiss, "Examining Massive Digital Libraries (MDLs) and Their Impact on Reference Services," *Reference Librarian* 57, no. 4 (2016): 291–92, doi:10.1080/02763877.2016.1145614.
19. DPLA, http://dp.la.
20. Google, http://www.google.com.
21. Bing, http://www.bing.com.
22. Yahoo, http://www.yahoo.com.
23. DuckDuckGo, http://duckduckgo.com.
24. Kelley Blue Book Online, http://kbb.com.
25. Stephen Abram, "Future World: Strategic Challenges for Reference in the Coming Decade," in *Reinventing Reference: How Libraries Deliver Value in the Age of Google*, ed. Katie Elson Anderson and Vibiana Bowman Cvetkovic (Chicago: American Library Association, 2015), 133–45, PDF e-book.
26. ProQuest, http://www.proquest.com.
27. EBSCO, Host, http://www.ebscohost.com.
28. Ex Libris, "Primo," http://www.exlibrisgroup.com/category/PrimoOverview.
29. OCLC, "WorldCat Discovery," https://www.oclc.org/en/worldcat-discovery.html.
30. Google Scholar, http://scholar.google.com.
31. Web of Knowledge, http://webofknowledge.com.
32. EndNote, http://endnote.com.
33. Zotero, http://www.zotero.org.
34. Google Translate, http://translate.google.com.
35. John Paul Anbu and Sanjay Kataria, "Reference on the Go: A Model for Mobile Reference Services in Libraries," *Reference Librarian* 57, no. 3 (2016): 236, doi:10.1080/02763877.2015.1132181.
36. Online Computer Library Center (OCLC), http://www.oclc.org.
37. QuestionPoint, http://www.questionpoint.org.
38. Ask a Librarian, http://askalibrarian.org.
39. NoveList, http://www.ebscohost.com/novelist.
40. LibGuides, http://www.springshare.com/libguides/.
41. Pinterest, http://www.pinterest.com/.
42. Paul Pival and Johanna Tunon, "NetMeeting: A New and Inexpensive Alternative for Delivering Library Instruction to Distance Students," *College and Research Library News* 59, no. 10 (1998): para. 4.
43. Collaborate, http://www.collaborate.org.
44. WebEx, http://www.webex.com.
45. Go To Training, https://www.gotomeeting.com/training.
46. Screencast-O-Matic, http://screencast-o-matic.com.
47. Jing, https://www.techsmith.com/jing.html.
48. "About Guide on the Side," *Code.library*, last modified 2017, http://code.library.arizona.edu/.
49. Thomas Pack, "Got Questions? Stack Exchange Has Answers," *Information Today* 32 (2015, January–February): 31.
50. Yahoo! Answers, http://answers.yahoo.com.
51. Erik Choi and Chirag Shah, "User Motivations in Asking Questions in Online Q&A Services," *Journal of the Association for Information Services and Technology* 67, no. 5 (2016): background para. 1, doi:10.1002/asi.23490.
52. WikiAnswers, http://www.wikianswers.com.
53. Quora, https://www.quora.com/.
54. LibAnswers, https://www.springshare.com/libanswers/.
55. Kay Ann Cassell and Uma Hiremath, "Chapter 21: Reference 2.0," in *Reference and Information Services: An Introduction*, third edition (Chicago: American Library Association, 2014), 430. See also

Marian S. Ramos and Christine M. Abrigo, "Reference 2.0 in Action: An Evaluation of the Digital Reference Services in Selected Philippine Academic Libraries," *Library Hi Tech News* 29, no. 1 (2012): 8, doi:10.1108/07419051211223426.

56. Courtney L. Young, "Crowdsourcing the Virtual Reference Interview with Twitter," *Reference Librarian* 55, no. 2 (2014): 173, doi:10.1080/02763877.2014.879030.

57. New York Public Library, 2017, *NYPL Blogs*, https://www.nypl.org/blog.

58. NYPL (Instagram account), https://www.instagram.com/nypl/.

59. New York Public Library, "What NYPL Is Reading Now," https://www.pinterest.com/nypl/what-nypl-is -reading/.

60. New York Public Library, "Literary Greats," https://www.pinterest.com/nypl/literary-greats/.

61. Kay Ann Cassell and Uma Hiremath, "Chapter 22: The Future of Information Service," in *Reference and Information Services: An Introduction*, third edition (Chicago: American Library Association, 2014), 465.

62. Michelle Holschuh Simmons, "Finding Information: Information Mediation and Reference Services," in *Information Services Today*, ed. Sandra Hirsh (Lanham, MD: Rowman & Littlefield, 2015), 130, PDF e-book.

63. Tyckoson, "What Is the Best Model of Reference Service?," 194.

64. Amy Paterson, "After the Desk: Reference Service in a Changing Information Landscape" (paper presented at IFLA WLIC, Lyon, France, July 15, 2014), 3–4, http://library.ifla.org/944/1/101-paterson-en.pdf.

65. Meredith Farkas, "High Tech, High Touch: The Personal Touch in a Digital World," *American Libraries* (September 29, 2014), https://americanlibrariesmagazine.org/2014/09/29/high-tech-high-touch. See also Cassell and Hiremath, eds., *Reference and Information Services*, 465.

66. Stephen P. Buss, "Do We Still Need Reference Services in the Age of Google and Wikipedia?" *Reference Librarian* 57, no. 4 (2016): 269–70, doi:10.1080/02763877.2015.1134377.

67. Rachel Applegate, "Whose Decline? Which Academic Libraries Are 'Deserted' in Terms of Reference Transactions?," *Reference & User Services Quarterly* 48, no. 2 (2008): 177.

68. Association of Research Libraries, "Service Trends in ARL Libraries, 1991–2012," last modified 2012, http://www.arl.org/storage/documents/service-trends.pdf.

69. John B. Horrigan, "Library Usage and Engagement," *Libraries 2016*, Pew Research Center, September 9, 2016, para. 2, http://www.pewinternet.org/2016/09/09/library-usage-and-engagement/.

70. Cassell and Hiremath, eds., *Reference and Information Services*, 461.

71. Madelynn Dickerson, "Beta Spaces as a Model for Reconstructing Reference Services in Libraries," *In the Library with the Lead Pipe* (2016): Beta Spaces, http://inthelibrarywiththeleadpipe.org/2016/reference-as-beta-space.

72. Lisa A. Ellis, ed., *Teaching Reference Today: New Directions, Novel Approaches* (Lanham, MD: Rowman & Littlefield, 2016), 41–44, PDF e-book.

73. Tyckoson, "What Is the Best Model of Reference Service?" 190.

74. Kealin M. McCabe and James R. W. MacDonald, "Roaming Reference: Reinvigorating Reference through Point of Need Service," *Partnership: The Canadian Journal of Library and Information Practice and Research* 6, no. 2 (2011): 2.

75. Pokémon Go, http://www.pokemongo.com.

76. "Pokemon Hunt in the Library," *Karissa in the Library: Learning and Thinking about Libraries, in Libraries* (blog), July 14, 2016, https://karissamlis.wordpress.com/2016/07/14/pokemon-scavenger-hunt-in -the-library; Chad Mairn, "Technologies to Watch: 2017 Edition," Slideshare presentation, posted January 2017, http://www.slideshare.net /chadmairn.

77. Hafuboti, "Libraries Are for Everyone," *Hafuboti* (blog), posted February 2017, https://hafuboti .com/2017 /02/02/libraries-are-for-everyone/.

78. Alex Mudd, Terri Summey, and Matt Upson, "It Takes a Village to Design a Course: Embedding a Librarian in Course Design," *Journal of Library and Information Services in Distance Learning* 9, nos. 1–2 (2015): 71–72.

79. Maryska Connelly-Brown, Kim Mears, and Melissa E. Johnson, "Reference for the Remote User through Embedded Librarianship," *Reference Librarian* 57, no. 1 (2016): 166, doi:10.1080/02763877.2015.1131658.

80. Cassandra Kvenlid et al., "Embedded Librarianship: Questions and Answers from Librarians in the Trenches," *Library Hi Tech News* 33, no. 2 (2016): 8, doi:10.1108/LHTN-11-20150878.

81. Brian T. Sullivan and Karen L. Porter, "From One-Shot Sessions to Embedded Librarians: Lessons Learned over Seven Years of Successful Faculty-Librarian Collaboration," *College and Research Library News* 77, no. 1 (2016), http://crln.acrl.org/index.php/crlnews/article/view/9431/10650.

82. Christopher Michael Rosser, and Tamie Willis, "Flip Over Research Instruction: Delivery, Assessment, and Feedback Strategies for 'Flipped' Library," *Theological Librarianship* 9, no. 1 (2016): 22, https://theolib.atla.com/theolib/article/view/413.

83. San José State University, http://www.sjsu.edu.

84. Christina Mune et al., "Developing Adaptable Online Information Literacy Modules for a Learning Management System," *Journal of Library and Information Services in Distance Learning* 9, nos. 1–2 (2015): 101–2, doi:10.1080/1533290X.2014.946351.

85. Lisa Peet, "Five Brand-New Jobs for Today's Librarians: Careers 2016," *Library Journal*, March 9, 2016, http://lj.libraryjournal.com/2016/03/careers/five-brand-new-jobs-for-todays-librarians-careers-2016.

86. Ibid.

87. Brian Kenney, "Where Reference Fits in the Modern Library: Today's Reference User Wants Help Doing Things Rather Than Finding Things," *Publishers Weekly*, September 21, 2015, http://www.publishersweekly.com/pw/by-topic/industry-news/libraries/article/68019-for-future-reference.html.

88. R. David Lankes, *The Atlas of Librarianship* (Cambridge, MA: MIT Press, 2011), 13–14.

89. John B. Horrigan, "Libraries at the Crossroads," *Pew Research Center*, September 15, 2015, http://www.pewinternet.org/2015/09/15/libraries-at-the-crossroads.

90. American Library Association, "Standards for the 21st-Century Learner," http://www.ala.org/aasl/standards/learning.

91. American Association of School Librarians, *Standards for the 21st-Century Learner*. American Association of School Librarians (2007), http://www.ala.org/aasl/sites/ala.org.aasl/files/content/guidelinesandstandards/learningstandards/AASL_Learning_Standards_2007.pdf.

92. Association of Colleges and Research Libraries, *Framework for Information Literacy for Higher Education*, January 16, 2016, http://www.ala.org/acrl/sites/ala.org.acrl/files /content/issues/infolit/Framework_ILHE.pdf.

93. Smart Horizons Online Highschool, http://smarthorizonsonline.org/.

94. Phoenix Public Library, "College Depot," http://www.phoenixpubliclibrary.org/collegedepot.

95. "Standards of Distance Learning Library Services," Association of Colleges and Libraries, last modified June 2016, http://www.ala.org/acrl/standards/guidelinesdistancelearning. See also Yu-Hui Chen and Mary K. Van Ullen, "Helping International Students Succeed Academically through Research Process and Plagiarism Workshops," *College & Research Libraries* 72, no. 3 (2011): 209; Daniel Doss et al., "Assessing Domestic vs. International Student Perceptions and Attitudes of Plagiarism," *Journal of International Students* 6, no. 2 (2016): 542–44; Mary Knowlton and Shawn Bryant Collins, "Foreign-Educated Graduate Nursing Students and Plagiarism," *Journal of Nursing Education* 56, no. 4 (2017): 211–14, doi:10.3928/01484834-20170323-04.

96. Phoenix Public Library, "PhoenixWorks: Job Help Resources," last modified 2016, http://www.phoenixpubliclibrary.org/phoenixworks/job-help-resources.

97. Madelynn Dickerson, "Beta Spaces as a Model for Reconstructing Reference Services in Libraries," *In the Library with the Lead Pipe* (2016), http://inthelibrarywiththeleadpipe.org/2016/reference -as-beta -space.

98. "Computers in Libraries: Chad Mairn," *Info Today*, 2011, http://www.infotoday.com/cil2011/speakers .asp?speaker=ChadMairn.

99. Innovation Lab on the Seminole Campus, "Pinellas Comic and Maker Con and a Maker Boot Camp," https://sandbox.spcollege.edu/index.php/2016/08/pinellas-comic-and-maker-con-at-spc-seminole/.

100. Chad Mairn, "Technologies to Watch: 2017 Edition," Slideshare presentation, modified January 2017, http://www.slideshare.net/chadmairn.

101. Paterson, "After the Desk."

12

Metadata, Cataloging, Linked Data, and the Evolving ILS

Mary K. Bolin

Chapter 12, "Metadata, Cataloging, Linked Data, and the Evolving ILS," provides essential definitions and an overview of the central trends that correlate to some of the foundational tools of library and information science including metadata, MARC cataloging, linked data, and the evolving ILS. Mary Bolin, a professor and cataloging librarian, is uniquely situated to highlight how these trends continue to influence information services. She moves from a discussion of MARC's history, with brief discussions of other types of metadata such as DublinCore and MODS and new standards including RDA and FRBR, to the Library of Congress's BIBFRAME (a replacement for MARC), providing ample examples and tables or figures.

Bolin's careful identification of the new standards, her use of examples, and the definition of key principles within these standards (such as location, collocation, interoperability, and the principle that metadata must describe attributes of information) helps to clarify an often confusing and overwhelming area of information science. Her discussion of linked data and its relationship to BIBFRAME elucidates one of the leading trends in information science. BIBFRAME ("Bibliographic Framework") is a project by the Library of Congress that will implement a linked data model in creating library metadata. While integrated library systems (ILSs) have been around for several decades, they are about to undergo significant changes as they adapt to accommodate linked data and the BIBFRAME model that incorporates FRBR.

Bolin concludes the chapter by briefly summarizing and defining descriptive and subject cataloging and provides key terms associated with both, such as "authority control," for those new to the field. The chapter is dense in terminology, but provides a solid introduction to how information is classified, recorded, and made available to the organization's user.

★ ★ ★

Cataloging is the acquisition or creation of bibliographic records for a library catalog or other discovery tool. These records are created according to standards that allow them to be stored in a database, shared, and used by many different libraries. Today's standards and practices are the descendants of those that emerged in the late nineteenth century when an Anglo-American tradition of librarianship was established (see also chapter 2: "Libraries, Communities, and Information: Two Centuries of Experience"). Cataloging practices were codified to give access to the growing body of scholarly literature that accompanied new models of research and higher education.[1]

The Library of Congress (LC) and the American Library Association (ALA), along with other national libraries and library associations, have been major forces in the creation and adoption of cataloging practices and standards. LC and ALA have participated in the committees that created the cataloging rules used in the twentieth and twenty-first centuries. LC has also distributed its catalog records (first as cards and later as records in online databases) since 1904.

This chapter provides an overview of important concepts related to organizing data in structured ways so that people can access that data using systems and tools. At the end of the chapter, the reader should have an understanding of:

metadata: the structured data that gives access to information,
cataloging: descriptive and subject cataloging, authority control, and shared standards,
linked data: a form of information architecture that will soon be the way cataloging data is organized, and
the evolving ILS: the changes that have happened and that are coming to integrated library systems (ILSs), the software modules that libraries use in nearly all their activities and services.

METADATA

Metadata (i.e., "data about data") is the structured data that enables people to find and access information. Metadata schemes give access to digital texts, images, and other objects. Library cataloging, which will be discussed in more detail later in the chapter, is one kind of metadata. The object of metadata is the same as that of traditional cataloging: to identify and describe resources and make them findable and available. This section discusses MARC, the most common metadata scheme used in libraries and the basis for library catalogs, and briefly discusses other metadata schemes.

> The object of metadata is the same as that of traditional cataloging: to identify and describe resources and make them findable and available.

MARC Format

For much of the twentieth century, libraries acquired, created, duplicated, and edited catalog cards that they filed into card catalogs. Users searched them to find material by author, title, or subject. In the late 1960s, the Library of Congress (LC) created the Machine-Readable Cataloging (MARC) format. MARC is a system for encoding and transmitting bibliographic records.[2] A bibliographic record is the metadata for one item, such as a book. The record can be loaded into a database and users can find that book using the metadata. MARC format "encodes" bibliographic records by applying MARC field and subfield tags to elements of bibliographic information. For example, the title of a resource is recorded in the MARC "245" field, as demonstrated below:

245 10 To Kill a Mockingbird / $c by Harper Lee.

The slash and $c indicate that the next subfield will contain the "statement of responsibility," the authorship statement as it appears on the resource.

In the 1970s, what was then called the Ohio College Library Center (OCLC) became the basis for the current OCLC database, which has tens of millions of records and more than 25,000 member libraries worldwide. OCLC provides many services, but the heart of its services is the WorldCat database, which reflects the collections of its member libraries. Behind WorldCat's public interface are MARC records that can be created, edited, and exchanged.[3]

When MARC was first implemented, it created a revolution in cataloging, and eventually allowed libraries to replace card catalogs with online public access catalogs (OPACs). Thomale describes research on machine-processing of MARC data, saying that "the contents of these 245s [title fields] looked and acted less like data from a structured data record and more like textual markup from a document."[4] MARC is more like textual markup—a profound assessment—because it was created to make catalog cards

Check This Out

OCLC WorldCat database. *Visit:* http://www.worldcat.org/.

to print text on a 3 × 5 card. Its prolonged success in creating databases to produce online catalogs is remarkable.

MARC will soon be replaced with a scheme called BIBFRAME, a model that will be described later in this chapter. BIBFRAME is more flexible and is suited to the current computing environment and the expectations of users.

Discussion Questions

The Library of Congress online catalog is available at catalog.loc.gov. Search there for some specific items, and for a topic you are interested in. Look at the different displays provided, including "MARC tags," which will show you the MARC record. In the non-MARC display, click on some of the hyperlinked names and subject headings. When you are finished, think about the things you encountered. What are the strong and weak points in searching, navigation, and display? What differences did you notice between the MARC display and the public display?

Other Schemes

MARC is used for library cataloging, but there are numerous other metadata schemes used for image collections, archival materials, and other types of materials. Some metadata schemes are based on MARC, such as Dublin Core (DC)[5] and Metadata Object Description Schema (MODS).[6] Many metadata schemes, particularly DC and Text Encoding Initiative (TEI),[7] are widely used to create digital archives of research material, special collections, and other collections of images, letters, memorabilia, and photographs, as well as repositories of research data and institutional repositories. While MARC format still uses numbered tags, such as 245 for the title of a resource, other metadata schemes use named elements (e.g., "title") and are often in the form of an Extensible Markup Language (XML) schema. An XML schema is any application of XML. The schema defines metadata elements such as title and places them in angle brackets. For example, DC is based on MARC, and a portion of a DC record for *To Kill a Mockingbird*, expressed as XML, would look like this:

```
<dc:title>To Kill a Mockingbird</dc:title>
<dc:creator>Harper Lee</dc:creator>
<dc:publisher>Lippincott</dc:publisher>
<dc:date>1960</dc:date>
```

Shared Standards

MARC, DC, MODS, and other metadata schemes are all standards that can be shared by a community, such as libraries. Shared standards are crucial in the world of cataloging, metadata, bibliographic control, and discovery. If data is created using a shared standard, it is more likely to be interoperable between systems. For example, if bibliographic records are created using MARC format, they can be imported and exported by many different systems. MARC is a carrier of bibliographic information. Shared cataloging codes, like the second edition of the Anglo-American Cataloging Rules (AACR2) and its successor Resource Description and Access (RDA),[8] are descriptive content standards that create consistent information that can be shared and repurposed. Subject content standards, like the Library of Congress Subject Headings (LCSH),[9] Library of Congress Classification (LCC),[10] and Dewey Decimal Classification (DDC),[11] express the "aboutness" (fields, subjects, time and place, etc.) of resources.

New Standards: RDF, FRBR, FRAD, and RDA

There are several key principles that standards are built upon. The first principle is location and collocation. The principle of location refers to finding something whose author or title is known. The principle of collocation refers to bringing together things by the same author or on the same subject. These principles are carried out through:

aggregation: like things together,
discrimination: unlike things distinguished,
disambiguation: things with the same name separated.

The second principle is interoperability. Cataloging information must be able to be loaded, read, and interpreted by any system that uses MARC or its replacement. The third principle is that metadata, including library cataloging, must describe attributes of information (e.g., title, author, subject, date, etc.). The "aboutness" of resources is represented by subject metadata. These principles underlie all cataloging codes from at least the nineteenth century onward.

New standards are bringing changes to discovery systems. The most recent and significant new standards are discussed in this section. One of these new standards is "Functional Requirements for Bibliographic Records" (FRBR—pronounced "ferber").[12] RDA, the current cataloging code, assumes that library catalogs are moving toward a FRBR environment. FRBR expresses the relationship between "works" and the various examples of those works. "Work" is a relatively abstract term. For example, *Pride and Prejudice* is a work that has been expressed as a novel, a play, several films, and in other formats. These standards, and how they relate to each other, are explained in more detail below.

Resource Description Framework (RDF)

Resource Description Framework (RDF)[13] is a language for representing knowledge and is expressed as an Extensible Markup Language (XML) schema. That means that XML is a kind of universal container for many metadata "languages." RDF is one of those languages, and it is used by many different fields and organizations, not just libraries. RDF may be the replacement for MARC's encoding of cataloging information, and RDA paves the way for such a change. RDF uses a language of "triples," statements with three constituent parts that declare the relationship between pieces of data and a unique identifier for each piece. An example of an RDF triple is shown below. Many examples of RDF expressed as XML are available on the Worldwide Web Consortium (W3C) website.[14]

The triples consist of a subject, predicate, and object, similar to the grammar of English and other languages. For example, figure 12.1 adopted from Wikimedia commons, is an RDF graph containing the statements, "there is a Person identified by http://www.w3.org/People/EM/contact#me, whose name is Eric Miller, whose email address is em@w3.org, and whose title is Dr." Each of the statements (elements of the triple) have a URL that points to that piece of information.[15]

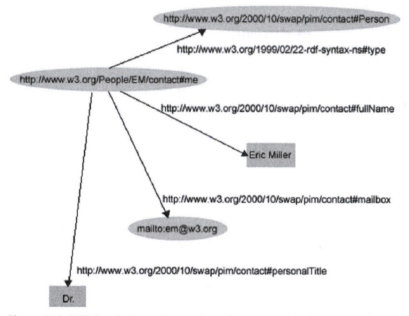

Figure 12.1 RDF Graph. *https://www.w3.org/Consortium/Legal/2015/doc-license.*

Other important shared standards include International Standard Bibliographic Description (ISBD, which has been incorporated into cataloging rules since the 1970s), RDA, and MARC.

Functional Requirements for Bibliographic Records (FRBR)

FRBR indicates what bibliographic records must do or be capable of. To identify what is required of bibliographic records, FRBR identifies user needs and user tasks, which are to find, identify, select, and obtain information. FRBR's entity-relationship model is a means for achieving those tasks. The records must show relationships between entities that will help information seekers find and use information. FRBR has three types of entities:

Group 1: Works, Expressions, Manifestations, and Items (WEMI).
Group 2: persons and organizations responsible for the creation of a work.
Group 3: subjects.

FRBR expresses relationships among entities. For example, Jane Austen's relationship to *Pride and Prejudice* is that she is the author. Figure 12.2 from an open-access textbook illustrates that relationship in general:[16]

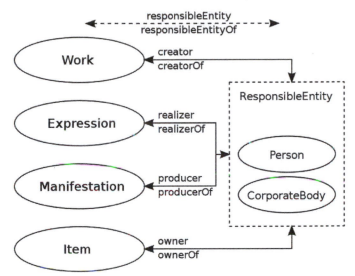

Figure 12.2 FRBR Example. *https://www.w3.org/Consortium/Legal/2015/doc-license.*

The work and its expressions and manifestations are linked to the "Responsible Entity," which can be a person, persons, or corporate body.

MARC can express some FRBR relationships and distinguish between the three groups of entities. For example, figure 12.3 is adopted from a MARC record of a particular edition of the novel *Pride and Prejudice* and shows the Group 1 entity (the manifestation of this work, shown by the title, edition statement, and publication information) and its author and editor (Jane Austen and Donald Gray, both Group 2 entities).

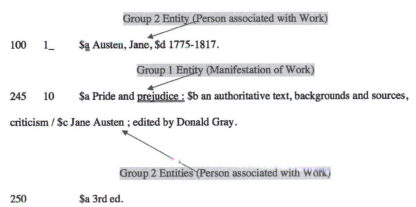

Figure 12.3 Examples of Group 1 and Group 2 Entities. *Created by author.*

Group 1 entities (WEMI) are intellectual and creative products that include books, journals, sound recordings, images, databases, and so on. The work entity is the most abstract of these. For example, there is a work called *Pride and Prejudice*. That work has been realized in many different expressions. The first expression of *Pride and Prejudice* was the novel by Jane Austen. It has also been realized as a play and more than one film. The novel, play, and films are all expressions of *Pride and Prejudice*. A manifestation is any version of an expression. For example, each of the many editions of the novel *Pride and Prejudice* is a separate manifestation, as is each of the scripts for each of the different films. An item is a single instance of a manifestation. Cataloging is done at the level of the manifestation.

Group 2 entities for *Pride and Prejudice* include Jane Austen, the author of the novel, but also any editors, playwrights, and screenwriters who created the play and film versions, performers, directors, and crew in a film, and so on. Group 2 entities also include organizations, such as the studio that produced the films.

Group 3 entities are the subjects that express the aboutness of resources. The following subject fields are from the same MARC record excerpted above, for an edition of *Pride and Prejudice*:

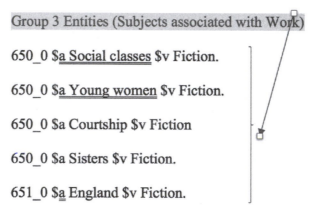

Figure 12.4 Example of Group 3 Entities. *Created by author.*

Functional Requirements for Authority Data (FRAD)

Functional Requirements for Authority Data (FRAD)[17] accompanies FRBR. The requirements for authority data are that it should uniquely identify a person, organization, topic, place, and other information, and should express the relationships between those entities and the WEMI entities (i.e., Who is the author of this book? Is this person the same as that person?). FRBR and FRAD are the foundations for RDA.

Resource Description and Access (RDA)

RDA does not represent a radical change in descriptive rules. Its general approach is to:

- transcribe elements exactly as they appear, including capitalization,
- avoid abbreviations, and
- follow the principles set out in FRBR (described above).

RDA contains guidelines for recording attributes (i.e., bibliographic elements such as title) and for expressing relationships between entities, such as that between title and author. RDA paves the way for a more revolutionary change, in which bibliographic records give way to the richer and more flexible concept of linked data.

RDA is a content standard, not a display standard. As a content standard, RDA has guidelines for what goes into an element (e.g., a title, an access point, etc.), but not what the element looks like when it is displayed in a public database. RDA is also not an encoding scheme—that is, it does not provide a method for preparing information to be loaded into a database. The current encoding scheme is MARC, which is used to encode bibliographic and authority information—that is, tag that information with MARC fields and subfields according to whatever content standard, or cataloging code, is in place. That means that currently RDA is used to create content of bibliographic records, and MARC is used to encode them.

CATALOGING

Cataloging uses tools and standards to create cataloging data. These include MARC format and the databases that use it, including OCLC and individual library catalog and computer systems, as well as things like the Library of Congress Subject Headings (LCSH), Library of Congress Classification (LCC), and so on. Cataloging has two main divisions: descriptive cataloging (including authority control) and subject cataloging. Descriptive cataloging deals with what a resource is and who is responsible for it. Subject cataloging deals with what the resource is about.

Descriptive Cataloging

Descriptive cataloging starts with bibliographic elements, which include title, edition, publication information, physical description, and series. The elements of description are found in the cataloging rules that are being used (e.g., RDA). MARC format provides for all those elements and has tags for all of them. The areas of description used by RDA are based on International Standard Bibliographic Description (ISBD), a standard that has been in place for nearly fifty years. ISBD prescribes which elements are standard and required when creating bibliographic information. Descriptive cataloging starts with FRBR Group 1 entities: works, expressions, etc. Next comes Group 2: persons and organizations responsible for the content. Finally, there is Group 3: subjects.

Authority Control

The creation of access points is also a part of descriptive cataloging. Access points are fields in a bibliographic record whose contents are authorized or controlled. The process of establishing and maintaining standardized access points is called authority control. An access point is a field that is indexed separately and specifically. In other words, a library catalog can be searched specifically by author, title, series, and subject.

Controlled access points include author, series, and some titles. The forms of those fields (e.g., the author's name) are standardized into a single form that becomes an index term. Many people, places, and things have the same name, and disambiguation is the first step in establishing an authorized name. Authority control includes identifying all the forms of names that a person or thing has used. Once the identity of a person or thing is established, and all names and forms of the name are compiled, one name is chosen as the authorized form. Users are then directed to the authorized form with cross-references from the forms that are not used. For example, if "Samuel Clemens" should be called "Mark Twain" in the library catalog, then someone who does an author search for "Clemens, Samuel" should be directed to search "Twain, Mark."

MARC 21 Format for Authority Data[18] is related but not identical to MARC 21 Format for Bibliographic Data.[19] The fields in the MARC authority format include the authorized headings, cross-references from other forms, and notes about where the information came from. MARC bibliographic and authority records are exported from OCLC or another source and imported into a library catalog in a batch or one at a time. Libraries search for authority records that match access points in bibliographic records and export and load these records into their catalogs. Loading authority records allows all the headings in bibliographic records that match an authority record to be linked to that authority record. An authorized name such as "Twain, Mark, 1835–1910" is stored just once in the database. The authorized name is stored in the authority record and then linked to bibliographic records that contain that access point.

The example below is an excerpt from the LC name authority file record for the author Harper Lee. The record uses MARC Format for Authorities.

100 1 $a Lee, Harper Authorized name that will be used in cataloging
370 | $a Monroeville (Ala.) **$b** Monroeville (Ala.) **$c** United States **$2** naf
372 $a Fiction **$2** lcsh
374 $a Novelists **$2** lcsh
375 $a female
377 $a eng
400 1 $a Lee, Nelle Harper
670 $a Her To kill a mockingbird, 1960: **$b** jacket (b. 1926 in Monroeville, Alabama)

Figure 12.5 MARC Format for Authorities. *Created by author.*

The bibliographic record for Lee's novel *To Kill a Mockingbird* shows the differences between MARC Format for Authorities and MARC Format for Bibliographic Records:

050 00 $a PS3562.E353

100 1 $a Lee, Harper. This is the only field shared by the MARC authority record and the MARC bibliographic record

245 10 $a To kill a mockingbird / $c Harper Lee.

250   $a 1st ed.

264 1 $a Philadelphia : $b Lippincott, $c 1960.

300   $a 296 pages ; $c 21 cm.

Figure 12.6 MARC Format for Bibliographic Records. *Created by author.*

Subject Cataloging

Subject cataloging uses controlled vocabulary and classification systems to express the aboutness of a book or other resource. Using a controlled vocabulary means that topics can be aggregated. Library of Congress Subject Headings (LCSH) is a widely used controlled vocabulary.

Subject authority records are encoded using MARC 21 Format for Authority Data. As with access points for the names of people and organizations, subject authority records can also be loaded into a library catalog so that users will be directed from terms that are not used as subject headings (e.g., "Arvicola amphibious") to the terms that are authorized (e.g., "European water vole"). LC creates new subject headings continuously and makes changes to older headings.

Classification is a single expression of a resource's aboutness. Classification has commonly been used as a way of arranging books on a shelf, but it can also be useful for electronic resources, particularly for browsing by classification and for statistical information about a library's collection. Resources can have multiple subject headings, but classification puts a resource in just one place, and its purpose is to put like things together. Library of Congress Classification (LCC) and Dewey Decimal Classification (DDC) are the two most widely used schemes in the United States.

DDC was created in the nineteenth century, and although it has been revised and updated continuously to add and change, it still retains a nineteenth-century worldview. DDC is used widely outside the United States, and by public libraries, school libraries, and some academic libraries in the United States.

LCC was developed by the Library of Congress in the early twentieth century. LCC uses a series of letters and numbers to express aboutness and create a unique place on a physical or virtual shelf. LCC uses letters to express the main subject and numbers to express subtopics. LCC uses nearly all the letters of the alphabet to divide up the world of knowledge, as it was conceived of more than one hundred years ago. Although there have been continuous revisions since then, the basic outline remains the same, and it displays the same nineteenth-century worldview as DDC, including an uneven distribution of topics.

Libraries and Publishers

Libraries have an important partnership with publishers in getting information to people. One way that librarians and publishers have worked effectively together is on cataloging and metadata initiatives. The oldest initiative is Cataloging in Publication (CIP). CIP information appears on the back of the title page of a printed book and corresponds to a MARC record created by LC.[20] LC catalogs most new books from mainstream publishers using prepublication information. The records are loaded into OCLC before the books are published, and libraries that use OCLC can find records for their books sooner.

Another important development is that publishers often supply MARC records for electronic resources, and when libraries purchase these resources, these MARC records can be batch loaded into the catalog. Publishers use a specialized metadata system, called ONIX (Online Information eXchange) for creating and exchanging bibliographic information about publications. ONIX is "an XML-based family of international standards intended to support computer-to-computer communication between parties involved in creating, distributing, licensing or otherwise making available intellectual property in published form, whether physical or digital."[21] An important trend is machine generation of bibliographic data, in which information from one database can be reused in another. Publishers can create ONIX metadata in this way, and libraries are preparing for machine-generated metadata as well. RDA requires catalogers to transcribe things as they appear to facilitate automated metadata creation.

LINKED DATA

Linked data is a concept that was originated by Tim Berners-Lee. He devised it as a way of making information more findable on the web. It is a model for bringing together different pieces of information about a person, place, or thing. Berners-Lee describes the rules of linked data as:

1. Use URIs [Uniform Resource Identifiers, of which a URL is one type, e.g., web addresses] as names for things.
2. Use HTTP URIs so that people can look up those names.
3. When someone looks up a URI, provide useful information, using the standards (RDF*, SPARQL).
4. Include links to other URIs so that they can discover more things.[22]

This means that metadata and cataloging information would no longer be in the form of bibliographic records, but would rather be discrete pieces of data linked together with URIs.

BIBFRAME ("Bibliographic Framework") is a project by the Library of Congress that will implement a linked data model in creating library metadata. It is part of the effort to find a replacement for MARC. LC's BIBFRAME initiative is deconstructing MARC and reconstituting it in a linked data format.[23] That means that each element of cataloging data, for example, the title or author of a work, would link to other pieces of data using a URI to show the relationship—that is, that this particular work has that particular author.

BIBFRAME would be a replacement for MARC, but it is also a process of rethinking cataloging to improve the discovery environment. BIBFRAME incorporates concepts from FRBR, including the idea of a work that is realized in specific physical (or electronic) entities housing the contents of the work (see textbox 12.3).

TEXTBOX 12.3

The BIBFRAME Model Core Classes

Creative Work: a conceptual essence of the cataloging resource.
Instance: an individual, material embodiment of the work.
Authority: key authority concepts that have defined relationships reflected in the work and instance.
Annotation: enhances our knowledge about another resource.[24]

BIBFRAME will transform MARC data to linked data, and will allow "cooperative cataloging at a far more granular level"[25] because whenever any library updates one piece of linked data, all other data that links to that piece will be updated as well.

Check This Out

For information on OCLC's work with linked data, see https://www.oclc.org/developer/develop/linked-data.en.html. VIAF can be found at http://viaf.org/, and information about FAST is at http://fast.oclc.org/searchfast/.

For cataloging to use linked data, each piece of information about a resource would be created as a piece of information with its own URL. These pieces of information can be associated, assembled, retrieved, and displayed in any number of ways. Search results could include information about a topic along with library resources concerning that topic. In other words, a search like "Barack Obama" could yield information about him (biographical data, for example), as well as books by and about him, journal articles, archival data such as presidential papers, government documents, videos, and so on. See figure 12.7 for this example.

Faceted Application of Subject Terminology (FAST) is a project of OCLC Research that "involves enumerative, faceted subject heading schema derived from the LCSH. The purpose of adapting the LCSH with a simplified syntax to create FAST is to retain the very rich vocabulary of LCSH while making the schema easier to understand, control, apply, and use . . . [A]ny valid set of LC subject headings can be converted to FAST headings."[26] FAST is designed to work in the linked data environment. Most library catalogs probably do not display FAST headings now, but they are present in LC MARC records.

Mary K. Bolin

Barack Obama

44th U.S. President

🌐 barackobama.com

Barack Hussein Obama II is an American politician who served as the 44th President of the United States from 2009 to 2017. He is the first African American to have served as president. Wikipedia

Born: August 4, 1961 (age 55), Kapiolani Medical Center for Women and Children, Honolulu, HI

Height: 6′1″

Parents: Ann Dunham, Barack Obama Sr.

Siblings: Maya Soetoro-Ng, Malik Obama, Auma Obama, More

Education: Harvard Law School (1988–1991), More

Figure 12.7 Google Linked Data Search for Barack Obama. *Screenshot from a Google search.*

THE EVOLVING ILS

Integrated library systems (ILSs) have been around for several decades, but they are about to undergo significant changes as they adapt to accommodate linked data and the BIBFRAME model that incorporates FRBR.

ILSs are computer systems with software modules that correspond to library services. They were developed starting in the 1980s and 1990s and are now poised for a significant change. Library catalogs in their present form do not express all FRBR relationships. Bibliographic records represent manifestations and do not directly express relationships among works, expressions, manifestations, and items. MARC format does not easily express those relationships. A catalog might have a record for the novel *Pride and Prejudice* and another record for a film based on the same work. The bibliographic records will give some indication that the different expressions are related, but the structure of current catalogs (i.e., the way bibliographic records are linked) does not express those WEMI relationships.

Integrated library systems were first developed in the 1980s and matured about twenty years later. They are "integrated" because they integrate library functions and the data used by those functions: cataloging, acquisitions, circulation, serials and electronic resources, and a public interface called the online public access catalog (OPAC). The structure of ILSs has a MARC database at its center, with a parallel database of borrower information that can interact with it (i.e., if something is checked out by a user, the record for that item and a patron record can be associated with each other). Those two databases have several types of records: the MARC database, for example, has bibliographic, order, and item records that are linked to each other.[27]

In the late 1990s, OPACs became web based, and library websites expanded beyond just the OPAC to also include links to full-text databases, digitized archival and research collections, the institutional repository, and other electronic resources. In about the mid-2000s, ILS vendors began creating and marketing discovery tools and layers that combined the MARC database (the OPAC) with other library collections and resources.[28] These discovery tools have an interface that is like the OPAC, but include information harvested or accessed from the institutional repository, image collections, selected periodical databases, and other resources. These discovery layers were a step forward since they combine resources and repositories that had been previously siloed. The underlying architecture allowed these siloed resources to be combined. That architecture included the MARC database and other databases that were either MARC-like or that could be mapped to DC for harvesting (and DC is based on MARC). None of these databases are FRBR-ized; that is, none of them can clearly link and distinguish the FRBR Group 1 entities (WEMI). It remains to be seen how discovery layers will fare in the linked data environment.

CONCLUSION

Information science was developed to deal with the explosion of scholarly publications[29] in the late nineteenth century, and this growth necessitated a way to organize this content and make it accessible to others. Cataloging and classification systems were developed to help address these needs. The principles of cataloging that were articulated in that era are the same principles followed today: that a user should be able to find something by author, title, or subject. These principles have been adapted in the past one hundred years to deal with many kinds of new materials and many kinds of technology, but the goals remain the same. The card catalog was revolutionary in its day because it could be easily updated. The form of the card catalog is found, in an expanded form, in MARC format and in the display of MARC records in library OPACs. In the 1970s, librarians became fluent in dealing with MARC and with OCLC, ILSs, and other metadata schemes. The same thing is occurring with FRBR, BIBFRAME, RDF, linked data, XML, and with any other standard, encoding format, language, syntax, or other tool or resource that is used for cataloging. The next change that comes will be discontinuous, based on a new model and a new concept. There are precursors and experiments that show what that new environment will be like. Information professionals will respond with creative problem solving and collaboration to give access to this data and to preserve it.

> " The principles of cataloging that were articulated in that era are the same principles followed today: that a user should be able to find something by author, title, or subject. "

Mary K. Bolin

NOTES

1. O. Lee Shiflett, *Origins of American Academic Librarianship* (Norwood, NJ: Ablex Publishing, 1981).
2. "MARC Standards," Network Standards and MARC Development Office, last modified March 16, 2017, https://www.loc.gov/marc/.
3. "WorldCat," OCLC, last modified 2017, https://www.oclc.org/en/worldcat.html.
4. Jason Thomale, "Interpreting MARC: Where's the Bibliographic Data?," *code{4}lib journal* no. 11 (September 21, 2010), http://journal.code4lib.org/articles/3832.
5. "Metadata Basics," Dublin Core Metadata Initiative, last modified 2017, http://dublincore.org/metadata-basics/.
6. "MODS, Metadata Object Description Schema," Library of Congress, last modified March 1, 2017, http://www.loc.gov/standards/mods/.
7. "TEI, Text Encoding Initiative," Text Encoding Initiative, last modified July 19, 2016, http://www.tei-c.org/index.xml.
8. "RDA-RSC," RDA Steering Committee, last modified February 8, 2016, http://www.rda-rsc.org/.
9. "Library of Congress Subject Headings," Library of Congress, Linked Data Service, last modified 2017, http://id.loc.gov/authorities/subjects.html.
10. "Library of Congress Classification," Library of Congress, last modified October 1, 2014, https://www.loc.gov/catdir/cpso/lcc.html.
11. "Dewey Services," OCLC, last modified 2017, http://www.oclc.org/en/dewey.html.
12. "Functional Requirements for Bibliographic Records," International Federation of Library Associations and Institutions, last modified April 5, 2016, https://www.ifla.org/publications/functional-requirements-for-bibliographic-records.
13. "RDF 1.1 Primer," World Wide Web Consortium, last modified June 24, 2014, https://www.w3.org/TR/2014/NOTE-rdf11-primer-20140225/.
14. Worldwide Web Consortium (W3C), https://www.w3schools.com/xml/xml_rdf.asp.
15. W3C, File: RDF graph for Eric Miller, PNG, last modified March, 2009, https://www.w3.org/TR/2004/REC-rdf-primer-20040210/.
16. Wikibooks, "Introduction to Library and Information Science/Information Organization," last modified May 2015, https://en.wikibooks.org/wiki/Introduction_to_Library_and_Information_Science/Information_Organization.
17. "Functional Requirements for Authority Data," International Federation of Library Associations and Institutions, last modified 2009, https://www.ifla.org/publications/functional-requirements-for-authority-data.
18. Library of Congress, MARC 21 Format for Authority Data, last modified May 2017, https://www.loc.gov/marc/authority/.
19. Library of Congress, MARC 21 Format for Bibliographic Data, last modified May 2017, http://www.loc.gov/marc/bibliographic/.
20. "Cataloging in Publication Program," Library of Congress, last modified 2017, https://www.loc.gov/publish/cip/.
21. "ONIX Overview," EDItEUR, last modified 2009, http://www.editeur.org/83/Overview/.
22. Tim Berners-Lee, "Linked Data," https://www.w3.org/DesignIssues/LinkedData.html.
23. "Overview of the BibFrame 2.0 Model," Library of Congress, last modified April 21, 2016, https://www.loc.gov/bibframe/docs/bibframe2-model.html.
24. Ibid.
25. "Model View: BIBFRAME Vocabulary," Library of Congress, http://bibframe.org/vocab-model.
26. "OCLC FAST," OCLC, last modified 2017, http://fast.oclc.org/.
27. Shea Tinn Yeh and Zhiping Walter, "Critical Success Factors for Integrated Library System Implementation in Academic Libraries: A Qualitative Study," *Information Technology & Libraries* 35, no. 3 (2016): 27–42, doi:10.6017/ital.v35i2.9255.
28. B. Thomsett-Scott and P. E. Reese, "Academic Libraries and Discovery Tools: A Survey of the Literature," *College & Undergraduate Libraries* 19, nos. 2–4 (2012): 123–43, doi:10.1080/10691316.2012.697009.
29. Shiflett, *Origins of American Academic Librarianship*.

13

Analog and Digital Curation and Preservation

Katherine Skinner

Chapter 13, "Analog and Digital Curation and Preservation," marks some of the most important events and shifts in thought regarding both theory and practice in curation and preservation. It also includes a look at the future as curation specialists grapple with evolving technology. Katherine Skinner brings deep familiarity with digital preservation and digital forensics practices in libraries, archives, and museums to provide a thorough overview of the key concepts, standards, principles, and decision-making processes involved in analog and digital curation as well as preservation theory and practices.

After defining the key terms associated with curation and preservation, Skinner explores the question of why preservation is important. She then provides a historical overview of preservation and the demand for action necessitated by the rise of technology and digital materials. Skinner also offers the reader an overview of early digital preservation efforts and highlights important digital preservation initiatives.

Skinner identifies the key concerns and the central debates and arguments in the field associated with digital preservation, including those affecting audiovisual materials, film, tape, and optical media. She further looks at the future and addresses the question: "What does preservation look like down the road?" Skinner enhances the chapter with resources and strategies for understanding the importance of curation and preservation of analog and digital content for their organization and the information user's access to that content in the future.

★   ★   ★

This chapter provides a broad overview of historical, theoretical, managerial, analytical, and practical aspects of curation and preservation. The chapter marks some of the most important events and shifts in thought regarding both theory and practice. It also provides a brief forecast of what might come in the near future as curation specialists continue to wrestle with difficult issues around the longevity, security, and authenticity of the content they manage. As with other aspects of the information profession, practitioners working in this subfield are grappling with new challenges as evolving technology continuously transforms the work they do and the issues they must address.

After completing this chapter, the reader should have an understanding of how to:

- describe the evolution of preservation theory and practice;
- identify the decision-making process involved in selection;
- summarize the causes of deterioration and loss for various types of information objects;
- identify key concepts and standards in digital preservation, including the OAIS model;
- define the principles of preservation policies;
- identify disaster planning, prevention, response, and recovery strategies; and
- locate and evaluate tools, research, and other resources on preservation.

DEFINING TERMS: CURATION AND PRESERVATION

Life cycle management. Curation. Preservation. Conservation. These terms describe actions information managers regularly undertake to ensure the longevity and accessibility of content. But what do these terms mean and how do they relate to one another?

Life cycle management refers to the full spectrum of activities a collections manager undertakes, from creation to disposal of an item or collection. The DCC Curation Life Cycle Model[1] offers one influential diagram to explain the broad range of tasks encompassed by this term.

Curation denotes the range of tasks involved in managing content, including such important steps as selection, acquisition, cataloging, and transformation. It is often conjoined with the term *digital* to mark the specific activities that are undertaken for digital objects.

Preservation overlaps with curation, and it designates the steps taken to ensure the long-term accessibility and usability of content, including (but not restricted to) activities that prevent content from deteriorating.

Conservation is the set of preservation practices used to rectify damages done to an object and/or the set of actions taken to slow an object's deterioration.

These terms sit in a hierarchy of sorts, with life cycle management at the broadest level, curation and preservation embedded within it as two essential, interrelated (and sometimes overlapping) sets of activities, and conservation as one way that preservation is accomplished.

Many practitioners use these terms interchangeably, but there are significant distinctions between them. For example, differentiating successfully between conservation and preservation requires an understanding of the role played by *change* in each. Preservation is about ensuring abiding access to an object or collection through whatever means is necessary. Conservation, as a subset of preservation, is ultimately about preventing or repairing changes to the object or collection.

Conservation practices include:

Preventive measures, such as placing a fragile document in a protective enclosure;
Remedial activities, such as paper repair and binding replacement; and
Collection-wide activities, such as fumigation and deacidification, meant to hinder decay and damage.

Preservation encompasses these actions but also includes practices that intentionally change an object or collection as is necessary to maintain it. Preservation includes conservation activities of all types (preventive, remedial, and collection-wide).

WHY DO INFORMATION MANAGERS PRESERVE CONTENT?

> " Preservation is about much more than memory; it is about reliable access. Information managers of all types—librarians, archivists, technologists, and curators—preserve content so that people living today and in the future can use it. "

The term *preservation* often takes on an antiquated quality, evoking a sense of memory. In reality, preservation is about much more than memory; it is about reliable access. Information managers of all types—librarians, archivists, technologists, and curators—preserve content so that people living today and in the future can use it.

The familiar adage "those who cannot remember the past are condemned to repeat it"[2] is one piece of the logic undergirding the impulse to preserve. Of equal importance, though, is the rationale that today's innovations depend on yesterday's discoveries. Limiting or losing access to content erodes the foundation of knowledge that is built iteratively. To say that more plainly, the ability to create new research, new services, or new products depends largely on the ability to remember and build upon what has come before. Accessing knowledge—both current and historical—is essential to this process.

Discussion Question

How might you justify an investment in preservation to your institution?

TEXTBOX 13.1

Preservation Activities

Refreshing: transferring content from one container to another container in the same format and media (e.g., copying a cassette tape to another cassette tape).
Reformatting: transferring the intellectual content of an object or collection from one medium to another (e.g., photocopying, microfilming, or digitizing).
Replication: making and distributing copies of content.
Emulation: creating an environment that enables digital content to be rendered in new software and hardware environments without changing the content file.

MILESTONES IN THE SUBFIELD OF PRESERVATION

The impetus for preserving content is far from new. Preservation practices can be traced back at least to the infamous Library of Alexandria in the third century BCE. Reformatting and repair examples date back to the earliest media forms and were certainly prevalent with efforts to repair the Library of Alexandria's collection of papyrus scrolls.

However, today's strong emphasis on preservation as a field of practice is a more recent phenomenon that dates back only to the 1950s and 1960s, when several occurrences prompted information managers to focus funding and attention on preservation in unprecedented ways. Notably, the preservation subfield as understood today has been undergirded by a sense of foreboding, threat, and destruction. Established in response to concerns about a crisis, a danger-driven sensibility continues to infuse much of the language around preservation, even today. The next subsections address several major milestones in the maturation of preservation as a subfield of practice in library and information science and demonstrate their connections to disaster relief and/or aversion.

Katherine Skinner

Brittle Books

The longevity of materials inscribed or printed on papyrus and linen/cotton rag-based paper was established over generations of use. In contrast, wood-pulp paper was a relatively unknown medium from a preservation standpoint, and chemists and specialists began to document their concerns about its stability by the early 1900s. Specifically, the highly acidic nature of wood-pulp paper differentiates it from its papyrus and linen/cotton rag predecessors, putting it at risk of deterioration. Pages become brittle and, when handled, in extreme cases will disintegrate into dust. The challenges associated with wood-pulp paper's stability drew early attention to the process of preservation.

The Florence Flood

In 1966, Italy's Arno River flooded Florence,[3] damaging thousands of library and museum collections. The international response to this catastrophe was dramatic.[4] Representatives from hundreds of libraries and museums around the world contributed to the salvage efforts. Conservators experimented with many different techniques to restore a wide variety of objects. The event provided a distressing example of the extensive damage flooding could do to collections. It also created a research environment where practices and protocols that greatly influenced the emerging field of preservation were established.

National Historic Preservation Act (United States)

The convergence of the brittle books crisis and the Florence flood helped to speed the professionalism of preservation practices (see also chapter 13: "Historical Context for Brittle Books" in the online supplement). The 1966 passage of the National Historic Preservation Act in the United States[5] emphasized preservation as a disaster response. As a consequence:

- key U.S. institutions[6] established preservation divisions by the early 1970s,[7]
- library science programs at U.S. universities developed and offered dozens of preservation courses,
- professional associations established new committees focused on preservation,[8] and
- numerous conservation programs and research labs were founded.[9]

In addition, continued concerns about the instability of acid-based paper drove additional activities throughout the field,[10] which focused on the preservation microfilming of endangered "brittle" papers and the advocacy campaign to promote acid-free paper adoption in the publishing industry.[11]

DIGITAL PRESERVATION

Although the earliest digital preservation efforts began in national archives and other cultural establishments in the 1960s,[12] concerns about the longevity (or the lack thereof) of digital content formats were raised to the level of national prominence in the United States in 1994, when the Research Libraries Group and the Commission on Preservation and Access cocreated the Task Force on Digital Archiving. This group was charged with studying how best to provide "continued access indefinitely into the future of records stored in digital electronic form."[13]

The Task Force, which included representatives from libraries, museums, foundations, archives, societies, government, and industry, published a groundbreaking report in 1996 *Preserving Digital Information.*[14] The report described the dire need for coordination of resources and infrastructure across broad communities of stewards to establish the digital preservation standards, certification procedures, and deep infrastructure necessary to preserve digital content.

Examples of International Collaborations

1998: Stanford University Library developed and released the Open Source software "Lots of Copies Keep Stuff Safe" (LOCKSS)[15]—the world's first community-based preservation network.

2000: The Consultative Committee for Space Data Systems (CCSDS)[16] produced the Reference Model for an Open Archival Information System[17] (first circulated as the Draft International Standard).

2004: The National Digital Information Infrastructure and Preservation Program (NDIIPP)[18] made multimillion-dollar preservation awards launched by the Library of Congress.

2005: The Preservation Metadata Implementation Strategies (PREMIS)[19] were developed to tie together the varied international efforts around preservation metadata standards development.

Funding provided by private foundations and federal agencies established a large number of initiatives around digital preservation methodologies and infrastructures by the late 1990s and early 2000s. Many of these initiatives stressed the need for collaboration, and most of the successful standards and early operations were developed through national or international collaborations.

Digital Preservation Milestones

Four key digital preservation initiatives bear significant influence in today's digital preservation practices:

Open Archival Information System (OAIS): describes both the organizational and technical aspects of a preservation approach and model. Released by the Consultative Committee for Space Data Systems (CCSDS) in 2000 and as an ISO standard in 2003,[20] it provides the core human- and system-level components of a preservation archive (analog or digital) and provides a set of standard vocabulary that is now used across many different information management fields to talk about the various roles and operations within a preservation system. Such commonly understood concepts as Submission Information Packages (SIPs) and producers were first established within this model.

Preservation Metadata Implementation Strategies (PREMIS): provides a data dictionary and resources to assist information managers in the implementation of preservation metadata efforts. Established as a working group by the Online Computer Library Center (OCLC) and the Research Libraries Group (RLG), with its report and data dictionary first released in 2005, PREMIS documentation is housed and maintained by the Library of Congress.

The Audit and Certification of Trustworthy Digital Repositories standard (ISO 16363):[21] provides metrics for certifying preservation archives. It is complemented by *Requirements for Bodies Providing Audit and Certification (ISO 16919)*,[22] which documents how to certify auditors to exercise this standard.

Digital Preservation Outreach and Education (DPOE):[23] developed by the Library of Congress in 2010 as a concerted effort to spread the knowledge and practice of digital preservation throughout the United States. A "Train-the-Trainer"[24] program developed in 2011 has reached thousands of practitioners throughout the United States and has fostered a national network of digital stewardship.

Digital content is notoriously ephemeral and easily compromised. Digital preservation focuses on a wide range of risk factors in order to offset the chances of unintended change to or loss of files. Key concerns addressed by digital preservation include the following:

Obsolescence: the way that both storage media and file types change so quickly that they may become unusable. Think, for example, about an eight-inch floppy disk with its WordPerfect files from the 1980s. Both the disk and the files may still be intact, but they are unrenderable due to a lack of the necessary equipment and software/operating system components to read them.

Media failure: the "death" of a media component (computer, server, hard drive, etc.) due to any system failure, especially from physical loss (e.g., a flood or fire that takes out a computer or server entirely).

Security threats: the theft, alteration, or deletion of historically significant content (e.g., a person changes a sensitive government document).

Approaches to digital preservation infrastructures vary widely, with some preservation archives adopting centralized infrastructures, and others adopting distributed infrastructures that intentionally spread risk by housing infrastructure elements (e.g., servers) in different physical locations. Debates and issues have raged within the community regarding the value and distinctions between bit-level preservation (preserving the strings of 0s and 1s that comprise a file) and other preservation components more commonly referred to as curation, including format migration and metadata creation. Currently, most libraries and archives address both of these essential components in their digital preservation planning and implementation efforts.

> Digital content is notoriously ephemeral and easily compromised. Digital preservation focuses on a wide range of risk factors in order to offset the chances of unintended change to or loss of files.

TEXTBOX 13.3

Timeline of Preservation Practices

Third century BCE: Library of Alexandria
Second century CE: paper (rag-based) invented in China
Eleventh century: Bi Sheng develops movable type printing technology in China
Twelfth century: paper carried to Europe by Arab traders
Fourteenth century: Europe primarily uses rag-based paper, not animal skins, for written content
Fifteenth century: Johannes Gutenberg develops the European printing press
1850s: shortage of linen and cotton rag paper; development of wood-pulp paper
Nineteenth century: steam-powered paper-making machines and the steam-powered rotary press together provide power for industrial-scale printing
1854: first U.S. public library founded in Boston, Massachusetts
1930: William J. Barrow first published information about acid paper issues
1950: Federal Records Act includes "machine-readable materials"
1966: Florence Flood and subsequent salvage/rescue missions; National Historic Preservation Act passed in the United States
1982: U.S. Newspaper Program launched (microfilm-based)
2001: OAIS Reference Model issued by CCSDS
2013: surpassed 4.4 Zetabytes of digital content (EMC)
2016: DataRefuge hackathons begin as a grassroots effort to preserve at-risk digital science datasets

---

AUDIOVISUAL CONTENT PRESERVATION

Audiovisual (A/V) content preservation refers to efforts to stabilize and maintain a wide variety of A/V content, or content that stores and/or reproduces sight and/or sound. The means to preserve and conserve audiovisual content vary widely, depending upon the recording format—film, tape, or digital media.

There are significant differences between these formats. Think, for example, of the media used for sound recordings over the last century, which include the tinfoil phonograph, wax cylinders, LPs, a range of magnetic tape devices, cassette tapes, CDs, and digital audio files. Within each of these formats are additional, substantive differences in quality that depend upon their manufacturers.

> The means to preserve and conserve audiovisual content vary widely, depending upon the recording format—film, tape, or digital media.

Concerns in A/V preservation range from the rapid obsolescence of media to the deterioration of the media themselves. For example, eight-track recordings became obsolete when companies ceased to manufacture the devices used to play them in the 1980s. The main cause of this shift away from the eight-track was the market's transition to cassette tapes and players. The cassette tape, however, soon proved to be a quick-loss media device, one that lost sound quality and fidelity upon each playback, each fast-forwarding, and each rewinding.

Although the mechanics of conservation and preservation in the audiovisual realm tend to be specific to the media type, common principles undergird their preservation efforts. For example, A/V preservation plans must include:

- specific steps around care and handling (limiting use, storing in cool, humidity-controlled, clean environments),
- making multiple copies (at least two copies,[25] stored separately), and
- careful monitoring to ensure deterioration is identified and rectified regularly.

Common Media Types and Their Preservation Challenges

Film

Film (negatives, reels, etc.) consists of three core components:

1. a layer of color dye or silver (black-and-white film),
2. gelatin emulsion that acts as a binder for the image dye, and
3. a clear plastic base.

A wide variety of chemical substances have been used in film production over time, and many of the preservation challenges inherent in films are caused by the deterioration of these substances.

Common film issues include:

Nitrate deterioration: Perhaps the most dramatic hazard in film preservation is that of nitrate deterioration. Used until the early 1950s, cellulose nitrate film stock deteriorates at moderately high temperatures (e.g., over 106°F) and will spontaneously combust and burn.[26] This process can be slowed through the use of cold storage.

Acetate Deterioration (vinegar syndrome): This safety film was introduced as an alternative to its highly flammable predecessor, nitrate film. Acetate was popularized in 35 mm, 16 mm, and 8 mm sizes, and has been used prevalently by professionals and amateurs alike. When stored in non-ideal conditions, acetate film quickly disintegrates through "vinegar syndrome." The symptoms of this deterioration are a vinegar scent, followed by shrinkage and buckling of the film. Many conservationists use A-D Strips to identify vinegar syndrome before the smell arises.

Fading: Color dye films, in particular, will fade due to chemical changes and decomposition, even in normal room-temperature environments. As with nitrate and acetate deterioration, this process can be slowed substantially by the use of cold storage.

Physical damage: Usage and storage can cause myriad forms of physical damage. Most can be avoided through applying archival standards to the handling of a collection.

Tape

Magnetic tape is composed of several layers of materials:

1. A top coat that is the polymer binder in which the magnetic "pigment" is embedded (the top coat also includes lubricant, a head-cleaning agent, and carbon black, all of which aid in playback).
2. The tape backing, which provides the substance to hold the binder and magnetic pigment. Sometimes a third layer called the "back coat" is added to cut down on friction and enable the tape to wind properly. The tape is stored on a reel and held in a tape pack.

Problems that regularly arise in the preservation of tape are as follows:

Lubricant loss: Lubricants are added to the binder of a tape during the manufacturing process. This helps to ensure friction does not compromise the tape. Over time, and with many playbacks of a tape, the lubricant wears down. Relubrication can sometimes salvage severely degraded magnetic tapes.

Dust damage: If magnetic tape becomes dusty, the dust will scratch the oxide layer of the tape during playback.

Binder break-down (sticky-shed syndrome): In the mid-seventies, half of the leading tape manufacturers changed the chemical composition of the binder used in their tape manufacturing processes. The new binder later proved unstable; the coating of the tape becomes sticky and sheds oxide on its playback equipment in humid conditions.

Optical Media

Compact Disks (CDs) and Digital Video Discs (DVDs) are digital optical disc data storage formats. The form includes a polycarbonate (usually) plastic component with a center spindle hole, upon which are multiple recording areas. These areas are encoded with data (machine readable) as "pits," or small indentations. This data layer may be metallic or dye-based. A layer of aluminum or gold is applied to the top surface, and is protected by a coat of lacquer.

CDs, in particular, were heralded as a preservation medium at their initial release; however, they have proven highly susceptible to multiple forms of damage and loss including scratches, label-based problems, and corrosion of the metal layer. Even archival-quality gold CDs and DVDs are no longer considered preservation media by most experts, though when they are stored in cold, dry conditions, they may survive up to a century. They are used most widely in memory institutions to provide users with access copies of digital material (they are no longer used as storage masters).

Problems that regularly arise in the preservation of CDs and DVDs are as follows:

Scratches: During normal handling, CDs and DVDs often become scratched. When the scratches occur on the clear side of the disc, they can often be repaired through plastic refills or polishing.

Dye-fading: When the data layer is made of dye (rather than metal), the dye sometimes fades over time, rendering the data unreadable.

Bonding failure: The bonding on the edges of CDs and DVDs is often unstable and fails over time, allowing moisture and gases to permeate the data area of the disc, causing failure.

Lack of production standards: CDs and DVDs are produced in many factories, with highly variable quality-control standards. As a result, a batch of CDs or DVDs may be compromised. Archivists are encouraged to ensure that they make multiple copies (one master, a working copy, and a safety copy is a good "rule of three") and use CDs or DVDs from different batches for these three copies whenever possible.

Check out a list of specific types of media (specifically film, tape, and optical media) and the specific preservation challenges they entail in chapter 13 of the online supplement.

PRESERVATION THEORY AND PRACTICES

The DPOE curriculum (funded by the Institute of Museum and Library Services and initially developed by Nancy McGovern in cooperation with the Office of Strategic Initiatives at the Library of Congress), provides a solid introduction to digital preservation theory and practice.[27] The mission of DPOE is to "foster national outreach and education to encourage individuals and organizations to actively preserve their digital content, building on a collaborative network of instructors, contributors, and institutional partners."[28]

DPOE curriculum focuses on six steps in the preservation workflow:

1. *Identify:* What digital content do you have? Focusing on this question, the identify module helps practitioners think about how to create an inventory of digital content.
2. *Select:* What portion of that content will be preserved? The select module helps practitioners determine what selection/appraisal/acquisition principles make the most sense for their local collections.
3. *Store:* How should your content be stored for the long term? The store module describes optimal content storage, including what content to store (files plus metadata, encoded as one object), describes what well-managed collections look like, and discusses the optimal storage media options and number of copies recommended for long-term archiving.
4. *Protect:* What steps are needed to protect your digital content? The protect module covers the major hazards for digital content (including change and loss, obsolescence of media, inappropriate access, and various disaster scenarios) and details best practices for ensuring content remains safe, authentic, and trustworthy over time.
5. *Manage:* What provisions are needed for long-term management? The manage module describes management roles—including what staff positions should be involved in preservation, how practices should be documented at the organizational level, how funding impacts preservation, and what standards conformance and good practice should include.
6. *Provide:* How should your content be made available over time? This final module focuses on good practices for long-term access to preserved content by users. It discusses organizational responsibilities, access policies, how to understand user needs and expectations (current and future), how to handle intellectual property (IP) and other legal issues, and how to effectively sustain both the preservation program and the collections it protects.

Discussion Questions

How does selection work as a principle of preservation? What effects (intentional or not) might selection have on historical perspectives of a particular moment in time?

FUTURE OF PRESERVATION

The future of preservation always includes great uncertainty regarding what formats will persist, but also great certainty that there will be a need for preservationists of all kinds across all types of information organizations. With our increased reliance on ephemeral digital content comes further emphasis on preservation across all government, commercial, cultural, and scientific sectors.

> The future of preservation always includes great uncertainty regarding what formats will persist, but also great certainty that there will be a need for preservationists of all kinds across all types of information organizations.

Some of the emerging concerns, efforts, and practices in today's preservation environment are described below. They provide a glimpse into how rapidly the preservation environment is changing, how quickly preservationists must grapple with new challenges, and new areas where preservationists will be working in the future.

Web Archiving

Web archiving is the process of capturing and preserving portions of the World Wide Web for historical purposes. Many experts argue that today, web archiving is among the least attended to and most important frontiers of preservation. Although tools and processes for web archiving are maturing, there are myriad hindrances to the process itself, including intellectual property barriers, variability in how pages render for different viewers, and the inaccessibility of the "Deep Web" (the majority of the web cannot be found, crawled, or indexed because it is in databases or other web service environments). The International Internet Preservation Consortium (IIPC)[29] is the broadest network of web archiving practitioners, and it serves as a hub where tools, standards, and practices are exchanged and documented by these practitioners. Some of the best established (and arguably most important) web archiving initiatives today include:

* The Wayback Machine,[30] a free historical resource provided by the U.S. nonprofit organization Internet Archive, making available a set of crawling and archiving snapshots of websites across the internet that date back to 1996.
* Human Rights Web Archive (Columbia University),[31] which captures and preserves at-risk websites that chronicle human rights violations.
* End of Term Web Archive, a project of the California Digital Library, Internet Archive, Library of Congress, University of North Texas, and U.S. Government Publishing Office,[32] in which these institutions crawl all of the U.S. federal web domains at each presidential transition.

"Data Rescue" Efforts

Concerns about the accessibility and preservation of federal data (including sources hosted by federal agencies) in the United States following the 2016 election prompted a grassroots response from many researchers, scholars, librarians, archivists, citizen scientists, and activists, who began collecting and distributing this data to ensure it remains available for future researchers. Two key examples are these:

* DataRefuge (University of Pennsylvania)[33] is building a refuge for federal climate and environmental data in the United States; it has hosted dozens of "Data Rescue" events worldwide in its first six months.
* Preservation of Electronic Government Information (University of North Texas, U.S. Government Publishing Office, University of North Carolina at Greensboro, Council for Research Libraries)[34] is focused on the preservation of at-risk government digital information.

Newspaper/News Preservation

For centuries, memory organizations—including libraries, archives, and historical societies—have dependably acquired, provided access to, and preserved print news for future researchers. As news has transitioned from print-only to multimedia, and as consolidation has transformed the news industry from small family-owned papers to large conglomerates, most of these preservation relationships and workflows have broken. Today's news exists primarily in digital forms that are created and disseminated using content management systems and e-publishing platforms. Contained in a cacophony of file types and bitstreams, this news content is more fragile and ephemeral than the print content of the recent past. Libraries today are grappling with how best to collect, organize, and preserve this content for tomorrow's researchers.

Compounding the problems presented by today's news sources, many libraries and archives have also now digitized their historical physical news collections, discarding the physical copies in the process. The resulting digital files, in many cases, represent the only extant copies of historical newspapers. Finding the resources (staff time, infrastructure, finances) to support the long-term preservation of these files is a key challenge for many libraries today—and their collections hang in the balance. The Reynolds Journalism Institute, the University of Missouri Libraries, and the Educopia Institute have worked in partnership to raise awareness of these issues in a series of projects; the Reynolds Journalism Institute also hosts the "Dodging the Memory Hole" annual conference to encourage newspaper owners, journalists, librarians, historians, and technologists to prioritize and collaborate on digital preservation.[35]

Digital Forensics

Digital forensic science is concerned with recovering data from digital devices. First prevalent in criminal investigations of computer-based crimes in the 1980s, applications of digital forensics tools now regularly extend to archival institutions. For these memory organizations, forensics tools and methods must address two fundamental issues that are not addressed by the digital forensics industry, but are part of the key practices of preservationists: workflows for incorporating forensic practices into the archival/library/museum content life cycle, and mechanisms for providing public access to the recovered data. The BitCurator Open Source software,[36] developed by the University of North Carolina at Chapel Hill School of Information and Library Science and the Maryland Institute for Technology in the Humanities, is the most prevalent set of forensics documentation, tools, and approaches in the library, archives, and museum fields.

Hypermedia and Digital Art

Documenting and preserving variable media, such as hypermedia and digital art installations, requires collective approaches that blend art, science, and technology. Many of the pathbreaking publications and artworks of the 1960s forward have occurred in digital forms, and they are notoriously difficult to archive due to the constant technological changes that impact their contexts and compromise their renderability. Efforts to address one of the most complex digital preservation challenges of the early twenty-first century thus far have yielded such experiments as the Archive of Digital Art (ADA, formerly known as the Database of Virtual Art).[37]

See textbox 13.4 for examples of Digital Art Preservation and Game Preservation.

Examples of Game Preservation

Game preservation has been a vibrant subfield of preservation activity since the 1980s. Such projects include:

- Preserving Virtual Worlds (University of Illinois, Rochester Institute of Technology, Stanford University, and University of Maryland)[38] work on computer gaming and interactive fiction as blurred genres of content.
- 1980-games.com and DOSGamesArchive.com emulate game environments of the past.
- The American Classic Arcade Museum[39] preserves the hardware and software environments in physical form.

Social Media

The challenges of preserving social media come in three main forms: intellectual property and legal issues around privacy for material that is produced in such a public arena; technological challenges; and volume/speed of creation. In 2010, one of the major social media sites—Twitter—donated all of its public tweets to the Library of Congress for preservation and research.[40]

CONCLUSION

Curation and preservation are information management "must knows" for caretakers of both analog and digital content types. This chapter has introduced these related concepts, highlighted key milestones in preservation development, and provided an overview of current preservation practices across a range of media types. It has also described various "real-world" scenarios in which curation and preservation take place on a routine basis and the significant work ahead for libraries, archives, and all other curation and preservation realms.

NOTES

1. "DCC Curation Life Cycle Model," Digital Curation Centre, 2017, http://www.dcc.ac.uk/resources/curation-lifecycle-model.
2. "George Santayana," *Wikipedia*, last edited January 22, 2018, https://en.wikipedia.org/wiki/George_Santayana.
3. "1966 Flood of the Arno," *Wikipedia*, last edited January 20, 2018, https://en.wikipedia.org/wiki/1966_flood_of_the_Arno.
4. Ibid.
5. National Historic Preservation Act of 1966, as amended through 2006, http://www.achp.gov/docs/nhpa%202008-final.pdf.
6. Library of Congress, Yale University, and the New York Public Library.
7. George Bobinski, *Libraries and Librarianship: Sixty Years of Challenge and Change, 1945–2005* (New York: Scarecrow Press, 2007), 105–10.
8. ALA's "Committee on Preservation of Library Materials," 1970; AIC's "Book and Paper Group," 1980; CLR's "Commission on Preservation and Access," 1986.
9. Bobinski, *Libraries and Librarianship*; NEDCC, "History of the Northeast Document Conservation Center," http://www.nedcc.org/about/history/overview; NEDCC, "What Is Preservation," Preservation 101, http://unfacilitated.preservation101.org/session1/expl_whatis-libraries.asp.

10. See, for example, the establishment of the National Endowment for the Humanities (NEH) U.S. News-paper Program in 1982. See also Paul Conway, *Preservation in the Digital World*, CLIR, Pub 62, 1996, available at https://www.clir.org/pubs/reports/reports/conway2/index.html.

11. Bobinski, *Libraries and Librarianship*.

12. Anne R. Kenney and Nancy Y. McGovern, "The Five Organizational Stages of Digital Preservation," 2003, https://quod.lib.umich.edu/cgi/t/text/text-idx?c=spobooks;idno=bbv9812.0001.001;rgn=div1;view=text;cc=spobooks;node=bbv9812.0001.001%3A11.

13. John Garrett and Donald Waters, *Preserving Digital Information: Report of the Task Force on Archiving of Digital Information* (Washington, DC: CLIR, 1996), iii, https://www.clir.org/pubs/reports/pub63waters garrett.pdf.

14. Ibid.

15. "LOCKSS: Lots of Copies Keeps Stuff Safe," LOCKSS, accessed September 18, 2017, https://www.lockss .org/.

16. "The Consultative Committee for Space Data Systems," CCSDS, 2017, https://public.ccsds.org/default .aspx.

17. "Reference Model for an Open Archival Information System (OASIS), CCSDS, 2012, https://public .ccsds.org/pubs/650x0m2.pdf.

18. "National Digital Information Infrastructure and Preservation Program," *Wikipedia*, lasted edited August 10, 2017, https://en.wikipedia.org/wiki/National_Digital_Information_Infrastructure_and_Preserva tion_Program.

19. "PREMIS," Library of Congress, accessed September 18, 2017, https://www.loc.gov/standards/premis/.

20. ISO 14721:2003. For the current version of ISO 14721:2012, https://www.iso.org/standard/57284.html, see the identical text here: Reference Model for an Open Archival Information System (OAIS), Recom-mended Practice, CCSDS 650.0-M-2 (Magenta Book) Issue 2, June 2012.

21. "Audit and Certification of Trustworthy Digital Repositories," CCSDS, 2011, https://public.ccsds.org/ pubs/652x0m1.pdf.

22. "ISO 16919:2014," accessed September 18, 2017, https://www.iso.org/standard/57950.html.

23. "Digital Preservation Outreach and Education," Library of Congress, accessed September 18, 2017, http://www.digitalpreservation.gov/education/.

24. Ibid.

25. U.S. Copyright law allows up to three copies of a work to be made by cultural institutions for works that are endangered or damaged, so long as a replacement is not easily available [17 USCA 108(c)], https:// www.gpo.gov/fdsys/granule/USCODE-2011-title17/USCODE-2011-title17-chap1-sec108.

26. "Care, Handling, and Storage of Motion Picture Film," Library of Congress, accessed September 18, 2017, http://www.loc.gov/preservation/care/film.html.

27. The Digital Preservation Outreach and Education curriculum, http://www.digitalpreservation.gov/edu cation/curriculum.html.

28. George Coulbourne, "DPOE handout," http://www.digitalpreservation.gov/education/documents/ DPOE_handout.pdf.

29. International Internet Preservation Consortium, http://netpreserve.org/.

30. "Wayback Machine," Internet Archive, 2014, https://archive.org/web/.

31. "Human Rights Web Archive," Columbia University Libraries, 2012, https://hrwa.cul.columbia.edu/.

32. "End of Term Web Archive, US Federal Web Domain at Presidential Transitions," accessed September 18, 2017, http://eotarchive.cdlib.org/.

33. "DATAREFUGE," PPEH Lab, accessed September 18, 2017, http://www.ppehlab.org/datarefuge/.

34. "Preservation of Electronic Government Information (PEGI)," Center for Research Libraries Global Re-sources Network, accessed September 18, 2017, https://www.crl.edu/preservation-electronic-govern ment-information-pegi.

35. Donald W. Reynolds Journalism Institute, https://www.rjionline.org/events/dodging-the-memory -hole-2017; Abbey Potter, "Dodge That Memory Hole: Saving Digital News," *Signal*, June 2, 2015, https://blogs.loc.gov/thesignal/2015/06/dodge-that-memory-hole-saving-digital-news/.

36. Christopher Lee and Kam Woods, BitCurator, 2017, GitHub repository, https://bitcurator.github.io/.
37. Archive of Digital Art, http://www.virtualart.at/nc/home.html.
38. "Preserving Virtual Worlds," Library of Congress, accessed September 18, 2017, http://www.digitalpres
    ervation.gov/partners/pvw.html.
39. American Classic Arcade Museum, http://www.classicarcademuseum.org/.
40. Matt Raymond, "How Tweet It Is! Library Acquires Entire Twitter Archive," *Library of Congress Blog*, April
    14, 2010, http://blogs.loc.gov/loc/2010/04/how-tweet-it-is-library-acquires-entire-twitter-archive/.

14

User Experience

Courtney McDonald

Chapter 14, "User Experience," focuses on the key product of the information organization: the user. To thrive as the community anchor, information organizations must have a keen understanding of how to serve users. Courtney McDonald, librarian and author of Putting the User First, *defines user experience, explores user-centered design principles and excellence in practice, and highlights essential techniques for identifying, implementing, and assessing improvements in user experience, online or in person. Her expert overview makes clear that information professionals must recognize that all aspects of the user experience have an impact on what feelings, thoughts, and judgments the end user takes away from the encounter. Thus, determining how to make the user experience successful is key to any information professional's education and experience.*

McDonald notes several central components of user experience, such as the importance of identifying and evaluating touchpoints and channels; maintaining a compatible, comfortable, and welcoming user space; utilizing design thinking; and engaging with the user. Perhaps most importantly, she reminds information professionals that the user is not "us."

McDonald moves beyond the technical expertise needed to craft the best user experience and focuses on the personal and social skills an information professional needs: curiosity, empathy, clear communication, and effective collaboration. Readers of this chapter come away with real-world techniques to help identify the user's needs. McDonald concludes that information professionals must be willing to continually evaluate the resources and services offered to users and invite users to help cocreate services. This is the best recipe for meeting user needs and providing a great user experience.

★   ★   ★

Each day, the places someone goes, the people they encounter, and the things they do combine in their perceptions to create an overall "experience." Information organizations are actively creating user experiences every day, intentionally or not. Information professionals create critical connections between end users and information organizations through the systems and data that describe the organization's services (e.g., collections, programs, facilities, and policies) and support its constituents (those directly and indirectly served by the organization).

User experience can be defined in different ways. Jesse James Garrett, in his seminal book *The Elements of User Experience*, defines user experience (UX) simply: "how the product behaves and is used in the real world."[1] Within library and information science (LIS) literature, Steven Bell describes UX as "crafting systemic library experiences designed to deliver totality."[2] This chapter focuses on user experience in both contexts and why these definitions matter when talking about information services and today's information user. After completing this chapter, the reader should have an understanding of:

- what is meant by user experience,
- the connections between user-centered design principles and excellence in practice within key areas of information practice, and
- essential techniques for identifying, implementing, and assessing improvements in user experience for information organizations, online or in person.

BEYOND THE WEB: DEFINING "USER EXPERIENCE" MORE BROADLY

While usability—how effectively, efficiently, and satisfactorily a user can interact with a user interface—is an important part of user experience, UX encompasses more than simply whether an interface is usable. In 2004, information architect Peter Morville visualized the complex relationships between various key factors for UX in the user experience honeycomb (figure 14.1).[3]

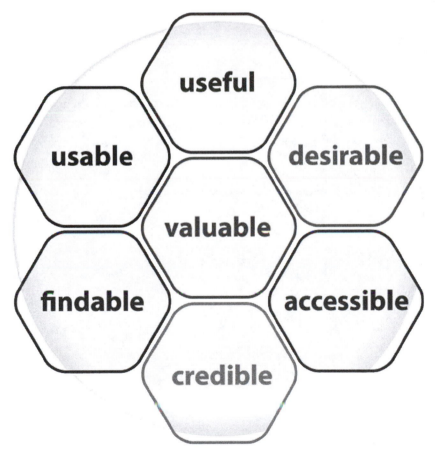

Figure 14.1 User Experience Honeycomb. *CC by 2.0. Peter Morville, "User Experience Design." Semantic Studios. 2004. http://semanticstudios.com/user_experience_design/.*

When designing for a good user experience, each of the facets within the honeycomb must be present. Steven Bell also echoes the call to go beyond usability: "The user experience, from my perspective, is about much more than usability. It's about designing an intentional, well-thought-out experience that ensures the community member has a consistently great library experience at every touchpoint."[4]

Touchpoints, Channels, and More

A touchpoint is a situated, specific task interaction between a person and an information organization via any one of a large number of possible static, virtual, or human agents.[5] These possible agents are described as channels: "the medium of interaction between a customer and an organization."[6] Not to be confused with devices, channels facilitate different modes of interaction or communication, even via a single device. To put this into perspective, check out textbox 14.1, which demonstrates the various modes of interaction via a single mobile phone.

> It is important to remember that while all the elements of the end user's experience may not be directly within the information organization's control, all aspects of the experience can and do have an impact on what feelings, thoughts, and judgments the end user takes away from the encounter.

Many techniques can be applied to help think through these various touchpoints, channels, and paths from the patron perspective. One of these is the journey map:

A customer journey map is a very simple idea: a diagram that illustrates the steps your customer(s) go through in engaging with your company, whether it be a product, an online experience, retail experience, or a service, or any combination. The more touchpoints you have, the more complicated—but necessary—such a map becomes.[7]

It is important to remember that while all the elements of the end user's experience may not be directly within the information organization's control, all aspects of the experience can and do have an impact on what feelings, thoughts, and judgments the end user takes away from the encounter. See also appendix 14.1: "Journey Mapping Exercise."

TEXTBOX 14.1

Mobile Phone Channels

A mobile phone allows users to select whether they interact with their information organization via any (or all) of these seven possible channels:

- mobile app
- website or web application, such as an online catalog
- social media
- e-mail
- text message
- telephone
- instant messaging service

That is a lot of channels!

User Experience and Physical Spaces

The physical location through which information organizations provide access to collections and services is an essential aspect of the overall user experience. Maintaining consistency for cross-channel experiences requires ensuring that physical and virtual environments are well integrated and present a compatible vocabulary, tone, and mood.

Information organizations may or may not directly manage services that are provided within their buildings; for example, a local business might run the café. Not infrequently, across all types of information organizations, the state of the facilities—well maintained, outdated, worn, convenient, awkward—is outside the direct control of the information professional. In this situation, initiating renovations, coordinating custodial services, or even improving signage might be the domain of a group external to the information organization. At Oregon State University, for example, information professionals have given time and attention to examining and improving "wayfinding," or how users find their way through a space, through revising signage and implementing a concierge service, among other efforts.[8]

In their recent article *Leading from the Library Loo: An Illustrated, Documented Guide to New York City Academic Library Bathrooms*, Jennifer Poggiali and Stephanie Margolin discuss the important role of restroom facilities in relation to an information organization's overall user experience, noting that modern, clean, and accessible facilities "promote the comfort of our students and enable them to study and learn within our libraries. That should be our goal for all the areas in our libraries—even the lowly restroom."[9]

Discussion Question

Recently some debate has arisen in the profession as to what terminology is most appropriate to refer to those people whom information organizations serve. What advantages or disadvantages do you see to adopting any of the following potential descriptors when referring to user experience?

- user
- constituent
- customer
- member
- patron

RELATED AREAS OF STUDY AND PRACTICE

Designing for great user experience relates closely to several areas of study and practice, situated across various disciplines and professional specializations. This section highlights just a few areas likely to provide insights that are applicable to the day-to-day work of information organizations and information professionals, specifically information architecture and interaction design, design thinking, service design, and content strategy.

Information Architecture and Interaction Design

Information architecture and interaction design share an emphasis on defining patterns and sequences in which options will be presented to users. Interaction design concerns the options involved in performing and completing tasks. Information architecture (IA) deals with the options involved in conveying information to a user.[10]

Information architecture is often covered as part of an information science curriculum and is closely related to library science, among other disciplines. Also related to IA is interaction design, which is "concerned with describing possible user behavior and defining how the system will accommodate and respond to that behavior."[11] In *About Face: The Essentials of Interaction Design*, Cooper et al. clarify what is meant by design in this context: "Interaction design isn't merely a matter of aesthetic choice; rather, it is based on an understanding of users and cognitive principles . . . quite amenable to a repeatable process of analysis and synthesis."[12]

Design Thinking

In the freely downloadable document *Design Thinking for Libraries: A Toolkit for Patron-Centered Design*, design thinking is defined as follows:

> Design thinking is a creative approach, or a series of steps that will help you design meaningful solutions for your library . . . a deeply empathic and intuitive process that taps into abilities we inherently all have but often overlook. In other words, you don't have to be a designer to use creative tools to solve problems. Instead, design thinking relies on our ability to be intuitive, to recognize patterns, to construct ideas that resonate emotionally and rationally, and to be expressive through action.[13]

Design thinking processes consistently involve three main phases: inspiration, ideation, and iteration (see also chapter 23: "Innovative Library and Information Services: The Design Thinking Process").

Check This Out

Design Thinking for Libraries: A Toolkit for Patron-Centered Design. Visit: http://designthinking forlibraries.com/.

Service Design

In a 2015 article on service design in libraries, Joe Marquez and Annie Downey define service design as "a holistic, co-creative, and user-centered approach to understanding customer behavior for the creation or refining of services."[14] By "co-creative," Marquez and Downey mean that information professionals work directly with patrons to identify issues, brainstorm solutions, create and test prototypes, and implement changes. They further note, "Within the context of service design in libraries, the collections and physical space of the library are services in the same way that reference and circulation are services. In order to evaluate these services, librarians need to focus on users' experiences."[15]

Content Strategy

Kristina Halvorson and Melissa Rach define content strategy quite succinctly: "Content is what the user came to read, learn, see, or experience. . . . Content strategy guides your plans for the creation, delivery, and governance of content."[16] Information professionals are deeply familiar with the idea that content exists in many forms in the context of collections—but what about content created on behalf of the organization? Finding a unified voice across a diverse group of colleagues with different interests, responsibilities, and availability can be challenging. A robust content strategy is an important tool in providing the best service to constituent communities of information organizations.

IN PRACTICE: INFORMATION ORGANIZATIONS AND USER EXPERIENCE DESIGN

While there are challenges and circumstances specific to the context of information organizations, the overarching principles and best practices for planning, creating, assessing, and maintaining a great user experience are the same as they would be for any other organization. In their 2014 book, *Useful, Usable, Desirable: Applying User Experience Design to Your Library*, Aaron Schmidt and Amanda Etches outlined eight "Principles of Library User Experience Design" (see textbox 14.3).[17]

TEXTBOX 14.3

Principles of Library User Experience Design

1. You are not your user.
2. The user is not broken.
3. A good user experience requires research.
4. Building a good user experience requires empathy.
5. A good user experience must be easy before it can be interesting.
6. Good user experience design is universal.
7. Good user experience design is intentional.
8. Good user experience design is holistic.

Several of these concepts have already been touched upon in this chapter, such as the importance of intentional, holistic design and the value in conducting research about and with users to develop effective, useful, desirable products, and services.

Expertise and UX Work: You Are Not Your User, and The User Is Not Broken

Organizing, finding, preserving, retrieving, managing, and evaluating information in a variety of formats through numerous and varied systems is a specific and situated expertise cultivated and developed by information professionals. There is a great deal of research outside the scope of this chapter that describes how differently experts and novices (in any subject domain, from information science to athletics) perceive questions, solve problems, and approach tasks. Here is a quick elucidation of this idea in the context of information organizations drawn from *Putting the User First*:

1. Information professionals (i.e., experts) *notice* more things than non-librarian users (i.e., novices), even expert ones. Proof: upon viewing a search results page cluttered with data, an information professional will instantly zero in on subject descriptor terms, like *Manhole covers in art* or *Boxing—Corrupt Practices—New Jersey*.
2. Information professionals (i.e., experts) *ignore* more things than non-librarian users (i.e., novices), even expert ones. Proof: an information professional will say, almost instantly upon scanning results, something like, "Oh no, not that one, it's only a review; and not that one either, it's from a questionable press."[18]

Bearing in mind the differences between information professionals' and end users' knowledge and approach to information retrieval helps in taking a broader, more holistic view of the journey of the end user, and forms the foundation of the principle "The User Is Not Broken." Ben Daigle stated in a 2013 article in *Public Services Quarterly*:

To develop services that are truly user-centered and, by extension, more compelling, useful, and valuable we need to validate our assumptions about how users discover information, how they manage what they do find, and how they use it by allowing them to show and tell us. We have to be prepared to act on what we learn and then validate whether or not those actions resulted in something better than it was before.[19]

Connections to Established Areas of Expertise in Information Practice

User experience design is, explicitly or implicitly, connected to all areas of expertise in information services including:

Access services: direct patron contact through a variety of venues, policies, signage, and stacks management (see also chapter 15: "Accessing Information Anywhere and Anytime: Access Services").

Cataloging and metadata creation: impact on patrons largely mediated through catalog and/or discovery interfaces; findability is a key UX issue (see also chapter 12: "Metadata, Cataloging, Linked Data, and the Evolving ILS").

Collection development and management: direct patron contact through a variety of venues; selection of materials (see also chapter 24: "Managing Collections").

Information and technology literacy instruction: direct patron contact through a variety of venues (see also chapter 16: "Teaching Users: Information and Technology Instruction").

Reference and research support services: direct patron contact through a variety of venues, reader's advisory policies, signage, etc. (see also chapter 11: "Information Intermediation and Reference Services").

KEY SKILLS: POTENTIAL TOOLS AND TECHNIQUES

While there are technical skills and specialized knowledge that can be helpful to the practice of user-centered design, several key competencies are not technical in nature. These include curiosity, empathy, clear communication, and effective collaboration. With attention and practice, these skills can be developed by any information professional in any role. The remainder of this chapter touches on each, and presents potential tools and techniques related to each competency.

Curiosity and the Five Whys

A genuine interest in people is invaluable in any UX-focused work and indeed is crucial to success in any customer service–oriented profession. This section presents a technique that relies on asking questions to reveal valuable data about user preferences and habits, called the "Five Whys."

As the name suggests, this technique focuses on asking "why" five times as a method of enabling deeper understanding. The answer to each question forms the content of the next. For example:

1. Why was the patron angry? Because she didn't expect the library to be closed when she arrived.
2. Why didn't she expect the library to be closed when she arrived? Because the holiday hours were not clearly posted online.
3. Why were the special holiday hours not clearly posted online? Because no information about hours is visible on the home page.
4. Why are the hours not visible on the library home page? Because the home page can only be edited by a web developer with server access, rather than through the content management system.
5. Why does the content management system have limited functionality? Because it was installed a decade ago.

For the scenario above, there are other lines of inquiry that could have been followed that might identify additional areas for improvement: Does the information organization have a social media presence where information related to special closures could also be shared? And so on.

Marquez and Downey point out, "The 'five whys' technique also allows the team to differentiate between actual problems and symptoms. . . . Understanding the difference between problems and symptoms can help the research team decide where to focus their questions and how to address symptoms."[20] In the example above, the symptom is a patron complaint about access to a building, but the underlying problem is that a crucial tool, the content management system, lacks sufficient functionality and needs to be updated.

The Five Whys technique requires no funding, and in some cases, can be conducted without the direct involvement of patrons (if the answers can be determined by information professionals from data already available such as e-mails or via knowledge of processes).

Empathy and Observation

In the context of user experience work, Indi Young defines empathy as follows:

> Empathy is an understanding you develop about another person. Empathizing is the use of that understanding—an action. Empathy is built through the willingness to take time to discover the deep-down thoughts and reactions that make another person tick. It is purposely setting out to comprehend another person's cognitive and emotional states. Empathy then gives you the ability to try on that person's perspective—to think and react as she might in a given scenario.[21]

In her excellent book, *Practical Empathy*, Young outlines a methodology for distilling insights gathered from interviews into actionable data that can be used in the process of designing or revising products and services.[22] This section describes a related technique that can be practiced by anyone at any time with useful results, called *observation*.

Observation involves passively inhabiting a space for a period of time, actively studying what takes place in the space, and recording those actions without reference to one's own judgments or evaluations. How do people move through the space? How are the furnishings arranged? Is the space staffed, and do staff interact with the people visiting? A consistent observation in the same space will reveal patterns in usage that vary daily, weekly, and seasonally; it will also reveal unexpected uses of space or furnishings that can give insights into unmet needs.

If observation is just paying close attention to what is going on, why is that a special technique? The more familiar a person is with a space or process, the less their active attention is given to that space or process. The effect of familiarity compounds in shared spaces. This could explain why an unsightly, jumbled display of boxes and materials arranged on shelves behind a checkout counter is noticeable to customers, but not to staff. Reasons may include:

1.   the staff are facing the opposite direction,
2.   the shelves have ceased to become an object of attention, and
3.   it may be unclear who is responsible for maintenance of that area.

Secondly, being able to actively observe and record details *without reference to one's own assessments, judgments, or feelings about a situation* is a valuable skill that must be consciously cultivated. Assessments by any individual are subject to that person's experiences, biases, and preferences; if acted upon prematurely, these individualized assessments of a space or process can lead to unnecessary, even costly, changes.

Observation may be practiced in any location. It may be undertaken at the spur of the moment or planned in advance. Observation also requires minimal tools (some method of note-taking) and few incidental costs (e.g., entry fees to a space, the price of a beverage), if any.

Clear Communication and Writing with Your Audience in Mind

Communication carries within its meaning both the act of sharing or transmitting information and the process by which the shared information is internalized by its intended audience. Ensuring that sent communications (e.g., writing an e-mail to colleagues, publishing a quarterly newsletter, preparing an annual report, etc.) clearly convey the intent of the communicator to the receiver is a matter of real concern at every level.

One technique, called "Writing with Your Audience in Mind," focuses on writing, but the principles can be applied to verbal communication as well:

> The fundamental purpose of scientific discourse is not the mere presentation of information and thought, but rather its actual communication. It does not matter how pleased an author might be to have converted all the right data into sentences and paragraphs; it matters only whether a large majority of the reading audience accurately perceives what the author had in mind. Therefore, in order to understand how best to improve writing, we would do well to understand better how readers go about reading.[23]

Professor George Gopen of Duke University transformed his expertise in rhetoric into a practical approach to clear, understandable writing for highly technical disciplines in the sciences and law through focusing on one essential UX question: How does *the reader* experience the writing?

In *Writing Effectively In Print and on the Web*, Rebecca Blakiston suggests that personas, the creation of fictional characters that represent your audience (a tool often used in other aspects of UX work), can also be useful when writing copy directed at end users: "When implemented well, you can bring personas into conversations and decision making to ensure you are always keeping the user in mind.[24]

As writers become aware of reader expectations, they can structure their writing to make their meaning more clear. Best practices before beginning a piece of writing of any size or complexity include asking the following three questions:

- For whom is the message intended? (consumer)
- What level of familiarity does the reader have with the information being conveyed? (context)
- What are the expectations for the method of transmission (e.g., e-mail, newsletter, report) chosen to communicate the message? (channel)

Good writing is a time investment, but it bears dividends in every part of one's work—and life.

Discussion Question

Effectively designing useful, usable, desirable experiences requires that information professionals put the user first. To be able to put the user first, information professionals must be able to answer this question: Who is our user? One cannot effectively serve "everybody," so information professionals must be able to identify a primary user group and define the characteristics of that user group. How would you go about doing this in a specific information organization?

Effective Collaboration and Agile Development Methodology

User experience work is commonly project based, even when ongoing, and frequently involves multiple stakeholders from within and outside the organization (colleagues and patrons). Skills such as strategic planning (see also chapter 19: "Strategic Planning"), data analysis (see also chapter 26: "Managing Data and Data Analysis in Information Organizations"), and change management (see also chapter 20: "Change Management") are essential to not just managing people but also to managing projects successfully. Successful projects require effective collaboration. Familiarity with project management techniques can establish a productive structure in which a project can move forward with fewer obstacles. One project management technique is called Agile.[25] Agile development methodology is a structured, collaborative, iterative process in which a product or service is developed incrementally with continuous feedback from the intended users.

> **Check This Out**
>
> A good basic introduction to the concepts of "scrum" agile development methodologies is *Scrum: A Breathtakingly Brief and Agile Introduction* by Chris Sims and Hillary Louise Johnson. *Visit:* http://www.agilelearninglabs.com/resources/scrum-introduction/.

While often associated with IT projects, agile methodologies (e.g., "scrum," "Kanban") can be adapted widely. In 2016, Galadriel Chilton presented at the Electronic Resources & Libraries (ER&L) Conference on how "using Scrum to develop a framework for a comprehensive review of e-resource collections kept the project on task, strengthened the project's deliverables, increased team morale, and resulted in equitable task distribution."[26]

TEXTBOX 14.4

Key Components of Agile Methodology

- User stories
- Discrete descriptions of tasks or features from the end user's point of view
- A set, repeating time frame in which work hours available to be used for the project are defined and in which work on user stories is scheduled accordingly
- Well-defined process and participant roles to facilitate clear communication and open collaboration

---

CONCLUSION

From the front door to the seating, lighting, and restrooms, to how the books or films are shelved or where someone clicks to find them, each aspect of the building and the environment and every interaction with an information professional or staff member is part of every patron's user experience. A user-centered approach enables information professionals to consider the spaces, materials, and services provided by information organizations from an outside perspective—the perspective of constituents—and to consciously work to construct experiences that engage with users wherever they are in terms of expertise in information retrieval.

Hallmarks of the user-centered information organization include a willingness to evaluate and reevaluate the content, scope, method, and extent of resources and services offered to patrons and an openness to inviting patrons to participate in co-creation of services. These qualities are also essential to the sustainability of information organizations in the future and therefore become essential competencies of today's information professional.

In *The Atlas of New Librarianship*, R. David Lankes pursues an overarching theme: "The mission of librarians is to improve society through facilitating knowledge creation in their communities."[27] He points out that "true facilitation means shared ownership," and goes on to say:

> Just as we share in the successes, responsibilities, and failures of our members, we must cede some of our own responsibilities to the members as well. As in a conversation, when you must stop and listen, so too must we allow our services to listen, that is, be influenced by our members. Doing so . . . builds trust and ultimately builds the relationship necessary for a new compact with our communities.[28]

> "A user-centered approach enables information professionals to consider the spaces, materials, and services provided by information organizations from an outside perspective—the perspective of constituents—and to consciously work to construct experiences that engage with users wherever they are in terms of expertise in information retrieval."

Without keeping those who are served by the organization on the forefront—learning from them, engaging with them, and allowing our services to be influenced by them—information organizations may risk their relevancy for the information user in the future.

An information organization exists for the benefit of a specific, situated community, and so any service, resource, or system must privilege their experiences and expectations: "We must remember always to question ourselves and our definitions of what makes a more usable system in order to hope to be trustworthy arbiters of what constitutes a great user experience."[29] In the long term, the relative success of the information organization must be in reference to its responsiveness to the needs of its own unique constituency—to developing a great user experience.

APPENDIX 14.1: JOURNEY MAPPING EXERCISE

Pause for a moment and think back to the last time you visited a store in person. When did you visit the store—at the beginning of your day, after a long workday, on an urgent errand, or perhaps just to browse? Was the weather pleasant that day, or was it very hot, cold, rainy, or windy? How easy or difficult was the process of actually getting to the store—by foot, using public transportation, or arriving in your own or a friend's automobile? What was your experience in the parking lot, and/or the entrance of the store? Were there ample carts or shopping baskets available to you, and were they all clean and in good repair? Did the store provide Wi-Fi, was there music playing, was the lighting neither too dim nor too bright? What was the demeanor of the various employees you encountered? What about the other customers? Were all the items you desired in stock and in good condition? Were they located where you expected to find them? How long did it take you to pay for your purchase, if you made one, and if you didn't, what were the reasons that kept you from purchasing?

Now that you have taken a moment to consider one specific personal journey of your own, you can begin to see how the planning, execution, and evaluation of "user-centered design" is quite complex.

- Briefly, describe the experience you had in mind when completing this practice exercise. Name at least one positive and one negative aspect that were specific to factors within the store's control; then, do the same for factors that were specific to your situation, mood, or schedule.
- Review the web presence of the store you visited. In what ways is it consistent with the physical experience of visiting? How does it diverge?

Courtney McDonald

- A crowded store on a very wet, blustery day in late afternoon around rush hour might have a number of disadvantages to overcome in order to produce a good user experience, yet many factors that could contribute to positive or negative elements of the potentially less-than-stellar experience are outside of the control of the store's employees and management. What actions could they take to mitigate these external factors and increase the likelihood that their customers have a good experience?

NOTES

1. Jesse James Garrett, *The Elements of User Experience: User-Centered Design for the Web and Beyond* (Berkeley, CA: New Riders, 2011), 10.
2. Steven J. Bell, "Staying True to the Core: Designing the Future Academic Library Experience," *Portal: Libraries and the Academy* 14, no. 3 (2014): 376, doi:10.1353/pla.2014.0021.
3. Peter Morville, "User Experience Design," Semantic Studios, 2004, http://semanticstudios.com/user_experience_design/.
4. Steven J. Bell, "Usability and User Experience—There Is a Difference," *Designing Better Libraries* (blog), May 29, 2012, http://dbl.lishost.org/blog/2012/05/29/usability-and-user-experience-there-is-a-difference/.
5. Chris Risdon, "Un-Sucking the Touchpoint," Adaptive Path, December 2, 2013, http://adaptivepath.org/ideas/un-sucking-the-touchpoint/.
6. Kim Flaherty, "How Channels, Devices, and Touchpoints Impact the Customer Journey," Nielsen Norman Group, December 4, 2016, https://www.nngroup.com/articles/channels-devices-touchpoints/.
7. Adam Richardson, "Using Customer Journey Maps to Improve Customer Experience," *Harvard Business Review*, November 15, 2010.
8. Meggie Wright and Valery King, "LEADing the Way: UX IRL @ OSU," *OLA Quarterly* 22, no. 3 (February 22, 2017): 31–36, doi:http://dx.doi.org/10.7710/1093-7374.1869.
9. Jennifer Poggiali and Stephanie Margolin, "Leading from the Library Loo: An Illustrated, Documented Guide to New York City Academic Library Bathrooms," in *ACRL 2017 Conference Proceedings* (Baltimore, MD: Association of College and Research Libraries, 2017), 384, http://www.ala.org/acrl/sites/ala.org.acrl/files/content/conferences/confsandpreconfs/2017/LeadingfromtheLibraryLoo.pdf.
10. Garrett, *The Elements of User Experience*, 87.
11. Ibid.
12. Alan Cooper et al., *About Face: The Essentials of Interaction Design*, fourth edition (Hoboken, NJ: Wiley, 2014), 11.
13. "Design Thinking for Libraries: A Toolkit for Patron-Centered Design," IDEO, 2015, https://www.ideo.com/post/design-thinking-for-libraries.
14. Joe Marquez and Annie Downey, "Service Design: An Introduction to a Holistic Assessment Methodology of Library Services," *Weave: Journal of Library User Experience* 1, no. 2 (2015), doi:http://dx.doi.org/10.3998/weave.12535642.0001.201.
15. Ibid.
16. Kristina Halvorson and Melissa Rach, *Content Strategy for the Web* (Berkeley, CA: New Riders, 2012), 28.
17. Aaron Schmidt and Amanda Etches, *Useful, Usable, Desirable: Applying User Experience Design to Your Library*, Chicago: American Library Association, 2014.
18. Courtney Greene McDonald, *Putting the User First: 30 Strategies for Transforming Library Services* (Chicago: Association of College and Research Libraries, 2014), 12.
19. Ben Daigle, "Getting to Know You: Discovering User Behaviors and Their Implications for Service Design," *Public Services Quarterly* 9, no. 4 (October 1, 2013): 331, doi:10.1080/15228959.2013.842416.
20. Joe J. Marquez and Annie Downey, *Library Service Design: A LITA Guide to Holistic Assessment, Insight, and Improvement* (Lanham, MD: Rowman & Littlefield, 2016), 84.
21. Indi Young, *Practical Empathy: For Collaboration and Creativity in Your Work* (New York: Rosenfeld Media, 2015), 18.
22. Ibid.
23. George Gopen and Judith Swan, "The Science of Scientific Writing," *American Scientist*, 1990, http://www.americanscientist.org/issues/pub/the-science-of-scientific-writing/99999.

24. Rebecca Blakiston, *Writing Effectively in Print and on the Web: A Practical Guide for Librarians* (Lanham, MD: Rowman & Littlefield, 2017), 13.
25. "Agile 101," Agile Alliance, accessed August 12, 2017, https://www.agilealliance.org/agile101/.
26. Galadriel Chilton, "Using the Scrum Project Management Methodology to Create a Comprehensive Collection Development Framework," *Electronic Resources & Libraries*, 2016, https://www.slideshare.net/gchilton/erl-2016-using-the-scrum-project-management-methodology-to-create-a-comprehensive-collection-assessment-framework.
27. R. David Lankes, *The Atlas of New Librarianship* (Cambridge, MA: MIT Press, 2011), 65.
28. Ibid.
29. Buddy Pennington et al., "Strategies to Improve the User Experience," *Serials Review* 42, no. 1 (January 2, 2016): 23, doi:10.1080/00987913.2016.1140614.

Courtney McDonald

15

Accessing Information Anywhere and Anytime

ACCESS SERVICES

Michael J. Krasulski

Chapter 15, "Accessing Information Anywhere and Anytime: Access Services," identifies the many services that go into everyday operations in providing access to the information organization's resources and services. Access services retains its historical roots in circulation and collection management but continues to change in response to technological and institutional changes. As a leader in access services and coeditor of Twenty-First Century Access Services: On the Front Line of Academic Librarianship, *Michael Krasulski brings his extensive knowledge of this topic to his well-rounded discussion of access services.*

Central to any discussion of access services is the integrated library system (ILS) because it handles various functions throughout the information organization (e.g., acquisitions, cataloging). Krasulski explains how the ILS works to facilitate a wide range of access services functions beyond collection management and circulation, such as maintaining privacy and managing the user database. Krasulski explains other technological changes in access services; for example, automated storage and retrieval systems have brought a technological solution to the shelving and housing of physical collections. The chapter covers other important topics including resource sharing and course reserves, as well as assessment.

Access services demands trained staff committed to creating positive interactions with users, notes Krasulski. Because of the multiplicity of roles often included in access services, information professionals in this field may need to be comfortable with everything from building maintenance to copyright, from security to signage. The takeaway from this chapter is that no matter what title the information professional possesses, this person will have a direct impact on the effectiveness of access services within his or her organization and therefore the user experience.

★　★　★

Access services is a catchall term to describe the circulation, course reserves, document delivery, collection management, and related tasks and functions found within an information organization.[1] See appendix 15.1: "Access Services Functions and Tasks." These often unseen and underappreciated functions are central to an information organization's daily operations, and have been for a very long time. The exact impetus for the creation of access services as a concept is unclear and debatable; for example, few information organizations used the term *access services* before 1981.[2] Regardless of its exact origins, there is some consensus that the creation of access services signaled "more emphasis on the user as a consumer of information who needs access to information in a variety of formats."[3] The implication is that access services help facilitate access to materials users need in a timely manner regardless of the source. After completing this chapter, the reader should have an understanding of circulation, collection management, resource sharing, course reserves, and related functions that are most common within information organizations, and have some familiarity with leading and assessing access services.

> Access services help facilitate access to materials users need in a timely manner regardless of the source.

FACILITATING ACCESS

Access services is a sum of many disparate parts, and its operations impact every user of the information organization. In reflecting upon his over thirty years of experience in the profession, James G. Neal, university librarian emeritus, Columbia University, and American Library Association president (2017–2018) once noted:

> Access services opens the library in the morning and secures it at night. It serves as our essential link to campus operations, like building maintenance, security, and food services. It oversees the quality and usability of library space. It manages our physical collections. . . . It circulates materials and technologies and supports the special facilities for distinctive formats, for group and class use. . . . It supports teaching and learning through traditional and electronic reserves, enabling a strong presence for libraries in course management systems and online education. It is the front line of our consortial relationships, managing an expanding array of regional, national and global interlibrary loan and document delivery services that support quality scholarship. It is the early warning system for building environmental issues and collection preservation and damage problems. It is the gatekeeper for the authorization and authentication of library users to the vast array of electronic resources we have leased and acquired. Access services is essential, fundamental, and pervasive.[4]

The functions that Neal details above are indeed essential—fundamental to and pervasive within the information organization. Besides a collection of functions and tasks, access services can also be an administrative umbrella where aforementioned tasks and functions reside within the information organization. The absence of access services from the organizational chart does not mean access services is absent from the information organization. Rather, access services functions can be diffused administratively across and throughout the organizational structure. As such, access services can appear to assume the persona of a refuge for services and functions that do not fall clearly under any other category.[5] The fluidity of access services means being all things to everyone. The various functions described in this chapter are found in information organizations, in varying incarnations, regardless of type.

> The absence of access services from the organizational chart does not mean access services is absent from the information organization. Rather, access services functions can be diffused administratively across and throughout the organizational structure.

Michael J. Krasulski

Circulation and the Integrated Library System

Circulation and access services are often used interchangeably since access services tends to be thought of as circulation activities plus other functions. Circulation fulfills the vital roles of administering who can use the information organization and what they can use therein, facilitating the access to physical items between the information organization and the user, and being able to identify the location of any item in the physical collection at all times. All of these roles are, in varying degrees, automated in and administered through the information organization's integrated library system (ILS) (see also chapter 25: "Managing Technology"). Different modules exist within the ILS to handle various functions throughout the information organization (e.g., acquisitions, cataloging). The ILS demonstrates the interdependency of access services with other departments within the information organization. For example, cataloging and acquisitions, often labeled together as technical services, process materials into the ILS, and the systems department administers the ILS (see also chapter 12: "Metadata, Cataloging, Linked Data, and the Evolving ILS").

The ILS manages the information organization's user database and tracks what items have been loaned out, to whom, and when those items are due back, as well as the locations of items within the building. Each user has a unique record in the user database containing the user's contact information, as well as information regarding any library use activity. The American Library Association's (ALA) "Library Bill of Rights," article IV, states, "Libraries should cooperate with all persons and groups concerned with resisting abridgement of free expression and free access to ideas"[6] (see also chapter 35: "Intellectual Freedom"). One interpretation of Article IV is "when users recognize or fear that their privacy or confidentiality is compromised true freedom of inquiry no longer exists"[7] (see also chapter 34: "Information Privacy and Cybersecurity"). The library has a responsibility to maintain the privacy and confidentiality of all user records. Not only is this a courtesy to the library's users, in the United States, forty-eight states require by law that libraries maintain user confidentiality in its records. Many other countries have adopted such laws as well.[8]

As well as managing the user database, the ILS automates the bookkeeping and recordkeeping aspects of circulation, which include overdue fines, item renewals, and communications to users concerning overdue and recalled material via various means, including e-mail or short message service (SMS). Each information organization has its own loan rules and policies that govern who can borrow what and for how long. For example, in academic libraries, undergraduate users may have twenty-eight days to borrow an item, while it is not uncommon for faculty to have a semester-long borrowing period. The ILS takes the guesswork out of managing, administering, and remembering these rules and policies since the ILS is customizable to handle such institutional variability. The ILS is not just for managing traditional book and journal collections. Information organizations that circulate e-reading devices, laptops, audiovisual materials, and even Wi-Fi hotspots and makerspace equipment can track these materials in the ILS.[9]

It is common for circulation functions to be located at or near an information organization's main entry/exit point. Consequently, access services, and circulation in particular, can be the first, and often only, point of contact between the majority of users and the organization.[10] To state this reality another way, access services *is* the information organization's original user interface. It is here that perceptions about the information organization are formed. Consider the variety of interactions at any circulation desk in any information organization on a given day. There is the potential for an interaction to go wrong. Such situations may be the result of a serious user infraction, like theft or mutilation of organizational property. Others are more benign, like enforcing fine policies. It is imperative for access services staff to be trained in creating a positive user experience (see also chapter 14: "User Experience"). Negative user interactions reflect poorly on the information organization. As corporations have learned in today's digitally connected age, negative customer interactions can become viral thanks to various Web 2.0 technologies, such as blogging, Twitter, Yelp, or Facebook. Experiences with access services staff often shape how users view the organization.

The increased availability of electronic resources and the decline in book circulation have led many information organizations to rethink the role of the circulation desk. There has been a movement toward one-stop shopping, particularly in college and university libraries, by combining the circulation desk with the reference or information desk[11] (see also chapter 7: "Learning and Research Institutions: Academic Libraries"). Streamlining service and freeing staff to do other things have been reasons for organizations to add self-check terminals at circulation desks, a change that can also improve service. These terminals allow users to check out materials with little or no staff involvement. However, no system is foolproof; errors may occur and staff intervention may be needed. Thus, self-check machines are typically placed in close proximity to the circulation desk. While technologies, such as the ILS and self-check, have drastically changed how a circulation department operates, what has remained the same is the need for outstanding user interactions—whether that interaction is in person, over the telephone, or online.

> " Access services *is* the information organization's original user interface. It is here that perceptions about the information organization are formed. "

Table 15.1. Keys to a Successful Circulation Operation.

Collection is accounted for.
Circulation records are in good order.
Positive user experience is provided.

Collection Management

The storage, retrieval, and maintenance of the organization's physical collections, also known as collection management, is a vital access services function (see also chapter 24: "Managing Collections"). Depending upon the organization, collection management functions may fall to volunteers, student workers, or paraprofessional staff. These employees typically:

- shelve returned items or new items added to the collection,
- check, from time to time, the items on the shelves to ensure items are shelved properly (often referred to as shelf-reading), and
- adjust items already on the shelves to accommodate changes in collection size, often referred to as shifting.

The decline of book circulation, the ubiquity of journals available electronically, and the calls to repurpose shelving space for other purposes have caused information professionals to experiment with various storage options that maximize existing space for the organization's collections. Compact shelving stores more materials than traditional shelving because the space between the shelving units is largely eliminated. Think about having the entire book stacks compressed together and then having the ability to open a section of stacks to retrieve a needed book or journal. That is essentially how compact shelving works. Users still go to the shelves, call number in hand, and retrieve the item. However, instead of walking into the stacks, users operate a manual or automatic shelving system to open up the exact access point where the needed item is located.

Michael J. Krasulski

Automated storage and retrieval systems (AS/RS) have brought a technological solution to the shelving and housing of physical collections. The first installation of such a system was at California State University, Northridge. The James B. Hunt Library at North Carolina State University is another example; it opened in January 2013 to much excitement. Because the building is designed to have more open and collaborative study and work space, the book stacks are largely removed and out of sight. Items are kept in a high-density storage facility within the library and retrieved using bookBot (a robotic, automated book delivery system). Users select the item they wish to use in the online catalog, and within minutes, the item is available for pickup near the library's entrance. The online catalog permits virtual browsing so users can view like items that would be on the shelves around the item requested. The bound journal collection also utilizes the bookBot system. Users place a request for an article, and the article is delivered by e-mail in about twenty-four hours. AS/RS technology allows the Hunt Library collection to take up about one-ninth the space it would if the same items were stored on traditional shelves. Another notable example of AS/RS technology at work is the book train at the New York Public Library.[12]

Remote storage, as the term suggests, is the removal of physical collections to a site separate from the information organization. The distances can vary by organizations, with the remote storage sometimes located in a building next door and other times in another state. Users locate items in the catalog, request them, and then have these items delivered to a service point, likely the circulation desk, for pickup. Remote storage meets the goal of opening space for other purposes; however, users lose the ability to browse the shelves and may experience a delay between the placement of the request and the delivery of the item.[13] While remote storage removes the serendipitous person's ability to interact with the books on the shelves, the long-term future for preservation of books is actually better because remote storage facilities are often newer and are usually designed with careful temperature and humidity controls in mind (see also chapter 13: "Analog and Digital Curation and Preservation").

Resource Sharing

Resource sharing, which is sometimes known as interlibrary loan (ILL), is the process that supplies users with materials not readily available at their own institution. A user places a request for a desired item. If the item is owned by another information organization, a request to borrow the item is sent; when the item is received, it is checked out to the patron for a loan period determined by the lending organization. Resource sharing complements materials owned by the information organization since the information needs of users are enhanced by the ability to obtain items outside those in their local collections. Increasingly, users are also allowed to request items that are owned in their local collections but that are otherwise unavailable. This allows multiple users to research the same topic without competing for resources,[14]

> Resource sharing complements materials owned by the information organization since the information needs of users are enhanced by the ability to obtain items outside those in their local collections.

Resource sharing services offered for those materials that are held locally is called document delivery. Document delivery services were first offered in large academic libraries as a convenience to save faculty users the time and trouble of coming into the library and pulling and copying print journal materials themselves. Document delivery services allow faculty users to place requests and have these materials delivered to faculty offices via campus mail or scanned and e-mailed directly to them. The growth of remote storage collections in both academic and public libraries and the popularity of distance education in academic institutions have expanded the need of document delivery services. Usually, users place requests through the same resource-sharing system used for items not owned locally. Document delivery is also a way to abate any criticism that items in remote storage are not accessible. Additionally, document delivery demonstrates in a clear and convincing way that access services contributes to the success of the information organization by supporting distance education users.

Resource sharing is not without its costs and requires a significant investment on the part of the information organization in both human and financial resources. Staff intervention is required to locate, pull, and scan materials, especially when an article or book chapter (rather than the full publication) is requested. Additionally, the arranging, tracking, and managing of requests can be labor intensive, and many large information organizations invest in a separate information management system to administer resource sharing tasks. Shipping costs, fees to acquire items, copyright fees, fees for lost or overdue items, and costs from article providers are often absorbed by the information organization.

Discussion Question

Resource sharing and course reserves activities can infringe on copyright. In what ways can access services practitioners mitigate these potential infringements?

While book circulation may be declining, the need for resource sharing in information organizations is growing. The reason for this paradox rests in the fact that users want to use the information organization and its services, but not necessarily the materials provided for them on physical shelves. Additionally, advances in resource-sharing technologies have often reduced turnaround times for article and other nonreturnable requests from days to mere hours.[15]

Course Reserves

Course reserves are commonly found in college and university settings. Reserves can be either physical objects available at a service desk or digital resources available remotely, typically through a password-protected portal (e-reserves). When available at the service desk, access services staff purchase new or retrieve already owned materials from the stacks at the request of faculty members and place these in a restricted area, often behind the service desk. The materials are added to the faculty members' course listings, and students can retrieve the items at the library. The loan period is generally short, typically no more than a few hours, and often accompanied by the threat of high late fees to ensure prompt return. Formats can include books, journal articles, DVDs, and even anatomical models. Course reserves can also utilize the academic library's laptop and e-reader or other nontraditional format item-lending programs when these types of programs are locally available. Placing materials on reserve provides an ideal solution to the problem of managing materials in high demand. The service allows users equal access to the same materials.

Discussion Questions

Some have called access services the original library user interface. How can access services shape, both positively and negatively, the user experience? In what ways can access services help provide a positive user experience?

The rise of distance education and the general desire to provide an excellent user experience have prompted many academic libraries to provide remote access to reserve materials in digital form. In terms of process, electronic reserves differ considerably from print reserves. Faculty still identify the materials they want placed on reserve, but instead of photocopying those materials and housing them behind a service point, library staff make digital copies and make them available online (either hosted by the library or in the college or university's course management system) or link directly to e-resource holdings.[16] The library is still involved in the processing and maintenance of this service but its efforts are largely unseen by the user.

Other Duties as Assigned

The persona of access services as being all things to all people is perhaps best evidenced through the myriad ways in which it supports the information organization. Access services, as a reflection of the needs and idiosyncrasies of the larger information organization, can make discussions about common experience across institutions difficult. Yet, it is not uncommon for access services practitioners to assume the personas of library security, copyright experts (see also chapter 31: "Copyright and Creative Commons"), and building managers within their information organizations.

Access services can take on the persona of library security since it is often responsible for enforcing and defending various policies of the information organization, such as entrance, fines, food and drink, noise, and usage policies. Given the omnipresent nature of access services, it makes sense for access services to take on these responsibilities. Sometimes enforcing these policies can result in conflict. Frontline access services staff are usually several administrative levels below where policy or decisions are made, so this can create frustration when the reasons behind the policy/change are not fully communicated to the staff and when frontline staff do not have the opportunity to provide feedback to the administration before a policy is implemented. To successfully navigate these proverbial minefields, access services practitioners need to be familiar with both the information organization's current policies and the various arguments made against said policies, and need training on the best ways to defuse potential conflicts with users.

Access services practitioners often have a fluency in copyright rules because of the very nature of resource sharing and course reserves. Within the information organization, it is not uncommon for others to look to access services staff to serve as the copyright "experts." At the very least, those working in document delivery or course reserves must have a working knowledge of fair use and the various guidelines around fair use. It has been over forty years since the last major changes to the American copyright laws were made. Ever since, content producers and information practitioners have attempted to draw up guidelines or model practices to no avail, since neither side could agree. Information organizations often argued for more conservative interpretations of copyright law to remain in the good graces of the content providers.

TEXTBOX 15.3

Copyright Clearance Center and Association of American Publishers v. Georgia State University

In 2008, several publishers, with the backing of the Copyright Clearance Center (CCC) and the Association of American Publishers (AAP) brought suit against Georgia State University, challenging the University's use of copyrighted material for electronic course reserves. The original ruling and the subsequent appeals largely agreed with Georgia State University's copyright interpretations. Even after this court case, many questions regarding copyright and resource sharing and course reserves remain. It is incumbent upon access services practitioners to continue to monitor the situation and apply any changes as necessary.

The persona of the building manager arises from access services staff being present during all the operating hours of the information organization. Access services often serves as the liaison between the information organization and the institution's facilities or physical plant department (see also chapter 23: "Innovative Library and Information Services: The Design Thinking Process"). Problems with the building are typically reported to access services staff first.[17] Additionally, access services staff possess a unique perspective from their frontline service point and are able to oversee certain facility-related issues within an information organization operation, for example, 24/7 staffing and the creation of signage for effective wayfinding.

Just as an information organization's electronic resources are available twenty-four hours a day, the demand for access to physical collections has resulted in many academic libraries remaining open for twenty-four hours for five, or in some cases seven, days a week. Providing twenty-four-hour access is no small undertaking. The barrier to providing such a service often comes down to staffing overnight hours. Sometimes full-time access services staff take the overnight shifts, while other times it is the responsibility of student assistants or students receiving work-study funding. If few or no services are provided in these overnight hours, a member of the organization's security department may be utilized to provide adequate staffing. The solution is based on local conditions, including funding (see also chapter 21: "Managing Budgets") and building design considerations.[18]

The creation and subsequent revisions of signage for the organization can fall to access services staff. Responsibility for signage is a result of maintaining the signage at the ends of ranges of shelving units indicating the first and last call numbers of each row. Additionally, access services professionals should think about signage as a response to frequently asked questions. Clearly worded and well-placed signage can greatly reduce the number of directional questions received at service points and communicates a welcoming and inclusive atmosphere.[19]

ASSESSING ACCESS SERVICES

The above sections serve as an introduction to the various access services functions and illustrate ways access services contributes to the success of the information organization. However, contributing to the success of the information organization is no longer enough to remain vital or essential since the continuing relevance of information organizations is being questioned as never before in many arenas (e.g., academia and local and state governments). Every function or department in the information organization, access services included, must demonstrate and document its contributions in purposeful and meaningful ways. The process of systematically evaluating and demonstrating success and implementing improvement as needed is called assessment. As information organizations strive to become more user-centric, they are paying increasing attention to assessing user needs and designing services to meet those needs. Access services functions are often at the center of these assessment efforts. Additionally, academic libraries, for example, are required to participate in formalized assessment efforts across their campuses since accrediting bodies mandate that institutions of higher learning organize, document, and sustain assessment activities in order to, as the Middle States Commission on Higher Education has instructed its member institutions, demonstrate "periodic assessment of mission and goals to ensure they are relevant and achievable"[20] (see also chapter 28: "Advocacy").

> Every function or department in the information organization, access services included, must demonstrate and document its contributions in purposeful and meaningful ways.

The most basic assessment measure is documenting use—that is, how and to what extent the services and functions of the information organization are being used (see also chapter 26: "Managing Data and Data Analysis in Information Organizations"). Put simply, gauging use involves gathering usage totals from various functions over a period of time, typically a year, compiling these data in a chart or table, and then comparing to data from the previous period. Such data can be gathered in a variety of ways, including entrance and exit counts or lending and borrowing statistics from both circulation and resource sharing.

Evaluating and tracking use over time are important; however, these data do not inform administrators if users are satisfied with the quality of services provided. User satisfaction studies, often performed via surveys, can answer such questions and help the organization measure the value of their services. Information organizations may choose to develop their own survey instrument or elect to use a standardized survey. Each approach has its own advantages. An instrument developed in-house is certainly cheaper and questions can be tailored specifically to the needs of the information organization. While a standardized survey is more expensive, these tools have the advantage of allowing for benchmarking across organizations. Two major survey instruments are LibQUAL+ and LibSat. LibQUAL+, developed by the Association of Research Libraries (ARL), asks respondents to rate a library on twenty-one different qualities that focus on quality of service, information access, and the library as place. Respondents also rate the minimum level of service they would expect versus the actual level received. ARL administers LibQUAL+ and provides initial analysis of the results for the library. LibSat, developed by Counting Opinions, is more focused on public libraries. LibSat is a continuous survey tool that measures user satisfaction and expectations and the importance of those expectations to users. Regardless of which instrument is used, user satisfaction studies provide valuable data that cannot be extrapolated from usage statistics alone.[21]

After collecting data, the information organization should close the assessment loop, that is, use the results to improve, change, or realign services. For example, knowing when users come to the building can be helpful in determining how much staffing is needed at a service point. Additionally, these data can also be useful in setting appropriate service hours or demonstrating the appropriateness of current levels of service should there be a clamor for additional service. User satisfaction data may reveal that underused services need to be promoted more heavily or are no longer needed. The utilization of assessment data varies from one information organization to the next. If improvements are made, the information organization should communicate those changes to the user.

LEADING ACCESS SERVICES

As stated earlier in this chapter, access services is both a collection of functions and tasks as well as an administrative umbrella within an information organization. Those tasked with leading access services may be paraprofessionals with significant experience or information professionals who have library and information science master's degrees. Generally speaking, a dedicated course in access services is not taught in ALA-accredited library and information science graduate programs, though aspects of access services may be covered elsewhere in the curriculum.[22] A recent study has shown that access services professionals typically learn the skills directly related to access services on the job.[23] That is not to suggest, however, that library and information science education has no role in the development of access services professionals.

The same study showed that higher order managerial skills are equally as important as access services specific skills to the success of the access services information professional. The overwhelming majority of respondents reported that the ability to formulate policies; delegate responsibilities (see also chapter 37: "Leadership Skills for Today's Global Information Landscape"); determine priorities; supervise and evaluate staff (see also chapter 22: "Managing Personnel"); utilize existing resources effectively; and collect, calculate, and analyze statistics were important to the success of the access services professional.[24] Practitioners are likely to be exposed to these types of management and statistical skills during their library and information science educational experience.

Additionally, respondents were asked about their professional backgrounds in information organizations before becoming access services professionals. The study found no clear path to becoming an access services professional.[25] Some of the respondents began their careers in access services paraprofessional positions and then moved into more administrative roles, while others began in other areas of the information organization, typically in reference or technical services, and moved into access services after sharpening their administrative skills. Although there is no single path leading to access services functions or units, the study demonstrates that both work experience and course work are necessary to acquiring the necessary skill sets. Students interested in access services should consider taking courses related to assessment, management, and statistics. Additionally, students should seek volunteer or intern opportunities in an access services unit. Having hands-on experience as well as the theoretical underpinnings gained from course work will provide a sound foundation for any access services practitioner.

CONCLUSION

Access services has moved well beyond the circulation desk to fill vital roles in the continued success of information organizations by connecting users with resources. As Trevor A. Dawes and the author of this chapter have argued, the present state of access services can be best summed up as "Like always, like never before," which was used in the short-lived tagline to the mid-2000s Saturn automobile commercial. "Like always" because access services retains its historical roots in circulation and collection management and "like never before" because access services continues to adjust and change in response to technological and institutional changes.[26]

These types of changes will continue as the information organization continues to find its place in a twenty-first-century reality. However, there are several clear trends in access services that are worth noting:

- Coupling of information or reference desks and circulation desks into one service point is increasing. In organizations that have coupled their service points, access services staff tend to be present at the desk.
- Resource sharing usage continues to increase as information organizations continue to cancel journal subscriptions due to ever-increasing costs.
- Information organizations are exploring shared remote storage spaces and collections.
- Course reserves in academic libraries are declining as the responsibility is shifted to faculty end users.
- Access services practitioners are expected to educate their users on the nature of fair use, specifically, and copyright law.
- Access services work is becoming more interdependent, further blurring the lines between the various access services tasks and functions.
- Excellent customer service skills continue to remain paramount.[27]

Regardless of whether these predictions prove correct, one can be assured that access services will continue to grow, change, and adapt to meet the needs of a robust twenty-first-century information organization, and access services will continue to assume new responsibilities, sometimes finding itself in unfamiliar territory.

Michael J. Krasulski

APPENDIX 15.1: ACCESS SERVICES FUNCTIONS AND TASKS

Table 15.2. Access Services Functions and Tasks.

Function	Tasks
Circulation	Check in/Check out Materials
	Answer Directional Questions
	Process Holds and Renewals
	Administer Overdue Fines
	Provide Superior Customer Service
Collection Management	Sort and Shelve Materials
	Shift Collections
	Shelf-Read
	Provide Superior Customer Service
Resource Sharing	Process Requests from Users
	Process Request from Other Libraries
	Monitor Copyright Issues
	Provide Superior Customer Service
Course Reserves	Process Reserve Requests from Faculty
	Check in/Check out Reserve Materials
	Post e-Reserves Materials in Locally Available Platform
	Instruct Users in How to Use Reserves
	Provide Superior Customer Service
Other Duties as Assigned	Liaise with Facilities Department or Physical Plant
	Liaise with Security Department
	Manage Physical Structure during All Operating Hours
	Maintain Signage

NOTES

1. Duane Wilson, "Reenvisioning Access Services: A Survey of Access Services Departments in ARL Libraries," *Journal of Access Services* 10, no. 3 (2013): 153.
2. Trevor Dawes, Kimberly Burke Sweetman, and Catherine Von Elm, *Access Services: SPEC Kit 290* (Washington, DC: Association of Research Libraries, 2005), 18.
3. Mary Anne Hansen, Jakob Harnest, Virginia Steel, Joan Ellen Stein, and Pat Weaver-Myers, "A Question and Answer Forum on the Origin, Evolution and Future of Access Services," *Journal of Access Services* 3, no. 2 (2005): 15.
4. James Neal, "Foreword," in *Twenty-First-Century Access Services*, ed. Michael J. Krasulski and Trevor A. Dawes (Chicago: Association of College and Research Libraries, 2013), vii.
5. Nora Dethloff and Paul Sharpe, "Access Services and the Success of the Academic Library," in Krasulski and Dawes, *Twenty-First-Century Access Services*, 174.

6. "Library Bill of Rights," American Library Association, June 30, 2006, http://www.ala.org/advocacy/intfreedom/librarybill.

7. "Privacy," American Library Association, July 7, 2006, http://www.ala.org/advocacy/intfreedom/library bill/interpretations/privacy.

8. "State Privacy Laws Regarding Library Records," American Library Association, May 29, 2007, http://www.ala.org/advocacy/privacyconfidentiality/privacy/stateprivacy; and see Zdzislaw Gebolys and Jacek Tomasczczyk, *Library Codes of Ethics Worldwide* (Berlin: Simon Verlag fur Bibliothekswissen, 2011).

9. Jenny Xie, "Two Major Public Library Systems Are about to Start Lending Wi-Fi Hotspots," *CityLab*, June 23, 2014, http://www.citylab.com/cityfixer/2014/06/two-major-public-library-systems-are-about-to-start-lending-wi-fi-hotspots/373233/; and Bringham Fay, "MIT Libraries and MIT MakerWorkshop Launch Equipment to Go," *MITNews*, March 9, 2017, http://news.mit.edu/2017/mit-libraries-and-mit-makerworkshop-launch-equipment-to-go-0309.

10. Mary Ann Venner and Seti Keshmiripour, "X Marks the Spot: Creating and Managing a Single Service Point to Improve Customer Service to Maximize Resources," *Journal of Access Services* 13, no. 2 (2016): 104.

11. Pixey A. Mosley, "Assessing User Interactions at the Desk nearest the Front Door," *Reference & User Services Quarterly* 47, no. 2 (2007): 160.

12. Jay Price, "NCSU's Hyper-Modern James B. Hunt Jr. Library Poised to Open," *News Observer*, December 18, 2012, http://www.newsobserver.com/2012/12/18/2553438/ncsus-hyper-modern-new-james-b.html; and Corey Kilgannon, "Below Bryant Park, a Bunker and a Train Line, Just for Books," *New York Times*, November 21, 2016, https://www.nytimes.com/2016/11/21/nyregion/new-york-public-library-book-train.html.

13. Dethloff and Sharpe, "Access Services," 180–81.

14. Bradley Tolppanen, "A Survey of Current Tasks and Future Trends in Access Services," *Journal of Access Services* 2, no. 3 (2004): 7–8.

15. John B. Horrigan, "Libraries 2016," September 6, 2016, *PewResearchCenter*, http://www.pewinternet.org/2016/09/09/libraries-2016/, 11; Shaneka Morris and Gary Roebuck, *ARL Statistics 2014–2015* (Washington, DC: Association of Research Libraries, 2017), 84, 89, 94 passim; Ian Reid, "The 2015 Public Library Data Service: Characteristics and Trends," May 2016, *Counting Opinions,* https://storage.googleapis.com/co_drive/Documents/PLDS/2015PLDSAnnualReportFinal.pdf, 2, 5.

16. Steven J. Bell and Michael J. Krasulski, "Electronic Reserves, Library Databases and Courseware: A Complementary Relationship," *Journal of Interlibrary Loan, Document Delivery, & Electronic Reserves* 15, no. 1 (2004): 85.

17. Stephanie Atkins Sharpe, "Access Services within Campus and Library Organizations," in Krasulski and Dawes, *Twenty-First-Century Access Services*, 129–30.

18. David W. Bottorff, Katherine Furlong, and David McCaslin, "Building Management Responsibilities for Access Services," in Krasulski and Dawes, *Twenty-First-Century Access Services*, 88–89.

19. Ibid., 90–91.

20. *Standards for Accreditation and Requirements of Affiliation* (Philadelphia: Middle States Commission on Higher Education, 2013), 4.

21. David K. Larsen, "Assessing and Benchmarking Access Services," in Krasulski and Dawes, *Twenty-First-Century Access Services*, 196–97.

22. David McCaslin, "Access Services Education in Library and Information Science Programs," *Journal of Access Services* 6, no. 4 (2009): 485.

23. Michael J. Krasulski, "'Where Do They Come From, and How Are They Trained?' Professional Education and Training of Access Services Librarians in Academic Libraries," *Journal of Access Services* 11, no. 1 (2014): 23.

24. Ibid., 21.

25. Ibid., 24.

26. Trevor A. Dawes and Michael J. Krasulski, "Conclusion," in Krasulski and Dawes, *Twenty-First-Century Access Services*, 243.

27. Ibid., 244–45.

16

Teaching Users

INFORMATION AND TECHNOLOGY INSTRUCTION

April D. Cunningham and Stephanie Rosenblatt

Chapter 16, "Teaching Users: Information and Technology Instruction," addresses the need for information and technology instruction across all types of information organizations. April Cunningham and Stephanie Rosenblatt, with their background as instructional librarians, focus on instruction in information organizations and how to achieve the goals of information and technology literacy. Given the importance of these goals, they note that many information organizations have developed sets of criteria and standards used for planning and assessing the acquisition of information and technological literacy instruction. The authors discuss how these standards and skills are essential across all types of information organizations and they address possible difficulties and obstacles, such as lack of access to technology or wireless infrastructure.

The authors also introduce the importance of critical information literacy, which recognizes that the practices that define the information environment are political and socially constructed, and can therefore be changed and questioned. They explain how information literacy and problem-solving skills remain vital competencies for success across many fields. They further address the importance of assessment of both the information setting and the learning outcomes in an instructional situation.

To round out their discussion, the authors go over the fundamental instructional principles and models useful for all information settings. Finally, the chapter details the types of professional development and trend watching needed to ensure that an information professional develops the competencies in instruction and funding for programs.

★ ★ ★

One of an information professional's core roles is teaching information users. Information professionals not only make sure that users know how to get the most they can from the organization's collections but also ensure that users develop effective information behaviors that apply in any environment. This chapter describes the development of information professionals' work as educators in various types of information organizations. It also argues for the continuing value of information and technology literacy in the twenty-first century. After completing this chapter, the reader should understand how information professionals can embrace their role as teachers and ensure that they achieve the goals of "new librarianship" by "facilitating knowledge creation in their communities."[1]

DEFINITION OF INFORMATION AND TECHNOLOGY LITERACY

In 1989, the American Library Association (ALA) formally defined information literacy as a person's ability "to recognize when information is needed and have the ability to locate, evaluate, and use effectively the needed information."[2]

This simple definition has been used by a number of organizations, such as the American Association of School Librarians (AASL),[3] the Association of College and Research Libraries (ACRL),[4] and the Public Library Association (PLA),[5] to define the skills and conceptual knowledge that information professionals should be teaching users at their institutions. Using this definition, these associations have developed sets of criteria used for planning and assessing the acquisition of information and technological literacy. These criteria, often presented as standards and performance objectives, and lately as threshold concepts, have informed the way information professionals have done their jobs, formalizing the information professional's teaching role and, more recently, adding an assessment component to the information professional's work.

Many organizations outside libraries have adopted the above definition of information literacy in order to legitimize their own conceptualizations of the intellectual skills needed by the populations they serve. Examples of these organizations include UNESCO,[6] the National Council of Teachers of English,[7] and the Association of American Colleges and Universities.[8]

The core concepts that define information literacy have largely remained constant, and there is evidence that information literacy was being taught in libraries for at least a century before ALA's definition was adopted.[9] However, the terms used to describe the ability to find and use information effectively have changed over time, as have the criteria used to identify the acquisition of this ability. These additional terms reflect growing concerns that citizens should be able to navigate and evaluate a wide range of resources both in and out of the library so they are able to participate in today's information society by creating as well as consuming information. These changes have also influenced how information professionals have tried to explain the concepts of information literacy to themselves and to outside groups.

As happens with any definition of a complex concept, multiple parties, including the task force of the ACRL, chafed at the limitations they saw in the 1989 definition of information literacy and the standards that followed. After months of drafts and public feedback, and despite vocal opposition from some librarians who felt unrepresented, a new definition of information literacy was proposed, and the *Framework for Information Literacy for Higher Education* was filed by the ACRL executive board in 2015; this was officially adopted in 2016 when the 2000 *Standards* were retired. The *Framework* defines information literacy as "the set of integrated abilities encompassing the reflective discovery of information, the understanding of how information is produced and valued, and the use of in-

---

TEXTBOX 16.1

Alternate Terms for Information Literacy Instruction

- User education
- Bibliographic instruction
- Library orientation
- Library instruction
- Information literacy instruction

Alternate Terms for Information Literacy

- Critical thinking
- Metaliteracy
- Information fluency

Alternate Term for Technology Literacy

- Digital literacy

---

formation in creating new knowledge and participating ethically in communities of learning."[10] The *Framework* outlines six concepts, outlined in textbox 16.2, and lists examples of the knowledge and dispositions that experts master as they come to a full understanding of each concept. Some consider these to be the threshold concepts of information literacy, which, once understood, change irrevocably our understanding of information. In 2017, the creators of the Threshold Achievement Test for Information Literacy published a set of learning outcomes and performance indicators inspired by the *Framework* in order to support librarians' efforts to teach and assess information literacy (IL) in the post-*Standards* era.[11]

Concerns about the limitations presented by early definitions of information literacy also led to recognition among information professionals that information literacy was not a neutral concept. This awareness is often called *critical information literacy*.[13] Critical information literacy recognizes that the practices/processes/intellectual products that define the academic information environment are politically and socially constructed and can therefore be changed, questioned, and contravened. Instead of just socializing students into current academic discourse and the information economy, the information professional should teach learners to also question its underlying principles.

> TEXTBOX 16.2
>
> **Six Concepts of the Framework for Information Literacy for Higher Education**
>
> 1. Authority is constructed and contextual.
> 2. Information creation is a process.
> 3. Information has value.
> 4. Research as inquiry.
> 5. Scholarship as conversation.
> 6. Searching as strategic exploration.[12]

TEACHING INFORMATION AND TECHNOLOGY LITERACY IN VARIOUS SETTINGS

Libraries in the United States have traditionally garnered support by tapping into the belief that people have an unlimited capacity to improve themselves through self-education. In 1757, Benjamin Franklin described the importance of social or subscription libraries to the birth of the new American republic:

> These libraries have improved the general conversation of Americans, made the common tradesman and farmers as intelligent as most gentlemen from other countries, and perhaps have contributed to some degree to the stand so generally made through the colonies in defense of their privileges.[14]

While information professionals have been consistently recognized as coaches for adults engaged in independent self-study, partners in developing collections supporting formal educational institutions, and champions for youth and adult literacy, their role as formal instructors of information users did not begin to be widely documented until the beginning of the twentieth century[15] (see figure 16.1). Support for information professionals as formal instructors waxed and waned during the middle of the century. Public librarians largely began to retreat from this role—with the exception of continuing to provide literacy-related programming to children and adults.[16]

In 1983, the National Commission on Excellence in Education report, *A Nation at Risk*, sounded the alarm about the tide of mediocrity flooding American education since the height of Cold War–era investment, and voiced fears that the country would soon lose its dominance in the world economy, baldly stating, "If an unfriendly foreign power had attempted to impose on America the mediocre educational performance that exists today, we might well have viewed it as an act of war."[17] ACRL's *Presidential Committee on Information Literacy: Final Report*, which formally defined information literacy in 1989, directly responded to *A Nation at Risk*, and proposed information literacy as the solution to the threat the National Commission identified.[18]

1910s	1920s	1930s	1940s	1950s	1960s	1970s	1980s	1990s
• According to U.S. Bureau of Education 20% of academic libraries surveyed offer some sort of IL instruction.	• Public libraries begin services for children. • ALA Commission on Libraries and Adult Education begins. School library standards published. • Some land-grant institutions offer credit-bearing IL courses.	• Public libraries join Adult Education Movement with mixed results. • The Great Depression reduces funding for libraries.	• World War II reduces funding for libraries.	• Russia launches Sputnik satellite in 1957 raising fears that the US has lost its technical and scientific edge. Nation responds by increasing funding for education.	• Rapid creation of community colleges with open admissions results in surge of "non-traditional" students into higher education.	• LOEX, the Library Instruction Roundtable (LIRT), and ACRL-IS are founded. • Academic librarians experiment with modes of instruction including peer coaching and the "workbook" course.	• *A Nation at Risk* points out that educational gains made during the Cold War have evaporated. • ALA defines information literacy. • Tim Berners-Lee develops the protocols that give birth to the World Wide Web and ushers in the Information Age.	• Public libraries ramp up their technology training in an effort to combat the growing digital divide. • *Information Power*, highlighting the importance of school libraries, is published.

Figure 16.1 Teaching Users in the Twentieth Century. *Created by editors.*

Academic libraries, school libraries, and, to a lesser extent, public libraries, used the release of the presidential report to galvanize efforts to prove libraries' relevance in the new Information Age born with the creation of the World Wide Web. ACRL released the *Information Literacy Competency Standards for Higher Education* in 2000.[19] AASL continued to promote best practices in school library service and teach with *Information Power: Building Partnerships for Learning* in 1998.[20] School and academic librarians began renewed efforts to collaborate with other faculty members to infuse information literacy across the curriculum. Colleges and universities showed support for information literacy programs by adding library instruction classrooms—dedicated computer labs with projectors and internet connections—to their buildings. Public libraries continued to provide the same types of programming as earlier in the century, but added programs to provide computer-use instruction and technology training.

Information literacy is a survival skill in the Information Age. Just as public libraries were once a means of education and a better life for many of the over 20 million immigrants of the late 1800s and early 1900s, they remain today as potentially the strongest and most far-reaching community resource for lifelong learning.[21] Instead of drowning in the abundance of information that floods their lives, information-literate people know how to find, evaluate, and use information effectively to solve a particular problem or make a decision—whether the information they select comes from a computer, a book, a government agency, a film, or any number of other possible resources. Libraries, which provide a significant public access point to such information and usually at no cost, must play a key role in preparing people for the demands of today's information society.

THE GROWING NEED FOR INFORMATION AND TECHNOLOGY LITERACY IN COMMUNITIES

Increasing people's access to information has not resulted in all the positive social outcomes that commentators of the twentieth century had hoped to see.[22] Instead, the current information environment has raised new concerns about how people think and learn, communicate with one another, and evaluate the information they find.[23]

The Digital Divide

The term *digital divide* first came to prominence in 1995 when the National Telecommunications and Information Administration published its study on the disparity in access to the internet;[24] emerging technologies had rapidly changed what it meant to be connected.[25] The causes of the digital divide have often been attributed to structural inequalities leading to disparities in socioeconomic status, which are further complicated by inequalities related to ethnicity and gender.[26] Other dimensions of

April D. Cunningham and Stephanie Rosenblatt

the digital divide besides access include disparities in the skills,[27] knowledge,[28] and interest[29] to use information technology and the web.

Twenty-First-Century Literacies

The need for a highly skilled workforce in the United States has been one of the driving concerns behind efforts to reduce the effects of the digital divide. Influential reports like *What Work Requires of Schools*, prepared by the Secretary's Commission on Achieving Necessary Skills in 1991 (SCANS), have identified the job skills that employers prize most.[30] These job skills include knowing how to acquire, evaluate, and communicate information, as well as how to use "efficient learning techniques to acquire and apply new knowledge and skills."[31] These skills also have strong connections to the fundamental attributes of information literacy as defined by ALA in 1989. Recent surveys of employers[32] show that information literacy and solving problems using information remain vital competencies for success in many fields, whether in the professional, service, or manufacturing sectors. Efforts to define the value of a college degree in the first two decades of the twenty-first century have focused on these core competencies that all students should expect to develop

> Recent surveys of employers show that information literacy and solving problems using information remain vital competencies for success in many fields, whether in the professional, service, or manufacturing sectors.

before graduation, regardless of their location, major, preparation, or standing. The *Degree Qualifications Profile*, developed in 2011 and updated in 2014 by the Lumina Foundation[33] as part of its efforts to increase college attendance and completion, defines the proficiencies that come from an effective undergraduate education. These include the intellectual skills associated with information literacy, like analytical inquiry, using information resources, "engaging diverse perspectives, ethical reasoning, quantitative fluency, and communicative fluency."[34]

Accountability Movement

Widespread concern about maintaining United States prominence in the global economy has resulted in increased scrutiny and control of educational and nonprofit organizations by the government and by reformers.[35] In the field of information science, the accountability movement inspired ACRL to commission the *Value of Academic Libraries Report* in 2010.[36] This report was a large-scale review of the existing research about the impact of academic libraries on higher education (see also chapter 7: "Learning and Research Institutions: Academic Libraries"). Many of its recommendations call upon academic librarians to investigate the effects of their teaching on users by comparing students who have had library instruction against students who have not. See textbox 16.3.

In 2014, the AASL launched a national assessment initiative to gather evidence of the impact of school libraries on students' success.[37] The initiative resulted in a planning guide, program assessment rubric, and program assessment tool kit to support school librarians in evaluating, advocating for, and improving their own instructional programs as well as models for collaborating with their counterpart librarians in colleges and universities to facilitate

TEXTBOX 16.3

Recommended Areas for Demonstrating Academic Libraries' Value

- Student enrollment
- Student retention and graduation rates
- Student learning
- Student achievement (e.g., GPA)
- Student experience
- Student success after graduation

students' transition to higher education. In 2015, AASL launched a research project to revise and update these guidelines so they would be more reflective of the work performed by information professionals today.[38] The study was completed in June 2016 and implemented in fall 2017. (Check out: http://www.ala.org/aasl/standards/revision for the latest update on these revised guidelines.)

CONTEMPORARY EXAMPLES OF TEACHING IN LIBRARIES

When information professionals talk about teaching, they are most often referring to formal teaching, such as when learners enroll in a course or attend a class or workshop taught by an information professional or staff member. In addition to formal teaching, there is also informal teaching, such as when information professionals teach patrons at their moment of need. Often referred to as "reference" by public services librarians, instruction librarians widely consider these services to be instructional, and they include the work information professionals do at the reference desk, in research consultations, or via online tutorials and videos that learners access when they get stuck while conducting their research (see also chapter 11: "Information Intermediation and Reference Services").

Literacy Training at Public Libraries

Information professionals recognize that reading is a foundational skill that facilitates all other learning.[39] Although not usually taught by information professionals, adult literacy training in libraries ensures that libraries are fulfilling one of their core roles. Many public policies that provide funding for adult literacy programs in libraries are supported because literacy has a social value as a work skill.[40]

TEXTBOX 16.4

Examples of Public Libraries Promoting Early Literacy and Family Literacy

- Libraries in Santa Monica, California; Pueblo, Colorado; and Halifax, North Carolina, are partnering with national organizations including ALA, the Institute of Museum and Library Services (IMLS), and ProLiteracy to provide online training to library staff about how to support adult learners.[41]
- The Casa Grande Public Library in Arizona used grant funding to begin a storytime using e-readers and promoted participation by reaching out to parents who were least likely to have access to e-readers themselves and were most likely to be looking for ways to give their children a chance to experience this new technology.[42]
- The San Diego Public Library offers a family literacy program throughout its branches where parents can attend with their children. The sessions introduce techniques parents can use when reading to their children, families receive free books to begin an in-home library, and parents learn about nutrition and healthy media habits for children.[43]

Technology Literacy Training: Public and Academic Libraries

Though closely related, information literacy and technology literacy are not synonymous. Technology literacy addresses users' abilities to problem-solve and build confidence with new technologies. There is an assumption that everyone now has the computer skills and internet access they need to complete basic tasks like applying for jobs, signing up for health insurance, and interacting with government agencies online. As a result, technology literacy is more important than ever. Despite wider dissemination of information technologies across populations in the United States, public libraries still play a significant role in reducing the negative effects of the digital divide by providing access to computers and other hardware for users.[44] Information professionals observe that library users are often five to ten years behind in developing the skills they need to effectively use all of the tools now available to them.[45] In order to make these tools more useful for creating and sharing knowledge, information professionals train users and teach them about the social practices around information technology.[46] Ever since personal computers became ubiquitous, public librarians have been offering basic sessions on using them for word processing and accessing the internet. Lafayette Public Library and Hennepin County Library, for example, also offer classes on creating websites, designing video games, editing photos, and using 3-D printers.[47]

> **Discussion Question**
>
> Imagine that you are assigned to create a new technology workshop for library users, what would be your first few steps in preparing a successful workshop?

In higher education, library users often already have access to personal computers so information professionals focus on emerging technologies instead. When Google Glass was first released in 2013, most people had no chance to try it out, so a handful of academic libraries became early adopters. Claremont College, for example, organized class visits, a lecture program, and symposia about Google Glass where users not only had a chance to encounter the technology but also to consider its meaning for their community.[48] More recently, librarians have been providing their users with access to video games and equipment, including virtual reality, to support academic programs.[49]

Information Literacy and Research Training

School Libraries

The Common Core Standards, initiated in 2010 and widely adopted by 2015, changed elementary and secondary education in the name of increasing students' readiness for careers and college. The standards required students to conduct research and integrate sources into their writing across content areas and much earlier in their education than they had in the past.[50] Although these new standards emphasized students' use of information, it made no provision for additional funding for school libraries or school librarians. Severely under-resourced libraries remained a pressing issue in states without a minimum requirement for school library staffing. The school librarians already on-site used the new Common Core curriculum to continue their work with classroom teachers to ensure libraries had materials to support students' inquiry and provided training to teachers, staff, and students about research fundamentals[51] (see also chapter 6: "Literacy and Media Centers: School Libraries"). Many school librarians implemented or adapted existing models like iSearch[52] and Big 6[53] to support students' growth as researchers.

Public Libraries

Public librarians teach users how to do research using the public library's more specialized collections (see also chapter 8: "Community Anchors for Lifelong Learning: Public Libraries"). Two common examples are business research and genealogical research. This instruction makes the library's collections more valuable to users who might not know how to get the most out of them or how to access them at all. This improves the library's return on investment by bringing more users to some of the collections that are costly for the library to maintain, providing information professionals with data that shows why the funding should continue.

Academic Libraries

Academic librarians introduce novice researchers to advanced techniques for thinking about information, framing questions for inquiry, and making meaning of what they find (see also chapter 7: "Learning and Research Institutions: Academic Libraries").[54] Recent surveys show that college professors and academic library directors highly value academic librarians' efforts to develop undergraduates'

> Recent surveys show that college professors and academic library directors highly value academic librarians' efforts to develop undergraduates' information literacy, including research and analysis, ranking it ahead of the support the library provides for faculty research.

information literacy, including research and analysis, ranking it ahead of the support the library provides for faculty research.[55] Academic librarians also provide research instruction for graduate students and teaching assistants to ensure that they have the skills they need to complete their own research and support their students' development.

When professors request information literacy instruction to prepare students to successfully complete specific assignments, communication is essential to ensure that the instruction will be relevant to students' needs. If faculty do not provide sufficient information to plan effective instruction, it is the academic librarians' responsibility to educate professors about their expectations, demonstrating to faculty how more collaboration will result in better learning.[56] At many institutions, academic librarians train new faculty about information literacy, library resources, and the standards information professionals have set for instruction.[57]

Communication between information professionals and faculty about research instruction can be as simple as brief e-mails or conversations to plan one-shot sessions that meet the information professional's and the professor's goals for students' learning.[58] But sometimes information professionals and faculty work more closely together to plan instruction. In these cases, information professionals may make suggestions to improve assignment instructions or may create new assignments for students to support their development as researchers and lifelong learners.[59] Academic librarians have also adapted a concept from special libraries called embedded librarianship.[60] Embedded librarians provide ongoing support to students and faculty by integrating themselves into learning environments, like courses and fieldwork, where they have more opportunities to intervene in students' learning and create experiences that reinforce positive research habits.[61]

Many academic librarians also teach for-credit courses. Innovative approaches include kYmberly Keeton's hip-hop-based curriculum, where students gain core IL concepts while engaging with the history and influence of hip-hop culture; and open pedagogy, where students apply IL concepts as they use, remix, and create open educational resources, often for the benefit of future learners or for the wider community.[62]

Research suggests that taking an information literacy course in college can improve students' graduation rates.[63] Some colleges and universities require students to take a course entirely on information literacy, while other campuses have identified one or more courses where information literacy is integrated into the existing curriculum in other disciplines. Some information professionals have found a middle path by co-teaching courses with other faculty or teaching in paired classes where their course is linked to a course in another discipline.[64]

EDUCATIONAL PRINCIPLES

All instruction librarians, regardless of the setting in which they work, need to apply the same basic instructional design principles when planning learning experiences.

Instructional Design Principles

- Identify the audience/students that will be taught.
- Determine the information needs of the students.
- Decide what will be taught.
- Decide how to formally or informally assess what the students have learned.
- Design the instructional experience.
- Reflect on the teaching.

Deciding what will be taught and how to assess the acquisition of the skill/concept before planning the instructional experience is common to all methods of instructional design. Models of instructional design commonly used by information professionals include Wiggins and McTighe's backward design method,[65] the ADDIE method,[66] and Char Booth's USER method.[67]

> One of the key steps to deciding what to teach a particular group of students is identifying desired outcomes for the class based on the users' immediate information needs as connected to broader ideas about information literacy.

One of the key steps to deciding what to teach a particular group of students is identifying desired outcomes for the class based on the users' immediate information needs as connected to broader ideas about information literacy. Identifying outcomes helps information professionals prioritize what to focus on during the lesson. This is especially important for information literacy instruction, as the majority of the teaching by information professionals still takes place in a one-shot session without any follow-up contact.

Assessing Instruction

One of the biggest changes in the work of instruction librarians in the twenty-first century is the increased expectation that information professionals document and assess the learning that takes place through their teaching efforts. Most often, information professionals assess users' learning during instruction or immediately after. When information professionals assess users' learning during the instruction session, often called formative assessment, the information professional can use what he/she discovers about learners' understanding to make informed decisions about what to emphasize and de-emphasize during the rest of the session. When information professionals conduct summative assessment at the end of the session or after learners have applied their skills to complete a research task, the information professional gains a sense of what users learned overall. Both types of assessment give the information professional the opportunity to find out if users can demonstrate the skills and knowledge that were the focus of the instruction.

There are many types of activities that get learners to engage with the content of instruction, whether during a one-shot session or throughout longer courses. Many educators share their active learning techniques online. Information professionals can also find examples in books and in professional periodicals like *College & Research Libraries News*. The foundational work on classroom assessment by Angelo and Cross, *Classroom Assessment Techniques: A Handbook for College Teachers*, provides an overview of the rationale behind classroom assessment, as well as strategies that can be adapted for the classroom.[68]

The decision about the type of assessment methods to use in a classroom should be based on what the information professional wants to know about students' learning and how they plan to use that knowledge. Assessment should be an ongoing process of learning about the information professional's effect on users and applying this learning to keep improving instructional efforts. Information professionals should select assessment methods that will elicit the most actionable information from learners so that the assessment results can lead to improved instruction and outcomes. Often in library instruction this means gathering data about learners' reaction to the session and their ability to recall key information.[69] Assessment of more lasting behavioral change or any long-term increase in learners' information literacy cannot be achieved during one-shot instruction, but it is possible for embedded librarians or librarians teaching credit-bearing courses.

Discussion Question

What evidence have you observed to support or refute the claim that the key role for information professionals going forward will be user education to enhance users' abilities to create knowledge in their own communities rather than the traditional stewardship of large library collections?

OPPORTUNITIES AND CHALLENGES

Pursuing Professional Excellence

It is impossible to become an effective instruction librarian without dedicating time and energy to professional development. Most information professionals learn how to teach by observing more experienced teachers, reading the professional literature, attending conferences that focus on information and technology literacy instruction, and joining local or national organizations for instruction librarians. A good method for ensuring continued improvement is to set aside time annually to reflect on satisfying and uncomfortable teaching experiences to identify areas of strength and those in need of improvement.[70] Once one or two goals for improvement are identified, make time for additional training to help meet those goals.

Scaling Up

Attention on information literacy development is increasing in the early twenty-first century. Evidence of this includes the 2014 UNESCO declaration on media and information literacy,[71] higher education accreditation standards that identify information literacy as a core outcome of a college education,[72] national policies that name the library as a site of workforce development because of the lifelong learning skills that librarians encourage,[73] and employer surveys that demonstrate their expectation that employees will apply advanced information processing and communication skills.[74] This presents an opportunity for information professionals because they have been developing their capacity for teaching users this set of skills that is now so sought after. In order to benefit from this opportunity, however, some information professionals have already found that they need to meet the challenge of scaling-up their efforts to reach more users without additional staff or increased funding.[75] Online instruction, particularly through web-based tutorials, has been embraced by many information professionals as a method for providing instruction to self-directed learners and learners who are looking for just-in-time instruction as they are encountering the limits of their research skills.

Research suggests that online and in-person instruction on information literacy skills result in similar learning gains.[76] Yet drawbacks remain. One drawback to online instruction is that some users

> Online instruction, particularly through web-based tutorials, has been embraced by many information professionals as a method for providing instruction to self-directed learners and learners who are looking for just-in-time instruction as they are encountering the limits of their research skills.

do not have access to the technology they need to access the materials. Another is that some do not prefer to learn online. Additionally, if users do not apply what they learn from these tutorials, it will not lead to lasting changes in their skills or habits. In order to get the most benefit from online instructional materials that information professionals create, professors, teachers, and employers must further facilitate users' learning by deliberately connecting the content the information professionals made to performance requirements in classes and on the job.

Stepping Up

In order to sustain instruction programs, information professionals need the ability to see opportunities to enter what has been called in organizational research the "arena of confrontation."[77] This is the location, sometimes physical and sometimes only symbolic, where institutional priorities are weighed and decisions are made about allocating limited resources. For information professionals who teach in public libraries, the arena of confrontation may be management meetings at their library or city council meetings where elected officials make budget decisions that will either enhance or hinder the library's ability to provide learning opportunities for users. In academic settings, information professionals benefit from volunteering for campus-level service opportunities, like organizing accreditation self-studies or serving on first-year-experience committees, because these are the sites where the values of the institution are defined and information professionals can influence decisions to benefit students' information literacy. School librarians can enter the arena of confrontation by accepting leadership roles on their campus and in their district, including becoming a teacher on special assignment who is responsible for building their colleagues' skills through professional development.

Information professionals must also stay alert for emerging cultural, political, and economic trends they can use to highlight the educational value of libraries. Media coverage of inflammatory and unsubstantiated news stories during the 2016 presidential election evolved into widespread concern about the creation and dissemination of "fake news" through social media in 2017.[78] This period of heightened awareness about media literacy, confirmation bias, and the economics of click-bait provided an opportunity for information professionals to highlight their role as educators working to create a more informed citizenry. Seizing the moment, some information professionals created new webinars, workshops, and credit-courses. The 2010 book *Blur: How to Know What's True in the Age of Information Overload* was rediscovered as a resource for defining the critical thinking necessary to evaluate information generally and news sources in particular.[79] Information professionals and other educators also took the "fake news" trend as an opportunity to reflect on their own role in contributing to the view that all information has some bias and the resulting nihilistic skepticism that some saw as the root cause of the trend.[80]

Information professionals must not wait to be asked to step into leadership roles or to take stands on challenging issues. Instead, they should seek out these opportunities for themselves. In every case, entering the arena of confrontation requires information professionals to transcend their day-to-day role and allows them to demonstrate their value to their institution and to the broader community. By challenging others' assumptions about the place of the information professional in their institution and in society, information professionals gain power and influence that they can use to create the circumstances that will result in the biggest benefit for learners.

CONCLUSION

The future holds exciting possibilities for information professionals who teach. Education is considered a growth area for information professionals.[81] Some believe that soon the buildings and collections that have traditionally constituted libraries themselves will no longer be the purpose and focus of information professionals' work.[82] The profession may already be in the process of orienting itself toward facilitating learning and communication, regardless of where users are finding information.[83] Teaching users in the future may prove to be one of the most stable aspects of a profession that no longer has to warehouse materials just in case they are needed. The value information professionals add to users' abilities to create knowledge in their own communities[84] and strengthen "civic ecologies"[85] may become our most recognizable trait. This chapter offered background, examples, and suggested techniques for teaching that information professionals will use as the foundation on which to build the future of librarianship.

NOTES

1. R. David Lankes, *The Atlas of New Librarianship* (Cambridge, MA: MIT Press, 2011).
2. Association of College and Research Libraries, *Presidential Committee on Information Literacy: Final Report*, last modified January 10, 1989, http://www.ala.org/acrl/publications/whitepapers/presidential.
3. American Association of School Librarians, *Information Power: Guidelines for School Library Media Programs* (Chicago: American Library Association, 1988), http://files.eric.ed.gov/fulltext/ED315028.pdf.; American Association of School Librarians, *Standards for the 21st Century Learner* (Chicago: American Association of School Librarians, 2007), http://www.ala.org/aasl/sites/ala.org.aasl/files/content/guidelinesandstandards/learningstandards/AASL_Learning_Standards_2007.pdf.
4. Association of College and Research Libraries, "Information Literacy Competency Standards for Higher Education," archived March 22, 2017, https://web.archive.org/web/20170322170540/http://www.ala.org/acrl/standards/informationliteracycompetency.
5. June Garcia and Sandra Nelson, *2007 Public Library Service Responses* (Public Library Association, 2007), http://ryepubliclibrary.org/wp-content/uploads/2012/05/ALAserviceresponses.pdf.
6. Forest Woody Horton, Jr., *Understanding Information Literacy: A Primer* (Paris: UNESCO, 2007), http://unesdoc.unesco.org/images/0015/001570/157020e.pdf.
7. "The NCTE Definition of 21st Century Literacies," *National Council of Teachers of English*, last modified February 5, 2013, http://www.ncte.org/positions/statements/21stcentdefinition.
8. American Association of Colleges and Universities, "Information Literacy Value Rubric," in VALUE: Valid Assessment of Learning in Undergraduate Education, last modified March 14, 2013, http://www.aacu.org/value/rubrics/InformationLiteracy.cfm.
9. Otis H. Robinson, "College Library Administration," in *Public Libraries in the United States: Their Condition and Management. Special Report, Department of the Interior, Bureau of Education*, part 1 35, no. 1187 (Washington, DC: Government Printing Office, 1876), 520–25, facsimile of the 1st edition with an introduction by Francis Keppel; Jacquelyn M. Morris, *Bibliographic Instruction in Academic Libraries: A Review of the Literature and Selected Bibliography* (Champaign, IL: University of Illinois, 1979), 1–48, http://files.eric.ed.gov/fulltext/ED180505.pdf.
10. "Framework for Information Literacy for Higher Education," *Association of College & Research Libraries*, last modified January 11, 2016, http://www.ala.org/acrl/standards/ilframework.
11. Rick Wiggins, "About the Threshold Achievement Test for Information Literacy" (Carrick Enterprises, 2017), https://thresholdachievement.com/the-test/about-the-test.
12. American Library Association, "Framework for Information Literacy for Higher Education," 2016, http://www.ala.org/acrl/standards/ilframework.
13. James Elmborg, "Critical Information Literacy: Implications for Instructional Practice," *Journal of Academic Librarianship* 32, no. 2 (2006): 192–99, doi:10.1016/j.calib.2005.12.004; James Elmborg, "Literacies, Narratives, and Adult Learning and Libraries," *New Directions for Adult and Continuing Education*, no. 127 (2010): 67–76, doi:10.1002/ace.382; Heidi L. M. Jacobs, "Information Literacy and

Reflective Pedagogical Praxis," *Journal of Academic Librarianship* 34, no. 5 (2008): 256–62, doi:10.1016/j
.acalib.2008.03.009; Debra Hoffman and Amy Wallace, "Intentional Informationists: Re-Envisioning
Information Literacy and Re-Designing Instructional Programs around Faculty Librarians' Strength as
Campus Connectors, Information Professionals, and Course Designers," *Journal of Academic Librarianship* 39, no. 6 (2013): 546–51, doi:10.1016/j.acalib.2013.06.004.

14. Benjamin Franklin, *The Autobiography of Benjamin Franklin* (Charlottesville, VA: University of Virginia
Library, 1995), 36.

15. Henry L. Cecil and Willard A. Heaps, *School Library Service in the United States: An Interpretive Survey*
(New York: H. W. Wilson Co., 1940). Reprinted in Melvin M. Bowie, *Historic Documents of School Libraries*
(Fayetteville, AR: Hi Willow Research & Publishing, 1986), 175–91; Robert Ellis Lee, *Continuing Education
for Adults through the American Public Library, 1833–1864* (Chicago: American Library Association, 1966),
1–13; Elise A. Rogers Halliday Okobi, "History and Development of Adult Services," in *Library Services for
Adults in the 21st Century* (Santa Barbara, CA: Libraries Unlimited, 2014), 19–28; Jesse H. Shera, "The
Social Library: I: Origins, Form, and Economic Backgrounds," in *Foundations of the Public Library* (Chicago:
University of Chicago Press, 1949), 68–85; John Mark Tucker, "User Education in Academic Libraries: A
Century in Retrospect," *Library Trends* 29, no. 1 (1980): 9–27.

16. Okobi, *Library Services for Adults in the 21st Century*.

17. David P. Gardner and the United States National Commission on Excellence in Education, *A Nation at
Risk: The Imperative for Educational Reform: A Report to the Nation and the Secretary of Education* (Wash-
ington, DC: Government Printing Office, 1983), 5, http://www.eric.ed.gov/contentdelivery/servlet/
ERICServlet?accno=ED226006.

18. ACRL, *Presidential Committee on Information Literacy: Final Report*.

19. American Library Association, *Information Literacy Competency Standards for Higher Education* (Chicago:
American Library Association, 2000).

20. American Association of School Librarians and Association for Educational Communications, *Information Power: Building Partnerships for Learning* (Chicago: American Library Association, 1998).

21. ACRL, *Presidential Committee on Information Literacy: Final Report*.

22. Vannevar Bush, "As We May Think," *Atlantic* (July 1, 1945), http://www.theatlantic.com/magazine/
archive/1945/07/as-we-may-think/303881/?single_page=true.

23. Siva Vaidhyanathan, *The Googlization of Everything (and Why We Should Worry)* (Berkeley: University of
California Press, 2012); David Weinberger, *Too Big to Know: Rethinking Knowledge Now That Facts Aren't
Facts, Experts Are Everywhere, and the Smartest Person in the Room Is the Room* (New York: Basic Books, 2011).

24. "Falling Through the Net: A Survey of the 'Have Nots' in Rural and Urban America," National Telecommunications & Information Administration, United States Department of Commerce, last modified
February 22, 2014, http://www.ntia.doc.gov/ntiahome/fallingthru.html.

25. Svanhild Aabø, "The Role and Value of Public Libraries in the Age of Digital Technologies," *Journal of
Librarianship and Information Science* 37, no. 4 (2005): 205–10, doi:10.1177/0961000605057855.

26. Eszter Hargittai, "Second-Level Digital Divide: Differences in People's Online Skills," *First Monday* 7, no.
4 (2002), doi:10.5210/fm.v7i4.942.

27. Ibid.

28. Mun-Cho Kim and Jong-Kil Kim, "Digital Divide: Conceptual Discussions and Prospect," in *The Human
Society and the Internet: Internet-Related Socio-Economic Issues* (New York: Springer, 2001), 78–91.

29. Michael Kende, *Internet Society Global Internet Report 2014* (2014), http://www.internetsociety.org/
sites/default/files/Global_Internet_Report_2014_0.pdf.

30. The Secretary's Commission on Achieving Necessary Skills (SCANS), "*What Work Requires of Schools:
A SCANS Report for America 2000*, U.S. Department of Labor (1991), http://wdr.doleta.gov/SCANS/
whatwork/whatwork.pdf.

31. SCANS, *What Work Requires of Schools*, 14.

32. Hart Research Associates, *It Takes More Than a Major: Employer Priorities for College Learning and Student
Success* (Washington, DC: American Association of Colleges and Universities, 2013), http://www.aacu
.org/leap/documents/2013_EmployerSurvey.pdf; Alison J. Head et al., "What Information Competencies Matter in Today's Workplace?," *Library and Information Research* 37, no. 114 (May 2013): 75–104,
http://www.lirgjournal.org.uk/lir/ojs/index.php/lir/article/view/557/593.

33. Lumina Foundation, https://www.luminafoundation.org/.
34. Lumina Foundation, *The Degree Qualifications Profile 2.0: Defining U.S. Degrees through Demonstration and Documentation of College Learning* (Indianapolis, IN: Lumina Foundation, 2014), 19–23, https://www.luminafoundation.org/files/resources/dqp-web-download.pdf.
35. F. King Alexander, "The Changing Face of Accountability: Monitoring and Assessing Institutional Performance in Higher Education," *Journal of Higher Education* 71, no. 4 (July–August 2000): 411–31, http://www.jstor.org/stable/2649146.
36. Megan Oakleaf, *Value of Academic Libraries: A Comprehensive Research Review and Report* (Chicago: American Library Association, 2010), http://www.ala.org/acrl/sites/ala.org.acrl/files/content/issues/value/val_report.pdf.
37. American Association of School Libraries National Research Forum, "Causality: School Libraries and Student Success," American Library Association (2014), http://www.ala.org/aasl/sites/ala.org.aasl/files/content/researchandstatistics/CLASSWhitePaperFINAL.pdf.
38. American Library Association, "Your Voice, Your Standards!," accessed September 19, 2017, http://www.ala.org/aasl/standards/revision.
39. Erlene Bishop Killeen, "Yesterday, Today, and Tomorrow: Transitions of the Work but Not the Mission," *Teacher Librarian* 36, no. 5 (2009): 8–13.
40. Kathleen de la Pena McCook and Peggy Barber, "Public Policy as a Factor Influencing Adult Lifelong Learning, Adult Literacy and Public Libraries," *Reference & User Services Quarterly* 42, no. 1 (2002): 66–75.
41. Alicia Suskin Muniz and Sarah Howell, "Adult Literacy through Libraries: Building a National Movement," New York Library Association (November 3, 2016), https://www.nyla.org/max/userfiles/uploads/NYLA_November_2016_without_notes.pdf.
42. "Digital Storytime Means Serious Fun—and Vital Learning—for Arizona Toddlers," *Institute of Museum and Library Services* (March 2013), http://www.imls.gov/digital_storytime_means_serious_fun_and_vital_learning_for_arizona_toddlers.aspx?CategoryId=2&pg=5.
43. "San Diego Public Library's Award-Winning Literacy Services," Support My Library San Diego (February 22, 2011), https://supportmylibrary.org/?attachment_id=516.
44. Paul T. Jaeger, et al., "The Intersection of Public Policy and Public Access: Digital Divides, Digital Literacy, Digital Inclusion, and Public Libraries," *Public Library Quarterly* 31, no. 1 (2012): 1–20, doi:10.1080/01616846.2012.654728.
45. Joseph McKendrick, *Funding and Priorities: The Library Resource Guide Benchmark Study on 2011 Library Spending Plans* (Chatham, NJ: Unisphere Research, 2011), http://lgdata.s3-website-us-east-1.amazonaws.com/docs/231/215960/Funding-and-PrioritiesThe-Library-Resource-Guide-Benchmark-Study-on-2011-Library-Spending-Plans.pdf.
46. Kimberly Pendell et al., "Tutor-Facilitated Adult Digital Literacy Learning: Insights from a Case Study," *Internet Reference Services Quarterly* 18, no. 2 (2013): 105–25.
47. Cynthia Matthias and Christy Mulligan, "Hennepin County Library's Teen Tech Squad: Youth Leadership and Technology Free-for-All," *Young Adult Library Services* 8, no. 2 (2010): 13–16; Richard Burgess, "South Regional Library to Give 3-D Printing, Electronic Kits Trial Run over Summer," *Advocate* (May 23, 2014), http://theadvocate.com/news/9184745-123/south-regional-library-to-give.
48. Char Booth and Dani Brecher, "Ok, Library: Implications and Opportunities for Google Glass," *College & Research Libraries News* 75, no. 5 (May 2014): 234–39, http://crln.acrl.org/content/75/5/234.full.pdf+html; Carolyn Bishoff, Shannon L. Farrell, and Amy E. Neeser, "Outreach, Collaboration, Collegiality: Evolving Approaches to Library Video Game Services," *Journal of Library Innovation* 6, no. 1 (2015): 92–109, https://conservancy.umn.edu/bitstream/handle/11299/174475/bishoff_farrell_neeser_joli_2015.pdf.
49. Bishoff, Farrell, and Neeser, "Outreach, Collaboration, Collegiality: Evolving Approaches to Library Video Game Services."
50. Liz Deskins, "Inquiry Studies: Needed Skills," *School Library Monthly* 28, no. 5 (February 2012): 20–23, http://transferfoster.pbworks.com/w/file/fetch/97619920/Inquiry%20Studies—Needed%20Skills.pdf.
51. American Association of School Librarians, *Implementing the Common Core State Standards: The Role of the School Librarian* (Chicago: American Library Association, November 2013), http://www.ala.org/aasl/sites/ala.org.aasl/files/content/externalrelations/CCSSLibrariansBrief_FINAL.pdf.

52. iSearch, "INFOhio," 2017, https://www.infohio.org/students/er/item/isearch.
53. Big 6, "The Big 6: Information and Technology Skills for Student Success," Accessed September 19, 2017, https://www.infohio.org/students/er/item/isearch.
54. Barbara Fister, "Smoke and Mirrors: Finding Order in a Chaotic World," *Research Strategies* 20, no. 3 (2005): 99–107, http://homepages.gac.edu/~fister/WILU2005.html.
55. Ross Housewright, Roger C. Schonfeld, and Kate Wulfson, *Ithaka S+R US Faculty Survey* (April 8, 2013), 69, http://www.sr.ithaka.org/sites/default/files/reports/Ithaka_SR_US_Faculty_Survey_2012_FINAL.pdf.
56. Yvonne Nalani Meulemans and Allison Carr, "Not at Your Service: Building Genuine Faculty-Librarian Partnerships," *Reference Services Review* 41, no. 1 (2013): 80–90, doi:10.1108/00907321311300893.
57. Betsy Baker, "Bibliographic Instruction: Building the Librarian/Faculty Partnership," *Reference Librarian* 24 (1989): 311–28.
58. Joan R. Kaplowitz, *Transforming Information Literacy Instruction Using Learner-Centered Teaching* (New York: Neal-Schuman Publishers, Inc., 2012); Ryan Sittler and Douglas Cook, *The Library Instruction Cookbook* (Chicago: Association of College and Research Libraries, 2009).
59. Daniel Brendle-Moczuk, "Encouraging Students' Lifelong Learning through Graded Information Literacy Assignments," *Reference Services Review* 34, no. 4 (2006): 498–508, doi:10.1108/00907320610716404.
60. David Shumaker, *The Embedded Librarian* (Medford, NJ: Information Today, Inc., 2012).
61. Cassandra Kvenlid and Kaijsa Calkins, *Embedded Librarians: Moving Beyond One-Shot Instruction* (Chicago: Association of College and Research Libraries, 2011); Amy Van Epps and Megan Sapp Nelson, "One-Shot or Embedded? Assessing Different Delivery Timing for Information Resources Relevant to Assignments," *Evidence Based Library and Information Practice* 8, no. 1 (2013): 4–18, http://ejournals.library.ualberta.ca/index.php/EBLIP/article/view/18027/14793.
62. kYmberly Keeton, "The Remix: Hip Hop Information Literacy Pedagogy in the 21st Century," in *Librarians with Spines: Information Agitators in an Age of Stagnation* (Los Angeles: Librarians with Spines, 2016); Michele Van Hoeck, "Wikipedia as an Authentic Learning Space," *LOEX Quarterly* 39 (Winter 2013): 4–8, http://commons.emich.edu/cgi/viewcontent.cgi?article=1188&context=loexquarterly.
63. Jean Marie Cook, "A Library Credit Course and Student Success Rates: A Longitudinal Study," *College & Research Libraries* 75 (May 2014): 272–83, http://crl.acrl.org/content/early/2012/12/19/crl12-424.full.pdf+html.
64. Hoffman and Wallace, "Intentional Informationists."
65. Grant Wiggins and Jay McTighe, *Understanding by Design* (Upper Saddle River, NJ: Merrill Prentice Hall, 1998).
66. Steven J. Bell and John D. Shank, *Academic Librarianship by Design: A Blended Librarian's Guide to the Tools and Techniques* (Chicago: American Library Association, 2007).
67. Char Booth, *Reflective Teaching, Effective Learning: Instructional Literacy for Library Educators* (Chicago: American Library Association, 2011).
68. Thomas A. Angelo and K. Patricia Cross, *Classroom Assessment Techniques: A Handbook for College Teachers* (San Francisco: Jossey-Bass Publishers, 1993).
69. Dominique Turnbow and Annie Zeidman-Karpinski, "Don't Use a Hammer When You Need a Screwdriver: How to Use the Right Tools to Create Assessment That Matters," *Communications in Information Literacy* 10 (2016): 143–62, http://www.comminfolit.org/index.php?journal=cil&page=article&op=view&path%5B%5D=v10i2p143.
70. Stephen Brookfield, *Becoming a Critically Reflective Teacher*, second edition (San Francisco: Jossey-Bass, 2017).
71. UNESCO, "Paris Declaration on Media and Information Literacy in the Digital Era. UNESCO," 2014, http://www.unesco.org/new/fileadmin/MULTIMEDIA/HQ/CI/CI/pdf/news/paris_mil_declaration.pdf.
72. Western Association of Schools and Colleges, "Core Competency FAQs," Senior College and University Commission, June 2014, http://www.wascsenior.org/content/core-competency-faqs.
73. American Library Association, "Workforce Innovation and Libraries," 2017, http://www.ala.org/advocacy/advleg/federallegislation/workforce.
74. Hart Research Associates, *It Takes More Than a Major*; Head et al., "What Information Competencies Matter in Today's Workplace?"

75. Lisa Kammerlocher et al., "Information Literacy in Learning Landscapes: Flexible, Adaptable, Low-Cost Solutions," *Reference Services Review* 39, no. 3 (2011): 390–400.

76. Kenneth J. Burhanna, Tammy J. Eschedor Voelker, and Julie A. Gedeon, "Virtually the Same: Comparing the Effectiveness of Online Versus In-Person Library Tours," *Public Services Quarterly* 4, no. 4 (2008): 317–38, doi:10.1080/15228950802461616; Joanna M. Burkhardt, Jim Kinnie, and Carina M. Cournoyer, "Information Literacy Successes Compared: Online vs. Face to Face," *Journal of Library Administration* 48, nos. 3–4 (2008): 379–89; Yvonne Mery, Jill Newby, and Ke Peng, "Why One-Shot Information Literacy Sessions Are Not the Future of Instruction: A Case for Online Credit Courses," *College & Research Libraries* 73, no. 4 (2012): 366–77, http://crl.acrl.org/content/early/2011/08/26/crl-271.full.pdf+html.

77. Michel Crozier and Erhard Friedberg, *Actors and Systems: The Politics of Collective Action*, trans. Arthur Goldhammer (Chicago: University of Chicago Press, 1980).

78. danah boyd, "Did Media Literacy Backfire?," *Medium: Points*, January 5, 2017, https://points.datasociety .net/did-media-literacy-backfire-7418c084d88d.

79. Bill Kovach and Tom Rosentiel, *Blur: How to Know What's True in the Age of Information Overload* (New York: Bloomsbury, 2010).

80. boyd, "Did Media Literacy Backfire?

81. Nancy Bolt, "Libraries from Now On: Imagining the Future of Libraries: ALA Summit on the Future of Libraries—Report to ALA Membership," *ALA Connect* (May 19, 2014), http://connect.ala.org/files/ LibrariesFromNowOn_ALASummitOnTheFutureofLibraries_FinalReport.pdf.

82. Barbara Fister, "Critical Assets: Academic Libraries, a View from the Administration Building," *Library Journal* (May 29, 2010), http://lj.libraryjournal.com/2010/05/academic-libraries/critical-assets-ac ademic-libraries-a-view-from-the-administration-building/#; Lankes, *The Atlas of New Librarianship*; Brian Mathews, "Librarian as Futurist: Change the Way Libraries Think about the Future," *Portal: Libraries and the Academy* 14, no. 3 (2014): 453–62, http://vtechworks.lib.vt.edu/handle/10919/49667.

83. Mathews, "Librarian as Futurist"; Frank Menchaca, "Start a New Fire: Measuring the Value of Academic Libraries in Undergraduate Learning," *portal: Libraries and the Academy* 14, no. 3 (2014): 353–67, doi:10.135/pla.2014.0020; Kelly E. Miller, "Imagine! On the Future of Teaching and Learning and the Academic Research Library," *portal: Libraries and the Academy* 14, no. 3 (2014): 329–51, doi:10.1353/ pla.2014.0018.

84. Lankes, *The Atlas of New Librarianship*.

85. Amy K. Garmer, *Rising to the Challenge: Re-imagining America's Public Libraries* (Washington, DC: Aspen Institute, 2014), http://d3n8a8pro7vhmx.cloudfront.net/themes/5660b272ebad645c44000001/ attachments/original/1452193779/AspenLibrariesReport.pdf?1452193779.

17

Hyperlinked Libraries

Michael Stephens

Chapter 17, "Hyperlinked Libraries," introduces a library model that is welcoming and participatory by encouraging user input and creativity to create a transformational anytime-anywhere service dynamic. Dr. Michael Stephens, author of The Heart of Librarianship *and the popular "Office Hours" column for* Library Journal, *emphasizes that the ability to share, collaborate, and reflect with information users while quickly responding to new technologies has become a necessary component of the information professional's skill set.*

Information professionals in this hyperlinked world must adopt and adapt, with a continuous eye on innovation and knowledge discovery. Mobile devices and social media are essential to this process because they create continuous, decentralized, and transparent participation across the world. This emphasis on technology, the author argues, is not doing away with the physical space, but changing and enriching it.

Stephens also stresses the importance of understanding that the hyperlinked library will not only exist in the cloud but will also continue as a physical place—with hyperlinked library services transforming the library into a classroom for learning and discovering new knowledge in community spaces. Hyperlinks, he notes, can also be individuals, who connect with people in the community and facilitate interactions with groups and individuals. The skills needed for this transformation include curiosity, creativity, and an always-learning approach that continually goes to the user for ideas, feedback, and engagement.

★ ★ ★

Emerging mechanisms for global communication and collaboration are changing the world and the way the world works. Businesses no longer demand employees and customers to be in any particular physical location to provide and receive premium services. Schools, colleges, and universities are offering courses virtually to students anywhere. Individuals are constantly engaged in conversation and expect to have their information needs satisfied immediately, on any device, and wherever they happen to be. Information is no longer bound to a form or a place. Information organizations such as libraries, housing unique and valuable collections, works, and artifacts of local significance as well as information sources not yet digitized must find ways to provide a seamless information experience between our hyperconnected virtual channels and our real-world facilities. Information professionals already providing online services and digital materials must constantly watch for innovative solutions that could be included in their information center services and web presences.

Historically, libraries have been advocates for the protection and expansion of information access (see also chapter 28: "Advocacy"). Today's libraries extend their foundational roles by becoming the primary inclusive space for the public to experiment with and use technological tools. In order to meet these changing needs and behaviors of their community, information professionals must now extend their knowledge and training into the online space—sharing, collaborating, and reflecting. Information professionals must think and act outside their organization, community, and even national boundaries to seek inspiration and support. A recent report from Pew Research Center indicated that 77 percent of Americans now own a smartphone, 73 percent have broadband access at home, 69 percent of U.S. adults are social media users, and half of the public own some type of tablet computer.[1] On the global level, industry analysts predict that by 2020 more than fifty billion mobile devices will be connected worldwide.[2] In the next few years, the world will be using mobile services and devices that cannot be imagined today. The information organization that builds value and thrives will be fluid enough to anticipate and quickly respond to new technologies and user expectations.

> Information professionals must now extend their knowledge and training into the online space—sharing, collaborating, and reflecting. Information professionals must think and act outside their organization, community, and even national boundaries to seek inspiration and support.

One such model, the hyperlinked library model, builds this value by being welcoming, open, and participatory while also incorporating user input and creativity. The hyperlinked library is human, and its communications and conversations, externally and internally, encompass a human voice. It is a playful model emphasizing collections, services, and spaces that evolve via user and staff participation in a transformational anytime-anywhere service dynamic. After completing this chapter, the reader should have an understanding of

- the hyperlinked library model and its qualities of transparency, openness, and participation,
- the current landscape of continuous computing,
- the influence of communication technologies on information organizations and information services both online and on-site, and
- the skill sets information professionals need to create viable, evolving information organizations.

THE HYPERLINKED LIBRARY

The Hyperlinked Library model is synthesized from data collected on emerging societal trends and burgeoning technologies used in information service as well as the writings of such authors as David Weinberger, Clay Shirky, and Seth Godin. Foundational to the model is Weinberger's "The Hyperlinked Organization" in 1999's *The Cluetrain Manifesto*, which explored how the internet was disrupting business and changing how things work within corporate structures.[3] Glenn calls the methodology used to build the evolving model "futures research," which is a blend of horizon scanning, trend research, and scenario planning.[4] In an article for *Serials Review*, the hyperlinked library model is defined as

> an open, participatory institution that welcomes user input and creativity. It is built on human connections and conversations. The organizational chart is flatter and team-based. The collections grow and thrive via user involvement. Information professionals are tapped in to user spaces and places online to interact, have presence, and point the way.[5]

Michael Stephens

A further exploration, from *The Heart of Librarianship*, defined hyperlinked library practice with these concepts:

- The library is everywhere—it is not just the building or virtual spaces.
- Hyperlinking subverts existing organizational structures.
- Our institutions should be flatter and team based.
- Seamless service should be available across all channels of interaction.
- We must reach all users, not just those who come through our doors.
- The most powerful information services to date are probably found in the palm of everyone's hand.
- The path forward will always be an evolutionary one.
- Inevitably, there will always be some amount of chaos.[6]

Hyperlinked library services are born from the constant, positive, and purposeful adaptation to change that is based on thoughtful planning and grounded in the mission of libraries. Information professionals embracing the hyperlinked model practice careful trend spotting and apply the tenets of librarianship, along with an informed understanding of emerging technologies' societal and cultural impact. Information professionals communicate with patrons and potential users via open and transparent conversations using a wide variety of technologies across many platforms.

The hyperlinked library model flourishes in both physical and virtual spaces by offering collections, activities, learning opportunities, and events that actively transform spectators into participants. In participatory cultures, everyone is in the business of advancing knowledge and increasing skill levels. The community is integrated into the structure of change and improvement.

The hyperlinked library is transparent when it talks and listens, practices inclusion, and keeps no secrets. The information organization activates processes to gather as much input from the entire community as possible, which heightens the patron's expectation that communications with the information organization will be open and equitable. The hyperlinked library encourages all types of conversation and feedback about the organization (see also chapter 27: "Communication, Marketing, and Outreach Strategies"). It is a move toward greater transparency when users are invited to share their opinions about how an information organization is performing, and when the information organization listens and responds. Management shows evidence of active listening and responding to users and staff by implementing requested changes and launching new services, using careful testing as part of the plan for solid, incremental growth.

> " The hyperlinked library encourages all types of conversation and feedback about the organization. It is a move toward greater transparency when users are invited to share their opinions about how an information organization is performing, and when the information organization listens and responds. "

Because of the easy and ubiquitous communications possible with mobile devices and social media, these technologies make transparency more attainable than ever. Information organizations can share information about current plans and solicit feedback on social networks, which utilize the more naturally transparent and trusted conversation channels developed among peers and families. Published updates, calls for community input, and beta tests of new services delivered to the devices in users' hands enable the hyperlinking of all stakeholders anytime and anywhere.

CONTINUOUS COMPUTING AND PARTICIPATION

The current landscape is one of continuous computing and of always being in a conversation. Information has an active social life; creating and sharing ideas play out across networks and social sites. World populations are moving toward this ubiquitous digital connectivity with anytime-anywhere access, mainly via mobile devices, such as tablets or phones. Organizations no longer have a monopoly on packaging information, and information control is decentralized and distributed. Anyone can curate information and publish collections from anywhere, deliver content anytime, and share on a wide selection of devices in many different formats and multiple languages. User preferences for particular technologies are unpredictable; the heavily promoted complex nano-computers, head-mounted displays, and other experimental devices may never make it to mainstream adoption, but handheld devices of all kinds have become the norm for connectivity.

Information professionals who establish free, open, and well-publicized communication channels on mobile platforms, and who build these channels for user interactivity, will be rewarded with a growing, engaged community base. With patrons and potential users thinking and interacting on the move, information professionals must constantly study how information services are discovered, accessed, and used. Communications have evolved from simple two-way interchanges into interconnected, multilayered flows. Adopting the hyperlinked library model means inviting patrons to partner with information professionals to revisit mission and value statements, set revised goals and objectives, and discuss the big ideas behind information services (see also chapter 19: "Strategic Planning"). Communication can flow between the organization, information users, and all stakeholders seamlessly between devices, between virtual space, and the physical space of the library.

TEXTBOX 17.1

**Five Concepts of
Knowledge Networking**

- Open up access
- Provide the hooks for intelligence (metadata)
- Link everything
- Leave no institutional knowledge behind
- Teach everyone

Throughout *Too Big to Know*, David Weinberger argues that the smartest person in the room is not the biggest brain or the whole group of people in the room, but the room itself. A poorly constructed room can result in echo chambers and groupthink, while a well-constructed room can enable constructive conversations and continuous knowledge discovery. Weinberger suggests five foundational concepts (see textbox 17.1) to "help make the networking of knowledge the blessing it should be."[7]

These tenets should guide the building of new outreach services with technology as well as participatory opportunities to learn and grow created by information professionals for their constituents. The "room," as Weinberger calls it, is not only virtual; it can also be in a physical space, wherever the community gathers. The following sections examine the hyperlinked library in mobile environments and as a physical space for learning, exchange, and growth. Technology creates a cyclical stream of opportunities that flow from mobile apps to brick and mortar and back again.

THE HYPERLINKED LIBRARY GONE MOBILE

When exploring the hyperlinked library model, the current state of continuous participatory computing, and the affordances of mobile technologies, information professionals must focus on what information organizations could develop as strategies for mobile access and participation. What avenues should be explored in relation to hyperlinked mobile services? How can information professionals find a place inside these emerging environments?

Collections Everywhere

A few years ago, the author discovered that a university library with a unique artifact from a song-writer in its special collection had digitized and showcased only one page of the lyrics on the library website. The rest is only available for visitors who travel to this distant institution. The university cited concerns about preservation and copyright as reasons why these documents could not be accessed digitally. Counter that unfortunate barrier to access with the impressive collection-focused apps from the British Library and the work done at New York Public Library highlighting various parts of the collection via iPad apps. The hyperlinked library opens up access to offer collections anywhere (see also chapter 33: "Open Access")—especially an information organization's most unique and interesting offerings. Mesa County Libraries in Colorado designed a mobile application intended to educate their community about local flora and fauna, and included capabilities for users in the field to add to the knowledge base via photos, notes, and shared updates posted directly from the app to social media.[8]

Information Professionals in the Cloud

As users spend more computing time on mobile devices and become increasingly familiar with saving and sharing content on cloud-based services, information professionals can harness the power of the data stored in the cloud to answer questions, share information, and collaborate with users. Huge amounts of data—images, status updates, reviews, and more—become a set of resources at our fingertips (see also chapter 10: "Digital Resources: Digital Libraries" and chapter 26: "Managing Data and Data Analysis in Information Organizations"). The groups and collections thriving at the image- and resource-sharing communities, Flickr, DeviantART, Instagram, and Pinterest, are examples of environments that hold opportunities for cloud content curation and management. For example, Flickr's *The Commons* partners with many organizations, including the Smithsonian Institution, to share photos and encourage users to tag, comment, and reuse the images.[9] These virtual storage houses can only become more findable and useful with the assistance of information professionals working to provide the *hooks to intelligence* via metadata and other organizational schema.

> " As users spend more computing time on mobile devices and become increasingly familiar with saving and sharing content on cloud-based services, information professionals can harness the power of the data stored in the cloud to answer questions, share information, and collaborate with users. "

Gamification

The *NMC Horizon Report: 2014 Higher Education* Edition placed the time-to-adoption for applying gaming dynamics to learning and research environments at two to three years.[10] Games and game-based learning have since dropped off the *Horizon Report* timeline of impactful technologies, but the concepts of games remain in a broader context of experience. Game-play is a portable activity that utilizes the combination of particular elements, mechanics, and frameworks to increase productivity, creativity, and problem solving.

Information organizations take advantage of game-play's ability to increase engagement by creating online environments with level-up properties that reward users. Information users can interact in experimental gamified spaces or become involved with larger regional, national, or even international gaming groups within the information organization. Information professionals can participate as on-demand expert scouts and guides. In a discussion of gamifying library experiences in *ACRL TechConnect*, Kim reported that applying game dynamics has the potential to raise levels of engagement with library services, especially when the objectives of games are not particular outcomes, but fun and enjoyable experiences.[11] An example of a gamified library service in the United Kingdom aimed at promoting a sense of play and excitement is Librarygame, "a bespoke library enhancement product that adds game elements directly into the library experience to make it more fun, engaging, and delightful."[12]

Hyper-local and Hyperlinked

An increasing number of the new social sharing apps on mobile devices incorporate geo-location in surprising and innovative ways. The interfaces can be messy, weird, and silly, but mapping content to location offers a promise of discovering hidden relationships within the content that can be used to spot trends and expand information services.

With the most rudimentary location-based apps, it is easy to find specialty menu restaurants within specific distances from any geographic point via localized search. It is also possible to tap into the wisdom of nearby hikers while exploring a national park via app services like "Find Twitter users near me." An interesting example that ties to archival practice and the sharing of images is History Pin, a mobile-enabled website that provides "a way for people to come together to share and celebrate local history."[13] The site includes a shared archive of a community's photos available via map interfaces.

Deciding how much information to share about personal location and situation on open platforms is an important privacy consideration (see also chapter 34: "Information Privacy and Cybersecurity"). Information professionals need to develop more understanding about how much is too much and how little is too little, and develop learning opportunities for users to help them understand these considerations as well.

THE HYPERLINKED LIBRARY AS PLACE

It is easy to think that mobile devices and continuous computing will be the future of information services, and information will work solely in the cloud, especially if one pays attention to the usual "who needs libraries in the age of Google?" inference in news reports. The information organization is and will always be just as important as its digital offerings. In fact, physical facilities have been in the midst of a pronounced shift from libraries as book warehouses to information organizations as centers for discovery, learning, and creation for a number of years. Consider the following as models of hyperlinked library service in the physical space.

Library as Classroom

The 2014 *Horizon Report* identified the Elements of the Creative Classroom Research Model, developed by the European Commission Institute for Prospective Technological Studies, as a method to frame the report's issues, challenges, and technologies impacting education.[14] The model presents the building blocks of a twenty-first-century technology-enabled classroom environment: learning by play/exploration/creation, collaboration with others, meaningful activities, and networking (see also chapter 6: "Literacy and Media Centers: School Libraries," chapter 7: "Learning and Research Institutions: Academic Libraries," and chapter 8: "Community Anchors for Lifelong Learning: Public Libraries"). Applying this model to all libraries means they can serve as creative classrooms outside of the formal classroom, supporting learners by em-

> " The hyperlinked model presents the building blocks of a twenty-first-century technology-enabled classroom environment: learning by play/exploration/creation, collaboration with others, meaningful activities, and networking. "

ploying the building blocks mentioned above (see also chapter 16: "Teaching Users: Information and Technology Instruction"). This includes academic, public, special, and K–12 libraries where community-learning spaces help learners of all ages achieve goals, acquire new skills, and understand more about how the world works. These initiatives make the library a laboratory for exploration, via formal and informal programming, group activities, and experiential opportunities of all kinds. Many facilities also feature creation zones with requisite digital and 3-D hardware to allow people to build things. Via the web and other communication technologies, there are potentially endless opportunities to connect virtually with people worldwide for discussions, lectures, and "field trips."

Programming in these spaces might be focused on enhancing or extending curricula in the academic environment, such as the initiatives described by Dean of Libraries Keith Webster, Carnegie Mellon University. These include makerspaces and gaming studios (see also chapter 18: "Creation Culture and Makerspaces"), while also maintaining attractive, quiet areas for reflection and study.[15] The focus does not have to be specifically on high-tech tools either. The Johnson County Public Library's successful "Books and Butchers" program offered a chance for library patrons to learn from two successful butchers how a pig becomes a pork chop.[16]

> **Discussion Question**
>
> What does the library as classroom concept mean for various information environments?

Library as Community Space

"We designed our libraries for people, not books," Marie Østergård, Project Leader, Dokk1, Aarhus Public Libraries, Denmark,[17] told an assembled group of librarians from all over the United States at the Public Library Association Conference in 2016. She was describing the multiyear process of redesigning and building the new public library in Aarhus.[18] The waterfront building design is based on the Model Programme for Public Libraries developed by Danish Royal School of Library and Information Science professors: inspiration space, learning space, meeting space, and performative space that overlap and intersect. Action words for each sector of the model included "Excite," "Explore," "Create," and "Participate."[19]

Østergård reported that an average of four thousand people visit Dokk1 each day, using the space for work, socializing, meetings, and relaxation. Offices for community services are also located within the library building. At the intersection of meeting space and performative space, community members attend programs in meeting rooms and open areas related to learning, politics, art, and self-expression. Dokk1 promotes open dialog between citizens and encourages the exchange of ideas.

> **Discussion Question**
>
> What ideas do you have to create a more community-focused library?

Imagine this model utilized by public libraries globally to extend the mission of what libraries have always done: to connect people to the information and knowledge they need throughout their lives.

Hyperlinks Are People Too

Simply, in current information environments of all kinds, and as reflected in the models above, information service first and foremost seeks to link people to information, each other, and the world. This means that hyperlinks can also be individuals. The information professional can be a connector, a facilitator, and a conduit for groups and individuals. They might lead in-person discussions/workshops on the timely topics of the day, and take a step back as conversations grow to nurture understanding between stakeholders. They let the topics and talk evolve. Holding community discussions around civic education/civic literacy can bring people together in ways not imagined before.

THE HYPERLINKED LIBRARIAN: SKILLS AND ROLES

Embracing the virtual and physical aspects of the hyperlinked library means that today's and tomorrow's information professionals need a skill set that reflects not only the foundations of library and information science but also the emerging trends related to the topics of this chapter (see also chapter 3: "Librarianship: A Continuously Evolving Profession").

Curiosity and Creativity

Two important qualities of an information professional working within these participatory spaces are that of curiosity and creativity. Curiosity about the world and how people create, use, and access information should define the field of information science. Curiosity should also drive ongoing evaluation of services and user needs (see also chapter 4: "Diverse Information Needs"). When an information professional looks for the path forward for new services, technology offerings, or materials to provide, curiosity should lead to "I will ask the users."

> Curiosity about the world and how people create, use, and access information should define the field of information science. Curiosity should also drive ongoing evaluation of services and user needs.

Creativity helps information professionals look outside the usual thinking about what libraries do and how they do it. Creativity helps new ideas to form, such as creating a space for users to express themselves as in the Idea Box service created by Oak Park Public Library in Illinois. Rotating interactive exhibits in a once unused café space engages the library's users monthly.[20] Creative information professionals across all types of libraries have remixed and reused the Idea Box concept within their facilities, adapting a bulletin board, white board, or similar to engage with constituents.

Always Learning

Information professionals should be competent, engaged, and always learning. Learning on the job should be steeped in experimentation and play as a means to problem-solve. Information professionals should also engage in lifelong learning by seeking out professional development opportunities often, both formal and informal opportunities. An information professional's education does not end with an MLIS degree but should continue always. Participation in staff development days, workshops, and conferences is just part of the equation. The web has enabled information professionals to learn with each other on a global scale through computers or mobile devices. Programs such as those based on the Learning 2.0 model for libraries, originating well over a decade ago, offer access to online communities centered on reflection and learning about mobile devices, research skills, and more.[21] Connecting with colleagues from around the world can enhance the information professional's career.

CONCLUSION

Information organizations continue to evolve and adapt as socio-technological changes occur. Exploring the hyperlinked library model as a platform for discovery, interaction, and participation is just one facet of the rich and varied possibilities for the future. Delivering easy-to-use, unique, and knowledge-extending services to users no matter where they are may be one of the most important goals information professionals address. The emerging participatory culture will need the traditional foundations of literacy (research skills and critical analysis), along with skills in networking, problem solving, and exploratory play. Information professionals can expand their practice by becoming knowledgeable guides in these new landscapes and seek to hyperlink opportunities for knowledge and growth for and with their communities.

NOTES

1. Aaron Smith, "Record Shares of Americans Now Own Smartphones, Have Home Broadband," Pew Research Center, 2017, http://www.pewresearch.org/fact-tank/2017/01/12/evolution-of-technology/.
2. Mark Wells, "A Growing World of Connected Devices," YouTube video, posted by CTIA, May 5, https://www.youtube.com/watch?v=HxK46CFsJeM.
3. David Weinberger, "The Hyperlinked Organization," in *The Cluetrain Manifesto*, by Rick Levine, Christopher Locke, Doc Searls, and David Weinberger (New York: Basic Books, 2017), http://www.cluetrain.com/book/hyperorg.html.
4. Jerome C. Glenn, "Introduction to the Futures Research Methods Series," *The Millennium Project Futures Research Methodology Version 2.0*, ed. Jerome C. Glenn and Theodore J. Gordon, August 21, 2009, http://www.millennium-project.org/millennium/FRM-v2.html.
5. Michael Stephens and Michael Collins, "Web 2.0, Library 2.0, and The Hyperlinked Library," *Serials Review* 33, no. 4 (2007): 253–56.
6. Michael Stephens, *The Heart of Librarianship* (Chicago: American Library Association Editions, 2016).
7. David Weinberger, *Too Big to Know: Rethinking Knowledge Now That the Facts Aren't the Facts, Experts Are Everywhere, and the Smartest Person in the Room Is the Room* (New York: Basic Books, 2012).
8. "Wild Colorado App," Mesa County Libraries, accessed March 27, 2017, http://mesacountylibraries.org/aboutus/wild-colorado-app/.
9. "The Commons," Flickr, accessed August 17, 2017, https://www.flickr.com/commons/institutions/.
10. Larry Johnson, Samantha Adams Becker, V. Estrada, and A. Freeman, *NMC Horizon Report: 2014 Higher Education Edition* (Austin, TX: The New Media Consortium, 2014), http://www.nmc.org/pdf/2014-nmc-horizon-report-he-EN.pdf.
11. Bohyun Kim, "Harnessing the Power of Game Dynamics," *College & Research Libraries News* 73, no. 8 (2012): 465–69.
12. "Engaging Libraries with Librarygame," last accessed August 17, 2017, http://librarygame.co.uk/.
13. "About History Pin," History Pin, https://about.historypin.org.
14. Johnson et al., *The NMC Horizon Report: 2014 Higher Education Edition*.
15. Keith Webster, "Reimagining the Role of the Library in the Digital Age: Changing the Use of Space and Navigating the Information Landscape," *LSE Impact Blog*, February 15, 2017, http://blogs.lse.ac.uk/impactofsocialsciences/2017/02/15/reimagining-the-role-of-the-library-in-the-digital-age-changing-the-use-of-space-and-navigating-the-information-landscape/?platform=hootsuite.
16. Books and Butchers," Johnson County Library, 2017, http://www.jocolibrary.org/newsroom/books-and-butchers.
17. "Dokk1 English," Dokk1, https://dokk1.dk/english.
18. Michael Stephens, "Dream Explore. Experiment: Office Hours," *Library Journal*, May 23, 2016, http://lj.libraryjournal.com/2016/05/opinion/michael-stephens/dream-explore-experiment-office-hours/.
19. "The Library's Spaces and Zones," Model Programme for Public Libraries, 2017, http://modelprogrammer.slks.dk/en/challenges/zones-and-spaces/.
20. "Idea Box," Oak Park Public Library, 2017, http://oppl.org/visit/idea-box.
21. Michael Stephens, "Exemplary Practice for Learning 2.0," *Reference & User Services Quarterly* 53, no. 2 (2013): 129–39.

18

Creation Culture and Makerspaces

Kristin Fontichiaro

Chapter 18, "Creation Culture and Makerspaces," highlights creative and engaging library spaces that are not only incorporating novel services and technologies but, perhaps more significantly, also developing communities of like-minded people who come to experiment, work, and collaborate within the library. Reviewing the brief history of makerspaces, Dr. Kristin Fontichiaro, coordinator of University of Michigan's mobile makerspace project, dives into "maker programming," which brings together technologies of the past with innovative cutting-edge technologies like artificial intelligence and the internet of things. She notes that makerspaces embody a culture that is community oriented and focused on supporting and teaching one another. She highlights the importance of developing and maintaining this culture to ensure makerspace success.

Fontichiaro discusses the skills and planning required to create makerspaces, such as a craft corner in the library. Information professionals need to be attuned to community needs and wants and to have the patience to create a sustainable space that supports creative and collaborative practice. Fontichiaro emphasizes the importance of always keeping an eye on what is coming next for makerspace activities. She offers guidance in planning for long-term success, including asking key questions for defining program goals and expectations. She also suggests documenting the plan and how to effectively disseminate it.

Fontichiaro shares successful makerspace experiences, demonstrating the possibilities available with open source and sharing or partnering. Her rich examples give information professionals excellent ideas on how to get started, what resources are available, and how to make makerspaces into a long-term option and not a quick fad.

★   ★   ★

Many generations grew up learning about Leonardo da Vinci, who could sketch, create scientifically correct diagrams, build inventions, paint frescoes, and more. For generations, da Vinci has been called a Renaissance man: someone who could blend art and science in potent and powerful ways. Today, he might be called a *maker*. Maker is an inclusive term for anyone who sews, solders, welds, creates, tinkers, prototypes, designs, cooks, codes, gardens, or otherwise transforms one set of materials into another (see also chapter 18: "What's in Your Patrons' Dream Makerspaces?" in the online supplement). One need only wander into the nonfiction section of a public library to see titles that reflect these traditional and new interests. From carving pumpkins to coding web pages, the creative possibilities have sat on library shelves for decades. What is different in today's information environment? Instead of checking out books and working alone at home, patrons increasingly find a community of like-minded neighbors working in the library itself.

"Creation culture," the democratization of digital tools and a community-based hunger for personal and creative connections in an era of unprecedented hurry and change, has given birth to new opportunities to reenergize and restimulate the creative impulses in patrons and citizens. Carving out temporary or permanent spaces, many information organizations continue experimenting with novel services to attract new patrons or a wider range of services for existing patrons. After completing this chapter, the reader should have an understanding of the big ideas behind the creation culture and how makerspaces can fulfill long-term strategic planning that supersedes fads or novel technology.

MAKERS AND MAKERSPACES

"All of us are makers," says Maker Media founder and CEO Dale Dougherty.[1] To use one's hands to create an object that is personally satisfying and helpful—is an inherently human instinct. At a time when an unprecedented number of people are doing sedentary screen-based work, there is a kind of latent hunger to use our hands to create and customize our world.

Beginning around 2011, many information organizations leveraged past authority as resource providers and extended into providing experiences in-house, shifting from "check out our DIY materials and leave" to "check in and linger." Forming spaces that may be named makerspaces, digital labs, or production studios, along with activities for creators known as "makers," many information organizations are experimenting with how to invite in new patrons while expanding services for existing patrons.

> " Forming spaces that may be named makerspaces, digital labs, or production studios, along with activities for creators known as "makers," many information organizations are experimenting with how to invite in new patrons while expanding services for existing patrons. "

In the early years of the maker movement, many pointed to the dramatic price drops in digital fabrication tools like 3-D printers as a sign of new manufacturing and prototyping opportunities that could be deployed in libraries. A 3-D printer was the most common tool one saw in early library or information center makerspaces, like Fayetteville Free Library's Fab Lab, the University of Michigan Library's 3-D Lab, the makerspace at the University of Nevada–Reno, and the Westport (Connecticut) Public Library's maker-in-residence program.

But high-tech tools were just the beginning. Soon, those expensive tools—whether a library owned them or was provoked to think about doing so—were brokering conversations between staff and patrons. The question shifted from "We know what patrons want" to "What other kinds of hands-on, open-ended learning do patrons want?" This expanded the range of creative avenues. For example, Chicago Public Library's Maker Lab might teach 3-D modeling one day and flower arranging the next. Free Library of Philadelphia's Maker Jawn initiative focused on creating with low-cost materials, investing instead in strong mentors to build a sense of community and supported exploration. School librarian Leslie Preddy's Perry Meridian (Indiana) Middle School, like Maker Jawn, used low-cost materials in her school library, publishing the field's first school library–focused guide.[2] The first tools to wear out at the Ann Arbor District Library's Secret Lab were not their 3-D printers, but their overworked sewing machines. In her library at New Milford High School, Laura Fleming added resources for curriculum-connected projects like molecular gastronomy.[3] The University of Michigan School of Information's after-school program for youth, Michigan Makers, started with Arduinos[4] and coding but later grew to include prototyping, sewing, circuits, and even a gift-wrapping tutorial.

Today, library "maker programming" is as likely to focus around STEM (science, technology, engineering, and math) as it is to embrace technologies of the past, like letterpress printing, spinning wheels, knitting, and sewing. These forms of making differentiate library-based spaces from community makerspaces, wood shops, and welding studios.[5]

MAKERSPACE CULTURE

Makerspaces are not just stuff or places. In thriving makerspaces, there is a culture as well, one that prioritizes community, mutual support, and a noncompetitive atmosphere. Massimo Banzi, world renowned for his work codeveloping the Arduino microcontroller—a low-cost, open-source microcontroller or "brain" that acts as home base for sensors, lights, and other future inventions—says,

> The whole idea of being a maker involves concepts of collaboration, community, and working with other people. It is very hard to be a maker and be by yourself locked in a room or even in a lab. It is really something that involves a lot of collaborations at different levels.[6]

This collaborative spirit is key to makerspace culture. Just as the information organization's resources help patrons bring together multiple perspectives, face-to-face making lets them merge their knowledge and experiences with others. This does not mean lockstep work in which everyone does the same thing at the same time; rather, as in the Renaissance guilds and studios, some may be novices and others, masters. The goal is for patrons to feel they are working at their "center of gravity"[7]—pursuing their interests and curiosities in a safe environment. A safe environment to explore new tools and methods, envision new creations, and persevere when early prototypes and attempts do not succeed is key in aligning the information organization with the goals of creation culture.

> A safe environment to explore new tools and methods, envision new creations, and persevere when early prototypes and attempts do not succeed is key in aligning the information organization with the goals of creation culture.

Melvil Dewey said, "The new library is active, an aggressive, educating force in the community."[8] School libraries have always fulfilled this role, as have academic libraries (see also chapter 6: "Literacy and Media Centers: School Libraries" and chapter 7: "Learning and Research Institutions: Academic Libraries"). Public libraries, too, build on long traditions as learning institutions via storytimes, book clubs, informational lectures, film showings, concerts, knitting circles, quilt guilds, digital literacy initiatives, and more (see also chapter 8: "Community Anchors for Lifelong Learning: Public Libraries"). Makerspaces do not replace these activities; they build on them and provide an overarching narrative that all making—from robots to running stitches—has value in satisfying the personal need to create and, perhaps, jump-starting new economic opportunities.

DEVELOPING DYNAMIC MAKERSPACES IN THE INFORMATION ENVIRONMENT

> Experienced maker facilitators know that it takes planning, attunement to community needs and wants, and patience to create a sustainable space that supports creative, collaborative practice.

Whether developing a new makerspace or envisioning future growth for an existing maker program, it can be easy to look to influential blog posts or conference presentations and assume that assembling a new coterie of equipment will convert the information organization into a thriving, collaborative space. Experienced maker facilitators know that it takes planning, attunement to community needs and

Kristin Fontichiaro

wants, and patience to create a sustainable space that supports creative, collaborative practice—even after the novelty of a new 3-D printer or tool has faded. This section will offer some guidance in planning for long-term success.

Identify Makerspace Goals and Expectations

When information professionals purchase books, multimedia, or online resources, they rely on their collection development policy (see also chapter 24: "Managing Collections") to guide their selections. When planning to buy maker tools, similar guidelines help to unify expectations and desired outcomes. Key questions to ask include:

- What is the purpose for having a makerspace in the organization? What are the desired outcomes? How will the organization know it has been successful?
- What other creative activities are going on in the community, and how does the information organization's program complement existing projects?
- Is the mission to provide a series of entertaining hands-on activities, an educational sequence of skills development, an enhancement or enrichment of school curricula, or something else?
- Is the information organization the only creative outlet in town, or does it serve, as Mark Anderson[9] says, as an "on-ramp," a place to explore a variety of activities before moving on to formal education or a professional makerspace?

The answers to these questions help define the goals and expectations of the makerspace and need to be documented in a charter or other planning document.[10] Not only is this a useful reference for sharing plans with supervisors and board members, but it also provides essential talking points for employees, marketing staff, and potential donors. Clarity up front can avoid a scenario in which some patrons expect CNC routers and laser cutters when your goal is, perhaps, STEM kits for youth.

Start Small and Expand Based on Patron Wants and Needs

A quick look through the Chicago Public Library Maker Lab's Flickr stream,[11] for example, can catapult one's dreams to a new zenith. Keep in mind, however, that this is one of the profession's most established makerspaces. It is tempting to think big—but just as important to start small. For example, the Michigan Makers service-learning project partners graduate-student mentors with K–8 makers in underserved communities; graduate students work with the same student maker cohort all year long. Developing a supportive community is a top priority. One strategy is to offer just three to five options per week (makers need choices!) that are low-cost, relatively low-tech activities such as origami, cardboard challenge, toy take-apart sessions, Snap Circuits kits,[12] LittleBits,[13] Squishy Circuits,[14] friendship bracelets, refashioning or fashion hacking, or junk box creations. These activities cluster makers around tables, maximizing eye contact and potential conversation. Conversations with mentors often reveal future topics of interest that the participants would like to explore—providing direct insight into the selection of future directions.

> **Discussion Questions**
>
> Good information centers keep tabs on what community members—both current and potential patrons—want and need. Planning around those wants and needs can help limited budgets be spent more wisely. What needs and wants do you see in your community? What systems are in place at the organizational level to find out this information in an ongoing way?

Embrace Open-Source Thinking

Many information professionals are familiar with the concept of Creative Commons licensing (see also chapter 31: "Copyright and Creative Commons"), which allows writers, photographers, and multimedia creators to retain copyright, but signal in advance that their work may be reused, remixed, or adapted under particular circumstances. Early makers adopted similar practices under the open-source label. Blueprints, design plans, and computer code can all be labeled as open source, meaning that they can be used, reused, added to, and adapted without gaining permission or paying royalties.

For example, one of the maker movement's most ubiquitous tools, the Arduino microcontroller mentioned earlier, is open source. Although they are available for purchase for about $35, one can construct an Arduino from scratch using freely available plans online or adapt the provided plan in new ways, as long as the new plans are released similarly. Not only is the hardware open source, but Arduino's code is as well. If a maker wants to make a plant sensor that tweets when it needs water, existing construction plans and open-source programming code just might be available online, shared by another maker. By sharing code and construction plans, future tinkerers can accelerate their growth because they build on the existing work of others—legally. As Arduino's coinventor Banzi writes,

> We believe in the open source movement and everyone should be really aware that it can develop successfully if everyone takes from it, but especially if people and companies contribute back. That's why it's important to highlight who creates a positive loop and nurture knowledge sharing and collaboration.[15]

While there are now many commercial maker and STEM products that eschew the open-source option, the commitment to shared knowledge should remain resonant in information spaces, where shared information has always been a core value.

Partner Rather Than Compete

There is an aphorism that says, "The rising tide lifts all boats." Makers feel the same, realizing that it is by helping fellow makers and maker-interested organizations grow that the entire ecosystem for making improves. As information professionals consider beginning or expanding the maker work in their organizations, seeking out maker partners can produce valuable results. For example, who in the community designs video games, comics, or yarn-bombing campaigns and would be willing to mentor others? These makers may be interested in partnering to expand outreach, promotion, learning, and community engagement.

> As information professionals consider beginning or expanding the maker work in their organizations, seeking out maker partners can produce valuable results.

Community makerspaces provide potential colleagues for maker efforts in information organizations, not competition. Partnering to seek funding and swap expertise and resources is a smart move forward. Often, information organizations have space and makers have skills; by trading, both institutions grow. Similarly, information organizations have access to grants that for-profit makerspaces do not. There are opportunities and advantages in seeing community makerspaces as colleagues, not as competition. Being connected to community colleagues helps maximize our potential instead of duplicating offerings.

Seek Mashups

Traditional programming in information organizations has relied on scheduling one activity at a time: Minecraft on Monday and weaving on Wednesday. Part of the excitement and innovation that makerspaces can create comes from putting people of diverse backgrounds and skill sets together at the same time and in the same place. Even though the maker movement is now about five years old in libraries and information centers, this aspect remains an area for growth. Community makerspaces are never simply single-activity workshops; thriving makerspaces encompass different people working on different things simultaneously. Partnering two or more activities at once can create new cross-disciplinary creations. For example, kids who like to sew stuffed animals plus programmers who love to control sensors with an Arduino discover that, by merging their skills, they could end up with a cuddly object that automatically illuminates when it gets dark or a stuffed animal that senses the temperature of a sick child. It is the twenty-first-century version of those 1980s Reese's Peanut Butter Cup commercials where a peanut butter lover's jar bumped into a chocolate fan's bar, yielding a tasty new creation: "Two great tastes that taste great together!" One strategy for making this work might be to host events where a wide variety of equipment and mentors are available for experimentation, or people can bring and work on their own projects in a communal setting. Whether these events are called "open lab," "studio time," or even a cheekily titled "maker happy hour," these events can help patrons enjoy personal creative time surrounded by others. They can turn solo making into a community event.

Cast a Wide Net: Welcome All Kinds of Makers

At the 2013 FabLearn conference at Stanford University, Leah Buechley shared some startling statistics regarding the cover photos for *Make* magazine, the leading popular magazine for makers. By her analysis of the forty people who had been featured on covers by that time, 85 percent were male and none was a person of color. Her review of *Make*'s editorial staff showed a similar homogeneity: 87 percent men, none of whom were of color. Buechley also found that the content of the photos showed a narrow range of maker activities. She found that just over half featured electronics: vehicles 31 percent, robots 22 percent, rockets 8 percent, and music 5 percent.[16] Sadly, little has changed in the years since her presentation. Making is still considered overwhelmingly white and middle class. In fact, *Make*'s 2016 media kit[17] describes its Maker Faire attendees as 61 percent male, having an average household income of $119,000 and a median age of thirty-seven.

Certainly, some makers will be interested and intrigued by those topics. However, an information organization has a responsibility to serve all. The first tenet of the American Library Association Code of Ethics states, "We provide the highest level of service to *all* library users through appropriate and usefully organized resources; equitable service policies; equitable access"[18] (see also chapter 5: "Diversity, Equity of Access, and Social Justice" and chapter 30: "Information Ethics").

Therefore, consider broadening the range of activities in order to welcome a broader swath of the population. Seeing something familiar reassures people that it is safe to enter the room to try something new. Once they are in the room, they may migrate to something new that would have been off-putting from the outside. A philosophy of having "something for everyone"[19] promotes inclusion. Often, a tool predicted to interest one gender may interest both. For example, in Michigan Makers, sewing machines are more popular among boys than girls!

Consider Activities That Both Echo and Expand Current Patron Interests

Embrace the concept of "windows and mirrors" when planning formal maker programming. Formal programming is a great introduction to making, but so is "open lab" time in which people put their new skills into practice on their own timeline and in their own way. And it is during open lab time that people become exposed to new materials or tools and broaden their sense of possibilities. Mirrors are makerspace activities that reflect existing or known patron/community interests. These draw in people with existing interests. For example, the community may have an existing group of drop spindle aficionados, woodcarvers, or weavers; early programming that welcomes and recognizes those activities brings early engagement. Window activities, on the other hand, introduce less familiar, less established, or newly launched activities. An example of a window in most communities is 3-D modeling, the process of designing objects that can be represented in multiple dimensions by a 3D printer. So are activities that add unfamiliar elements to familiar objects, such as pasting circuits into paper books or digitizing images for use on electronic embroidery machines.

Another way to welcome all makers is to balance short- and long-term projects for skills acquisition. Especially in under-resourced communities, some patrons may feel intimidated by novel or high-tech tools or uncertain about their ability to achieve success. Activities that can be completed in a single visit can help minimize frustration, work around unpredictable schedules, and eliminate the challenge of returning multiple times to create a product. Some short-term tasks—like learning to fold an origami cup or decorating unfinished pottery—can be accomplished in a single sitting. These can boost confidence and demonstrate to novices that they are capable of success in new arenas.

As success and interests grow, makers may become more willing to take on new challenges that take longer to accomplish, such as learning to code in Python, building a robot, or tackling alterations. Additionally, some people are more comfortable in formal learning settings than others. Some like to putter independently while watching others out of the corner of their eye, so having some activities that require no instruction at all, or for which videos or instructional sheets are provided, is an effective strategy for makerspaces.

Another way to promote inclusivity is by embracing peer mentorship and leadership. Rather than avoiding certain maker activities because staff are not experts, look to the community of makers and tap them for expertise. Teens with parental permission can teach Minecraft, for example. In a makerspace, experience determines expertise, not age. And the more sharing of expertise that is developed among the participants, the more sustainable the makerspace will be. Peer mentorship is key in developing a community of learners in the information organization.

Discussion Questions

What is the advantage of focusing a makerspace on STEM tools, digital tools, and/or a wide variety of tools and materials? What could some unintended consequences be of limiting the range of maker activities offered?

Celebrate Progress

Along with the collective enthusiasm for making among makers, celebrating the patron's achievements along the way promotes the organization's services and provides openings for newcomers to join in. Design challenges, in which participants are asked to solve a problem or put unusual materials to work, offer a short-term involvement for familiar faces and new ones. Consider a cardboard challenge, in which discarded boxes from the recycling center or appliance store provide raw materials for who can build the tallest or widest building, animal, or robot. For kids, Rachelle Doorley of Tinkerlab has an archive of challenges[20] for one-off events, such as creating something new from cupcake liners. Hackathon challenges focus on using computer programming to solve a problem, and there are emerging trends in developing challenges around low-cost prosthetics design and other world-changing maker practices.

> Along with the collective enthusiasm for making among makers, celebrating the patron's achievements along the way promotes the organization's services and provides openings for newcomers to join in.

Information organizations need to establish a formal sharing time both during workshops and in showcase events. Each community is different in this regard, and the desire to share publicly can vary, so choose a sharing pathway that feels right to patrons—and is designed with their input. Some groups enjoy taking the last few minutes of a workshop to see how everyone else interpreted a new task. Completed projects can be placed out on a table or participants can sit in a circle to admire what has been made, depending on the size of the creation. Other recommendations include:

- keeping a physical photo album, bulletin board, or video monitor slideshow of inspiring works in progress or completed objects;
- taking advantage of social sharing platforms like the organization's Facebook page, Flickr site, blog, or Instagram feed; and
- setting up a semiannual maker event, such as a MAKE Media–licensed Maker Faire[21] or a customized MakerFest event (an event title for which no licensing agreement is required).

These efforts can garner attention from the wider community of makers and those who admire their efforts.

TEXTBOX 18.1

Think into the Future

Information professionals should consider these questions moving forward as they consider the next phase of their maker programs:

- Who remains underserved in the maker programs your organization offers?
- What is the potential for entrepreneurship around making in the community so there is an economic impact in addition to personal satisfaction?
- What keeps the maker work centered on a broad group of creators in the community?
- How can information professionals be more intentional about showing how their programs change patrons?

CONCLUSION

Information organizations have a long tradition of supporting their community's intellectual and personal interests through rich collections available for checkout and interactive activities online and in the physical space. This chapter explored creation culture and the maker movement in information organizations as pathways to expand on those traditional activities. It considered the questions and issues that boost makerspace success (see also chapter 18: "Makerspace Virtual Tour" in the online supplement). By unifying the how-to collections of the information organization with the let's-do energy of the community, information organizations can create maker learning communities and opportunities that delight, motivate, and inspire communities.

NOTES

1. Dale Dougherty, "We Are Makers," January 2011, TED Talks video, 11:47 min., http://www.ted.com/talks/dale_dougherty_we_are_makers.
2. Leslie Preddy, *School Library Makerspaces, Grades 6–12* (Santa Barbara, CA: ABC-CLIO, 2013).
3. Laura Fleming, "Worlds of Making @ NMHS," *Worlds of Making*, 2013, http://worlds-of-learning.com/2013/11/26/worlds-of-making-nmhs-3/.

4. Arduino, "Tutorials," 2017, https://www.arduino.cc/en/Tutorial/HomePage.
5. Dale Dougherty, *Free to Make: How the Maker Movement Is Changing Our Schools, Our Jobs, and Our Minds* (Berkeley, CA: North Atlantic Books, 2016).
6. Massimo Banzi, "Making Is Best When It's Done Together," *Make*, 2014, http://makezine.com/magazine/making-is-best-when-its-done-together/.
7. John Dewey, "The School and the Life of the Child," *School and Society: Being Three Lectures* (Chicago: University of Chicago Press, 1900), https://books.google.com/books?id=5c5wDDTNHAIC.
8. Melvil Dewey, "Why a Library Does or Does Not Succeed," in *Library Notes: Improved Methods and Labor-Savers for Librarians, Readers and Writers* (Boston, MA: Library Bureau, 1887), 47.
9. Mark Anderson, personal communication, September 23, 2013.
10. Kristin Fontichiaro, "A Charter for Your School Makerspace?" *Active Learning*, 2014, http://www.fontichiaro.com/activelearning/2014/09/04/a-charter-for-your-school-makerspace/.
11. Flickr, "Chicago Public Library Makerspace," accessed, August 7, 2017, https://www.flickr.com/photos/cpl_makerspace/sets/.
12. Snapcircuits, "Home," 2014, http://www.snapcircuits.net.
13. LittleBits Electronics, "Home," 2014, http://littlebits.cc.
14. Squishy Circuits, "Squishy Circuits Project Page," July 26, 2014, http://courseweb.stthomas.edu/apthomas/SquishyCircuits/.
15. Banzi, "Making Is Best When It's Done Together."
16. Christina Quattrochi, "MAKE'ing More Diverse Makers," *EdSurge*, 2013, https://www.edsurge.com/n/2013-10-29-make-ing-more-diverse-makers.
17. Maker Media, "2016 *Make*: Media Kit," http://makermedia.com/wp-content/uploads/2013/01/2016-Make-Media-Kit-Final.pdf.
18. American Library Association, "Code of Ethics of the American Library Association," 2008, http://www.ala.org/tools/ethics.
19. Kristin Fontichiaro, "Reflections on North Quad MakerFest," *Active Learning blog*, December 18, 2013, http://www.fontichiaro.com/activelearning/2013/12/18/reflections-on-north-quad-makerfest/.
20. Tinkerlab, "Challenges," 2014, http://tinkerlab.com/challenges/.
21. Maker Faire, "How to Make a Maker Faire," 2014, http://makerfaire.com/mini.

Part IV

Managing Information Organizations

Management Skills for the Information Professional

It helps leaders to harness their own creative potential, but they should also pay attention to creating the right culture and environment that lead to a creative library organization as a whole.

—Steven Bell[1]

Information professionals use their skills to meet the needs of their community and users, as well as to advance, develop, and manage information resources and services. They do this across a broad range of roles within their organizations—whether their role is that of a manager or is focused more specifically on managing collections, data systems, budgets, facilities, or user experience. While management skills are applicable across all types of organizations, information professionals need to be dynamic thinkers, creative visionaries, and innovators who are also adept at gathering evidence to support decision making, communicating the value of their organization to key stakeholders, and applying design thinking approaches to providing new services. These skills are essential to ensuring the information organization stays viable and can sustain its services while it continually adapts to change.

Part IV introduces readers to the range of management roles from developing a strategic plan to managing data analysis, from the budgeting process to onboarding personnel. But it goes beyond these organizational roles to look also at how to manage the rapidly changing information organization and to foster innovation, outreach, and advocacy to make the information organization continually relevant to its community.

NOTE

1. Steven Bell "Leading the Creative Library," *Library Journal*, August 25, 2016, http://lj.libraryjournal .com/2016/08/opinion/leading-from-the-library/leading-the-creative-library-leading-from-the-li brary/#_.

19

Strategic Planning

Lisa Rosenblum

Chapter 19, "Strategic Planning," offers both theoretical and practical applications in understanding the essential role strategic planning plays in the organization's ability to create a thriving, well-funded system that meets the needs of its staff, users, and the community. In the rapidly evolving information landscape where the whole purpose of information organizations is sometimes called into question and the organization must continuously redefine the programs and services it provides, the need for strategic planning is more critical than ever. As director of the King County Library System, Lisa Rosenblum is aptly positioned to highlight the importance of strategic planning for information organizations. She explains how to prepare and implement a strategic plan, how to anticipate potential changes, and how to measure an organization's success in accomplishing its strategic goals.

Strategic planning, Rosenblum notes, focuses on the organization's mission as the driving force for collecting input from all key stakeholders, identifying places where resources might be more effectively applied, and reinforcing a sense of teamwork that directs the organization to focus on areas most critical to their long-term success. She details a four-stage, ten-step process for strategic planning and includes an explanation of how to use both an environmental scan and a strengths, weaknesses, opportunities, and threats (SWOT) analysis for needs assessment.

For the information organization, strategic planning requires determining which of the many programs and projects to support in order to most effectively accomplish the organization's goals. Strategic planning is not without its problems, and Rosenblum explores these while offering useful suggestions for effectively overcoming these obstacles. However, strategic planning remains an essential tool to ensure that today's information organizations continue to adapt and thrive well into the future.

★ ★ ★

Every organization must have a strategy to be successful. This is especially true for businesses in rapidly changing sectors with challenging fiscal models that serve diverse constituencies. Nowhere is the need for strategic planning more critical than in modern libraries and information organizations. A generation ago, when print was the only game in town and the availability of books was limited by the inventory of the local bookstore, libraries could prove their worth by loaning out collections and providing reference expertise. However, things are different today, as books are now widely available in a multitude of digital formats and the answer to every query is "Google it." Today's information professionals scramble to keep up with the latest trends in media while policy makers and budget-conscious taxpayers repeatedly ask them, "Why do we even need libraries?"[1] Within this dynamic environment, where the whole purpose of the enterprise is called into question and the organization must continuously redefine its core competency, strategic planning really proves its worth.

> "If you don't know where you are going, you'll end up someplace else."—Yogi Berra

In times like these, a solid, consensus-based strategic plan can mean the difference between a thriving well-funded system in a culturally resurgent city on the one hand, and deteriorating branches out of step with the information needs of their patrons on the other. This chapter outlines the steps needed for information professionals to create a flexible yet comprehensive strategic plan to better serve their communities. After completing this chapter, the reader should have a better understanding of:

- the importance of strategic planning,
- the steps required to prepare and implement a strategic plan, and
- an approach to measuring an organization's success in achieving its strategic goals.

WHAT IS STRATEGIC PLANNING?

According to Lawrence Freedman, author of *Strategy: A History*, strategy is "about maintaining a balance between ends, ways, and means; about identifying objectives; and about the resources and methods available for meeting such objectives."[2] In short, strategy exists to solve a problem—specifically, the problem of how an organization can accomplish its goals with available resources.

Strategic planning has its origins in military history; the word *strategy* itself is derived from the Greek word for commander, and many scholars cite the martial textbook of Sun Tzu, *The Art of War*, as the first to describe the practice.[3] True to its military roots, modern strategic planning came into vogue in the middle of the twentieth century when (like the internet) it was embraced by the U.S. Defense Department. The Department of Defense adopted strategic planning after it "began to look for better and more useful ways to plan for its long-term needs while at the same time achieving cost savings."[4] By the mid-1980s, dozens of local governments had jumped on the bandwagon. A host of business books (Osborne and Gaebler's *Reinventing Government*[5] was among the most popular) promised that by identifying core functions and measuring outputs, organizations could achieve a higher level of performance with greater customer satisfaction at a reduced cost.

> Strategy exists to solve a problem—specifically, the problem of how an organization can accomplish its goals with available resources.

From the standpoint of the information professional, strategic planning is an essential element of organizational management. The process of creating and implementing a strategic plan focuses the attention of the organization on its mission and identifies places where resources might be more effectively directed while at the same time reinforcing a sense of teamwork. But there is another reason that the most agile and admired corporations routinely perform strategic planning exercises—namely, so that they can be sure that their best efforts are applied to those areas most critical to their long-term success. Information organizations, including public and academic libraries, can no longer afford to continue repeating past practices without checking to see that they are meeting the needs of their constituents. This is especially critical for those institutions that are publicly funded and are thereby insulated from market forces that might otherwise require greater accountability from their "shareholders."

STRATEGIC PLANNING AND OPERATIONAL IMPROVEMENT

While the concept of strategic planning and operational improvement remains sound, the challenge lies in performing both tasks together and continuously. Management professor Henry Mintzberg differentiates between strategic thinking, which he considers visionary, and strategic planning, which "as it has been practiced, has really been strategic programming, the articulation and elaboration of strategies, or visions, that already exist."[6]

A similarly important distinction may also be made between strategic planning and planning to continuously improve operations, which is widely recognized as a subordinate activity. Operational effectiveness, which is the ability to do things well and to continuously improve them, is not a strategy but the consequence of a strategy. According to Porter, "Operational effectiveness means performing similar activities *better* than rivals perform them."[7] By contrast, he defines strategy as the process of creating a unique and valuable position for an organization from a variety of possible alternatives, each of which involves tradeoffs: "Strategy is making tradeoffs in competing. The essence of strategy is choosing what *not* to do. Without trade-offs, there would be no need for choice and thus no need for strategy."[8] For the information organization, strategic planning involves deciding which of the many programs and projects to embrace—or reject—in order to use limited resources most effectively to accomplish the organization's goals.

THE IMPORTANCE OF STRATEGIC PLANNING FOR INFORMATION ORGANIZATIONS

Within the context of library and information management, a strategic plan allows an information organization to achieve its goals and objectives by identifying those projects, programs, and activities that are essential to and consistent with its core mission and overarching vision. Because strategic plans are focused on high-level outcomes rather than immediate outputs, they tend to be fairly long term in scope, often in the range of three to five years. Given this long-range perspective, strategic plans anticipate potential changes in future conditions and prescribe alternative actions that may be implemented as required. They also involve extensive stakeholder input to ensure that the information organization continues to fulfill its mandate for service to the community.

For these and many other reasons, a well-developed strategic plan can be of immense benefit to an information organization. The strategic plan can enhance external communication between the information organization and the communities it serves while simultaneously ensuring that the information organization's staff work together to accomplish their common goals. In addition, by relating the information organization's vision to its activities, a well-articulated plan can justify the budget for mission critical programs, and, if those resources are not available, the plan will direct the development of alternative methods for accomplishing the same essential result.

> Within the context of library and information management, a strategic plan allows an information organization to achieve its goals and objectives by identifying those projects, programs, and activities that are essential to and consistent with its core mission and overarching vision.

For example, a strategic plan can help a public library effectively express to its supporters (including donors and foundations) how tax dollars, contributions, and other resources are put to work. Internally, a plan that clearly illustrates how each program contributes to the organization's mission helps managers and staff understand the need for cooperation between the various departments.

Perhaps nowhere is the value of a strategic plan more fully realized, however, than during the budgeting process (see also chapter 21: "Managing Budgets"). Regardless of economic conditions, a strategic plan provides a solid position from which to direct the allocation of resources to core activities, even when those resources turn out to be limited or unavailable through traditional channels. For example, if a strategic plan has identified adult literacy as a primary objective, the information organization might reasonably plan to hire additional staff to teach literacy classes. However, if the organization's budget is cut due to lack of funds and thus eliminates the proposed positions, the strategic plan would direct management to look for other ways to further this critical activity. Inspired by that direction, staff might decide to partner with a nonprofit that shares the same mission by providing space in the information organization for comparable classes, or by collaborating on grant applications to provide an alternate source of funding for these services.

> The strategic planning process serves to focus the attention of directors, managers, and staff on the same priorities, optimizing the organization's ability to achieve its goals.

Alternatively, if the strategic plan has identified as a community priority the maintenance of a large collection of digital materials, it may be preferable to reduce hours rather than cut back on materials to meet the community needs. By the same token, managers looking for programs to cut would be directed by the strategic plan toward other, less essential services. In either case, the strategic planning process serves to focus the attention of directors, managers, and staff on the same priorities, optimizing the organization's ability to achieve its goals.

STRATEGIC PLANNING: AN OVERVIEW

With an understanding of what strategic planning is, the rest of the chapter discusses some of the practical benefits of strategic planning and describes in some detail the steps necessary to formulate and implement a strategic plan for today's information organization.

When to Create a Strategic Plan

Some management experts hold that strategic plans are like investments, in that the best time to make them is five years ago, while the second-best time is now. In practice, strategic plans are often developed when there has been a change in leadership at the highest level of the organization. Many incoming board chairs and newly appointed directors recognize that the strategic planning process can be the catalyst necessary to move the organization forward, correcting outdated practices and gaining consensus around new initiatives. Other times, a strategic planning process is a continuation of an ongoing effort, restarted when the previous plan has expired or is out of date. Strategic planning can also be undertaken for the specific intent of practical problem solving, when an organization seeks to solve recurring issues in a systematic way.[9]

In all cases, one of the first benefits realized during the strategic planning process is the inclusion of internal stakeholders (i.e., library management and staff). Staff involved in identifying key projects and programs—the first part of every strategic plan—understand and appreciate their value and are more likely to work together to achieve their goals. The same holds true for the community at large (e.g., donors and the tax paying public); when their voices are heard and their suggestions are acknowledged during the planning process, they become library advocates who are invested in the system's success (see also chapter 28: "Advocacy").

Given the need to involve so many stakeholders, it is no surprise that a successful strategic planning process involves a significant investment of both time and money. Often an outside consultant is hired to run the many meetings required and to direct all or part of the process. This has some advantages, especially when strategic planning is initiated to change the organizational culture, since a third party may be seen as more neutral or objective by those vested in the status quo (see also chapter 20: "Change Management"). But even when the process is managed in-house, there is a considerable investment in staff time preparing for and conducting meetings with internal and external stakeholders and writing reports, as well as the cost of the training required to distill and interpret the results and incorporate them into a structured plan.

Unfortunately, these upfront costs mean that the processes may be deferred when budgets are tight (see also chapter 21: "Managing Budgets"). During times of economic constraint, strategic planning is often considered a frill and is among the first items cut. This is regrettable because, as noted above, a good strategic plan can be of particular value in hard times by helping the organization retain its focus on critical programs and activities.

THE STRATEGIC PLANNING PROCESS

According to Bryson,[10] the strategic planning process can be divided into ten steps that fall within four primary stages as demonstrated in figure 19.1.

Stage 1: Preparing to Plan
- Step 1: Initiate and agree on a strategic planning process
- Step 2: Identify organizational mandates
- Step 3: Clarify organizational mission and values
- Step 4: Assess the external and internal environments to identify Strengths, Weaknesses, Opportunities and Threats (SWOTs)

Stage 2: Developing the Plan
- Step 5: Identify the strategic issues facing the organization
- Step 6: Formulate strategies to manage the issues
- Step 7: Review and adopt the strategic plan or plans
- Step 8: Establish an effective organizational vision

Stage 3: Implementing the Plan
- Step 9: Develop an effective implementation process

Stage 4: Measuring the Results
- Step 10: Reassess strategies in the strategic planning process

Figure 19.1 The Strategic Planning Process.
Created by editors.

These steps, while distinct, are interrelated, and the process involves a certain amount of back-and-forth and recurrence, so it may seem more like painting a picture than building a bridge. In order to create a strategic plan, the organization must first develop and gain consensus around a mission statement, as well as inventory existing programs and activities. In the process of completing this preparatory stage, it is likely that certain of the inventoried programs will emerge as mission critical because they are clearly seen to support the organization's main purpose. When later on during the development of the strategic plan, staff must identify core activities, these programs can serve as good examples.

The remainder of this chapter provides additional details and suggestions for each of the stages of the strategic planning process.

Stage 1. Preparing to Plan

"Would you tell me please, which way I ought to go from here?"
"That depends a good deal on where you want to get to," said the Cat.
"I don't much care where," said Alice.
"Then it doesn't matter which way you go," said the Cat."
Alice's Adventures in Wonderland—Lewis Carroll

Not surprisingly, as with many significant efforts (house painting comes to mind), a good deal of the work in strategic planning goes into the preparation. Key elements in preparing for a strategic plan are the development of a mission and vision; stakeholder interviews (both internal and external); and a needs assessment, including an environmental scan and strengths, weaknesses, opportunities, and threats (SWOT) analysis.

The Foundation of the Plan: Mission, Vision, and Values

Chief among these preparations is the organization's development of mission, vision, and value statements. These types of statements form the foundation of the strategic planning process and have been differentiated as follows: "A mission statement is a statement of purpose, a vision statement is a vivid image of the future you seek to create, and a value statement outlines your organization's guiding concepts and beliefs."[11]

Much information is available regarding the process of identifying and gaining consensus around an organization's mission and vision, which involves an effort very similar to strategic planning itself. Even if the organization already has a mission, vision, and value statement, it is a good idea to review it with appropriate staff and stakeholders to validate or revise the team's understanding of the organization's purpose.

A mission statement should be short and memorable. It is difficult to create concise mission statements, but they are so much more effective than diffuse "baskets of good ideas." See textbox 19.1 for examples of mission statements from three information organizations that have successfully mastered this stage.

Note that all three statements describe the core purpose of the organization in very few, well-chosen words.

Lisa Rosenblum

Examples of Strong Mission Statements for Information Organizations

- "The Seattle Public Library brings people, information, and ideas together to enrich lives and build community."[12]
- "Multnomah County (Oregon) Library's mission: Empowering our community to learn and create."[13]
- "The Harvard Library advances scholarship and teaching by committing itself to the creation, application, preservation, and dissemination of knowledge."[14]

Vision statements may be somewhat longer if they help provide a clearer context for the activities that follow. Vision statements should be lofty and aspirational, describing the world as it will be when the organization has reached its potential, as shown in textbox 19.2.

Examples of Strong Vision Statements for Organizations

- "A world where everyone has a decent place to live," Habitat for Humanity.[15]
- "To become the world leader at connecting people to wildlife conservation," San Diego Zoo.[16]
- "Our vision is an educated, connected community of readers, learners, doers and dreamers," Pima County (Arizona) Public Library.[17]

Value statements connect the information organization to its users by reflecting the organization's core beliefs. They are sometimes called guiding principles. Examples of value statements are shown in textbox 19.3.

Examples of Strong Value Statements for Organizations

- "Sell good merchandise at a reasonable profit, treat your customers like human beings, and they will always come back for more," L.L. Bean.[18]
- "Freedom. We are free and open to all. We treat everyone with respect and compassion." The New York Public Library.[19]
- "The Library values all customers and is responsive to their service needs. The customer's opinion and input is welcomed in all initiatives and undertakings. We consider the impact on the customer in all decisions," The Public Library of Cincinnati and Hamilton County.[20]

Well-developed mission, vision, and value statements like the ones shown above provide the planning team with a blueprint to which it can refer, to ensure that the strategic plan supports the organization's goals.

Reviewing the Organizational Structure: A Transparent Process

Before creating a strategic plan, it is also necessary to review the organization's structure with respect to its ability to accomplish its mission and vision. This review will also suggest which key divisions and groups of employees need to be responsible for the development of a successful plan, and which stakeholders (including patrons and other community members, etc.) should be selected to participate in the process.

A good plan includes external stakeholders. In fact, communication with community stakeholders served by the organization (and also not served by them) can provide additional input on how well the plan is helping the information organization to accomplish its ultimate goals (see also chapter 27: "Communication, Marketing, and Outreach Strategies"). For example, in public libraries, typical external stakeholders may include any library support groups, such as a Friends of the Library or other tax exempt 501(c)(3) groups; government officials, including the mayor or council person; local business owners or business associations (e.g., Chambers of Commerce); school boards; and nonprofit organizations that focus on underserved communities, including the homeless and new immigrants. This extensive outreach should be designed to elicit general and detailed comments from representatives of all segments of the community about:

- how well the library is currently meeting the community's needs,
- which library services are of value to the community and why,
- what policies or practices make it less likely that they would use the library, and
- what services or programs should be offered in the future.

Community open houses are often held, and the community is also surveyed.

Internal stakeholders, including all levels of library staff and board members, are also included in the strategic planning process. The same process of eliciting feedback is held to solicit insight on the current and future role of the organization. Frontline staff are especially valuable to the process, contributing their insight to how people are currently accessing the organization, what services people use, and what trends and changes they are seeing as people walk through the doors or access information services online.

Performing Needs Assessment Exercises

Once stakeholder input has been gathered and reviewed, the next step is to conduct a needs assessment, which further analyzes the data to determine the gaps between how the information organization serves its community and how the organization should be serving the community in the future. There are two types of needs assessment:

Environmental scans: These consist of an analysis of near-term and long-term trends and behaviors that may help or hinder the organization's progress.

SWOT analysis: The focus here is on both internal and external factors influencing the group. SWOT stands for: strengths, weaknesses, opportunities, and threats.

The terms *environmental scanning* and *SWOT analysis* are often used interchangeably, but they are different. The environmental scan is more objective. It looks at current conditions and is outward focused. The SWOT analysis is comparatively more subjective. Both internal and external stakeholders are asked to identify the positive and negative aspects of the organization.

Typically, the first part of the SWOT analysis focuses inwardly; participants are asked what the strengths and weaknesses are of the organization. The next step focuses on the external: "What are the outside forces that influence the organization?" Responses could vary as widely as a downturn in

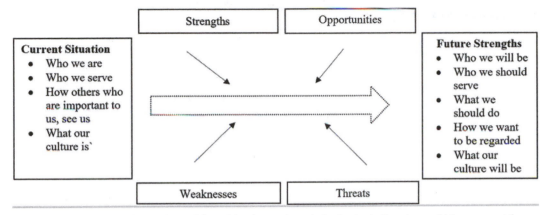

Figure 19.2 SWOT Analysis adopted from Matthews, Joseph R., *Strategic Planning and Management for Library Managers. Created by editors.*

the economy, a new school built across the street, an emerging technology, and so on. The chart above shows a graphical representation of a SWOT analysis.

The University of British Columbia[21] provides a simple summary of questions to ask during a SWOT analysis:

- What conclusions can we draw about priorities for action from this SWOT Analysis?
- What should we do more of? What should we stop doing?
- What should we do less of? What should we start doing?
- What are the priorities for action in each area?

With respect to environmental scans, it is worthwhile to recall Mintzberg's statement that "strategies are plans for the future and patterns from the past."[22] The environmental scan, then, is performed in part to recognize past patterns with an eye toward determining how they limit or enhance future practices: "The purposes of scanning the environment is to ground your strategic plan in the realities of the world around you."[23]

Finally, preparation for a strategic plan requires a comprehensive inventory of existing programs as well as an assessment of their outcomes. Even if a mission and vision statement has already been adopted, it is important to meet with both internal and external stakeholders before beginning the process to hear their opinions about which activities are most effectively meeting the needs of the community. All of this information is crucial to the development of the plan as the team considers which current activities support the group's mission and which are peripheral to its key goals.

> Even if a mission and vision statement has already been adopted, it is important to meet with both internal and external stakeholders before beginning the process to hear their opinions about which activities are most effectively meeting the needs of the community.

Once the data are gathered from the stakeholder interviews and the needs assessment, one can begin to develop the strategic plan. To ensure that the plan is aligned with the overall mission, vision, and values, the strategic plan should identify the organization's key purposes, including its goals and objectives. This sets the groundwork for the planning process. The strategic plan may also provide a summary of the library's organizational structure, highlighting those departments and divisions that are responsible for designing and implementing specific programs.

Stage 2. Developing the Plan

The strategic planning team has gone through all the preparatory exercises: There is data about usage and input from internal and external stakeholders. The organization's mission, vision, and values have all been discussed and articulated, and the organization is ready to enter the heart of the strategic planning process. This consists of defining the specific goals and objectives that support the mission, selecting a planning horizon, assessing available resources, and identifying and describing key projects.

Defining Goals, Objectives, and Core Competencies

While the definition of goals and objectives is one of the more challenging exercises within the strategic planning process, some consider it the most creative. This is the moment when the strategic planning team begins to evaluate its research from the perspective of the organization's mission and vision.

For example, inspired by a mission "empowering our community to learn and create,"[24] the Multnomah County planning team might consider what its constituents are currently learning, and how well the library is supporting their efforts. Conversely, the team might look at where the creativity of certain segments of the community are hindered. Key questions at this stage include:

- How can the library enhance the community's ability to realize its potential as it relates to the library's mission?
- Where does the community fail to meet the lofty expectations of the library's vision, and what obstacles prevent the community from progressing toward this goal?
- In what way is the library competent to help solve these problems, and which solutions require partnerships or are the responsibility of other organizations?

The result of this exercise is a list of goals and objectives consistent with the library's mission, which allow it to address the identified needs of the community. Goals are the big picture, where the library wants to go; objectives are the steps the library must take to get there. These objectives will in turn suggest a range of programs and activities that translate those goals into action, which will be further articulated in the library's operating plan. Table 19.1: Santa Clara University Library's Strategic Goals and Objectives is an example of a goal and its objectives.[25]

Note how broad the first goal is, while the objectives are more specific and address how to accomplish the goal. Another feature of the objectives is that each one suggests a whole range of activities. This is, in fact, one of their chief virtues in that they form a kind of bridge between the library's goals and the programs that support them, as specified in more detail in the development of the list of strategic projects and in the operational plan, which drills down even further and lists specific steps.

Table 19.1. Santa Clara University Library's Goals and Objectives.

GOAL: **Expand the presence of Archives & Special Collections in our community.**
Objective 1: Implement an outreach and marketing strategy for Archives & Special Collections.
Objective 2: Pursue strategic gifts and acquisitions that reflect our collection development philosophy.
Objective 3: Adopt best practices for description, discovery, and preservation to improve access to our unique collections.
Objective 4: Create a strategy for acquiring and curating born-digital materials.

Lisa Rosenblum

Planning Horizon

The plan should describe the programs and projects the information organization will undertake during the planning period to fulfill its mission and accomplish its goal. While it is not necessary to provide too much detail, the strategic plan should, at a minimum, address the organization's signature programs, ongoing services, and new initiatives and explain how they will accomplish its goals and objectives.

> " While it is not necessary to provide too much detail, the strategic plan should, at a minimum, address the organization's signature programs, ongoing services, and new initiatives and explain how they will accomplish its goals and objectives. "

There is no rule on the time range that a strategic plan should cover, but because of the time and resources spent to create a plan they typically are long range—at least five years and longer. A lot can happen in five years within the information landscape.

Discussion Question

Why is a strategic plan particularly important during a fiscal crisis or in economic downturns?

Project Selection

The selection of key projects can be considered a continuation of the process of defining "Goals and Objectives" consistent with the organization's mission. It differs, however, in that this is the part of the planning process that draws most deeply on staff knowledge and experience as they identify and prioritize the actual programs, products, and services that the information organization will provide to meet their objectives.

For example, one of the Santa Clara University Library's objectives is to "Implement an Outreach and Marketing Strategy" to support the library's goal to "Expand the presence of Archives & Special Collections."[26] The library might form a new staff marketing team focused on designing a marketing campaign. Similarly, to accomplish the objective of "pursue strategic gifts and acquisitions that reflect our collection development philosophy," the library would benefit from partnering with the development department in the University to create a list of possible donors. These projects will be developed further in the operational plan, along with specific measurements for their success (e.g., "Acquire a certain amount of contributions per year for collections"). However, at this stage, the initial list of candidate projects that accomplish organizational goals is often best developed as a brainstorming exercise, capturing as many ideas from the team members as possible before screening them for feasibility.

Resource Assessment

Once the prospective project list has been developed, the team must consider what resources are needed to implement them. A detailed budget is not required, but there should be some assessment of the level of resources required, in terms of financial resources as well as staff time. In addition, consideration should be given to the need for potential partnerships for activities requiring collaboration with other entities. For example, the team may determine that significant progress toward a key goal will require more time than is included in the original planning horizon and decide to extend the range of dates the plan will cover. This may, in turn, impact the resources needed to support the selected program. Also, during the development of the strategic plan, many suggestions will be developed that have a narrower tactical focus, which is more appropriate to the operations plan. These ideas should be captured and recorded so they can be utilized during the implementation phase.

Stage 3. Implementing the Plan

After all this effort, it is important for the information organization to introduce the plan to the community and gain the support of the decision makers who will provide the resources (including funding) required for its implementation. Just as important, managers must share the plan with the staff ultimately responsible for its implementation, so they can translate the objectives and selected programs into measurable actions.

Documenting the Strategic Plan

Since the strategic plan sets the direction of the information organization for a significant period of time, it should serve both internal and external stakeholders. A planning report should be written and organized in such a way that it is readily comprehensible by the widest possible audience. Typical components of the planning document include an introduction referencing the mission, vision, and values of the organization, a description of the planning process, a report on the goals and objectives, and a road map for implementation. Sometimes information organizations will use different terms and phrases in their strategic plan, but these typically refer to the same concepts. For example, a goal can be referred to as a service priority. A guiding principle is used interchangeably with a value statement and a library action means the same as an objective.

The report should also include an executive summary, with key points distilled into a one-page graphically enhanced handout to market and communicate the plan to an even broader audience. Simplified graphics and other communications strategies can help make the plan more understandable to the community.

Rollout to the Community

Completion of strategic planning often provides an opportunity for a marketing campaign to gain additional support for the organization (see also chapter 27: "Communication, Marketing, and Outreach Strategies"). The strategic plan can be announced via a press release distributed to all social media channels. The marketing campaign can also include additional community meetings to introduce the strategic plan and solicit input for refinements to the operational plan, which can be further modified to include appropriate programs and services. Reconvening the stakeholder groups can also help generate buzz around the strategic plan and create new champions to advocate for its successful implementation.

> " All staff in the organization should be involved in communicating the plan, even those not directly accountable for any one specific goal or objective, since all staff contribute (in one way or another) to the overall success of the organization. "

Just as important to the external presentation is rolling out the plan to staff responsible for implementing the plan. One mistake directors often make is to discuss the strategic plan only at the time it is first created, and then only with high-level managers. All staff in the organization should be involved in communicating the plan, even those not directly accountable for any one specific goal or objective, since all staff contribute (in one way or another) to the overall success of the organization. An organization may develop a formal training program to introduce the plan with a facilitated process for eliciting feedback from staff.

Too often a strategic plan is created, placed on the shelf, and no one looks back at it until it is time to start planning again. Instead, the strategic plan should be considered "a living document," charting the information organization's direction throughout the planning horizon. It should be featured front and center on the organization's website, and management and staff should refer to it often.

Putting the Plan into Action

In conjunction with the strategic plan, the information organization must also prepare an operating plan to identify the steps necessary for implementation. Also known as a tactical plan or short-range plan, the operational plan links the organization's strategic goals and objectives to specific projects, programs, and services the organization provides and performs in its day-to-day operations. Shorter in time frame and often aligned with the fiscal or budget year, the operational plan also allocates the resources needed to implement specific programs and officially incorporates them in the annual budget.

Based on the strategic plan, the team identifies projects and programs that can be accomplished within a budget year, given the available budget and other resources. These manageable programs should be accompanied by appropriate measurements that relate the programs to the organization's mission and vision. The operational plan also identifies the roles and responsibility of staff, and the time frame for accomplishing each program.

One common mistake information organizations make is not providing adequate resources to implement the objectives identified in their strategic plan into their operational plan. While robust budgets are always preferred, the history of funding for information organizations testifies to the fact that budgets rise and fall. In fact, one of the advantages a strategic plan gives an information organization is the ability to continually allocate resources based on greatest impact. For example, if the staffing budget has been cut but the strategic plan directs the information organization to provide homework help centers to meet their goal to "encourage lifelong learn-

> ### Discussion Question
>
> Why is it important to engage an organization's stakeholders in the strategic planning process?

ing," the organization can find a way to fulfill its commitment through volunteers who can provide the assistance (see also chapter 22: "Managing Personnel"). Alternatively, the information organization can partner with a nonprofit that provides tutoring to underserved students. In all cases, the strategic plan identifies which services are key to its mission to guide the budget process.

Stage 4. Measuring Performance and Adjusting the Plan

The best way to ensure the successful implementation of a strategic plan is to create measurable objectives. While this may sound simple, when related to high-level strategies, objectives often tend to be difficult to quantify. Objectives may be broad, but they should also be clear: vague objectives that are too general are too easy to ignore and may never get accomplished. Objectives should align with the goals and the overarching mission, vision, and values of the organization, but they should also suggest programs that can be implemented and attained within a reasonable amount of time.

Chapter 20 speaks more specifically about data analytics, but the measurement of *efficiency* and *effectiveness* are key to strategic planning (see also chapter 26: "Managing Data and Data Analysis in Information Organizations"). As management guru Peter Drucker famously explained, "Efficiency is doing things right; effectiveness is doing the right things."[27] While both are important, *output*, which is a measure of efficiency, should not be confused with *outcome*, which is a measure of effectiveness.

Measuring Output and Outcome: Breaking It Down

Literacy Objective: "All children in the community use the library for education and recreation."

Output efficiency measures:

- the "percent of third graders who have a library card by the end of the fiscal year"
- how many children participate in a summer reading program

Outcome effectiveness measures:

- how often third-graders utilize their library cards
- how often they access materials
- how participation in the program helped improve their reading level

As can be seen from textbox 19.4, efficiency and output are much easier to measure than effectiveness and outcomes. However, the latter are ultimately more meaningful and relate most closely to the goal of the strategic planning process, which is to align the organization's activities to its mission.

To paraphrase Drucker,[28] the effective manager wants to manage not only what the information organization does, but how it transforms the lives of the library patrons and the entire community.

Performance measures—especially measures of efficiency—are typically modified during the life span of a strategic plan. A good plan accommodates these changes without losing its spirit and vision.

CONCLUSION

Strategic planning is a time-consuming process, requiring energy, time, and resources. However, if done well and implemented consistently, strategic plans have the potential to transform an organization. Just the process of involving community stakeholders alongside staff to discuss the future direction of the information organization creates a synergy that cannot be accomplished by staff alone.

Once developed, it takes discipline to follow a strategic plan. Tradeoffs must be made to promote high-priority, core programs at the expense of other less central activities. Sometimes, despite everyone's best effort, only parts of a plan are implemented, or the plan fails altogether. For instance, if in year three of a five-year plan a popular program emerges, it may be tempting to support it by redirecting resources from a strategic goal. The temptation may even be stronger when a mayor or a board member pushes for a pet project. Another common pitfall is the failure to involve key staff—not just upper management—in the planning process from the start. If a strategic plan is perceived as "just another management idea," the staff will not be committed to its success.

> If a strategic plan is perceived as 'just another management idea,' the staff will not be committed to its success.

Sometimes a beautifully written plan is developed and then sits on the shelf. When this happens, it is a sure sign that the organization's managers failed to appreciate that strategic planning is essential to organizational development and requires the same level of effort as other "change management" initiatives (see also chapter 20: "Change Management").

Today's information organization is a busy place: the frantic pace of *doing* allows little time for reflection. It is also a place filled with the voices of many telling the organization what to do—such as fiscal agents and politicians, even their own traditions and past practices. Strategic planning forces an organization to step back and think about *why* they do what they do. If, in the final analysis, the only thing gained is the opportunity for the organization's staff to ask the important questions—*What is our purpose? Why are we here? Who are we serving?*—and if the answers to those questions help direct their activities to reach those goals, then the time was not wasted, and the effort will have been worthwhile.

NOTES

1. John Palfrey, *BiblioTech: Why Libraries Matter More Than Ever in the Age of Google* (New York: Basic Books, 2015).
2. Lawrence Freedman, *Strategy: A History* (New York: Oxford, 2013), xi.
3. See, for example: http://www.strategies-tactics.com/suntzuchp1.htm; http://www.easy-strategy.com/strategic-planning.html; https://suntzublog.wordpress.com/2009/12/17/the-importance-of-planning/.
4. Richard D. Young, "Perspectives on Strategic Planning in the Public Sector," University of South Carolina, Institute for Public Service and Policy Research, http://www.ipspr.sc.edu/publication/perspectives%20on%20strategic%20planning.pdf., 2.
5. David Osborne and Ted Gaebler, *Reinventing Government* (New York: Plume, 1993).
6. Henry Mintzberg, "The Fall and Rise of Strategic Planning," *Harvard Business Review*, January 1994, 1, https://hbr.org/1994/01/the-fall-and-rise-of-strategic-planning.
7. M. E. Porter, "What Is Strategy?," *Harvard Business Review* 74, no. 6 (November–December 1996): 62.
8. Ibid., 70.
9. Freedman, *Strategy*, 72.
10. John Bryson, *Strategic Planning for Public and Nonprofit Organizations* (San Francisco: Jossey-Bass, 2011), 46.
11. Michael Allison, *Strategic Planning for Nonprofit Organizations: A Practical Guide for Dynamic Times* (Hoboken, NJ: Wiley, 2015), 77.
12. Seattle Public Library, "Mission Statement," 2017, http://www.spl.org/about-the-library/mission-statement.
13. Multnomah County (OR) Public Library, https://multcolib.org/about/priorities.
14. Harvard Library, "Mission and Objectives," 2017, http://library.harvard.edu/objectives-priorities.
15. Habitat for Humanity, "Our mission, vision and principles," 2017, https://www.habitat.org/about/mission-and-vision.
16. San Diego Zoo, "San Diego Zoo Global Mission and Vision," 2017, http://zoo.sandiegozoo.org/content/san-diego-zoo-global-mission-and-vision. Note that in June 2017, the mission of this organization was changed to, "We will lead the fight against extinction."
17. Pima County Public Library, "Vision, Mission, and Values," 2017, https://www.library.pima.gov/mission/.
18. L.L. Bean, "Company Values," 2017, https://www.llbean.com/customerService/aboutLLBean/company_values.html.
19. The New York Public Library, https://www.nypl.org/help/about-nypl/mission/core-values.
20. The Public Library of Cincinnati and Hamilton County, "About Us: Mission Statement," 2017, http://www.cincinnatilibrary.org/info/mission.asp.
21. University of British Columbia Library, "*UBC Library SWOT Analysis*," UBC Library Planning, Vancouver: 2000, 1, http://www.ryerson.ca/~itm700/Attachments/UBCLibraryswot-analysis.pdf.
22. Henry Mintzberg, "Crafting Strategy," *Harvard Business Review* 65, no. 4 (July–August 1987): 66–75.
23. Allison, *Strategic Planning for Nonprofit Organizations*, 99.
24. Multnomah County (OR) Public Library.
25. Santa Clara University Library, https://www.scu.edu/library/strategicplan/collections/.
26. Ibid.
27. Peter F. Drucker, *The Effective Executive: The Definitive Guide to Getting the Right Things Done* (New York: Harper Collins, 2006).
28. Ibid.

20

Change Management

Ruth Barefoot

Chapter 20, "Change Management," illustrates how and why organizational change management and leadership is a core skill among professionals in the information field today. Ruth Barefoot, a longtime library manager and instructor teaching change management, starts by defining change and change management, using the term "change leader" to identify those involved with change management. After establishing this foundational understanding, Barefoot explains the skills needed for change management, defines how to apply these skills in diverse environments, and explores current change management trends within information organizations.

Within information organizations, notes Barefoot, the focus is on organizational change, including its mission, values, policies, procedures, technology, and people. Change leaders are central to change management and use a three-step process that involves identifying why change is needed, how to enact change and facilitate the process with the change recipients, and when to make the change for optimal and sustainable outcomes.

Barefoot identifies key skills that change leaders need to have, which include developing, communicating, and implementing a vision; understanding change drivers; analyzing organizational change; engaging and supporting people through change; assessing change leadership traits and perceptions; and demonstrating change leadership. Change management is an important topic for all information professionals because effective change leaders help their organizations adapt to the ever-evolving information landscape while remaining relevant and essential to their community.

★   ★   ★

Societal needs and norms are constantly changing. It is imperative that information organizations change as well to meet the evolving needs of their users and communities. Without proactive change in the service offerings provided by information organizations, information professionals will lose contact and become less effective in serving the needs of their users. But what is change? How is it managed? Who is responsible for managing that change? Information professionals need to have the skills to manage change and lead their information organizations through the often difficult, uncertain, and risky processes that are necessary to adapt to those changes. This chapter illustrates how and why organizational change management and leadership is a core skill among professionals in the information field today.

After completing this chapter, the reader should have an understanding of:

- the definition of change, change management, and the different types of people who engage with the change management process;
- the skills and competencies needed throughout the change management process;
- the application of change management skills in information environments; and
- industry trends.

> "Twenty years from now, you will be more disappointed by the things you didn't do than by the things you did do. So throw off the bowlines. Sail away from safe harbor. Catch the tradewinds in your sails. Explore. Dream. Discover."—Mark Twain

DEFINING CHANGE, CHANGE MANAGEMENT, AND CHANGE PLAYERS

It is first important to define the key terms related to change management, specifically: organizational change, change management, change manager, change leader, and change agent.

Organizational change is "a planned alteration of organizational components to improve the effectiveness of the [library] organization."[1] Organizational components, such as mission, values, policies, procedures, technology, and people, are important elements that bind an organization together. Some of the biggest changes in information services today are not driven by new and emerging technologies but by ideological questions; for example, why are libraries essential and how are they providing core services to the communities they serve and/or the organizations they support (e.g., university systems, city governments, hospitals, etc.)?

John P. Kotter, a well-recognized expert in the field of change management and author of *Leading Change*,[2] defines change management as "a collective term for all approaches to preparing and supporting individuals, teams, and organizations in making organizational change." Kotter developed a well-known eight-step process for enacting change that includes:

1. creating a sense of urgency,
2. building a coalition,
3. creating a change vision,
4. communicating a vision for change,
5. removing obstacles,
6. creating short-term wins,
7. building upon the change, and
8. anchoring the change in the organization.

> " When using any model to enact change, information professionals need to provide the *structure* for change to take root, flourish, and thrive. This will further require the information professional to become the custodian of the change process. "

(See also chapter 37: "Leadership Skills for Today's Global Information Landscape" for more on Kotter's Model in table 37.2.)

When using any model to enact change, information professionals need to provide the *structure* for change to take root, flourish, and thrive. This will further require the information professional to become the custodian of the change process. High-tech guru, Guy Kawasaki, urges change leaders to make the change and the messages involved with that change easy for the stakeholders involved to follow and accept, especially for those people who are directly impacted by the change.[3] Clearly, change management is a complex process that will require several people to help facilitate the change. Key players in this process are the change managers, change leaders, and change agents.

Change managers are individuals tasked with the responsibility to:

- see that change happens,
- play a primary role in evaluating the effectiveness of the change,
- identify and analyze what change is needed, and
- apply the tools to create positive and lasting change.

Change leaders are more often identified as:

- out front in the change process,
- first adopters,
- the first to test-drive change, and
- the first to deal with the nebulous nature of initial change in the organization.

A change leader may be assigned a project office, coupled with cross-departmental support personnel, or a team of people who can affect needed change while fostering a stable environment. This situation is not often prevalent, but if they are lucky to have assigned staff, it will only add to the stability of the big change work planned for the organization. Change may happen more swiftly due to their workload being focused on their specific project work. These dedicated staff will minimize the impact on frontline staff workload, increase collaboration, improve grassroots buy-in, and foster stability.

Change agent is a general term to describe any staff person, titled or not, although most often not holding a position of power in the organization. The change agent is often someone leading change by attitude and personality, rather than by position in the organization.

While each of these key players performs a different role in the change management process, this chapter will use a single term, *change leaders*, to represent all main people involved in the change process.

Change leaders help to set the framework for change management for their organizations. They use a three-step identification process to define the change process that asks the following questions:

1. Why is the change needed?
2. How will this change get accomplished? What specific tools will be applied to enact change and facilitate the process with the change recipients (e.g., employees in the organization)?
3. When will the change get implemented for optimal and sustainable outcomes?

CASE STUDY

Applying the Three-Step Process to Define the Change Process

Imagine that a change leader is working on enhancing access to the organization's collection of e-audio books. By using the three-step process, the change leader would develop an understanding about the overarching need for change and the process that would need to be followed:

1. *Why is the change needed?* The existing downloadable e-audio book collection is available even when the [physical] library is closed but not enough users are aware of this service. The library wants to enhance awareness of and access to this collection.
2. *How will this change get accomplished?* The library will change the way it promotes the collection to improve visibility of the e-audio book collection; specifically, the library will increase funding to purchase more titles and then will promote these new titles to the user community.
3. *When will this change get implemented?* The library will begin selecting new e-audio book titles immediately and aggressively market this popular collection to users.

ESSENTIAL CHANGE MANAGEMENT SKILLS FOR THE INFORMATION PROFESSIONAL

Given the dynamic and continuous change within the information landscape, information professionals can anticipate being involved with the organization's change process at least once throughout their career. Information professionals can prepare themselves, and the organizations they work in, to successfully deal with change by adopting seven key competencies:

1. Develop a vision
2. Communicate and implement a vision
3. Understand change drivers
4. Analyze organizational change
5. Engage and support people through change
6. Assess change leadership traits and perceptions
7. Demonstrate change leadership

These skills are explained in greater depth below.

Skill 1: Develop a Vision

Developing a vision begins by exploring and envisioning opportunities and possibilities for the organization, while also identifying the challenges. Being both a dreamer and a pragmatist is characteristic of all great leaders. Effective change leaders devise a vision that is resilient in the face of changing resources, build on a new direction but utilize gains from the past, and provide common ground or an opportunity for the entire organization to be included. A great vision challenges the status quo and inspires leaders to get on board to help facilitate the steps needed to reach the new vision.

> Effective change managers devise a vision that is resilient in the face of changing resources, build on a new direction but utilize gains from the past, and provide common ground or an opportunity for the entire organization to be included.

Change leaders, as "agents of change," must take every opportunity to promote the new changed vision in everyday activities and with each person in the organization. Some of the ways that change leaders can successfully get people in the organization to buy into the changed vision include:

- adding financial resources to promote the vision such as by hosting events and developing marketing materials (see also chapter 21: "Managing Budgets"),
- hiring and retraining staff who embrace innovation as central to the library's mission (see also chapter 22: "Managing Personnel"),
- developing metrics that demonstrate the benefits that individuals and the organization will realize as a result of the vision and then track and report on that data (see also chapter 26: "Managing Data and Data Analysis in Information Organizations"), and
- creating a culture in the organization that empowers everyone involved to become agents of change.[4]

Discussion Questions

Think of a time you experienced organizational change in an organization you worked for (library related or not). Who were the early adopters of the change? How did their behavior influence the effectiveness of that change? What types of skills, competencies, or behaviors did these early adopters demonstrate that helped influence the success of that change?

Skill 2: Communicate and Implement the Vision

One of the ways to communicate and implement the vision for change is through framing. Framing is the process of capturing an idea or image of a process within the larger organizational framework to redefine it within the organizational role, re-assimilate it, and give it new purpose. Understanding how to capture and communicate an idea by framing a message assigns meaning to the everyday course of organizational life to enhance organizational effectiveness. Framing language can shape or modify how an event is viewed, and how the change leader wants their staff to see the event. Many different interpretations can be construed. Change leaders can shape ideas and modify understanding as an organization through framing. Leaders and managers can frame through use of stories, myths, and metaphors of an organization (see figure 20.1).

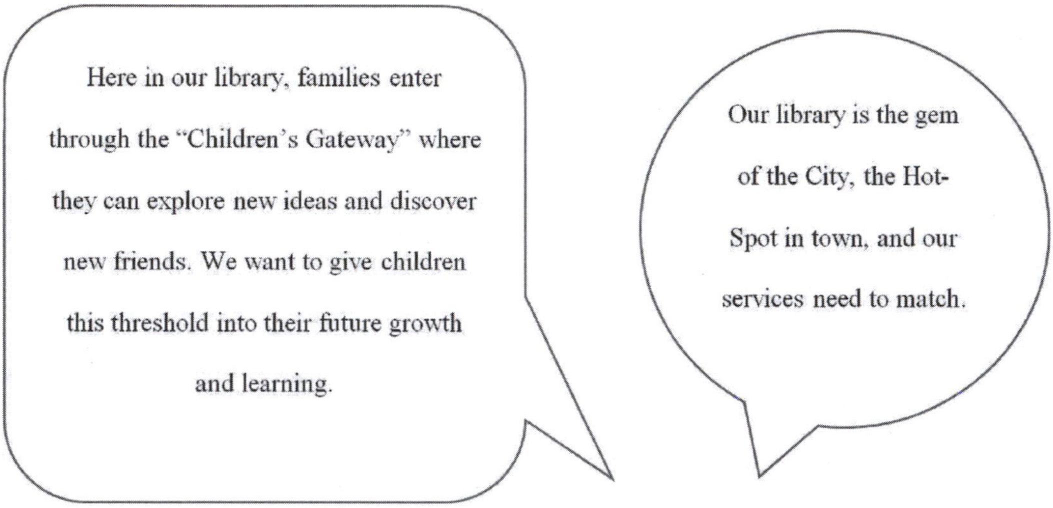

Figure 20.1 Examples of Framing Messages. *Created by editors.*

Framing through metaphors, such as the statement on the left in figure 20.1, extends the library from a place to explore books to a "children's gateway" of discovery and growth. Framing can also rally staff efforts by building a sense of unity, purpose, and urgency, as is demonstrated in the quote to the right where the message emphasizes the essentialness of the library to the community. Framing is a great tool and often goes underutilized in management efforts.

Discussion Questions

What framing opportunities have gone unnoticed in information organizations? How should leaders better frame the messages they want staff to hear?

Skill 3: Understand Change Drivers

What is driving organizational change? Globalization is among the chief drivers for organizational change. This means that competition for services comes from anywhere, anytime. Cawsey and Deszca highlight how organizations are now influenced by several global and fundamental forces that impact the information environment, often triggering the need for change in information organizations. These change drivers include:

- "changing social, cultural, and demographic patterns;
- spectacular technological achievements that are transforming how we do business;
- a global marketplace that sends us competing worldwide and brings competition to our doorsteps; and
- continued political uncertainty in many countries that have the potential to introduce chaos into world markets."[5]

Other forces that play a role in driving change in information organizations today include the availability (or lack) of resources, changing social, cultural, and demographic patterns, technological advancements, and the political climate.

How can organizations adapt to these drivers of change? In order for organizations to evolve and grow, they must be dynamically engaged with the individuals and environments they serve. It is equivalent to Stern's "evolutionary fitness,"[6] defined as the capacity to accept or adopt change in a gradual way, often collaboratively from or through the grassroots of an organization (see also chapter 28: "Advocacy"). This evolutionary fitness of an organization entails the growth of more reluctant or resistant staff who become more resilient over time. Taking small steps every day helps, although sometimes the organization must leap into action. Information professionals can also prepare for change by keeping up with global and societal trends; this can help them stay ahead of the change curve and remain aware of the various factors that directly and indirectly impact the climate of their organizations (see also chapter 3: "Librarianship: A Continuously Evolving Profession").

Being caught by surprise by change may have the greatest negative impact on an organization because the process of responding, catching up, and reconfiguring the organizational structure to accommodate change may be more strenuous—and even more costly. The shift to outsourcing services has become a more attractive option for many information organizations trying to solve this gap in organizational readiness. For instance, the Library Systems and Services, Inc.'s (LSSI)[7] business model provides an alternate management system that is "for-profit" instead of the traditional nonprofit models that many city and county governments use. This permits LSSI managers to approach change management projects with a strict cost-based strategy as the driver for change.

Change leaders are tasked with the responsibility to accept that change happens and play a primary role in evaluating the effectiveness of the change. They remain aware and analyze what change is needed. Their goal is to apply the tools and processes necessary to create positive and lasting change. An organization's evolutionary fitness for change will depend on how well this initial analysis is done.

Skill 4: Analyze Which Type of Change to Apply to Organizational Change

When tackling an organizational change—whether it is a big or small one—a change leader must think through what is needed before setting out on the journey of transformation. As shown in table 20.1, there are four types of organizational change: tuning, adapting, reorienting, and re-creating.[8]

Change that is incremental and continuous can be relatively easy to adapt to through simple tuning or adjusting within the organizational departments; these types of changes require less organizational shifting in processes and policy. Change that is aimed at reorienting or re-creating within an organization is

> " Allowing those on the front lines of the organization to process the change in the way that helps them adopt a sustainable day-to-day work environment will strengthen the organization's change muscle. "

much more challenging, as this involves major strategic change, often making changes to a vast array of policies and procedures, and is most likely to shift the climate in the organization.

Table 20.1. Types of Organization Change.

	Incremental/Continuous	Discontinuous/Radical
	Tuning	*Redirecting or Reorienting*
Anticipatory	• Incremental change is made in anticipation of future events; implementation is the major task • Need is for internal alignment • Focuses on individual components or subsystems • Middle management role Example: a quality improvement initiative from an employee improvement committee	• Strategic proactive changes are based on predicted major changes in the environment • Need is for positioning the whole organization for a new reality • Focuses on all organizational components • Senior management creates sense of urgency and motivates the change Example: a major change in product or service offering, in response to opportunities identified
	Adapting	*Overhauling or Re-creating*
Reactive	• Incremental changes are made in response to environmental changes • Need is for internal alignment • Focuses on individual components or subsystems • Middle management role Example: modest changes to customer services, in response to customer complaints	• Change is in response to a significant performance crisis • Need is to reevaluate the whole organization, including its core values • Focuses on all organizational components to achieve rapid, system-wide change • Senior management creates vision and motivates optimism Example: a major realignment of strategy, involving plant closures and changes to product and service offerings, to stem financial losses and return the firm to profitability

Source: Adapted from D. Nadler and M. Tushman, "Organizational Frame Bending: Principles for Managing Reorientation," *Academy of Management Executives (1987–1989)* 3, no. 3 (August 1989): 197–204.

Appropriately analyzing which type of change is needed will make the change smoother to adopt with a higher degree of sustainability among those resistant to the change. Allowing those on the front lines of the organization to process the change in the way that helps them adopt a sustainable day-to-day work environment will strengthen the organization's change muscle. Consequently, the next change will be easier for them to assist in the analysis, problem-solving, and standardizing of new processes of doing things for a more optimal outcome. That is not to say all change may be steered through small, slow incremental steps to avoid staff disorientation and overall unhappiness with change. Some large and systemic changes cannot be parsed up, delayed for more opportune times, or held off until all staff are "ready" for the leap of change. The larger climate of change and changing resources may dictate how and when to move.

Skill 5: Engage and Support People through Change

Finding the right staff to help with change in the organization involves spotting the early adopters. Early adopters are curious and excited to solve challenges; they are risk takers and can see long-term gains by trying something new in the short term. Encouraging early adopters to work with the change leaders on the small components of changing processes or policy is a great first step in the change management process. Once these early adopters are identified and confirmed as being participators in the change activities, they can be folded into the change leadership development and move forward more steadily on various change projects they participate in. These early adopters assist in fostering an atmosphere of acceptance and transparency. They help model the new path of changed behaviors for the organization, although they do not have any more answers than the change leaders—often fewer.

> " Early adopters are curious and excited to solve challenges; they are risk takers and can see long-term gains by trying something new in the short term. "

Skill 6: Assess Change Leadership Traits and Perceptions

Change leaders often need to perform some self-diagnosis before engaging in change management activities. They must know themselves, understand why they want to lead the specific change, and identify what their inspiration is for instilling the change in the organizational environment. They must know themselves before they can genuinely encourage others to embrace a climate of change. Leaders can do this by taking personality tests such as the popular Myers-Briggs[9] or the short quiz through the Mindful Leadership Institute.[10] In addition, change leaders may seek out a 360-Degree Feedback,[11] a substantial blind review received from colleagues and bosses where they work. This feedback can be very revealing of how the organization's leadership comes across, not just because the feedback is given anonymously but most significantly because the evaluations are completed by those most impacted by the change. Without this feedback, fears may undermine the change leaders' effectiveness as they try to implement any change at all. Each change, viewed in a positive or negative light, contributes to the climate or environment of change, which directly contributes to the resiliency of the organization's change muscle. Building the organization's evolutionary fitness for change places a role of "innovator" on the change leader. In fact, many leaders correlate change with innovation.

Skill 7: Demonstrate Change Leadership

Cawsey and Deszca stated in *Toolkit for Organizational Change*, "Change capability has become a core managerial competence."[12] Change leaders are often the first to adopt an entrepreneurial mind-set, exhibit a high degree of comfort with risk taking, and lead pilot projects happily and with a true interest in finding sustainable answers.

Library leaders are embracing creative thinking models such as design thinking, an approach that was developed by IDEO[13] (see also chapter 23: "Innovative Library and Information Services: The Design Thinking Process"). Design thinking has three modes:

1. Inspiration (framing a challenge).
2. Ideation (based on the challenge to generate ideas).
3. Iteration (putting ideas out to the world, often through co-creation).

By embracing design thinking, library staff are building multidisciplinary teams that can pop up strategically as needs arise and can help to implement change in the organization. Library leaders are using these three modes of design thinking to develop risk-taking cultures for supporting change, such as due to budgetary challenges and technological developments, in their organizations. These design thinking models can produce optimal and sustainable results (see Case Study: Change Management in the Library Setting as an example).

Change Management in the Library Setting

Library staff noticed customers were frustrated that they could only print documents from library desktop computers. Customers wanted to print straight from their cell phones, laptops, or tablets. A library crew quickly volunteered to come up with a set of alternative solutions that enabled customers to print directly from their devices to the printer wirelessly. The capability was already present in their equipment settings. They tested the printing capability for usability and reliability and prepared a proposal for management. Management approved the service changes and the adoption of the new wireless printing service began. With a few adjustments to the initial proposed plan, this new service was offered within a few days. The library crew that developed this change in service was asked to review other service enhancements and make recommendations. This staff created optimal results for the most sustainable outcome through their thrifty and easy-to-implement solution. The customers immediately began using the wireless printing service. They told their friends and the service nearly promoted itself. The change had very high ROI (return on investment) for optimal results.

The above case study illustrates how a team is capable of exploring new and innovative solutions to common challenges in the organization. The case study exemplifies how organizational change can build the change muscle needed for future changes. The change process followed in one scenario can build the change muscle needed to be applied to other challenges in the organization. The more the staff can apply this process to small projects, the more their change muscle can be tested on more involved and complex change projects. The organization needs to consistently build the change muscle and apply it when opportunities and needs arise. This is also an example of how evolutionary fitness is exercised when the organization not only allows, but also promotes, change leadership.

Developing Change Leadership Skills

How can change leaders develop the right skills for the job? One step toward becoming an innovative change leader is to perform informational interviews with proven successful leaders to learn about their best practices in change leadership. Change leaders can also explore completed change management projects and search out success stories that feature effective change management processes.

CONCLUSION

Change is not only possible but also necessary. Information organizations are endlessly evolving environments. More organizations are decentralizing, leaving leaders and managers to accomplish the goals of the organization. Yet, despite the abundance of change management information, there remains a scarcity of good change leaders to do the actual work of meeting fast-paced changing needs.

Learning to be a change leader starts with knowing oneself better. Exploring situations that will foster a more resilient nature in personal and professional life, especially when one is leading change in an organization, prepares information professionals to affect smoother transitions. Change in work environments causes the biggest shifts in organizations in that these changes often re-create or reorganize how organizations operate.

Information professionals should develop a change agent's tool kit that includes the seven skills shared above, such as how to craft a vision and utilize the framing tool to help shape ideas and modify understanding throughout the organization. As a result of using these skills, communicating with staff is more genuine and encourages staff effort, urgency, and unity. A great vision challenges the status quo and inspires leaders to get on board to help facilitate the steps needed to reach the new vision. Effective change leaders begin by fostering an atmosphere of acceptance and transparency.

Having a climate or environment where change happens more readily and is more accepted by its stakeholders depends on how the organization views change. Providing a format to appreciate change and the work that goes into it will be the strongest contributing factor to how employees embrace change now and in the future.

NOTES

1. Tupper Cawsey and Gene Deszca, *Toolkit for Organizational Change* (Los Angeles: Sage Publications, 2007), 2.
2. John Kotter, "Leading Change: Why Transformation Efforts Fail," *Harvard Business Review* (March–April 1995): 59–67.
3. Guy Kawasaki, *Enchantment: The Art of Changing Hearts, Minds, and Actions* (New York: Portfolio/ Penguin, 2011), 45.
4. Amy K. Garmer, "Libraries in the Exponential Age: Moving from the Edge of Innovation to the Center of Community" (Washington, DC: Aspen Institute, 2016), 39, https://csreports.aspeninstitute.org/docu ments/Libraries_Exponential_Age.pdf.
5. Cawsey and Deszca, *Toolkit for Organizational Change*, 10.
6. Michael D. Stern, "Patrimony and the Evolution of Risk-Taking," *PLoS ONE* 5, no. 7 (July 2010): 5.
7. Libraries Systems and Services, Inc. (LSSI), http://www.lsslibraries.com.
8. Cawsey and Deszca, *Toolkit for Organizational Change*, 10.
9. The Myers and Briggs Foundation, "MBTI Basics," 2017, http://www.myersbriggs.org/my-mbti-person ality-type/mbti-basics/.
10. Institute for Mindful Leadership, "Why Us," 2017, https://instituteformindfulleadership.org/.
11. 360-Degree Feedback, http://www.testsonthenet.com/atctests/360-Degree-Overview.htm.
12. Cawsey and Deszca, *Toolkit for Organizational Change*, 4.
13. IDEO, https://www.ideo.com/.

21

Managing Budgets

Sara F. Jones

Chapter 21, "Managing Budgets," provides a solid introduction to budget management for the information organization. Sara Jones, director of library services at the Marin County Free Library, opens the chapter with a discussion on understanding types of budgets and the budget process. She outlines line-item budgets as being the most common type of budget but also discusses program budgets, performance budgets, and zero-based budgets. She then takes the reader through the budget process, noting that these processes are ongoing, cyclic, and should align with the organization's strategic plan. The budget process includes preparing the budget, approving the budget, implementing the budget, and evaluating the budget.

Jones highlights that while some information organizations receive most of their funding from government sources (such as tax revenue), other information organizations are funded by a parent organization's general fund. Many organizations also find the need to support a program or fill the gap in their funding through supplemental funds, often made possible through fund-raising, Friends of the Library organizations, grants, and so on. No matter the type of funding, it is up to the budget manager and other organizational leaders to demonstrate the value of the organization and its services to support the funding, as well as the budget.

Throughout the chapter, Jones notes that most information professionals will be involved in the budgeting process at some point in their careers; therefore, it is essential that information professionals understand budgets and best practices. Additional competencies relating to effective budgeting practices addressed by the author include strategic planning, leadership, and effective communication.

★ ★ ★

Managers of information organizations are not usually accountants or financial experts. Many enter the profession with no accounting training and little expertise in managing professional budgets. They often learn how to manage budgets on the job, through trial and error. In today's challenging economic times, it has become increasingly apparent that in order to effectively manage any information organization, unit, or program, an information professional needs to be able to effectively manage a budget. The basic financial principles and practices remain the same, whether managing a budget of $15 million or $15 hundred. After completing this chapter, the reader should have an understanding of how to plan a budget aimed at helping an information organization achieve its strategic objectives.

UNDERSTANDING BUDGETS

A budget is a plan that allocates money to specific elements of income (revenue) and expenses over a certain period of time. It is the foundation for any organization's planning process and the basic tool used to track and control spending. A budget is a fairly universal tool used by business, nonprofit organizations, and all forms of government.

Budgets typically cover a calendar year or a fiscal year, which for many institutions runs from July 1 through June 30, and for the federal government runs from October 1 through September 30. In some cases, budgets are biennial, which means they cover two years.

It is important to learn as much as possible and ask questions about the budgeting process. The more information professionals know about budgeting, the more they can advocate for funding aimed at meeting specific organizational objectives. Understanding budgets also makes it more likely that an information professional can take on additional leadership responsibilities, as managing budgets is a part of all leadership positions in an information organization.

> The more information professionals know about budgeting, the more they can advocate for funding aimed at meeting specific organizational objectives. Understanding budgets also makes it more likely that an information professional can take on additional leadership responsibilities.

Budgets and Revenue

It is a common misconception that information organizations only deal with the expense side of the budget equation. That is rarely the case. Even in an organization where the majority of income is derived from tax revenue, a budget must be used when requesting funds from a parent entity and determining how much revenue was allocated to the organization. Many information organizations (such as public libraries, academic libraries, special libraries, school libraries, etc.) are government entities that receive the majority of their funding from a parent agency, such as a city government, school district, or university.

> The ability of an information organization's leader to demonstrate the value of the services it provides and advocate for funding is an important part of ensuring that the organization receives adequate funding from the parent entity.

There are two types of funds typically used to provide revenue to these publicly funded organizations, and it is important to understand the distinction. *General fund* is a term used to describe funding that supports government agencies by drawing from the parent organization's general ledger account. A *special purpose fund*, which some organizations have, describes funding (usually from a dedicated tax source) that is collected and set aside specifically for the organization's purposes (see textbox 21.1). In a general fund, there is usually competition for scarce funding across all departments in a government organization, often including mandated public safety services like fire and police. Thus, the ability of an information organization's leader to demonstrate the value of the services it provides and advocate for funding is an important part of ensuring that the organization receives adequate funding from the parent entity.

In addition to an entity's general funds, many information organizations also benefit from supplemental types of income, which usually vary from year to year. These supplemental financial resources include contributions, such as direct donations by individuals or corporations, as well as grant funds awarded by government agencies or private foundations. In addition, several groups typically associated with information organizations (e.g., Friends of the Library organization, a group of volunteers, or a library foundation) either provide direct contributions or assist in raising funds for the organization. Some information organizations also receive revenue through fines (e.g., on overdue materials) and fees (e.g., fees paid by college students used to fund an academic library).

Budgets and Expenditures

In addition to using budgets to understand and plan for revenue, budgets are tools managers can use to plan allocations prior to implementing the budget, and then track and control expenditures. Through ongoing monitoring of the budget, managers can view actual amounts for each expenditure and identify any variance between the budget and the actual expenditures. Budget expenditures can be planned and controlled for the overall organization, as well as by department, location, or program. As an example, the organization might have a budget for a specific branch of a library system, or a budget for particular services or programs.

TEXTBOX 21.2

Budgeting Activities

- managing employees
- scheduling employees
- managing hardware and software
- ordering supplies
- ordering books
- reviewing materials or resources for selection
- building management
- programming

Types of Budgets[1]

Line-item budgets are the most common type of budget. This type of budget lists expenses item by item, grouped by the type of expense (e.g., personnel, materials, training, travel). Line-item budgets are fairly simple to manage as the amount of funds allocated for each line item makes it clear to the manager the total amount allocated for the line item. In addition, as managers review budget updates during the year, they can watch spending for each line item as time progresses.

Line-item budgets have several management limitations. First, when funds are spent all at once for a specific line item (e.g., purchasing a database) early in the year, it suggests budgeting amounts are more than they should be early in the year. For the governing or oversight authority, this type of cash flow always needs explaining. They will need to know why the total amount for that line item was spent in the first month of the year. Another limitation of a line-item budget is it gives little information linking expenses to programs or service goals. For example, salaries are usually listed together in a single line item, rather than listed by program or service, so actual costs for a program cannot be determined.

Sara F. Jones

Other types of budgets include:

Program Budgets: Program budgets group expenses by program (e.g., literacy program budget). The program budget then follows the line-item budget format, listing expenses such as employee's salaries, benefits, and operating expenses. In addition, program budgets include a cost allocation for shared overhead expenses, like use of facility space or utilities, and administrative functions, such as accounting and human resources. Program budgets are very effective for assessing funding allocations by program or service, which can be helpful when making budget-cut decisions or deciding to expand an existing program.

Performance Budgets: Performance budgets attach funds to performance objectives. This type of budget directly connects the input of resources with the output of services. Performance budgets are used to demonstrate the link between funding provided by the public and the outcomes of services provided to the public.

Zero-Based Budgets: Zero-based budgets rebuild all the budget numbers from zero. Zero-based budgeting requires managers to analyze every function within an organization to determine its needs and expenses. The largest downside of zero-based budgeting is it can be very time consuming, and justifying every expense can be a waste of resources. The benefit of zero-based budgeting is that it prevents managers from keeping budget categories year after year; this makes it possible for managers to create budget categories that are in better alignment with the organization's current strategic objectives.

THE BUDGETING PROCESS

The budgeting process is ongoing and is often described as a four-phased cycle.

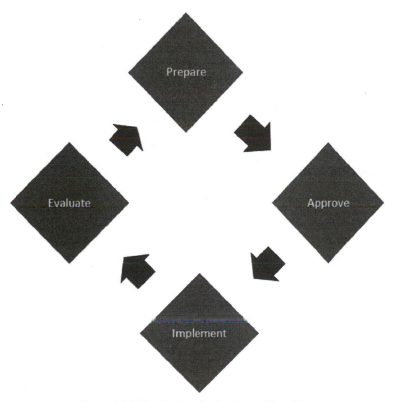

Figure 21.1 The Budget Cycle. *Created by editors.*

Preparing the Budget

Good budget preparation starts with a meaningful strategic plan (see also chapter 19: "Strategic Planning"). Decisions regarding what to include in a budget must be based on that plan, ensuring that funds are focused on helping the organization achieve its strategic objectives. Unfortunately, some budgets are not based on updated strategic plans, but instead are created by adding a new layer to an old budget, keeping older budget items in place. Using this approach, an organization may have several budgeted items they no longer need, which remain in the budget year after year because leaders do not take the time to examine existing budget items and decide if they are still appropriate.

> With a strategic plan in place before budget preparation, the plan provides guidance regarding how budget allocations can support strategic objectives and the types of expenses departments should plan for in the upcoming budget year in order to achieve those objectives.

With a strategic plan in place before budget preparation, the plan provides guidance regarding how budget allocations can support strategic objectives and the types of expenses departments should plan for in the upcoming budget year in order to achieve those objectives. The process of generating the budget for the next year (or the next two years, if using a biennial time frame) should start with careful thought regarding what programs, services, and resources need to continue and what new initiatives fit the goals and objectives of the strategic plan. Each department provides recommendations regarding what to include in the budget, and sends their requests to decision makers for inclusion in, or exclusion from, the final document.

Discussion Question

What are some items information professionals should include in a strategic plan for budget preparation, and why?

Approving the Budget

There are a variety of ways budgets are approved, ranging from a process that may involve relatively few steps to a process that has many steps. The type of approval process is driven by the governing laws of the organization, including which parent organization (if any) is involved in the approval process.

To describe the budget approval process simply, after the information organization finalizes the budget, it is shared with an oversight agency (e.g., Library Board or Commission) or an elected official. For public agencies, the budget is usually filed in some manner with the state government, and there are usually public hearings and notices involved. Managers responsible for budget oversight must understand the steps needed to get a budget approved, as well as the timelines, to ensure that each step is completed on time.

Sara F. Jones

Types of Budget Expenditures

Salaries and benefits usually require coordination with other entities. Health benefits might be handled by the organization, by the government entity, or in a pool of similar organizations. Retirement benefits also are coordinated with the public entity. In most cases, a public employment retirement system is in place that covers full-time employees and excludes them from contributing to Social Security. Part-time employees are usually included in Social Security contributions.

Employee raises for performance or a cost-of-living adjustment, often called a COLA, are also managed together. Compensation is often determined by a union agreement, so there are many factors needed to accurately calculate salaries and benefits. This portion of the budget is, in most cases, set for this type of spending and not easily or readily moved to services and supplies spending categories.

Services and supplies line items will have a variety of categories.

Implementing the Budget

Once the budget is approved, an online or printed document verifies what has been approved and provides details regarding approved expenditures. There are standard areas in virtually every budget, and they include:

- salaries and benefits for personnel;
- services and supplies, such as purchasing materials for the collection, employee training expenses, and utilities; and
- capital expenditures for tangible assets valued over a certain amount (e.g., $5,000) or building improvements.

Evaluating the Budget

A critical component of the budgeting process is ongoing evaluation. As important as it is to have a strategic plan when creating a budget, it is even more important to use the strategic plan to evaluate the budget's effectiveness. This evaluation should be ongoing, occurring monthly or quarterly. Performance-based budgeting is very common for information organizations, and funding authorities often ask how funding directly affects desired performance outcomes. Ongoing budget evaluation allows a manager to explain the connection between budget expenditures and performance outcomes.

Managers at every level should spend time on budget evaluation. Since it is necessary for them to monitor the budget and make sure costs do not exceed amounts budgeted, that time can also be spent ensuring the resources and services provided through the organization's budget are meeting expectations.

Because funding is very limited for many information organizations, it is important for managers to identify expenditures they no longer need. For example, libraries may have a line item in their budget for the preservation of books or periodicals, including tasks such as microfilming or periodical binding, when these services are no longer necessary. Managers should plan to take those unnecessary allocations out of future budgets. And during the current budget year, these unnecessary allocations can be shifted from one line item to another, ensuring that budgeted funds are reallocated to more relevant needs.

FUNDING SOURCES

Information organizations receive revenue from a variety of sources. Some of the revenue is fairly consistent, with the organization receiving stable funding levels year after year. Other types of revenue are not as stable, and the organization cannot rely on receiving this funding. In addition, some funding comes with specific restrictions regarding how it can be spent, while other funding allows the organization's leaders to determine how it is spent.

It is important for a manager to understand where revenue comes from, and how much of the organization's funding comes from supplementary funding sources that may be variable in terms of how much money is received, and how often it is received. The best practice is to integrate these variable resources into budget forecasts and expenditure plans, allowing managers to account for them in the budgeting process.

Discussion Questions

List the types of funding sources for information organizations. Which sources offer consistent funding for the organization? Which sources are inconsistent?

Government Funding Sources

Many information organizations rely extensively on public funding. For example, the majority of funding for public libraries, as well as publicly supported academic libraries and school libraries, comes from tax revenue. In some cases, the tax revenue is dedicated for libraries from a taxing district, in the form of a rate or a levy. Thus, libraries funded through a taxing district can be assured they will receive all funds raised through the levy. In other publicly funded libraries, the tax revenue is not directly raised to benefit a library, but instead funds a range of local services, with the library representing just one entity that can receive funds. In this funding model, tax revenue is placed first in a general fund for a city, county, or state, and then decisions are made regarding how much of that revenue to allocate to library operations.

TEXTBOX 21.4

Funding through Tax Revenue

In some cases, organizations, primarily public libraries, are their own government organization and are typically called a district or special district. When funded as a district, the formation, governance, and structure is found in state law. Each state has some variations, but library districts exist in most every state. In a district, there are set taxes collected for the specific purpose of supporting the library.

There are a variety of other types of public library governance structures that dictate how they are funded, and they could be town, township, municipal, city, county, consolidated city and county, multicounty, or any of a large array of possible variations. However, in the end, they are most distinctly separated by whether they have a dedicated tax stream or they compete with other parts of the government organization for their funding. In these cases, they are funded from the parent organization's general fund.

Supplementary Funding Sources

There are a wide variety of supplementary funding sources for information organizations. One type of supplementary funding is direct sources, such as fines and fees. This type of revenue is often a small portion of the budget, although it can be a more substantial portion of an academic library budget, which receives revenue from fees paid by college students. In addition to fines and fees, supplementary funding is often generated by organizations created to support the library. These include Friends of the Library organizations, volunteers dedicated to raising funds for the library, and library foundations.

Many information organizations also pursue grant funding, another source of supplementary revenue. Grant funding is typically used to develop and pilot new programs, expand or digitize collections, purchase new technology, train personnel, or update facilities. In academic libraries, grants can also be used to fund research conducted by information professionals. Grants are awarded for a short amount of time, for a very specific purpose, with grant funders indicating how funds are to be allocated. Grant funders range from small, local private foundations with minimal guidelines regarding how funds are to be spent, to large national private foundations or government agencies that have very specific guidelines regarding how grant funds can be spent by the organization. Grants range from very small amounts disbursed for a single year, to multiyear awards for substantial amounts. Also, proposals requesting a grant award must include a budget; thus, budgeting skills are used in grant seeking, as well as administering grant awards.

A major source of federal grant funding for libraries is the Institute of Museum and Library Services (IMLS).[2] The IMLS awards grant funds directly to libraries through several highly competitive grant programs. In addition, libraries can receive grant funds through a formula-based program called the Library Services and Technology Act (LSTA).[3] State libraries receive LSTA funds from IMLS, and then decide how to use the funds, either to support statewide initiatives or by distributing funds through sub-grants or cooperative agreements to libraries located in their state.

AUDITS

It is fairly common for audits to occur. An audit is a systematic examination of financial or accounting records by a specialized inspector, called an auditor, to verify the accuracy and truthfulness of those records. Sometimes a financial audit examines a specific part of an organization's budget, such as one library program. Other audits involve a review of the entire budget for the information organization, while some audits may involve a review of certain financial information regarding the library as part of an audit of the parent organization. Audits can be a very positive part of an organization's budgeting process, as they can show a manager where funds can be managed more effectively. Audits can also foster development of good internal controls, methods that ensure all resources are used effectively and efficiently. Controls ensure that money is handled properly, including funds received (e.g., how cash and checks are handled and deposited), and how funds are spent (e.g., the purchasing process).

> Audits can be a very positive part of an organization's budgeting process, as they can show a manager where funds can be managed more effectively. Audits can also foster development of good internal controls, methods that ensure all resources are used effectively and efficiently.

FINANCIAL MANAGEMENT PRINCIPLES

It is impossible to be an effective manager of financial resources without having a comprehensive knowledge of the budgeting process. In some cases, managers are promoted within an organization and are able to learn the budgeting process incrementally and thoroughly. This gradual process to learn about budgeting provides many advantages, as managers take on new oversight responsibilities and manage larger aspects of the organization's resources. However, in many cases, managers come from other organizations that take a different approach to budgeting. There are almost always some variations in budgeting processes across organizations. For example, although many public libraries may follow a similar budgeting process, the process can look quite different when comparing the process used in a public library with the budgeting process of an academic library. Regardless of the type of institution, many budgeting process elements are the same, and managers need to be competent in their knowledge and abilities to understand the process and be accountable for the financial actions of the organization.

Another critical component of financial management is having a full awareness of the level of accountability that comes with being responsible for a budget. When a manager does not fully understand all the financial aspects of their organization, they are more likely to make critical mistakes.

> When a manager does not fully understand all the financial aspects of their organization, they are more likely to make critical mistakes.

While having accounting professionals and financial departments to support managers is a tremendous asset, the ultimate responsibility for financial management still rests with the organization's top leader (e.g., a library director). Also, any leader who is part of the financial management process and has authority to approve expenditures carries the responsibility for those decisions. Mishandling public funds is a criminal offense, so budget responsibilities should not be taken lightly. All leaders who are responsible for approving expenditures must understand approved budget allocations and policies regarding how budget allocations can be disbursed. Handling public finances means being responsible and accountable to the public. Being unaware of budgeting practices or being poorly informed will never be an acceptable excuse for mismanagement of funds, whether done intentionally or as a result of incompetence.

Credibility is also a central element of successful financial management. Managing resources effectively means keeping spending within budgets. It also means following all legal requirements for purchases and making good decisions regarding any large investment, such as a major technology upgrade.

The organization needs to have one person who is ultimately responsible for budget oversight, ensuring that budget decisions help the organization achieve its strategic objectives and that resources are managed effectively. Also, having one person responsible for oversight of the organization's budget allows key stakeholders, including the public, to trust that their investment is well spent, whether the investment is tax revenue, student fees, donations, grant funds, or other resources.

Even with due diligence, budget crises can and do occur. These can come from a variety of directions, and many are outside a manager's control. Natural disasters can completely destroy collections and buildings. Many cities have been forced to declare bankruptcy, and information organizations have found it extremely challenging to continue offering services at any level. And just as there has been fraud and embezzlement in private corporations, there have been cases of fraud and embezzlement in information organizations. After a crisis, leaders must manage day-to-day operations as efficiently as possible and meet with all affected stakeholders to explore solutions aimed at returning the organization to a healthy and stable financial future.

Discussion Question

What are some best practices for leaders in responding to and resolving a budgeting crisis?

Finally, an entire chapter could be written on handling budget cuts. In recent years, budget cuts have been a very common part of budget management for information organizations. Budget cuts can range from a few percentage points to cases where the organization needed to reduce spending by more than 50 percent. The same principles used to build budgets are used when making decisions regarding where to make budget cuts, and should begin and end with a meaningful strategic plan.

CONCLUSION

Budgeting is an important part of managing an effective information organization. As with any important responsibility, having a solid knowledge of the process is a critical element of success. It is also important to utilize input from every resource available and accept full accountability for decisions.

NOTES

1. National Center of Education Statistics, "Chapter 3: Budgeting," in *Financial Accounting for Local and State School Systems*, 2003, last modified July 2, 2013, http://nces.ed.gov/pubs2004/h2r2/ch_3.asp.
2. Institute of Museum and Library Services (IMLS), last modified August 28, 2014, http://www.imls.gov/. The mission of IMLS is to inspire libraries and museums to advance innovation, lifelong learning, and cultural and civic engagement. IMLS provides leadership through research, policy development, and grant making.
3. Library Services and Technology Act (LSTA), last modified August 14, 2014, http://www.ala.org/advocacy/advleg/federallegislation/lsta. LSTA is also known as the Grants to States Program and is the largest grant program run by IMLS; it provides funds to State Library Administrative Agencies (SLAAs) using a population-based formula. SLAAs may use federal funds to support statewide initiatives and services; they also may distribute the funds through sub-grant competitions or cooperative agreements to public, academic, research, school, and special libraries in their state. The program has the benefit of building the capacity of states to develop statewide plans for library services, and to evaluate those services every five years.

22

Managing Personnel

Robert Goch, Bruce Haller, Dawn DiStefano, and Maureen L. Mackenzie

Chapter 22, "Managing Personnel," focuses on the skilled and talented people who provide the content, programs, and services that fit the needs of their communities. Managing these people is a key skill for information professionals, and Robert Goch, Bruce Haller, Dawn DiStefano, and Maureen Mackenzie, all from Molloy College, bring together their expertise in personnel management to highlight each step of the management process. Starting with hiring employees, this chapter then moves to discussing onboarding and managing employees, separating an employee, and understanding major legal issues related to personnel.

Throughout the chapter, the authors remind us of the importance of ensuring diversity throughout the organization—from volunteers who restack the shelves to upper management. The authors also emphasize the importance of ensuring that employees understand and buy into the mission and values of the organization as this helps organizations have strong contributors working toward the same goals.

Effective information organizations are only as good as the people who staff them, so it is important that information organizations hire the right people for the organization, and once hired, then effectively manage them. All information professionals should have some knowledge of personnel policies and practices—even if they are not a manager. The authors further emphasize that information professionals also should know their rights as an employee and should consider that management opportunities may be in their future as well.

★   ★   ★

People are at the heart of every successful organization. Information organizations are no exception. As new technologies are introduced, communities change, and information access evolves; the information organization's staffing needs also change. Information organizations need staff with varied skills, experiences, and backgrounds who can provide the content, programs, and services that fit the needs of their communities. But how do information organizations find and recruit those employees? What do information organizations need to do to retain strong employees? What are some of the challenges involved in managing personnel in information organizations today?

Developing the knowledge and understanding of personnel policies and practices is an essential competency for all information professionals. No matter what career pathway an information professional may choose, the opportunity to manage others is sure to arise—whether as a director of a library, manager of a department, team leader, or volunteer coordinator. After completing this chapter, the reader should have an understanding of hiring, onboarding, training, motivating, evaluating, and at times, separating an employee from the organization. The chapter further delves into some of the legal aspects of managing personnel that all information professionals—whether in a management role or not—should be aware of.

HIRING PERSONNEL FOR THE INFORMATION ORGANIZATION

The information world continues to evolve as a result of accelerated digitization and how consumers retrieve and use information. In addition, both the breadth (broadening functions) and depth (specialization) of information continue to develop. Specialization can be dictated by the type of organization (e.g., public library, academic library, special library, corporate, not-for-profit, etc.) and function (e.g., information and knowledge creation, organization and classification, acquisition, preservation, analysis, evaluation, communication, etc.). As a result, the recruitment and hiring of information professionals who fit the needs of the organization are critical. The process begins with creating a precise job assessment and drafting an accurate job description.

Once the job assessment and job description are created, it is important to attract and recruit a strong applicant pool—one that reflects the social, racial, and ethnic composition of the workforce. Attracting and retaining a diverse pool of applicants is critical to the strength of the organization and to its customers/patrons. Applicants should reflect a diverse populace with differing needs. The American Library Association (ALA) recognizes this and states:

> In order to ensure that libraries are both reflective of and relevant to the communities they serve, the American Library Association encourages and supports recruitment and continuing education initiatives that facilitate the hiring and promotion of a diverse workforce in libraries of all types and at all organizational levels.[1]

Recruiting a more diverse workforce is an important priority for the information professions, as it is in all professions.

Attracting and recruiting the right candidates also present challenges, as the library and information science (LIS) field continues to evolve. Posting jobs in traditional outlets (e.g., classified newspaper ads, general job boards such as Monster.com or Indeed.com) may not reach the widest range of candidates with the critical skill sets needed for today's information roles; therefore, human resource (HR) professionals may need to broaden their outreach and recruitment efforts to more technical/specialized job boards.

After assembling a pool of potential candidates, the HR professional must be cognizant of each candidate's disposition and organizational cultural fit. This is critical for job retention and mitigating employee turnover.

Essential topics to be discussed in this section include:

- conducting a job analysis, creating a job (person) specification, and drafting a job description;
- attracting and recruiting candidates; and
- conducting the job interview and offering employment.

Job Analysis, Specification, and Description

Textbox 22.1 differentiates between the job analysis, job description, and job specification, which are explained in further detail below.

Comparing the Job Analysis, Description, and Specification

Job description: essential tasks and functions required for the job
Job analysis: skills needed to perform those tasks and functions
Job specification: minimum qualifications needed to be considered for a position

The job analysis process identifies and determines, in detail, the job duties and requirements, and the relative importance of these duties, for any given job. Therefore, a job analysis is centered on the job and not the potential person to fill that job. The first step in a job analysis is to determine if there is, in fact, a need for the prospective job. Even if the opening is a replacement position, the needs may have changed due to a range of factors, such as technology or organizational focus. Therefore, a job analysis is still necessary for a replacement position. Similarly, even if the need of an impending new position is well articulated, it still needs to be further scrutinized.

> Skills are not synonymous with qualifications; skills relate to the job, and qualifications relate to the candidate.

Many methods can be utilized to effectuate a job analysis. They include, but are not limited to, incumbent interviews, supervisor interviews, expert panels, structured questionnaires, and task inventories. If work logs were kept, they should also be reviewed.

A job description relates to the scope of tasks, working condition, hours, salary range, and such factors (see also chapter 22: "Job Description for a Reference Librarian" in the online supplement). It is important to note that skills are not synonymous with qualifications; skills relate to the job, and qualifications relate to the candidate. This brings us to the job (person) specification, which outlines the minimum qualifications needed to be considered for a position (i.e., minimum educational attainment, licensing/certificate requirements, specialized abilities, etc.).

Attracting and Recruiting Candidates

After completing the job description and specification, the phase of attracting and recruiting potential candidates commences. A search committee is formed and a chairperson is identified. It is imperative that the committee is mindful of diversity and inclusiveness. As such, the committee itself should be reflective of both the organization's and the society's diversity. This is of special importance in the LIS field, which has historically been underrepresented by racial minorities.[2]

There is a critical difference between a job description, a job posting, and a job advertisement. The job description is an in-house document that describes job responsibilities, scope of tasks, skills, etc. Job descriptions are also detailed and factual in nature. The purpose of a job posting, which is a shortcut to the job description, is to inspire a potential candidate to apply. A job advertisement, on the other hand, is an external document intended to engage, motivate, and inspire. To achieve this, the job advertisement needs to be brief and appealing, highlighting the main positive attributes of the position (see also chapter 22: "Job Advertisement for a Reference Librarian" in the online supplement).

It is important that the search committee be continually mindful of inclusiveness throughout the entire process, including the drafting of the job advertisement (see also chapter 5: "Diversity, Equity of Access, and Social Justice"). Therefore, language emphasizing the organization's commitment to diversity should be utilized (e.g., "our organization has a strong commitment to the principle of diversity and actively encourages applications from underrepresented groups").

After the job advertisement is completed and approved, it needs to be publicized. While there are many national internet job sites used in the LIS field,[3] in order to cast a wide net and encourage underrepresented groups to apply, the committee should also publicize the job advertisement in specialized job sites. There is a multitude of such sites geared toward recruiting racial, ethnic,[4] gender,[5] and sexual minorities.[6]

The Job Interview and the Offer of Employment

After receiving a sufficient number of applications from a diverse pool of candidates, the next task is to select candidates for interviews, either on-site, by phone, or more often using a virtual meeting application such as GoToMeeting or Skype. Preliminary interviews often take place on the phone or via a virtual meeting application. Telephone interviews are helpful in initially assessing a candidate's knowledge, interest, availability, and salary expectations, and clearing up any résumé ambiguities. Virtual meeting applications allow for a face-to-face interaction that can include multiple individuals from the search committee. The decision to invite a candidate for an on-site interview should be made within two weeks of the phone or virtual interview.

The on-site interview is where the real work begins. While exploring the candidate's credentials, education, and qualifications is a given, many interviewers also try to discern how well a candidate would fit into the organizational culture, as well as his or her operating, leadership, and decision-making style. It is often best to query the candidate with both behavioral descriptive and situational descriptive questions. Behavioral descriptive questioning involves asking a candidate to describe past stories and how he or she reacted, such as asking a candidate to describe a time when he or she disagreed with the supervisor. Situational descriptive questioning looks into the future at a hypothetical situation and asks the candidate to predict how he or she would react to that situation, such as asking a candidate what he or she would do if the candidate disagreed with the supervisor. See also textbox 22.2 for examples of behavioral descriptive and situational descriptive questioning. Both behavioral and situational descriptive questioning techniques assess the candidate's preparedness, thought processes, intelligence, knowledge, and problem-solving skills. Under no circumstances should an interviewer ask candidates questions related to age, race, national origin, religion, marital or parental status, gender/gender expression, or sexual identity.

TEXTBOX 22.2

Examples of Behavioral Descriptive and Situational Descriptive Interview Questions

Behavioral

- Tell me about a time you had to make a quick decision.
- Tell me about a time you had too many things to do and had to prioritize.
- Tell me about a situation where you failed. Why did you fail and what did you learn from it?

Situational

- You are a team leader. What would you do if the work of one of your subordinate team members was not up to expectations?
- You have reason to believe that a coworker is preparing to divulge company secrets to a rival corporation. These secrets have the potential to significantly damage the company. How would you deal with this situation?
- How would you handle a customer who is not happy with your service even though you have done nothing wrong and the customer is actually the one who has made the mistake?

After interviewing a broad and diverse pool of applicants, the committee narrows the candidate pool to those whom they want to offer second interviews or recommends to make an offer of employment to one selected candidate. It should be noted that, in many instances, candidates reject employment offers for a host of reasons. Therefore, employment offers should be made in a timely and courteous fashion and the terms of any offer should not differ from what was discussed during the interview phase.

ONBOARDING AND MANAGING PERSONNEL[7]

Once the hiring process is complete, the priority becomes the onboarding of the new employee.[8] Onboarding allows the new employee to transition from an outsider to one who becomes part of the organizational culture. The culture should promote continuous learning and be mission-driven. An early investment in effectively onboarding a new employee will pay dividends for years to come. Essential topics to be discussed in this section include:

- training,
- motivating, and
- evaluating performance.

Training

TEXTBOX 22.3

Examples of Paperwork for Onboarding

- I-9 Employment Eligibility Verification
- Verification of a Social Security number
- State-specific tax withholding form
- W-4 Employee's Withholding Allowance Certificate
- Emergency contact information
- Benefit-related paperwork

When onboarding, new hires complete the paperwork needed (see textbox 22.3) as defined by the terms of employment.[9] The employee should also attend an orientation prior to or upon starting with the information organization. Instilling the mission and the vision of the organization into a new hire's frame of reference makes it easier for the new employee to assimilate the range of information that will be shared. Training is essential.[10] Reducing the opportunity for the employee to make a work-related error, or to feel insecure, increases the employee's confidence in becoming a contributing member of the workplace community. Technical training, coupled with a healthy organizational culture, allows the employee to acclimate and succeed. A successful technique is to allow the employee to shadow a more experienced employee. Organizational learning that is linked to strategic plans creates alignment among the employees and the goals of the information organization. This alignment is especially important for organizations that are adapting to significant amounts of technological change,[11] which is common in information organizations (see also chapter

> Organizational learning that is linked to strategic plans creates alignment among the employees and the goals of the information organization.

3: "Librarianship: A Continuously Evolving Profession"). Also, a healthy organizational culture is a key influence that allows employees to integrate more successfully.

Within a patron-oriented organization, it is helpful for departments to coordinate training efforts so that employees from across the organization get to know each other and can avoid departmental silos. For example, having acquisition services and technical services employees train together allows relationships to develop that benefit the larger mission of the organization.

Motivating Employees

How might management motivate its employees? Primary to understanding what motivates an individual is knowing what the person wants. People work for different reasons: money, achievement, affiliation, or power. This understanding is foundational to effectively managing and leading employees.[12]

Once a supervisor understands what an employee desires, then the supervisor can establish work goals that link to recognition and rewards aligning with the employee's desired outcomes (e.g., workplace relationships, public recognition, or promotion). For example, an individual who resonates with power is generally seeking professional advancement, perhaps to an executive level. The supervisor can motivate this employee by encouraging him or her to further enhance his or her qualifying credentials (e.g., graduate degree), while further developing managerial skills (e.g., time management, multitasking). Employees who are motivated by affiliation desire friendly relationships with coworkers, subordinates, and senior management. The supervisor can motivate this employee by assigning responsibilities that lead to noncompetitive working relationships (e.g., creating community programs, organizing blood drives). Supervisors who can effectively motivate employees will meet and exceed organizational goals, retain talent, and create a healthy organizational culture that will serve its patrons.

> Supervisors who can effectively motivate employees will meet and exceed organizational goals, retain talent, and create a healthy organizational culture that will serve its patrons.

Performance Evaluation/Reward and Recognition[13]

A successful employee evaluation system reflects focus, simplicity, and clarity. A supervisor should start with the job description and job duties. Performance standards should be established that make clear to the employee what is expected both short term (e.g., day to day) and long term (e.g., strategic initiatives).

Feedback is essential so that the employee can adjust his or her performance to meet the standards expected. Therefore, the supervisor should formalize the performance evaluation process. Supervisors should meet with the employee one-on-one to assess whether or not varying performance criteria are being met. This could take place quarterly or semiannually, but at least annually.

Elements for discussion should refer back to the job duties, and they might include employee attendance, punctuality, completion of day-to-day tasks, progress toward long-term projects, participation in team projects, completion of higher degrees and/or managerial training, assessment from patrons, and perhaps peer evaluation.

The outcome of the evaluation process should be a written assessment that establishes a plan. This plan may include training and other performance developmental activities, as well as goals for the next evaluation period. Rewards, based on merit, should motivate the employee to improve skills, knowledge, and disposition that support the mission of the organization. Outcomes of the performance evaluation might include a monetary salary increase, promotion, induction into a management-training program, or recognition award. The reward need not be made solely on a monetary basis (e.g., salary increase or promotion). Rewards can include ceremonial rituals in nonmonetary forms (e.g., employee of the month) or awards to employees that complete advanced certifications or industry-relevant degrees (e.g., MLIS).

SEPARATING AN EMPLOYEE FROM THE INFORMATION ORGANIZATION

The prior sections of this chapter provide a road map to information organizations with regard to identifying, hiring, onboarding, and managing an employee. The goal is to recruit and retain an individual who effectively transitions from an outsider to a contributing member of the organization. Unfortunately, there are times when an employee must be separated from the information organization. Essential topics to be discussed in this section include:

- positive discipline and progressive discipline;
- reasons for separation of an employee from an organization;
- documentation: before, during, and after;
- legal issues related to human resource management in information organizations;
- Fair Labor Standards Act; and
- discrimination laws.

Positive Discipline and Progressive Discipline

As soon as an employee's performance reflects a gap or a derailment in relation to his or her job duties, the supervisor should intervene. Therefore, a progressive discipline policy,[14] properly implemented and managed, will minimize wrongful termination litigation and is the most likely way to correct employee performance issues. Progressive discipline should be based on the principles of fairness, consistency, and proportionality. The rules, and all consequences for their violation, should be effectively communicated to all employees, independent contractors, interns, volunteers, and vendors.

Policies, rules, and procedures should be neutrally enforced. Progressive discipline systems should be designed to facilitate enhanced management-employee communication, improve morale, and ensure that no disparate impact or other legal issues arise.

Many information organizations operate in an environment with a unionized workforce to consider. If this is the case, discipline policies and procedures will be incorporated into the collective bargaining agreement and should not be unilaterally implemented. Public sector employees, such as public libraries (see also chapter 8: "Community Anchors for Lifelong Learning: Public Libraries"), state universities (see also chapter 7: "Learning and Research Institutions: Academic Libraries"), and public high schools (see also chapter 6: "Literacy and Media Centers: School Libraries") are often operating under the constraints of a collective bargaining agreement; thus, any discipline, up to and including discharge, is considered government action. Government action results in additional constitutional protections for the potentially impacted employee.[15]

Tenure is another job security protection that many academic libraries provide to certain employees. A tenure system extends a right to due process; this means that a college or university cannot discipline, up to and including termination, a tenured employee, which for many organizations includes academic librarians, without following a required process. Nationally, about 2 percent of tenured faculty are dismissed in a typical year.[16]

Reasons for Separation of an Employee from the Organization

Employee separation occurs when the employee ceases to be a legal member of the organization. The separation may be temporary (e.g., layoff), permanent (e.g., termination), voluntary (e.g., retirement or resignation), or involuntary (e.g., dismissal). Each type of separation comes with associated costs and benefits that the supervisor must consider.[17] Separated employee costs, new employee recruitment costs, and training costs must be weighed against the potential benefits of reduced labor costs, increased diversity, and an infusion of new ideas. Information organization managers need to consider the financial, ethical, and productivity ramifications of any separation. If the separation is involuntary, the supervisor must be detail oriented and document that all legal, contractual, and organizational policies and procedures were complied with. Involuntary separation requires strategic planning and careful adherence to all relevant policies (see also chapter 19: "Strategic Planning").

> Separated employee costs, new employee recruitment costs, and training costs must be weighed against the potential benefits of reduced labor costs, increased diversity, and an infusion of new ideas.

Terminations for cause and layoffs are the separations most fraught with union, legal, and procedural requirements.[18] Documenting what rises to the judicial requirement of just cause for terminating union or contract employees should be reviewed by legal experts. Layoffs should be a last resort to reducing labor costs. Alternatives to layoffs, such as early retirement incentive programs, reducing compensation packages across the board, and reducing costs through cross-training and job redesign, may have less of a negative influence on morale and productivity.

Documentation: Before, During, and After

Managers of information organizations should clearly and objectively document all relevant facts related to human resource management issues. This is an essential step in any process that may lead to discipline or separation.[19] Clear and objective communication with the employee during any investigation, will result in a more fact-based document, allow employees to engage in corrective action, and avoid additional legal complications.

The objectives of proper documentation (e.g., establishing an official record of the incident or conduct) are to benefit the employee and meet the requirements of the legal and contractual disciplinary process. The manager should not include his or her opinions or feelings in the document. Personnel-related documents should focus on objective facts and should precisely and accurately record the information gathered along with the source and context of the data. If the information organization manager's role includes recommending a specific disciplinary action or separation, he or she should include in the documentation specific reference to the company's policies, handbook provisions, employment contract, or collective bargaining agreement.

Discussion Questions

What is a progressive discipline policy? What are the advantages of implementing one?

LEGAL ISSUES RELATED TO PERSONNEL MANAGEMENT IN INFORMATION ORGANIZATIONS

Legislation regarding personnel management exists mainly to protect the rights of employees. This section provides an overview of the major factors defining the legal system that supervisors must navigate. The Fair Labor Standards Act,[20] Civil Rights Act,[21] and Americans with Disabilities Act[22] are among the statutes briefly covered, as the private and public sector institutions are both impacted.

Fair Labor Standards Act

The Fair Labor Standards Act (FLSA)[23] is the primary federal statute governing minimum wage, overtime compensation, and child labor constraints. Most information organizations, such as school, academic, and public libraries, are likely covered by the act. Employees are either exempt from provisions of the act or nonexempt. Nonexempt employees must be paid the higher of the federal minimum hourly wage or the applicable state minimum wage depending upon the relevant jurisdiction.[24] Most employees are entitled to minimum wage and overtime under the FLSA. These workers must be paid at least one and one-half times their hourly pay for all hours worked greater than forty hours in any workweek. Substitute compensation options, such as additional time off (e.g., comp time), are generally not allowable under the act. Numerous exemptions exist under the FLSA, the most common being for executive, administrative, and professional employees.[25]

Discrimination Laws

Discrimination based on race, color, national origin, religion, and many other less publicized protected classes must be removed from all employment decisions.[26] Jokes, comments, or pictures based on a protected class such as race, religion, or sex, that are severe and pervasive according to a reasonable person so as to create a hostile environment, are also illegal.[27]

Sexual harassment in the workplace is another far too common occurrence that can be damaging to workplace morale, productivity, talent recruitment, and retention efforts.[28] Information organization managers should understand what sexual harassment in the workplace is, how to minimize its occurrence, and what the employer's legal obligations are when allegations of sexual harassment are reported (see also chapter 22: "Sexual Harassment Procedure Flowchart" in the online supplement).

Harassment based on race, religion, national origin, or sex is actionable under federal and state discrimination laws. Harassment is always unethical, unacceptable, and harmful to an information organization. Sexual harassment under most state statutes and the Civil Rights Act of 1964 as amended by the Civil Rights Act of 1990 is actionable if the alleged conduct is based on sex, is unwelcomed, and affects a tangible or intangible condition of employment. The information organization should create a sexual harassment policy and effectively disseminate the policy to all workers. The policy should define harassment, give examples, provide a clear and easy to access grievance procedure for reporting the harassment, and clearly state the consequences for the prohibited behavior.[29]

Protecting the information organization from liability is important. The best way to avoid liability for illegal harassment is to take all steps necessary to prevent harassment from occurring. Discrimination based on sex, as currently interpreted under federal law, does not prohibit discrimination based on sexual orientation or identity in the private sector.[30] However, some states, local governments, and individual organizations may provide workers protection against discrimination based on sexual orientation and/or identity.[31] These protections must be appropriately incorporated into the information organization's policies and procedures.

Information organizations are also prohibited from discriminating against qualified individuals who are defined as disabled under federal or state law. The Americans with Disabilities Act (ADA)[32] attempts to level the employment playing field for disabled individuals. Which applicants and employees are disabled under the act can be subjective. Information organization managers should consult with human resource professionals to correctly identify the protected parties.[33]

An employee's legal off-site recreational activities, military service, marital status, and numerous other behaviors may also be protected activities against workplace discrimination.[34] Managers should create employment processes and procedures, in consultation with legal and human resource professionals, to ensure compliance.

CONCLUSION

As the complexity of the information world increases, the skills, knowledge, and disposition of those individuals who serve in the information professions, must also increase. At the heart of all successful information organizations are the talented, dedicated, knowledgeable, patron-focused employees. Yet, employees bring their *individual* differences, creativity, desires, problems, and more, into the workplace. Effective human resource strategies lead to sustainable workplace policies and practices. These practices create a healthy workplace culture where individuals can make a contribution that allows them to be part of the success of the information organization.

This chapter provided a high-level overview and road map of what managers and supervisors need to know to ensure that effective HR practices exist that benefit *all* stakeholders. Hiring, new employee onboarding, training, motivating, evaluating, and at times separating employees requires thoughtful care and commitment to policy and process; but it also requires the essential focus on the people.

NOTES

1. American Library Association, ALA Policy Manual Section B: Positions and Public Policy Statement, 2012/2013, http://www.ala.org/aboutala/sites/ala.org.aboutala/files/content/governance/policy manual/cd_10_2_Section%20B%20New%20Policy%20Manual-1%20%28final%205-4-2016%20 with%20TOC%29.pdf.
2. According to 2010 Census data and data for the American Library Association's Diversity Counts Report, Latinos (16.3 percent of the population) compose just 3.1 percent of credentialed librarians and 9 percent of library assistants. African Americans (12.6 percent of the population) compose 5.1 percent of credentialed librarians and 9.3 percent of library assistants. Asian and Pacific Islanders (5 percent of the population) compose 2.7 percent of credentialed librarians and 5.5 percent of library assistants. Native Americans (less than 1 percent of the population) were 0.2 percent of credentialed librarians and 0.7 percent of library assistants. See http://www.ala.org/news/2012/09/american-library-association-releases-new-data-update-diversity-counts-report.
3. These include, but are not limited to, http://joblist.ala.org; http://inalj.com; www.lisjobnet.com; www.libraryjobpostings.com; and www.hiringlibrarians.com. In addition, there are many state-specific LIS job sites.
4. Sherika Hill, *Diversity Websites to Increase Racial/Ethnic Representation*, MCH Training, October 2009, http://66.165.155.81/email/MCHtrainfund/documents/2009.12weblist.pdf.
5. Holly Reisem Hanna, "The Best Career Websites for Women," *Work at Home Woman*, May 7, 2014, http://www.theworkathomewoman.com/career-websites-women/.
6. LBGT Connect.com, last accessed on August 1, 2017, http://lgbtconnect.com/?gclid=CjwKEAiA8dDE BRDf19yI97eO0UsSJAAY_yCSr6jcuwqy8yv_YQrOya4Tc9b-JLE_w3ZWeSc465fhYBoC1fPw_wcB.
7. Kaylee L. Pike, "New Employee Onboarding Programs and Person-Organization Fit: An Examination of Socialization Tactics," *Seminar Research Paper Series, Schmidt Labor Research Center at* DigitalCommons@ URI, Paper 24, 2014, http://digitalcommons.uri.edu/lrc_paper_series/24; K. Bugg, "Best Practices for Talent Acquisition in 21st-Century Academic Libraries," *Library Leadership & Management, NYC College of Technology at CUNY Academic Works* 29, no. 4 (2015): 1–14; Adam H. Lisbon and Megan E. Welsh, "New Librarians: Building Culture and Connections—Onboarding, Training, and Manuals," *University Libraries Faculty & Staff Contributions, CU Scholar* 72 (2014), http://scholar.colorado.edu/libr_facpapers/72.

8. Jolie O Graybill, Maria Taesil Hudson Carpenter, Jerome Offord, Mary Piorun, and Gary Shaffer, "Employee Onboarding: Identification of Best Practices in ACRL Libraries, *Library Management* 34, no. 3 (2013): 200–218, doi: 10.1108/01435121311310897.

9. Internal Revenue Service, "Hiring Employees," Small Business/Self-Employed Topics, 2017, https://www.irs.gov/businesses/small-businesses-self-employed/hiring-employees.

10. Dennis R. Defa, "Recruitment of Employees in Academic Libraries: Advice from the HR Perspective," *Library Leadership & Management* 26, no. 3 (2012): 1–10.

11. Philip B. Evans and Thomas S. Wurster, "Strategy and the New Economics of Information," *Harvard Business Review* 75, no. 5 (1996): 70–82; Sona Macnaughton and Mary Medinsky, "Staff Training, Onboarding, and Professional Development Using a Learning Management System," *Partnership: The Canadian Journal of Library and Information Practice and Research* 10, no. 2 (2015): 1–8.

12. David McClelland, *Human Motivation* (Cambridge: Cambridge University Press, 1987).

13. L. Rutledge, S. LeMire, and A. Mowdood, "Dare to Perform: Using Organizational Competencies to Manage Job Performance," in *Creating Sustainable Community—ACRL Conference, 2015*, ed. D. Mueller (Chicago: Association of College and Research Libraries), 160–67, http://www.ala.org/acrl/sites/ala.org.acrl/files/content/conferences/confsandpreconfs/2015/Rutledge_LeMire_Mowdood.pdf.

14. HR Specialist, "Designing a Progressive Discipline Policy," 2017, http://www.thehrspecialist.com/2880/Designing_a_Progressive_Discipline_Policy.hr?cat=tools&sub_cat=white_paper.

15. Marnie Larson, "Avoiding HR Disasters. Employee Discipline in a Union Workplace," *LinkedIn*, 2015, https://www.linkedin.com/pulse/avoiding-hr-disasters-employee-discipline-union-workforce-larson.

16. National Education Association, "The Truth about Tenure in Higher Education," Higher Education Departments of the National Education Association and the American Federation of Teachers, 2002–2015, http://www.nea.org/home/33067.htm.

17. Kim Lachance Shandrow, "10 Questions to Ask When Firing an Employee," *Entrepreneur*, 2015, https://www.entrepreneur.com/article/243632; Heather Boushey and Sarah Jane Glynn, "There Are Significant Business Costs to Replacing Employees," *Center for American Progress*, 2012, https://www.americanprogress.org/issues/economy/reports/2012/11/16/44464/there-are-significant-business-costs-to-replacing-employees/.

18. Bridget Miller, "What Does At-Will Employment Really Mean?," *HR Daily Advisor*, May 1, 2014, accessed April 30, 2017, http://hrdailyadvisor.blr.com/2014/05/01/what-does-at-will-employment-really-mean/; National Labor Relations Act 29 U.S.C. Sec. 201-219, 1978; Jonathan Fineman, "The Inevitable Demise of the Implied Employment Contract," *Berkeley Journal of Employment and Labor Law* 29, no. 2 (2008): 345, doi:10.15779/Z38K63D; Katherine V. W. Stone, "Revisiting the At-Will Employment Doctrine: Imposed Terms, Implied Terms, and the Normative World of the Workplace," *Industrial Law Journal* (March 2007): 84–101; Keynen J. Wall Jr. and Jacqueline Johnson, "Colorado's Lawful Activities Statute: Balancing Employee Privacy and the Rights of Employers," *Colorado Lawyer* (December, 2006).

19. Flora Richards-Gustafson, "What Elements Must Be Included in Documenting an Employee for Termination?," *Chron*, accessed August 1, 2017, http://smallbusiness.chron.com/elements-must-included-documenting-employee-termination-17686.html; Anne Williams, *How to Discipline Employee Behavior* (Brentwood, TN: M. Lee Smith Publishers, 2002).

20. United States Department of Labor, "Wage and Hour Division (WHD): Handy Reference Guide to the Fair Labor Standards Act," 2016, https://www.dol.gov/whd/regs/compliance/hrg.htm.

21. U.S. Equal Employment Opportunity Commission, Title VII of the Civil Rights Act of 1964, accessed April 30, 2017, https://www.eeoc.gov/laws/statutes/titlevii.cfm.

22. United States Department of Justice, Civil Rights Division, "Information and Technical Assistance on the Americans with Disabilities Act," accessed April 30, 2017, https://www.ada.gov/; ADA National Network, home page, last accessed August 1, 2017, https://adata.org/.

23. United States Code, Title 29, "Fair Labor Standards Act of 1938," June 25, 1938, 29 USC §201 et seq.; United States Department of Labor, Employment Law Guide Fair Labor Standards Act of 1938, "Minimum Wage & Overtime Pay," 29 CFR Parts 510 to 794.

24. United States Department of Labor, "Wages and Hours Worked: Minimum Wage and Overtime Pay," accessed April 30, 2017, https://www.dol.gov/compliance/guide/minwage.htm.

25. Michael Cardman, "How to Classify an Employee Under FLSA," *XPert HR*, 2017, http://www.xperthr .com/how-to/how-to-classify-an-employee-under-the-flsa/9341/.
26. United States Equal Employment Opportunity Commission, "Federal Laws Prohibiting Job Discrimination, Questions and Answers, last accessed August 1, 2017, https://www.eeoc.gov/facts/qanda .html; "Federal Discrimination Laws in the Workplace: The Basics," *FindLaw*, 2017, http://employment .findlaw.com/employment-discrimination/federal-laws-prohibiting-job-discrimination-questions-and .html; "State Laws on Employment-Related Discrimination," National Conference of State Legislators, 2017, http://www.ncsl.org/research/labor-and-employment/discrimination-employment.aspx; "Past LGBT Nondiscrimination and Anti-LGBT Bills across the Country," *ACLU American Civil Liberties Union*, 2017, https://www.aclu.org/other/past-lgbt-nondiscrimination-and-anti-lgbt-bills-across-country.
27. United States Equal Employment Opportunity Commission, "Harassment," accessed April 30, 2017, https://www.eeoc.gov/laws/types/harassment.cfm; U.S. Equal Employment Opportunity Commission, "Laws Enforced by EEOC," accessed April 30, 2017, https://www.eeoc.gov/laws/statutes/index.cfm; Renea I. Saade, "When Does a Workplace Qualify as Being Hostile," *Seattle Business*, http://www.seat tlebusinessmag.com/business-corners/workplace/when-does-workplace-qualify-being-hostile.
28. United States Equal Employment Opportunity Commission, "Sexual Harassment," accessed April 30, 2017, https://www.eeoc.gov/laws/types/sexual_harassment.cfm.
29. "Sexual Harassment—Legal Standards," *Workplace Fairness: It's Everyone's Job*, 2017, accessed April 30, 2017, http://www.workplacefairness.org/sexual-harassment-legal-rights; "Know Your Rights: Workplace Sexual Harassment," AAUW, http://www.aauw.org/what-we-do/legal-resources/know-your -rights-at-work/workplace-sexual-harassment/; U.S. Department of State, "Sexual Harassment Policy," https://www.state.gov/s/ocr/c14800.htm.
30. United States Equal Employment Opportunity Commission, "You Should Know about EEOC and the Enforcement Protections for LGBT Workers," accessed April 30, 2017, https://www.eeoc.gov/eeoc/ newsroom/wysk/enforcement_protections_lgbt_workers.cfm.
31. "Past LGBT Nondiscrimination and Anti-LGBT Bills across the Country," ACLU, https://www.aclu.org/ map/non-discrimination-laws-state-state-information-map; Jennifer Calfas, "Employment Discrimination: The Next Frontier for LGBT Community," *USA Today*, July 31, 2015, https://www.usatoday.com/story/ news/nation/2015/07/31/employment-discrimination-lgbt-community-next-frontier/29635379/.
32. 42 U.S.C. 12101 et seq.
33. The Americans with Disabilities Act of 1990 and Revised ADA Regulations Implementing Title II and Title III, ADA.gov. accessed April 30, 2017, https://www.ada.gov/2010_regs.htm; United States Department of Justice, "Disability Rights Section," https://www.justice.gov/crt/disability-rights-section.
34. "Your Rights against Workplace Discrimination and Harassment," *NOLO*, 2017, http://www.nolo.com/ legal-encyclopedia/workplace-rights.

23

Innovative Library and Information Services

THE DESIGN THINKING PROCESS

Rachel Ivy Clarke

Chapter 23, "Innovative Library and Information Services: The Design Thinking Process," defines design, explains how the design thinking process works, and highlights what the future of design looks like for information professionals. Dr. Rachel Ivy Clarke, professor and researcher of design thinking, asserts that information professionals need to utilize design thinking principles to create tools and services that are better aligned with user needs and interests. She explores the four major phases of design thinking: investigative phase, planning phase, development phase, and evaluative phase, and then includes case studies that demonstrate these phases across diverse information environments.

Design thinking is important because of its creative, problem-solving approach. Clarke looks carefully at some of the components of design, defining each component: repertoire; problem finding, framing, and reframing; design rationale; and reflection. Design thinking is an essential competency in helping information organizations adapt to change, problem-solve, remain innovative, and evolve with the information and user-centric landscape.

Design thinking, Clarke shows, creates possibilities for new management approaches, staff positions, and roles in library and information organizations that include design-based roles. She concludes the chapter advocating for including design in MLIS education and provides the reader with resources for professional development in design thinking.

★ ★ ★

In recent years, design has emerged at the forefront of various industries. While many people think of design in specific, applied contexts, like fashion design or architecture, a well-established record of research shows that design is a creative, problem-solving approach that differs from other approaches, such as science.

For more than a hundred years, American information professionals have been creating tools and services to solve information problems and connect people with information—an innate form of design. This chapter illustrates the relevance of design perspectives and methods to library and information services and outlines one particular design approach—the design thinking process—and how it can be used to help libraries and information organizations.

After completing this chapter, the reader should have an understanding of:

- the meaning of design in the context of library and information services;
- the design thinking process and approach; and
- the design-related competencies relevant for future information professionals, including suggestions for how to build those competencies.

WHAT IS DESIGN?

Ask ten people for a definition of *design* and you are likely to receive eleven different answers. By dictionary definition, design means "to create, fashion, execute, or construct according to plan; to conceive and plan out in the mind; to have as a purpose; to devise for a specific function or end."[1] People typically think of this creation in terms of specific industries or applications, like graphic design, fashion design, architecture, and technology (like software design or website design), just to name a few. Yet from the 1960s, when the first formal investigations of processes and methods of design began, to the present day, scholars have identified commonalities and consistent factors and aspects of design processes across these various applied disciplines.[2]

In this chapter, design is defined not as a niche-applied practice, but as an overarching creative discipline with its own ways of working and knowing. Just as fields like biology and genomics rely on higher-level scientific perspectives, applied fields like architecture

> The fundamental difference between traditional science and design worldviews stems from the idea that science is about *what is*, while design is about what *could be* (or arguably what *should be*).

and graphic design draw on broader shared design perspectives. The fundamental difference between traditional science and design worldviews stems from the idea that science is about *what is*, while design is about what *could be* (or arguably what *should be*).[3] While science focuses on observing and describing the existing world with the goal of replicability and prediction, knowledge in design stems from creating artifacts[4] and addressing problems.[5] Therefore, the different goals and focus of design requires a different approach: what Cross calls a "designerly way of knowing."[6]

TEXTBOX 23.1

Review across a wide body of design scholarship reveals a common set of fundamental elements and competencies that underlie design approaches. These include:

- Creating artifacts
- Finding, framing, and reframing problems to be solved
- Applying iterative processes
- Using repertory knowledge
- Providing a rationale for decision making
- Engaging in reflection during and after creation
- Critiquing

A NEW PERSPECTIVE: LIBRARY AND INFORMATION SERVICES AS DESIGN ARTIFACTS

Upon examination, the work of information professionals demonstrates many of these characteristics of design.[7] Information professionals do not observe and describe the existing library and information world in order to predict what may happen next; rather, they create things (called "artifacts" in design parlance) with the intention of solving problems. These artifacts may be tangible, physical objects like printed indexes, handouts like pathfinders, or even coloring book pages for passive programming. These artifacts may also be intangible, such as digital products, new classification schemes for special interests, curricula for library and information science instruction, or event planning. With such an emphasis on making tools and services, the field of library and information science can be served well by design and its focus on making things that solve problems in the world.

Beyond this fundamental similarity of creation, examples of library and information services also demonstrate aspects of fundamental design elements. For example, repertoire (i.e., the name given in design to previous experiences and bodies of knowledge) in library and information services manifests in the work of readers' advisory, a service requiring information professionals to supply reading recommendations to patrons.[8] There is not one authorized list that information professionals memorize and use to suggest reading materials. Rather, to perform this work, information professionals must draw on their personal repertoire of knowledge, such as from reading the books and book reviews themselves; hearing recommendations and reports from other professionals, friends, and family; and seeing advertisements in various media.

The element of problem finding, framing, and reframing (i.e., the process of identifying and viewing a problem from different angles or points of view) occurs in many reference interviews, where information professionals are trained to delve, explore, and determine a patron's true underlying information need because it is not necessarily directly stated[9] (see also chapter 4: "Diverse Information Needs" and chapter 11: "Information Intermediation and Reference Services"). For example, a patron may ask an information professional, "Do you have *Time* magazine?" Solving the direct problem as presented, the answer would be a simple "yes" or "no." However, the patron may be a student looking for articles about the U.S. war in Iraq and associate *Time* magazine with articles of that genre and topic. Or the patron may be a senior citizen looking for a recent article about new cancer treatments who recalled the article being published in *Time* magazine, but it actually appeared in *Newsweek*.[10] It is the explicit job of the information professional to reframe the problem in order to give the patron more than what they have expressed as their need.

Design rationale refers to the reasons and justifications for decisions made during the creation of an artifact and serves to explain why an artifact is the way it is.[11] A prime example from library and information services is the notion of *warrant*, or the justification and verification of decisions in the creation of classification systems[12] (see also chapter 12: "Metadata, Cataloging, Linked Data, and the Evolving ILS"). Most classification schemes and subject headings are based on the idea of literary warrant; that is, any class or term in the scheme must have appeared in the text of the resources comprising the collection. A classification scheme for a small public library may contain descriptors for animals like *Cats* and *Dogs*, but is unlikely to contain terms appearing in collections of literature in a library of veterinary medicine such as *Felines* and *Canines*. Decision making about which term should be included in the vocabulary—*Cats* or *Felines*—rests on rationale.

Reflection is the idea that people look back on a completed project or past situation with serious thought and consideration, such as a reflective essay students might write for English class. This type of after-the-fact *reflection-on-action* is familiar to most people.[13] It is arguably designers' engagement in "reflection-in-action," or the ongoing, continual reflection throughout the process of creation, that distinguishes design.[14] Although this type of reflection can be difficult to observe, there is evidence that it occurs in library storytimes. Storytime providers use purposeful reflection when debriefing and reviewing their performances after the fact to continually improve for future events.[15] They also may draw on reflection during the storytime itself, making adjustments in tone, posture, and other interactions as necessary.[16]

Library and Information Professionals as Designers

If library and information services are indeed design artifacts, then information professionals need to explicitly harness principles, techniques, and methods of design to create more robust and successful tools and services. Yet most information professionals do not think of their work as design. User experience (UX) librarians—people in positions that are directly inspired by fields like interaction design—consider their role specifically as a research role rather than a design one, de-emphasizing design-related tasks and relegating design to other staff and departments[17] (see also chapter 14: "User Experience"). Design research methods are conspicuously absent from textbooks on research methods for information professionals, even recent publications.[18] When design is discussed in the context of library and information science, it is often relegated to architecture and space planning, such as *Library Journal*'s annual Design Showcase, which highlights architectural and interior design.[19] In addition to this emphasis on architecture, discussions and discourse of design in library and information science literature often reflect technology (such as "web design") and printed material formats (such as the design of book jackets).[20] But design in library and information science is much more than physical spaces and web pages. As demonstrated in this chapter, information professionals design all manner of tools and services to enable access to and use of information resources. Such a disconnect means that elements of design knowledge, if drawn on by information professionals when creating problem-solving artifacts, are implicit, and thus not harnessed to their full potential.

> If library and information services are indeed design artifacts, then information professionals need to explicitly harness principles, techniques, and methods of design to create more robust and successful tools and services.

Discussion Question

Multiple examples of design elements in library tools and services are discussed in this chapter, such as the use of repertory knowledge in readers' advisory and the use of rationale in controlled vocabulary. What other examples of library and information services include the elements of design identified in this chapter?

DESIGN METHODS FOR LIBRARY INNOVATION

How can information professionals create better tools and services by explicitly incorporating design ways of knowing into their work? There are numerous frameworks drawn upon by designers, such as user-centered design or participatory design, and many concrete methods that designers partake in, from A/B testing to word clouds.[21] Entire books can (and have) been written on these varying approaches. Because of this, the focus here is instead to discuss how information professionals use the design thinking process to help their information organizations.

The Design Thinking Process

The design thinking approach is a problem-centered, iterative process for finding problems and creating solutions to them. Although the process has always been employed in design work, most people drawing on this method agree that the explicit articulation of the steps in the process was first codified and popularized by David Kelley, cofounder of the product design firm IDEO and creator of the Hasso Plattner Institute of Design (a.k.a. the "d.school") at Stanford University.[22] Since its original explicit articulation, many variations on the process have emerged. Although the specific verbiage varies, the design thinking process consists of four major phases that are not linear but form an iterative cycle (see figure 23.1), allowing constant reflection and improvement.

> The design thinking approach is a problem-centered, iterative process for finding problems and creating solutions to them.

analyze
define
empathize
identify
inquire
investigate
research
understand

brainstorm
develop
ideate
generate
plan

assess
evaluate
reflect
test

build
create
deploy
develop
implement
realize
solve
take action

Figure 23.1 Design Thinking Process. *Created by author.*

The four phases are given below.

The investigative phase encourages a problem-solving mind-set by finding patterns, clearly identifying and articulating issues and goals, and emphasizing empathetic understanding of users and customers by seeing things from their perspective.[23] Empathetic understanding of users is a key component to understanding and framing problems.

The planning phase encourages collaboration and innovation. This phase relies on divergent thinking and brainstorming to generate as many ideas as possible, no matter how absurd they may seem. Because design thinking emphasizes multiple approaches to solving a problem, it generates more—and more innovative—solutions.[24]

The development phase encourages creativity in the most literal sense, through the creation of problem solutions, but also encourages adaptation and flexibility, as designers find themselves navigating constraints and restraints. This includes creating prototypes, or low-fidelity preliminary mock-ups, to test ideas and gather more feedback before committing to full development. Sometimes prototyping is delineated as a separate phase between ideation and development.

The evaluative phase encourages leaders to communicate value clearly and feeds back into investigation for continued improvement. In addition to merely judging a product's reception and use, this phase is used to expose and identify new problems, thus connecting to the investigative phase and starting the cycle anew.

All of these phases play a role in fostering twenty-first-century leadership skills (see also chapter 37: "Leadership Skills for Today's Global Information Landscape"). All of the skills and abilities drawn upon in the design thinking process are critical if future libraries and information organizations are to remain valuable entities and thrive in future environments. A recent report on the future of MLIS education notes an increasing need to foster graduates who are collaborative, creative, socially innovative, flexible, and adaptable problem solvers—characteristics that are demonstrated by people with backgrounds in design.[25] The Aspen Institute's recent report on the future of public libraries emphasizes the need for libraries to foster new organizational cultures that emphasize innovation, calling out design thinking as an integral part of this paradigm shift.[26]

Examples of the Design Thinking Process in Libraries

Case Study 1: Chicago Public Library Co-Lab[27]

A team of library staff and design professionals used the design thinking process to create a new coworking space at Chicago Public Library's Bezazian Branch. First, in the investigative phase, the team visited diverse examples of existing coworking spaces—many of them outside of library contexts. They interviewed users of those spaces to understand their needs and desires. They also interviewed library patrons for similar information. After synthesizing what they found out about people's' coworking needs, they brainstormed ideas for coworking spaces in the library (planning phase). Next, they created a prototype space in the library (development phase) and observed how people used it (evaluative phase). Observed aspects of the space that were not working were either modified or eliminated entirely and replaced with other approaches, thus beginning the cycle anew. New perspectives surfaced, such as the need to support job seekers. Additional coworking spaces as well as services to assist with employment will be developed based on what they learned from the original prototype.

Case Study 2: The eXtensible Catalog Project at the University of Rochester[28]

Librarians at the University of Rochester observed that students faced problems using the library catalog. To understand the frame and context of the problem, they brought in Nancy Fried Foster, an anthropologist, for an investigative phase exploring exactly what, how, and why undergraduate students conducted research and scholarship. To generate ideas for solutions to the problem, the library held participatory design workshops in which teams of students were asked to design an app that would assist them with group work. The ultimate goal of these workshops was not to build an app, but to produce ideas about what students needed to perform and complete their scholarly work:

> We didn't want their app design, we wanted to understand the work that they needed to be able to do through the ideas that they came up with in designing their apps. . . . All we care about is knowing the work they need to be able to do. And sure, their apps had good ideas in them, but we weren't building an app. We were learning about their work. And we were learning about their work by having them do a creative design activity that would create something to support their work.[29]

The knowledge gleaned from these design sessions revealed that students work with a variety of materials and sources, which led to the creation of a new metadata schema that allowed records for materials of various formats to be united together into one collection and seamless user interface, enabling students to search one location rather than multiple silos.

Case Study 3: ASK Desk at Ohio State University Health Sciences Library[30]

Librarians at the John A. Prior Health Sciences Library at Ohio State University explicitly drew on the design thinking process when planning a renovation of the physical library space. Library staff observed faculty and staff at work in the library, noticing the increase in problem-based learning, original research, and collaborative projects, as well as combined use of analog and digital tools from skeletal models to laptops and PDAs. They also watched where and for how long patrons waited for library assistance. In addition to observations, library staff solicited direct feedback via informal surveys and oral and written suggestions. Brainstorming solutions to the identified issues ranged from roving reference to library-produced podcasts. Ultimately, the team refined possible solutions and implemented a single service point—the ASK desk, which served as a one-stop shop for information, circulation, and computing services. However, the process did not end with implementation. True to the design thinking process, ongoing evaluation and investigation led to additions and revisions, such as downsizing the area for photocopying as the demand ebbed and increased availability of staff with copyright expertise to field increasing questions on that topic.

Discussion Question

In this chapter, the design thinking cycle is described as having four phases: investigate, plan, develop, and evaluate. However, other descriptions of the design thinking cycle identify five phases: empathize, define, ideate, prototype, and test. How do the two models differ, and how might the differences affect your approach to a design project?

LOOKING FORWARD: THE NEED FOR LIBRARY AND INFORMATION DESIGNERS

Although it is but one approach, the design thinking process supports an information organization's need to remain creative, innovative, and technologically advanced through the use of empathetic understanding, teamwork and collaboration, creativity and innovation, adaptation and flexibility, and communicative ability. Explicitly and proactively engaging with elements of design knowledge like repertoire, reflection, and other elements described above will help shift from a mind-set of service *provision* to one of service *creation*—to library and information designers. This new positioning opens up possibilities for new management approaches, new staff positions, and new roles in library and information organizations. As Bradburn notes, information professionals cannot create new and innovative library services if they cannot understand and articulate the profession's new, design-based roles.[31]

How can current and future information professionals gain and strengthen their design skills and competencies to be successful in these new evolving roles? As the future of library and information science progressively hinges on reimagining the profession in a design mind-set, education for this perspective needs to be considered. Clarke and Bell argue that the current MLIS degree should be reinvented as an "MLD": a master's of library design degree.[32] Yet none of the top ALA-accredited master's-level library education programs require coursework in design.[33] However, a few schools show interest in incorporating design thinking and methods into their program offerings. At the time of

Rachel Ivy Clarke

writing, San José State University, Simmons College, University of Maryland, and University of Washington are all developing and piloting courses incorporating aspects of design and design thinking.

Meanwhile, other options of design education abound. Traditional design schools may be one option. In addition to degree programs, many of these schools offer online modules, MOOCs (Massive Open Online Courses), and other more easily accessible options for self-education. For example, Stanford University's d.school offers a number of downloadable modules.[34] Other nonacademic organizations offer introductory tool kits and online mini-courses in basic design thinking approaches and methods. A few are even specifically tailored for libraries, such as IDEO's "Design Thinking For Libraries" tool kit, which offers information professionals a step-by-step guide to adopting design thinking as a staff-driven process for change.[35] Prior workshops from the Council on Library and Information Resources (CLIR) offered academic librarians opportunities to learn and apply the methods and techniques of participatory design, a form of design process that supports cooperation and collaboration between users and designers. Although the workshops have ceased, reports summarizing activities and offering further suggested reading are still available.[36] In 2016, the *Library Journal* Design Program, which initially focused on architectural design challenges that united information professionals and architects to explore the use of design to improve library services, began to offer a design thinking workshop in conjunction with the Chicago Public Library, which itself contributed to the rise of design thinking.[37] Other online tools, like the blogs at the Blended Librarians Online Learning Community[38] and Designing Better Libraries,[39] offer information professionals opportunities to participate in discussions and information exchange.

Both new and experienced information professionals can benefit from attaining competencies in design thinking. Students just beginning a degree on their path to becoming an information professional should consider programs that offer courses or other opportunities to learn design skills like the design thinking process, or, lacking such opportunities, seek out their own educational resources. Current information professionals wishing to update their skills and delve deeper into design can seek out formal postgraduate education opportunities, such as advanced certificates or professional workshops and trainings. A list of resources to help new and current information professionals can be found in chapter 23 of the online supplement.

CONCLUSION

This chapter illustrates the relevance of design perspectives and methods, especially design thinking, to library and information services. Although design is commonly defined in the context of specific applied fields, like graphic design or architecture, design is actually a unique way of thinking. The characteristics of this way of thinking—including elements like artifact creation, problem finding, framing and reframing, iteration, reflection, repertoire, rationale, and critique—are evident in library and information services, although implicitly and passively applied.

One introductory way of applying design more explicitly to library and information services is through the design thinking process. The phases of the design thinking process—investigation, planning, developing, and evaluating—draw on the elements of design knowledge to create artifacts like library tools and services. Additionally, to support explicit application of design, information professionals require an expanded set of competencies beyond those traditionally taught in MLIS education. Future information professionals need to explicitly embrace their positions as library and information designers and the accordant ways of thinking to remain valuable and thrive in future environments.

NOTES

1. *Merriam-Webster Dictionary*, s.v. "design," accessed March 25, 2017, http://www.merriam-webster.com/dictionary/design.

2. See, for example, Herbert Simon, *The Sciences of the Artificial* (Cambridge, MA: MIT Press, 1969); Donald A. Schön, *The Reflective Practitioner: How Professionals Think in Action* (New York: Basic Books, 1983); Nigel Cross, *Design Thinking* (Oxford: Berg, 2011).

3. Jeanne Liedka, "Design Thinking: The Role of Hypothesis Generation and Testing," in *Managing as Designing*, ed. Richard J. Boland Jr. and Fred Collopy (Stanford, CA: Stanford University Press, 2004).

4. Silke Konsorski-Lang and Michael Hampe, "Why Is Design Important? An Introduction," in *The Design of Material, Organism, and Minds* (Berlin: Springer, 2010), 3–18.

5. A. Telier, *Design Things* (Cambridge, MA: MIT Press, 2011).

6. Cross, *Design Thinking*.

7. Rachel I. Clarke, "Toward a Design Epistemology for Librarianship," *Library Quarterly: Information, Communication, Policy* (forthcoming).

8. Joyce Saricks, *Readers' Advisory Service in the Public Library*, third edition (Chicago: American Library Association, 2005), 1–13.

9. Anne M. Fields, "Ill-Structured Problems and the Reference Consultation: The Librarian's Role in Developing Student Expertise," *Reference Services Review* 34, no. 3 (2006).

10. Example from Stephanie W. Brown, "The Reference Interview: Theories and Practice," *Library Philosophy and Practice*, 2008, http://www.webpages.uidaho.edu/~mbolin/willenbrown.htm.

11. Thomas P. Moran and John M. Carroll, "Overview of Design Rationale," in *Design Rationale: Concepts, Techniques, and Use* (Mahwah, NJ: Lawrence Erlbaum Associates, 1996), 8–9.

12. Claire Beghtol, "Semantic Validity: Concepts of Warrant in Bibliographic Classification Systems," *Library Resources and Technical Services* 30, no. 2 (April/June 1986): 110.

13. Schön, *The Reflective Practitioner*.

14. Ibid.

15. "Storytimes Matter! Building Early Literacy in YOUR Public Libraries," *VIEWS2*, 2017, http://views2.ischool.uw.edu/welcome-directors/.

16. J. Elizabeth Mills, Kathleen Campana, and Rachel I. Clarke, "Learning by Design: Creating Knowledge through Library Storytime Production," *Proceedings of the Association for Information Science and Technology* 53, no. 1 (2016): 1–6, doi:10.1002/pra2.2016.14505301115.

17. Craig M. MacDonald, "User Experience Librarians: User Advocates, User Researchers, Usability Evaluators, or All of the Above?," *Proceedings of the Association for Information Science and Technology* 52, no. 1 (2015): 1–10, doi:10.1002/pra2.2015.145052010055.

18. See, for example, Susan E. Beck and Kate Manuel, *Practical Research Methods for Librarians and Information Professionals* (New York: Neal-Schuman Publishers, 2008); Lynn S. Connaway and Marie L. Radford, *Basic Research Methods in Library and Information Science*, sixth edition (Westport, CT: Libraries Unlimited, 2017); Alison Jane Pickard, *Research Methods in Information*, second edition (Chicago: Neal-Schuman, 2013).

19. Phil Morehart, "2015 Library Design Showcase," *American Libraries*, September 1, 2015, https://americanlibrariesmagazine.org/2015/09/01/2015-library-design-showcase/.

20. Rachel I. Clarke, "Designing Disciplinary Identity: An Analysis of the Term 'Design' in Library and Information Science Vocabulary," *Proceedings of the Association for Information Science and Technology* 52, no. 1 (2015): 1–4, doi:10.1002/pra2.2015.145052010074.

21. Word Cloud, last accessed August 9, 2017, Q, http://wiki.q-researchsoftware.com/wiki/Word_Cloud.

22. Hasso Plattner Institute of Design, last accessed August 9, 2017, https://dschool.stanford.edu/.

23. Kevin Clark and Ron Smith, "Unleashing the Power of Design Thinking," *Design Management Review* 19, no. 3 (2008): 8–15, doi:10.1111/j.1948-7169.2008.tb00123.x.

24. Jimmy Guterman, "How to Become a Better Manager . . . by Thinking Like a Designer," *MIT Sloan Management Review* 50, no. 4 (2009): 39–42.

25. John C. Bertot, Lindsay C. Sarin, and Johnna Percell, "Re-envisioning the MLS: Findings, Issues, and Considerations," College of Information Studies, University of Maryland, College Park, 2015, http://mls.umd.edu/wp-content/uploads/2015/08/ReEnvisioningFinalReport.pdf.

26. Amy K. Garmer, "Libraries in the Exponential Age: Moving from the Edge of Innovation to the Center of Community," The Aspen Institute, 2016, http://csreports.aspeninstitute.org/documents/Libraries_Exponential_Age.pdf.

27. Rebecca T. Miller and Meredith Schwartz, "What Wallets Have to Do with Libraries," *Library Journal*, January 3, 2014, http://lj.libraryjournal.com/2014/01/opinion/design4impact/what-wallets-have-to-do-with-libraries-design4impact/#_.

28. Rachel Clarke, "It's Not Rocket Library Science" (PhD diss. University of Washington, 2016), https://digital.lib.washington.edu/researchworks/bitstream/handle/1773/37159/Clarke_washington_0250E_15974.pdf.

29. Ibid., 174–75, quote from interview with David Lindahl, March 2, 2016.

30. Pamela S. Bradigan and Ruey L. Rodman, "Single Service Point: It's All in the Design," *Medical Reference Services Quarterly* 27, no. 4 (2008): 367–78, doi:10.1080/02763860802367755.

31. Frances B. Bradburn, "Redesigning Our Role While Redesigning Our Libraries," *Knowledge Quest* 42, no. 1 (2013): 52–57.

32. Rachel I. Clarke and Steven Bell, "Transitioning from the MLS to the MLD: Integrating Design Thinking and Philosophy into Library and Information Science Education," in *Re-Envisioning the MLS: Perspectives on the Future of Library and Information Science Education*, ed. L. C. Sarin, J. Percell, P. T. Jaeger, and J. C. Bertot (Bingley, UK: Emerald Group Publishing, forthcoming).

33. Rachel I. Clarke, Jin Ha Lee, J. H., and Katie Mayer, "Design Topics in Graduate Library Education: A Preliminary Investigation" (paper presented at the annual meeting for the Association for Library and Information Science Education conference, Atlanta, Georgia, January 17–20, 2017).

34. "Tools for Taking Action," Stanford d.School, accessed August 10, 2017, https://dschool.stanford.edu/resources/.

35. "Design Thinking for Libraries: A Toolkit for Patron-Centered Design," IDEO, last accessed August 9, 2017, http://designthinkingforlibraries.com.

36. Council on Library and Information Resources, "Participatory Design in Academic Libraries: Methods, Findings, and Implementations," Council on Library and Information Resources, 2012, https://www.clir.org/pubs/reports/pub161.

37. "Designing the Future: A Design Thinking Workshop," *Library Journal*, last accessed August 10, 2017, http://learn.libraryjournal.com/designing-the-future-a-design-thinking-workshop/.

38. *Blended Librarian* (blog), last accessed August 9, 2017, http://blendedlibrarian.org.

39. *Designing Better Libraries*, 2017, http://dbl.lishost.org.

24

Managing Collections

Wayne T. Disher

Chapter 24, "Managing Collections," offers an essential component of information services that requires strategic planning, innovation, trend forecasting, and community analysis to successfully meet the needs of the community. Collection development is continually evolving, particularly as new technologies are introduced and the expectations and needs of users are changing as they interact with collections. Wayne T. Disher, author of several textbooks including Crash Course in Collection Development *and past director of Library Services at Hemet Public Library, explains how and why collection management took its current shape and discusses why it is necessary for collection managers to create new and innovative ways to offer collections to users.*

To survive, Disher argues, information organizations must broaden their mandate beyond "the book brand" to prepare for a "post-print world" and to include other benefits and services to communities, such as providing critical support for information literacy. Collection managers must adopt a strategic planning process that attends to external trends such as reader preferences and demands, emerging technologies, and challenges such as limited resources for collections purchases.

Disher elaborates that collection managers need to remain innovative and technologically advanced, recognize collection development models that help meet user demand and increase the relevancy of an information organization's collections within the community, and follow consumer and industry trends to help identify potential opportunities to advance the information organization. By engaging in these activities, collection managers will ensure information organizations provide collections—both print and digital—that are well aligned with and continually evolving to meet the needs and interests of the communities they serve.

★   ★   ★

Collection management is a complex process that involves strategic planning, innovation, change management, and community analysis. This chapter discusses those responsibilities through an exploration of how collections have evolved over time and how they are likely to evolve even further in the digital future, especially as users interact with technology in new ways and have different demands and expectations regarding how they access and use collections. Since the publication of the first edition of this book in 2015, there have already been significant changes in the way users interact with library collections. As more and more data about collections are updated and analyzed, collection managers are now able to better understand user behaviors and are getting a clearer picture of what users' expectations regarding collections are likely to be in the future. This chapter examines some of the new data, offering potential explanations of what it means to collection managers in the Digital Age. After completing this chapter, the reader should have an understanding of how and why collection management took its current shape. Readers will also acquire an understanding of why it is necessary for managers to create new and innovative ways to offer information collections to users. This chapter also presents recommendations to help deal with the challenging issues in developing the best possible collection. See also appendix 24.1, "Basics of Building a Collection" at the end of this chapter for a summary of basic collection management activities.

HOW COLLECTIONS HAVE EVOLVED OVER TIME

Perhaps as far back as when Ptolemy collected papyrus scrolls and stored them at the ancient Library of Alexandria, collection developers have focused most (if not all) of their attention and budget on the printed word (see also chapter 2: "Libraries, Communities, and Information: Two Centuries of Experience"). Modern-day collection developers have not been immune to equating a society's cultural knowledge solely to the physical content of printed books. As technology and publishing innovation made it easier and less costly to mass-produce the printed word, the number of books collected in information organizations across the United States increased exponentially. The publication of printed books went from 78,000 in 1948 to nearly 2 million in 2005.[1] While that industry growth is certainly impressive, the growth rate continued to accelerate. A report from the Association of American Publishers reported that 2.7 billion books (in all formats) were published and sold in 2014.[2] Printed material remained the focus of collection managers, even as collections expanded in the 1950s and 1960s to include media. Although user demands for music and film certainly pressed collection managers to turn attention to alternative material formats, 85 percent of information organizations' collections were still comprised of books.[3] This occurred at a time when mass communication and media professionals like Marshall McLuhan were proclaiming the death of printed material.[4] Collection developers most certainly saw community expectations and behavioral patterns change (see also chapter 4: "Diverse Information Needs"). However, much of the evidence suggests that they either ignored these changes or chose to collect the material they were most comfortable with providing—books.

Society changed even more drastically, during the 1980s and 1990s. Television, video gaming, and of course the internet instilled new user behaviors that favored a preference for visual stimulation, virtual environments, and the ability to think and be entertained in a far less linear fashion than that provided by the printed word. While collection managers did begin to address community demand and shifting user preferences by adding small collections of film, music, and other formats, they did not turn their primary focus away from the printed book. In fact, the Institute of Library and Museum Services reported that, in 2010, the proportion of print materials in the information organization's collections—at least in the public library—had increased to 87 percent.[5] Meanwhile, in the retail world, business managers understood the need to adapt to new behaviors and were responding to the public's shifting reading habits. For example, as the availability of e-books increased, online bookseller Amazon reported in 2011 that it was selling more e-books than printed ones.[6] The consumer world changed, but the information organization's collections, for the most part, did not.

THE BOOK BRAND

Collection managers can point with at least a modicum of pride to the success of branding "the book" as a professional product. This collecting activity has taken a firm hold in the mind of information users. In 2005, the Online Computer Library Center, Inc. (OCLC) conducted an extensive survey of users around the world on their perceptions of libraries.[7] The published report revealed roughly 70 percent of respondents first thought of "books" when they thought of a library. Another more recent study[8] conducted by the Pew Research Center revealed that 80 percent of survey respondents cited books as the library's major resource. While businesses and organizations spend millions on advertising and marketing campaigns to achieve a high level of brand recognition that books already enjoy, it should pose serious concerns for information managers. If an organization relies only on one product or service, what happens when it becomes unnecessary?

Fortunately, communities also recognize the role information organizations play in creating an information literate society. *Libraries and Learning*, a recent study by the Pew Research Center,[9] reported that nearly 80 percent of survey respondents had used their library over the past twelve months, and 93 percent of them said they were visiting the library to use the library's internet access. The report indicated that more than two-thirds of those surveyed fit the category of "lifelong learners" seeking information about what is happening in their community and society. Clearly, there is support from people to utilize libraries when seeking to become more information literate.

This thirst for information in communities should provide collection managers with strategic direction in collection planning. Whether by supporting tax measures or by visiting information organizations in record numbers, society—for the time being—respects the relationship between communities and information organizations. Information professionals must continue to exhibit their expertise in retrieving the most useful information while teaching others to do the same, proving their positive role in the advancement of information literacy.

> " With the information organization's focus on information literacy, collection managers must not only maintain collections that work seamlessly with their role as teachers, coaches, and partners in the information exchange process, but they must do much better in promoting these collections so users are aware of them. "

The *Libraries and Learning* report also stated that most libraries are focusing on their information literacy responsibilities. In 2016, over 90 percent of libraries were offering e-book borrowing and online digital audio books.[10] Over 60 percent offered online career guidance and job resources. Additionally, a third of libraries were offering programs on starting a new business and improving educational skills. With the information organization's focus on information literacy (see also chapter 16: "Teaching Users: Information and Technology Instruction"), collection managers must not only maintain collections that work seamlessly with their role as teachers, coaches, and partners in the information exchange process, but they must do much better in promoting these collections so users are aware of them. Certainly, the things collection managers have done in the past have been incredibly valuable—even critically important—to the successful expansion of information literacy in our society.

The collecting activities that served that purpose well in the past, however, could soon reach their expiration date. At this time, there seems to be a need for a new approach to collection management if information collections are to remain meaningful to the communities they serve. The new approach involves a strategic planning process that includes substantial thought about new trends, technology, and changes in user behavior.

STRATEGIC PLANNING AND THE COLLECTION

Studies in professional journals attest to the importance of strategic planning in organizations, including information organizations (see also chapter 19: "Strategic Planning"). It is a critical aspect of collection management as well. Although collection managers spend a considerable amount of time evaluating the internal value (the strengths and weaknesses) of collections, their planning efforts all too often stop there, without considering the external impact (the opportunities and threats) of their decisions. The collection manager must pay attention to external trends, such as reader preferences and emerging technologies, and visualize how those trends will affect what would be best to include in the collection (see also chapter 3: "Librarianship: A Continuously Evolving Profession"). At the same time, an analysis of current collection practices in light of those trends should be made to determine if the direction of that trend is aligned with the collection development plan. The desired result is that the trend and current practice are converging, rather than diverging.

> The collection manager must pay attention to external trends, such as reader preferences and emerging technologies, and visualize how those trends will affect what would be best to include in the collection.

Divergence is exemplified in the practice of inventory control, a process that involves much labor. So much time is spent accounting for printed material that the information manager loses sight of the shift in user demands. Inventory control, although necessary to keep the collection relevant, needs to take into account new trends for immediate access in any format.

Strategic planning helps collection managers recognize when user demands are shifting, enabling them to respond to those shifts by adapting their collection management plans. The lesson here is that having prior knowledge of possible new trends and thinking strategically about those trends gives one a tactical advantage. If collection management practices fail to focus on today's user needs and anticipate future trends, information organizations could be in real trouble. Managers must continuously reposition their collections and keep them viable in a technologically and information literate society.

The collection development policy seems the most likely document to compel information professionals to include strategic planning into the core decision-making process of the library. Most every library has a collection development policy. Using the library's mission, vision, and values, these policies provide a framework for the growth, selection, and scope of materials the library collects. However, libraries need to continually evaluate their collection development policies to ensure that current trends and practices are included in the planning of what the collection should include. Unfortunately, the collection development policy becomes less and less useful to a library if information professionals do not use and update it with strategic changes in direction. Collection development policies in many libraries do not even include the words "digital," "e-book," or "online."

> Libraries need to continually evaluate their collection development policies to ensure that current trends and practices are included in the planning of what the collection should include.

Certainly, this is an indication that the library's collection development process is not addressing its community's current wants, needs, and demands. A collection development policy that places a larger emphasis on strategic direction will more effectively establish collection priorities that match future community trends. When developing a collection plan, policies that embrace—rather than ignore—specific steps for including strategic direction will ensure that collections are relevant and useful to their community well into the future.[11]

CAN STRATEGIC PLANNING REALLY HELP COLLECTION MANAGERS?

The use of a collection development plan to help librarians plot a strategic course for the future cannot be overemphasized. While more and more libraries in recent years have included e-books as part of their collection in response to growing demand, new reports seem to show user demand tapering off—if not declining due to "digital fatigue."[12] Some might see this issue as a reason for alarm. However, the Association of American Publishers reported that while the use of e-books had plateaued in 2015, consumers were spending more on other digital content such as streaming video and music.[13] This obviously seems like a contradiction. Can demand for e-books be wavering even as the market for other digital content seems to be increasing? This is where strategic planning and updating collection development plans may help library collection developers prepare—by forcing information professionals to focus and notice user behavior and trends.

Much like the societal changes mentioned earlier that spurred changes in the early days of book printing and those brought about by television and video gaming in the 1970s and 1980s, e-book preference early in the first part of the twenty-first century can be tied to users who owned dedicated e-readers (such as the Amazon Kindle and the Nook). Collection developers continued to struggle with the compatibility, licensing, and pricing issues that plagued the industry as they tried to determine into which e-reader path to invest its collection funds. Inflexible collection development plans often trapped library selectors into purchasing one particular format, contrary to expressed concerns of device limitations by the library's users. A collection plan that specifies the need to tie digital content to growing trends and behaviors would certainly seem more appropriate.

TOMORROW'S COLLECTIONS: PREPARING FOR A POST-PRINT WORLD

Will the post-print world be completely paperless? The answer is not clear, and the debate rages on. The question as to whether society will (or should) become paperless can be left for others to debate. While there is still a significant user base for print collections, particularly for children, tomorrow's collections will (and should) necessarily look quite different from yesterday's collections. Current trends indicate a much larger demand for access to electronic content. Even if society should decide to become completely paperless and to produce and exchange informational content only in electronic form, the change will not happen quickly.

However, the change that will happen quickly (if it has not happened already) is in user perception regarding information collections. Because electronic information is delivered to almost anywhere more quickly and more conveniently than other resources, users may perceive that the electronic format is the most valuable resource for their information needs. In a post-print world, digital information resources can no longer be a secondary priority for collection managers. Furthermore, forward-thinking managers move beyond inventory control (e.g., check in, check out, shelve, and re-shelve) as a primary focus and instead work to increase information literacy by helping communities access and use collections more creatively.

COMMUNITY EXPECTATIONS AND THE ROLE OF THE COLLECTION MANAGER

Strategic planning and evaluation are important parts of collection management. So, too, is the principle that the collection effectively serves the community that supports it. The success of the information organization and users' perception of the collection's relevance is built on understanding the user community today and anticipating its needs for tomorrow. For example, collection managers must realize that most users want to access information without physically visiting buildings. Saving the reader's time is one of the five laws of library science proposed by S. R. Ranganathan[14] back in 1931. See table 24.1.

Each year, *Library Journal* magazine reports e-book usage statistics at U.S. public libraries. The magazine does the same with e-book usage statistics at U.S. academic libraries. A look at these annual reports over just the last five or ten years can be very frustrating. Usage statistics for one year can point to slowing circulation in one library environment while other library environments report healthy demand. The trend may seem to reverse itself the next year. A quick look at the 2016 survey of *eBook Usage in U.S. Academic Libraries* illustrates some of the frustration present when trying to make

Table 24.1. Ranganathan's Laws of Library Science.

1. Books are for use
2. Every reader his [or her] book
3. Every book its reader
4. Save the time of the user
5. The library is a growing organism

Source: R. S. Ranganathan, *The Five Laws of Library Science* (London: Edward Goldston, 1931).

firm implications on the meaning of each year's e-book data.[15] For example, while the report reveals that librarians believed that use of e-books would slow down, the same report also revealed that few respondents could actually confirm how—or if—usage was measured. The report further revealed that e-book demand at academic libraries is influenced by ease of access, device compatibility, or how easy the student feels it will be to cite a print source versus an electronic source (see also chapter 7: "Learning and Research Institutions: Academic Libraries"). Even so, librarians across all types of environments still see demand rise from time to time. Such statistics illustrate that information users are placing more and more value on access to digital material in the post-print society. They expect information organizations to provide access to it, not debate its staying power.

Many collection managers are repositioning information organizations to take advantage of electronic resources and to meet the digital demand. However, the pace may be frustratingly slow for a society that has become more and more tech savvy. Collection content has become user-driven. A collection manager must convince key stakeholders to invest and support the strategic direction for the collection. The current community of information users is demanding collections with a great deal more electronic material, and the format of that material will continue to evolve rapidly. As such, managers need to be open to the evolving nature of information formats and focus on the users' learning experience and information needs when making collection management decisions.

CHALLENGES AND OPPORTUNITIES IN COLLECTION MANAGEMENT

Resources are an organization's most important asset—a means to meet its mission. The same is true with the resources available to a collection manager, which are usually scarce, and must be appropriated to specific goals prudently. As has repeatedly been shown in public, academic, and school financing for information materials, the resources needed by collection managers to meet their organization's mission will likely be greater than the funds available. So, how should the collection manager reconcile the gap between the need for more collection formats and the need for more money to keep the collection current and accessible? Remaining innovative and technologically advanced is the key (see also chapter 21: "Managing Budgets"). Collection managers looking toward innovation must take advantage of newer collection

> " With limited resources, it is critical for the collection manager to adopt a more 'demand-driven' philosophy and look for collection-building processes that focus first on community demand before considering other selection criteria. "

development models (such as patron-driven acquisition and cooperative collection development) that help meet demand, provide wider access, and increase the relevancy of an information organization's collections within the community.

With limited resources, it is critical for the collection manager to adopt a more "demand-driven" philosophy and look for collection-building processes that focus first on community demand before considering other selection criteria. Patron-driven acquisition models, while not necessarily new to the information environment, do seem to be gaining popularity with collection managers across all information environments. In adopting these models, collection managers emphasize to the users that user needs and user wants are the core of their collection building efforts.

Complex licensing policies (see also chapter 32: "Information Licensing") and expensive pricing from vendors and publishers may prevent many information organizations from providing electronic content on their own. Therefore, efforts must be made to find opportunities to create collection partnerships and share information resources cooperatively as members of a consortium. Two examples of very successful collection partnerships are the California Digital Library and the Northeast Research Libraries Consortium. Both cooperatives provide best practices models in sharing collections, negotiating licenses, and providing optimal consortia services. Fortunately, technology advances have made participating in consortia and resource sharing easier, and offer the collection manager a promising approach to building access and relinquishing the burden of ownership.

> **Check This Out**
>
> Examples of successful collection partnerships: California Digital Library, http://www.cdlib.org, and Northeast Regional Libraries Consortium, http://www.nerl.org.

> **Discussion Question**
>
> Libraries currently use "patron-driven acquisition"—a model of library collection development in which a library only purchases digital content, like e-books and e-journals, when it is clear that a user wants, needs, and demands them. What are your reactions to this collection development model?

RELEVANT COLLECTIONS IN A CHANGING WORLD

There are more subtle changes a collection manager can make when looking toward innovation and technology. Although community expectations are not always apparent, the collection manager must be able to anticipate those changes. Business managers follow consumer and industry trends to help identify potential opportunities to advance their market share. Collection managers should do the same.

In the past, communities looked to information organizations as windows into a world they knew little about. Users turned to information organizations as natural vehicles to increase awareness of the world around them. However, today, a user's natural first step in meeting their information need is to turn to the internet. For example, many current consumer trends reveal that community members are now embracing hyper-localism: the clamoring for information regarding local events, local photographs, and local information as they strive to gain a local identity and perspective of their neighborhood. If the user's information need includes their immediate community and local environment, the user will find a far less successful online experience. However, collection managers could well capitalize on this trend by enriching their local history offerings by providing digitalized collections of local history photographs, curated data of local events, and localized content. In doing so, they expand the way their collections meet changing community needs (see also chapter 14: "User Experience").

Wayne T. Disher

CONCLUSION

The twenty-first century will undoubtedly continue to be a time of great upheaval and change for institutions. As the ground shifts underneath collection managers, it is even more important for them to remember the management skills relevant to handling change. They must now consider new formats, as well as new ways of reading and learning, for which many in the profession have not, up to this point, adequately planned. Collection managers must revisit strategic plans and chart new directions that meet the demands of a changing society. Having a strategic plan in place will increase consumer confidence that information organizations are relevant to their changing information needs.

The information professional must employ managerial skills most suited to deal with current and future collection challenges, plan strategically, embrace innovation, and analyze community trends. Collection managers can then capitalize on the organization's role in fostering information literacy, rather than solely being content providers. The collections they build accelerate learning, increase global access, improve convenience, and add value to the user experience.

APPENDIX 24.1: BASICS OF BUILDING A COLLECTION

What are the basic activities involved in building a collection? This section provides an overview of some of the key aspects of collection management, ranging from access to community analysis to weeding.

Access: When collection development professionals talk about access, they are usually referring to how an information organization's materials are made available to its users (see also chapter 15: "Accessing Information Anywhere and Anytime: Access Services"). Traditionally, information professionals focused on providing physical access to information by placing an item on the organization's shelves—thus allowing a user to come into the facility to look at or borrow it. Technology has provided alternative ways of providing access to the organization's users. Information can now be delivered digitally over the internet or via electronic devices (see also chapter 10: "Digital Resources: Digital Libraries"). Users are trending toward a preference for this type of access due to the fact it can be delivered to them more conveniently and quickly.

Allocations: Allocations are the amounts of money given to a particular service, product, or department. The information organization's budgeting process is usually a complex undertaking by which the total amount of money available is distributed and allocated among the various departments and collections (see also chapter 21: "Managing Budgets"). To track collection expenditures in more detail, the total amount of money allocated to the organization's collection is usually subdivided into smaller allocations, with a portion of the total amount given, for example, to children's material, a portion of the total amount given to young adult material, and so on. Collection development professionals follow allocation expenditures closely—using this information to measure performance, monitor trends, and project future budget needs.

Collection building: Collection developers in information organizations are continually identifying, selecting, and acquiring materials to include as part of their collection. Often, a need arises for the information professional to select information meant for a specific purpose, a specific group of people, a specific location, and a specific time. This requires collection building, which is a more specific part of the entire collection development process focusing on building specific areas of the collection on an as-needed or emergency basis. As an example, many information professionals found themselves needing to build collections to help children understand the topics of Islam and Muslims following the terrorist attacks on the World Trade Center on 9/11.

Collection development: An information organization needs a method by which it can make decisions about what material it should spend its money on. Collection development best describes this method. It is that part of the larger collection management that includes the process of identifying the strengths and weaknesses of a collection in terms of user needs and community resources and then attempting to correct any weaknesses found.

Collection management: Collection management is the management-related processes and procedures involved in developing and building the collection, such as planning, budgeting, controlling, and evaluating.

Community analysis: An information organization does not exist for any other purpose than to serve the wants, needs, and demands of those in its community of users. To determine what the community's wants, needs, and demands are, a collection developer must define the community—its legal boundaries; its residents; and its demographic, economic, political, geographic, and sociological composition. By utilizing various community analysis tools, such as U.S. Census data, surveys, state and local statistical analysis, and personal observations, a collection developer can qualitatively and quantitatively determine current community demands and predict future ones.

Consortia: A consortium is a legal partnership formed of local, regional, statewide, or interstate information organizations cooperating with one another to coordinate specific information-related activities. Information organizations may form a consortium to pool their resources, negotiate improved licensing agreements, and share professional expertise in order to reap service benefits for each of their user communities.

Digital content: Also known as e-content, e-resources, and virtual content, digital content refers to most any collection of data in digital format that can be stored and transmitted electronically, for example, over the internet (see also chapter 10: "Digital Resources: Digital Libraries"). Unlike print material, digital content requires another medium to store, retrieve, and/or open the digital data in order for a user to see and use it. However, digital content can be made instantly available at any time to almost any user who has the appropriate technical capability to access it. Forms of digital content include computer files, e-books, computer databases, streaming media, audio files, and websites.

E-books: One of the most popular forms of digital content, electronic books (or e-books) are digital versions of the print book that can be read using a personal computer, smartphone, or proprietary e-book readers such as a Kindle or Nook. Publishers sell the rights to their material to vendors who then transfer the book into a digital format. Information professionals work with these vendors to purchase subscriptions to popular e-book collections and license this content to allow limited access to their users via an online authentication process (see also chapter 32: "Information Licensing). With few exceptions, e-books are exact replicas of their print versions. Trends are showing that users prefer e-books because they can be distributed over computer networks, thereby improving accessibility.

Selection: The basic process of collection development involves information professionals looking at the immense breadth of materials available, and then deciding what is (and what is not) appropriate for the community that the organization serves. In almost every case, the amount of appropriate material is still too large for any single information organization to afford, so a selection process is put in place to identify the *most* appropriate material. Collection developers utilize an established collection development policy and develop criteria for selection that often include established need; author/publisher reputation; and suitability for the intended audience in terms of authoritativeness, scope, and price.

Selection tools: Collection development professionals are often called upon to select material about which they have limited knowledge. There is some risk in spending funds to purchase material the information professional knows little about. To reduce risk, collection developers use selection tools to help obtain information about material they may be considering adding to the organization's collection. The most common selection tool is a journal providing current book reviews. Journals such as *Publisher's Weekly, Library Journal, Booklist,* and *Choice* offer current reviews of material. Information professionals, with an understanding of the needs, wants, and demands of information organizations and their users, often write reviews.

Weeding: Material contained in an information collection is rarely—if ever—needed forever. Community needs, wants, and demands constantly evolve. For an organization's collection to remain relevant to the users it intends to serve, information professionals must continually evaluate material contained in the facility to ensure it is still useful, in good condition, not outdated, and appropriate for the community. This process is called weeding. Collection developers develop a weeding plan that involves, in many cases, a book-by-book appraisal in which information professionals evaluate condition, use, and appropriateness. Books that do not meet preset criteria are deleted from the collection.

NOTES

1. George Bobinski, *Libraries and Librarianship* (Lanham, MD: Scarecrow Press, 2007), 8.
2. Marisa Bluestone, "U.S. Publishing Industry's Annual Survey Reveals $28 Billion in Revenue in 2014," Association of American Publishers, June 10, 2015, http://publishers.org/news/us-publishing-industry%E2%80%99s-annual-survey-reveals-28-billion-revenue-2014.
3. Bobinski, *Libraries and Librarianship*, 11.
4. Alden Whitman, "Marshall McLuhan, Author, Dies; Declared 'Medium Is the Message,'" *New York Times*, January 1, 1981, http://www.nytimes.com/books/97/11/02/home/mcluhan-obit.html.
5. "IMLS 2010 Public Library Survey Results Announced," last modified April 10, 2014, http://www.imls.gov/imls_2010_public_library_survey_results_announced.aspx.
6. "Amazon.com Now Selling More Kindle Books Than Print Books," Amazon, accessed June 2, 2014, http://phx.corporate-ir.net/phoenix.zhtml?c=176060&p=irol-newsArticle&ID=1565581&highlight.
7. OCLC, *Perceptions of Libraries and Information Resources 2005* (Dublin, OH: OCLC, 2005), 3–31, accessed July 6, 2014, http://www.oclc.org/content/dam/oclc/reports/pdfs/Percept_all.pdf.
8. Kathryn Zickuhr et al., "How Americans Value Public Libraries in Their Communities," Pew Internet and American Life Project, December 11, 2013, http://libraries.pewinternet.org/2013/12/11/libraries-in-communities.
9. Lee Raine, "Libraries and Learning," Pew Research Center, April 7, 2016, http://www.pewinternet.org/2016/04/07/libraries-and-learning/.
10. Ibid., 4.
11. Contra Costa Public Library, "Collection Development Plan," 2011, http://ccclib.org/aboutus/ThePlan3.pdf.
12. Jim Milliot, "As E-book Sales Decline, Digital Fatigue Grows," *Publisher's Weekly*, June 17, 2017, http://www.publishersweekly.com/pw/by-topic/digital/retailing/article/70696-as-e-book-sales-decline-digital-fatigue-grows.html.
13. Ibid.
14. S. R. Ranganathan, *The Five Laws of Library Science* (London: Edward Goldston, 1931).
15. "2010 eBook Usage Reports: Academic Libraries," *Library Journal*, 2016, http://lj.libraryjournal.com/downloads/2016academicebooksurvey/.

25

Managing Technology

Marshall Breeding

Chapter 25, "Managing Technology," provides a clear understanding of how technology can be employed to better serve information communities. Specifically, it examines the scope of technologies used to manage print and digital collections and enable discovery and access to those materials, and the important trends in information technology that provide context for the development and architecture of these tools. Marshall Breeding, an expert in information technology, a columnist for Computers in Libraries, *and author of the annual Library Systems Report in* American Libraries *magazine, examines current trends in software applications used by information organizations and evaluates proprietary products governed by commercial licenses or contracts and open-source options.*

Breeding also explores cloud computing and its use in information organizations. Breeding further addresses how technology can be incorporated for managing resources and automating operations. He provides explanation and examples of the major technologies used including the integrated library system (ILS) and Library Services Platforms. Breeding explains the differences between these two resource management systems and also highlights how other technologies interact with these new products. In addition to these technologies, Breeding discusses the adoption of mobile and e-book technologies, as well as other emerging and innovative technologies like virtual reality.

Technology leaders need to be aware of this vast and evolving array of tools, understand when to apply each tool, and know how to operate and manage these systems. They need a diverse range of skills—from programming to metadata to computer architecture. Information organizations especially need forward-looking leaders who are keeping an eye on emerging technologies and who are willing to pilot and evaluate new and often cutting-edge technology.

★ ★ ★

Technology permeates almost every aspect of libraries, archives, museums, corporations, and other organizations where information professionals carry out their work. All information professionals make use of technology tools in their portfolio of responsibilities. A clear understanding of how technology can be employed to better serve their communities will help information professionals use these tools more effectively. Beyond using technology as part of their daily tasks, some information professionals are responsible for managing some aspect of their organization's technology tools and infrastructure, making it even more important for these leaders to develop deeper expertise in the various ways technology can be used today, and how knowledge of technology trends can guide their decision making.

Technology remains in constant flux, so no discussion of trends or how technology is currently used will endure for long (see also chapter 3: "Librarianship: A Continuously Evolving Profession"). While this chapter aims to provide information and insight into the current technology landscape, it can provide only a baseline that must be continually updated throughout the career of an information professional. After completing this chapter, the reader should have an understanding of the scope of technologies used to manage print and digital collections and enable discovery and access to those materials. Readers will also learn about some of the important trends in information technology that provide context for the development and architecture of these tools.

TRENDS THAT IMPACT HOW INFORMATION ORGANIZATIONS MANAGE TECHNOLOGY

The constantly turning cycles of technology mean that information organizations have to continually adapt to changes, including broad trends affecting all businesses, as well as technology trends specifically oriented to information organizations. These ongoing trends have broad implications for information organizations, including the kinds of technology tools used by the organizations, the forms of content that comprise their collections, and the ways that organizations deliver access to these collections. This section discusses some of the major technology trends that currently warrant attention: open-source software, cloud computing, mobile technology, and voice-activated technology. While it is helpful to note the features of the current landscape, the overarching message involves continually surveying the field for each next phase of change.

From Proprietary to Open-Source Software

In the current technology environment, software applications oriented for information organizations are provided in two ways: (1) as proprietary products under the control of a specific vendor; and (2) as open-source software, where users of the software can use, modify, and share it freely (see also chapter 33: "Open Access").

Defining Proprietary and Open-Source Software

Proprietary software is governed by a commercial license or contract that specifies the terms under which it can be used and the fees required to use it. The source code for proprietary software is usually not made available to those who use the software, and all development is conducted under the control of the vendor. The overwhelming majority of business software is developed as proprietary software. The commercial terms of this type of software have been generally well accepted in the business and consumer sectors. The majority of the integrated library systems are licensed as proprietary software, though open-source alternatives make up a growing segment. See textbox 25.1 for examples of integrated library system providers.

In contrast, open-source applications provide access to source code, allowing users to use the software without licensing fees, and to modify it. Licenses apply to this type of software as well. To qualify as open source, the licenses must include terms that require the provision of the source code, the ability to make modifications, and the redistribution of the modified software. These general provisions apply to all open-source software, but different licenses entail different specific terms. Open-source software usually involves a more distributed development paradigm. Rather than remaining under the control of a single vendor, many individuals and organizations can participate in developing an open-source application. Some open-source projects involve broad, international development efforts, while for others, activity takes place within a more limited or tight-knit community or even by a single individual. Many technical infrastructure components have been developed as open-source software, including the Linux operating system, search technologies such as Elasticsearch[1] and Solr,[2] database management systems, and programming languages. Many open-source licenses allow inclusion within proprietary products.

The flexibility associated with open-source software can be accomplished within proprietary software, at least to a limited extent, by exposing application programming interfaces (APIs). These APIs enable programmers to extend the functionality, create connections with other systems, or extract and manipulate data without the need to work with the underlying source code of the application. APIs have become a general expectation for any larger-scale application, whether it was developed as open-source or proprietary software.

Managing Proprietary and Open-Source Software

Information professionals involved in managing technologies need to understand the differences between open-source and proprietary software, as well as the varying roles they will perform in managing the use of these tools in their organizations. For example, proprietary software comes with comprehensive support from a vendor, and the contract specifies the up-front costs for the software, as well as annual software and support fees. In return for these fees, the organization is entitled to make use of the software, receive ongoing updates made to the application, and accept help from the vendor with problem resolution. Information organizations are not able to directly reprogram the internal workings of the software, but most major applications offer a wide set of customization options. Most vendors of proprietary software sponsor user groups that provide additional avenues for training, and many user groups develop lists of desired enhancements for the vendor to address.

Adopting applications based on open-source software does not obligate an organization to participate in its development. Organizations that use open-source applications can opt to participate in its development, engaging in a wide range of technical and nontechnical activities. Those who have adequate technical expertise may join the coordinated development community for the project and work on programming new features or bug fixes for the application. Others may contribute their efforts toward less technical tasks, such as writing documentation or testing. Rather than managing the installation directly, some organizations opt to implement open-source products through support contracts with commercial companies. These commercial contracts bring the use of open-source applications within the reach of libraries without programmers or technical personnel. While proprietary applications are tied to a single vendor, open-source applications allow multiple vendors to offer service and support.

The tools and methodologies generally associated with open-source software development can be applied to other types of projects. Document repositories with version control find a variety of use cases beyond the management of computer source code. Environments such as GitHub[3] have become well established in the technical community for managing the source code for programming projects. Designed to support distributed teams of programmers, these code repositories have collaborative capabilities to manage multiple versions, or forks, of project files, with features to synchronize or reconcile changes. As information professionals collaborate on projects with large numbers of files or documents, they can be managed using GitHub or other repositories. Examples of projects might include collections of metadata, website component files, XML documents, or documentation and procedures.[4]

Discussion Questions

What are some of the tools or technologies that an information organization can implement to provide access to its collections? How do these tools compare with those that people use, such as Google or Google Scholar, to find information?

Evolving Software Development Approaches

The software development arena has seen a major shift in project management away from waterfall to Agile methodologies. A waterfall approach creates new products or versions for release in large increments. These packages may be the result of many months of effort, with a fully functional product meeting a broad set of functional requirements released at the end of the initial development stage. New versions with enhanced features would then be produced in another large development project. This waterfall methodology has become less favored in the technical realm since many factors may have changed during the course of a long development timeline.

Most technical communities instead follow Agile[5] development methodologies. Agile processes organize development into short, well-defined sprints that focus on a set of tasks for features that can be accomplished in a few weeks. The features produced in each sprint can be evaluated and tested more efficiently than an entire finished application. Agile processes approach development in manageable increments, enabling the overall project to be more responsive to end-user needs. Problems with any given area of functionality can be addressed before they are deeply embedded within a complex application.

Agile methodologies also can be applied to nontechnical projects. Rather than treating a lengthy or complex task as a whole and evaluating it when all aspects are complete, Agile methodologies can be followed to break it into smaller activities called sprints. The work associated with each sprint can be evaluated as completed, and the goals or expectations of the overall project can be adjusted as needed.

Transition to Cloud Computing

In today's technology environment, most software applications are used through some form of cloud computing. In previous phases of computing, it was common for organizations to operate software on local servers, but this arrangement is rapidly being replaced. While some remnant legacy implementations remain, all new software applications are developed for deployment on cloud infrastructure, and existing implementations are moving from local servers to some form of hosted infrastructure. This transition from local computing to what is informally called cloud computing brings many fundamental changes in the way that information organizations manage technology.

Cloud computing encompasses a variety of technologies, each with their own distinct characteristics and functionality. Each form of cloud computing in turn comes with different implications for those responsible for managing technology for information organizations. In general, cloud technologies mean less need for the organization's personnel to deal with low-level hardware and software components, enabling them to focus on technical work with more immediate impact. The following section provides an overview of key types of cloud computing: local computing, vendor hosting, and multitenant software-as-a-service (SaaS). For additional context, see also chapter 25: "Cloud Computing Technologies" in the online supplement.

Local Computing

Cloud computing in general contrasts with local computing, a model of technology deployment that depends on servers that reside on the premises of the organization. For major products, such as the integrated library system (ILS), the software would be installed on a server and accessed by information organization personnel through client software installed on their desktop or laptop computers. These systems may also have web-based interfaces that avoid this requirement to install special client software. The client/server architecture distributes the overall set of computer tasks involved for an application between what is handled by the server and others that take place within the client software.

In a local computing environment based on client/server technologies, the functional modules connect to the server component physically housed on the premises of the organization. These modules may be in the form of software installed on desktop or laptop computers or the interfaces may be provided through web browsers. Client/server applications have been developed to serve organizations of all sizes. A consortium can implement a client/server ILS that supports many libraries or branches. The server might, for example, be housed in a facility managed by the consortial office or in a lead institution within the consortium. The users of that system would connect their client applications via the local network or the internet to that server.

Sometimes the server is not necessarily housed directly in the information organization, but may reside in the data center of its parent organization. It is common for a university or municipal IT department to operate a data center for the applications it manages directly and those managed by other departments or units.

The model of local computing comes with a substantial burden for those that manage technology. Some of the key components of a local system requiring attention include the following:

Server, Storage, and Network Hardware: The initial deployment of the system requires the procurement, installation, and configuration of a variety of hardware components. Technical management tasks include tasks such as physical installation of the servers in the data center, updates and configuration of firmware, configuration of storage systems, and establishing connectivity with the local network.

Server Operating System: A locally managed application runs on a specific server operating system such as Microsoft Windows Server or Linux. The operating system must be installed, configured, and optimized according to the specifications of the application. Network security tasks include the configuration of internal and external firewalls to protect the server from external attacks, malware, and other potential problems.

Database Engines: High-performance business applications typically depend on third-party relational database management systems, such as the proprietary products from Oracle or open-source tools like MySQL[6] or PostgreSQL.[7] Management tasks include basic table configuration, resource allocation, and optimization.

Disaster Planning and Recovery: Any business application managed on a local server demands careful attention to implementing measures to protect data in the event of any possible hardware or software failure or through human error. Data must be backed up regularly with the ability to quickly restore data following a failure.

Application Management: In addition to all the components of the operating environment mentioned above, the application itself requires significant attention. The initial installation includes tasks such as configuration of each of the modules to match to organizational structure, business rules, and circulation policies.

The paradigm of local computing and the client/server architecture is declining rapidly. Although legacy installations remain, most new implementations of large-scale systems are based on web-native, multitenant platforms, deployed through hosted infrastructure components. This shift means that many of the areas of specialization needed for individuals working in information organizations will be oriented less on infrastructure and more on user experience, domain functionality, user workflows, and other higher-level concerns.

Vendor Hosting or Application Service Provider

One alternative to the local computing mentioned above involves the same basic configuration of system, but with the server equipment housed and managed by the vendor of the software. The fundamental architecture of how the instance of the software serves the organization remains in place, including the configuration of what information organizations and branches are served by an instance of the software. The only difference is that the server resides in the vendor's data center rather than in that of the information organization. Any client software remains in place, but connects via the internet rather than the network of the information organization or consortium. The model of vendor hosting is recently marketed as a form of software-as-a-service (SaaS), but it was originally described as an application service provider (ASP) arrangement. Library automation vendors have offered their products via ASP since around 1999.

The application service provider model of deployment relieves the information organization of all of the responsibilities that come with a locally managed server as described above. The vendor takes responsibility for the physical hardware platform and all its subsequent components, systems administration for the operating system and network connectivity, security patches, database administration, and some aspects of the management of the application itself. In most cases, the vendor assumes responsibility for disaster planning and recovery and for general data security issues.

A significant set of tasks remains in the domain of technology management in the information organization relative to the vendor-hosted model of application deployment. The systems librarian, for example, might continue to have responsibility for maintaining circulation policy tables, performing data loads, and other routine tasks.

Moving to a hosted arrangement allows the information organization to redirect its technical personnel away from low-level infrastructure management to higher-level activities that potentially focus on tasks with more direct impact to the information organization and its customers. Support of low-level technical infrastructure may not necessarily be a core competency of the information organization and can be provided more efficiently and effectively by specialized organizations that manage large numbers of server instances.

Multitenant Software as a Service (SaaS)

A more current flavor of cloud computing technology is based on a natively web-based platform designed to simultaneously support all the institutional or individual users of an application. Multitenant applications organize the functionality in order to segregate the data and functionality of the software as needed, but all use is supported through a unified platform. A multitenant platform relies on a large number of servers and other hardware components often deployed in data centers distributed across multiple geographic regions, but these components remain entirely transparent to its users.

The multitenant SaaS model simplifies how new versions of an application are deployed. Since there is a single instance of the software that serves all users simultaneously, the concept of needing to install updates on a given server do not apply, at least not from the perspective of the information organization or its users. The provider of the platform can apply bug fixes once that are immediately available for all users. Updates to the software are deployed frequently, providing a continual improvement in capabilities and new features. In most cases, new features are initially provided for testing before they are activated for production use.

From a technology management perspective, the multitenant SaaS model comes with the least need for direct technology management support relative to other deployment models. Most of the support is directed toward functional tasks rather than those relating to technical infrastructure. Tasks related to institutional options for business rules, customized policies, and data loading routines may be required.

Multitenant SaaS platforms involve different methodologies for reporting, data access, and interoperability than those operating on dedicated servers. Since the data of multiple organizations reside within the platform, access to data must be handled through APIs rather than through native access to relational databases or other data stores. Systems librarians or programmers working with older technologies routinely created data extractions or reports using SQL directives. While this was an efficient mechanism for single-tenant implementations, modern platforms expose APIs or have built-in reporting or analytics engines to enable organizations to work with their data.

Widespread Adoption of Mobile Technologies

The ever increasing adoption of smartphones and tablets is a trend that has major implications for the ways information organizations provide access to their collections and deliver their services to their clients. When most software and content products used by information organizations were developed, they were primarily oriented toward web browsers on full-sized devices—laptop and desktop computers. Consumer technology has reshaped itself, with smartphones and tablets now dominating access to the web.

To adequately accommodate mobile devices, all interfaces used by clients, including websites and online catalogs, must follow the principles of responsive design. Responsive sites are not optimized for any specific device, but instead detect the size and capabilities of the device and adapt accordingly. This approach not only adjusts presentation features, such as layout, font size, and orientation, but it can also selectively present functionality according to the capability of the device.

Individuals responsible for managing their organization's use of technology must also monitor usage statistics for each of its web-based services. Either through analysis of usage logs or through services such as Google Analytics, information organizations can analyze very detailed data regarding the client use by each category of mobile device and operating system. Armed with these data, technology managers can focus their attention toward ensuring that each service the organization offers is well optimized for delivery via the most popular devices.

Responsive design can be accomplished in different ways. For example, organizations that directly control their websites can modify the interfaces themselves to incorporate responsive design. This work may require some training and expertise with the content management system used to deploy the site, as well as general web technologies and protocols, such as HTML5, JavaScript, and CSS. Web developers can also incorporate libraries such as Bootstrap,[8] originally created by Twitter, or jQuery[9] to create sophisticated user experience features. Both of these frameworks have been released as open source and are well documented, enabling rapid development of web-based user interfaces. In addition, managers can draw upon experts or develop expertise in the domain of user experience (UX)[10] to ensure that the redesigned site can be easily understood and used (see also chapter 14: "User Experience").

Voice Activated Technology

Consumers increasingly engage with services through voice-activated technologies. Rather than typing commands on a phone or computer keyboard, many systems are now able to process voice commands with exceptional accuracy. This technology has entered the consumer mainstream through a variety of popular services, including:

Siri: the voice-activated digital assistant built into iOS and available on iPhones and iPADs.[11]

Alexa: the voice-activated device created by Amazon capable of performing a wide variety of tasks, ranging from providing answers to questions, playing music, managing smart devices in the home or office, and placing orders on Amazon.[12]

Google Home: the voice-activated device programmed with a rapidly growing set of features, tapping into Google's services. Google Home is able to distinguish voices, enabling it to perform personalized services.[13]

Cortana: the voice interface built into recent versions of Microsoft Windows.[14]

Bixby: the voice-activated assistant available for Android-based mobile phones.[15]

Voice-activated services have not yet seen wide deployment in products created specifically for libraries and related organizations. Voice interfaces can be implemented with existing products and services. The ability to handle voice commands has become an inherent interface in modern desktop and mobile operating environments. Voice command interfaces are routinely used to assist users with disabilities or in support of staff workflows to avoid repetitive motion injuries.

TECHNOLOGIES FOR MANAGING RESOURCES AND AUTOMATING OPERATIONS

Information organizations rely on specialized business applications to automate many aspects of their operations and to describe and manage their collections. From the earliest years of computing, software has been developed to help information organizations automate their work. These systems have evolved through every generation of computer technology, from the early systems based on punch cards, to mainframe computers, to distributed systems based on client/server technology, and most recently to those based on cloud computing technologies. This section discusses key technologies for managing resources and automating operations in information organizations, specifically: integrated library systems, electronic resource management systems, and library services platforms.

Integrated Library Systems

The integrated library system (ILS) emerged as the basic model for information organization automation as computing technologies matured, and it continues to be a core business system used by information organizations to manage their collections. The ILS brings together multiple areas of functionality (e.g., cataloging and circulation) into a single application, in order to operate as an efficient and cohesive system. The ILS emerged prior to the advent of electronic resources, and thus was primarily oriented to the management of print materials. Many different vendors developed ILS products, each with a variety of distinguishing characteristics and relative strengths and weaknesses.

The ILS products available today offer very mature and sophisticated functionality, with thousands of discrete features and options (see textbox 25.2). Understanding the general features of these

Features of Integrated Library Systems

- Cataloging modules provide the capability to create the bibliographic records that describe each item of content.
- Public catalog modules allow clients to interact with the collection.
- Circulation modules manage the lending of physical materials in the collection.
- Acquisitions modules manage the procurement of materials and include placing orders for materials, managing funds used to purchase material, maintaining a database of current suppliers, and other transactions related to the financial component of collection management.
- Serials-control modules are used to manage journals, newspapers, and other subscription-based materials.

systems provides a basic framework for information organizations to identify how they can best use library automation tools and make decisions regarding which new ILS technology to adopt.

Electronic Resource Management Systems

Since integrated library systems are primarily oriented to the management of print resources, these products are not necessarily well equipped to manage the growing number of electronic resources in the collections of most information organizations.

The management of e-journals and other electronic resources involves specialized functionality not available in the standard feature set of the ILS. As a result of this gap in functionality, a number of vendors launched electronic resource management products that offer tools for managing procurement, tracking license terms, analyzing use statistics, identifying overlap of coverage among content packages from different aggregators, and other related tasks. Electronic resource management systems were usually integrated with the knowledge base of a link resolver to provide a repository of titles associated with each information product to enable portfolio-level management rather than title by title.

Despite the gap in functionality in the ILS and the major investments in electronic resources in academic and research libraries, this genre of software saw fairly limited adoption. Many academic libraries found the products on the market cumbersome and challenging to use in parallel with their integrated library systems. Operating an ILS and an electronic resource management system in parallel often meant considerable redundancy in processing workflows. The genre of electronic resource management systems as a separate application has largely given way to the inclusion of this functionality in the new genre of library services platforms discussed below.[16]

Library Services Platforms

As the universe of information resources shifts toward electronic forms of content, the framework of automation ingrained in the ILS may become strained. A new genre of business system for information organizations was developed more recently based on a new framework. These systems, generally termed library services platforms, aim to address the needs of organizations that manage collections comprised of materials in diverse formats, deployed using modern technology architectures. The conceptual designs of the library services platform began to be discussed as early as 2009 with products put into production use beginning in 2011. A considerable portion of the functionality available through library services platforms overlaps with integrated library systems, but there are important differences including the following:

Inherent design to manage multiple types of information organization content: Library services platforms take a comprehensive resource management approach that accommodates multiple types of formats, including different metadata formats, procurement processes, business rules, and access methods for the many different categories of print and digital materials. These platforms at a minimum support comprehensive workflows for electronic resources and print materials; as the genre matured, it has also become used more frequently for managing digital assets and as a publishing platform.

Web-based multitenant platforms: Library services platforms are primarily deployed using web-based, multitenant platforms, aimed at serving multiple types of users. A single global instance of the platform serves many different organizations. This type of deployment enables sharing of common resources, such as knowledge bases, as institutional and personal data are appropriately segregated.

Shared metadata and knowledge bases: These new systems have a sharper focus on bodies of metadata that can be shared globally among all the users of the product.

Service-oriented architecture: Library services platforms tap into the current global IT trend toward service-oriented architecture, which means that software products are built from very small units of functionality, called services, that can be composed to assemble more complex workflows, modules, complete applications, or interoperable product suites.

Robust APIs (application programming interfaces): Robust APIs enable organizations implementing these platforms to create additional functionality as needed, exchange data with other business systems, and create customized data extractions or reports.

Integrated library systems continue to evolve, in many cases gradually reshaping themselves into library services platforms. Organizations that continue to be primarily oriented toward the management of print collections will continue to find that integrated library systems are well suited for their requirements.

Discussion Questions

What are the key differences between library services platforms and integrated library systems?
What kinds of information organizations would be best suited for library services platforms?
What kinds of information organizations are best suited for integrated library systems?

Managing Technology Using New Resource Management Models

These evolving business applications mean that the approach to technology management for information organizations needs to change. For example, to the extent that these new products are deployed through cloud computing, technology managers need to focus on higher-level functionality and services, rather than on administration of hardware, operating systems, and other infrastructure components. The new resource management models require that technology managers think and work more collaboratively as they engage with other organizations using the platform, with less emphasis on self-sufficiency and isolation. Technology managers need to be well versed in many different types of metadata structures, processing workflows, and other characteristics inherent in complex collections spanning diverse formats.

For example, libraries have been deeply engaged in exposing library resources as linked data (see also chapter 12: "Metadata, Cataloging, Linked Data, and the Evolving ILS"). A major initiative is under way to create a linked data implementation for bibliographic description. The Library of Congress, with the support of many partners, has created BIBFRAME as a mapping of MARC21 into linked data.

Although the future of BIBFRAME as the foundation of bibliographic data in the library realm is not certain, it has gained substantial momentum. Most of the developers of integrated library systems and library services platforms have participated in the BIBFRAME initiative and are building support for it as one of the supported metadata formats. Other linked data techniques, such as schema.org, have also been incorporated into online catalogs and discovery interfaces. This evolution will further impact the way that technology managers need to change the way that they do their work.

NEW GENERATIONS OF RESOURCE DISCOVERY TOOLS AND PATRON PORTALS

As information organizations seek new ways to facilitate access to collections and discovery of resources by clients, new tools are continuously developed (see also chapter 25: "Examples of New Generations of Resource Discovery Tools and Patron Portals" in the online supplement). This section addresses a few of these resource discovery tools and patron portals, specifically online catalogs, discovery interfaces, index-based discovery services, library portals, and discovery technologies.

Online Catalog: The online catalog is a long-standing tool for providing client access to resources. In recent years, online catalogs have been redesigned to include more intuitive interfaces. For example, many online catalogs have been extended to provide discovery and lending of e-books through integration with the e-book lending platforms.

Discovery Interfaces: Discovery interfaces are tools designed to provide access to resources through a more modern interface with a scope of search often beyond those accessible through the organization's ILS. Instead, web-based discovery interfaces rely on their own indexes or connectors with external content sources to provide access to an information organization's resources. The interfaces aim to provide a more intuitive user experience and usually follow well-established conventions seen within other web-oriented services, such as a single search box, relevancy-ordered result lists, and facets to narrow results according to applicable categories (e.g., author, subject, date, language, format). Many discovery interfaces depend on integration with the ILS, such as looking up the status of an item in the ILS (e.g., available or checked out to another borrower). Discovery interfaces can also provide access to many other categories of content not included in the ILS, including access to other content repositories maintained by the information organization or resources maintained externally. The distinguishing characteristic of these vendor-based discovery interfaces lies in their independence from any specific ILS.

Index-based Discovery Services: These products are based on a central index that can be used to explore the broad universe of scholarly publishing to enable searchers to discover and access scholarly articles. An alternative term, web-scale discovery services, has also been widely used to describe these products. The indexes of these products address many hundreds of millions if not billions of individual content items, represented by citations, full text, abstracts, or discipline-specific controlled vocabularies. The index-based discovery services are especially oriented to academic libraries, but may be of interest to any organization that makes major investments in access to electronic scholarly content.

Library Portals: Library portals provide a content management environment and other specialized tools to replace the entire information organization website, not just the online catalog. These portals provide an integrated experience for information organization customers, instead of a jarring separation that is often seen between an information organization's website and its online catalog or discovery service.

Discoverability Technologies: In addition to dedicated interfaces for discovery and access of information resources, many organizations are also implementing technologies that strengthen their exposure in non-library interfaces such as Google Scholar, Google Search, Microsoft Academic Search, and other environments. Building on the search engine optimization (SEO) techniques routinely used in the e-commerce realm, libraries can expose their resources as structured data optimized to funnel researchers to the information resources made available by their library. These discoverability techniques include encoding catalog or resource pages according to schema.org so that search engine bots can index the content and use geocoding elements for location-aware services.

Technology Managers and Resource Discovery Tools

Any product used by an information organization to offer client access to resources is a critical part of the services offered by the organization, and as such, professionals responsible for managing technology need to understand how it functions. Technology managers must therefore devote intense attention to these discovery interfaces, portals, and other related tools. This aspect of the information organization's infrastructure is subject to even more rapid change than the tools used by personnel behind the scenes. Organizations may change discovery services, for example, as their collection profile evolves. Since discovery services do not involve transactional data that would need to be migrated, shifting to a new discovery service can be accomplished without significant disruption. While an information organization may retain its integrated library system for a decade or two, it needs to refresh its customer-facing services on a much more accelerated schedule.

> This arena of customer-facing interfaces and tools provides the greatest opportunities for information professionals charged with managing technology to make a positive impact for their institution.

Not only do client expectations continually change, such as the current movement toward using mobile technologies to access resources, but the products available in this space likewise evolve rapidly. Information professionals must be constantly vigilant to ensure that the organization's web presence remains as close as possible to the state of the art for these types of tools. In recent years expectations for web design have changed dramatically. Previous conventions such as placing all important information "above the fold" to be visible on any web browser no longer hold. Instead, many sites are moving to an infinite scroll where information is continuously appended to the bottom of the page. This interface style works well for mobile devices where scrolling is the simplest form of navigation.

This arena of customer-facing interfaces and tools provides the greatest opportunities for information professionals charged with managing technology to make a positive impact for their institution.

EMERGING AND INNOVATIVE TECHNOLOGIES

Many information organizations are relatively conservative in their decisions regarding which technologies they rely on to support their internal operations and manage their collections. The technology that supports their mission-critical infrastructure must be well proven and reliable. Although it is important to ensure that the organization's technology infrastructure is reliable, it is also essential for information professionals to be well versed in new cutting-edge technologies so they can take advantage of useful new technology, implementing these new tools early in their development and adoption cycle (see also chapter 3: "Librarianship: A Continuously Evolving Profession"). Forward-looking leaders show an interest in providing personnel with opportunities to try out new technologies and make them available to clients. After piloting and evaluating new technology, the technologies that organizations incorporate into their operations must be well proven and reliable.

Innovation labs help information professionals identify new technology that may benefit their organization and their clients, providing an opportunity to investigate how the technology could be used by the organization and its clients. For example, many information organizations now have facilities where their clients and their personnel can gain hands-on experience with new and emerging technologies. Such a facility might be thought of as an innovation lab or sandbox to try out new technology products that may or may not eventually move into the mainstream. In innovation labs, explorations of new technology can spark ideas by personnel regarding new services the organization could offer that incorporates use of this new technology. Likewise, clients appreciate opportunities to try out new technologies that may not yet be widely available or affordable. In addition, an innovation lab helps position the organization as cutting edge, willing to continuously explore how to improve its services. The specific technologies that might be part of an innovation lab are naturally going to change frequently. Examples of emerging technologies of current interest to information organizations include iBeacon,[17] which is a technology from Apple that uses low-powered transmitters to interact with persons within an indoor space, and near field communications (NFC),[18] which is technology that enables devices such as smartphones to carry out payments or other transactions.

> Although it is important to ensure that the organization's technology infrastructure is reliable, it is also essential for information professionals to be well versed in new cutting-edge technologies so they can take advantage of useful new technology, implementing these new tools early in their development and adoption cycle.

A related concept comes in the form of what is often called makerspaces (see also chapter 18: "Creation Culture and Makerspaces"). These facilities provide tools that enable clients to design and create content or objects. A makerspace might include a variety of software tools for graphical or physical design, video editing or production, as well as more traditional tools for creating and editing textual information.[19]

Virtual reality technologies continue to mature and are increasingly seeing use in information organizations. These technologies can power impressive virtual tours of an organization's physical facilities and digital collections. Many libraries include virtual reality technologies as part of a makerspace, enabling community members to experience their capabilities. These organizations may also provide assistance and equipment to enable users to develop their own virtual spaces.

MANAGING THE PEOPLE WHO MANAGE TECHNOLOGY

All information organizations' employees are touched by technology due to the nature of their work. Information professionals involved directly in the support and implementation of technology naturally need to have the most in-depth skills and expertise. Some of the categories of skills that an information professional focused on technology might include in their portfolio include:

Programming: Some information professionals may decide to gain proficiency with programming and scripting languages. Programming languages are flexible tools that can be applied to solve an almost infinite array of problems, such as creating customized tools for the organization and interacting with databases and other software applications deployed by the organization (e.g., the ILS). Which programming languages might be of interest will depend on the local environment and the interests of the information professional. Python[20] and Ruby on Rails[21] currently stand out as preferred general-purpose languages. R[22] finds use in many projects involving text analysis; those involved in development of iOS apps for Apple devices might work with Swift. Go,[23] developed by Google, has seen considerable adoption for web application development. Those needing to support legacy sites or products may need to become familiar with programming languages such as PHP[24] or Perl.[25]

Systems Administration: Information professionals should understand the tasks associated with the management of local server installations. These activities span multiple aspects or layers of technology, such as operating systems, network connectivity, security, and configuration of software applications that run on the server. In many organizations, an IT professional will be responsible for these categories of activities. As organizations shift to cloud computing, these skills will become less of a priority.

Metadata: Information professionals should understand metadata and the general concepts and syntactical structures that might be involved in scenarios such as the exchange of data between information systems. Technologists should also have a strong understanding of XML, since it is the underlying syntactical carrier for most metadata and many forms of content. Information professionals must also have a strong grasp of linked data and semantic web technologies. Library metadata formats are increasingly shifting from unit record concepts, such as MARC, to BIBFRAME, a bibliographic description framework based on linked data (see also chapter 12: "Metadata, Cataloging, Linked Data, and the Evolving ILS").

Library Standards and Protocols: Information professionals involved in technology benefit from a basic familiarity with the major standards, such as those provided by the National Information Standards Organization (NISO),[26] plus more detailed understanding of those that are relevant to the key systems used within the organization.

Web Standards and Protocols: Information professionals involved with technology should be familiar with at least the most common and broadly implemented standards overseen by the W3C,[27] which define the basic building blocks of the web. Good starting points are HTML, XML, and CSS, since they are used in almost all content-oriented applications.

Computer Architectures: Information professionals involved in the creation of software will have detailed knowledge of the concepts and implementation details related to development frameworks, such as the services-oriented architecture. The microservices architecture has emerged in recent years as the preferred approach for developing software to support large-scale and complex organizations.

Security and Privacy: Information professionals must have sufficient knowledge of the technologies involved in protecting sensitive data, especially that related to personally identifiable patron data. Organizations must provide their services via secure technologies, such as https, to ensure patron search and display activity cannot be intercepted (see also chapter 34: "Information Privacy and Cybersecurity").

Even a very basic introductory level of knowledge in each of these categories will foster a better understanding of how computer and information systems work. From this foundation of basic concepts, an information professional may need to selectively explore some of the technologies or concepts in more depth, according to areas of interest or focus of responsibility. It is generally not feasible to achieve expert-level mastery of all aspects of technology, but a well-rounded technology professional will have both broad general knowledge in many different areas and deep expertise in a selected area of specialization (see also textbox 25.3).

> It is generally not feasible to achieve expert-level mastery of all aspects of technology, but a well-rounded technology professional will have both broad general knowledge in many different areas and deep expertise in a selected area of specialization.

TEXTBOX 25.3

Essential Competencies for Technology Managers

- Graphic design
- User experience
- Information architecture
- Programming languages
- Content management environments (e.g., Drupal)
- Coding standards (e.g., HTML5 and CSS)

Job Titles Requiring Expertise in Computing Models

- Hardware and network engineers
- System administrators
- Database administrators
- Systems librarians

CONCLUSION

This chapter discussed a wide range of topics that information professionals involved with managing technology will face. The topics covered are not meant to be comprehensive, but to give a selection of real-world examples of the categories of technology currently in place and trends that shaped the current environment. The discussion focused primarily on larger-scale technology that is especially relevant to information organizations, such as integrated library systems, library services platforms, customer-facing discovery services, and e-book lending technologies. Cloud computing has ushered in a new genre of products and services for resource management and discovery. For those charged with managing technology, cloud computing dramatically redefines the profession, shifting away from the need to manage low-level infrastructure to working at a level closer to the users, both clients and the personnel in the organization who depend on these tools to carry out their work. We are now in a new phase where microservices architecture is beginning to take precedent over the service-oriented architecture and development of monolithic applications.

Just as important as the specific trends and technologies described, readers should take away the inevitability of ongoing change in technology and be attuned to shifts in the priorities and strategies of their organizations. The chapter illustrated how some of the products and technologies in place today displaced tools used in earlier generations. Likewise, those tools in place today cannot be considered as final solutions. Rather, they are interim steps along the path to yet another phase in the ongoing quest of information professionals to leverage technologies to support their work. Practitioners in the field should expect to continually master new skills and adapt to each new cycle of technology to avoid stagnation in their career path and enable them to contribute positively to the profession.

NOTES

1. "Elastisearch," Elastic, 2017, https://www.elastic.co/products/elasticsearch.
2. "Solr," Apache Solr, 2017, http://lucene.apache.org/solr/.
3. "Built for Developers," Github, Inc., 2017, https://github.com/.
4. R. Davis, "Git and GitHub for Librarians," *Behavioral & Social Sciences Librarian* 34, no. 3 (2015): 159–64, http://academicworks.cuny.edu/cgi/viewcontent.cgi?article=1034&context=jj_pubs, accessed July 18, 2017.
5. "Agile 101," Agile Alliance, 2015, https://www.agilealliance.org/agile101/.
6. MySQL, 2017, https://www.mysql.com/.
7. PostgreSQL, 2017, https://www.postgresql.org/.
8. Bootstrap, accessed September 9, 2017, http://getbootstrap.com/docs/3.3/.
9. jQuery, 2017, https://jquery.com.
10. Aaron Schmidt and Amana Etches, *User Experience (UX) Design for Libraries*, The Tech Set Series, 18 (Chicago: ALA TechSource, 2012).
11. "Hey Siri, Show Me My Life Goals List," Apple, Inc., 2017, https://www.apple.com/ios/siri/.
12. "Alexa," Amazon Developer, 2017, https://developer.amazon.com/alexa.
13. "Google Home: Voice-Activated Speaker," Made by Google, accessed September 9, 2017, https://madeby.google.com/home/.
14. "Cortana Is Your Truly Personal Digital Assistant," Microsoft, 2017, https://www.microsoft.com/en-us/windows/cortana.
15. "Bixby," Samsung, accessed September 9, 2017, http://www.samsung.com/global/galaxy/apps/bixby/.
16. Marshall Breeding, "The Many Facets of Managing Electronic Resources," *Computers in Libraries* 24, no. 1 (2004): 25; Marshall Breeding, "The Year of ERM," *Smart Libraries Newsletter* 25, no. 3 (2005): 2.
17. "iBeacon," Apple, Inc., 2017, https://developer.apple.com/ibeacon/.
18. "Near Field Communications," NFC, 2017, http://nearfieldcommunication.org/.
19. Erin Fisher, "Makerspaces Move into Academic Libraries," *ACRL TechConnect Blog*, 2012, http://acrl.ala.org/techconnect/?p=2340.
20. Python Software Foundation, 2017, https://www.python.org.

21. "Imagine What You Could Build If You Learned Ruby on Rails," RAILS, accessed September 9, 2017, http://rubyonrails.org.

22. "What Is R?," accessed September 9, 2017, https://www.r-project.org/about.html.

23. "Try Go," The Go Programming Language, accessed September 9, 2017, https://golang.org.

24. "What is PHP?," 2017, http://php.net/manual/en/intro-whatis.php.

25. "About PERL," 2017, https://www.perl.org/about.html.

26. "Welcome to NISO," 2017, http://www.niso.org/home/.

27. "Standards," W3C, 2017, http://www.w3.org/standards/.

26

Managing Data and Data Analysis in Information Organizations

H. Frank Cervone

Chapter 26, "Managing Data and Data Analysis in Information Organizations," defines data management and the basic concepts of data analysis, points out the differences and similarities between administrative and research data management, and explains why data recovery and disaster planning are critical aspects of a data management program. Dr. Frank Cervone, director of information technology and college information security officer for the School of Public Health at the University of Illinois at Chicago, brings his sharp lens to the major issues and concerns related to data management, analysis, and governance in today's information organizations.

Key terms and functions in data management, such as curation, data analysis, and compliance, are critical to the sustainability of the information organization. Organizations use data to help identify both opportunities (e.g., in products, programming, and services) as well as threats (e.g., changed behaviors, economic impacts). With this in mind, the author discusses preservation and business continuity planning, disaster recovery planning, and data cleansing within the information organization. He also delves into the topic of research data management (RDM), a method for managing the life cycle of data in research projects. He then describes data analytics (including predictive analytics) and data mining, two of the essential steps for RDM.

While the focus of data management and analysis may differ across information organizations, Cervone argues that the fundamental concepts remain the same. It is only through these processes that information professionals can better understand information organizations and how they function—greatly increasing the value of their service to their organizations.

★   ★   ★

Data management and data analysis are critical functions in organizations. Without careful curation and analysis of organizational data, organizations cannot effectively function. Data provide the information critical to run organizations' daily operations as well as identify gaps within existing products and services. Perhaps more importantly, data are essential for planning how to evolve to meet future needs and take advantage of opportunities the organization may have to enhance and expand the scope of their products and services.

This chapter focuses on the major issues and concerns related to data management and data analysis in libraries and information organizations. Over a decade ago, data management and data analysis were identified as important skills for information professionals to have.[1] While information professionals have been seen as curators of external scholarship and resources, the volume of administrative data within organizations as well as internal scholarship at universities and research institutions has grown significantly in the past few decades.[2] The strategic gap in many organizations related to data management and analysis was identified as a critical role where information professionals could make a significant contribution.[3]

As this new role has evolved, much of the work related to data management is occurring with partners outside the library or information organization. This evolution is not limited to academia. In the public library, members of the user community increasingly turn to the library with questions related to managing their personal data. In the corporate world, there are similar changes in expectations of the information organization and its staff.[4] One of the striking differences related to work in data management and analysis is that it requires the information professional to venture out into the larger organization and work on projects as a collaborator rather than within the silo of the information organization.

Data management and data analysis are critical competencies for information professionals. After completing this chapter, the reader should have an understanding of:

- what data management means in its various contexts,
- the differences and similarities between administrative and research data management,
- why data recovery and disaster planning are critical aspects of a data management program,
- the basic concepts of data analysis, data visualization, and data governance, and
- some of the more commonly used tools in each of these functional areas.

WHAT IS DATA MANAGEMENT?

Data management is quickly becoming a major service as academic libraries help faculty and researchers manage, store, and share their research data in accordance with governmental and funder requirements (see also chapter 7: "Learning and Research Institutions: Academic Libraries"). Data management is also of interest to public librarians because helping citizens manage and curate their personal data offers a major opportunity for service to the community (see also chapter 8: "Community Anchors for Lifelong Learning: Public Libraries").

The Data Management Association (DAMA) has defined data management as the "development, execution and supervision of plans, policies, programs and practices that control, protect, deliver and enhance the value of data and information assets."[5]

DAMA's definition leads to the question, "What is a data and information asset?" The answer is not as straightforward as it may seem. In a corporate environment, data and information assets typically originate in applications that are used to run the business (see also chapter 9: "Working in Different Information Environments: Special Libraries and Information Centers"). For example, data from an order entry system or a human resource system are a data asset. A locally developed database that contains competitive analysis of other organizations' information, such as sales and financial data, could be a strategic data asset.

A data asset is also derived from applications, but in an educational environment, these applications are often considered differently than they are in the commercial sector. In the university setting, for example, faculty would not consider the student information system (SIS) as an application used to "run the business" even though it performs many of the functions relating to the management of students and their academic programs. The same is true of learning management systems (LMS). While much of the information in an LMS is learning material, the data collected about student and faculty interactions with the material and each other function as information assets, which can be used to help understand issues related to the effectiveness of learning materials as well as curriculum pathways.

In libraries and information organizations, the situation is further complicated because data assets may be external to the organization and out of direct control. Research literature databases that libraries subscribe to are clear examples of this. These databases would be considered data assets. In fact, they are often the primary "product" of the library. They differ from organizational applications in that the data in research literature databases are often not directly manageable by the organization. This can create limitations because information related to the data assets may not be readily available for analysis by the library or information organization.

TEXTBOX 26.1

Data Assets in a Library

Data assets in a library include a wide variety of electronic information, each of which has different requirements for acquisition and management. Examples include:

- catalog records in a library management system;
- catalog records in a shared utility such as OCLC;
- journal article databases;
- e-book collections;
- bibliographies created by the library;
- digitized special collections;
- course reserves;
- interlibrary loan materials;
- streaming media;
- circulation, acquisition, and payment data in an LMS; and
- configuration data in discovery layer tools such as Primo or Summon.

How data management and data analysis functions are implemented within an organization depends on the organization size, type, and structure. In the library or in large organizations with a library, administration of electronic resource information is a shared responsibility with the cataloging or technical services department taking the lead in capturing and maintaining bibliographic types of information.

Outside of libraries, the situation is quite different. In smaller organizations, both data management and data analysis are often performed by a single department located within the information technology function. In mid-sized organizations, or large organizations that are highly centralized, the responsibilities may be divided between several departments with data management usually situated within information technology and data analysis housed in a business analysis unit, which may be organizationally accountable to the IT organization. In very large organizations, such as a major research university or a large multinational corporation, both functions are often distributed throughout the organization in various local or line-of-business IT and analysis units.

Regardless of whether data are sales information, library database usage statistics, or student interaction information from an LMS, this type of data is known as "run the business data" because it is the raw information collected at the application level.[6] It is subsequently used to integrate data across an organization, such as matching student enrollment data from an SIS to learning objectives in courses within an LMS. This can then be extended to analysis by correlating patterns in student enrollment data from the SIS with achievement of learning outcomes from courses in an LMS. Another example would be when a library compares the number of citations in student theses and dissertations to the usage statistics of databases they subscribe to in order to make collection development decisions.

ADMINISTRATIVE DATA MANAGEMENT

While there are many factors to consider in administrative data management, the two most critical functions are ensuring that data are recoverable and that data are accurate.

Depending on the organization, data preservation means different things. From an administrative perspective, and certainly in the corporate environment, data preservation is focused on business continuity planning and disaster recovery (BCP/DR). While this aspect is also important in libraries and information organizations, the scope of data preservation is often more broadly construed to include ensuring that data remain accessible for extended periods. This difference in accessibility is important because this is not necessarily a goal in many corporate systems.

> While there are many factors to consider in administrative data management, the two most critical functions are ensuring that data are recoverable and that data are accurate.

Regardless of the context, the goals and outcomes of business continuity planning (BCP) are the same: ensuring the organization can survive a catastrophic event. BCP is the methodology used to create and validate a plan for maintaining operations before, during, and after a disruptive event.[7] Disaster recovery is a component of a BCP. Information technology organizations are typically focused on addressing the immediate recovery of data assets after a specific type of event so that the organization can implement its business continuity plan.

Viewed another way, disaster recovery provides for recovery of information technology after a disruptive event, whereas BCP is "the process of ensuring your organization can continue doing business even when its normal facilities or place of business is unavailable"[8] (see also chapter 25: "Managing Technology").

Data Recovery and Disaster Recovery Planning

A fundamental component of planning for data recovery after a disaster is developing a disaster recovery plan (DRP). A disaster recovery plan documents how an organization will recover from data loss in the event of a major incident related to information technology.

In some environments, especially those that are highly reliant on large-scale processing of database transactions, data recovery may be facilitated by *replication*, which is the process of frequently copying data from one storage medium to another. This safeguards that there is always a duplicate copy of the data available. Replication can be performed in three ways: snapshot, transactional, and merge replication.[9] More information about these replication processes is available in chapter 26 of the online supplement.

In most environments though, data recovery is implemented through a more traditional "back up and restore" function.[10] While conceptually the process is simple—back up data on a regular basis so that it can be restored in the event it is accidentally deleted, corrupted, or destroyed—the implementation of a viable and robust strategy for data recovery is usually quite complex, involving many different decisions on the part of the organization.

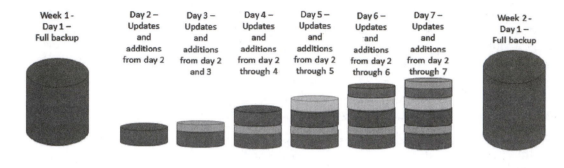

Cumulative differential backup series

Incremental differential backup series

Figure 26.1 Data Backup Schemes—Cumulative Differential versus Incremental Differential. *Created by author.*

Depending on the nature of the data, it may not be feasible to take a full backup of all data every day. In this case, an organization may choose to use an alternate method of data backup to expedite backup processing (see figure 26.1: Data Backup Schemes—Cumulative Differential versus Incremental Differential). For large administrative systems, differential incremental or cumulative incremental backups are often used to minimize the time required for daily backups as well as minimize the overall storage requirements of backup media. In a cumulative incremental backup, every new cumulative backup includes all of the new or changed data since the last full backup. Consequently, the amount of time each subsequent cumulative backup takes will increase as the amount of accumulated data increases. In a differential incremental backup, only the new or changed data since the last backup is included, regardless of whether the last backup was full or differential. Therefore, the amount of time a differential incremental backup takes tends to remain consistent from backup to backup since it is only capturing the new or changed data since the last backup. The primary factor in deciding between which method to use is often a balance between recovery time in the event of a disaster versus the amount of time needed on a regular basis to perform the incremental backup.

For most applications, a retention cycle is also defined. Particularly when using a differential incremental backup scheme, a retention cycle must take into account the retention of all backups that might be required if data needs to be restored. A commonly used scheme is the daily-weekly-monthly-yearly cycle.

H. Frank Cervone

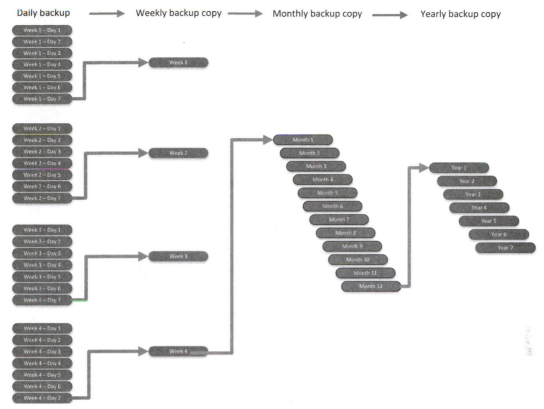

Figure 26.2 Data Backup Retention Schemes. *Created by author.*

In the scheme presented in figure 26.2, the cycle starts with a full backup, then an incremental (either cumulative or incremental) backup is taken each day. At the end of the week, another full backup is taken. This backup is retained as the weekly backup. The last weekly full backup in a month is retained as the monthly backup. Finally, the last monthly full backup is stored as the yearly backup. This scheme provides the organization with the ability to restore data from the past if questions should ever arise related to past activity related to the data.

An organization's DRP documents state, in writing, all of the decisions made regarding the data backup cycle methodology used as well as any exceptions or modifications to that plan that apply to specific circumstances. In addition, a DRP documents the specific procedures that must be used to recover data and information systems in the wake of a disaster.

Business Continuity Planning

While data recovery is a critical function of data management, it is not sufficient for ensuring organizational continuity after a disaster. An organization should also develop a business continuity plan (BCP) that outlines how to restore and maintain operations after various *types* of disaster scenarios, including:

- natural disasters, such as hurricanes, tornadoes, earthquakes;
- human-caused problems, such as accidental file deletion, data corruption due to an incorrect sequence of processing commands; or
- accidents and technological hazards, such as those that involve a water main burst or accidental discharge of a fire suppression system.

The organization must consider how quickly data need to be restored, known as recovery time objectives, as well as what the objectives of specific types of recovery are (recovery point objectives). For example, the objective of a recovery in the event of a disaster may be to simply provide basic services by the end of the second day after the disaster with other specified services restored according to a predefined timetable, whereas the recovery point objective for an accidental file deletion might be full recovery of data within four hours.

When developing either a disaster recovery plan or business continuity plan the organization also must consider the legal and regulatory obligations under which they operate. For example, hospitals and health care systems in the United States must meet stringent recovery and resumption expectations that are required under the Health Insurance Portability and Accountability Act (HIPAA).[11]

Check This Out

More information about constructing business continuity plans is available from professional organizations such as DRI International in the United States: https://www.drii.org/ and the Business Continuity Institute in the United Kingdom: http://www.thebci.org/.

Data Cleansing

The other major function of data management is ensuring that data are accurate. This is typically referred to as *data cleansing* or *data scrubbing*—a set of processes used to ensure data quality and integrity.[12] Specific techniques used to clean data vary widely depending on the nature of the data itself. They can, however, be grouped into several broad categories[13] and include:

- validation of constraints to ensure validity, such as ensuring course numbers are within correct ranges (bachelor's courses 100–499, master's 500–699, doctoral 700–799);
- normalizations to ensure that data inconsistencies are corrected, such as changing an incorrect code to a correct one;
- format transformations to enforce a consistent standard on structured data (such as dates, times, or telephone numbers); and
- de-duplication of records that are functionally equivalent.

In general, systems should be designed to avoid the need for data cleansing. An example of proactive data management would be to create a taxonomy to be used for a specific data element. Library of Congress subject headings (see also chapter 12: "Metadata, Cataloging, Linked Data, and the Evolving ILS") are an example of this as would be a predefined list of codes, such as the standard state abbreviations. Where complex relationships exist between data elements, such as when the selection of a particular value in one data element implies selection of a set of specific values in another data element, an ontology might be more appropriate.

RESEARCH DATA MANAGEMENT

While research data management (RDM) is not a new concept, it has gained more attention in recent years due to the increased interest on the part of governments in promoting data sharing from grant-funded research, particularly in the sciences.

In its most basic form, RDM is a method for managing the life cycle of data in research projects, from project inception to dissemination of research results. A major focus of information organizations that

H. Frank Cervone

are involved in RDM initiatives is on the archiving and preservation of research data. From the researcher's perspective, the most important aspect of RDM is how the plan facilitates making the research process more efficient.[14] RDM also has to meet the expectations and requirements of the funding organization, the research institution, and any regulations or legislative rules that may apply. In the majority of cases, the goals of these stakeholders focus on ensuring the reliable verification of results, as well as providing easy access to data to further build upon the existing research.[15]

> " A major focus of information organizations that are involved in RDM initiatives is on the archiving and preservation of research data. From the researcher's perspective, the most important aspect of RDM is how the plan facilitates making the research process more efficient. "

Data Management Plans

To facilitate RDM objectives, many research projects now require that a data management plan (DMP) be submitted with any funding proposal. The DMP must describe how the research team will create data, share data with collaborators, protect and store data, and make data available to other researchers.

For example, the National Science Foundation (NSF)[16] requires researchers in computer and information science to develop a DMP (check out chapter 26: "National Science Foundation's Data Management Plan Requirements" in the online supplement).

While the basic elements of a DMP are similar across disciplines, the vast majority of work academic libraries perform in conjunction with researchers focuses on DMPs in the STEM (science, technology, engineering, and math) fields. Different funding agencies often have unique sets of requirements, which vary in level of complexity and detail required. For example, the Institute of Museum and Library Services (IMLS) currently does not have any specific requirements other than that some type of DMP should exist. NSF has very detailed and specific requirements, but these requirements vary depending on the discipline. As such, NSF has different requirements for DMPs in the biological sciences, education and human resources, engineering, geosciences, and so on.[17]

What Is Data Analysis?

Data analysis, sometimes also referred to as *data analytics*, is the practical application of quantitative and qualitative techniques in order to extract and derive meaning from collected data. While much of the current literature is focused on business applications, data analysis can be used in a wide variety of organizations to identify and analyze behavioral data and patterns.

A well-known application of data analysis in the commercial sector is Amazon's "other customers bought" suggestions. In libraries, recommender services (such as Ex Libris's bX product) use search and retrieval data gathered from hundreds of academic institutions to develop individualized recommendations for other relevant literature in response to a researcher's search inquiry. In higher education, analysis of student behavioral patterns within an online course can be compared to their performance outcomes to understand how learning activities may be better ordered to enhance learning. These same data, in

---

TEXTBOX 26.2

Functions for Data Analysis

In most organizations, data analysis is used to

- improve productivity,
- gain a better understanding of an organizational issue, and
- predict future outcomes.

---

aggregate, can be used to analyze overall academic performance in programs to determine the best sequence in which students should take courses.

Various types of tools can be used for data analysis. The original data analysis tools were programming languages, such as COBOL.[18] Report generators, such as IBM's RPG programming language, were developed to ease the creation of reports and analyses of data.[19] Today, data analysis is a much more sophisticated and complex undertaking, encompassing a number of specialized tools and techniques.

A critical component in facilitating the analysis of data across the organization is a data warehouse. Sometimes referred to as an online analytical processing system (OLAP), a data warehouse is used for the long-term storage of data and usually provides a common system for reporting and analyzing data. Essentially a database of databases, it provides a stable, wide range of historical information in a normalized manner that can be analyzed in depth.

The normalization of the data occurs as a result of the extract, transform, and load process (ETL). ETL is often discussed as a singular entity, but the process involves several different component processes. In the first step, data are extracted (unloaded) from a source database, such as a library management system or an organization's accounting system.

In the second step, the data are transformed in various ways. The data may be standardized in terms of permissible values, size of the data elements, or format. These transformations are defined through *business rules* that describe how data are to be modified based on various conditions. Other transformations are possible as well. Data from one or more source databases may be combined to create new data elements. Records from an original source may be summarized to create a "golden" record that is the preserved record. For example, in a student information record in the data warehouse, individual grade change records (i.e., midterm grade, incomplete, withdrawal, final grade) in the SIS may be summarized to only reflect the final status and grade at the end of a semester.

Finally, when the data have been appropriately transformed, they are loaded into the data warehouse. This may be a simple process or it may be quite complex, particularly if data are being added to an existing data warehouse. In this case, integrity checks, such as ensuring that duplicate data are not loaded, are required to maintain the validity of the data within the warehouse.

While a data warehouse is not a prerequisite for *data mining*, this is one of the primary applications of a data warehouse. Data mining is a process that an organization uses to analyze large amounts of data to discover relationships and patterns that may not be obvious. The end goal in searching for these relationships is to have a better understanding of organizational issues or foster new insight into how to deliver better services or products. In a library, data mining could be used to understand how various segments of the user community use the resources of the library. An example of this would be to analyze patterns in circulation data with the goal of more clearly tailoring services and resources to specific communities based on their usage patterns.

The biggest area of interest in data analytics today uses artificial intelligence (AI) and machine learning to implement *predictive analytics*, which help an organization understand what might happen in the future. While there are many techniques that can be used to provide predictive analytics, some of the most common include the following:

Text mining is the analysis of natural language, often using statistical techniques, to uncover patterns and meaning that can only be discovered through context and patterns of relationships.

Pattern discovery is the recognition of occurrences or sequences that frequently arise in an effort to understand how these occurrences and sequences are related and therefore relationships within the data.

Cluster analysis is the process of analyzing data elements to understand both how data coalesce into groups (clusters) based on how they share similar characteristics as well as how clusters differ from each other.

Data Visualization

Closely associated with analytics is data visualization, which, as one might expect, presents information in image form rather than traditional text-based formats. Data visualization has been rapidly adapted for many types of applications because of the significant advantage it provides in highlighting issues of note within a data set.

Consider the example of capacity utilization in a hospital that is the primary trauma center for a region. Trauma victims are sent to these facilities first as they are best equipped to deal with such cases. However, as multiple patients may arrive in quick succession during times of crisis, it is extremely important for the hospital to know at all times whether it has the capacity to serve additional trauma victims. In many hospitals, there is a hierarchy of capacity ranging from situations where

- the patient load is manageable (optimal),
- the hospital is approaching maximum capacity (warning),
- patients that are not in critical condition should be diverted to other hospitals (critical), and
- any arriving patient must be sent elsewhere because there is no capacity (diversion).

When these data are presented in a traditional tabular format (figure 26.3), the actual status is not immediately evident. The person viewing the table must know from memory where the critical cutoff points are.

Time	Utilization
12:00 AM	470
1:00 AM	474
2:00 AM	465
3:00 AM	480
4:00 AM	482
5:00 AM	482
6:00 AM	484
7:00 AM	486
8:00 AM	480
9:00 AM	479
10:00 AM	483
11:00 AM	486
12:00 PM	490
1:00 PM	496
2:00 PM	500
3:00 PM	503
4:00 PM	506
5:00 PM	503
6:00 PM	515
7:00 PM	503
8:00 PM	506
9:00 PM	490
10:00 PM	480
11:00 PM	464

Figure 26.3 Hospital-Bed Utilization Presented as Text in a Table. *Created by author.*

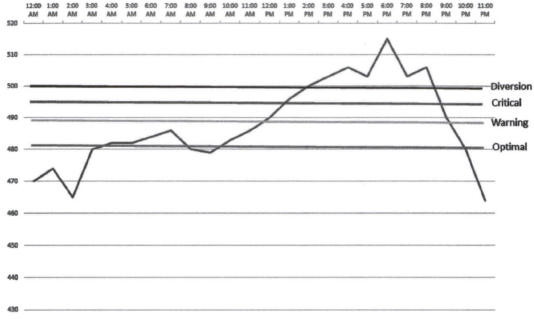

24 Hour Utilization Trend

Figure 26.4 Hospital-Bed Utilization Presented in Visual Form. *Created by author.*

Compare this to figure 26.4, where the data are presented visually. It is immediately clear when there are no capacity-related issues: where the trend count remains below the optimal line. As the number of patients increases, it is immediately evident when capacity concerns elevate, crossing over the warning, critical, and diversion lines.

Visualizations are often combined onto a single page known as a *data dashboard*. With a dashboard, a person can see the status of several *key performance indicators* (KPIs) and make assessments quickly. KPIs are measures an organization collects systematically to evaluate factors they believe are critical to meeting service expectations. In figure 26.4, the obvious KPI is utilization. However, this visualization also indicates that patient discharges do not follow the normal pattern. Typically, the goal is to have patient discharges as early in the day as possible. The visualization, in this case, tells the hospital that something is awry, and the cause of the late discharges should be investigated.

TEXTBOX 26.3

Key Performance Indicators

Key performance indicators (KPIs) are used in a broad range of contexts in the information organization setting. Examples include:

- Ninety-eight percent of all copy cataloging transactions will be completed with only a single editing session.
- Ninety percent of eligible digitization requests will be fulfilled within three working days.
- Uptime for the resource discovery system will be maintained at 99.9 percent availability 24/7 except for scheduled downtimes.

H. Frank Cervone

Qualitative Versus Quantitative Data

In general, the measures on a dashboard are *quantitative data*, which are data that can be measured in some objective manner, such as web page views per month, the number of completed applications, or the average duration in minutes of a patient visit. This is in contrast to *qualitative data*, which are data that are not directly measurable but can be categorized, such as perception of smells or physical attractiveness; this term is also used to refer to data that must be interpreted in some way, such as free-form text in an open-ended survey question or the transcript of an interview.

Traditionally, data types have been further categorized based on how the data may be analyzed. For quantitative data, there are two data types:

1. *Discrete data* are typically measured in integers (i.e., whole numbers). Discrete data are things that are counted, and the count cannot be made more precise. Often, the values are finite. For instance, the number of page views on a website is discrete data because this is counting an action (page views) that cannot be further divided. That is, it is not possible to have 2.5 page views.
2. *Continuous data* are often measured in real numbers because the data points represent a continuous range of values. For example, distance is a continuous value because there is always a more accurate measure, such as miles vs. yards vs. feet vs. inches vs. millimeters vs. micrometers, etc. The accuracy of continuous data is limited only by the level of precision used.

For qualitative data, there are three basic data types:

1. *Binary (dichotomous) data* can take only one of two values such as true/false, yes/no, or on/off.
2. *Ordinal data* can be categorized, often based on quantitative data, where there is an inherent relationship between categories. For example, class letter grades are based on a numeric value and categorized in levels such as A, B, C, D, F.
3. *Nominal data* can be categorized, but there is no inherent order or relationship between the categories. For example, media types might be categorized as CD, DVD, Blu-ray, and streaming. There is no inherent order to these types.

STATISTICAL BASIS OF DATA ANALYSIS

Being familiar with the basic concepts of statistics is critical to understanding the underlying characteristics of data, which in turn is a prerequisite to success in analytics, as well as data visualization. Analyses in a dashboard or visualization are based on statistical analysis of the data points in a data set. The individual data points are referred to as *observations*.

Statistical analysis is either descriptive or inferential. Descriptive statistics report on the characteristics of data. They are used to report on the current state of affairs. Descriptive statistics measures include a broad range of techniques:

> Being familiar with the basic concepts of statistics is critical to understanding the underlying characteristics of data, which in turn is a prerequisite to success in analytics, as well as data visualization.

- *Central tendency*, which includes the
  - mean (the average value within a set of values),
  - median (the value in the middle of a range of measures), and
  - mode (the most commonly occurring value in a set of numbers);

- *Measures of dispersion*, such as
  - quartile analysis (where a value falls, assuming a distribution of all observations into four equally divided ranges),
  - deviation (the difference between an individual observation and the average of all observations),
  - variance (the amount of deviation within the data set as a whole), and
  - the standard deviation (the amount of deviation within which an observation can vary before falling outside a "normal" range in the data set); and

- *Data shape*, which includes skewness (how symmetrical the distribution of data are in relationship to the mean) and kurtosis (how much the data tend to cluster around the mean).

Descriptive statistics are often used to identify *outliers* (observations that lie outside of the typical range within a set of observations). Identification of outliers is important because it allows the researcher to find observations that are unusual or noteworthy. For example, in the set {31, 39, 40, 32, 1, 35, 37, 43, 102, 44, 32, 32, 37}, the values of 1 and 102 are clearly outliers as they are, respectively, much smaller and larger than the values in the rest of the set. Often, outliers are indicative of incorrect data.

In comparison, inferential statistics are used for hypothesis testing and to predict outcomes or relationships. When used in hypothesis testing, inferential tests are used to determine if there is (the alternative hypothesis, H1) or is not (the null hypothesis, H0) an association or difference between variables. Inferential tests are also used to predict outcomes with techniques, such as a trend analysis. Inferential statistics may be either *parametric* or *nonparametric*, the difference being whether the data to be analyzed are normally distributed (parametric) or they are not (nonparametric).

Discussion Questions

What are the distinguishing characteristics of descriptive and inferential statistics? Why are each critical to comprehensive data analysis?

Finally, the sample size is a critical factor in ensuring that statistical tests, and the analytics derived from them, are valid. In an ideal world, every single observation would be included in an analysis. In many big data projects, this is possible. However, in many situations, only a sample of the data may be available for analysis. In this case, the researcher must ensure that the data to be analyzed are representative of the total population. If the sample of data available to the researcher is too small, it will likely not be representative. This can be a major problem because errors in sampling may lead the researcher to incorrect conclusions.

TOOLS FOR DATA MANAGEMENT AND ANALYSIS

When looking at tools for data management, there is a considerable range of software that is used, depending on the nature of the data and the point in the data life cycle in which the tool is being used.

Cleaning and transforming data can be complicated. In general, data cleansing and transformation are performed with specialized tools that are usually associated with the underlying database or data system used to store the data. However, an independent tool used in many environments, especially in research contexts, is OpenRefine.[20] Originally developed by Google and now a community-supported open-source project, it is a multifunctional tool that can:

- import and convert data in various formats,
- transform data (from text to numeric, etc.),
- extract and reduce data elements that contain multiple values,
- filter and partition data, and
- perform advanced operations using the General Refine Expression (GRE) language.

For administrative data, perhaps the most familiar tool for data analysis is Microsoft's Excel. While often thought of as "just a spreadsheet" program, Excel has been enhanced over the years to incorporate very sophisticated analytic capabilities and is the basis for much of Microsoft's online analytics platform. Excel has extensive statistical analysis capabilities as well. For many administrative staff, particularly in the corporate environment, Excel is a suitable platform for their needs.

However, in the world of research, there are several different platforms that are used for statistical analysis, such as the following:

- SAS,[21] often used in public health, government, and business.
- SPSS,[22] often used in social science fields.
- Stata,[23] often used in the sciences in general.
- Minitab,[24] often used in a teaching environment to familiarize students with basic statistical concepts.
- An open-source solution to statistical analysis is available in the R programming language.[25]

While many of these statistical tools also have add-on modules that provide data mining and visualization functionality, many organizations use stand-alone tools to perform these functions. In the commercial sector, Tableau[26] is a popular tool for creating visualizations given its streamlined and intuitive user interface. For data mining, many organizations use tools with open-source options, such as KNIME or RapidMiner,[28] both for philosophical and financial reasons. Additionally, Microsoft's Power BI tool set[29] is popular in academic and nonprofit environments that have a discounted licensing agreement with Microsoft.

Some tools incorporate options that allow an organization to host and analyze their data in the cloud. For example, while Power BI can be used stand-alone, when combined with the cloud-based Azure platform[30] the organization can store their data in the cloud and display analyses in web-accessible dashboards.

With the increasing reliance on cloud-based solutions, some data management tools are solely cloud-based. Qualtrics Research Core[31] provides a data collection and statistical analysis tool hosted entirely in the cloud. For many researchers, having the ability to use one tool, managed by a trusted provider, to both gather and analyze data is a significant advantage. In addition to alleviating issues related to errors introduced when transferring responses from one tool to another, it also helps ensure data security by having a single, trusted platform. Similarly, many libraries use tools such as Counting Opinions[32] to gather survey and performance data for many of the same reasons.

In many research environments, an additional concern is how to manage and archive research data for long-term storage. Funding agencies increasingly require data to be made available for analysis and validation for a period of time, often up to ten years, after research funding has ended. As a result of this need, consortiums of universities and research institutions have formed to address the many issues related to this. Check out various examples of digital management plans in chapter 26 of the online supplement.

In the area of long-term data management and storage, the CKAN project[33] is a data management system that provides tools to publish, share, and find data. In a similar vein, the DataVault platform[34] is a joint project of the University of Manchester and the University of Edinburgh under the auspices of JISC[35] to provide similar functionality.

DATA GOVERNANCE

Running a library, or any organization, on a series of unconnected and disparate information assets, such as locally managed Microsoft Access databases, is unacceptable in today's world.[36] Therefore, organizations with a mature data management model also have a data governance model in place because it is a vital component of an effective overall data management process and because the data governance model is the major factor in ensuring that repeatable and compliant practices are used[37] throughout the organization.

The overarching purpose of data governance is to manage data assets using a holistic perspective in order to ensure data can be trusted. In addition, data governance helps ensure data within the organization meet the needs of the entire organization rather than specific or idiosyncratic requirements of a single organizational unit. Balancing the needs at the local and organizational level can be complicated, but a data governance model provides an agreed-upon structure allowing multiple stakeholders' needs to be met (see textbox 26.4).

TEXTBOX 26.4

Data Governance Initiatives

Examples of data governance initiatives driven by external requirements:

- Ensuring the copyright law is maintained in relationship to materials the library may provide.
- Protection of health data as required by HIPAA regulations in the United States.
- The GDPR (General Data Protection Regulation) to protect personal information in the European Union.

In the typical data governance model, there are two major foci: designating accountability for information quality and defining how data can be used and by whom. In some cases, lines of accountability are clear as in the case of the library being responsible for the management, maintenance, and preservation of information in the online public access catalog (OPAC). However, in other areas, it may not be as clear cut, such as in a large multinational corporation that may require multiple accounting systems because of differing local requirements. A good data governance model would provide a clear framework for managing, maintaining, and preserving the data at the organization level, regardless of which local system the data are in or came from.

Implementing data governance is not simple—nor is it something that emerges as a fully conceptualized plan. Rather, it is an incremental process an organization engages in to fully realize the benefits of their data assets.[38] A good data governance program "encourages the understanding and management of data from both business and technical perspectives, plus it promotes the importance of data as a valuable resource, allowing the organization to use its data confidently to satisfy regulatory and other business needs."[39]

Discussion Questions

Within your organization, what do you see as the major benefits of implementing a data governance plan? What challenges might you anticipate to implementing such a plan?

CONCLUSION

Data management and data analysis are critical functions in organizations of all types. Within information organizations, traditional roles related to data management have focused on curating bibliographic records and, especially in academic libraries, materials related to external research. As information professionals take on new roles to better meet the needs of the larger organizations in which they work, an additional focus of data management has evolved that concentrates on the management of internally created data resources. These resources may be related to research within the organization or simply the data used to manage and guide the organization's operations. Regardless of the focus in a particular context, data management and data analysis are important skills for today's information professional.

While the conception and focus of data management differ among public, academic, and corporate environments, the fundamental concepts are consistent. Correct classification of data, whether through metadata or other means, is desirable across all environments. Data recovery, particularly in the context of disaster recovery planning and business continuity planning, is a critical function in ensuring both library and organizational data assets are preserved in a sustainable manner.

Data analysis is closely related to data management. Through the use of both quantitative and qualitative techniques, information professionals extract and derive meaning from collected data. While often thought of as a "business" function, data analysis is a critical skill for other information professionals because it is only through data analysis that information professionals can better understand information organizations and how they function. With this understanding, information professionals can identify and analyze data for patterns of behavior that might provide insight into how to improve products and services.

Data management and data analysis are critical competencies for information professionals today. By combining these skills with an understanding of data governance frameworks and how to implement them, information professionals can greatly increase the value of their service to their organization.

NOTES

1. Tony Hey and Jessie Hey, "e-Science and Its Implications for the Library Community," *Library Hi Tech* 24, no. 4 (2006): 515–28.
2. Taylor Stang, "Librarians: The New Research Data Management Experts," *Elsevier Connect* (blog), 2016, https://www.elsevier.com/connect/librarians-the-new-research-data-management-experts.
3. Neil Rambo, "Research Data Management: Roles for Libraries," Issue Brief, *Ithaka S+R*, October 22, 2015.
4. James Matarazzo and Toby Perlstein, "New Management Realities for Special Libraries," *Online Searcher* 40, no. 3 (2016), http://www.infotoday.com/OnlineSearcher/Articles/Features/New-Management-Realities-for-Special-Librarians-110761.shtml.
5. Mark Mosley and Michael Brackett, eds., *The DAMA Guide to the Data Management Body of Knowledge (DAMA-DMBOK)*, first edition (Middletown, DE: Technics Publications, 2010), 4.
6. T. Hammergren, *Data Warehousing for Dummies*, second edition (Hoboken, NJ: John Wiley & Sons, 2009).
7. Susan Snedaker, *Business Continuity and Disaster Recovery Planning for IT Professionals*, second edition (Waltham, MA: Syngress-Elsevier, 2014).
8. Thomas R. Peltier, Justin Peltier, and John Blackley, *Information Security Fundamentals* (Boca Raton, FL: CRC Press, 2004), 171.
9. "Types of Replication: Microsoft Docs–SQL Relational Databases," Microsoft, last accessed May 1, 2017, https://docs.microsoft.com/en-us/sql/relational-databases/replication/types-of-replication.
10. David B. Little and David A. Chapa, *Implementing Backup and Recovery* (Hoboken, NJ: John Wiley & Sons, 2003).

11. Under HIPAA §164.308(7)(i).

12. Jonathan Maletic and Andrian Marcus, "Data Cleansing: A Prelude to Knowledge Discovery," in *Data Mining and Knowledge Discovery Handbook*, ed. Oded Maimon and Lior Rokach, second edition (New York: Springer, 2010), 19–32.

13. Felix Naumann and Melanie Herschel, *An Introduction to Duplicate Detection* (San Rafael, CA: Morgan & Claypool Publishers, 2009).

14. Binny Krishnankutty et al., "Data Management in Clinical Research: An Overview," *Indian Journal of Pharmacology* 44, no. 2 (2012): 168–72, doi:10.4103/0253-7613.93842.

15. Angus Whyte and Jonathan Tedds, "Making the Case for Research Data Management," Digital Curation Centre, last accessed May 10, 2017, http://www.dcc.ac.uk/resources/briefing-papers/making-case-rdm.

16. "CISE Data Management Guidelines," National Science Foundation, last modified May 15, 2015, https://www.nsf.gov/cise/cise_dmp.jsp.

17. "Dissemination and Sharing of Research Results," National Science Foundation, last accessed May 13, 2017, https://www.nsf.gov/bfa/dias/policy/dmp.jsp.

18. Jean E. Sammet, "The Early History of COBOL," *ACM SIGPLAN Notices* 13, no. 8 (1978): 121–61, doi:10.1145/960118.808378.

19. W. C. McGee, "Data Base Technology," *IBM Journal of Research and Development* 25, no. 5 (1981): 505–19, doi:10.1147/rd.255.0505.

20. OpenRefine, http://openrefine.org.

21. SAS, http://www.sas.com.

22. SPSS, http://www.spss.com.

23. Stata, http://www.stata.com.

24. Minitab, http://www.minitab.com/en-US/.

25. R programming language, https://www.r-project.org/.

26. Tableau Software, http://www.tableau.com.

27. KNIME, http://www.knime.org.

28. RapidMiner, https://rapidminer.com/.

29. Power BI, https://powerbi.microsoft.com/en-us/.

30. "What Is Azure?," Microsoft Azure, https://azure.microsoft.com/en-us/overview/what-is-azure/.

31. Qualtrics Research Core, https://www.qualtrics.com/research-core/.

32. Counting Opinions, http://www.countingopinions.com/.

33. CKAN Data Management, https://ckan.org/.

34. Jisc Data Vault, http://datavaultplatform.org/.

35. Jisc Digital Solutions, https://www.jisc.ac.uk/.

36. John Ladley, *Data Governance: How to Design, Deploy, and Sustain an Effective Data Governance Program* (Waltham, MA: Morgan Kaufmann, 2012).

37. Tibor Koltay, "Data Governance, Data Literacy and the Management of Data Quality," *IFLA Journal* 42, no. 4 (2016): 303–12, doi:10.1177/0340035216672238201.

38. Steve Sarsfield, *The Data Governance Imperative: A Business Strategy for Corporate Data* (Ely, UK: IT Governance Pub., 2009).

39. David Marco, "Understanding Data Governance and Stewardship, Part 1," *DM Review* 16, no. 9 (2006): 28.

H. Frank Cervone

27

Communication, Marketing, and Outreach Strategies

Susan W. Alman

Chapter 27, "Communication, Marketing, and Outreach Strategies," identifies different types and models of communication and highlights the value of communicating effectively using a variety of techniques depending on the message and the intended audience. Effective communicators understand the factors that impact communication and possess the strategies to deal effectively with many situations. Strategies include marketing, outreach, and interpersonal communication with colleagues, the community, and stakeholders. Dr. Susan W. Alman, who teaches interpersonal communication and is the author of Crash Course *in Marketing for* Libraries, *identifies and explains communication techniques for effective interaction. In addition, she includes resources for further development of communication skills.*

Alman discusses the importance of soft skills for building interpersonal relationships, such as effective speaking and writing and nonverbal cues, and for helping with effective communication. She also identifies a range of impact factors that are essential for understanding individual perspectives, such as civility, conflicts, cultural diversity, and generational differences. Understanding these impact factors and how they affect communication can lead to more effective communication.

While many may not think of outreach and marketing as part of communication, Alman notes that they certainly are, and, as such, she discusses the planning techniques and tools needed to effectively communicate and promote a positive vision of the information organization. Assessment is also essential in providing evidence about the value of the information organization in an ever more competitive environment. The chapter is wrapped up with resources and guidance for developing effective communication, marketing, and outreach strategies as part of the information professional's repertoire.

★ ★ ★

Gathering, organizing, analyzing, and distributing information resources and providing services without understanding the needs of the organization's internal and external communities is an incomplete endeavor. It is incumbent on information professionals to interact with individuals, groups, and organizations through oral, written, and nonverbal communication to learn how to better serve their communities. These interactions enable knowledgeable decisions to be made regarding the provision of resources and services deemed valuable by the constituents.

Some of an information professional's routine interactions with the community include guidance and instruction, marketing, public relations, and outreach for a variety of constituent groups. Interactions also occur throughout the information organization with staff and administration. Being an effective communicator entails an understanding of the factors that impact communication and possessing the strategies to deal effectively in many situations. Employees who have these skills will be needed even more in the future as information organizations continue to evolve. Information professionals will also need to interact with the organization's constituent groups to plan and promote new processes, procedures, and technologies.

> Being an effective communicator entails an understanding of the factors that impact communication and possessing the strategies to deal effectively in many situations.

This chapter provides an overview of some of the most critical communication skills necessary for effective interactions through face-to-face, virtual, oral, and written strategies within and outside an information organization. The chapter introduces skills that are of paramount importance for effective communication, marketing, and outreach. After completing this chapter, readers should have an understanding of the factors that affect interpersonal communications and the types of communication that are integral to the information professional's interactions with a variety of audiences including users, nonusers, colleagues, administrators, and funders. Recognizing impact factors and learning communication techniques can lead to more effective personal and professional communication. For a more in-depth investigation of the communication techniques, the author has provided several resources in chapter 27 of the online supplement with the recommendation that further study will lead to mastery of the communication skills needed to lead the information profession (see also chapter 37: "Leadership Skills for Today's Global Information Landscape").

COMMUNICATION MODEL AND TYPES OF COMMUNICATION

Communication occurs when an individual (sender) delivers a message to others (receivers) by employing a variety of oral, written, and nonverbal techniques. Employing a variety of communication tools, messages can be exchanged with an information organization's colleagues, administrators, users and nonusers, collaborators, and funders. Communication is successful when others receive the exact message that was intended by the sender. As easy as that sounds, many factors impact the successful transmission of the message.

In two-way communication, the receiver should respond to the sender's message to prevent miscommunication. In many instances, however, there is no opportunity for the receiver to ask for clarification. There may be other factors that prevent the intended message from being interpreted correctly, as noted below.

One-way communication can occur in a variety of personal and professional interactions, and this communication practice should be avoided in all instances. Within all communication scenarios, it is worth allowing extra time for discussion of oral and written communication to avoid possible errors or misunderstandings. The notable exception to this rule is when immediate action is required (such as in an emergency situation) and instructions need to be followed (see also chapter 27: "Basic Communication Model" in the online supplement). Table 27.1 highlights how individuals engage in verbal and written communication activities.

Although everyone uses verbal, nonverbal, and written communication to send their messages to others, some people seem to have natural interpersonal skills and are considered effective communicators while others struggle to be understood and to understand the intended message. It is important that information professionals have positive interactions and use communication techniques that

Table 27.1. Types of Communication: Interpersonal, Organizational, and Marketing.

	Interpersonal Communication	Internal Organizational Communication	External Marketing Communication
VERBAL			
Person-to-person	X	X	X
Phone	X	X	X
Meetings	X	X	X
Presentations	X	X	X
WRITTEN			
E-mail	X	X	X
Memos	X	X	X
Newsletters		X	X
Print Materials		X	X
Electronic Materials		X	X
Website		X	X
Social Media		X	X

will enable them to effectively transmit and receive messages. These communication characteristics, known as soft skills, are highly valued by employers.

VALUE OF EFFECTIVE COMMUNICATION: SOFT SKILLS

One of the most important managerial responsibilities is selecting and hiring candidates who have the technical and interpersonal skills needed to support the mission and goals of the organization (see also chapter 22: "Managing Personnel"). Both technical and interpersonal skills may be gained through academic and practical experiences; however, many individuals have not learned about effective communication techniques. The lack of soft skills can have a negative impact on the success of the organization because of miscommunication.

Soft skills are critical to forming interpersonal relations, and information professionals need to communicate effectively using many different techniques depending on the message and the intended audience. These techniques include effective speaking and writing, active listening, understanding nonverbal cues, and the ability to work independently and in groups. It is important to learn effective communication techniques through self-study, formal courses, and an ongoing review of resources focused on interpersonal communication.

Effective Speaking and Writing

Information professionals are expected to uphold the literacy gold standard by having a solid mastery of oral and written skills to interact effectively with their communities and stakeholders for interpersonal communication, marketing, and outreach. Professionals prepare documents, teach classes, deliver presentations, write marketing and promotional materials, and interact with small and large user, peer, and outside groups. Public service positions require more interpersonal interactions than technical services, but all employees need to speak and write clearly. These skills can be honed through writing and public speaking classes along with instruction in effective interpersonal communication (see also chapter 27: "Top Skills for Tomorrow's Librarians" in the online supplement).

Active Listening

> " Effective listening skills require the receiver to stay focused on the message through mental concentration or taking notes. "

Learning how to listen is usually an informal and lifelong process. Society expects individuals to understand how to speak and interact effectively with others, often without formal instruction. Depending on the situation, children usually rely on modeling behavior they have observed. Directives children receive early on, such as, "Sit still and listen" or "Speak up," do not provide them with information on exactly *how* they are to behave or communicate. This process continues throughout people's lives as they observe the behavior of others at home, school, or work, and in social activities. There is a need to distinguish between hearing and listening. While one may hear the words spoken, that person might be mentally multitasking causing him or her to miss key points of the message. Effective listening skills require the receiver to stay focused on the message through mental concentration or taking notes. The International Listening Association[1] provides excellent resources for the self-improvement of listening skills.

Check This Out

The International Listening Association. *Visit:* https://www.listen.org/.

Understanding Nonverbal Cues

Nonverbal cues are those unspoken messages that influence the understanding of the intended communication. The messages that are sent and received are often impacted by the nonverbal cues that may or may not be perceived. Examples of nonverbal behaviors include body posture and movement; use of personal space; vocal qualities (e.g., pitch, rate, loudness, tone of speech); timing of speech; personality preferences; physical appearance (e.g., clothing, hair, body art, cosmetics); eye contact; and, smiling and nodding (for example, nodding is *not* the same in all cultures). It is important to be aware that these nonverbal behaviors can greatly impact the understanding of the intended message more than the actual words that are spoken or written.

Research findings have indicated that nonverbal behaviors account for 60 percent or more of the message that is transmitted from the sender. These findings indicate that 40 percent or less of the spoken words have an impact on the message that is actually received. Understanding nonverbal behavior can provide information professionals with insights into interpreting and improving face-to-face communication[2] (additional information about nonverbal cues appears in chapter 27 of the online supplement).

Working Independently and in Groups

Managers value employees who have the skills and flexibility to work alone on projects and also to be effective team players depending on the situation and the organization's needs. Although it may take less time to complete a project when working alone, there are many advantages to working on a team. The shared responsibility of a group often results in a greater number and complexity of ideas generated, a shared workload, and satisfaction from comradery. Successful teams include a balance of social and technical skills for a strong structure, acceptance of a common goal, and support for attaining rewards,

Susan W. Alman

training, and resources.[3] Effective teams also need to have open lines of communication that can help to guard against interpersonal conflicts created by the impact factors listed below. Being a member of a group requires an individual to assume one of many possible roles and to work toward keeping communication open among team members (see also chapter 27: "Working in Groups" in the online supplement).

Other soft skills desired by managers include the ability to build strong relationships, effectively manage conflict, adapt to new situations and technologies, solve problems, and possess a strong work ethic. It is important for employees to understand the organizational culture and expectations for attire, personal use of devices, and performance.

> " Successful teams include a balance of social and technical skills for a strong structure, acceptance of a common goal, and support for attaining rewards, training, and resources. "

IMPACT FACTORS

Understanding situations and personal differences can provide insights about ways to deal effectively with human actions and interactions. Impact factors are individual perspectives that have been developed through experiences, beliefs, teachings, and preferences, which can influence the interpretation of the message. Examples of impact factors that the information professional should be knowledgeable about include civility, conflicts, cultural diversity, generational differences, group dynamics, noise, nonverbal cues, disabilities (see also chapter 5: "Diversity, Equity of Access, and Social Justice"), and personality type. Understanding these impact factors and practicing communication techniques can improve the soft skills that are highly valued in organizations.

Civility

Civility, the practice of politeness and courtesy in everyday interactions, is a topic of concern in politics, higher education, and many organizations including libraries and information organizations. Nearly 75 percent of the population believes that more people are ruder now than they were twenty to thirty years ago, according to a study conducted in 2016 by the Associated Press–NORC Center for Public Affairs Research.[4] Sometimes rudeness can be observed in libraries through the actions and interactions of both users and library personnel, and it is the responsibility of information professionals to engage in civil discourse in all instances. A recommended source for practicing civility can be found in *Miss Manners' Guide to Excruciatingly Correct Behavior*.[5] While not related to libraries or communication, the book is recommended as essential for anyone who deals with others in any capacity. Practicing courtesy and politeness in every interaction, as the example in textbox 27.1 shows, models the behavior for others to copy.

TEXTBOX 27.1

Practicing Courtesy and Politeness

A library user who is having a loud conversation on a cell phone and is disturbing others in a quiet area of the library becomes agitated when asked to either end the conversation or move to a public area. Here is a suggested response by the information professional to the user's uncivil behavior: "When you speak in a loud voice it disturbs others who are trying to concentrate on their materials. You are welcome to continue your conversation in the center hall." If the user continues to be disruptive, it would be appropriate to bring in another staff member and/or security in order to end the uncivil behavior.

Conflicts

Conflicts can occur when dealing with one or more individuals who strongly disagree with one another and who are immovable in their position. The relationships or situations can be very uncomfortable and stressful, and the conflict can create deep rifts between individuals and within the organizational environment. There are, however, techniques that can be used to facilitate conflicts and reach resolution. The organizational leader should foster an open environment that supports employees to voice their concerns or discuss disagreements, but also permit individuals to approach the manager for conflict mediation.

When conflicts arise with a library user or colleague, it is important to remove the emotion from the argument and examine the situation objectively. Rather than allowing themselves to get pulled into a heated discussion, information professionals may choose among a couple of options to ensure that the disagreement does not develop into a hostile situation. Such strategies include:

- lowering their voice and speaking slowly and thoughtfully, and
- asking another individual to join them in the discussion.

TEXTBOX 27.2

Internal Conflict Example

A staff member is perpetually late to work and other staff must cover for her by opening the technology lab. There is growing hostility on the part of the staff that arrives on time. The supervisor discusses the situation with the staff member by asking if there are extenuating circumstances that prevent her on-time arrival. If the response is "yes" then the supervisor works with her on a solution to the situation. If the response is "no" then the supervisor must point out the duties that others are assuming in her absence, explain why that is a problem, and impress the importance of coming to work on time or face the penalty (as noted in the organizational policies and procedures manual).

Cultural Diversity

Cultural norms dictate actions and expectations. Cultural differences are not only observed in people who were born in other countries or speak various languages. Lifelong friends can exhibit different cultures based on the actions and expectations observed in their families. For example, loud talking may be the norm in one family while another family requires each member to speak softly without interruption. Is one communication style more correct than the other? No, each style is acceptable in the respective family culture. Cultural differences may be evident between individuals, groups, and organizations. The differences in communication style and tone may cause friction when exhibited with users, colleagues, or even departments in the workplace.

Each culture has expectations for communicating, and deviations from the norm may result in misunderstanding. Information professionals can create positive interactions with the communities they serve by becoming knowledgeable about the various cultures within that community. Understanding the cultures within the community not only improves verbal one-on-one communications but can also enhance the communication experience by knowing how to use appropriate communication strategies such as:

nonverbal cues: eye contact, personal space, and gestures;
emotional responses: volume and tone of voice and display of emotions;

frame of reference: anticipation of outcome; and
language: understanding of written or spoken message.

Steps toward effective communication across all cultures when teaching users or colleagues new skills include the following:

- Explain the technique with verbal *and* written instructions.
- Allow the person to complete a task on their own under supervision to make certain they do understand.
- Offer assistance if they have additional questions.

TEXTBOX 27.3

Understanding Cultural Communication Differences

Yes, does not always mean *yes*. Sometimes people will respond with "yes" when asked if they understand the process or situation because it is unacceptable in their culture to say "no," or perhaps they do understand the instructions that are given at that moment, but may not retain them after the session ends.

Generational Differences

Generational differences have been the focus of research, and there is evidence to suggest that the five generations represented in today's workforce do exhibit different attitudes toward work.[6] The groupings include:

traditionalists: born before 1946,
baby boomers: born between 1946 and 1964,
Gen X: born between 1965 and 1976,
Millennials: born between 1977 and 1997, and
Gen 2020, born after 1997.

Rather than focusing on characteristics that may be divisive in the workplace, it is more productive to establish a respectful work environment and encourage cross-generational collaboration that fosters the free exchange of information and ideas.

Group Dynamics

Groups are an integral part of organizations, and it is likely that employees will work with a variety of groups that are face-to-face as well as virtual. The same factors that impact individual communication also affect group communication, but there can be additional dynamics evidenced in group settings. Working in a group can be more time consuming than working alone, but the outcome of decisions or projects developed by groups can be stronger. The communication style and commitment to the project may be different for each member of the group. Having a designated group leader who conveys the group's goal and keeps everyone on task will guide the group process to a successful conclusion.

Key Points for Group Decision Making

- Have a clearly defined goal and timeline for the desired outcome.
- Take time to gather input from each group member before reaching a decision, and discuss the pros and cons of each suggestion.
- Each group member should have an individual or shared responsibility.

Noise

Noise refers to factors that create a disturbance and impede the sender's message from being interpreted as it was intended. Such factors that can be described as noise are:

- actual noise that is louder than the message, such as motors, loud voices, and ambient noise from a phone, and
- the attitude of the sender or receiver that distracts from the message.

Disabilities

Communication may be impeded if either the sender or the receiver has a disability. It is important that information professionals treat all individuals with civility and respect, talk to them directly (and not to someone who is accompanying them), use positive language, and listen to their response to identify clues on how to be of assistance.[7]

Check This Out

See also chapter 27 in the online supplement for additional guidance on how to communicate with individuals with disabilities, including:

- visual impairments or blindness
- hearing impairments or deafness
- mobility impairments
- speech impairments
- cognitive disabilities

Personality-Type Preferences

Each person's communication style is unique, and personality type is another factor that impacts understanding the intended message. The numerous personality-type self-assessments readily available online provide a framework to understand individual communication preferences (for a list of self-assessment personality tests, check out chapter 27 in the online supplement). The results of these assessments provide insights about the ways someone may prefer to interact with others. For example, each person in a group will have an individual preference on the way to approach the planning of a project. Some people in the group may want to engage in a brainstorming discussion and list the possibilities while others in the group may want to think about the possibilities before discussing them. Thus, there can be disparities in the preferred ways to approach the project. Neither approach is wrong or right—just a different preference.

Although people may have a communication preference, they can also change their behavior to accommodate the requirements of the situation. Understanding the varying communication preferences will enable individuals to modify communication behaviors that should lead to more effective interpersonal communication exchanges.

MARKETING AND OUTREACH

Marketing, public relations (PR), and outreach are all forms of communication. In today's competitive environment, information organizations need to promote the resources and services that are available and to provide evidence that they add value to the communities served. Information professionals engage in marketing and public relations whenever there is a need to inform the targeted segments of the community served by a particular message, service, or program. Marketing and outreach efforts extend to both internal and external markets including staff, administrators, legislators, collaborators, media outlets, and funding agencies.

There are many ways to provide evidence of the value of information organizations through public relations tools. The development of a planning document is the first step in marketing and outreach to promote the information organization's resources and services. This section of the chapter provides an introduction to some of the planning techniques and tools that are needed for an effective communications campaign.

Marketing Overview

A solid marketing plan is built from the organization's strategic plan (see also chapter 19: "Strategic Planning") using the established goals and objectives. Marketing should be directed by a formal plan with information targeted to specific populations using multiple formats, informal encounters, and community input. Above all, marketing should employ communication techniques that send the intended message to new and existing market segments.

While a marketing plan is needed to guide the organization, it is imperative that each employee, from the director to the custodian, projects a positive image of the organization. Each employee impacts the public—either positively or negatively—and negative perceptions can undermine the efforts of an otherwise flawless marketing and public relations campaign.

Marketing Plan

A marketing plan follows the same steps as an organization's strategic plan, although the scope is tailored to at least one of the strategic plan's goals. Information professionals have access to numerous strategic planning guides and community analysis techniques.[8] An individual (or department) within the organization needs to be the designated communication strategist who is tasked with oversight of the organization's marketing, public relations, and outreach. Often this area of responsibility is among many other duties, and the individual(s) must develop skills to manage the process effectively.

The following discussion provides a focus on the communication plan and assessment measures that promote and record the value-added resources and services available in the information organization.

Check This Out

Check out these resources in chapter 27 of the online supplement:

- ALA Marketing @ Your Library
- Market Plan and Cycle
- Library Marketing Plan Workbook
- Marketing Library Video

Communication Plan and Branding

A communication plan is a vital outreach working document within the marketing plan that provides resources for promoting the organization to a variety of constituencies. The American Library Association's materials on Building a Communication Plan provide an excellent template.[9] The details of the communication plan need to be customized for each organization; however, the components remain the same. The communication plan components include the following:

Media List: The list includes contact information for individuals and groups that will promote the organization through news outlets. The focus of this list is to indicate the preferences of each contact for receiving information (e.g., press releases, calendar of events, photos, or feature stories) and the format and time frame in which they are to be received. Keeping this list up to date needs to be a priority.

Press Release and Public Service Announcement (PSA): Promote the organization's events through press releases and PSAs and send these to the appropriate contacts on the media list.

Media Kit: This is a set of materials developed for a featured program or service that includes the complete information needed by the media for full coverage of the event.

Newsletter: A print or electronic newsletter may include a calendar of events, news features, recommended readings, and/or donor list. There are many issues to consider in terms of time and costs, but if an organization decides to produce a newsletter it needs to be viewed as a marketing tool.

Promotional Materials: These are items used to promote the organization and/or its programs. Examples of promotional materials include print pieces (e.g., pamphlets, flyers, posters, stickers, newsletter), swag (e.g., pens, mugs, book bags, etc. with the organization's name or logo on it), social media, and electronic resources (e.g., the organization's website, Facebook, Twitter, Instagram, e-newsletter).

Annual Report: As a unique communication tool, this report should showcase the resources and services achieved throughout the year in either print or electronic format.

Branding: Synonymous with an organization's identity, a brand is the first thing that someone thinks of when the name of the organization is heard or when the logo or icon is viewed. The brand should be created after the organizational vision has been developed. Think about the message that is projected when the name or logo of an organization is recognized. The brand needs to be a consistent message.

Elevator Pitch: This short message (forty-five seconds to a minute) should include information about the organization's accomplishments or plans for new resources and services. It can be given during an impromptu meeting with a potential funder or member of a constituency.

Social Media: These provide an effective way to communicate, but it is impossible for an information organization to be actively involved and effective in managing all of the options. The marketing plan must focus on the segments of the information organization's community that will be reached by social media and must select the appropriate tools. Conducting an environmental scan will identify the market segments in this community and identify the most popular social media outlets. An environmental scan is an analysis that gathers data about the community to assist in planning with a purpose. Information about user demographics, economic factors, and trends can be gathered through organizational data, surveys, census data, scenario creation, focus groups, literature reviews, and consultation with administrators or peers. A common form of data gathering is through a SWOT exercise to analyze the strengths, weaknesses, opportunities, and threats that are in-

---

Check This Out

Social Media Apps

- Facebook
- Flickr
- Instagram
- Pinterest
- Snapchat
- Tumblr
- Twitter
- WordPress
- YouTube
- Flipboard

Susan W. Alman

ternal and external to the organization. A relevant example of a SWOT analysis from the American Library Association[10] is available online in chapter 27 of the online supplement.

The strategic planning process for marketing and PR begins after the environmental scan/community analysis.

Social media used in information organizations is not an effective communication tool unless monitored and updated on a regular basis. A social media policy is necessary, and it should "include clear expectations for how often your sites will be updated, when you will check for comments and responses, and what kind of content is appropriate to post."[11]

EVALUATION AND ASSESSMENT

Implementing a strategy for tracking and measuring the success of a project is an inherent component of a marketing plan. The assessment measures developed before the implementation of the plan enable the organization to gauge the impact of the project. The data can be used to determine if revisions in the marketing plan or project need to be made or if the intended results have been achieved. The results can provide tangible evidence to demonstrate the value of libraries and the return on investment (ROI). Measures of assessment can be quantitative or qualitative depending on the type of project, and they may include head counts at events, an increase in circulation or participation in programs or services, focus group/survey data, correlations between factors, and ROI analyses.

Assessment of marketing and outreach activities will continue to be of major importance for future activities. Information organizations and the communities served by them are changing in academic, public, school, corporate, and archival settings. Providing evidence about the value of the information organization serves as a stabilizer in an ever more competitive environment (for an example, check out chapter 27, figure 27.1 in the online supplement). Several organizations maintain websites that include reports and resources related to ROI for libraries.[12]

These materials provide bibliographies, studies, reports, white papers, marketing tools, and ROI calculators that can be adapted for individual information organizations.

MARKETING RESOURCES

There are many useful online tools for information professionals to use in personal marketing and in market research, analysis, and assessment. These resources include the websites of professional associations, big data banks, online tools, research services, and professional conferences. A descriptive list of the tools is available in the online supplemental text, and a few are highlighted below.

Marketing Research, Analysis, and Assessment Resources

Census Data: American Fact Finder and FedStats
Online Surveys: Survey Monkey and Google Forms
Big Data Banks: Think with Google and Google Analytics
LibQual: Library Assessment Conference

Library Marketing and Communications Conference
American Library Association: Library Leadership and Management Association John Cotton Dana Library Public Relations Award
American Library Association: LLAMA PR Xchange

CONCLUSION

Communication is multifaceted, and it requires knowledge and practice to become an effective communicator. Soft skills will become increasingly important for information professionals as the complexity of information organizations increases with the expansion of new programs, services, and technologies. Virtual communication will continue to expand for internal and external communities served by the information organization. The information in this chapter provides a wide overview of communication techniques and factors that affect interpersonal and organizational communication. Having an increased awareness of these factors is the first step toward gaining the communication skills that are required for interacting with others to meet the challenges of the evolving information profession. The next steps include lifelong self-study and professional development to improve communication techniques.

NOTES

1. International Listening Association, https://www.listen.org/.
2. Esther Grassian and Joan R. Kaplowitz, *Learning to Lead and Manage Information Literacy Instruction* (New York: Neal-Schuman, 2005); Nancy M. Puccinelli, "Nonverbal Communicative Competence," in *APA Handbook of Interpersonal Communication*, ed. David Matsumoto (Washington, DC: American Psychological Association, 2010), 273–88.
3. Martine Haas and Mark Mortensen, "The Secrets of Great Teamwork," *Harvard Business Review*, June 2016, https://hbr.org/2016/06/the-secrets-of-great-teamwork.
4. "Rude Behavior in Everyday Life and on the Campaign Trail—Issue Brief," Associated Press-NORC Center for Public Affairs Research, 2016, http://www.apnorc.org/projects/Pages/HTML%20Reports/rude-behavior-in-everyday-life-and-on-the-campaign-trail.aspx.
5. Judith Martin, *Miss Manners' Guide to Excruciatingly Correct Behavior* (New York: W.W. Norton & Company, 2005).
6. Jeanne C. Meister and Karie Willyerd, "Are You Ready to Manage Five Generations of Workers?," *Harvard Business Review*, October 16, 2009, https://hbr.org/2009/10/are-you-ready-to-manage-five-g.
7. United States Department of Labor Office of Disability Employment Policy, https://www.dol.gov/odep/pubs/fact/communicating.htm.
8. Susan W. Alman and Sara Gillespie Swanson, *Crash Course in Marketing for Libraries* (Santa Barbara, CA: Libraries Unlimited, 2015).
9. "Building a Communication Plan," American Library Association, accessed August 9, 2017, https://www.ala.org/ala/pio/campaign/prtools/marketing_wkbk.pdf.
10. American Library Association, SWOT Analysis Chart, accessed August 20, 2017, http://www.ala.org/advocacy/swot-analysis-your-librarys-strengths-weaknesses-opportunities-and-threats.
11. Alman and Swanson, *Crash Course in Marketing for Libraries*, 44.
12. "Return on Investment for Public Libraries," Library Research Service Research and Statistics about Libraries, accessed August 9, 2017, https://www.lrs.org/data-tools/public-libraries/return-on-investment/; "Value of Academic Libraries Toolkit," Association of College & Research Libraries, accessed August 9, 2017, http://www.ala.org/acrl/issues/value/valueofacademiclibrariestoolkit. "The ROI of Corporate Libraries & Research Solutions—White Paper," EBSCO, accessed August 9, 2017, https://help.ebsco.com/interfaces/EBSCO_Guides/General_Product_FAQs/ROI_of_Corporate_Libraries_Research_Solutions.

28

Advocacy

Cheryl Stenström

Chapter 28, "Advocacy," highlights the information professional's essential advocacy role in demonstrating the value that information organizations provide to their community. The main goal of advocacy is to gain stable support for a well-funded organization, but it is also useful for developing support for other information-related issues and programs—from information literacy to privacy and intellectual freedom. Dr. Cheryl Stenström, who teaches on advocacy and conducts research on advocacy for public libraries, continues the focus from the previous chapter on effective and persuasive communication and the essential role it plays in advocacy in convincing key stakeholders to fund and support the organization. She notes that successful advocacy campaigns are built on an understanding of decision making, context, timing, economic trends, and the individuals involved in funding information organizations.

Advocacy, Stenström notes, is a full-time process of promotion of the information organization's brand and programs, public relations, marketing, networking, persuasion, and lobbying. She provides a model of how these processes can work in diverse organizations. Effective messaging is key to showing stakeholders how the organization will help them achieve their vision, objectives, and goals and, as such, advocacy must be oriented toward the experiences, attitudes, beliefs, and perspective of those key stakeholders.

Defining value is also essential to advocacy and should include both qualitative and quantitative measures of user satisfaction and social impact. Research findings must be conveyed in a meaningful way to target audiences, clearly and appropriately. Stenström ends her discussion by providing the reader with strategies for creating their own advocacy plan.

★   ★   ★

In today's evolving information landscape, the information professional's ability to advocate for the profession while demonstrating the value that information organizations provide their communities is one of the most important skills needed. To the surprise of many managers, much of a skilled leader's time is spent communicating with decision makers about the important role modern information services and organizations play in their local and global communities. While gaining support for well-funded information organizations is the most frequent reason information professionals engage in advocacy and advocacy-related activities, advocacy can also help:

- bolster cases involving issues such as intellectual freedom,
- develop more integration of literacy instruction in the classroom,
- build new library spaces and innovative services (such as the need for creative and collaborative spaces), and
- strengthen services that support diversity.

Being able to effectively communicate the essential role that information organizations play to decision makers who control funding and support is equally as important as other management functions involved in running an efficient organization, such as budgeting, planning, and performance monitoring. Indeed, being able to effectively manage the operations of an information organization as well as successfully garner external support are two aspects of management that work synergistically. After reading this chapter, the reader should have an understanding of:

- the advocacy process, including key concepts such as influence, persuasion, marketing, promotion, lobbying, and networking;
- the foundations of decision making;
- perceptions and target audiences; and
- how to develop an advocacy plan for an information organization.

ADVOCACY: DEFINITIONS AND MISCONCEPTIONS

For many information professionals, uncertainty about the financial decisions made by those who fund their organizations can make it difficult to plan and engage in the daily operations of their information organizations. As a result, interest has grown within the library and information (LIS) field on how to advocate for stable and increased funding, as is evident through the increased attention given to advocacy campaigns. While each information organization is unique, a systematic examination of these campaigns shows that they are rarely evaluated on their success.[1] Successful advocacy campaigns are built on an understanding of decision making, context, timing, the economic climate, and the individuals involved in funding information organizations.

> **TEXTBOX 28.1**
>
> **Advocacy Defined**
>
> Ken Haycock defined advocacy as a "planned, deliberate, sustained effort to develop understanding and support incrementally over time."[2]

Often when people hear the word *advocacy*, they think of a one-shot deal or something that can be done once in reaction to an event. But advocacy is so much more than a one-time action item. Each component of Haycock's definition is important, including the part about *incrementally over time*. In other words, a group cannot go out and "do advocacy" just for one day; rather, a holistic approach is needed. Advocacy also includes:

Promotion: the activities that raise awareness, generate interest, and build the brand for an organization, product, service, or issue aimed at a target group or the general public. Promotional activities include developing and distributing branded materials, deploying an attractive web page, and managing special events. Promoting services and collections can feed into the image portrayed by an information organization (see also chapter 27: "Communication, Marketing, and Outreach Strategies").

Public relations: the process for managing communication between an organization and the public. The public relations process includes several discrete components including positioning the organization, defining the audience, developing key messages, creating a cohesive plan, evaluating effectiveness, working with the media, creating a welcoming environment in the building, and reaching out to users and other stakeholders.[3]

Cheryl Stenström

Marketing: the process of proactively reaching out to those outside the organization. Through marketing, advocacy becomes visible. Here the continuum of activities moves from a one-sided approach to a two-way dialogue with a target audience. Advocacy can be viewed as marketing an issue. The effective advocate uses marketing to home in on a specific audience and think about their needs in a way that responds to them, rather than an interpretation of what might be important to the target groups.

Networking: the deliberate effort to develop meaningful relationships with as many people as possible within the community that an information organization serves (also known as relationship marketing). Effective networking extends itself to the individual level and leads directly to the sister concepts of social influence and persuasion. Social influence reflects the "change in the belief, attitude, or behaviour of a person which results from the action, or presence of another person."[4]

Persuasion: the process of using factual or values-based appeals with a target audience to shift previous ways of thinking. The process begins with a person who has a goal who delivers a message to a target audience. The process is complete when the target complies with, commits to, or rejects the message.[5]

Lobbying: the activities undertaken with the intent of influencing government. Lobbying is often associated with advocating for an issue, particularly within the political realm. Lobbying efforts fall into three categories and are hierarchical in their level of aggressiveness. Specifically, the lobbying categories include engaging in:

1. Collaboration with another group that shares similar concerns and interests.
2. Grassroots lobbying (see textbox 28.2). This can include the dissemination of information about the policies in question, rallies, and demonstrations. Grassroots techniques are designed to inform and influence members of the public.
3. Direct lobbying, such as financially supporting a campaign or meeting directly with elected officials to discuss specific issues.[6] Direct lobbying is the most aggressive set of techniques.

TEXTBOX 28.2

Grassroots Lobbying

Grassroots activities are used to get the word out about an issue to a wide group of people with the hope of gaining widespread support. Ideally, with this new understanding, people are then willing to speak on behalf of the information organization and its goals. Keeping messages simple and unified is important when many people are speaking to address "what is it?" The strength of this technique lies in large numbers. If there is a ballot issue at hand, the hope is that this approach will translate into votes. For non-ballot issues, grassroots campaigns do not always translate into a positive outcome on the part of the decision makers; the reality is that these formal decisions make up a small part of the overall decision landscape. This is not to say that grassroots campaigns are ineffective, but they should not be the "go-to" technique for all settings.

None of these techniques on their own constitute an advocacy plan, but each can have a place in the plan depending on the context of the organization and the organization's goals. Each type of activity can be used to achieve different objectives; aligning techniques with those objectives to produce the desired outcome is key. To help inform the planning process from a practical viewpoint, each of these activities can be put into context and expanded with examples. See appendix 28.1: "Example of an Advocacy Plan."

ADVOCACY AND INFLUENCING DECISION MAKERS

The above definitions are important when thinking about *alignment* in the activities carried out on a day-to-day basis in an information organization. When developing a strategic plan (see also chapter 19: "Strategic Planning"), it is important to align the organization's mission, vision, values, and goals with its objectives as well as the activities undertaken on a day-to-day basis. Failure to do so can result in unfocused efforts, wasted energy, and poor results. The same principles of alignment apply when taking a message outside the information organization. While the development of a strong mission and vision creates a stable internal foundation, effective messages will resonate with an audience when the audience can see how it will help them achieve their vision and goals.

Those who make decisions that can positively affect information organizations will do so when it makes sense from their perspective. For those advocating for an organization, the ability to solve the problems of those funding the organization is imperative when making a case for support. In these cases, a "problem" does not mean a crisis; rather a "problem" is effectively used as part of the messaging to meet the stakeholders' goals. Many factors contribute to a decision maker's decision to support an organization, such as their:

- prior experience as a decision maker (e.g., personal background, knowledge of information organizations and their mission and purpose, the perception of information professionals, etc.);
- attitude about supporting such information organizations, which could include societal and organizational influences;
- image of the information organization; and
- confidence that a certain alternative will be implemented.

To understand advocacy, a closer look at decision making is key.

Understanding Decision Making

There are some fundamental principles that guide how people gather and use information for decisions, including those decisions that affect information organizations. The logic behind decision-making theory is based on a hierarchy of "means-ends" decisions leading to objectives and goals (i.e., a rational decision is based on selecting the most appropriate means to an end, which is a part of reaching an objective). In the mid-twentieth century, Herbert Simon described the limits of this model in the concept of bounded rationality. Briefly, the concept is described as rational actors choosing the best of all possible alternatives in a decision (e.g., in economics, the choice that yields the highest profit), but recognizing that knowing all alternatives and their consequences is impossible. Therefore, decision makers look for simplified models of alternatives, using their imaginations to fill in some of the gaps of the unknown. Often, decision makers select the best, first alternative made available to them (a concept Simon called satisficing),[7] rather than seeking the most efficient alternatives with the most advantageous outcomes.

All decision makers rely on common shortcuts, such as incorporating their previous knowledge and experience to create a complete profile of situations lacking in sufficient detail. In other words, they use stereotypes of people or situations to fill in the information gaps. The more familiar the decision maker is with the characteristics in a given situation, the easier they will find the situation to be feasible and rational. They can assess options but must rely on a personal set of beliefs and experiences in the absence of complete information about each option.[8] The ultimate decision is a complex interplay between personal beliefs, attitudes toward the object in question, and the decision maker's intention leading to behaviors.[9]

Influence and Power

The most important factor a leader must consider when trying to make a positive impact on a decision maker is interpersonal influence. The effective use of interpersonal influence affects the way decision makers access, process, and ultimately use information to make a decision. Cialdini developed a common framework of influence that is a critical part of the advocacy process.[10] This influence framework has six features: consistency, authority, reciprocity, relationship building, social proof, and scarcity. However, early research on the use of influence in information organizations indicates that when decision makers consider funding requests, they most often use three distinct lenses:

Consistency: influenced by one's values.
Authority: influenced by someone with hierarchical power requesting or demanding action.
Relationships: influenced by how much the person likes and knows about the organization and the requester. This is the most important lens for the decision maker.[11]

> **Discussion Question**
>
> What are some examples where an information organization can help decision makers meet their goals?

More than any other tactic, the concept of relationship building is present in the work of those advancing requests for funding, whether pertaining to library funding or non-library-related issues. The networks used to support the requests are most often created over lengthy periods of time.

CRAFTING EFFECTIVE MESSAGES

Effective advocacy is about crafting messages that will resonate with those who an information professional is aiming to influence. The following questions can guide the development of an effective message:

*   Who is the target audience? What do they already know and what additional information do they need?
*   How can the message be made clear and credible?
*   Will this information help them? If it will cause problems, are there solutions to propose?

Defining Audience

Developing a diverse network from all corners of the community the organization serves is paramount because other information professionals are not typically the target audience for advocacy messages. Target groups can include:

*   teaching faculty and academic administrators (e.g., deans and vice provosts);
*   city councilors or community members who sit on a board;
*   patrons and community groups;

- department heads or community leaders with subject expertise (e.g., medical doctors);
- school superintendents; and
- regional, national, and international policy-making bodies and elected politicians.

Different aspects of a message are emphasized when dealing with diverse audiences. It is important, therefore, to imagine the background of each of the members of these different groups. For example, the same message would be delivered in different ways to a supervisor than to colleagues in other departments or to a supervisor's boss, and so on.

Many people could be considered to have influence over an information organization, the kind of support it receives, and its reputation in the community. All organizations have some form of reporting structure. In a university setting, the academic library dean is responsible to the provost as well as an advisory body, and, ultimately, the president and board (see also chapter 7: "Learning and Research Institutions: Academic Libraries"). In a corporate setting, often the knowledge center lies within a particular work unit with responsibility falling to a vice president and ultimately the CEO and, in some cases, shareholders (see also chapter 9: "Working in Different Information Environments: Special Libraries and Information Centers"). And in a public library, the library director or chief librarian directly reports to the appointed board and has formal relationships with a myriad of funders including local, state, and federal bodies (see also chapter 8: "Community Anchors for Lifelong Learning: Public Libraries").

Also, there are other influencers, both within and outside the organization, with broad leadership roles within each community. For the public library, the influencer could be a popular small business owner, the president of the Chamber of Commerce, a well-known doctor, or a local high school principal. In the university, perhaps the influencer is the student union president, the professor whose latest book is getting a lot of media attention, or the development manager who could have significant influence on the organization. In a business library setting, the influencer could be the manager of a department strategically related to the information center, the director of finance, or the CEO's brother who ends up impacting the organizations in some unknown way.

Developing Clear and Credible Messages

With a picture of an audience firmly secured, the successful advocate should start to get a clearer idea of the message that may be most meaningful to that audience. It is imperative to think about what the audience might already know and what they need to know and understand when "less is more."

Broadly speaking, messages should be aligned with how an information professional can help solve a decision maker's problems and should be focused on the desired outcome: simple and repeatable, and flexible and adaptable (recall the points about alignment made earlier in the chapter). Table 28.1 offers examples of using effective messaging to solve an organization's problems.

Demonstrating Value

Understanding the various ways users perceive value is important, as is understanding options for measuring the impact of services. In the twentieth century, information organizations typically gathered statistics on all kinds of inputs and outputs, such as funding, books purchased, items circulated, or the number of visits to the building. These statistics were used to make statements like, "Last year, the average number of books borrowed by each patron of the library was 5.2." More recently, information professionals are recognizing that numbers showing outputs, such as the number of books someone borrows, are not all that meaningful. Drawing on the example above, the average borrower might find that the true value comes from the content found in those books. Indeed, the number of items borrowed might have no bearing on whether or not people have found the *right* information to meet their needs.

Cheryl Stenström

Table 28.1. Examples of Using Effective Messaging to Solve Organizational Problems.

Type of Organization	Problem	Case for Support
Academic Library	Providing access to scholarly information that would otherwise be both disorganized and unaffordable	Needed in order for faculty and students to produce high-quality research
Public Library	Providing civic spaces to citizens in which they feel welcome	Needed as part of the suite of services and amenities they expect from their city as voters
School Library	Teaching students how to find resources and critically evaluate information	Needed so students can achieve high academic results/grades
Corporate Library	Disseminating the latest results of competitors' earnings and other research	Needed so the corporation is better positioned to increase profits

Thinking about the impact of the organization's services and collections on the user leads to a discussion of outcomes and gets much closer to the concept of value. Unlike the previous example where only quantitative measures were used, both qualitative and quantitative measures can and should be used to measure outcomes. Both direct and indirect value can be considered when looking at services and collections provided by an information organization:

Direct value: to the user, for example, as measured by increased skills, knowledge, enjoyment, or financial savings (with an emphasis on user satisfaction).

Indirect value: to society, for example, as measured by greater levels of education, generalized trust, job creation, or support of the publishing cycle and national cultural growth (with an emphasis on the broader social impact).

Simply gathering output data about an organization's operations allows managers to answer questions such as, "How many hours of instruction does the library provide?" or "How many computers are available to the public?" However, these questions fall short of answering the question of how an information organization provides indirect and direct value to its users and the wider community. More significant questions allow managers to explore and express value, such as, "What impact has the library's instructional program had on student achievement?" or "In what ways did the library's public access computers enhance the quality of users' lives?"

Since the mid-1990s, there has been a growing trend of evaluating libraries from a broad community and, more frequently, an economic view. Whether the organization in question is a special, public, academic, or school library, many stakeholders are thinking about value from a neoliberal, economic-growth mind-set. It is nearly impossible to talk about the value of information organizations and libraries strictly in terms of economic outputs. Information professionals need to ensure they are informed of the issues from various perspectives in order to craft effective messages for different stakeholder audiences.

All the best research is useless unless the findings can be conveyed in a meaningful way to target audiences. To effectively demonstrate value, information professionals must be able to speak about data clearly and appropriately (see also chapter 26: "Managing Data and Data Analysis in Information Organizations"). In this regard, both qualitative and quantitative data matter, and statistical measurements can be contextualized through storytelling.

Consider this example of a public librarian using both qualitative and quantitative data in presenting different aspects of early literacy to targeted groups. To her boss, she presented an informal but thorough report covering the types of activities undertaken in the library, the use of preschool services, and the demographics of the city. For a group of elementary school teachers, she prepared a PowerPoint presentation that pulled out some of the most technical aspects of how pre-literacy skills are acquired. To the group of elected town council members, she simply held up a board book (the kind with the thick cardboard pages you would read to babies and toddlers) in one hand and a calculus textbook in the other hand and said, "It is a long road from here [referring to the board book] to here [referring to the calculus text]."

> Sometimes value is shown over long periods of time or in multiple ways rather than through a single program or initiative.

A challenge in conveying the value propositions of information services lies in the complexity of the impact. Sometimes value is shown over long periods of time or in multiple ways rather than through a single program or initiative. Caution and sense must be exercised when crafting messages. Information professionals should avoid sweeping, unbelievable statements like, "Storytimes reduce crime; therefore, money should be taken from the police force and given to children's librarians." A more appropriate way of expressing this might be, "Law enforcement personnel recognize the role high literacy rates play in reducing crime. The public library is the best place for young children to get a head start in developing strong literacy skills in their preschool years."

> Local, regional, national, and international venues are important targets for demonstrating impact, and key relationships should be developed at each of these levels to ensure the message is heard.

Recognition of the need to align the impact of the organization with the values of decision makers is growing. Local, regional, national, and international venues are important targets for demonstrating impact, and key relationships should be developed at each of these levels to ensure the message is heard.

THE ADVOCACY PLAN

It is worth noting a couple of important factors in the advocacy planning context. In his article "Advocacy in Organizations: The Elements of Success," MacConnell states: "Advocacy is about moving from 'what is' to 'what should be' and that it is accomplished by, among other things, drawing attention to underlying or 'submerged' issues, influencing public attitudes, and changing policies and practices."[12] While many strategic plans focus on one, three, or maybe five years, it is difficult to suggest this is realistic when looking at shifting attitudes and the complexity of working in multiple political settings. The ability to "develop understanding and support incrementally over time" accentuates the need for a long-range view here. If an information organization is looking to align its goals with the values of particular decision makers, the reality is that sometimes these leaders have to wait for the right decision maker to come to power. LIS professionals need to be consistently working toward advocacy goals, but they may need to be more flexible than when executing operational, strategic plans.

> While many strategic plans focus on one, three, or maybe five years, it is difficult to suggest this is realistic when looking at shifting attitudes and the complexity of working in multiple political settings.

The most sophisticated plans encompass a plan within a plan! This applies in the advocacy context as well. How can a communications plan reflect advocacy goals? Can a staff training plan be

Cheryl Stenström

applicable? How does work in the community affect relationships and the image of the information organization? It is important to avoid spending too much time planning at the expense of implementation, but advocacy goals are complex, and the planning process should recognize the long run.

CONCLUSION

This chapter defined various activities in an information organization that make up the advocacy process. The definitions help information professionals distinguish the singular components of an advocacy plan from a successful campaign. The single most significant activity that can help information professionals advocate successfully is their ability to develop meaningful relationships with decision makers. Within those relationships, care must be taken to develop and carry out effective messaging about information organizations, whether in a general sense or when communicating about a specific organization.

As with any complex process, thorough planning and consideration of the alignment of activities with an organization's mission and vision, as well as those of key decision makers, should be undertaken deliberately. Resources and training that support an advocacy plan can help ensure its success. It goes without saying that good planning is part of a cycle that includes an evaluation stage. Over time, few organizations have taken the time to appropriately evaluate their advocacy efforts; advocacy based on evidence needs to become a stronger priority within the information profession. Looking ahead, information professionals might consider undertaking more action-based research projects and working in ways that can help develop leaders who understand and exercise social influence as a key part of the advocacy process. Information professionals who are persuasive, good communicators, able to set strategies, able to understand what drives decision makers, and are good at engaging with the public will have the greatest success at advocating for their information organizations.

APPENDIX 28.1: EXAMPLE OF AN ADVOCACY PLAN

At the beginning of this chapter, the definitions of different activities that are often lumped under the advocacy umbrella were presented: promotion, public relations, marketing, networking, persuasion, and lobbying. To help inform the planning process from a practical viewpoint, this sample advocacy plan for a rural public library that is trying to secure a new library building to provide expanded spaces for the community is shown below.

I. Setting
    A rural public library trying to secure a new building.
II. Problem/Solution Statement
    Providing spaces to citizens in which they feel welcome as part of the suite of services and amenities they expect from their city as voters.
III. Activities
    A. Promotion
        a. *Branding:* The library's logo and branding strategy convey vibrancy and confidence in the institution as a good place for a long-term investment. The image speaks to a dynamic and growing organization rather than a slow-moving, old-fashioned service. A key component of the branding strategy would include making the existing space as attractive as possible—a place where people want to be.
        b. *Website and social media:* Technology is used not only to promote the library's services and programs but also to reinforce the library's vision and values and provide a means for the library staff to be instantly and consistently responsive to citizens.

B. Public relations
  a. *Press releases:* Notices about community-based programs and events are regularly sent to local media outlets, affirming the frequent demand for and use of the existing building as a community space.
  b. *News items:* Calls from the local media and requests for interviews are used as an opportunity to talk about the constant buzz that takes place in the library building, whether at a storytime or community event, in the computer lab, or when neighbors meet and catch up.
C. Marketing
  a. *Survey:* The library's annual customer satisfaction survey includes questions about the community's public space needs, as well as some questions that measure its desire for a new library building.
  b. *Reports and services:* Research results are incorporated into the design, implementation, and promotion of new and existing services. Reports of "You told us . . ." are used to bolster the impression that the library belongs to the community.
D. Networking
  a. *Local committees:* The library's director is a member of the local Chamber of Commerce, Rotary Club, etc. and can act as a resource for other committee members. However, the library director primarily plays the role of active participant and is seen as a competent, trustworthy community member.
  b. *Formal meetings:* The library's director and senior staff actively engage with and participate in other citywide committees and help implement the city council's non-library-related initiatives.
E. Persuasion
  a. *Board and staff members:* While key messages and talking points about the new library proposal are shared with all board and staff members, those who have existing relationships with powerful community members are noted; when opportunities arise, these board and staff members are asked to assist with communication, including learning about any concerns those community members have about the city and library.
  b. *Connecting agendas:* When invited to deliver formal presentations, the message emphasizes the expectations of the citizens, the ability of a new library to enhance the suite of services and amenities offered in the area, and the value it can provide the city council expressed in terms of meeting their goals.

NOTES

1. Cheryl Stenström and Ken Haycock, "Influence and Increased Funding in Canadian Public Libraries: The Case of Alberta in 2009–10," *Library Quarterly* 84, no. 1 (2014): 49–68.
2. Ken Haycock, "Advocacy and Influences," Ken Haycock and Associates Organizational Development, 2011, http://kenhaycock.com/advocacy-and-influence/.
3. Lisa A. Wolfe, *Library Public Relations, Promotions, and Communications: A How-To-Do-It Manual* (New York: Neal-Schuman Publishers, 2005).
4. Bertam H. Raven, "Political Applications of the Psychology of Interpersonal Influence and Social Power," *Political Psychology* 11, no. 3 (1990): 493–520.
5. William L. Benoit, *Persuasive Messages: The Process of Influence* (Malden, MA: Blackwell, 2008).
6. Jill Nicholson-Crotty, "The Stages of Nonprofit Advocacy" (PhD diss., Texas A&M University, 2005).
7. Herbert Simon, "A Behavioral Model of Rational Choice," *Quarterly Journal of Economics* 69, no. 1 (1955): 99–118.

8. Amos Tversky and Daniel Kahneman, "Judgment under Uncertainty: Heuristics and Biases," in *Judgment under Uncertainty: Heuristics and Biases*, ed. D. Kahneman, P. Slovic, and A. Tversky (Cambridge: Cambridge University Press, 1982), 3–20.

9. Martin Fishbein and Icek Ajzen, *Belief, Attitude, Intention, and Behavior: An Introduction to Theory and Research* (Reading, MA: Addison-Wesley, 1975).

10. Robert B. Cialdini, *Influence: Science and Practice*, fourth edition (Boston: Allyn & Bacon, 2001).

11. Stenström and Haycock, "Influence and Increased Funding in Canadian Public Libraries."

12. Stephen MacConnell, "Advocacy in Organizations: The Elements of Success," *Generations* 28, no. 1 (April 2004): 25–30.

Part V

Information Issues
Influences and Consequences

Information professionals have indeed been leaders in the fight for policies that reflect the profession's core values, such as equity of access and intellectual freedom, sometimes at great personal and professional risk.

—Kate Marek, chapter 29

Information professionals have an almost sacred responsibility to uphold the values and principles of intellectual freedom, freedom of access, and the free flow of information, but this responsibility is not without its tensions and challenges. Balancing ethical codes, organization values and principles, and one's own beliefs, particularly in the face of rapid technological change, is a difficult but critical skill. Users and the community rely on information organizations to provide useful information, but they also expect accuracy, reliability, and equity.

Part V addresses these critical issues and how information professionals incorporate them into their organization in the face of a changing world. Information ethics, licensing, open access, privacy, copyright, cybersecurity and intellectual freedom are all considered. The authors examine the state of these central issues today, the challenges that one may expect, and the impact of rapid changes in technology, never losing sight of the central responsibilities of information professionals to uphold the rights of information users.

29

Information Policy

Kate Marek

Chapter 29, "Information Policy," addresses the role of information policy in a society that values important foundational ideas such as civil liberties, intellectual freedom, intellectual property, and equity of access to resources. Dr. Kate Marek, with her background as director and professor at the School of Information Studies at Dominican University and her expertise in information policy, introduces information policy as it pertains to information professionals, provides a framework for policy analysis and awareness, and highlights the important role of information policy issues in a democratic society.

Marek raises and explores two key questions: What are the key value questions and what are the key issues with establishing information policy? These foundational issues, such as who owns information and who decides how it is shared, create persistent value conflicts, and Marek delineates the central values that shape information policy examining the strengths and limits of each. She emphasizes, however, that these value conflicts must also be taken into consideration in conjunction with the mission and values of the information organization itself.

Information professionals' roles in the arena of information policy include awareness, advocacy, and activism. Marek emphasizes the importance of information professionals staying up to date on and engaged with information policies that impact the profession's core values. She notes that it is part of information professionals' responsibility to participate in national policy conversations that impact information use while also being aware of their workplace's position and recognizing that there could be legal issues involved. Marek addresses these roles and provides the reader with insight and resources regarding information policy issues and concerns in their organization and their community.

★   ★   ★

Our contemporary society runs on information, from the day's weather and stock prices to details about international terrorism. It therefore stands to reason that the policies, rules, and processes that govern information—called information policies—are fundamental to the tenor of society.

The emergence of this information-based society has profoundly shaped the development of laws, rules, and policies that govern information use and flow. Information policies enable civil liberties, such as privacy, intellectual freedom, and equity of access to resources, and impact economic issues, such as intellectual property and commercial performance. Each of these issues, however, is as complex as today's complex society and involves conflicting priorities that must be balanced simultaneously. For example, today's critical discussion of national security versus citizen privacy is an information policy issue. Another example is the economic benefit of intellectual property and the right to information ownership, which must be balanced with society's need for a healthy public domain to enable creativity. In her seminal work, *Change of State*, Sandra Braman asserts that the very nature of power has shifted from the ability to manipulate the physical, structural, and symbolic aspects of society to the ability to control and manipulate the informational bases of all three of the other forms of power.[1] Thinking about information policy in today's dynamic world is challenging and exciting, and information professionals are called to be key contributors to the public discussion.

This chapter provides a brief introduction to information policy, specifically for information professionals, to provide a framework for policy analysis and awareness in key areas that are relevant to the information field. After completing this chapter, the reader should have an understanding of information policy as a concept, the role of values in policy formulation, the policy-formulation process, the frameworks for analyzing policy decisions, some specific information policies in the United States, and how information professionals play an important role regarding information policy issues in a democratic society.

CONCEPTUAL ELEMENTS OF INFORMATION POLICY DEVELOPMENT

While the field of information policy studies can be expansive and multidimensional,[2] for the purposes of this chapter, information policies are defined simply as the rules, regulations, laws, and tacit processes that direct and govern the information cycle: creation, ownership, dissemination and flow, access, use, and legacy storage. When considering this definition, two broad questions arise:

- What are the *key value questions* that need to be asked when establishing information policy?
- What are the *key issues* that must be addressed when establishing information policy?

For example, is information accessible by everyone or only by a select few? Under what circumstances is information accessible, and at what price? What power do government agencies have to limit ownership of and access to information? Who owns information? Who decides what information is created and shared, and how are those decisions made? What power inequities exist as a result of decisions regarding information access and control, and to what extent are those power inequities acceptable in a democratic society?

Decisions regarding information policy can have profound impacts on daily life and may involve personal privacy (see also chapter 34: "Information Privacy and Cybersecurity"), intellectual freedom (see also chapter 35: "Intellectual Freedom"), or even workplace effectiveness. For example, who has access to people's medical information? Who has access to people's electronic book purchases? What protections should be in place regarding information collected through internet-based learning programs and apps? What information barriers exist in people's workplaces?

Values as the Foundation for Policy Formulation

Values drive the creation of information policy. Overman and Cahill[3] list seven values that shape the information policy debate. See textbox 29.1.

An examination of the strengths and limits of each of these values within the context of freedom, security, and the nation's capitalistic economic structure provides a framework for policy analysis in a democratic society.

Kate Marek

Information Issues That Drive Policy Formation

A society's values provide an important context for establishing information policies, and specific types of issues must be addressed when establishing information policies. While information policy issues are always changing, textbox 29.2 provides a list, by no means exhaustive, of current information policy issues. These issues may have conflicting priorities; they may overlap; they may have political, social, and bureaucratic implications; and they may be temporary (ceasing to be an issue as technology and society evolve).

Policy Making in Light of Organizational Mission

Just as solutions to information policy issues differ depending on the values of society, they also differ based on the mission and goals of the information organization (see also chapter 19: "Strategic Planning"). An organization's institutional mission adds nuance to information policy discussions.

For example, a public library might be concerned with the chilling effect on patron privacy of national legislation, such as the USA PATRIOT Act,[4] which limits information privacy (see also chapter 8: "Community Anchors for Lifelong Learning: Public Libraries"). Public libraries may also seek to balance a desire for patron privacy with many patrons' desire for customized information services via social media. An academic library might be hypervigilant about government surveillance of faculty research, and also concerned with open academic content weighed against author recognition for academic tenure and review policies (see also chapter 7: "Learning and Research Institutions: Academic Libraries"). Similarly, an information service within a corporate environment might be concerned with intellectual property from the perspective of protecting corporate assets, as well as with legal uses of information for competitive advantage (see also chapter 9: "Working in Different Information Environments: Special Libraries and Information Centers").

A FRAMEWORK FOR EVALUATING POLICY DECISIONS

One helpful framework for evaluating information policy decisions was developed by Ian Rowlands, who designed a four-quadrant matrix[5] based on standard conflicting aspects of information (for the public good and as a tradable commodity) and two extremes of access (open and closed). Figure 29.1 offers examples of current information issues in each quadrant and provides a tool for policy makers to better visualize the impact of their decisions.

Information as Public Good

INFORMATION FOR CITIZENSHIP
- Free public libraries
- Open Internet
- User privacy
- Information for civic discourse
- Barrier free access to resources
- Strong public domain

INFORMATION PROTECTIONISM
- Restricted data access
- National security
- Data collection / surveillance
- Censorship Commercial secrecy

Open, unrestricted Information flows ——————— Closed, restricted Information flows

INFORMATION FOR CONSUMER CHOICE
- Freedom of the press
- The mass media
- Universal service
- Public-private partnerships
- Fee-based information services and Internet Infotainment

INFORMATION FOR COMPETITIVE ADVANTAGE
- Intranets
- Competitive intelligence
- Patents
- Strict intellectual property rights; long rights terms
- Proprietary information
- Work for hire

Information as a Tradable Commodity

Figure 29.1 Matrix of Information Issues. *Created by author; adapted from Ian Rowlands, "Understanding Information Policies,"* Journal of Information Science *22, no. 1 (1996): 13–25.*

Kate Marek

Rowlands's concept of information as a public good emphasizes the perspective that information is needed for an open society. However, the matrix also represents the competing priority to limit openness in order to ensure both personal privacy (e.g., can anyone access my Social Security number?) and national security (e.g., can anyone access our government's emergency security plans?). Information as a tradable commodity acknowledges the role of information in a capitalistic, knowledge-based society, where potential profit from information ownership must be balanced with consumer access for ongoing discovery and quality of life (see also chapter 33: "Open Access").

As depicted in figure 29.1, there are tensions when weighing policy decisions in light of the public good (individual rights and social justice) versus the private good (ownership and economic growth). There are also tensions when evaluating policy decisions in light of the need for open/unrestricted flows of information (no cost, no limits) and closed/restricted flows (fee-based, tight limits).

Information professionals will not always choose policies from the open/public good quadrant. For example, information centers within commercial organizations, particularly those that are developing products or are highly competitive, will select information policies that restrict flows of information outside the organization and perhaps even will practice very restrictive information flows within the organization. It is important to consider the mission, purpose, and overall values of the organization or the society when analyzing whether a policy is appropriate.

Another twenty-first-century example of an information policy issue involving the need to address two equally desirable goals is the use of electronic surveillance and encryption, which can foster national security while potentially violating personal privacy rights without the knowledge or consent of the individual. What kind of information policies can best address this tension, maximizing national security but also ensuring citizens' civil liberties?

Discussion Question

A typical example in today's society of conflicting policy values is the tension between national security versus information privacy. Discuss the issue of broad government access to citizens' information in a world where personal communications, including, for example, medical reports from your doctor and financial information from your bank and investment adviser, are all conducted electronically. Then, discuss the same issue from the perspective of access to your personal electronic information by private companies via your internet service provider.

THE PROCESS OF GOVERNMENT POLICY MAKING

Information policies are necessary at all levels of society: global, national, regional, state, local, organizational, and personal. As already discussed, an organization's mission drives its decision making regarding information policies, and society's values impact how information issues are addressed. However, government agencies play a key role in information policy making. The policy making process in the United States takes place within the three branches of government: executive, legislative, and judicial. Each of the branches of government may play a role in the policy process. There are five stages to the policy formulation process. See textbox 29.3.

TEXTBOX 29.3

Policy Formulation Process

Once values are identified, a standard policy formulation process in government and business typically includes the following stages:

- Problem identification and agenda setting
- Policy formulation / policy making
- Budgeting
- Policy adoption and implementation
- Evaluation

Stage 1: Problem Identification and Agenda Setting

When an issue in society develops, an agenda or broad plan to address the issue may take shape within the government or in response to a vocal public urging government officials to take action. Values emerge as drivers of suggested government action. This stage of the process is considered the time of problem identification and agenda setting.

Stage 2: Policy Formulation/Policy Making

The next stage of the process is policy formulation, where an approach to the issue is designed and articulated. Policy formulation often includes extensive debates based on contrasting values and intended outcomes. To be effective, policy formulation must involve compromise.

In her book, *Policy Paradox: The Art of Political Decision Making*, Deborah Stone describes policy formulation using the metaphor of dividing a chocolate cake for a classroom of students. The cooperative goal may be to divide the cake fairly, but disagreements arise on seemingly ceaseless aspects of the question. In particular, there are "competing values of an equitable distribution."[6] Many factors are brought into the decision-making process and are part of the values definition that precedes policy formulation, such as whether the cake should be divided equally among the students based on weight and size of the pieces, or whether extenuating circumstances and preexisting external conditions should influence the definition of "equitable." Stone identifies eight potential scenarios that might influence the division of the cake, including the possibility that a student already had some chocolate cake and indeed has lots at home (external conditions), that a student contributed more actively to class discussions (merit), or that a student might or might not receive a portion because of her absence that particular day (requirements for benefits).[7]

> To be effective, policy formulation must involve compromise.

In the United States, this policy formation stage takes place most often in the legislative branch but may also come from a president's executive order or a Supreme Court ruling. For example, the Freedom of Information Act (1967)[8] was enacted by Congress and had subsequent modifications through various executive orders. An example of policy made through a Supreme Court ruling is the 1965 landmark case *Griswold v. Connecticut*,[9] where a state ban on contraceptives was declared unconstitutional based on a citizen's right to marital privacy. This decision has had broad ramifications guaranteeing Americans a constitutional right to privacy.

Kate Marek

Stage 3: Budgeting

After policy formulation/policy making, budget issues associated with the policy need to be resolved. Keep in mind the power of the purse. Adequate funding is required for policy implementation, and the level to which a policy is (or is not) funded is a powerful political tool in the policy process (see also chapter 21: "Managing Budgets").

Stage 4: Policy Adoption and Implementation

The stage of policy adoption takes place when legislation is passed, when an executive order or a new regulation goes into effect, or when the Supreme Court issues a ruling. This is followed by policy implementation, which frequently happens through government agencies, individual state governments, or even local jurisdictions, depending on the nature of the policy or of the ruling.

Stage 5: Evaluation

The final stage of the process is evaluation, allowing decision makers to examine the impact of the policy and whether it is still relevant. For example, a policy may need to be updated or revised based on broad changes in public opinion, developments in technology or new research, or the more pragmatic basis of a cost-benefit analysis in situations where it may no longer be financially feasible to continue with the policy. When considering possible policy solutions to an issue, it is useful to think not only of the intended outcomes (e.g., welfare payments to ease hunger) but also potential unintended consequences (e.g., the welfare system perpetuates dependence on government payments rather than building self-sufficiency). Unintended negative outcomes of a policy are frequently the rationale for policy reconsideration and revision.

Discussion Question

Explore the concept of "unintended consequences" of a government or organizational policy by thinking about a particular government policy such as the Family Educational Rights and Privacy Act (FERPA) or the Health Insurance Portability and Accountability Act of 1996 (HIPPA). How might unintended consequences of a policy be avoided and/or mediated?

INFORMATION PROFESSIONALS: RESPONSIBILITIES AND OPPORTUNITIES

Information professionals' roles in the arena of information policy include awareness, advocacy, and activism. Information professionals have indeed been leaders in the fight for policies that reflect the profession's core values, such as equity of access and intellectual freedom, sometimes at great personal and professional risk (see also chapter 35: "Intellectual Freedom").

An example of one of those heroes is Ruth Brown (1891–1975) who, in the mid-twentieth century, took a stand on equity of access within her community. As the longtime director of the Bartlesville, Oklahoma, Public Library, Brown gradually but relentlessly opened the library's programming and collections to African Americans. Despite the strong support of many community members as well as the Oklahoma Library Association, the American Library Association (ALA), and the American Civil Liberties Union (ACLU), growing political opposition cost Brown her job; she was fired in 1950.[10]

Activist Zoia Horn (1918–2014) is considered a hero for her work protecting privacy rights and intellectual freedom. Horn, who worked in academic and public libraries, spent twenty days in jail in

1972 because of her refusal to testify against the Harrisburg Seven, priests, and nuns who were peace activists and protested against involvement in the Vietnam War. She asserted that being forced to testify would violate her professional principles of privacy and intellectual freedom.[11] Throughout her life, Horn continued her activism in support of intellectual freedom and against all barriers to information services.

Something as subtle, but as fundamental, as standardized subject headings used to classify library materials can support or question a cultural point of view. The efforts in the 1970s of the ALA Task Force on Gay Liberation (now the Gay, Lesbian, Bisexual, and Transgender Round Table)[12] provide a case history of policy activism as it relates to simple, but highly visible, language changes. By moving the topic "homosexuality" from the Library of Congress Subject Heading "Sexual Deviations" to "Sexual Life" in 1972, the Library of Congress made a significant contribution to shifting cultural norms.[13] Bowker and Star explore the issue of "classification and its consequences" in depth in their book on this topic, *Sorting Things Out*.[14]

The value of information privacy came to the forefront in a 2005-2006 court case involving the "Connecticut Four," where four librarians from a Connecticut library database co-op challenged a national security letter demanding USA PATRIOT Act-sanctioned access to patron records without a court order. A significant component of the case was the mandatory gag order associated with the delivery of the national security letter and thus the broad restrictions on freedom of speech. Engaging the American Civil Liberties Union to fight the gag order, the Connecticut Four fought the gag order and continued to fight to protect their patrons' privacy. The case, officially titled *Doe v. Gonzales*,[15] was finally resolved in 2006 when a federal court lifted the gag order, and, shortly thereafter, the FBI dropped its demand for the patron records. The Connecticut Four, George Christian, Barbara Bailey, Peter Chase, and Janet Nocek, were subsequently recognized by the American Library Association with the 2007 Paul Howard Award for Courage.[16]

> Information professionals have indeed been leaders in the fight for policies that reflect the profession's core values, such as equity of access and intellectual freedom, sometimes at great personal and professional risk.

As these examples demonstrate, information professionals benefit from knowing federal and state laws affecting information organization, access, and use, and it is important for information professionals to stay engaged with policy developments that impact our core values. For example, net neutrality[17] is a complex issue that pits preservation of the open internet and equitable information access against commercial gain through the creation of fee-based internet "fast-lanes." Information professionals should consider it their responsibility to participate collectively in this critical national policy conversation.

Information professionals should also be aware of their own organization's policies and be a part of the evaluation and review of those policies. Information professionals should always consult an attorney when they are confronted with a challenge to an information policy issue. The American Library Association and state library associations also have structures to help defend citizens' rights to access and privacy.

CONCLUSION

As the role of information in our society has expanded in recent decades, so too has the work of information professionals as information stewards. The questions regarding information policy introduced in this chapter should trigger an awareness of the critical role information professionals play in the formulation of information policy. Indeed, as all aspects of the information cycle (creation, distribution, analysis, collection, use, and curation) shift from analog to digital, many of our policy mechanisms, and even our conceptions upon which policy is based, are outdated. Information professionals must act collectively through partnerships and professional organizations to bring our voices to the policy-making table, emphasizing the essential democratic value of universal equitable access to information.

NOTES

1. Sandra Braman, *Change of State* (Cambridge, MA: MIT Press, 2006).
2. Sandra Braman, "Defining Information Policy," *Journal of Information Policy*, no. 1 (2011): 1–5.
3. Sam E. Overman and Anthony G. Cahill, "Information Policy: A Study of Values in the Policy Process," *Policy Studies Review* 9, no. 4 (1990): 803–18.
4. USA PATRIOT Act of 2001, Pub. L. No. 107-56, 115 Stat. 272 (2001), http://thomas.loc.gov/cgi-bin/query/z?c107:H.R.3162.ENR:%20.
5. Ian Rowlands, "Understanding Information Policies," *Journal of Information Science* 22, no. 1 (1996): 13–25.
6. Deborah Stone, *Policy Paradox: The Art of Political Decision Making*, revised edition (New York: W.W. Norton & Company, 2002).
7. Ibid.
8. Freedom of Information Act of 1967, Pub. L. 89-487, 80 Stat. 250 (1967), http://www.foia.gov/.
9. Griswold v. Connecticut, 381 U.S. 479 (1965), http://www.pbs.org/wnet/supremecourt/rights/landmark_griswold.html.
10. Louise S. Robbins, *The Dismissal of Miss Ruth Brown: Civil Rights, Censorship, and the American Library* (Norman: University of Oklahoma Press, 2000).
11. John N. Berry III, "Library Freedom Fighter Zoia Horn Remembered," *Library Journal*, August 19, 2014, http://lj.libraryjournal.com/2014/08/people/library-freedom-fighter-zoia-horn-remembered/.
12. American Library Association, "Gay, Lesbian, Bisexual, and Transgender Round Table," http://www.ala.org/rt/glbtrt.
13. Melissa A. Adler, "The ALA Task Force on Gay Liberation: Effecting Change in Naming and Classification of GLBTQ Subjects," *Advances in Classification Research Online* 23, no. 1 (2013), https://journals.lib.washington.edu/index.php/acro/article/viewFile/14226/12086.
14. George C. Bowker and Susan L. Star, *Sorting Things Out* (Cambridge, MA: MIT Press, 2000).
15. Doe v. Gonzales, 546 U.S. 1301 (2005), http://www.supremecourt.gov/opinions/05pdf/05a295.pdf.
16. "2007 Paul Howard Award for Courage Recipient Named," *ALA.org*. 2007, http://www.ala.org/Template.cfm?Section=archive&template=/contentmanagement/contentdisplay.cfm&ContentID=157765.
17. Two key sources that explain and discuss net neutrality are "Network Neutrality," American Library Association, at http://www.ala.org/advocacy/telecom/netneutrality, and "Network Neutrality, an Internet Society Public Policy Briefing," at https://www.internetsociety.org/sites/default/files/ISOC-Policy Brief-NetworkNeutrality-20151030-nb.pdf.

30

Information Ethics

Martin L. Garnar

Chapter 30: "Information Ethics" offers a foundation for understanding the ethical principles that lie at the core of the information professions. Martin L. Garnar, past chair of the ALA Intellectual Freedom Committee and Committee on Professional Ethics, defines the terminology for discussing ethics, explains and identifies different ethical theories and principles that inform the profession's ethical codes, discusses options for decision making, and highlights future trends and implications for ethical thinking.

Garnar defines ethics "as a set of principles that guide decision making in a specified setting." He notes that when ethics are shared, the underlying principles must also be shared and agreed upon by those involved. Within the information professions, professional ethical codes have been established by several professional associations. Garnar examines the shared ethical principles across four professional associations in the information field. He further raises the issue of how well these ethical codes have held up given all the technological changes. He carefully examines issues pertinent to changes in technology, including filtering, net neutrality, and equality of access, and raises questions about the ethical issues involved. These questions lead to more questions, which, Garnar notes, is often the state of ethical dilemmas.

These ethical codes provide a useful framework that can assist in decision making on central issues in the information professions. However, knowing ethical codes does not necessarily give answers, particularly since the ethical codes are intentionally lacking in specificity. Given this challenge, information professionals need to think carefully before applying ethical principles to current situations, and they may need some help. Knowing when and where to get this help is important. Garnar provides the reader with resources that information professionals may access for guidance.

★   ★   ★

Information ethics is "a field of applied ethics that addresses the uses and abuses of information, information technology, and information systems for personal, professional, and public decision making."[1] For information professionals, this subset of ethics has the most direct application to their daily work, and its primary concerns are well represented in the profession's ethical statements. By understanding the ethical principles at the core of the information science profession and by referring to those principles when making decisions or facing dilemmas, information professionals can strive to ensure that their everyday actions are consistent with the field's professional values. In addition, discerning how those principles apply to new trends and situations helps keep the profession vital and relevant in a constantly changing world. After completing this chapter, the reader should have an understanding of how to:

- define the terminology for discussing ethics,
- explain different ethical theories,
- review the principles that inform the profession's ethical codes,
- identify evidence of those principles, and
- discuss future trends and implications for ethical thinking.

INFORMATION ETHICS: KEY CONCEPTS

Defining terms is the first step in understanding ethics. For the purposes of this chapter, ethics is defined as a set of principles that guide decision making in a specified setting. Ethics can be personal or shared, which impacts the source of the principles at the heart of an ethical system. Principles may also be referred to as morals, values, or beliefs—and people may have these instilled by their family, culture, and society. People may also choose to adopt their own principles based on personal experience and study. When ethics are shared, such as in a professional setting, the underlying principles must also be shared and agreed upon by those involved. As different settings may have distinct areas of concern, there are subsets of ethics, such as information ethics, which may be tailored to various fields.

ETHICAL THEORIES

Before ethics can be approached from a professional perspective, it is important to understand different theories for applying ethics. Though there are multiple ethical theories, this chapter focuses on three dominant schools of thought: utilitarianism, deontology, and the ethics of care.

Utilitarianism

As defined by Henry R. West, utilitarianism is "the theory that actions, laws, institutions, and policies should be critically evaluated by whether they tend to produce the greatest happiness."[2] First espoused by Jeremy Bentham, utilitarianism is associated closely with John Stuart Mill, whose writings popularized the concept.[3] A layperson's approach to utilitarianism may be summed up by the exchange between Captain Kirk and Mr. Spock in *Star Trek II: The Wrath of Khan*, when Spock tells Kirk why he is sacrificing his life in the damaged engine room: the needs of the many outweigh the needs of the few [or the one]. Something that is beneficial for the majority is ethically acceptable if the people disadvantaged by such a decision are in the minority. Critics of utilitarianism observe that negative consequences can too easily be justified in this system of thought.

> The utilitarianism theory emphasizes that 'something that is beneficial for the majority is ethically acceptable if the people disadvantaged by a decision are in the minority.'

Deontology

Deontology, from the Greek *deon* meaning duty, refers to an ethical system based on adherence to rules (i.e., duty-bound to follow the rules). Immanuel Kant[4] is considered to be the preeminent proponent

> In contrast to utilitarianism, deontology focuses not on the consequences of a decision, but on the rightness of the action taken.

of a deontological approach to ethics. In contrast to utilitarianism, deontology focuses not on the consequences of a decision, but on the rightness of the action taken. An action is ethical if the rule guiding the action depends on an underlying principle of validity as applied to everyone regardless of the consequences.[5] Deontology falls short when all the choices of action are right, leaving the actor in the difficult position of having to decide which rule to break in order to preserve another rule.

Ethics of Care

Another approach to ethical thinking is care-based ethics, which may be easily summed up with what is commonly known as the *Golden Rule*: "Do unto others as you would have them do unto you." Though often associated with Christianity, this tenet can be found throughout a variety of world religions and philosophical traditions, including Confucianism, Hinduism, Islam, Judaism, Buddhism, and classic Greek and Latin texts, so considering it a universal value is not beyond reason.[6] Additionally, the "ethics of care"[7] is a feminist concept offered as a corrective to the dominant paradigms of utilitarianism and deontology, as both of those approaches represent the patriarchal hegemony in modern ethical thought.

> Given the service orientation of the library and information science professions, a care-based approach to ethical thinking can be seen as complementary to overall goals.

Given the service orientation of the library and information science professions, a care-based approach to ethical thinking can be seen as complementary to overall goals. However, as with other approaches to ethics, flaws can be found with care-based thinking. "Do unto others" stops being effective when the other is an evildoer. Even the *Platinum Rule* ("Do unto others as they themselves would have done unto them," or more simply, "Treat people how they want to be treated") coined by Milton Bennett[8] has its critics, as some people may wish others to do them harm or may not have the capacity to make appropriate decisions, so there are limits to the universal applicability of care-based thinking.

All the aforementioned approaches to ethics can be discredited with examples of scenarios that fall outside of their paradigms. Rather than focus on the merits or deficits of a specific ethical approach, it is helpful to know that there are multiple ways of approaching ethical dilemmas, as specific situations may require the consideration of a variety of solutions before a decision can be made.

PROFESSIONAL ETHICAL CODES

Having a clearly defined ethical code is a hallmark of a true profession.[9] In the library and information science profession, there are several ethical codes that correspond with specialties within the profession. The Code of Ethics of the American Library Association (ALA), the earliest professional code for information professionals, was first adopted in 1939 and establishes broad principles to "guide the work of librarians [and] other professionals providing information services."[10] The Code of Ethics for Archivists from the Society of American Archivists (SAA) and the Code of Ethical Business Practice from the Association of Independent Information Professionals (AIIP) cover many of the same topics, but also address issues that are unique to their respective situations.[11] A relative newcomer on the scene, the IFLA Code of Ethics for Librarians and Other Information Workers from the International Federation of Library Associations and Institutions (IFLA) was first adopted in 2012 and is the most detailed of these four examples, as it must establish some principles that are taken for granted in individual countries.[12] While these statements cannot provide guidance in every situation, they serve as reminders of the principles that are the foundation of the information profession. See textbox 30.1.

The Profession's Shared Principles

When faced with an ethical dilemma, one of the first steps is to determine what principles are in conflict. In a professional setting, it is imperative for shared principles to be identified and articulated. Of the four professional codes mentioned previously, only the SAA Code of Ethics for Archivists is explicitly paired and presented with a statement of core values: the SAA Core Values of Archivists.[13] This statement is essential to understanding the full commitment of archivists to their principles. Though not presented in tandem with the ALA Code of Ethics, the ALA Core Values of Librarianship statement is a good starting point for a broad list of shared principles and is used as the framework for comparing how these principles are represented in the four ethical codes.[14] Table 30.1 presents these comparisons in a side-by-side format with detailed comparisons following.

Table 30.1. Shared Principles: Side-by-Side Comparison.

Shared Principles	ALA	SAA	AIIP	IFLA
Access	Y	Y	Y	Y
Confidentiality and Privacy	Y	Y	Y	Y
Democracy	Y	N	N	Y
Diversity	Y	Y	N	Y
Education and Lifelong Learning	Y	Y	N	Y
Intellectual Freedom	Y	N	N	Y
Preservation	Y	Y	N	N
Professionalism	Y	Y	Y	Y
Public Good	Y	Y	Y	Y
Service	Y	N	Y	Y
Social Responsibility	Y	Y	N	Y

Y = included principle. N = not included. Implied principles are indicated as included.
Comparison of shared principles across the ALA, SAA, AIIP, and IFLA Codes of Ethics.

Access

ALA mentions equitable access in the very first article, denoting its importance among principles.[15] Likewise, the first section of the IFLA code is titled "Access to Information" and details why access is so important.[16] "Access and Use" is an entire section within the SAA code and includes an acknowledgment that access may be restricted due to donor agreements based on protecting confidential information, thus highlighting how competing principles may sometimes cause an ethical dilemma.[17] Though access does not necessarily apply to the client of an independent information professional, AIIP's code includes "giv[ing] clients the most current and accurate information," which is similar to ensuring good access to information[18] (see also chapter 15: "Accessing Information Anywhere and Anytime: Access Services").

Confidentiality/Privacy

All four codes reference confidentiality and privacy for users regarding information use.[19] As it did with access, the SAA code spells out special responsibilities for both donor and user privacy (see also chapter 34: "Information Privacy and Cybersecurity").

Democracy

Alone among the codes, the preamble to the ALA code notes that information professionals are in a "political system grounded in an informed citizenry" and states that the profession has a "special obligation to ensure the free flow of information."[20] Given the specialized roles of archivists and independent information professionals, and given that democracy is not the only form of government in countries represented by IFLA, the absence of a specific mention in the other three codes is not a surprise. It is worth noting that the SAA Core Values of Archivists statement does make a clear reference to the relationship between democracy and archives when they document "institutional functions, activities, and decision-making" for purposes of accountability.[21]

Diversity

The IFLA code has the only explicit reference to diversity, noting "that equitable services are provided for everyone whatever their age, citizenship, political belief, physical or mental ability, gender identity, heritage, education, income, immigration and asylum-seeking status, marital status, origin, race, religion or sexual orientation"[22] (see also chapter 5: "Diversity, Equity of Access, and Social Justice"). The IFLA code also calls for respect for language minorities. Though the SAA code's preamble states that archives "provide evidence of the full range of human experience" and the ALA code mentions serving "all library users," these references to diversity are implicit at best.[23] However, the SAA core values statement includes an entire section on diversity.[24] The AIIP code does not address diversity.

Education and Lifelong Learning

Article VIII of the ALA Code notes the importance of continuing education for members of the profession.[25] IFLA includes education as one of the core missions of libraries and specifically mentions increasing reading skills and teaching information literacy and also notes the importance of professional development.[26] Though the SAA code does not mention education and lifelong learning, it is part of the SAA core values statement[27] (see also chapter 16: "Teaching Users: Information and Technology Instruction").

Martin L. Garnar

Intellectual Freedom

The ALA code specifically states, "We uphold the principles of intellectual freedom," while the IFLA code references the importance of "freedom of opinion, expression and access to information"[28] (see also chapter 35: "Intellectual Freedom"). Neither the SAA code nor its core values statement makes explicit reference to intellectual freedom, though elements of intellectual freedom such as privacy and access have been noted above. The AIIP code does not mention intellectual freedom.

Preservation

Not surprisingly, multiple sections of the SAA code and core values statement refer to the importance of preservation[29] (see also chapter 13: "Analog and Digital Curation and Preservation"). The ALA code implies that preservation is a responsibility in its preamble when it states that librarians have "a special obligation to ensure the free flow of information and ideas to present and future generations."[30] While the need to publicize preservation policies is mentioned in the IFLA code's section on neutrality and professionalism, the purpose of preservation is not discussed.[31] The AIIP code does not include preservation.

Professionalism

All codes include professionalism as a concept. ALA, SAA, and IFLA all call for fairness and respect when dealing with other members of the profession, while AIIP gives clear direction about respecting the rules of libraries, not accepting projects that would be "detrimental" to the profession, and upholding the profession's reputation.[32] The SAA core values statement also includes a section on professionalism.[33]

The Public Good

This core value may not be easily understood without some context. The ALA core values statement affirms that "libraries are an essential public good" in light of movements to outsource and/or privatize library services.[34] In this sense, none of the codes address this value beyond previous mentions of connections to democracy. The SAA core values statement does explicitly mention the public good with reference to social responsibility, but in the context that archives have a responsibility *to* the public good, not that archives *are* a public good.[35]

Service

All codes except SAA highlight service as a primary value of the profession, though SAA's core value statement does include a section devoted to service.[36]

Social Responsibility

Like the concept of the public good, this concept may benefit from context. The ALA core values statement says that "The broad social responsibilities of the American Library Association are defined in terms of the contribution that librarianship can make in ameliorating or solving the critical problems of society."[37] The IFLA code is the only one that specifically mentions social responsibility as inherent to the profession because of the importance of information service to "social, cultural and economic well-being."[38] The SAA core values statement includes a section on social responsibility, explaining that archivists are responsible not only to their employers and institutions but also to the greater society because of their custody of the cultural record.[39]

Reflecting on the four professional codes, the choice between brevity and detail can make a big difference in what principles or values are clearly stated and what needs to be inferred. IFLA, with the longest code at almost 1,600 words, has the most inclusive approach when it comes to explicating shared principles. The choice to pair an ethical code (of just over 800 words) with a core values statement (of just over 1,400 words) allowed SAA to have a shorter code, though some of those core values were not reflected in that shorter code. That some issues were still not covered in the combined statement shows that a specialized professional statement can get into great detail on matters of special concern while still ignoring areas of broader concern. The AIIP code shows a very different approach to a specialized statement. At 187 words, it is the shortest of the four and is focused exclusively on the concerns of this subset of the profession. Finally, the ALA code favors brevity over detail at 380 words. Twelve of those words were added in the latest revision to expand upon an issue not previously discussed in this chapter, as this topic (intellectual property) was not included in either of the core values statements. Yet, three of the four codes (ALA, IFLA, and AIIP) state that information professionals should respect intellectual property, and ALA and IFLA go on to discuss the rights of information users (IFLA, of course, in much greater detail).[40] This is an example of how codes of ethics may sometimes include principles of how information professionals ought to act regarding a topic that may not be at the spiritual heart of a profession but nevertheless is vital to the profession's work. It is also an example of how ethical codes can adjust and change in response to current trends.

> **Discussion Questions**
>
> The principal, in response to a parent's complaint about a book in the school library, removes the book and puts it in her office without following the official policy for handling challenges. Do you say anything? If so, what and to whom?

KEEPING PACE WITH A CHANGING WORLD

As noted earlier, the ALA Code of Ethics was first created in 1939. Though it has been revised three times since its adoption to address necessary changes, is it possible that some of the values are no longer relevant? In other words, do print-based principles apply to a digital world? The short answer is yes, but not without recognizing how the world has changed or explaining why the principles are still relevant.

Digital Content

Information organizations continue to shift their collections from print/analog to digital content. While some library users provide their own devices for accessing the content, there will always be some people who need to use or borrow library-provided devices, as they do not have anything suitable (or at all). It may be technically equal access to say that everyone has the same right to download content, but the professional ethical codes call for equitable access, which means that information professionals need to bridge the gaps created by individual needs. Whether those needs take the form of equipment, skills deficits, or other barriers to accessing content, information professionals must do their best to remove those barriers. At the same time, if information organizations spend too much money on devices, they will have less money for increasingly expensive content. Meanwhile, licensing continues to supplant purchasing as the model for acquiring content, especially when it is in digital form. If information professionals leave behind the limits on copyright that allowed their organizations to lend and reproduce portions of purchased content, how are they ensuring the free flow of information to future generations?

Diversity

A 2012 study of diversity in the library profession showed a 1 percent increase (from 11 percent to 12 percent) of ethnic and racial minorities working as degreed librarians. In response, ALA president Maureen Sullivan observed that, "Although the findings show some improvement in the diversity of the library workforce, [the profession] clearly has a long way to go. . . . To continue to serve the nation's increasingly diverse communities . . . libraries and the profession must reflect this diversity."[41] Is the profession actively recruiting underrepresented people? Can users truly feel they are receiving the highest level of library service when no one speaks their language or if they cannot find materials that are relevant to their communities? Is digital content accessible to those using adaptive equipment? If diversity is one of the profession's shared principles, then it is imperative the information professional move beyond statements of openness and learn how to live it. The adoption of equity, diversity, and inclusion as a fourth strategic direction of the ALA[42] is a promising development and may signal a commitment to action, but it is still too early as of this writing to judge the success of this initiative.

Internet Filtering

Since the upholding of the Children's Internet Protection Act[43] in 2003, the use of internet filters in public (see also chapter 8: "Community Anchors for Lifelong Learning: Public Libraries") and school libraries (see also chapter 6: "Literacy and Media Centers: School Libraries") has become ubiquitous. A recent study by the ALA reveals a tendency for information organizations to over-block content beyond what is required by law and that the use of internet filters has a disproportionate impact on access to information for those library users without internet access at home.[44] Additionally, filters continue to be imperfect, blocking appropriate content and letting other materials through, so there are still concerns about censorship. How do information professionals balance the desire to save money through the e-rate discounts that come with adopting a filter with the ethical imperative to ensure equitable and unfettered access to information?

User-Created Content

Information organizations have become places where users interact with and create content, rather than just consume it (see also chapter 18: "Creation Culture and Makerspaces"). If information organizations allow users to add their own reviews and comments to library materials in the catalog or through library social media outlets, is it censorship to remove a racist or sexist remark? At what point do organizations place limits on the use of 3-D printers and other makerspace equipment? When does someone's hobby turn into a library-supported business? What obligations do information professionals have to educate users about the copyright implications of their latest video mashup made on library equipment?

Privacy

Many pundits have stated that privacy is dead, and the continuing convergence of online services and resources makes it increasingly difficult to maintain a private persona without opting out of the online world completely. Social media allows individuals to broadcast and document the minutiae of their lives, and many do so voluntarily. Yet, the profession still invests significant resources and political capital in the public defense of privacy, and the public outcry over revelations of the National Security Agency's data collection practices demonstrates that not everyone undervalues privacy. Is it right for ALA to continue to invest in educational efforts like Choose Privacy Week[45] when its resources are stretched thin? Is it right to abandon a principle that has been enshrined in the Code of Ethics since its inception?

Service Models

The first article of the ALA Code of Ethics states: "We provide the highest level of service to all library users through . . . equitable service policies [and] equitable access."[46] The term "service" can be looked at in several ways. A move toward self-service has freed up staff to work on other projects. Some users might like the increased sense of privacy that comes with using a self-check machine, while others are concerned that their materials on open hold shelves are identified with their names for all to see (see also chapter 14: "User Experience"). Information organizations of all types have seen an increase in online users, including those who never step foot in a physical library. Do online users get the same level of service as walk-up users? Alternatively, if information professionals move away from the traditional reference desk to a more centralized service center, are they offering the highest level of service to the technology-averse user encouraged to "live chat" with their reference questions? How do information organizations strike a balance between supporting traditional services and testing innovative ideas? How do information professionals evaluate services and programs when funding is tight and cuts must be made?

Discussion Question

A vendor recently changed its platform to restrict printing of documents to one page at a time. You discover a work-around that restores the ability to print in larger quantities. Do you share this information with your colleagues? Your users? The vendor?

Neutrality

Article VII of the ALA Code of Ethics states, "We distinguish between our personal convictions and professional duties and do not allow our personal beliefs to interfere with fair representation of the aims of our institutions or the provision of access to their information resources."[47] This has often been interpreted to mean that information professionals must be neutral and cannot take positions on any issue. However, while the profession has aimed to be neutral about what is included in the content of collections, the profession has not been neutral about who should be able to access the content of those collections. In an increasingly divided political climate, some information professionals have called for restricting hate speech in their institutions, whether that means placing restrictions on user conduct or removing (or not adding) materials deemed to be hateful to others. When does selection turn into censorship? How can an organization support equity, diversity, and inclusion while keeping or adding materials that contradict those values? Should racists or any other group promoting hatred feel welcome at the library?

For all of these trends, there is a common theme: rather than finding answers, more questions arise. This is usually the case with ethical dilemmas. As noted in the preamble of the ALA Code of Ethics, the "principles of this Code are expressed in broad statements to guide ethical decision making. These statements provide a framework; they cannot and do not dictate conduct to cover particular situations."[48] Therefore, being comfortable with the profession's ethical principles is important to good decision making, as is knowing when to seek assistance.

GETTING HELP

Ethical dilemmas are by nature difficult to resolve—if it is easy to resolve, it is not truly a dilemma. There are resources from ALA that can help. The Office for Intellectual Freedom offers assistance to the library profession when dealing with ethical challenges and other issues related to core principles. The ALA Committee on Professional Ethics provides guidance on ethical issues through interpretative statements of the ALA Code of Ethics in a question-and-answer format, covering such topics as social media, conflicts of interest, and workplace speech, and in 2014 issued the first-ever interpretation of the Code of Ethics on copyright.

The best strategy for resolving ethical dilemmas is preparation. All information professionals should be aware of policies and procedures at their institutions, and regular reviews of policies and procedures serve as both a refresher on content and an opportunity to address new developments. Since professional values should be at the heart of these policies and procedures (e.g., access, privacy, balancing copyright and fair use), openly discussing these issues can educate new staff as well as remind others about what is truly important. In addition to knowing policies and procedures, an effective training method for resolving ethical dilemmas is by using scenarios. Participants are given a scenario that poses an ethical dilemma and are asked to discuss all the issues before deciding on what they would do. In addition, managers should keep track of issues happening in the workplace and discuss them at regular staff meetings to evaluate what was done well and what could have been done differently. It does not have to be a life-or-death situation to be good practice of how to resolve a dilemma.

> **Check This Out**
>
> The Office for Intellectual Freedom and the ALA Committee on Professional Ethics provides guidance on ethical issues through interpretative statements of the ALA Code of Ethics. *Visit:* http://www.ala.org/oif.

THINKING AHEAD

As the challenges facing information professionals continue to change and evolve, it is essential to stay on top of the latest news, updates, and resources so that actions can be forward thinking and not just reactive. There are many ways that information professionals can be proactive in the ethical realm:

- Join a professional organization (local, state, regional, national, international) and get involved, as active participation provides opportunities to learn about the latest trends facing the information professions through committee work and networking.
- Attend professional conferences, webinars, and other educational opportunities to stay current in the field and discover how colleagues are addressing shared concerns. Likewise, read blogs, articles, and books to continue learning in an informal setting.

> **Check This Out**
>
> The Intellectual Freedom Committee of the Colorado Association of Libraries has developed many scenarios that are freely available through their website, along with other training materials. *Visit:* www.cal-webs.org/?page=IFCTraining.

- Subscribe to updates from organizations devoted to job-related issues, such as the ALA Washington Office Newsline[49] for the latest on government policies and legislative initiatives or the ALA Office for Intellectual Freedom's Intellectual Freedom News[50] for news on censorship, privacy, and information access.

- Develop and use professional networks for regular conversations about ethical concerns and to learn from each other's experiences.

By staying connected and current, information professionals will be better prepared to fight for their communities' right to access information and to address ethical issues as they arise.

CONCLUSION

Change is a constant in the library and information science profession (see also chapter 20: "Change Management"). Information organizations are constantly adapting to new technologies, new demands on services, and new opportunities for serving their communities. At the same time, tradition plays an important part in what the profession represents. Collections represent the cultural heritage of society, and many information organizations have been at the heart of their communities for time immemorial. Along with the need to balance the competing needs of change and tradition comes the need to balance the competing interests of the latest ethical dilemma. Ethical codes serve as a reminder of the industry's principles, but the intentional lack of specificity requires information professionals to think before applying these principles to current situations. Reviewing past challenges and current issues demonstrates that there have been ample opportunities to apply ethical principles, and the future will surely bring new and unpredicted controversies. Information professionals can, however, depend upon these principles to remain applicable to whatever comes their way, provided they face each ethical dilemma as it comes and not rely on past practice to supply the only answer.

NOTES

1. Edwin M. Elrod and Martha M. Smith, s.v. "Information Ethics," in *Encyclopedia of Science, Technology, and Ethics* (Detroit: Macmillan Reference USA, 2005).
2. Henry R. West, "J. S. Mill," in *The Oxford Handbook of the History of Ethics*, ed. Roger Crisp (New York: Oxford University Press, 2013), doi:0.1093/oxfordhb/9780199545971.013.0025.
3. John Stuart Mill, *Utilitarianism* (London: Parker, Son, and Bourne, 1863).
4. "Immanuel Kant Biography," Who2Biographies, accessed August 12, 2017, http://www.who2.com/bio/immanuel-kant/.
5. Andrews Reath, "Kant's Moral Philosophy," in *The Oxford Handbook on the History of Ethics*, ed. Roger Crisp (New York: Oxford University Press, 2013), doi:10.1093/oxfordhb/9780199545971.013.0021.
6. Andrew H. Plaks, "Golden Rule," in *Encyclopedia of Religion* (Detroit, MI: Macmillan Reference USA, 2005).
7. Virginia Held, "The Ethics of Care," in *The Oxford Handbook of Ethical Theory*, ed. David Copp (New York: Oxford University Press, 2009), doi:10.1093/oxfordhb/9780195325911.003.0020.
8. Milton J. Bennett, *Basic Concepts of Intercultural Communication: Selected Readings* (Yarmouth, ME: Intercultural Press, 1998), 212–13.
9. Kenneth McLeish, ed., "Profession," in *Bloomsbury Guide to Human Thought* (London, UK: Bloomsbury, 1993).
10. "Code of Ethics of the American Library Association," American Library Association, last modified January 22, 2008, http://www.ala.org/tools/ethics.
11. "Code of Ethics for Archivists," Society of American Archivists, last modified January 2012, http://www2.archivists.org/statements/saa-core-values-statement-and-code-of-ethics; "Code of Ethical Business Practice," Association of Independent Information Professionals, last modified April 20, 2002, http://aiip.org/About/Professional-Standards.
12. "IFLA Code of Ethics for Librarians and Other Information Workers," International Federation of Library Associations and Institutions, last modified August 2012, http://www.ifla.org/news/ifla-code-of-ethics-for-librarians-and-other-information-workers-full-version.
13. "Core Values of Archivists," Society of American Archivists, last modified May 2011, http://www2.archivists.org/statements/saa-core-values-statement-and-code-of-ethics.

14. "Core Values of Librarianship," American Library Association, last modified June 29, 2004, http://www.ala.org/advocacy/intfreedom/corevalues.
15. "Code of Ethics of the ALA," art. I.
16. "IFLA Code of Ethics," art. 1.
17. "Code of Ethics for Archivists," Access and Use.
18. "Code of Ethical Business Practice."
19. "Code of Ethics of the ALA," art. III; "IFLA Code of Ethics," art. 3; "Code of Ethics for Archivists," Privacy; "Code of Ethical Business Practice."
20. "Code of Ethics of the ALA," preamble.
21. "Code of Ethics for Archivists," preamble.
22. "IFLA Code of Ethics," art. 2.
23. "Code of Ethics for Archivists," preamble; "Code of Ethics of the ALA," art. I.
24. "Core Values of Archivists," Diversity.
25. "Code of Ethics of the ALA," art. VIII.
26. "IFLA Code of Ethics," arts. 1, 2, and 5.
27. "Core Values of Archivists," Professionalism.
28. "Code of Ethics of the ALA," art. II; "IFLA Code of Ethics," preamble.
29. "Code of Ethics for Archivists"; "Core Values for Archivists."
30. "Code of Ethics of the ALA," preamble.
31. "IFLA Code of Ethics," art. 5.
32. "Code of Ethics of the ALA," art. V; "IFLA Code of Ethics," art. 6; "Code of Ethics for Archivists," Professional Relationships; "Code of Ethical Business Practice."
33. "Core Values of Archivists," Professionalism.
34. "Core Values of Librarianship," The Public Good.
35. "Core Values of Archivists," Social Responsibility.
36. "Code of Ethics of the ALA," art. I; "IFLA Code of Ethics," preamble, arts. 1, 2, and 5; "Code of Ethical Business Practice"; "Core Values of Archivists," Service.
37. "Core Values of Librarianship," Social Responsibility.
38. "IFLA Code of Ethics," preamble.
39. "Core Values of Archivists," Social Responsibility.
40. "Code of Ethics of the ALA," art. IV; "IFLA Code of Ethics," art. 4; "Code of Ethical Business Practice."
41. "Diversity Counts," American Library Association, accessed August 1, 2017, http://www.ala.org/offices/diversity/diversitycounts/divcounts.
42. "About ALA," American Library Association, accessed August 1, 2017, http://www.ala.org/aboutala/.
43. "The Children's Internet Protection Act (CIPA)," American Library Association, accessed August 12, 2017.
44. Kristen R. Batch, "Fencing Out Knowledge: Impacts of the Children's Internet Protection Act 10 Years Later," American Library Association, last modified June 2014, http://connect.ala.org/files/cipa_report.pdf.
45. "Choose Privacy Week," American Library Association, accessed August 1, 2017, https://choosepri vacyweek.org.
46. "Code of Ethics of the ALA," art. I.
47. Ibid., art. VII.
48. Ibid., preamble.
49. "#ALAWO Newsline," American Library Association, accessed August 1, 2017, http://ala.informz.net/ala/pages/ALAWON.
50. "Intellectual Freedom News," American Library Association, accessed August 1, 2017, http://ala.in formz.net/ala/profile.asp?fid=3430.

31

Copyright and Creative Commons

Mary Minow and Liz Hamilton

Chapter 31, "Copyright and Creative Commons," addresses one of the central balancing acts performed by information professionals—protecting intellectual property rights and providing access to content. Mary Minow, attorney and copyright expert, and Liz Hamilton, copyright librarian, provide an overview of key copyright provisions as well as developments concerning digitization. They note that American copyright law comes from the U.S. Constitution and is intended as a social good that protects creativity while benefiting society. Users need to know how they can use what is created by others, and information professionals need to understand how to help them while staying out of legal trouble themselves.

Minow and Hamilton review the pertinent laws noting what is included in copyright and relevant exceptions while providing illustrative examples. They go over public domain works, which is when works enter the public domain after copyright expires. Minow and Hamilton are careful to delineate differences across types of works and licenses, including the recently developed Creative Commons license.

Licensing is also important for information professionals to understand. Click-wrap licenses, negotiated licenses, and Creative Commons licenses are three types that impact information professionals, and the authors discuss them in detail. Information professionals who find themselves in the position of helping users with copyright will be relieved to know many resources and protections are available. However, it is imperative that information professionals understand what their rights are. This chapter aims to provide that understanding.

★   ★   ★

The Code of Ethics of the American Library Association (ALA) states: "We respect intellectual property rights and advocate balance between the interests of information users and rights holders."[1]

To support this balance, the information professional must first know what rights are reserved to copyright owners and what exceptions to those rights exist for users. This chapter provides a basic introduction to copyright, outlining its origins, what works are legally protected, the exclusive rights of copyright owners, and important exceptions that pertain to information organizations: the first-sale doctrine, Section 108 (the library exception), and fair use. Essential topics such as the Digital Millennium Copyright Act, Creative Commons licenses, and click-through and negotiated licenses and their relationship to copyright are discussed. The chapter also looks ahead to developments concerning mass digitization, course packs, orphan works, accessibility, and changes in the Copyright Office. After reading this chapter, the reader should have an understanding of the information professional's role as it relates to copyright today, from preserving copyrighted materials to teaching communities about the basics of copyright law in the United States, current developments in copyright law, and the importance of copyright law to the information professional.

COPYRIGHT

To explain why copyright matters to information professionals, it is important to first look at what copyright is. American copyright law is drawn from the U.S. Constitution, which grants Congress the power to "promote the Progress of Science and useful Arts, by securing for limited times to authors and inventors the exclusive right to their respective writings and discoveries."[2]

> Constitutional copyright is intended as a social good. By allowing owners to profit from their works for a limited period of time, Congress hoped to encourage creativity and expand the quantity of published works that would benefit society.

Congress, thus empowered, enacted U.S. Copyright Law, now in Title 17 of the U.S. Code.[3] The U.S. Copyright Office promulgates and implements regulations in Title 37 of the Code of Federal Regulations.[4] Constitutional copyright is intended as a social good. By allowing owners to profit from their works for a limited period of time, Congress hoped to encourage creativity and expand the quantity of published works that would benefit society. By limiting the periods of time, or the length of copyright protections, Congress intended to expand the public domain, which refers to works that can be used freely by everyone.

COPYRIGHT AND THE EXCLUSIVE RIGHTS OF OWNERS

Copyright protection extends to "original works of authorship fixed in any tangible medium of expression,"[5] according to Section 102 of the 1976 Copyright Act. It is worth noting that, although originality is necessary for copyright protection, ideas cannot be copyrighted. Poems, songs, stories, and so forth are protected by copyright only when the expression is fixed in a tangible medium, and even then, only the expression itself (not the underlying idea) is protected. Works that qualify for copyright protection include literary, musical, dramatic, artistic, choreographic, pictorial, graphic, sculptural, audiovisual, sound-recording, and architectural works.[6] Both published and unpublished works may be protected by copyright law.[7]

Check This Out

For more information about labeling the copyright status of works for which your information organization is not the copyright owner, *visit:* RightsStatements.org, a joint initiative of Europeana and the Digital Public Library of America (DPLA).

Section 106 of the 1976 Copyright Act grants several exclusive rights to copyright owners (see textbox 31.1).[8] Copyright owners may either exercise these rights on their own or authorize others to do so. While these rights are exclusive, they are balanced with a series of limitations and exceptions, detailed in 17 U.S. Code, Sections 107–22.[9]

The Exclusive Rights of Copyright Holders

1. To reproduce the copyrighted work in copies or phonorecords.
2. To prepare derivative works based upon the copyrighted work.
3. To distribute copies or phonorecords of the copyrighted work to the public by sale or other transfer of ownership, or by rental, lease, or lending.
4. In the case of literary, musical, dramatic, and choreographic works, pantomimes, and motion pictures and other audiovisual works, to perform the copyrighted work publicly.
5. In the case of literary, musical, dramatic, and choreographic works, pantomimes, and pictorial, graphic, or sculptural works, including the individual images of a motion picture or other audiovisual work, to display the copyrighted work publicly.
6. In the case of sound recordings, to perform the copyrighted work publicly by means of a digital audio transmission.[10]

For example, if a local high school wants to stage a play written by playwright Anita Page, they would have to ask her for permission to publicly perform it (the fourth enumerated exclusive right enjoyed by copyright owners), unless there is a limitation or exception that would allow them to do so without permission. Likewise, a publisher who wants to print copies of the play and sell it as a book would, absent an exception, needs the copyright owner's permission, as both the (1) reproduction and (2) distribution rights are implicated. If Professor Smith wanted the library to post a copy of Page's play on his public website for a class to read, the library would also need her permission beforehand, unless an exception applies.

The copyright owner's permission is *not* necessary if the work has entered the public domain, if a specific exception in the law allows someone other than the copyright owner to undertake a specific use, or if a broad license has already been granted, such as through the Creative Commons.[11] For information professionals, the most important exceptions to the protections of copyright law include Section 109 (the first sale doctrine), Section 108 (the library exception), and Section 107 (fair use). Each is discussed in turn.

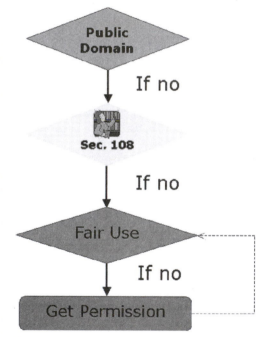

Figure 31.1 Exceptions to Copyright Law. *Created by author.*

THE PUBLIC DOMAIN

One of the most common cases where permission is not needed occurs when a work is in the public domain. A work typically enters the public domain after its copyright protection expires. Unpublished works have a copyright term of the author's lifetime plus seventy years. The duration of a published work's copyright protection will vary depending on the circumstances of its publication. For works created on or after January 1, 1978, the copyright endures for the life of the author plus seventy years following the author's death. This protection occurs automatically. For anonymous and pseudonymous works, and works made for hire (either works created by employees as a part of their employment, or created under contract and specified as work for hire), the duration of copyright is ninety-five years from publication or 120 years from creation, whichever is shorter.[12] Historically, other factors that have dictated the length of copyright protection have included the date the work was originally published, whether the work was published with a copyright notice (for example, "Copyright © 1970 by Toni Morrison"), and whether the work was registered after publication.[13]

A copyrighted work can also enter the public domain in other ways. U.S. Government works are in the public domain by statute 17 U.S.C. § 105.[14] A copyright owner may also dedicate a work to the public domain by adding a statement to that effect. An example of a public domain dedication is the Creative Commons CC0 license, which allows a creator to waive the rights to a work that would otherwise be protected by copyright.[15] This allows others to use that work as freely as possible. Other Creative Commons licenses allow creators to permit some uses of their works but not all of them, as discussed later. Creative Commons also offers a Public Domain Mark, placed on works identified as having safely entered the public domain.[16] Note that simply being free online does not make a work in the public domain; it is still subject to the rules of copyright law.

> **Check This Out**
>
> Peter Hirtle's *Copyright Term and the Public Domain in the United States* chart is highly recommended as a resource for determining whether a given work has passed into the public domain. *Visit:* https://copyright.cornell.edu/resources/publicdomain.cfm.

Specific Limitations and Exceptions

The First-Sale Doctrine

The first-sale doctrine, codified in Section 109 of the copyright law, does not translate well into today's digital world. What it does is allow the owner of a particular physical copy of a copyrighted work to *redistribute*—that is, sell, give away, or lend that copy. It was not written to allow the *reproduction* of that work.[17] For example, if someone possesses a legitimately obtained copy of *The Bluest Eye*, he can sell, give, or lend his copy to a friend when he is done reading it. However, he cannot scan or photocopy the book to give away, as that would infringe on the author's right of reproduction. The first-sale doctrine is what allows Amazon to sell vinyl records, Netflix to rent DVDs by mail, and—what is most important for information professionals—information organizations to lend books and other copyrighted materials.

The first-sale doctrine does not neatly apply in the digital realm because (1) the nature of digital media means reproductions are made in the course of distribution, and (2) in the digital marketplace, licenses, rather than sales, are the norm. In 2013, a federal district court in New York ruled against ReDigi, an online marketplace for used MP3s, in a lawsuit brought by Capitol Records. Even though ReDigi's customers were required to delete the MP3 from their computers when selling it to another customer, the court ruled that the initial act of reproduction infringed the copyright owners' rights.[18] At the time of this book's publication, the case is on appeal. The Library Copyright Alliance filed an amicus brief in February 2017 in support of ReDigi, supporting an interpretation of first sale to allow the reselling of used MP3s. They made two main arguments: first, that the first factor in the court's fair use analysis should favor uses with the same underlying purpose as first sale itself; and second, that a positive fair-use determination for ReDigi would allow libraries to provide innovative new digital services.[19] Information professionals should pay attention to developments in this case that may impact first sale.

Section 108

Section 108[20] of Title 17, sometimes called the library exception, allows information organizations to use copyrighted works without permission. Though complex, Section 108 is immensely important to information professionals in library and archival settings, as it allows these information organizations to create up to three preservation and replacement copies for themselves, in addition to a single distribution copy for their patrons. In both cases, the law requires certain conditions to be met:

1. The information organization must be either open to the public or open to researchers unaffiliated with the information organization or its host institution who are doing research in a specialized field.
2. The reproduction or distribution must be made without the purpose of commercial advantage.
3. The reproduction must contain a notice of copyright, either the notice printed on the original or, if none, a generic notice that the work may be protected by copyright.
4. Incidents of reproduction and distribution must be isolated and unrelated; that is, information organizations cannot systematically copy and distribute copyrighted materials.
5. The types of work to which Section 108 applies are sometimes limited, as outlined below.[21]

Preservation and Replacement

Information organizations are allowed to make up to three copies of works for purposes of preservation or replacement. The specific rules differ slightly for published and unpublished works. Replacement copies of a published work are permissible if it is damaged or missing or if its format has become obsolete and an unused replacement copy cannot be found at a fair price. Preservation copies of an unpublished work may be made solely for purposes of preservation and security or for deposit for research use in another information organization, and only if the original is currently in the copying organization's collection. Digital preservation or replacement copies can be made regardless of a work's publication status, but the copies may not be distributed in that format beyond the premises of the information organization (see also chapter 13: "Analog and Digital Curation and Preservation").

Copies for Patrons

Information organizations may also make single copies of materials for distribution to individual patrons. They may make a copy of an article or other small portion of a copyrighted work; or, if a copy of the complete work cannot be obtained at a fair price, the entire work may be copied. In both cases, the copy must become the property of the user, and the institution cannot have had notice that the copy would be used for any reason besides private study or research. The information organization must also display a standard warning of copyright, with prescribed wording from the Code of Federal Regulations. This warning must be displayed at the location where orders for copies are taken, as well as on the order form itself.[22]

Unlike preservation and replacement copies, these study copies are limited by the type of work. Information organizations may not use this provision to make copies of musical works (i.e., the musical composition and score); pictorial, graphic, or sculptural works; or motion pictures or other audiovisual works that do not deal with news. They may, however, use the provision to share materials with patrons at other institutions through interlibrary loan, provided these copies do not substitute for a subscription to or purchase of such work. The receiving library is responsible for keeping track of these copies.[23]

Last Twenty Years of Copyright: An Unusual Exception

During the last twenty years of any published work's copyright term, information organizations and nonprofit educational institutions gain additional privileges under Section 108(h). If the work is not subject to normal commercial exploitation, it cannot be obtained at a reasonable price, and the copyright owner has not provided notice that either of these conditions is false, the institution can reproduce, distribute, display, or perform copies of that work for preservation, scholarship, or research. This exemption does not extend to users beyond the information organization or educational institution.

Other Provisions of Section 108

Section 108(f) includes some notable provisions for information organizations. First, it protects these institutions from patron-induced liability for unsupervised use of reproduction equipment on its premises, so long as that equipment displays a notice that the reproduction may be subject to copyright law. No specific language is mandated by law. Second, it notes that Section 108 does not negate fair use. This is important for information organizations because some actions not permitted under Section 108 may be allowed under the fair-use provisions in Section 107.[24] For example, copying a stand-alone photograph from a collection for a researcher is not allowed under Section 108 but might be acceptable as fair use. Finally, any contract the information organization signs may overrule its abilities under Section 108. Information organizations should read contracts with vendors carefully so as not to give away any of their privileges under this exception[25] (see also chapter 32: "Information Licensing").

Section 108 is a vital protection for information organizations in preserving their materials and connecting their patrons with information. All information professionals should familiarize themselves with its provisions. There have been discussions to revise Section 108 in the Section 108 Study Group,[26] the 2013 Symposium on Section 108 held at Columbia Law School,[27] and most recently through a Notice of Inquiry in the summer of 2016 that led to a series of meetings between the Copyright Office and interested parties.[28] As of yet, no legislation has been proposed. Some libraries and information organizations are opposed to amending Section 108. The Library Copyright Alliance is opposed for four main reasons: Section 108 is not obsolete; fair use supplements 108

> **Discussion Questions**
>
> How might your information organization use Section 108 (the "library exception") in its operations? In cases where 108 doesn't apply, how might you use fair use?

where necessary; attempts to revise 108 could limit its current usefulness; and reform of 108 would require many resources from both libraries and Congress.[29] Information professionals should pay attention to this issue and advocate for the interests of their organizations and their users.

Section 107: Fair Use

Fair use is a critical exception to copyright law that allows information professionals and others to use copyrighted materials without permission. Fair use is outlined in Section 107 of the copyright law, and its exceptions are available to information organizations in addition to the provisions in Section 108. Section 107 states that the fair use of a copyrighted work "for purposes such as criticism, comment, news reporting, teaching (including multiple copies for classroom use), scholarship, or research, is not an infringement of copyright."[30] (See also chapter 31: "Section 107: Fair Use" in the online supplement.)

> **Check This Out**
>
> The Columbia Copyright Advisory Office is a great resource for model forms and for help in navigating the copyright permissions process. *Visit:* http://copyright.columbia.edu/copyright/permissions/.

RECENT DEVELOPMENTS

Recent developments in the copyright arena that are especially relevant to library and information professionals include updates to the exceptions in the Digital Millennium Copyright Act,[31] as well as Copyright Office reports and professional practices concerning mass digitization and orphan works. Case law regarding the scanning of books has developed positively with regard to accessibility and nonconsumptive research in the Google Books case[32] and the HathiTrust case.[33] Librarians and information professionals should also pay attention to ongoing developments affecting the accessibility of copyrighted materials, as well as developments in the structure of the Copyright Office itself. As of this writing, the House of Representatives has voted 378–48 to shift the power to appoint the next Register of Copyrights from the Librarian of Congress to the U.S. president.[34]

The Digital Millennium Copyright Act

The Digital Millennium Copyright Act (DMCA) was signed into law on October 28, 1998. The first title of the DMCA implements two World Intellectual Property Organization (WIPO) treaties of 1996: the WIPO Copyright Treaty and the first title of the WIPO Performances and Phonograms Treaty. It also addresses a variety of other copyright issues.[35]

The DMCA has two parts that are particularly relevant to information organizations and information professionals. The first is a prohibition on circumventing technological protection measures (such as encryption) and the second is a safe harbor for potentially infringing user-generated content.

Circumventing Technological Protection Measures: Challenging for Libraries

The DMCA's major significance to information professionals is its prohibition against circumventing "technological protection measures" that protect DVDs, online works, and the like, essentially prohibiting format transfers such as ripping a DVD to an MP4 format. The one exception written into the law for nonprofit libraries, archives, and educational institutions is not terribly useful because it allows circumventing access controls solely to make a good-faith determination about whether to obtain authorized access to the work.[36] Vendors are likely to offer samples or other evaluative information to make circumvention unnecessary. More important is the DMCA's prohibition that essentially forbids the format-shifting that is often needed as media formats evolve.

In 2013, a We the People White House petition garnered over 114,000 signatures complaining that "consumers will no longer be able [to] unlock their phones for use on a different network without carrier permission, even after their contract has expired." This uproar led to legislation to specifically allow cell phone unlocking.[37] The cell phone unlocking prohibition was a direct result of the DMCA that, by default, prohibits circumvention of the technological protection measures that safeguard copyrighted material. Every three years, the Library of Congress holds public hearings to examine exceptions to the DMCA. The national debate on cell phone unlocking sparked discussion as to whether the DMCA provisions that govern *all* technological protection measures guarding copyrighted content (including e-books, digital journals, DVDs, etc.) should undergo narrow legislative fixes or a major overhaul. Legislative reforms were initiated, with details available in Jonathan Band's "The Cell Phone Unlocking Saga,"[38] but as of this writing, it appears more likely that a narrow retooling is in store rather than broad changes.[39]

One positive result for information organizations to come out of the triennial public hearings mentioned above is the exemption from the prohibition against circumvention of technological protection outlined by Section 1201[40] for assistive technologies. Blind people and other people with disabilities can circumvent this protection in order to use screen readers or other assistive technologies, as long as the copy of the work has been lawfully obtained and the rights owner is remunerated for the price of a mainstream copy of the work, or when the work is a lawfully obtained nondramatic literary work.[41] This is a key gain for accessibility and will help many information professionals connect their users to works they could not use previously.

Safe Harbor: Helpful to Information Organizations

The DMCA also created a protection for information organizations and other service providers in Section 512 of the Copyright Act,[42] which offers them safe harbor from liability for infringing materials that users might store on their systems. To qualify for this protection, a service provider must:

1. accommodate standard technical measures for identifying and protecting copyright,
2. designate an agent to receive notices of claimed infringement (and file this designation with the U.S. Copyright Office),
3. take down or block infringing material expeditiously upon receiving proper notice, and
4. adopt and implement a policy of ending the accounts of users who are repeat copyright infringers.

Also, the information provider must not have prior knowledge of the infringing activity and must not receive a financial benefit directly from the infringing activity if they have the right and ability to control it. This system also creates a procedure for the copyright owner to give notice of infringement and for the user who originally posted the material to respond with a counter-notification.[43]

In 2013, the U.S. Department of Commerce's Internet Policy Task Force (IPTF) released a Green Paper on "Copyright Policy, Creativity, and Innovation in the Digital Economy" in an effort to examine the notice and takedown system established under the DMCA.[44] On March 20, 2014, IPTF held a first Public Meeting to discuss the practical operation of the existing notice and takedown system. This roundtable emphasized a multi-stakeholder approach based on consensus, in which the group would select substantive topics to work on for the future, as well as establish the process by which to proceed.[45] After a series of meetings throughout 2014, the group released a document outlining agreed-upon practices intending to improve the operation of the notice and takedown system under the DMCA. This document, called "DMCA Notice-and-Takedown Processes: List of Good, Bad, and Situational Practices," outlines best practices agreed on by consensus among the stakeholders over the course of these conversations.[46]

Mass Digitization

Mass digitization especially affects information organizations and information professionals. In the context of books, mass digitization usually means large-scale scanning projects conducted systematically.[47]

These range from smaller initiatives to scan images and short documents organized by libraries and other cultural heritage institutions to collaborative projects scanning full books on a massive scale.[48]

Mass digitization projects have many stakeholders: copyright owners (such as authors and artists), libraries, archives, museums, technology companies, educators, users of copyrighted works, and the general public.[49] Different groups take different approaches to copyright issues. The Internet Archive, an online library, initially digitized only public domain materials, thereby keeping themselves safely within the bounds of copyright law. Later, it began to add twentieth-century books still in copyright to its open library lending program.[50] The Internet Archive uses a "one-book, one-user" model, with the original print book stored safely in an inaccessible location. Their new Library of 2020 project plans to expand this work by curating, digitizing, and making available in digital form four million books, providing a digital copy to any library in the country that owns the print copy of the book.[51] Google Books has scanned all books regardless of their copyright status and returned the print copies to library shelves. Google has argued that their book-scanning project falls under fair use, since they only display snippet excerpts of books still under copyright.[52] Not all stakeholders agreed with this assessment. In 2005, authors and publishers brought a class action lawsuit against Google, claiming the Google Books project constituted willful copyright infringement.[53] The publishers settled the case with Google, but the authors continued the fight. After eight years of litigation, the U.S. District Court for the Southern District of New York dismissed the case, finding that Google had engaged in fair use.[54] The Authors Guild appealed to the U.S. Court of Appeals for the Second Circuit, which affirmed the district court's opinion, finding Google Books to be a fair use. The Supreme Court declined the Guild's request for it to review the case in April 2016, leaving intact the lower-court rulings in the case—that the scans making snippets available were fair use.[55]

In 2011, the Authors Guild sued five university libraries and the HathiTrust Digital Library over the six libraries' intention to offer access to book scans provided by Google.[56] In June 2014, the U.S. Court of Appeals for the Second Circuit released its opinion in the *Authors Guild v. HathiTrust* case,[57] which addressed the HathiTrust Digital Library's use of copyrighted material and whether it was protected under the doctrine of fair use. The court was particularly concerned with the following issues: the full-text search of HathiTrust's collection, access to the collection for print-disabled users, and the digital preservation of materials already owned by participating libraries. The court concluded that digitization for both full-text search and access for print-disabled patrons constituted fair use, while it vacated the district court's judgment on preservation and remanded to the district court the question of whether the plaintiffs had grounds to challenge the preservation use.[58]

In 2011, the Copyright Office published an analysis and discussion document of legal issues in mass digitization, addressing many of the issues at play in these projects.[59] The current copyright and licensing legal framework looks at the balance between the exclusive rights of the copyright owner, which aspects of digitization are (or should be) covered by fair use and library exceptions, the problem of orphan works (which will be discussed in depth shortly), and what licensing options are now, or could soon be, available. While reliance on fair use supports many digitization projects, it is not a solution for all circumstances. Licensing is proposed by some to help fill the gap between the current exceptions and the resolution of copyright law and mass digitization. Information professionals should pay close attention to developments in this area.

Orphan Works

An orphan work is a work for which the copyright owner cannot be located or identified by an individual who wishes to use that work in a way that would require the copyright owner's permission. Because they are unable to locate the copyright owner, users of these works may face liability for infringement if the owner should later surface. Even though it is in the public interest to make many of these works available, many information organizations will not digitize them because of the risk.

In January 2006, the Copyright Office issued a "Report on Orphan Works," which discusses the problem in detail and offers recommendations to Congress for how to proceed with orphan works legislation. The Copyright Office recommended that such legislation incorporate two requirements: that a potential user must conduct a reasonably diligent search for the copyright owner before using the work and that the user must provide attribution to the original author and copyright owner throughout the work in use. The Copyright Office also recommended limitations on monetary and injunctive relief that the original copyright owner can take in the event they discover the use, a clause making clear that the new legislation does not affect other rights and limitations to copyright elsewhere in the act and a sunset for the provision after ten years so that Congress can evaluate its effects.[60] Despite legislative efforts in 2008, none of these recommendations were implemented.

In 2012 and 2014, the Copyright Office solicited public comment and held roundtables to give orphan works legislation another chance.[61] The roundtables were held on March 10–11, 2014, and combined discussions on both orphan works and mass digitization. The views presented by the varying stakeholders showed the wildly divergent opinions on how to proceed; the only real consensus was caution toward extended collective licensing, though even that was mitigated by previously submitted comments favoring such licenses. After the roundtables, it seems unlikely that all groups will be able to find a mutually acceptable solution to the orphan works question.[62]

Developments in Accessibility

Copyright is designed to increase the quantity of available works for the benefit of society. However, less than 10 percent of all published materials are produced in a format that is accessible to blind or print-disabled people.[63] A recent development designed to help alleviate this problem is the Marrakesh Treaty to Facilitate Access to Published Works for Persons Who Are Blind, Visually Impaired, or Otherwise Print Disabled. The Marrakesh Treaty uses copyright systems as part of the solution to improve access to printed works for people with print disabilities. The treaty requires two obligations:

1. the provision of a limitation or exception to copyright that allows authorized organizations and persons with print disabilities to undertake any necessary changes to make a copy of a work in an accessible format for those persons, and
2. that those accessible copies can be exchanged across borders according to the provisions of the treaty.[64]

The treaty text was adopted on June 27, 2013, and entered into force on September 30, 2016, three months after twenty eligible countries ratified or acceded to the treaty. Only minor modifications of U.S. law would be necessary to implement the Marrakesh Treaty,[65] but as of this writing, the treaty has not been ratified by the United States.[66] Informational professionals should watch for further developments that will allow them to better serve their print-disabled users.

Developments in the Copyright Office

Copyright law in the United States saw its last major revision in 1976, before any of the copyright issues of the digital age came into play. The 1976 revision codified the fair-use doctrine, affirmed the first-sale doctrine, and created exceptions especially for information organizations.[67] However, even at the time of its creation, the 1976 Act had not thoroughly considered the needs of emerging technologies.[68] The Next Great Copyright Act is a useful way of referring to the next major revision of U.S. copyright law. The phrase was coined by the then-Register of Copyrights and Director of the U.S. Copyright Office, Maria Pallante, in a lecture at Columbia Law School, during which she outlined the many reasons the existing Act needs revision and asserted that now is the time for those revisions to be made.[69] In the lecture, Pallante stressed again and again that any revision to the Act must be forward thinking but flexible and must also serve the public interest.[70] As discussed earlier in this chapter, constitutional copyright is intended as a social good, and this idea should inform future revisions of the law.

Pallante called for revision for several reasons. She pointed out that Congress has always had a valuable role in reviewing the larger policies involved in copyright law. In the age of the internet, these overarching reviews should happen more frequently.[71] Since the turn of the century, the Copyright Office has prepared many background documents to guide Congress through relevant issues impacting the Next Great Copyright Act. These include completed research on digital first sale, orphan works, statutory licenses for cable and satellite retransmission, pre-1978 contract termination provisions, mass digitization, and pre-1972 sound recordings,[72] as well as resale royalties for visual artists and small copyright claims. There are also active policy reports on Section 108, moral rights of attribution and integrity, and the DMCA, particularly Section 1201 and Section 512.[73] These background reports shed light on many of the issues that would be addressed in a large-scale revision of the Copyright Act. Court decisions also call on Congress to legislatively address these issues as they are presented in case law. For example, in *Kirtsaeng v. John Wiley & Sons*, the court pointed out that Congress should decide whether copyright owners should have more than ordinary commercial power to divide international markets when it comes to first sale. Similarly, in *Capitol Records, LLC v. ReDigi, Inc.* (now on appeal), the district court stated it was up to Congress to determine whether the limitation of first-sale exceptions to physical copies, rather than digital, is outmoded.[74] As copyright issues affect more people in the digital age, the Act needs to be clarified for a wider audience.

Discussion Questions

Former Register of Copyrights Maria Pallante has argued for copyright reform in "The Next Great Copyright Act." What do you think is the most important area in need of reform? Why?

Revisions to copyright law will need to address many issues that have emerged or expanded since the 1976 Act. These include the disadvantages faced by owners of sound recordings, the creation of incidental copies over the course of digital commerce, the enforcement of copyright in the digital marketplace, a review of the DMCA, the application of first sale to digital materials, exceptions and limitations (such as Section 108, exceptions for print disabilities, higher education, and personal use), licensing issues (especially for music), mandatory deposit in the Library of Congress, copyright term, and the need for the new act to be as clear to the layperson as possible. In addition, the Copyright Office must fully become a twenty-first-century agency in order to support a revised Copyright Act.[75] Information professionals should take particular note of revisions to digital first sale, the DMCA, licensing of copyright materials, and the exceptions currently granted to information organizations. To ensure the best results for information organizations and their patrons, it is important to pay close

Check This Out

One ongoing case of importance to academic institutions that provide course packs is the litigation of *Cambridge University Press v. Georgia State University. Read more about it here:* http://www.arl.org/focus-areas/court-cases/106-cambridge-press-v-georgia-state-university#.

attention to any progress made in copyright law, and voice support for the revisions that support positive results for information users and organizations.

In October 2016, Carla Hayden, the Librarian of Congress, reassigned Pallante from her role as register of copyrights to an advisory position. Pallante declined this reassignment and resigned from the Library of Congress shortly afterward.[76] As of this writing, a new register has not been appointed. Despite Pallante's departure, efforts at copyright reform continue. In December 2016, House Judiciary Committee chairman Bob Goodlatte and Ranking Member John Conyers Jr. released the first policy proposal from the Committee's review of U.S. Copyright Law, reporting that other policy proposals will follow.[77] The first policy proposal called for making the register position subject to a nomination-and-consent process with a ten-year term limit, the addition of several advisory positions within the Copyright Office, the creation of Copyright Office Advisory Committees, information technology upgrades for the Copyright Office, and the implementation of a small claims system that would handle low-value infringement cases and bad faith Section 512 notices.[78] In March 2017, Chairman Goodlatte and Ranking Member Conyers introduced the Register of Copyrights Selection and Accountability Act, which would require the register to be nominated by the president of the United States, subject to confirmation by the U.S. Senate, and would limit the register to a ten-year term, renewable by another round of nomination and confirmation.[79] The Library Copyright Alliance released a statement opposing this Act, out of concern that the politicization of the position would lead to delays in the installation of a register, engage the register more in policy development than modernization of the Office, and lead to less accountability of the register to Congress and the public.[80]

> Now more than ever, information professionals must act in favor of copyright legislation that supports the work of information organizations and their users.

Further developments may have taken place since this writing, but it is clear that multiple parties are working to make changes to both the Copyright Office and the copyright law itself. Now more than ever, information professionals must act in favor of copyright legislation that supports the work of information organizations and their users.

LICENSES

Licenses add another layer of complexity to copyright issues. Click-wrap licenses, negotiated licenses, and Creative Commons licenses are three types that impact information professionals and are discussed in more detail below.

Click-Wrap and Negotiated Licenses

Today, virtually all electronic content is regulated by private licenses, a layer of control that generally overrules copyright law. That is, if a term in a license agreement differs from the rights laid out in copyright law, the license will prevail in nearly every instance. If the license is silent on an issue, then copyright law still regulates who owns what and when.

Creative Commons

The Creative Commons (CC) organization,[81] founded in 2001, provides licensing that works alongside copyright law and that can be advantageous to libraries. Creative Commons is a nonprofit organization that promotes the sharing of creative works and knowledge. In addition to the public domain dedication (CC0) and Public Domain Mark, CC offers a free suite of standardized licenses that allow copyright owners to keep their copyrights yet give the public permission to use their works under set conditions.[82] CC licenses benefit information organizations both as copyright creators who wish to more freely share their work, as well as users who wish to find sources they can use or adapt freely for their own purposes. Figure 31.2 demonstrates the compatibility of the different types of Creative Commons licenses.[83]

	PUBLIC DOMAIN	PUBLIC DOMAIN	CC BY	CC BY SA	CC BY NC	CC BY ND	CC BY NC SA	CC BY NC ND
PUBLIC DOMAIN	✓	✓	✓	✓	✓	✗	✓	✗
PUBLIC DOMAIN	✓	✓	✓	✓	✓	✗	✓	✗
CC BY	✓	✓	✓	✓	✓	✗	✓	✗
CC BY SA	✓	✓	✓	✓	✗	✗	✗	✗
CC BY NC	✓	✓	✓	✗	✓	✗	✓	✗
CC BY ND	✗	✗	✗	✗	✗	✗	✗	✗
CC BY NC SA	✓	✓	✓	✗	✓	✗	✓	✗
CC BY NC ND	✗	✗	✗	✗	✗	✗	✗	✗

Figure 31.2 License Compatibility Chart. *"License Compatibility Chart" from the Creative Commons Wiki [https://wiki.creativecommons.org/wiki/Wiki/cc_license_compatibility] is licensed under CC BY 4.0 [https://creativecommons.org/licenses/by/4.0/].*

Information organizations can use works with CC licenses without the need to negotiate further or pay money in cases where the use is nonprofit. One example of this is academic libraries that collect works in an institutional repository. These libraries can freely acquire works issued under CC licenses. Libraries can also create works and use CC licenses to share the works in a seamless manner, so long as the library does not need to get remuneration for nonprofit use of the works. For example, materials on the University of Michigan Library website authored by staff and librarians are licensed under a

Creative Commons Attribution 4.0 International License, granting free permission for the use of their content provided proper attribution is provided to the University of Michigan Library.[84]

COPYRIGHT AND THE INFORMATION PROFESSIONAL

The changing nature of information requires knowledge of copyright. Information professionals need to keep current on copyright issues so they can help their users with their copyright needs, use the material to the greatest extent possible, and protect themselves from liability. As copyright issues become more widespread and more complex, particularly as social media sharing of material flourishes, there is a greater need for information professionals to answer users' copyright questions. Users need to know what they can do with materials created by others, as well as what rights they hold in work they have created themselves.

Assisting users with copyright issues both remotely and on-site has become easier than ever. Many resources are now freely available online to use, and many of those also have Creative Commons licenses, making it possible to copy and reuse the resources in trainings or for other nonprofit purposes. If users approach the information organization remotely—for example, by e-mail or chat reference—the information professional can connect them with a wealth of resources available for free online wherever they are.

In addition to educating users, information professionals need to be aware of the protections available to them under copyright law. If libraries follow the procedures for safe harbor with DMCA agent registration, they can get protection from liability for user-generated content on their sites.[85] Information organizations also receive protection for designated uses of material under Section 108. It is also important to remember that information professionals are not copyright cops. Placing copyright warning signs near photocopiers insulates the information organization and information professional from liability for user copying. The same warning should be placed near all reproducing equipment, from scanners to computers to 3-D printers. Users can be educated about copyright law, but it is up to them to follow the rules.

> **Check This Out**
>
> Websites for assisting users with copyright issues. *Visit:* The Stanford Office of Fair Use Website http://fairuse.stanford.edu/ and Nolo.com.

CONCLUSION

Copyright, as formulated in the U.S. Constitution, is a social good. By providing a limited period of time in which creators can profit from their work, Congress hoped to encourage creativity and expand the quantity of works available to the public. Copyright owners have the exclusive right to reproduce and distribute their works, publicly perform and display their works, prepare derivative works, and perform their works publicly by digital audio transmission. These rights are balanced by exceptions, such as the first-sale doctrine, Section 108, and fair use. At the end of a work's copyright term, it enters the public domain, where it may be freely used by anyone, with no exceptions necessary. Before that time, if no exception fits a particular use, one can always ask the copyright owner for permission to use their work.

Recent developments in copyright law have been numerous. The Digital Millennium Copyright Act created two new elements of copyright law relevant to information organizations: a prohibition on the circumvention of technological protections and a safe harbor for user-generated infringing content. Mass digitization, orphan works, and accessibility are other areas that have received much attention by information organizations and others, as technology continues to make the digitization of materials easier. Given the advances in technology, copyright reform is needed now more than ever.

Information professionals should pay close attention to developments in copyright legislation and advocate for the interest of their organizations and users.

As more copyrighted materials become available digitally, information professionals need to be aware of licensing agreements and negotiate for licenses that do not inhibit their traditional rights under copyright law. Information professionals should also become familiar with Creative Commons licenses, which allow them to both use more material and create material that others can freely use in turn.

Information professionals need to know about developments in copyright law. The law offers them protection and valuable exceptions that they can use to connect users to the information they seek. It is important for information professionals to be familiar with the law, both so they can use materials to the fullest extent possible and educate their users about copyright.

ACKNOWLEDGMENTS

Special thanks to Henry Cohen and Amy Grace.

NOTES

1. "Code of Ethics of the American Library Association," American Library Association, accessed August 24, 2014, http://www.ala.org/advocacy/proethics/codeofethics/codeethics.
2. United States Constitution, Art. 1, Section 8, cl 8.
3. United States Copyright Act, 17 U.S.C., http://www.copyright.gov/title17/circ92.pdf.
4. Code of Federal Regulations, Title 37—Patents, Trademarks, and Copyrights, Subchapter A-Copyright Office and Procedures, https://www.copyright.gov/title37/.
5. United States Copyright Act, 17 U.S.C. § 102, http://www.copyright.gov/title17/circ102.pdf.
6. Ibid.
7. "Circular 1: Copyright Basics," United States Copyright Office, 2012, 3, http://www.copyright.gov/circs/circ01.pdf.
8. United States Copyright Act, 17 U.S.C. § 106.
9. United States Copyright Act, 17 U.S.C. § 107–22.
10. United States Copyright Act, 17 U.S.C. § 106 (1976).
11. Ibid.
12. "Circular 1: Copyright Basics," 2, 5.
13. Ibid., 3–6.
14. United States Copyright Act, 17 U.S.C. § 105.
15. "CC0" Creative Commons, accessed July 5, 2014, http://creativecommons.org/about/cc0.
16. "Public Domain Mark," Creative Commons, accessed August 24, 2014, http://creativecommons.org/about/pdm.
17. United States Copyright Act, 17 U.S.C. § 109.
18. Capitol Records, LLC v. ReDigi Inc., 934 F. Supp. 2d 640 (SD New York Dist. Court, 2013), http://digitalcommons.law.scu.edu/cgi/viewcontent.cgi?article=1334&context=historical.
19. "Internet Archive Files Amicus Brief in Support of Fair Use and Innovation in Libraries," *Internet Archive Blog*, last modified February 20, 2017, https://blog.archive.org/2017/02/20/internet- archive-files-amicus-brief-in-support-of-fair-use-and-innovation-in-libraries/.
20. United States Copyright Act, 17 U.S.C. § 108.
21. Ibid.
22. For actual wording required, see Code of Federal Regulations, title 37, sec. 201.14, http://www.copyright.gov/title37/201/37cfr201-14.html.

§201.14   Warnings of copyright for use by certain libraries and archives.

    (a)   *Definitions.*

        (1)   A *Display Warning of Copyright* is a notice under paragraphs (d)(2) and (e)(2) of section 108 of title 17 of the United States Code. As required by those sections the "Display Warning of Copyright" is to be displayed at the place where orders for copies or phonorecords are accepted by certain libraries and archives.

        (2)   An *Order Warning of Copyright* is a notice under paragraphs (d)(2) and (e)(2) of section 108 of title 17 of the United States Code. As required by those sections the "Order Warning of Copyright" is to be included on printed forms supplied by certain libraries and archives and used by their patrons for ordering copies or phonorecords.

    (b)   *Contents.* A Display Warning of Copyright and an Order Warning of Copyright shall consist of a verbatim reproduction of the following notice, printed in such size and form and displayed in such manner as to comply with paragraph (c) of this section:

- notice warning concerning copyright restrictions.
- The copyright law of the United States (title 17, United States Code) governs the making of photocopies or other reproductions of copyrighted material.
- Under certain conditions specified in the law, libraries and archives are authorized to furnish a photocopy or other reproduction. One of these specific conditions is that the photocopy or reproduction is not to be "used for any purpose other than private study, scholarship, or research." If a user makes a request for, or later uses, a photocopy or reproduction for purposes in excess of "fair use," that user may be liable for copyright infringement.
- This institution reserves the right to refuse to accept a copying order if, in its judgment, fulfillment of the order would involve violation of copyright law.

    (c)   *Form and manner of use.*

        (1)   A Display Warning of Copyright shall be printed on heavy paper or other durable material in type at least 18 points in size, and shall be displayed prominently, in such manner and location as to be clearly visible, legible, and comprehensible to a casual observer within the immediate vicinity of the place where orders are accepted.

        (2)   An Order Warning of Copyright shall be printed within a box located prominently on the order form itself, either on the front side of the form or immediately adjacent to the space calling for the name or signature of the person using the form. The notice shall be printed in type size no smaller than that used predominantly throughout the form, and in no case shall the type size be smaller than eight points. The notice shall be printed in such manner as to be clearly legible, comprehensible, and readily apparent to a casual reader of the form. (Pub. L. 94-553; 17 U.S.C. 108, 702)

23. For guidelines, see the "Commission on New Technological Uses of Copyrighted Works (CONTU) Guidelines for Interlibrary Loan Photocopying," American Library Association, accessed June 6, 2017, http://www.ala.org/advocacy/sites/ala.org.advocacy/files/content/copyright/GLsInterlibLoan.pdf.

24. United States Copyright Act, 17 U.S.C. § 107.
25. United States Copyright Act, 17 U.S.C. § 108, https://www.copyright.gov/policy/section108/.
26. The Section 108 Study Group, last modified February 7, 2014, http://www.section108.gov.
27. "Section 108 Reform," Columbia Law School, last modified December 11, 2013, http://web.law.columbia.edu/kernochan/symposia/section-108-reform.
28. United States Copyright Office, "Revising Section 108: Copyright Exceptions for Libraries and Archives," 2017, https://www.copyright.gov/policy/section108/.
29. Library Copyright Alliance, "Statement of the Library Copyright Alliance on the Copyright Office's Notice of Inquiry Concerning Section 108 of the Copyright Act," 2016, http://www.librarycopyrightalliance.org/storage/documents/108noiposition2.pdf.
30. United States Copyright Act, 17 U.S.C. § 107.
31. Copyright Office, "The Digital Millennium Copyright Act of 1998, U.S. Copyright Office Summary," 1998, http://www.copyright.gov/legislation/dmca.pdf.
32. Authors Guild, Inc. v. Google Inc., 954 F. Supp. 2d 282 (SD New York Dist. Court, 2013), http://scholar.google.com/scholar_case?case=6510192672912362556&hl=en&as_sdt=6&as_vis=1&oi=scholarr.
33. Copyright Alliance, "Second Circuit Decision on Authors Guild v. HathiTrust," 2014, http://www.copyrightalliance.org/2014/06/second_circuit_decision_authors_guild_v_hathitrust#; Authors Guild, Inc. v. HathiTrust (Court of Appeals, 2nd Circuit 2014).
34. HR 1695, https://www.congress.gov/bill/115th-congress/house-bill/1695.
35. Copyright Office, "The Digital Millennium Copyright Act of 1998, U.S. Copyright Office Summary," 1998, http://www.copyright.gov/legislation/dmca.pdf.
36. United States Copyright Act, 17 U.S.C. § 1201 (d), https://www.copyright.gov/1201/.
37. Ezra Mechaber, "Here's How Cell Phone Unlocking Became Legal," *The White House Blog*, August 15, 2014, http://www.whitehouse.gov/blog/2014/08/15/heres-how-cell-phone-unlocking-became-legal.
38. Jonathan Band, "The Cell Phone Unlocking Saga," Infojustice.org, 2014, http://infojustice.org/wp-content/uploads/2014/03/band04132014.pdf.
39. Brett Snider, "Is It Legal to 'Unlock' Your Cell Phone?," *Law and Daily Life Blog*, May 2014, http://blogs.findlaw.com/law_and_life/2014/05/is-it-legal-to-unlock-your-cell-phone.html.
40. U.S. Copyright Act, 17 U.S.C. § 1201, https://www.copyright.gov/1201/.
41. Copyright Office—Library of Congress, "Exemption to Prohibition on Circumvention of Copyright Protection Systems for Access Control Technologies," *Federal Register* 80, no. 208 (October 28, 2015): 65944–64, https://www.copyright.gov/fedreg/2015/80fr65944.pdf.
42. United States Copyright Office, "Chapter 5: Copyright Notice, Deposit, and Registration," https://www.copyright.gov/title17/92chap5.html#512.
43. "The Digital Millennium Copyright Act of 1998 U.S. Copyright Office Summary," 8–13.
44. The Department of Commerce Internet Policy Task Force, "Copyright Policy, Creativity and Innovation in the Digital Economy," United States Patent and Trademark Office, 2013, http://www.uspto.gov/news/publications/copyrightgreenpaper.pdf.
45. "Department of Commerce Multistakeholder Forum: Improving the Operation of the DMCA Notice and Takedown Policy First Public Meeting," United States Patent and Trademark Office, 2014, http://www.uspto.gov/ip/global/copyrights/First_Public_Meeting-Improving_Operation_of_DMCA_Notice_and_Takedown_Policy.pdf.
46. United States Patent and Trademark Office, "U.S. Commerce Department Announces Digital Millennium Copyright Act Multistakeholder Forum Results," 2015, https://www.uspto.gov/about-us/news-updates/us-commerce-department-announces-digital-millennium-copyright-act.
47. Office of the Register of Copyrights, "Legal Issues in Mass Digitization: A Preliminary Analysis and Discussion Document," United States Copyright Office, 2011, 8–9, http://www.copyright.gov/docs/massdigitization/USCOMassDigitization_October2011.pdf.
48. Ibid., 4–5.
49. Ibid., 9.
50. "Borrow eBooks," Open Library, 2014, https://openlibrary.org/borrow/about.
51. "Internet Archive's Library of 2020," Internet Archive, 2017, http://library2020.blog.archive.org/.
52. Office of the Register of Copyrights, "Legal Issues in Mass Digitization," 22.

53. Ibid., 6.
54. Authors Guild, Inc. v. Google Inc., 954 F. Supp. 2d 282 (SD New York Dist. Court, 2013), http://scholar.google.com/scholar_case?case=6510192672912362556&hl=en&as_sdt=6&as_vis=1&oi=scholarr.
55. Electronic Frontier Foundation, "Authors Guild v. Google, Part II: Fair Use Proceedings," 2017, https://www.eff.org/cases/authors-guild-v-google-part-ii-fair-use-proceedings.
56. Office of the Register of Copyrights, "Legal Issues in Mass Digitization," i.
57. "Second Circuit Decision on Authors Guild v. HathiTrust," Copyright Alliance, June 2014, http://www.copyrightalliance.org/2014/06/second_circuit_decision_authors_guild_v_hathitrust#; Authors Guild, Inc. v. HathiTrust (Court of Appeals, 2nd Circuit 2014).
58. Ibid.
59. Office of the Register of Copyright, "Legal Issues in Mass Digitization."
60. Marybeth Peters, "Report on Orphan Works: A Report of the Register of Copyrights," United States Copyright Office, 2006, 92–127, http://www.copyright.gov/orphan/orphan-report-full.pdf.
61. "Orphan Works and Mass Digitization," Copyright.gov, 2014, http://copyright.gov/orphan/.
62. "Recap of the Copyright Office's Roundtables on Orphan Works and Mass Digitization," ARL Policy Notes, accessed August 13, 2017, http://policynotes.arl.org/?p=51.
63. The Marrakesh Treaty in Action," World Intellectual Property Organization, 2017, http://www.wipo.int/pressroom/en/stories/marrakesh-treaty.html.
64. World Intellectual Property Organization, "Main Provisions and Benefits of the Marrakesh Treaty (2013)," 2017, http://www.wipo.int/edocs/pubdocs/en/wipo_pub_marrakesh_flyer.pdf.
65. The most significant difference in implementing Marrakesh would be permitting cross-border exchange of accessible copies. Ratifying the treaty would also require the United States to broaden the definition of beneficiaries, and to expand the types of copyright subject matter covered by the limitation. Neil Yap, "Welcoming the Marrakesh Treaty into a Consequentialist Framework," *JIPEL Blog*, last modified February 23, 2017, http://blog.jipel.law.nyu.edu/2017/02/welcoming-the-marrakesh-treaty-into-a-consequentialist-framework/.
66. "Treaties Pending in the Senate," United States Department of State, 2016, https://www.state.gov/s/l/treaty/pending/.
67. Maria A. Pallante, "The Next Great Copyright Act," *Columbia Journal of Law and the Arts* 36 (2012): 315–44, http://www.copyright.gov/docs/next_great_copyright_act.pdf.
68. Ibid., 344.
69. Ibid., 315.
70. Ibid., 323.
71. Ibid., 320.
72. Ibid., 320–22.
73. U.S. Copyright Office, "Active Policy Studies," 2017, https://www.copyright.gov/policy/.
74. Pallante, "The Next Great Copyright Act," 322–23.
75. Ibid., 324–39.
76. "Pallante Resignation May Indicate New Approach at Copyright Office," *Library Journal*, November 1, 2016, http://lj.libraryjournal.com/2016/11/industry-news/pallante-resignation-may-indicate-new-approach-at-copyright-office/.
77. House of Representatives Judiciary Committee, "Goodlatte, Conyers, Grassley, Feinstein, Leahy Call for Quick Action on Legislation to Provide Selection Process for Register of Copyrights," press release, March 23, 2017, https://judiciary.house.gov/press-release/goodlatte-conyers-grassley-feinstein-leahy-call-quick-action-legislation-provide-selection-process-register-copyrights/.
78. "Reform of the U.S. Copyright Office," House of Representatives Judiciary Committee, 2017, https://judiciary.house.gov/wp-content/uploads/2016/12/Copyright-Reform.pdf.
79. House of Representatives Judiciary Committee, "Goodlatte, Conyers."
80. "National Library Groups Oppose Bill to Make Register of Copyrights a Presidential Appointee," *ACRL Insider*, March 24, 2017, http://www.acrl.ala.org/acrlinsider/archives/13478#.WNapkbdNHJU.
81. Creative Commons, accessed September 22, 2017, http://www.creativecommons.org.
82. Ibid.

83. Creative Commons, "License Compatibility Chart" from the Creative Commons Wiki, https://wiki
.creativecommons.org/wiki/Wiki/cc_license_compatibility, is licensed under CC BY 4.0, https://
creativecommons.org/licenses/by/4.0/.

84. "Library Copyright Statement," University of Michigan Library, 2016, https://www.lib.umich.edu/
library-administration/library-copyright-statement.

85. "Online Service Providers," Copyright.gov, 2014, http://copyright.gov/onlinesp/.

32

Information Licensing

Celeste Feather, Sharla Lair, and Jill Grogg

Chapter 32, "Information Licensing," focuses on the ways that digital content can be shared and used by many through different licensing agreements. Understanding licensing is particularly important for information professionals given the proliferation of online content. Authors Celeste Feather, Sharla Lair, and Jill Grogg, all from digital services company LYRASIS, explore the development of best practices in creating license agreements.

Feather, Lair, and Grogg provide tables that depict usage terms and key licensing concepts. In crafting licensing agreements, information professionals need to understand who can use materials and under what conditions, the relevant legal issues, specific details of the business relationship, and technical aspects. All of these components are combined when creating either an individual or group Licensed Business Model that includes pricing. The authors explain several of these options—from a one-year licensing model to perpetual access with flat rates or rates based on usage.

While the authors note that most publishers' worries have been overblown, there are still issues that are problematic for publishers such as the technological advances in interlibrary loan, specifically e-books, which make lending of materials much easier. Licensing is an ever-evolving field that will continue to change and adapt with digital advances. Information professionals will need to stay abreast of these changes to best run their information organizations and serve their communities.

★   ★   ★

Information licensing is a maturing specialization in the information professions. For centuries, information professionals purchased printed materials in a straightforward purchase model from content providers. Even in more recent decades as information moved beyond the printed word, physical copies of images, video, and audio materials were still being acquired on microfilm, cassette, CD-ROM, and DVD. These items were placed on shelves and in storage cabinets to be used by one user at a time, similar to printed materials.

Digital content was well established in information organizations at the arrival of the twenty-first century. The acquisition of digital content, now mostly delivered to desktops and devices via the internet, is a transaction with different dimensions between the information organization and the content provider. As information organizations began to move into the realm of digital acquisition, one of the key aspects of the changing work was that the newly acquired content could be used by more than one user at a time. Use of digital content is also not necessarily limited by a user's physical access to a building. As a consequence of the explosion of information via the internet and the ease of information access, user expectations increased dramatically. Many information organizations now choose to license digital content rather than purchase content in traditional physical formats. The dynamics and techniques of content licensing continue to evolve along with information technology.

After completing this chapter, the reader should have an understanding of the origins and development of information licensing, key terms in license agreements, the underlying business models for structuring digital content for acquisition, and the critical evolving drivers of this field of work. With this introduction, the new information professional will be positioned to understand the dynamics of licensing in information organizations.

TEXTBOX 32.1

New Issues in Licensing

Without the constraints of use that were present in the print environment, new realities needed to be addressed by publishers and information organizations. These include:

- How would access to online content be controlled and limited to the appropriate clientele? In what ways could the content be used?
- How would the quality and reliability of content delivery be ensured?
- Absent a physical copy of information, how would continuing rights to purchased content be guaranteed?
- How would the information be archived and preserved?

THE ORIGINS OF LICENSING

Commercial online information services originated from technology developments during the 1970s. Some of the earliest services such as Dialog,[1] LexisNexis,[2] and Westlaw[3] remain major players in the licensed information services marketplace today. In the late 1980s and 1990s, several factors drove information licensing forward rapidly. Widespread adoption of the internet, the development of personal computers and user-friendly interfaces, the proliferation of information available on the World Wide Web (WWW), and a corresponding rise in user expectations all encouraged information providers to make online content available to information organizations under a new set of business practices. After centuries of stable business models, libraries and publishers had to adapt quickly to meet the demands of a world in which online content became the primary means of information exchange (see also chapter 20: "Change Management").

A specialized field of digital content licensing emerged during the 1990s as information professionals began to address new challenges. Publishers and information organizations were accustomed to one-time acquisition of physical content based on the first-sale doctrine.[4] The new availability of online content presented new challenges for accessibility, usability, and deliverability due to constantly evolving technology. Business relationships had to be reconfigured to support fast, flexible access to continually updated content.

Sales of physical volumes declined as subscriptions to online content increased, ensuring access to the most recent information. Since the presentation of information was no longer bound to the physical page, content was reformatted in ways that enhanced access and usability in the online environment. Dictionaries and encyclopedias became online databases of content, and journal articles were accessible via links from large multi-publisher online indexes. One-time purchases of content in the print era turned into annual subscriptions to online resources.

Legal contracts, or licenses, between content providers and information organizations became the norm as all parties endeavored to reach agreement on these critical questions related to online information. Specialized information professionals obtained the skills necessary to conduct these negotiations with content providers, often with support from legal teams at their organizations. The points of negotiation increased as technology and user expectations evolved.

In the late 1990s and early 2000s, information organizations and content providers focused on usage statistics as a key tool to analyze the impact and effectiveness of online content delivery for their clientele. Efforts by the International Coalition of Library Consortia[5] (ICOLC) and Project COUNTER[6] led to the creation of guidelines for gathering and reporting usage in standardized ways. Compliance with the Americans with Disabilities Act (ADA)[7] of 1990 and other accessibility issues entered the discussions and negotiations between information organizations and content providers as time passed (see also chapter 5: "Diversity, Equity of Access, and Social Justice" and chapter 29: "Information Policy"). The full array of terms that are now commonly considered in content licenses is discussed later in this chapter.

The arrival of abundant online information delivered immediately with flexible and user-friendly interfaces forever changed the world of information organizations in significant ways. The model of individual organizations acquiring separate collections was no longer effective or efficient. The demands by users required information organizations to create new ways to expand access to content (see also chapter 4: "Diverse Information Needs"). In response to these demands, information organizations joined group purchasing collaboratives to leverage buying power with better prices and terms of use. Content providers shifted costs from print production to digital hosting, and business models now focus on content creation costs as there are no longer significant ongoing production costs. As a result, opportunities increased for group purchasing with creative business models. The variety of current purchasing and business models is discussed later in this chapter.

Discussion Questions

Information organizations always need to maximize their purchasing power and obtain the best terms of use. What strategies will be most effective when negotiating licenses? Can these goals best be accomplished by individual organizations or groups?

TERMS OF A LICENSE

License documents range from short and simple to lengthy and complex. However, four major types of license terms are commonly included in the document: usage, legal, business, and technical. Through years of experience, the library and information professional community has established best practices that address these major license issues.[8] Nevertheless, information professionals should forge partnerships with all local stakeholders, including the procurement office and general counsel, to stay apprised of local requirements related to licenses and to negotiate appropriate language as needed.

Elements of a License

- Usage terms
- Legal terms
- Business terms
- Technical terms

Usage Terms

The usage terms of a license define who is permitted to use the content and what they are allowed to do with the content. How many pages of the content can be printed? Is interlibrary loan allowed? Can alumni access the content? It is important to note that usage terms override national copyright law in the United States (see also chapter 31: "Copyright and Creative Commons"). Therefore, license negotiators should be careful not to sign away existing rights under copyright law and thereby narrow the ways that users are permitted to use the digital content.

Licenses always include a definition of authorized users, the persons who are permitted to use the content. Employees, card holders, faculty, staff, and students are generally in the core group of users. Other authorized users can include the extended community such as on-site guest users or "walk-ins," alumni, and temporary contract research staff.

Lists of authorized and restricted uses in the license establish what can and cannot be done with the content. If there is a statement that a use is not permitted unless explicitly listed, information organizations may be giving up rights normally permitted under copyright law. Key usage concepts and reasons why they are important appear in table 32.1.

Table 32.1. Usage Terms in Licensing.

Usage Term	Description
Commercial vs. Noncommercial use	Limits the purposes for which the content can be used. Generally, users at educational organizations are restricted to noncommercial uses.
E-reserves and Course Management Systems	Permits content to be linked or temporarily stored (cached) in educational courseware for assignment to students in classes.
Printing and Downloading	Allows a user to obtain a printed or digital copy in addition to reading in a browser. There may be issues with how much can be printed and the ease of printing usable portions.
Remote Access	Allows authorized and authenticated users to access content when they are not in the library.
Resource Sharing and Interlibrary Loan	Allows libraries to share resources in compliance with Section 108 of U.S. Copyright Act (https://www.copyright.gov/title17/92chap1.html#108), and CONTU Guidelines (http://digital-law-online.info/CONTU/contu24.html).
Scholarly Sharing	Permits users to share limited content occasionally with scholarly colleagues who are not authorized users.
Text and Data Mining	Permits researchers to use computer-based services to search, index, and extract information from the licensed content and load the results onto their own servers. The purpose is to discover new knowledge from existing information.

Legal Terms

Other terms in a license relate to legal matters such as liability, warranty, and which jurisdiction's law governs the contract. How will a dispute related to the license be resolved? Under which state's laws

Celeste Feather, Sharla Lair, and Jill Grogg

will the agreement be interpreted if there is a dispute? Who, if anyone, is liable if a natural catastrophe restricts either party from fulfilling obligations outlined in the license? Sometimes these terms need to be customized to meet the requirements of local or state laws. When no agreement can be reached on the precise language to address these matters, one negotiation strategy can be to omit some of the clauses, also known as "being silent." Under this strategy, if a dispute ever arises, the parties will address the conflict at that time. Legal terms that are common points of negotiation and the reasons they deserve special attention appear in table 32.2.

Table 32.2. Legal Terms in Licensing.

Legal Term	Description
Breach	Violation of the license terms by either party or an end user. The terms specify how to cure the breach as well as what happens if it is not cured.
Confidentiality	License terms may be subject to open records laws and Freedom of Information Act requests in a state organization. The license may need to acknowledge an organization's need to disclose. User confidentiality is often stated explicitly.
Dispute Resolution	Procedure to follow if parties to license cannot resolve a conflict.
Force Majeure	French for "Act of God," acknowledging that certain events are out of the control of human beings, such as catastrophic weather-related system downtime.
Governing Law and Jurisdiction	Designates the law and court system that will be used to govern the license and address any related legal matter.
Indemnification	Protection by paying for the cost of damage or loss. Vendors generally indemnify licensees in the event that a third party sues the licensee for violating copyright in their use of the content. Many state laws prevent public organizations from indemnifying vendors for misuse of the content by users.
Warranty	Guarantees that specific facts are true. Vendors will warrant that they have the right to license all content and use of the content as specified will not violate any copyright.

Business Terms

Practical aspects of business relationships are also established in licenses. What fees are required and when will they be paid? Does the license cover a one-time purchase of content or an annual subscription? When can an organization cancel a subscription? Under what arrangements will the organization be able to access content in the future after it makes a one-time purchase?

The purpose of carefully negotiated business terms in a license is to ensure that both parties know the conditions that will govern their relationship in the present and future. Some contracts have a definite termination date, some renew annually unless one party decides to cancel, and others establish conditions for content licensed with perpetual access rights such as annual hosting fees that extend indefinitely. Table 32.3 provides key business terms to consider.

Table 32.3. Business Terms in Licensing.

Business Term	Description
Cancellation	In a multiyear agreement, specifies the conditions under which a library can cancel the contract, including budget reductions and the date by which vendor must be notified.
Fees and Payment	Specifies amount of fees to be paid, payment deadlines, and offsetting credits due, such as those for an increasing amount of open-access content in licensed collections.
KBART	For journal content, vendor will supply a title holdings list with metadata in compliance with the KBART (http://www.uksg.org/KBART) initiative.
License Grant	States type of acquisition: annual lease, one-time purchase with perpetual access, etc.
Post-license Access	Methods through which content acquired with perpetual rights will be accessible if license is canceled, including third-party archiving and rights to create/obtain local backup copy.
Preservation	Provides for the long-term accessibility of content on a known preservation-hosting platform, including data format migration as technology continues to evolve. Also provides assurance that content will remain accessible if the current publisher or host ceases to exist. Portico (http://www.portico.org/digital-preservation/) and LOCKSS (https://www.lockss.org/) are two established preservation organizations.
Transfer	When journal content moves from one vendor to another, the original vendor is obligated to make certain that the access and perpetual rights transfer to the new site. The Transfer Code of Practice (http://www.niso.org/workrooms/transfer/) provides guidance.
Withdrawal of Content	If content is removed that renders the product significantly less useful, specifies how licensee will be compensated.

Technical Terms

Licenses also include clauses that address the technical aspects of how the online content will be provided (see also chapter 25: "Managing Technology"). What are the responsibilities of the actual hosting site and the content provider to make the content available? How will users receive support and technical troubleshooting? Will the content be available in a way that is accessible to all users? How is usage data gathered and shared? Can the content be linked to other services that will help users discover information of interest?

Users now have high expectations about online availability, linking, and accessibility of digital content. Table 32.4 lists key technical issues that merit careful attention by license negotiators so that acquired online content meets users' needs.

Table 32.4. Technical Terms in Licensing.

Technical Term	Description
Authentication Procedures Supported	The technical means by which users will be permitted to have access, usually either by password and/or IP address recognition.
Disabilities Compliance	Vendor may state compliance with the Americans with Disabilities Act and provide a VPAT (https://www.state.gov/m/irm/impact/126343.htm) form to show compliance with federal standards.
Hosting Platform, Access Requirements, and Compatibilities	Establishes the technical requirements for accessing the content at the host site.
Persistent Links	Vendor will comply with the OpenURL (http://www.niso.org/apps/group_public/project/details.php?project_id=82) standard and provide durable links to licensed content.
Providing Metadata to Discovery Systems	Vendor is obligated to make licensed material accessible for indexing and retrieval by the discovery service used by the licensee.
Required Performance and Remedies	Establishes the acceptable level of downtime in a year and what remedies are appropriate if a vendor does not meet this requirement.
Usage Data	Vendor will provide information about available usage reports. COUNTER and SUSHI (www.niso.org/workrooms/sushi) are the current usage data collection and reporting standards.
User Support	Hours during which vendor will provide user support and the expected response time.

BUSINESS MODELS AND PRICE STRUCTURES

Key components of a license are establishing what resource(s) will be accessed, for what period of time, by which organizations and users, and the price to be paid. The combination of these components is a licensed-content business model. As digital resources, organizational needs, and budgets evolve, business models and price structures must as well. Currently, there are several common business models for digital resource licenses.

> Key components of a license are establishing what resource(s) will be accessed, for what period of time, by which organizations and users, and the price to be paid.

While an annual license for one resource is the most common approach, there are other variations. Table 32.5 includes variations for licensing and indicates when they typically are used. These variations can apply to content licensed either by annual subscription or by one-time purchase with perpetual access rights. They also apply whether the license is one year or several years in duration or for single institution or group licenses. These variations do not always stand alone, but can be combined to create a hybrid license.

Table 32.5. Business Models in Licensing.

Business Model	Description
Title Level	Access to one title; typically a single e-book or e-journal title. These types of licenses are typically negotiated directly with the publisher at the single-institution level.
Database	Access to one electronic database. May be established directly with the publisher or via a third party. A relationship with a single publisher may include multiple databases covered by the same license. A publisher may bundle multiple databases together and offer more attractive pricing.
Aggregation	Database(s) of content from multiple publishers selected based on subject matter or a spectrum of interests to be covered. Content access may vary widely depending upon embargoes from publishers and will typically not provide perpetual access or the complete range of a publisher's content.
Collection	Multiple e-books, e-journals, or other digital content, including streaming audio or video, from a single publisher typically selected based on subject, interest, year, or any other criteria and sold as a single collection or database. This includes both current and archive content.

Pricing Models

Agreement as to how the price for a resource will be determined is a vital part of licensing digital resources. Some digital content may be priced at a flat rate regardless of library size, type, or other attributes, but many resources are priced based on one or more attributes of the licensing entity. The most common of these are full-time enrollment (FTE), for academic/school/special libraries, and size of population served, for public libraries. The price may be calculated based on the exact value of the attribute (e.g., FTE is exactly 1,534) or arranged in tiers (e.g., all libraries with FTE from 1,000 to 1,999 pay the same price).

Frequently used attributes, often in combinations, are included in Table 32.6 along with the type(s) of library/information organization or licensing institution(s) to which it is typically relevant.

Table 32.6. Pricing Attributes.

Attribute	Definition	Organization Type
Full-Time Enrollment (FTE)	Number of students enrolled at a given point in time, typically measured annually. Can also be a subset of FTE, applied to a specific school or program(s) of study for more specialized resources.	• Academic • Community/ Technical Colleges • K–12
Population Served	Number of eligible users of the library or institution's resources.	• Public
Cardholders	Number of registered patrons with a library card.	• Public
Carnegie Classification	Institutional assigned level based on established methodology; only for accredited, degree-granting institutions in the United States (http://carnegieclassifications.iu.edu/index.php).	• Academic

Attribute	Definition	Organization Type
Simultaneous User	Number of users able to access the resource at the same time. Most suitable for specialized databases and user groups.	• All
Specific User/Seat	Assigned to specific users. While this is a potential model in all types of libraries/institutions, it is largely applied to corporate libraries.	• Corporate
Budget(s)	Typically annual materials or operating budgets.	• All
Buildings/Sites	Number of physical buildings or locations (branch libraries or campuses) where the resource will be accessed.	• All
Hospital Beds	Number of beds in a hospital.	• Medical
Faculty	Number of full-time faculty.	• Academic • Community/Technical College
Historical Spending	The current level of spending for publisher content is used as a basis for establishing the price to be paid. This attribute was the widespread basis for many group licenses to publisher electronic journal collections. Often referred to as the "Big Deals."	• All

Single Institution versus Group Licensing

The growth of group-based approaches to purchasing content has been a hallmark of the licensing evolution. Library groups (most commonly known as consortia but also networks or systems) are plentiful and diverse. Most institutions are members of more than one group through which licensing options are available, and membership in multiple consortia allows a single organization to take advantage of various opportunities for group licensing. All of these groups' licensing activities are intended to help organizations extend their purchasing power over individual approaches. When making a purchase, it is important to consider not only the price, but all the license terms negotiated via each group before entering into any agreement. The lowest cost might come with license terms that do not meet the needs of an individual organization in other areas.

Consortia can be based on geography, areas of focus, member attributes, or any other criteria that might help to create a beneficial relationship for the members of the consortia. Types of consortia range from loosely affiliated small groups with one or two common goals and no centralized staff or resources, to a large group with highly centralized and well-funded resources (county and regional systems, state libraries, and state-based education and higher education systems are prominent examples). Groups that engage in licensing are diverse, and so are the ways in which they fashion their business models.

Through a consortium, each information organization may, regardless of what other members of the group decide, choose to license a resource at a reduced price. Commonly, this approach is called an opt-in group license. An opt-in group license may include terms that encourage higher participation among members via even more favorable prices and terms. Another type of group license is known as an all-in license, where common decision making may be required across group members and may offer the widest access and greatest price efficiency across the group if all the members participate. Consortia vary in their use of the opt-in, all-in, and other licensing techniques. They also vary in whether administration and payment of the license will be direct between each library and the publisher or coordinated through the consortium.

Group licenses may also be paid by a group centrally on behalf of constituent members. State libraries are a prime example, as they may provide statewide access to some resources. Such access may include public, K–12, and academic libraries in some combination. Other consortia may also fund group licenses all or in part, especially if they are affiliated with publicly supported education or higher education systems.

CONCLUSION

How will licensing evolve? Licensing is far from a static enterprise. Technological innovations and economic developments will continue to drive licensing evolution, as will changes in pricing models and core terms.

With time, many initial publisher fears about the economic threats related to the sale of digital content have been overcome or never materialized. However, some issues remain contentious, such as technological advances in interlibrary loan (ILL), specifically e-books. New supporting technologies for ILL provide different capabilities, and publishers are increasingly interested in finding a way to capture revenue for the temporary use of their content. While licensing terms regarding ILL and other types of content sharing have been negotiated and discussed since the advent of digitized materials, issues surrounding both are not settled and require continued dialogue between publishers and libraries. Other user demands, such as data mining, force all stakeholders to remember that as access to and use of digitized content mature, so do the accompanying technologies.

Discussion Question

There is a growing pressure for information organizations to license digital products and services that are outside of traditional purchasing parameters. How might this phenomenon impact the development of licensing for information professionals?

Economic developments, such as publisher consolidation and large company mergers, also affect how libraries license materials. While the number of libraries and consortia remain relatively constant, there are fewer and fewer independent companies on the other side of the negotiation table. Entities such as EBSCO and ProQuest continue to diversify and purchase smaller content providers, as well as other service-based companies including book jobbers and integrated library system (ILS) products, among others. Additionally, increased publisher consolidation introduces challenges. When two previously independent publishers with unique cultural and business norms merge, libraries can find themselves renegotiating terms once thought settled and standard.

Pricing models will continue to evolve to meet changing user expectations, organizational needs and budgets, and publisher needs and product offerings. This arena will likely be very active as organizations work to meet rising user expectations with limited resources. New and evolving collaborations among groups of libraries will continue to form for this purpose. Publishers will continue to package their content as effectively as possible to maximize purchases and subscriptions. Yet publishers and libraries both continue to feel the effects of open-access (OA) initiatives (see also chapter 33: "Open Access"), both established and emerging. Traditional pricing and usage models do not apply in the OA realm, and it remains to be seen how radically OA will alter the licensing landscape.

The basics of licensing have fallen into place since the 1990s, and evolution of core terms will continue based on changing needs (e.g., text mining) and technology changes (e.g., mobile technolo-

Celeste Feather, Sharla Lair, and Jill Grogg

gies). With this maturity and widespread prevalence of licensing as the primary avenue through which organizations acquire access to information, there is a movement to use the license as a vehicle to advocate for, and obtain new, organizational and user rights that may not be in current licenses. Author publishing rights beyond those offered directly by publishers to authors is one example. Consortia have become the strongest voices in advancing best licensing practices through their consolidated representation of many information organizations.

Perhaps the familiar axiom, "the only constant is change," best describes licensing in the twenty-first century. Terms that information organizations thought were settled become unsettled; what was once unambiguous in licensing becomes less so, and vice versa. Unforeseen changes in technology and economics ensure that licensing remains a vital and imperative core function.

NOTES

1. "ProQuest Dialog," Wikipedia, 2015, https://en.wikipedia.org/w/index.php?title=ProQuest_Dialog&old id=695448199.
2. "LexisNexis," Wikipedia, 2017, https://en.wikipedia.org/w/index.php?title=LexisNexis&oldid=76593 3156.
3. "Westlaw," Wikipedia, 2017, https://en.wikipedia.org/w/index.php?title=Westlaw&oldid=766510750.
4. United States Department of Justice, "1854. Copyright Infringement—First Sale Doctrine," 1854, *U.S. Attorneys' Manual*, 2017, https://www.justice.gov/usam/criminal-resource-manual-1854-copyright-infringement-first-sale-doctrine.
5. "Guidelines for Statistical Measures of Usage of Web-Based Information Resources, 1998, revised 2001, 2006," International Coalition of Library Consortia, 2006, http://icolc.net/statement/guidelines-statistical-measures-usage-web-based-information-resources-1998-revised-2001-0.
6. "COUNTER," Project COUNTER, 2017, https://www.projectcounter.org/.
7. United States Equal Employment Opportunity Commission, "Americans with Disabilities Act of 1990," 2017, https://www.eeoc.gov/eeoc/history/35th/1990s/ada.html.
8. "Liblicense: Licensing Digital Content," Center for Research Libraries, 2014, http://liblicense.crl.edu/licensing-information/model-license/.

33

Open Access

Heather Joseph

Chapter 33, "Open Access," emphasizes that the value of the scholarly work is in its intention to share and grow ideas. Open access provides the opportunity to do just that easily and freely. Heather Joseph, executive director of the Scholarly Publishing and Academic Resources Coalition, highlights the importance of open access and the role information professionals play in its development.

Policy makers and research funders around the world realize that open access creates the ability to increase innovation, improve education, and revolutionize the research process. Joseph discusses the dominant open-access model that relies on article processing charges (payments made prior to an article's publication, designed to cover the publisher's full costs), which has demonstrated success in North America and Europe. Joseph describes the long-standing climate of peer-reviewed research and how this culture and its associated ever-escalating costs contribute to its resistance to open access. Joseph argues that this current situation has further led to other challenges, such as the rise of predatory journals and confusion by authors of their intellectual property rights.

Information professionals are key to increasing open access by redirecting library funds from journal subscriptions to open-access publication models, helping authors understand their publishing options, and informing funders of opportunities to offer broader access to research findings through open-access publishing options. These approaches and the overarching role information professionals play in open access are discussed throughout this chapter.

★   ★   ★

The advent of the internet brought to light both significant opportunities and new challenges for information organizations. This has become especially evident in the evolution, theory, and practice of how the results of research are communicated and shared. The movement toward open access—the free, unrestricted accessibility and utility of scholarly articles online—has been under way for more than a decade, and has made significant strides in improving how scholars and researchers share their work. From the proliferation of open-access journal outlets to the burgeoning number of open-access digital repositories in higher education institutions and research facilities around the globe, scholars have promising new options for maximizing the impact of their work. While awareness of the potential benefits of increasing the digital reach of scholarly articles continues to grow, significant misconceptions and cultural barriers remain. These barriers must be addressed before open access can be widely accepted and become the norm in the communication of scholarly research.

After completing this chapter, the reader should have an understanding of the potential benefits and challenges that open access presents to the traditional system of scholarly communication, as well as how information professionals can play a key role in addressing today's challenges and fostering a continued transition to a truly open system of sharing scholarly work.

WHY OPEN ACCESS?

The internet has significantly changed the way people communicate with one another, from how people get their news to how they shop, from how they stay in touch with their families to how they work. As information organizations are keenly aware, it has also had a tremendous impact on how scholars and researchers conduct and share scholarly and scientific research. Scholarly work, in all fields, is increasingly digital, and now requires new, online solutions to optimize both individual and collective efforts. For researchers, the digital environment offers the very real opportunity to increase the global reach of the results of their work.

This appealing and very immediate possibility of expanding the circulation of knowledge has directly led to the open-access movement. This movement envisions a new way for scholars and researchers to share their own works, specifically peer-reviewed journal articles, and to access the works of their colleagues freely and immediately online—anytime, anywhere. Authors, researchers, funders, academic institutions, and publishers are actively engaged in exploring new ways of using the internet to make more of their research available in this way.

TEXTBOX 33.1

Why Scholars and Scientists Conduct Research

Scholars and scientists conduct research so that new ideas can be generated, new discoveries can be uncovered, and the collective understanding of the world and the interactions with it can be enhanced. Scientists and the organizations that fund their research rightly consider the communication of the results of their research to be an essential, inextricable component of the research itself.

There is a wonderful quote by the playwright and essayist, George Bernard Shaw that illustrates this concept:

> If you have an apple and I have an apple, and we exchange these apples, then you and I will still each have only one apple. But if you have an idea and I have an idea, and we exchange these ideas, then each of us will have two ideas.[1]

Scholarly research is conducted with the express purpose of sharing ideas and new knowledge as rapidly and as broadly as possible for just this reason. And so, given the development of the internet and its ability to deliver digital information rapidly to a global audience at very little marginal cost, one would think that this information—in particular, scientific research results—should be easily and broadly available. However, the current reality looks very different.

Financial Barriers in the Traditional System of Scholarly Communication

There are very real barriers to gaining access to information regarding much of the research that scholars and scientists conduct. For decades, the primary mechanism for communicating the results of research has been through the publication of articles in peer-reviewed journals. Researchers have traditionally written articles for publication in journals, sharing their research findings. They have also contributed their expertise and time to review (and often edit) their colleagues' work for journals—all without the expectation for payment. And yet, when the time comes to access and read articles (their own, as well as their colleagues' articles), they are nearly always required to pay a subscription fee or pay-per-view fee.

The cost to access journal content presents significant barriers to making scholarly communication widely available. Over the past several decades, the journal publishing market has undergone significant consolidation, with a handful of large, multinational publishing firms dominating the landscape. Journal publishing has become big business, with annual revenues from English-language science, technology, and medical journals totaling about $10 billion.[2] As commercialization has increased, so have journal subscription prices, with many costing thousands to tens of thousands of dollars each year, and prices escalating at an astounding pace. Research has shown that journal subscription prices have outstripped the pace of inflation by more than 250 percent over a thirty-year period.[3] Information organizations, which are the primary subscribers to journals on behalf of scholars and researchers, cannot keep pace with rising costs (see also chapter 21: "Managing Budgets").

This has become a global problem, affecting nearly all information organizations. Perhaps one of the most striking illustrations of this occurred in 2012, when Harvard University, arguably one of the most well-funded research universities in the world, issued a memo to its faculty that jolted the academic world. It read (in part):

> We write to communicate an untenable situation facing the Harvard Library. Many large journal publishers have made the scholarly communication environment fiscally unsustainable and academically restrictive. Harvard's annual cost for journals now approaches $3.75M (U.S dollar). . . . Prices for online content from two providers have increased by about 145% over the past six years, which far exceeds not only the consumer price index, but also the higher education and the library price indices. These journals claim an ever-increasing share of our overall collection budget. . . . The Faculty Advisory Council to the Library, representing university faculty in all schools and in consultation with the Harvard Library leadership, reached this conclusion: major periodical subscriptions, especially to electronic journals published by historically key providers, cannot be sustained: continuing these subscriptions on their current footing is financially untenable.[4]

This begs the question: If the situation is this dire for Harvard, what is it like for the tens of thousands of other academic and research institutions with budgets that do not come close to that of Harvard? What is it like for scientists and scholars on those campuses who are trying to conduct research? Researchers readily acknowledge that when they are conducting literature searches to further their research, they routinely run into abstracts of papers that they think might be of interest to them. While there is no cost to them to read the abstracts, they often do not read the full articles because their organization does not cover the cost to provide them with access to the full text. It is common practice for them to simply skip to the next paper where full text is available. Rather than reading all relevant articles, they only read the articles where there are no barriers to access. This has become the status quo in research, but should be unacceptable to scholars, educators, and information professionals.

The status quo means that there are scientists conducting research based only on the previous studies they have access to, rather than all prior studies relevant to their research. They are missing information they might need to inform their current research. Perhaps even more damaging, the instruction they provide to students is based on the information they have access to, not on what the students might truly need to know.[5]

The Phenomenon of the Digital Information Explosion

While the financial pressure alone might be enough to spur information organizations to search for a better solution, the world has also been simultaneously experiencing another phenomenon that further fuels the fire for change: an information explosion (see also chapter 3: "Librarianship: A Continuously Evolving Profession").

The move to digital has been happening just about everywhere and in just about every discipline. From the biological sciences to physics and from anthropology to the humanities, work is increasingly conducted online, and the amount of data generated from research is increasing exponentially. Similarly, the number of articles reporting on research is skyrocketing, with nearly two million new articles generated annually.[6] The only way to truly make sense of this welcome, if overwhelming, glut of information is to find new ways for these digital articles (and ideally, the data underlying these articles) not only to be accessed but also to be fully used.

In today's information environment, simply removing the financial barrier to access and enabling researchers to read an article is not enough. With so many articles being generated annually, the ability of individuals to deal with this explosion of information by sitting down and reading through researchers' papers one by one is untenable. Scholars and researchers want to be able to find that one article in a million that might be of interest in an unrelated discipline—the paper that uses a technique or methodology that otherwise would not have been considered. They want to be able to mine the text of digital articles to quickly find the information they seek, without needing to read an entire article. Better yet, they want to access the whole corpus of digital articles to find semantic connections and relationships among research papers that cannot be readily seen by reading a single paper at a time. They want to be able to analyze digital articles, using new cutting-edge computational techniques (and techniques not yet imagined), to find the most relevant articles without having to read each one of them. They need to be able to apply the power of networks to this information search, enable computers as a new category of "user," and help scholars fully unlock the value contained within this explosion of scholarly content. See textbox 33.2.

TEXTBOX 33.2

Computers as "Users"?

The concept of enabling the computer as a new category of "user" correlates to the concept of "machine readable" scholarly outputs. One nice illustration of this comes from John Wilbanks and Jamie Boyle. In their "Introduction to Science Commons" paper,[7] they talk about a researcher working on one aspect of malaria research (a specific protein called glycophorin A). A literature search turns up nearly two thousand papers that might be relevant; trying to read each one herself would take her, quite literally, years to complete. She needs to be able to use computer-enabled tools to do the kind of semantic and relational text mining that will help her identify key papers. She simply cannot do it alone.

OPEN ACCESS: THE NEW PARADIGM

With every crisis comes opportunity. These pressures have sparked conversations about new ways to revolutionize how scholarly research is shared, remove access barriers (i.e., financial, technical, and legal barriers), take advantage of the power of the internet, and come up with a vision for a new system that better serves scholarship and research. In short, the question that needs to be asked is this: If an ideal system could be created from the ground floor up for sharing scientific and scholarly information, what would it look like?

That question was the impetus behind the meeting that ultimately gave rise to the concept of open access. In 2001, the Open Society Foundations convened a small meeting in Budapest. The participants represented diverse points of view, academic disciplines, and geographical and geopolitical areas. A main outcome of the meeting was the expression of a vision to develop such an optimal system—a system that the participants termed "open access."

The participants eloquently prefaced the definition of open access by succinctly framing the broad issues, saying, in part:

> An old tradition and a new technology have converged to make possible an unprecedented public good. The old tradition is the willingness of scientists and scholars to publish the fruits of their research in scholarly journals without payment, for the sake of inquiry and knowledge. The new technology is the internet. The public good they make possible is the worldwide electronic distribution of the peer-reviewed journal literature and completely free and unrestricted access to it by all. Removing access barriers to this literature will accelerate research, enrich education, share the learning of the rich with the poor and the poor with the rich, make this literature as useful as it can be, and lay the foundation for uniting humanity in a common intellectual conversation and quest for knowledge.[8]

This new open-access paradigm involves the immediate, free availability of scholarly articles on the public internet, coupled with the rights to use articles fully in the digital environment, without financial, legal, or technical barriers. The drafters of this Budapest Open Access Initiative (which marked its fifteenth Anniversary in February of 2017)[9] were also careful to clearly articulate that the only role for copyright in this domain should be to give authors control over the integrity of their work and the right to be properly acknowledged and cited when others refer to the author's work in their own publications.

FIRST STEPS TO ACHIEVING OPEN ACCESS: BUILDING THE INFRASTRUCTURE

Open access is a simple and powerful concept. But can it become a reality? The framers of the Budapest Open Access Initiative initially envisioned two concrete strategies that the scientific and scholarly research community could immediately pursue. These two strategies have been crucial in building the global infrastructure over the last decade needed to support an open-access system of scholarly communication.

> " Open digital repositories and open-access journals have been crucial in building the global infrastructure over the last decade needed to support an open-access system of scholarship communication. "

The first strategy is the establishment of *open digital repositories* where authors can deposit journal articles to make them freely available to the world—a practice commonly called "self-archiving." When these open digital repositories conform to specific, uniform interoperability standards, search engines and other tools can treat separate archives as one, creating a globally networked system of archives, where articles can be readily located and accessed.

Heather Joseph

These types of interoperability standards, known as Open Archives Initiative (OAI) protocols, have already been developed and are used by many institutions, facilitating efficient content sharing and dissemination. Academic and research libraries, along with other institutions, have embraced this strategy of open digital repositories, and more than twenty-six hundred open repositories are currently in operation around the world.[10] In early 2017, the importance of repositories as a crucial piece of global open-access infrastructure was underscored with the release of an International Accord,[11] spearheaded by the Confederation of Open Access Repositories (COAR) and signed by representatives from repository networks around the world, committing to closer collaboration on interoperability, standards, and global services in the repository arena.

The second strategy involves another key piece of infrastructure—the establishment of *open-access journals*. In order for scholars and scientists to truly embrace the concept of open access, they need viable, sustainable, high-quality open-access journal options where they can publish their articles.

Open-access journals function in the same manner as traditional subscription-access journals from an editorial and peer-review standpoint. However, they differ in two key ways that serve to remove the barriers identified earlier. First, open-access journals do not use copyright to restrict access to and use of the material they publish. Instead, they use open licenses (such as Creative Commons licenses) to ensure permanent access to and full use of the articles they publish (see also chapter 31: "Copyright and Creative Commons"). Second, open-access journals do not charge subscription or access fees of any kind. Instead, they use a variety of other methods, such as article process charges, to cover their publishing costs up front. Since the definition of open access was first articulated, more than nine thousand open-access journals have been established.[12]

New business models continue to emerge to support these journals, along with new sources of support. On college and university campuses, libraries are using new strategies, such as redirecting library funds from paying for journal subscriptions to supporting open-access publication costs (see also chapter 7: "Learning and Research Institutions: Academic Libraries"). Academic libraries are also establishing separate pools of money, often called campus open-access funds, setting aside financial resources expressly to support open-access publication models. Outside of higher education institutions, foundations and government agencies that fund research are establishing policies that allow researchers to include open-access publishing charges in their research budgets, paying for those publishing charges with grant funds.

While many not-for-profit publishers are experimenting with new ways to support open-access journal publishing, including profits from the sale of add-ons to basic texts, membership fees, and other sources of revenue, the dominant model currently in use relies on article processing charges (APCs), payments made prior to an article's publication, designed to cover the publisher's full costs. While the use of this model is growing in North America and Europe, there is growing debate over the suitability of the APC model for regions with developing/emerging economies. This debate is particularly visible in the context of a number of newly proposed initiatives

> **TEXTBOX 33.3**
>
> **Open-Access Journal versus Traditional Subscription**
>
> Open-access journals differ from traditional subscription access in that they:
>
> - do not use copyright to restrict access to and use of material they publish, and
> - do not charge subscription or access fees.

> **Discussion Questions**
>
> What are the primary barriers to open access at your institution? What strategies might be useful for removing these barriers?

to conduct large-scale "flips" of journals from the subscription-based model to open access—by converting library subscription payments into APC payments.

ADDITIONAL CHALLENGES TO ACHIEVING OPEN ACCESS

While these initial strategies to provide open access form a strong foundation to encourage the transition to a new way of sharing scientific research, they are not enough. Over the past decade, it has become evident that simply building infrastructure is not sufficient to encourage the kind of widespread culture change that is needed for researchers—and institutions—to fully move toward embracing open access. More is needed.

Predatory Journals

As the popularity of open-access journals has grown, a new phenomenon has come on the scene: the emergence of predatory journal publishers. Predatory publishing refers to a set of exploitative practices employed by individuals or organizations that target individual researchers via e-mail, soliciting articles for publication and charging authors publication fees without providing any of the editorial services associated with legitimate scholarly journals, including peer review and editorial review. These publications are simply money-making schemes that often employ additional nefarious tactics including listing prominent academics as members of their editorial board without permission, mimicking the style of an established journal or publisher's website, misusing ISSNs, and making up impact factors.

The rapid proliferation of these predatory publications has caused a great deal of confusion and uncertainty in many scholars' minds about the legitimacy—and quality—of open-access publishing in general. In an attempt to call attention to this problem, Jeffrey Beall, a librarian at the University of Colorado at Denver, established a list of questionable publishers, widely known as "Beall's List."[13] While this list, which was recently discontinued, was somewhat controversial, it did serve to raise awareness of the problem and led to the open-access community taking stronger steps to combat it.

These steps included the Directory of Open Access Journals (DOAJ) re-reviewing all ten thousand-plus open-access journals it had indexed to ensure that they met rigorous editorial and peer review standards, and subsequently removing nearly one thousand titles from the directory.[14] They also included the collective establishment of a resource called "Think, Check, Submit" that walks authors through the process of determining if an open-access publication is legitimate or if it is to be avoided.[15]

Author Rights

Authors, who control the rights to their research articles unless and until they choose to sign them over to a third party using copyright transfer, are, by and large, unaware of their rights. They are leery of open access, not fully understanding what it means to forgo signing a traditional copyright transfer form in favor of publishing an article under an open license. They worry that they are being asked to "give up" something that may have value for them in the future. They also do not understand that they are actually strengthening their ability to reach new audiences, who may not only read but also cite their articles. Many authors are nervous about treading into what they perceive to be a complex legal territory.

Additionally, while standardized open licenses have been established and are widely adopted, specifically the Creative Commons[16] set of open licenses, their adoption is not yet universal. Indeed, one of the major points of contention in the open-access community is the ongoing debate about the establishment of the Creative Commons Attribution Only (or CC BY) license as the gold standard for open-access journals (see also chapter 31: "Copyright and Creative Commons").

For open-access strategies to succeed, authors need to understand their intellectual property rights and the implications of each publishing option available to them. While authors want to ensure that their articles are available to audiences that would benefit from the content, many authors do not fully understand the value of their work, all the ways their content can be used by various audiences, and which approach to publishing is the best option for enabling each type of use.

Incentives to Publish in Open-Access Journals

For the status quo to truly change, scientists and scholars employed by higher education institutions must be incentivized to make their articles available under open-access terms in journals or digital repositories. As long as they fear that they will not be adequately rewarded—in either the tenure and promotion process or the evaluation of research grant funding—by making their work openly accessible, they will choose to continue to follow traditional routines and publish their articles solely in subscription-access journals with high-impact factors.

Collectively, higher education institutions must review their priorities and decide to actively pursue new measures for judging the impact of a researcher's contribution to their discipline. Initiatives to measure the impact of a researcher's publications should explicitly take into account the value that is added when researchers pursue open-access avenues for sharing their work.

In the open-access environment, new measures are emerging, broadly termed Alternative Metrics (sometimes also referred to as "Altmetrics"), that can provide information about how often an article is read and cited, as well as the types of individuals who are reading and using articles. Alternative metrics can also provide insight regarding how an article is being used. These article-level alternative metrics have the potential to offer a rich suite of tools to better understand the full story of the utility and value of research articles. These tools can be applied to articles wherever they are located—either in open-access journals or in collections in open-access repositories.

Information organizations are well positioned to play an active role in helping to change this dynamic and help authors better understand their publishing options. For example, information professionals who work in academic libraries can work closely with faculty to help them understand their options regarding how to publish their articles, including how their choices impact their intellectual property rights, as well as the option to publish content in an open repository hosted by the institution. Research funders are also interested in ensuring that findings are broadly shared, and typically expect researchers to share findings via articles published in scholarly journals. However, these funders must also be educated about opportunities to offer broader access to findings through open-access publishing options so they do not place undue restrictions on access and reuse. Institutions that have explored the idea of supporting the distribution of articles created by their faculty and researchers via an open repository supported by an institutional copyright policy have found that it raises the visibility of their institution's intellectual output and enhances their institution's brand as well.[17]

New Policy Frameworks

A final challenge relates to the need to create a new policy framework to support the transition to open access. Specifically, there is strong evidence that establishing a robust policy framework—on an institutional, national, and international level—to support the transition to open access is a crucial requirement for ensuring a successful transition. While a growing number of open-access policies have been proposed and mandated, challenges remain to see that they are successfully implemented.

Over time, widespread understanding regarding how open access can play a key role in stimulating economic development, innovation, and competitiveness has grown markedly, leading to national and global efforts to establish new policies regarding open access. In 2005, the International Organization for Economic Cooperation and Development considered the issue of open access, and concluded it was a strategic necessity, stating:

> Governments would boost innovation and get a better return on their investment in publicly funded research by making research findings more widely available. . . . And by doing so, they would maximize social returns on public investments.[18]

This conclusion has been taken seriously by policy makers and research funders around the world. They realize that these returns include the ability to accelerate the pace of new ideas and discoveries, improve education, empower entrepreneurs to translate research into commercial ventures and jobs, and help revolutionize the research process.

In the United States, the National Institutes of Health (NIH) established its landmark open-access policy in 2008, requiring all grant recipients to make articles reporting on the results of their funded research freely available through NIH's digital repository, PubMed Central.[19] And in 2013, the White House Office of Science and Technology Policy issued an Executive Directive requiring two dozen other federal agencies to create plans for implementing policies similar to that of the NIH.[20]

Policy adoption has been global, with new policies emerging from the UK to the European Union, and from Argentina to South Africa. Perhaps no one has articulated the drivers behind this policy adoption more succinctly than Neelie Kroes, EU commissioner for Europe's Digital Agenda, who successfully led the call and required that all research funded by the European Commission be made available under open-access conditions. In 2012, she noted:

> Open access to research results—both publications and research data—is not just a luxury—it is a must for Europe if we are to be able to compete internationally. Access to knowledge, information, and data is essential in higher education and research, and using it provides the basis for knowledge transfer and knowledge generation.[21]

As a result of this growing understanding, national policies that ensure open access to research articles are proliferating, with more than one hundred research funders and government policies now on the books worldwide.[22]

> Many institutions are becoming aware of the advantages that can be accrued by retaining digital assets resulting from research and are establishing policies ensuring that locally generated research articles, data, and educational resources are housed in campus repositories.

These national policies are crucial, but the development of institutional or campus-wide open-access policies also play an important role. Many institutions are becoming aware of the advantages that can be accrued by retaining digital assets resulting from research and are establishing policies ensuring that locally generated research articles, data, and educational resources are housed in campus repositories. Information organizations have played a key role in championing these policies and in providing ongoing expertise and support to ensure their successful implementation. However, for open access to become the norm, more widespread adoption and cohesive implementation of such policies are needed.

Heather Joseph

CONCLUSION

The collective understanding of the benefits to be gained by enabling open access as the default mode for sharing research articles is growing worldwide, and a robust infrastructure of journals and repositories to support this vision has been established. Information organizations have played a key role in educating faculty, researchers, students, and administrators on the advantages of fast, barrier-free communication of research results, and in advocating for the successful adoption of open access-policies and practices (see also chapter 28: "Advocacy"). Significant challenges remain, particularly around the rise of predatory publishers, understanding how the adoption of open licenses impacts intellectual property rights, the establishment of incentives encouraging open-access publication, and the development and implementation of cohesive open-access policies on the institutional and national levels. These challenges provide information organizations with the opportunity to take on new roles, develop solutions to today's open-access challenges, and encourage the continued evolution toward the vision of a truly "open-access" system of sharing research findings and other scholarly activity.

NOTES

1. Lewis Hyde, *Common as Air: Revolution, Art and Ownership* (New York: Farrar, Strauss, and Giroux, 2010).
2. Mark Ware and Michael Mabe, "The STM Report," *International Association of Scientific, Technical and Medical Publishers*, March 2015, http://www.stm-assoc.org/2015_02_20_STM_Report_2015.pdf.
3. "Research Library Expenditure Trends," Association of Research Libraries, https://comminfo.rutgers.edu/~tefko/Courses/e553/Readings/ARL%20statistics%202006-07.pdf.
4. "Harvard Faculty Advisory Council Memorandum on Journal Pricing," Harvard University, 2012, http://isites.harvard.edu/icb/icb.do?keyword=k77982&tabgroupid=icb.tabgroup143448.
5. Gary Ward, "Press Conference: Congressman Doyle to Address New Bill to Unlock U.S. $60 Billion Investment in Research," *Alliance for Taxpayer Access*, 2010, http://www.taxpayeraccess.org/issues/frpaa/frpaa_resources/press-conference-congressman-doyle-to-address-new-.shtml.
6. Ware and Mabe, "The STM Report."
7. John Wilbanks and Jamie Boyle, "Introduction to Science Commons," *Science Commons*, 2006, http://sciencecommons.org/wp-content/uploads/ScienceCommons_Concept_Paper.pdf.
8. "Read the Budapest Open Access Initiative," 2002, http://www.budapestopenaccessinitiative.org/read.
9. "Budapest Open Access Initiative: Fifteenth Anniversary," 2017, http://www.budapestopenaccessinitiative.org/boai15-1.
10. "Directory of Open Access Repositories," OpenDOAR, 2014, http://www.opendoar.org.
11. Confederation of Open Access Repositories, May 2017, https://www.coar-repositories.org/activities/advocacy-leadership/aligning-repository-networks-across-regions/aligning-repository-networks-international-accord/.
12. Directory of Open Access Journals, 2014, http://www.doaj.org.
13. The original website is still up though discontinued, http://beallslist.weebly.com/.
14. See www.doaj.org.
15. Think, Check, Submit, accessed August 8, 2017, http://thinkchecksubmit.org/.
16. Creative Commons, "About the Licenses," last accessed August 8, 2017, https://creativecommons.org/licenses/.

17. "Open Access Policies," Harvard University Library Office of Scholarly Communication, 2014, https://osc.hul.harvard.edu/policies.

18. "Governments Should Improve Access to Publicly Funded Research, Finds OECD Report," Organisation for Economic Co-operation and Development (OECD), 2014, http://www.oecd.org/general/governmentsshouldimproveaccesstopubliclyfundedresearchfindsoecdreport.htm.

19. "NIH Public Access Policy Details," U.S. Department of Health and Human Services, March 27, 2014, http://publicaccess.nih.gov/policy.htm.

20. "Open Data Policy—Managing Information as an Asset," Executive Office of the President, Office of Management and Budget, 2013, http://www.whitehouse.gov/sites/default/files/omb/memoranda/2013/m-13-13.pdf.

21. Neelie Kroes, "Dutch Open Access Week Address," uploaded by Neelie Kroes, October 18, 2011, 4:00 min., YouTube video, https://www.youtube.com/watch?v=taux1l0Vgek.

22. Registry of Open Access Repositories Mandatory Open Access Policies (ROARMAP), 2014, http://roarmap.eprints.org.

Heather Joseph

34

Information Privacy and Cybersecurity

Cherie L. Givens

Chapter 34, "Information Privacy and Cybersecurity," introduces readers to key information about privacy concepts and laws, Fair Information Practice Principles (FIPPs), threats to personal data and measures for protection, and the role of information professionals in advocating for information privacy and cybersecurity within their organization. Dr. Cherie L. Givens, an attorney specializing in cybersecurity and privacy issues and author of Information Privacy Fundamentals for Librarians and Information Professionals, *begins the chapter with clearly defined terms. She then delineates information privacy rights in the United States and Canada, which, she notes, are protected through legislation, regulation, and self-regulation. She briefly discusses the federal agencies involved in preserving privacy rights and then focuses on federal laws that affect information organizations, such as the Children's Online Privacy Protection Act of 1998, the Family Educational Rights and Privacy Act, Protection of Pupil Rights Amendment, Gramm-Leach Bliley Act, Fair Credit Reporting Act, Health Insurance Portability and Accountability Act, and the Privacy Act of 1974.*

Throughout the chapter, Givens demonstrates how information professionals play a critical role in implementing data protection measures within their organizations. Specifically, information professionals help ensure information privacy and security by tracking and evaluating how data is collected, used, stored, shared, secured, and disposed of; performing privacy audits; and training employees. A key takeaway for the reader is a keen understanding of the complex information environment, the growing demand for information privacy experts, and the resources that help information professionals develop competency in this area.

★   ★   ★

Information privacy and cybersecurity threats have become regular news topics. Changes in technology and the rampant efforts to collect personally identifiable information (PII) from consumers have increased concerns about privacy and the need for improved security. Highly publicized data breaches such as the Equifax breach, which exposed the sensitive personal data of 143 million Americans,[1] and breaches of major retailers, health insurers, and universities give credence to these concerns.[2] Recent ransomware attacks[3] on businesses and hospitals show that attacks are increasing in sophistication. Sometimes the motive is not financial, as demonstrated by attacks on adult websites such as Penthouse's Adult Friend Finder and Ashley Madison.[4] The posting of PII of users of the Ashley Madison website caused embarrassment and untold amounts of grief for users and their families.

Data breaches affecting millions of patient health records[5] and the massive federal data breach of the records of 1.8 million federal workers and contractors[6] held by the U.S. Office of Personnel Management (OPM) have increased concerns about the security of personal data and the need for increased cybersecurity. Changing information privacy protections for social networking sites such as Facebook,[7] the large-scale data collection by the National Security Agency (NSA),[8] and Congress's recent approval of a bill to overturn the Federal Communications Commission's (FCC) Broadband Consumer Privacy Rules, which limit an internet service provider's (ISP) ability to use and share consumers' sensitive personal information,[9] have left many wondering what has happened to information privacy rights in the United States.

Americans have good reason to be concerned about online privacy and security. According to a 2017 PEW study,[10] 64 percent of survey participants "have personally experienced a major data breach."[11] The majority of those surveyed have an online account that contains sensitive information such as banking or health data.[12] The statistics are not surprising, given the move to online banking, health portals, and the explosion of online shopping options. The PEW studies highlight a growing lack of trust that businesses and the government will be able to keep our sensitive personal information secure.

A 2013 PEW[13] study that focused on online anonymity, information privacy, and security found that "86 percent of Internet users have tried to use the Internet in ways to minimize the visibility of their digital footprint" and 55 percent of them "have taken steps to avoid observation by specific people, organizations, or the government."[14] The study showed that confidence in legal privacy protections is low, with 68 percent of internet users reporting that they find current privacy laws inadequate to protect privacy online. Participants cited a variety of information privacy concerns, including compromises to e-mails or social networking accounts, theft of PII, and damage to reputations.[15] These studies confirm that Americans are feeling less secure about sharing and entrusting their PII in the online environment.

After completing this chapter, the reader should have an understanding of:

- key information privacy concepts, as well as an awareness of laws that protect information privacy and may limit information privacy;
- Fair Information Practice Principles (FIPPs) and how these principles influence international agreements and guidelines to safeguard information privacy;
- threats to personal data, the role of government in improving cybersecurity, and basic measures information professionals can take to help ensure information privacy and security; and
- how and why information professionals should be involved in ensuring information privacy and assisting in cybersecurity efforts.

DEFINITIONS

Before discussing information privacy and cybersecurity further, it is important to define key terms.

Information privacy: Information privacy focuses on "the right of individuals and organizations to control the collection and sharing of their personal information without consent."[16] Failing to protect information privacy can impact the daily lives of individuals whose information is stolen or compromised, damage professional reputations, and inhibit the free exercise of our civil liberties.[17] Protecting information privacy requires implementing physical and virtual security measures.

Information security: Information security refers to the protection of data, in any form, from unauthorized access, disclosure, alteration, or destruction. This protection involves assessing and monitoring threats and risks to data, as well as establishing policies, procedures, and controls to preserve the confidentiality, integrity, and availability of data. It is easy to see how information privacy and information security work together.

Cybersecurity: Cybersecurity is a form of information security. The U.S. Department of Homeland Security defines cybersecurity as the "activity or process, ability, or capability, or state whereby information and communications systems and the information contained therein are protected from and/or defended against damage, unauthorized use or modification, or exploitation."[18] Cybersecurity can be thought of as information security in the online environment. The practice of cybersecurity is necessary to ensure information privacy in online environments.

THE RIGHT TO INFORMATION PRIVACY

Information privacy issues exist in a wide range of information environments, including libraries, government agencies, hospitals, businesses, institutions of higher education, and any environment where personal data is collected. Individuals in most parts of the world, including the United States, Canada, and the European Union, enjoy privacy rights and expect that those rights will be protected when they provide or seek information in information environments and when they use websites that purport to have privacy policies and security. Every individual needs to feel free to seek and share information and ideas without scrutiny or other negative effects.[19] Information professionals are tasked with managing information and will benefit from an understanding of the laws affecting the collection, use, and storage of personal data.

Although the word "privacy" does not appear in the U.S. Constitution, the language in the Bill of Rights reflects a focus on protecting privacy. Amendments I,[20] IV,[21] V,[22] and XIV[23] address aspects of privacy. In 1890, in their seminal essay "The Right to Privacy," Samuel Warren and Louis Brandeis defined privacy as "the right to be let alone."[24] Brandeis, who later became a U.S. Supreme Court Justice, affirmed this definition of privacy in the context of government action in his dissent, in *Olmstead v. United States*.[25]

INFORMATION PRIVACY PROTECTIONS IN THE UNITED STATES

In the United States, information privacy rights are protected through a combination of legislation, regulation, and self-regulation. Most of these protections are focused on particular industries or business sectors. This type of approach to privacy protection is known as a sectoral approach. Several federal laws provide protections for different sectors of information privacy, including the activity of children online, as well as education records, financial records, health information, and records containing PII kept by the federal government.

Some federal agencies assist in preserving privacy rights by exercising regulatory functions related to privacy, including the Federal Trade Commission (FTC) and the Federal Communications Commission (FCC). Some agencies are involved in federal privacy policy making, including the U.S. Department of Commerce, the U.S. Office of Management and Budget, and the U.S. Department of Justice. Others, such as the Office of Civil Rights of the U.S. Department of Health and Human Services, are empowered to enforce actions. Private sector industries also engage in self-regulation providing guidance on privacy practices to members of their associations or groups.[26]

Federal Laws That Protect Information Privacy

Information professionals work in a variety of settings and manage a range of types of information that often includes personal data. The information they manage, the clients they serve, and their activities concerning data collection and sharing may be governed by federal laws that protect information privacy. The following discussion introduces important U.S. laws that protect information privacy.

Children's Online Privacy Protection Act of 1998 (COPPA)

COPPA is a federal law created to protect the online information privacy of children under the age of thirteen.[30] It regulates the collection and use of information that children under the age of thirteen provide to commercial website operators. The Act applies to operators of commercial websites and online services such as mobile apps. The Act applies to websites that do not specifically target children but have "actual knowledge" that information they are collecting is from children under the age of thirteen and from "websites or online services that have actual knowledge that they are collecting personal information directly from users of another website or online service directed to children."[31] Website operators for whom COPPA is applicable must adhere to rules for collecting and notifying users about the collection of personal data.

Family Educational Rights and Privacy Act (FERPA) and the Protection of Pupil Rights Amendment (PPRA)

Information professionals working in education settings or with access to education records should be aware of the privacy protections provided by the Family Educational Rights and Privacy Act (FERPA). FERPA limits the disclosures of information from education records that are allowed without the student's consent. Disclosure without written consent is generally only allowed for legitimate educational uses, health and safety emergencies, and release of records to state and local authorities to whom such disclosure is allowed pursuant to state statutes.[32] Directory information may be released without consent if students, or the parents of students under the age of eighteen, are notified ahead of time and given a reasonable time to request that the information not be disclosed.[33]

The Protection of Pupil Rights Amendment (PPRA) amended FERPA in 1978. PPRA is applicable to educational programs receiving funding from the U.S. Department of Education. Under PPRA, written consent must be obtained from parents of minor children before those children can participate in surveys, analyses, or evaluations seeking information about sensitive subjects.[34] The No Child Left Behind

Act of 2001 expanded PPRA's protections that limit the collection and disclosure of sensitive information to federally funded elementary and secondary schools. These schools must enact policies regarding collection and disclosure, allow parents access to inspect surveys, provide notice of survey activities, and make available to parents the right to opt out of sharing student information for commercial purposes.[35]

Gramm-Leach-Bliley Act and the Fair Credit Reporting Act

The Gramm-Leach-Bliley Act of 1999 applies to private financial records. It requires that financial institutions protect the consumer information they collect. Financial institutions are also required to inform customers about their information sharing practices.[36]

The Fair Credit Reporting Act (FCRA) is another consumer protection act. Enacted in 1970, it was created to ensure that consumer reporting agencies adopt reasonable procedures for credit reporting and provide consumers with the ability to access and correct the information about them that is contained in credit reports. Under the FCRA, the use of consumer credit reports is limited to certain "permissible purposes" such as those related to employment, the underwriting of consumer insurance, or other legitimate business need for the information.[37]

The FCRA was amended by the Fair and Accurate Credit Transaction Act (FACT Act) of 2003: "The FACT Act requires that the three major credit reporting agencies provide consumers with free copies of their credit reports every 12 months" and allows individuals who may have been the victim of credit fraud to place alerts in these files.[38]

The Health Insurance Portability and Accountability Act of 1996 (HIPAA)

The Health Insurance Portability and Accountability Act of 1996 (HIPAA) was established to protect health information. HIPAA's "privacy rule" addresses how health information may be used and disclosed. It functions to balance privacy with the need to transmit health information.[39] HIPAA applies to health care providers of all sizes, providers of health care plans, and health care clearinghouses.

Under HIPAA, all individually identifiable health information is considered "protected health information" (PHI).[40] HIPAA includes a security rule that mandates how PHI must be secured and it contains a "notice of breach" requirement, which requires that notice be given to those individuals whose PHI has been breached. Information professionals seeking positions in health-related environments will benefit from reviewing HIPAA's privacy and security requirements.[41]

The Privacy Act of 1974

The Privacy Act of 1974 (Privacy Act) regulates the U.S. government's collection, use, and disclosure of personal information about individuals contained in systems of records that allow data to be searched and retrieved through the use of personal identifiers, such as individuals' names or Social Security numbers. It provides individuals with a right to review information about themselves and amend or correct incorrect information.[42] An *individual* under the Privacy Act is defined as "a citizen of the United States or an alien lawfully admitted for permanent residence."[43]

While the Privacy Act does not extend protection to visitors or aliens, it has been the policy of the Department of Homeland Security (DHS) to extend Privacy Act protections to the PII of these non-U.S. persons that is contained in mixed systems (systems containing records of individuals covered by the Privacy Act and those of non-U.S. persons). This policy gave non-U.S. persons the right to access their PII and amend their records absent an exemption under the Privacy Act, although it did not extend or create a right of judicial review.[44] The practice of extending Privacy Act protections to records of non-U.S. persons in mixed systems appears to be coming to an end. On January 25, 2017, President Trump signed an Executive Order[45] requiring federal agencies "to the extent consistent with applicable law, ensure that their privacy policies exclude persons who are not United States citizens or lawful permanent residents from the protections of the Privacy Act regarding personally identifiable information."[46]

Some non-U.S. persons still enjoy limited Privacy Act protections that were imparted to them through the Judicial Redress Act (JRA), passed by Congress in 2015. The JRA extends certain rights of judicial redress established under the Privacy Act protections to citizens of most European Union countries. These protections apply to information that is shared with the U.S. government from a designated country for law enforcement purposes. The JRA enables a person covered by the Act to bring suit in the same manner and to the same extent as a U.S. citizen or permanent resident alien with respect to intentional or willful unlawful disclosure of covered records and improper refusal to grant access to or amendment of covered records under the Privacy Act.[47]

Diminishing Privacy Protections

U.S. citizens may also be poised to lose some existing privacy protections. As mentioned earlier, in March 2017, both the Senate and the House of Representatives approved a bill to repeal the FCC's Broadband Consumer Privacy Rules that limits an ISP's ability to use and share consumer data. On March 31, 2017, Commissioners of the FTC and FCC joined forces to pen an Op-Ed piece in the *Los Angeles Times* expressing their concern for Americans' online privacy. They explained that both agencies have a role in protecting consumer privacy and that removing the power from the FCC to protect consumers when they sign up for broadband coverage will leave a hole that the FTC cannot fill. It would allow broadband providers to collect sensitive data and sell it to third parties without our knowledge or consent. They urged President Trump to veto the legislation.[48]

In January 2017, President Trump issued an Executive Order (EO) focused on reducing regulation.[49] It is unclear, at this time, what impact his EOs or future congressional decisions may have on the role of the FTC in investigating violations of law by individuals and businesses and on its federal rule-making authority to issue industry-wide regulations, both of which have helped to protect consumer privacy.

According to the Electronic Frontier Foundation (EFF), searches of electronic media at U.S. borders have increased fivefold in fiscal year 2016, impeding on the privacy of device holders.[50] Several instances of cell phone searches have been reported in the media. EFF explains that the justification for these searches is the federal government's claim of broad powers to search and seize travelers' digital information at the border.[51] Although EFF recently issued a guide for travelers seeking to protect the data on their devices and in the cloud from such searches at the U.S. border, options for resisting these types of searches are limited.

Federal Laws That May Limit Privacy

In addition to the laws that protect information privacy, there are some to be aware of that may limit information privacy. These include the Foreign Intelligence Surveillance Act (FISA)[52] and the USA PATRIOT Act,[53] which pertain to terrorism investigations.

"Under FISA the government may conduct electronic surveillance to collect foreign intelligence in the United States. FISA establishes standards for the use of electronic surveillance and government requests."[54] The USA PATRIOT Act expands the ability of the U.S. government to seek information under administrative subpoenas and "expands the powers of law enforcement for surveillance and investigation to deter terrorism. Its enforcement accordingly places limits on information privacy protection."[55]

State Level Protection of Information Privacy

States have also enacted privacy protections. Although the level of these protections varies by state, in some instances these protections may be more comprehensive than existing federal laws. Privacy protections may be found in a number of state constitutions and statutes. The following states address privacy specifically in their state constitutions: Alaska, Arizona, California, Florida, Hawaii, Illinois, Louisiana, Montana, South Carolina, and Washington.[56]

INFORMATION PRIVACY PROTECTIONS IN CANADA

Like the United States, Canada works with businesses toward the goal of privacy compliance. Its approach to privacy is more comprehensive than that of the United States. Sections 7 and 8 of Canada's *Charter of Rights and Freedoms* have been interpreted to offer privacy protections. They provide that: "Everyone has the right to life, liberty and security of the person and the right not to be deprived thereof except in accordance with the principles of fundamental justice. Everyone has the right to be secure against unreasonable search or seizure."[57]

Canada has two main federal laws that govern the handling of personal data: the Privacy Act of 1983 and the Personal Information Protection and Electronic Documents Act of 2000 (PIPEDA). The Privacy Act governs the handling of personal data by federal agencies and departments. It provides individuals with a right to access personal information about themselves in the government's possession and request correction of incorrect information. PIPEDA governs the private sector's collection, use, and disclosure of personal data. PIPEDA allows individuals to request access to information collected about them and correct inaccuracies.[58] Information professionals working in Canada should consult the Office of the Privacy Commissioner of Canada and provincial privacy offices' websites, which offer a wealth of privacy information, tutorials, and teaching materials on the topic of information privacy.

FAIR INFORMATION PRACTICE PRINCIPLES

Fair information practice principles (FIPPs) "are the widely accepted framework for evaluating and mitigating privacy impacts."[59] The FIPPs provide guidance concerning the handling of personal data. "Understanding and being able to apply recognized fair information practice principles is necessary for responsible handling of personal information."[60]

The FIPPs have their origins in a 1973 report by the U.S. Department of Health, Education, and Welfare's advisory committee on Automated Personal Data, which indicated that an individual's privacy was "poorly protected" under the law and existing record-keeping practices. The 1973 report recommended that a federal code of information practice be enacted.[61]

The impact of the FIPPs is documented in a 2011 White House report on enhancing privacy and security in cyberspace. In it, the FIPPs were identified as the basis for trust and confidence in online transactions.[62] The eight FIPPs and the White House's guidance on implementing them are reproduced below.

Transparency: Organizations should be transparent and notify individuals regarding collection, use, dissemination, and maintenance of personally identifiable information (PII).

Individual participation: Organizations should involve the individual in the process of using PII and, to the extent practicable, seek individual consent for the collection, use, dissemination, and maintenance of PII. Organizations should also provide mechanisms for appropriate access, correction, and redress regarding use of PII.

Purpose specification: Organizations should specifically articulate the authority that permits the collection of PII and specifically articulate the purpose or purposes for which the PII is intended to be used.

Data minimization: Organizations should only collect PII that is directly relevant and necessary to accomplish the specified purpose(s) and only retain PII for as long as is necessary to fulfill the specified purpose(s).

Use limitation: Organizations should use PII solely for the purpose(s) specified in the notice. Sharing PII should be for a purpose compatible with the purpose for which the PII was collected.

Data quality and integrity: Organizations should, to the extent practicable, ensure that PII is accurate, relevant, timely, and complete.

Security: Organizations should protect PII (in all media) through appropriate security safeguards against risks such as loss, unauthorized access or use, destruction, modification, or unintended or inappropriate disclosure.

Accountability and auditing: Organizations should be accountable for complying with these principles, providing training to all employees and contractors who use PII, and auditing the actual use of PII to demonstrate compliance with these principles and all applicable privacy protection requirements.[63]

TEXTBOX 34.2

Global Information Privacy and Security Practices

Fair information practice principles have influenced the development of international guidelines such as the Organization for Economic Co-operation and Development's *Guidelines Governing the Protection of Privacy and Transborder Data Flows of Personal Data* (OECD Guidelines).[64] They are widely recognized and applied by the OECD's thirty-four member countries, including the United States and Canada. Fair information practice principles have been implemented by other international associations and countries to ensure the privacy and security of personal data and to assist in the free flow of data across borders. Examples include the European Union's Data Directive[65] and its successor, the EU General Data Protection Regulation (GDPR),[66] which replaces it in 2018, as well as the Asia-Pacific Economic Cooperation (APEC) Privacy Framework.[67]

CYBERSECURITY AND THREATS TO DATA PROTECTION

The importance of cybersecurity continues to grow in response to our expanding reliance on the internet. The number of individuals who perform daily activities online, including shopping, banking, teleworking, scheduling appointments, and completing online forms that request personal data continues to grow. This increased use of the internet is bringing increasing dangers from cyber criminals, including phishing attacks, viruses, malware, and more. Rising numbers of successful cyberattacks are being reported in the media, and these attacks continue to grow in sophistication.

Given these online dangers, the need to practice cybersecurity and educate others about threats to personal data and the need to practice online security is imperative. Individuals need training to understand the dangers of clicking on unknown links in e-mails and unknown attachments, as well as downloading programs and suspicious content from the web. Users need to be made aware of the dangers of providing too much information on social media sites and the security threats posed by malware and hackers that can compromise an entire organization and place proprietary/trade secret information and personal data at risk. Information professionals can play important roles supporting cybersecurity efforts and educating others about information security.

> Information professionals can play important roles supporting cybersecurity efforts and educating others about information security.

Government Cybersecurity Initiatives

Recognizing the importance of information security to economic and national security interests, the U.S. government enacted the Federal Information Security Management Act (FISMA) in 2002. FISMA, Title III of the E-Government Act,[68] requires that federal agencies develop and implement agency-wide information security programs to safeguard information and information systems that support "the operations and assets" of agencies. FISMA applies to the operations and assets of the agencies themselves and those provided by another agency, contractor, or another source.[69] FISMA represents one of the earliest cybersecurity initiatives of the federal government.

A Framework for Improving Cybersecurity

In February 2013, President Obama issued Executive Order 13636, Improving Critical Infrastructure Cybersecurity.[70] This order directed the National Institute of Standards and Technology (NIST) to work with stakeholders, including those from private industry, to create a voluntary framework to reduce cyber risks to the U.S. critical infrastructure. In February 2014, NIST released the initial version of the *Framework for Improving Critical Infrastructure Cybersecurity*. The framework represents a collaboration between government and industry. It is based on existing standards, guidelines, and practices, as well as input from professionals in the security and privacy communities.[71]

The framework includes a methodology to address the privacy implications of cybersecurity activities. While not mandatory, it includes advice for organizations to "consider how . . . their cybersecurity program[s] might incorporate privacy principles."[72] These include measures that are in keeping with the fair information practice principles (FIPPs) discussed earlier. The framework helps organizations to assess and improve their cybersecurity programs. Information privacy and security professionals have already begun using the framework to assess and improve their cybersecurity programs.

Big Data Concerns

In May 2014, the Executive Office of the President released a report describing their findings based on a ninety-day review of big data and privacy. The study focused on how big data is used by private industry, academia, and the government.[73] As part of the study, the administration solicited public opinion about these issues through a survey. The findings indicated that most of the 24,092 respondents felt strongly about data use and collection practices. They were specifically concerned about data storage and use; the need for transparency about data use; legal standards and oversight; and the collection of video, audio, and telecommunication data. Based on their analysis of survey results, the administration concluded that "respondents were most wary of how intelligence and law enforcement agencies are collecting and using data about them, particularly when they have little insight into these practices."[74]

This report highlighted potential benefits of big data analytics while acknowledging concerns about data protection in online environments. One concern is that data brokers are unregulated and their profiles of consumers can include information that is both factual and inferred. This information may be collected without the knowledge or consent of the individual and can be used in ways that are discriminatory.[75] There is also no consensus on "do not track" policies, leaving online users in limbo about what to expect when they ask not to be tracked. The report's findings indicate the need to address these issues related to big data and privacy.

BASIC MEASURES TO HELP ENSURE INFORMATION PRIVACY AND SECURITY

Organizations can take basic measures to help ensure information privacy and security such as tracking and evaluating how an organization collects, uses, stores, shares, secures, and disposes of data; performing privacy audits; and providing training to employees. Documenting these data practices through policies (see also chapter 29: "Information Policy") made available to customers or users demonstrates transparency and emphasizes the organization's commitment to information privacy and security.

Privacy and Security Policies

Every organization that collects personal information should provide its privacy policy to customers or users. This policy should document the organization's data practices, including security measures, and provide assurance to users that the organization takes privacy seriously. A well-written privacy policy explains what information is being collected, how the information is used, and with whom it may be shared. It should be easy to understand and readily accessible. Documenting and following a privacy policy assists in good customer relations and sends a message to regulators that information privacy is a priority for the organization.

Businesses often have multiple privacy and security policies for a variety of reasons, including multiple locations, websites, and differing services. Some privacy policies are internal and serve to guide those working in a company, while others are designed to inform both internal and external audiences. All policies directed to and shared with customers and other outside individuals must be understood and supported by employees. External-facing policies and internal procedures must align. Privacy programs should encompass all of the organization's privacy practices and actions necessary to ensure privacy.

Track and Evaluate Data Collection, Use, Risk, and Security

Tracking and evaluating how an organization collects, uses, stores, shares, secures, and disposes of data is a necessary initial step in planning a privacy policy. Employees from all divisions must be involved in this process to help determine where data is housed and how it is used. Information assets should also be clearly identified and inventoried, and their sensitivity levels need to be determined. Security measures should be implemented in accordance with the level of risk and the sensitivity of the information.

Privacy Audit

Performing a privacy audit,[76] or assessment of how an organization manages privacy risks, is a necessary task to get a baseline assessment of how well an organization is protecting personal data. Privacy audits involve reviewing all documentation addressing privacy, including privacy policies, procedures, and checklists. The flow of data through an organization and data handling practices are assessed. Audits may also focus on compliance and examine whether privacy policies and procedures are being followed. Privacy audits can determine areas for improvement and identify gaps in security or compliance.

Cherie L. Givens

Training

All employees should receive privacy training at the time of hire and at least annually thereafter. Everyone working in an organization needs to have access to a copy of the privacy policy. In addition to ongoing privacy training, employees must be accountable for implementing the organization's privacy policies and

Discussion Question

How can information professionals take a greater role in information governance and security?

procedures. Periodic specialized training sessions focused on the work of individual units and the implementation of accountability measures can help ensure that privacy remains a high priority.

THE ROLE OF INFORMATION PROFESSIONALS

Information professionals are in an opportune position to take the lead in information privacy education and management and to assist in cybersecurity efforts to ensure privacy rights. They are on the front lines addressing information privacy and security issues. By educating themselves and others, information professionals can improve privacy and security decision making and the protections that their organizations establish to safeguard the PII they collect. Information professionals can prepare clients and coworkers for the threats they will encounter online by providing a basic understanding of vulnerabilities and measures that can be taken to protect users while online. The role of information professionals is to set policy, ensure information privacy, and educate others. They should seek ways to be involved in the decision making and implementation of information privacy and cybersecurity efforts. Demonstrating knowledge and taking an interest in privacy and secu-

> The role of information professionals is to set policy, ensure information privacy, and educate others. They should also seek ways to be involved in decision making and implementation of information privacy and cybersecurity efforts.

rity discussions can place information professionals in positions to shape privacy policy and impart professional values. They can apply their expertise in managing information to identify and understand information privacy issues, apply fair information practice principles, create privacy policies, manage privacy programs, and instruct others in privacy literacy.

Self-educating and creating awareness about information privacy and security creates opportunities to demonstrate knowledge, shape policy, and advance careers. There are many opportunities to create a culture of information privacy awareness. Information professionals can increase information privacy awareness through various means including intranet postings, creating informative posters to boost staff and users' awareness, giving brown-bag lectures on current information privacy or security issues as well as core concepts, revising privacy notices, and sharing best practices with management and executives.

The privacy and security fields continue to grow, and there is an expected shortage of skilled professionals. Obtaining privacy expertise can increase a professional's value, earnings, and leadership opportunities. There are several avenues to seek privacy education, including the International Association of Privacy Professionals (IAPP),[77] which offers information privacy news, networking opportunities, resources, web conferences, and courses for those seeking certification as an information privacy professional. IAPP also has an extensive network of knowledgeable members who can provide mentorship to others seeking to increase their information privacy knowledge.

Subscribing to information privacy and security news feeds, listservs, and groups can increase baseline knowledge and provide an understanding of current issues in the field. Some useful sites that information professionals may wish to consult include: the National Cyber Security Alliance,[78]

Electronic Frontier Foundation (EFF),[79] the Electronic Privacy Information Center (EPIC),[80] and the Center for Democracy and Technology.[81] There are also many informative LinkedIn groups that budding information privacy professionals can join, including the International Association of Privacy Professionals; Privacy Professionals; CyberSecurity, Law, Policy, and Technology; Cyber Privacy Risk Advisors; and Privacy and Data Security. Information professionals should consider obtaining a privacy certification through IAPP if they wish to establish themselves as information privacy experts.

> **Discussion Question**
>
> How can information professionals assess the current level of information protection?

CONCLUSION

The fields of information privacy and cybersecurity continue to grow and change in response to changes in technology, threats to data, laws, and industry practices. Information professionals knowledgeable about information privacy can take leading roles in shaping policy, advocating for privacy rights, and instructing others in how to safeguard their personal information. It is time to take an active role in information privacy by getting involved in discussions aimed at shaping information privacy and security policies, best practices, and laws.

NOTES

1. Seena Gressin, "The Equifax Data Breach: What to Do," Federal Trade Commission, Consumer Information, last modified September 8, 2017, https://www.consumer.ftc.gov/blog/2017/09/equifax-data-breach-what-do.
2. Sara Kuranda, "The 10 Biggest Data Breaches of 2015 (So Far)," CRN, last modified July 25, 2015, http://www.crn.com/slide-shows/security/300077563/the-10-biggest-data-breaches-of-2015-so-far.htm/pgno/0/7.
3. Ransomware attacks generally involve the installation of malware onto a victim's computer that then encrypts the user's data. Cyber criminals demand money for the return of the data, but, even if paid, the data may be corrupted and unusable.
4. Andrea Peterson, "Adult FriendFinder Hit with One of the Biggest Data Breaches Ever, Report Says," *Washington Post*, November 14, 2016, https://www.washingtonpost.com/news/the-switch/wp/2016/11/14/adult-friendfinder-hit-with-one-of-the-biggest-data-breaches-ever-report-says/?utm_term=.5422f9dbb40a.
5. Erin McCann, "Hipaa Data Breaches Climb 138 Percent," *Healthcare IT News*, February 6, 2014, http://www.healthcareitnews.com/news/hipaa-data-breaches-climb-138-percent.
6. "Cybersecurity Resource Center," Office of Personnel Management, 2017, https://www.opm.gov/cybersecurity/cybersecurity-incidents/.
7. Brian Fung, "Your Facebook Privacy Settings Are about to Change. Again," *Washington Post*, April 8, 2014, http://www.washingtonpost.com/blogs/the-switch/wp/2014/04/08/your-facebook-privacy-settings-are-about-to-change-again/.
8. Electronic Frontier Foundation, "How the NSA's Domestic Spying Program Works," 2017, https://www.eff.org/nsa-spying/how-it-works.
9. Alina SelyukIt, "As Congress Repeals Internet Privacy Rules, Putting Your Options in Perspective," NPR, *All Tech Considered*, March 28, 2017, http://www.npr.org/sections/alltechconsidered/2017/03/28/521813464/as-congress-repeals-internet-privacy-rules-putting-your-options-in-perspective.
10. Kenneth Olmstead and Aaron Smith, "Americans and Cybersecurity," PEW Research Center, January 26, 2017, http://www.pewinternet.org/2017/01/26/americans-and-cybersecurity/.
11. Ibid., 2.
12. Ibid., 8.

Cherie L. Givens

13. Lee Rainie et al., "Anonymity, Privacy, and Security Online," Pew Research Internet Project, September 5, 2013, http://www.pewinternet.org/2013/09/05/anonymity-privacy-and-security-online/.

14. Ibid., 2.

15. Ibid.

16. Cherie Givens, *Information Privacy Fundamentals for Librarians and Information Professionals* (Lanham, MD: Rowman & Littlefield, 2014), 115.

17. Ibid., chap. 1.

18. "Cyber Glossary," National Initiative for Cybersecurity Careers and Studies, Department of Homeland Security, 2017, http://niccs.us-cert.gov/glossary#cybersecurity.

19. Givens, *Information Privacy Fundamentals*, 117.

20. U.S. Const. amend. I, http://www.usconstitution.net/const.pdf: "Congress shall make no law respecting an establishment of religion, or prohibiting the free exercise thereof; or abridging the freedom of speech, or of the press; or the right of the people peaceably to assemble, and to petition the government for a redress of grievances."

21. U.S. Const. amend. IV: "The right of the people to be secure in their persons, houses, papers, and effects, against unreasonable searches and seizures, shall not be violated, and no warrants shall issue, but upon probable cause, supported by oath or affirmation, and particularly describing the place to be searched, and the persons or things to be seized." http://www.usconstitution.net/const.pdf.

22. U.S. Const. amend. V (1787), http://www.usconstitution.net/const.pdf: "No person shall be held to answer for a capital, or otherwise infamous crime, unless on a presentment or indictment of a grand jury, except in cases arising in the land or naval forces, or in the militia, when in actual service in time of war or public danger; nor shall any person be subject for the same offense to be twice put in jeopardy of life or limb; nor shall be compelled in any criminal case to be a witness against himself, nor be deprived of life, liberty, or property, without due process of law; nor shall private property be taken for public use, without just compensation."

23. U.S. Const. amend. XIV, § 1, http://www.usconstitution.net/const.pdf: "All persons born or naturalized in the United States, and subject to the jurisdiction thereof, are citizens of the U.S. and the state wherein they reside. No state shall make or enforce any law which shall abridge the privileges or immunities of citizens of the United States; nor shall any state deprive any person of life, liberty, or property, without due process of law; nor deny to any person within its jurisdiction the equal protection of the laws."

24. Samuel Warren and Louis Brandeis, "The Right to Privacy," *Harvard Law Review* 4, no. 5 (1890): 193, http://groups.csail.mit.edu/mac/classes/6.805/articles/privacy/Privacy_brand_warr2.html.

25. Olmstead v. United States, 277 U.S. 438, 478–79 (1928), Justia, 2017, https://supreme.justia.com/cases/federal/us/277/438/case.html.

26. Givens, *Information Privacy Fundamentals*, chap. 3.

27. Givens, *Information Privacy Fundamentals*, glossary.

28. Ibid.

29. Ibid.

30. Bureau of Consumer Protection Center, "The Children's Online Privacy Protection Act of 1998 (COPPA)," 5 U.S.C. 6501–6505, Federal Trade Commission, 2017, http://www.ftc.gov/ogc/coppa1.htm.

31. Ibid., complying with COPPA.

32. Family Educational Rights and Privacy Act (FERPA), 20 U.S.C. § 1232g, http://www.gpo.gov/fdsys/pkg/USCODE-2012-title20/pdf/USCODE-2012-title20-chap31-subchapIII-part4-sec1232g.pdf.

33. U.S. Department of Education, "Family Educational Rights and Privacy Act (FERPA)," 2017, http://www.ed.gov/policy/gen/guid/fpco/ferpa/index.html.

34. Protection of Pupil Rights, 20 U.S. Code § 1232H, GPO, http://www.gpo.gov/fdsys/granule/USCODE-2010-title20/USCODE-2010-title20-chap31-subchapIII-part4-sec1232h/content-detail.html.

35. No Child Left Behind (NCLB) Act of 2001, Pub. L. No. 107-110, § 115, Stat. 1425 (2002), http://www2.ed.gov/policy/elsec/leg/esea02/107-110.pdf.

36. Gramm-Leach-Bliley Act, Pub. L. 106-102, 113 Stat. 1338, The Bureau of Consumer Protection provides information for institutions on how to comply with the Gramm-Leach-Bliley Act as well as helpful information for consumers at http://business.ftc.gov/privacy-and-security/gramm-leach-bliley-act.

37. The complete text of the Fair Credit Reporting Act (FCRA), 15 U.S.C. § 1681 et seq. is available at http://www.ftc.gov/os/statutes/031224fcra.pdf.
38. Givens, *Information Privacy Fundamentals*, 42.
39. "OCR Privacy Brief: Summary of the HIPAA Privacy Rule," United States Department of Health and Human Services, May 2003, 1, http://www.hhs.gov/ocr/privacy/hipaa/understanding/summary/privacysummary.pdf.
40. Ibid., 3–4.
41. Givens, *Information Privacy Fundamentals*, 43.
42. Office of Privacy and Civil Liberties, "Privacy Act of 1974 5 U.S.C. § 5529." The United States Department of Justice, http://www.gpo.gov/fdsys/pkg/USCODE-2012-title5/pdf/USCODE-2012-title5-partl-chap5-subchapII-sec552a.pdf.
43. 5 U.S.C. § 552a(a)(2).
44. Hugo Teufel, "Privacy Policy Guidance Memorandum Number: 2007-1 (as amended from January 19, 2007)," Department of Homeland Security, https://www.dhs.gov/xlibrary/assets/privacy/privacy_policyguide_2007-1.pdf.
45. "Executive Order: Enhancing Public Safety in the Interior of the United States, Sec. 14," Privacy Act, The White House, January 25, 2017, https://www.whitehouse.gov/the-press-office/2017/01/25/presidential-executive-order-enhancing-public-safety-interior-united.
46. Exec. Order No. 13768, 82 Fed. Reg, 8799 (July 25, 2017), Sec. 14.
47. U.S. Department of Justice, Judicial Redress Act of 2015, https://www.justice.gov/opcl/judicial-redress-act-2015.
48. Terrell McSweeny and Mignon Clyburn, "The Commissioners of the FTC and FCC are Worried about Your Online Privacy," Op-Ed, *Los Angeles Times*, March 31, 2017, http://www.latimes.com/opinion/op-ed/la-oe-mcsweeny-clyburn-internet-privacy-20170331-story.html.
49. "Presidential Executive Order on Reducing Regulation and Controlling Regulatory Costs," the White House, January 30, 2017, https://www.whitehouse.gov/the-press-office/2017/01/30/presidential-executive-order-reducing-regulation-and-controlling.
50. Sophia Cope et al., "Digital Privacy at the U.S. Border: Protecting the Data on your Devices and in the Cloud," Electronic Frontier Foundation, March 10, 2017, 5, https://www.eff.org/files/2017/03/10/digital-privacy-border-2017-guide3.10.17.pdf.
51. Ibid., 7.
52. Foreign Intelligence Surveillance Act (FISA), 50 U.S.C. §§ 1801–1811 (1978), http://www.gpo.gov/fdsys/pkg/STATUTE-92/pdf/STATUTE-92-Pg1783.pdf.
53. The full text of the PATRIOT Act Pub. L. 107-56 (Oct. 26, 2001) is available through the U.S. Government Printing Office at http://www.gpo.gov/fdsys/pkg/PLAW-107publ56/pdf/PLAW-107publ56.pdf.
54. Givens, *Information Privacy Fundamentals*, 4.
55. Ibid, 45.
56. National Conference of State Legislatures, "Privacy Protections in State Constitutions," NCSL, 2015, http://www.ncsl.org/research/telecommunications-and-information-technology/privacy-protections-in-state-constitutions.aspx.
57. Canadian Charter of Rights and Freedoms (CCRF), §§ 7–8, Part I of the Constitution Act, 1982, http://laws-lois.justice.gc.ca/eng/const/page-15.html.
58. Office of the Privacy Commissioner of Canada, "The Personal Information Protection and Electronic Documents Act (PIPEDA)," Office of the Privacy Commissioner of Canada, 2017, https://www.priv.gc.ca/en/privacy-topics/privacy-laws-in-canada/the-personal-information-protection-and-electronic-documents-act-pipeda/.
59. "White House, National Strategy for Trusted Identities in Cyberspace: Enhancing Online Choice, Efficiency, Security, and Privacy," Executive Office of the President, 2011, https://obamawhitehouse.archives.gov/sites/default/files/rss_viewer/NSTICstrategy_041511.pdf.
60. Givens, *Information Privacy Fundamentals*, 99.
61. Secretary's Advisory Committee on Automated Personal Data Systems, "Records, Computers, and the Rights of Citizens," No. (OS) 73-94. U.S. Department of Health, Education and Welfare, 1973, http://www.justice.gov/opcl/docs/rec-com-rights.pdf.

62. "White House, National Strategy for Trusted Identities in Cyberspace: Enhancing Online Choice, Efficiency, Security, and Privacy," Executive Office of the President, 2011, https://obamawhitehouse.archives.gov/sites/default/files/rss_viewer/NSTICstrategy_041511.pdf.
63. Ibid., appendix A.
64. Organization for Economic Co-Operation and Development, "Recommendations of the Council Concerning Guidelines Governing the Protection of Privacy and Transborder Flows of Personal Data" (2013), *OECD Privacy Framework*, www.oecd.org/sti/ieconomy/2013-oecd-privacy-guidelines.pdf.
65. "Directive 95/46/EC of the European Parliament and of the Council of 24 October 1995 on the Protection of Individuals with Regard to the Processing of Personal Data and on the Free Movement of Such Data," http://eur-lex.eu/LexUriServ/LexiUriServ.do?uri=CELEX:31995L0046:en:HTML.
66. The General Data Protection Regulation, Regulation EU 2016/679, represents a modernization of EU data protection law. It takes effect May 25, 2018. Full text is available at https://gdpr-info.eu.
67. *APEC Privacy Framework*, (Singapore: APEC Secretariat, 2005), http://www.apec.org/Groups/Committee-on-Trade-and-Investment/-/media/Files/Groups/ECSG/05_ecsg_privacyframewk.ashx.
68. Federal Information Security Management Act, Title III of the E-Government Act, Public Law 107-347.
69. National Institute of Standards and Technology, "Framework for Improving Critical Cybersecurity Infrastructure, Version 1.0." 2014, http://www.nist.gov/cyberframework/upload/cybersecurity-framework-021214.pdf.
70. Critical Infrastructure includes the systems and assets that are critical to national security, economic security, and health and safety. Jaikumar Vijayan, "Obama Executive Order Redefines Critical Infrastructure," *Computerworld*, February 14, 2013, http://www.computerworld.com/article/2494979/security0/obama-executive-order-redefines-critical-infrastructure.html.
71. National Institute of Standards and Technology, "Framework for Improving Critical Cybersecurity Infrastructure, Version 1.0," 2014, http://www.nist.gov/cyberframework/upload/cybersecurity-framework-021214.pdf.
72. Ibid., 16.
73. "Big Data: Seizing Opportunities, Preserving Values," Executive Office of the President, 2014, http://www.whitehouse.gov/issues/technology/big-data-review; 2015 update at https://obamawhitehouse.archives.gov/sites/default/files/docs/20150204_Big_Data_Seizing_Opportunities_Preserving_Values_Memo.pdf.
74. Ibid., 79.
75. Ibid., 45.
76. "An assessment that focuses on privacy risk which includes evaluation of all privacy documentation and examines how data flows through an organization as well as data handling practices," Givens, *Information Privacy Fundamentals*, 111.
77. International Association of Privacy Professionals, 2017, https://iapp.org/.
78. National Cyber Security Alliance, "Stay Safe Online," 2017, https://staysafeonline.org/about/.
79. Electronic Frontier Foundation, accessed September 19, 2017, https://www.eff.org/.
80. Electronic Privacy Information Center (EPIC), 2017, https://www.epic.org/.
81. Center for Democracy and Technology, 2017, https://cdt.org/.

35

Intellectual Freedom

James LaRue

Chapter 35, "Intellectual Freedom," addresses how the First Amendment to the U.S. Constitution—the right to intellectual freedom—is not only upheld but defended by today's information organizations. In the information landscape, intellectual freedom is defined as the right to speak freely, receive or access the speech of others, and peaceably assemble, as well as the right to confidentiality and privacy. As director of the Office for Intellectual Freedom, James LaRue is in an excellent position to provide guidance on intellectual freedom. He explains intellectual freedom as it relates to the American Library Association's Bill of Rights and how both relate to access, use, and engagement with all types of information organizations. Collection development policies can be key to maintaining intellectual freedom, and LaRue emphasizes the need for these policies to be free of bias, resist censorship, and represent all views. He further defends the request for reconsideration process as being one of the most effective tools against censorship as it allows information organizations to resist local outrage over library materials through a formal process.

Looking forward, LaRue notes the upcoming concerns for intellectual freedom, including the expansion of content and the opportunities, threats, and diversions attendant with this expansion. Specifically, he notes challenges in intellectual freedom such as the rise of self-publishing, hateful or fake content, and issues over net neutrality. Finally, he harkens back to the information organization's most foundational defense: the fundamental right to read. LaRue leaves readers with strategies for advocating for intellectual freedom, provides a list of key cases that address intellectual freedom issues, and shares essential resources to help information professionals understand and defend intellectual freedom in the communities they serve.

★   ★   ★

The American Library Association defines intellectual freedom as the freedom to hold, receive, and disseminate ideas without restriction.[1] The Office for Intellectual Freedom states that intellectual freedom provides all information users "the right to seek and receive information on all subjects from all points of view without having the subject of one's interest examined or scrutinized by others" and that "the role of libraries in America today is shaped by our constitutional legacy."[2] The First Amendment to the U.S. Constitution grants this right to intellectual freedom:

Congress shall make no law respecting an establishment of religion, or prohibiting the free exercise thereof; or abridging the freedom of speech, or of the press; or the right of the people peaceably to assemble, and to petition the Government for a redress of grievances.[3]

In the library context, the right of "free speech" encompasses four broad dimensions:[4]

The right to "speak freely." Speech is protected whether it be aloud, in writing, or in music, film, or art. This is the commonly held understanding of intellectual freedom.

The right to receive or access the speech of others. This is a traditional function of the library and the foundation of collection development policies. This right includes the collection of religious speech as long as the collection does not favor one religion to the exclusion of others and political speech, even when it is "dissenting."

The right to peaceably assemble.[5] This protection guides the information organization's public program and meeting policies. The information organization may provide limited public fora (free speech zones limited by time, place, and manner) in which even the most controversial or politically charged topics can be discussed.

The right to confidentiality and privacy. From "Right to Privacy,"[6] an article written by attorney Samuel D. Warren and future U.S. Supreme Court Justice Louis Brandeis in 1890, information professionals have derived the implicit need to protect records of individual library use, including but not limited to circulation records, research requests, and internet use (see also chapter 34: "Information Privacy and Cybersecurity").

This chapter explores intellectual freedom as it relates to access, use, and engagement with the library and information organization, its resources (including the resources created within), and the information professionals who work in these organizations. After completing this chapter, the reader should have an understanding of:

- intellectual freedom and the American Library Association's (ALA) Library Bill of Rights,
- the importance of a collection development policy and a request for reconsideration process,
- the names and importance of some of the information profession's key non-library allies,
- some of the most oft-cited cases in intellectual freedom law,
- the relevance of six key trends that will impact intellectual freedom now and in the future, and
- the fundamental competencies required of today's information professionals to be an effective advocate for intellectual freedom.

INTELLECTUAL FREEDOM AND THE LIBRARY'S BILL OF RIGHTS

The ALA's Intellectual Freedom Committee (IFC)[7] was founded in 1940 after member Forrest Spaulding noted that "indications in many parts of the world point to growing intolerance, suppression of free speech, and censorship affecting the rights of minorities and individuals."[8] In response to the events culminating in World War II and challenges around the nation to such works as *Grapes of Wrath* by John Steinbeck and *Mein Kampf* by Hitler, Spaulding drafted the "Library's Bill of Rights,"[9] which was approved by his board. A year later, he introduced it to the ALA Council, which amended and adopted it for the entire association.

> **Check This Out**
>
> Check out the American Library Association's Library Bill of Rights at http://www.ala.org/advocacy/intfreedom/librarybill.

The adoption of the Library Bill of Rights in 1939 marks the true beginning of ALA's commitment to intellectual freedom. ALA has amended and reaffirmed the bill several times since then, with the last revision in 1996. ALA's Intellectual Freedom

Committee (IFC) is responsible for upholding the Library Bill of Rights and assisting the Office for Intellectual Freedom (OIF)[10] with offering interpretations of the bill (check out chapter 35: "Library Bill of Rights: Protections for LGBT" in the online supplement as an example of such interpretations).

Check This Out

A great text for learning more about the ALA Bill and Rights and its interpretations, as well as additional statements such as the Freedom to Read, the Freedom to View, and Libraries: An American Value, can be found in the *Intellectual Freedom Manual*, ninth edition.[11]

INTELLECTUAL FREEDOM AND THE LAW

Intellectual freedom is rooted in the First Amendment. There are many significant U.S. Supreme Court decisions that address free speech—too many to cover here. Textbox 35.1 lists some of the most notable court cases mentioned in the Office for Intellectual Freedom's "Notable First Amendment Court Cases."[12]

TEXTBOX 35.1

Notable First Amendment Cases

The Right to Read Freely

- *Counts v. Cedarville School District*[13]
- *Evans v. Selma Union High School District of Fresno County*[14]
- *Rosenberg v. Board of Education of City of New York*[15]
- *Todd v. Rochester Community Schools*[16]
- *Minarcini v. Strongsville (Ohio) City School District*[17]
- *Creamer v. Bureau of Police for Morristown*[18]
- *Case v. Unified School District No. 233*[19]

Minor's First Amendment Rights

- *Interactive Digital Software Association, et al. v. St. Louis County, Missouri, et al.*[20]
- *American Amusement Machine Association, et al., v. Teri Kendrick, et al.*[21]

The Internet

- *American Library Association v. U.S. Department of Justice* and *Reno v. American Civil Liberties Union*[22]
- *United States, et al. v. American Library Association, Inc. et al.*[23]
- *Mainstream Loudoun, et al. v. Board of Trustees of the Loudoun County Library*[24]

Freedom of Expression in Schools

- *Tinker v. Des Moines Independent Community School District*[25]
- *Zana v. Warsaw (Indiana) Community School Corporation and Warsaw School Board of Trustees*[26]
- *Board of Education, Island Trees Union Free School District No. 26 v. Pico*[27]
- *Mozert v. Hawkins County Board of Education*[28]

Those who do not follow intellectual freedom law are often surprised to discover that:

- neither liberal nor conservative views may be banned with impunity,
- school boards do not have unlimited authority,
- parents' rights also have boundaries over their children's right to read and speak,
- minors have intellectual freedom rights,
- school journalists walk a sometimes difficult path,
- religious works are permitted in public institutions,
- pornography by itself is not illegal, or necessarily obscene,
- even obscene materials may be legally owned by adults,
- the act of filtering can itself violate the Constitution, and
- the only thing that was found illegal in the Children's Internet Protection Act (CIPA) was the transmission of *images* that fall into the categories of child obscenity, obscenity, and harmful to minors.

IMPORTANT DOCUMENTS THAT SUPPORT INTELLECTUAL FREEDOM

Following the Library Bill of Rights and interpretations, the most important documents guiding information professionals in their support of intellectual freedom are the collection development policy and request for reconsideration process.

The Collection Development Policy

Collection development policies[37] typically state the library's policy for making a good faith effort to avoid bias, resist censorship, and represent all views when selecting and curating content, within the limits of budget, space, and public interest (see also chapter 29: "Information Policy" and chapter 24: "Managing Collections").

A recurrent question about collection development is this: What is the difference between selection and censorship? In brief, collection development seeks to match available funds to general goals and community interest. Censorship avoids content because of specific topics or perspectives. As stated in the Intellectual Freedom and Censorship Q & A, "Selection is an inclusive process. Censorship is an exclusive process."[38]

Yet information professionals recognize that sometimes there is systemic bias that skates along the edge of censorship. That is, often popularity is at least partially due to being advertised. This favors the larger companies, which may bear undue influence over topics. Also, some viewpoints—books by or about diverse populations, for instance—have trouble surfacing in existing power structures. On the other hand, not every heavily advertised book or movie is successful. Finding a representative sampling of the content of our culture is a dynamic endeavor and remains more of an art than a science.

The Request for Reconsideration Process

The request for reconsideration process is among the information profession's most potent tools to resist censorship. When challenges arise to library materials, leaders may succumb to pressure, reacting too quickly to local anger or outrage, choosing to remove materials to resolve the problem as rapidly as possible. A request for reconsideration helps guide the process while protecting the intellectual freedom of the community served, and should include at least the following:

File a formal challenge. The person filing the complaint fills out a "Request for Reconsideration" form,[40] in which the item or service is identified, and the nature of the complaint recorded. Alternatively, the complaint might be some other public demand, such as a letter to the editor or plea at a public meeting.

Report the challenge to the Office for Intellectual Freedom.[41] The purpose is twofold. First, the Office of Intellectual Freedom can help the information professional gather any supporting materials that may be needed, such as reviews, history of previous challenges, advice, media statements, and more. Second, these reports enable ALA to better track and report on emerging trends across the country. Confidentiality of the original report, other than the title and reason for challenge, is assured, unless explicit permission is granted to talk about other details, such as type of library and state in which the challenge occurred.

Establish a review committee. The makeup of a review committee varies by type of institution. But the idea is this: away from the pressure of the moment, the committee or administrator reviews the item or service in its entirety (e.g., by reading the whole novel, considering the entire lecture series, etc.) and then thoughtfully considers the item in light of the collection development policy. Finally, the committee makes a recommendation to the institutional leader. Typically, the choices are: retain (keep it as is), reclassify (move to another location), restrict (place in a special collection or require permissions), replace (update with a more current title), or remove (withdraw from the collection). Restriction and removal are often clear recommendations for censorship.

Accept or reject recommendation. The institutional leader accepts or rejects the recommendation.

Appeal the decision. The decision may be appealed to some higher public entity. The appeal is typically reviewed by a school or public library board, whose decision is ordinarily final, unless challenged in court.

Information organizations that do not have a collection development policy and a request for reconsideration process are by far the most likely to fall prey to censorship, followed only by those organizations that have them, but do not follow them. Adoption of these two processes is the single best defense that an information organization has against censorship.

INTELLECTUAL FREEDOM ALLIES

Information organizations in the United States have a unique mission in regard to the First Amendment in terms of providing equal access to all, opposing censorship, and ensuring public access to organized content. To fulfill these roles, ALA has established not only the Office for Intellectual Freedom and the Intellectual Freedom Committee but also the Committee on Professional Ethics (COPE)[42] and the Intellectual Freedom Roundtable (IFRT).[43] COPE deals with practical applications of the Code of Ethics in much the same way as the IFC explicates the Library Bill of Rights. Defense of intellectual freedom is a key ethical concern (see also chapter 30: "Information Ethics"). IFRT provides a forum for the discussion of many intellectual freedom issues and oversees or participates in the granting of awards to IF champions (check out chapter 35: "List of IF Awards" in the online supplement).

Moreover, ALA chapters[44] often have their own intellectual freedom committees. Many information professionals begin their intellectual freedom work through the association committees, or IFRT, then work their way over to the IFC and COPE. Through their ongoing discussions, publications, and programs offered on the web and at conferences, these allies maintain a professional focus on the importance of intellectual freedom issues and help cultivate successive generations of leaders (see also chapter 37: "Leadership Skills for Today's Global Information Landscape").

Libraries, information organizations, and professional organizations are not the only defenders of intellectual freedom. There are many external allies who demonstrate both commitment and advocacy to defending intellectual freedom, such as the Freedom to Read Foundation,[45] Banned Books Week Coalition,[46] and many others (learn more about these allies in chapter 35: "External Allies for Intellectual Freedom" in the online supplement). It is the responsibility of the information professional, personally and institutionally, to support and work with as many of these allies as they can, depending, of course, on their time, overlapping interest, and resources.

TEXTBOX 35.2

Banned Books Week

Banned Books Week, the annual observance of the freedom to read, generates consistent and comprehensive media coverage. Every year, hundreds of libraries promote the event with programs, displays, posters, bookmarks, and other collateral. Many bookstores also get involved with the initiative. Banned Books Week was celebrated internationally for the first time in 2016. Learn more at http://www.bannedbooksweek.org/.

INTELLECTUAL FREEDOM HORIZONS

What is on the horizon of intellectual freedom? Here are six key trends that will profoundly affect the landscape of intellectual freedom in the next decade:

- Greatly expanded content
- Publishing and diversity
- Social and political change
- Pressure on educational institutions
- Internet-related issues
- Advocacy for intellectual freedom

See also chapter 3: "Librarianship: A Continuously Evolving Profession" for more trends that will impact the information landscape, including intellectual freedom.

Greatly Expanded Content

Before 2008, publishing in the United States was dominated by a few large publishing houses, now aggregated into the Big Five (Penguin Random House, Macmillan, HarperCollins, Hachette, and Simon & Schuster). They also dominated public library purchasing. Together, the Big Five and other mainstream publishers generated approximately 300,000 new ISBNs a year.[47]

Things have changed. While mainstream publishing continues to produce about 350,000 new ISBNs a year,[48] the volume has been almost equaled by small and independent presses, which are now able to create and distribute their books electronically. These bypass the barriers of print production and distribution.

The greatest increase in publication has occurred in self-publishing. According to Bowker (an organization which tracks publishing activity in the United States), "ISBN registrations for self-published titles have grown more than 375 percent since 2010, climbing from 152,978 ISBNs to 727,125 ISBNs."[49] The output of new titles carried by Amazon, Smashwords, and other emerging publishers and distributors now outstrips the number of new titles from mainstream and small and independent publishers combined.[50] There are several reasons for this growth. First, this growth of self-published works is due to the rise of electronic publishing generally, which allows books to be produced and distributed swiftly. Second, this growth of self-published works is due to the increased share of revenue for the author, generally 70–85 percent for self-published titles compared to 8–15 percent in mainstream publishing.[51]

However, self-published work presents several challenges. First, self-published work is often published as e-books through providers that do not sell to libraries. A second challenge is that, even if available to libraries, the self-published work often skips the usual gatekeeping of traditional publishing because the author put the work on a platform and sold it directly to customers. In other words, there is no agent, acquisitions editor, or publisher to copyedit, market, or promote the work in publisher catalogs. There are also no book reviews authored by librarians. An example of this situation is *Fifty Shades of Grey*, which, as a self-published book series, bypassed traditional editorial review processes and challenged mainstream publishing in new ways.[52]

Most of the challenges now reported by American libraries still concern the ostensibly vetted content from the mainstream publishing world. What will happen as more and more breakaway titles come not from the typical suppliers of library materials but from an increasingly wide-ranging field that no longer goes through the publishing gatekeeping process? There is the potential for increased challenges to these works, but also the chance for these works to represent changing demographics of authors and readers alike.

Publishing and Diversity

As America's population diversifies, libraries must respond to the changing needs of the communities they serve (see also chapter 5: "Diversity, Equity of Access, and Social Justice"). If the library's collection does not reflect a range of diverse cultures and identities, and users can find few books in the library about people that look or act like them, they will conclude that the library simply is not interested in them and is not "theirs." This absence of diversity in most library collections reflects the lack of diversity in the information profession's traditional publishing partners; it is also an intellectual freedom issue (see textbox 35.3). Information professionals and the profession at large need to seek out and build new systems of review and acquisition to ensure that libraries offer a broader and more inclusive range of content to meet the diverse interests and needs of the communities they serve.

1994 Cooperative Children's Book Center Survey

In 1994, the Cooperative Children's Book Center surveyed mainstream publishing to determine the percentage of books that featured diverse content, specifically, children's books featuring characters of color. At that time, it was about 10 percent.[53] Twenty-five years later, Lee and Low took another look.[54] The disappointing result was that the percentage of titles representing characters of color was *still* 10 percent. Part of this may be because the staff of mainstream publishing houses, especially among the acquisition editors, has remained largely white, straight, and female. However, the population of America has changed. As of 2014, over half of the population under the age of five was nonwhite;[55] by 2044–2055, that will be true of the entire nation.

Social and Political Change

In addition to fundamental demographic shifts, two social and political changes are currently shaping the cultural landscape: child-rearing styles and polarization in political stances.

The first trend is the difference in child-rearing styles, which has been pronounced from generation to generation, and has implications for the content that information organizations make accessible. For example, while baby boomers had to check in at home at key times (e.g., dinner, nightfall) and Gen-Xers (also referred to as "latchkey children") were often home alone, Millennials had supervised playdates and regimented sports activities. Child-rearing styles continue to evolve, with the next generation's parents complaining about sexual content in books read by high school seniors who are just a year or so away from other adult activities, such as the freedom to marry, serve in the military, or vote.[56] The overwhelming percentage of challenged content in the library's collection tends to come from parents and tends to target content of interest to newly literate children and coming-of-age teenagers.

A second trend has to do with increasing polarization of political stances and the implications this has for the role of information organizations in providing balanced information and fighting against censorship. In the 2016 U.S. presidential election, repeated accusations of "fake news," statements that the mainstream media is "the enemy," and calls for more stringent libel laws have raised the specter of censorship. Brexit (the withdrawal of Great Britain from the European Union) and the rise of far-right groups in France, Germany, Holland, Turkey, and elsewhere may mark a broader, global shift. What is the obligation of information professionals in such a tense time? The answer is clear: to continue to uphold the value of intellectual freedom in library collections and programs.

> **Discussion Question**
>
> Free speech, even "hate speech," may be protected by the Constitution. What is the obligation of the information professional to reflect these views in the balanced collection?

Pressure on Educational Institutions

All types of educational institutions are fielding challenges and pressures that have implications for intellectual freedom.

K–12 School Environments

One of the biggest issues in the intellectual freedom arena is challenges to materials in K–12 classrooms and school libraries. In fact, schools have long been hot spots for public challenges to school library and curricular materials (see also chapter 6: "Literacy and Media Centers: School Libraries"). In one respect, that is not surprising. Unlike other types of libraries and institutions, public schools are "in loco parentis"—acting in place and on the behalf of parents. Parents assume the institution will enforce their own personal values—even when those values conflict with those of other parents.

Among the most frequent censorship activities reported to the OIF involve principals and superintendents who receive a single verbal complaint and then unilaterally withdraw books from a school library or curriculum. The *School Library Journal* reported that 19 percent of public schools around the country still do not have policies for collection development, requests for reconsideration, or challenges to educational materials.[57] In such cases, short of public pressure, which often exposes the school librarian or teacher to employer discipline or punishment, there is not much that can be done. Even when policies are in place, it may take the threat or reality of a lawsuit to preserve intellectual freedom.

This trend is exacerbated by the continuing decline in the number of trained school librarians in the country. Often politically isolated in their districts, their positions are first to be cut when money is tight. They are replaced (*if* they are replaced) with computer technicians or volunteers. These replacements do not understand collection development policies, reconsideration practices, or the responsibility to report censorship attempts to the Office for Intellectual Freedom.

Check This Out

A tense atmosphere breeds the suppression of free speech and often punishes those brave enough to persist. Librarians who find themselves in financial distress because of their stand for intellectual freedom should be aware of the LeRoy C. Merritt Humanitarian Fund, which can provide some short-term support. *Visit:* http://www.ala.org/groups/affiliates/relatedgroups/merrittfund/merritthumanitarian.

Another trend in the school environment impacting intellectual freedom is the battle to retain K–12 textbooks that do not shy away from the darker or controversial parts of United States history. The economics of textbook sales require the key markets of Texas and California. For many years, largely under the two-person operation of the Gablers who challenged the content of textbooks under consideration by public schools,[58] Texas succeeded in spooking textbook publishers away from any discussion of religion, American bigotry, or minority rights. Now, there is some evidence that even novels may not survive; at least one school district, fielding a challenge to *The Kite Runner*,[59] is considering replacing all novel-based instruction with an electronic platform that only features snippets of the books, likely pruned of "offensive" content.

College and University Environments

American colleges and universities are not immune. While few report challenges to textbooks and academic library materials, there are several trends that challenge intellectual freedom.

Among them are the firing of, or withdrawal of job offers for, professors who are seen as politically incorrect. This has been true even for tenured professors, and even for articles written for scholarly publications (see textbox 35.4).

Another trend is the invitation, then disinvitation or cancellation, of controversial speakers. Most of them have been conservative speakers, such as Milo Yiannopolous[60] and Ann Coulter.[61] Student

University of Colorado Tenured Professor Fired for Article

In Ward Churchill's article, "'Some People Push Back': On the Justice of Roosting Chickens,"[62] he stated that some of the more imperialistic financial dealings of some of the people in the World Trade Towers, the target of 9/11 terrorist attacks, made many financiers complicit, made them "little Eichmann." (Adolf Eichmann was a mild-mannered bureaucrat under Hitler, responsible for the logistics of internment and extermination of Jews.) Churchill lost his job at the University of Colorado, was censured by the governor and state legislature (which threatened to withhold funding from the school if the professor was *not* fired), and lost a court appeal to get his job back.[63]

groups protest the speaker and threaten or (in the case of Yiannopolous) actually do commit acts of violence.[64] Library-initiated programs "should not be proscribed or removed [or canceled] because of partisan or doctrinal disapproval" of the contents of the program or the views expressed by the participants, as stated in Article II of the Library Bill of Rights;[65] however, many of these programs are not initiated by libraries or presented in library buildings.

A related trend is "trigger warnings." Some professors and students think it is perfectly reasonable that a professor should announce verbally or in the class syllabus that some difficult topics will be discussed. Announcing that an English class will be showing a film with war scenes might seem prudent for students that are war veterans. Others see this sensitivity to the possibility of class content "triggering" personal trauma (about issues as varied as spiders or death)[66] a repudiation not just of intellectual freedom, but of education.

The same positions are taken about the idea of "safe spaces," places on campus in which no one says anything challenging or offensive about, for instance, the Islamic faith, or in which no one other than people of color are allowed to congregate. Some would argue that this is merely correcting, through the provision of sanctuary, of historic bigotry or oppression. Others see it as the politics of victimization and a new call for segregation.

PEN America, in a 2016 study *And Campus for All*,[67] found that, generally, support for intellectual freedom was falling among college students. The same study noted rising support for social justice, righting historic wrongs, and greater inclusivity as a community and a culture. But free speech and justice are not opposites, although they may on occasion come into conflict. Free speech means the same rights are offered to every voice, even those who say things that may be controversial.

Discussion Questions

In what ways is social justice an intellectual freedom issue? In what ways do these values come into conflict?

Internet-Related Issues

The promise of internet technologies can be seen in the unrivaled access to information—whether through text-message-based newspapers in India or tweets in real time from people amid riots. One element of the early internet was the promise of a democratization of publishing, with everyone able to speak and find willing listeners. This trend identifies intellectual freedom issues related to the continuing rise and evolution of the internet and social media.

One challenge is the type of information that people share. While much valuable information is shared, some voices may spew hate speech, overwhelm earnest discourse with crudity and personal attacks, or threaten personal violence. Some people may simply be uninformed and barely articulate, but others may deliberately mislead and manipulate. Sorting out the real from the fake—the truth from the noise—is increasingly difficult.

Another challenge is the issue of net neutrality. Net neutrality aims to ensure that internet service providers provide consumers with access to content and applications on an equal basis, rather than creating "fast lanes" for some kinds of preferred traffic. In other words, net neutrality "is the principle that the company that connects you to the internet does not get to control what you do on the internet."[68] Without net neutrality, internet providers could prevent users from accessing certain websites, or even redirect them to other websites preferred by the internet provider in order to prevent the user from accessing a site the provider does not want the user to access (e.g., a competitor site). While the Obama administration demonstrated a strong commitment to net neutrality, the "Trump FCC"[69] threatens it. Information professionals should remain aware of these trends and the potential interference of the information user's right to access information.

Another version of the same problem is filtering: software, governed by proprietary algorithms, that permits or prevents people from accessing information through our internet connections. Since the Children's Internet Protection Act (CIPA),[70] libraries that accept federal money (e-rate and some grants) are required to install filtering. The selection, installation, and maintenance of such filters are often made by non-librarians, and reach far beyond the restriction of images that fall into the categories of child pornography, obscenity, and harmful to minors. While ALA does not recommend the use of filters, in some states filtering is required by state law. Others may choose or be forced by their governing authorities to accept the money. In 2017, the Intellectual Freedom Committee's Privacy Subcommittee created "Guidelines to Minimize the Negative Effects of Internet Content Filters on Intellectual Freedom."[71] At this writing, some politicians are pushing the idea that all public wireless networks, all internet service providers, and even all internet-capable devices, should be required by law to be filtered.[72] Encryption—secure connections between your browser and a particular website—is a necessary function of library catalogs and personal web surfing habits.[73]

The internet remains the frontier of intellectual freedom. It continues to have almost unimaginable power to assist information professionals in the fulfillment of their mission; misused, it compromises user privacy and withholds or manipulates information for financial or political gain (see also chapter 34: "Information Privacy and Cybersecurity").

Advocacy for Intellectual Freedom

The last trend concerns advocacy efforts to demonstrate the value of libraries in the internet age by focusing on intellectual freedom (see also chapter 27: "Communication, Marketing, and Outreach Strategies"). With OCLC's *From Awareness to Funding*,[74] information professionals began to grasp that their marketing over the past generation has served to increase the library's use, but use has little correlation with support. Going forward, information professionals must assert a proposition of value—and intellectual freedom is at the core of it.

In the area of advocacy for intellectual freedom (see also chapter 28: "Advocacy"), information professionals have several key approaches.

> **Check This Out**
>
> Choose Privacy Week, held annually May 1–7, focuses attention on current threats to patron privacy. *Visit:* https://chooseprivacyweek.org/.

Participation in local media. Information professionals should always work to develop strong and positive ties with area journalists and reporters. Providing a steady stream of calendar information and promotion of the organization is one approach. But there is another level of participation. Many information professionals write regular newspaper articles. Some host radio or cable TV shows. Being a relaxed and familiar presence on media outlets helps information professionals get out the word of our importance to the intellectual vitality of our communities.

Outreach. Libraries are respected institutions, with buildings that reflect the values of a community. But information professionals need to recognize that they must also leave the building and advocate for the freedom to read at schools, business meetings, churches, political events, civic clubs, social groups, and other community gatherings. This means more than just showing up, giving a spiel, and leaving. True advocacy for the value of intellectual freedom means the management of relationships and working to make the community better in many ways. Those relationships will matter when there is a library challenge.

Litigation. ALA and the Freedom to Read Foundation[75] join with publishers, the ACLU, and others to file amicus briefs (friend-of-the-court statements) to articulate how various laws violate free speech.

In today's wired culture, there is constant competition for attention. To secure that mindshare and to build an awareness of brand, it is important for information professionals to understand and apply what a half century of brain research has revealed: we need to know how to tell short, compelling stories about the extraordinary value of the right to free inquiry, then anchor those stories in succinct data and a compelling phrase. A good example is the messaging that ALA has adopted:[76]

- Libraries transform lives.
- Libraries transform communities.
- Librarians are passionate advocates for lifelong learning.
- Libraries are a smart investment.

CONCLUSION

Information professionals must understand, claim, and proclaim their history as defenders of the First Amendment. Professional competencies in addressing issues related to intellectual freedom require a persistent mindfulness and recommitment to these ongoing issues—as well as the trends that impact everyday decisions (see textbox 35.5). To that end, information professionals need to not only adopt and regularly review their library's collection policy but also think critically about the choices that they make in day-to-day purchases, the in-filling of collection gaps, and the weeding of outdated and unused content. They must be close social observers and understand the impact of technology on society.

To remain vibrant and vital, libraries and other information organizations must be players in emerging systems of publishing, news, public discourse, and social change. Libraries are keepers of a value essential to individual fulfillment and civic engagement and improvement. They must continue to offer common ground for the minds and hearts of our communities and our nation, where everyone has a seat at the table, and everyone is heard.

Professional Competencies Supporting Intellectual Freedom.

The following competencies fall under "Ethics and Values" in the OCLC report *Competency Index for the Library Field*,[77] and are most applicable for adhering to the principles of intellectual freedom:

- Understand the history of information organizations and their role in society, both in general and in the particular community.
- Understand and act in accordance with the basic values and ethics of library and information service.
- Understand [the] relationship between laws and ethics and apply relevant state and federal laws.
- Demonstrate familiarity with the Library Bill of Rights and the ALA Code of Ethics, and articulate the relevance to library and information service.
- Apply a fundamental understanding of the ethical/legal issues surrounding the access and use of information technologies.
- Understand privacy issues and protect user confidentiality.
- Understand and promote intellectual freedom and freedom of information.
- Provide equitable services to all users.
- Recognize, respect, and address the diverse nature of information users and the community.
- Apply a fundamental understanding of the ethical and legal issues surrounding the access and use of information technologies.

NOTES

1. "Intellectual Freedom and Censorship Q&A," American Library Association, 2017, http://www.ala.org/advocacy/intfreedom/censorship/faq.
2. Office for Intellectual Freedom, *Intellectual Freedom Manual* (Chicago: American Library Association, 2010), 3.
3. First Amendment to the U.S. Constitution, Legal Information Institute, accessed June 17, 2017, https://www.law.cornell.edu/constitution/first_amendment.
4. "The Universal Right to Free Expression: An Interpretation of the Library Bill of Rights," American Library Association, accessed September 24, 2017, http://www.ala.org/Template.cfm?Section=interpretations&Template=/ContentManagement/ContentDisplay.cfm&ContentID=8662.
5. Jenny S. Bossaller and John M. Budd, "What We Talk about When We Talk about Free Speech," *Library Quarterly* 85, no. 1 (January 2015): 26–44.
6. Samuel D. Warren and Louis B. Brandeis, "The Right to Privacy," *Harvard Law Review*, 1890, accessible at http://groups.csail.mit.edu/mac/classes/6.805/articles/privacy/Privacy_brand_warr2.html.
7. American Library Association, Intellectual Freedom Committee (IFC), 2017, http://www.ala.org/aboutala/committees/ala/ala-if.
8. "First Library Bill of Rights?," American Library Association, 2016, http://www.ala.org/tools/first-library-bill-rights; cited in Louise Robbins, *Censorship and the American Library: The American Library Association's Response to Threats to Intellectual Freedom, 1939–1969* (Westport, CT: Greenwood Press, 1996). The Library Bill of Rights has evolved over the years, with several revisions and amendments, as well as interpretations of the Library Bill of Rights.
9. American Library Association, "Library Bill of Rights," 2016, http://www.ala.org/advocacy/intfreedom/librarybill.
10. American Library Association Office for Intellectual Freedom, 2017, http://www.ala.org/aboutala/offices/oif.

11. Office for Intellectual Freedom, *Intellectual Freedom Manual: Ninth Edition* (Chicago: American Library Association, 2015).
12. "Notable First Amendment Court Cases," American Library Association, 2017, www.ala.org/advocacy/intfreedom/censorship/courtcases.
13. Counts v. Cedarville School District, 295 F.Supp.2d 996 (W.D. Ark. 2003).
14. Evans v. Selma Union High School District of Fresno County, 222 P. 801 (Ca. 1924).
15. Rosenberg v. Board of Education of City of New York, 92 N.Y.S.2d 344 (Sup. Ct. Kings County 1949).
16. Todd v. Rochester Community Schools, 200 N.W.2d 90 (Mich. Ct. App. 1972).
17. Minarcini v. Strongsville (Ohio) City School District, 541 F.2d 577 (6th Cir. 1976).
18. Kreimer v. Bureau of Police for Morristown, 958 F.2d 1242 (3d Cir. 1992).
19. Case v. Unified School District No. 233, 908 F. Supp. 864 (D. Kan. 1995).
20. Interactive Digital Software Association, et al. v. St. Louis County, Missouri, et al. 329 F.3d 954(8th Cir. 2003).
21. American Amusement Machine Association, et al., v. Teri Kendrick, et al., 244 F.3d 954 (7th Cir. 2001); cert.denied, 534 U.S. 994; 122 S. Ct. 462; 151 L. Ed. 2d 379 (2001).
22. American Library Association v. U.S. Department of Justice and Reno v. American Civil Liberties Union, 521 U.S. 844, 117 S.Ct. 2329, 138 L.Ed.2d. 874 (1997).
23. United States, et al. v. American Library Association, Inc. et al., 539 U.S. 194, 123 S.Ct. 2297, 156 L.Ed.2d 221 (2003).
24. Mainstream Loudoun, et al. v. Board of Trustees of the Loudoun County Library, 24 F.Supp.2d 552 (E.D. of Va. 1998).
25. Tinker v. Des Moines Independent Community School District, 393 U.S. 503, 89 S.Ct. 733, 21 L.Ed.2d. 731 (1969).
26. Zykan v. Warsaw (Indiana) Community School Corporation and Warsaw School Board of Trustees, 631 F.2d 1300 (7th Cir. 1980).
27. Board of Education, Island Trees Union Free School District No. 26 v. Pico, 457 U.S. 853, 102 S.Ct. 2799, 73 L.Ed.2d 435 (1982).
28. Mozert v. Hawkins County Board of Education, 827 F.2d 1058 (6th Cir. 1987).
29. In Stanley v. Georgia, 394 U.S. 55, 22 L. Ed. 2d 542, 89 S. Ct. 1243 (1969).
30. McIntyre v. Ohio Election Commission, 514 U.S. 334, 115 S.Ct. 1511, 131 L.Ed.2d. 426 (1995).
31. Tattered Cover, Inc. v. City of Thornton, 44 P.3d 1044 (Colo. Sup. Ct., 2002).
32. Miller v. California, 413 U.S. 15, 93 S.Ct. 2607, 37 L.Ed.2d. 419 (1973).
33. Butler v. Michigan, 352 U.S. 380, 1 L. Ed. 2d 412, 77 S. Ct. 524 (1957).
34. Ginsberg v. New York, 390 U.S. 62, 20 L. Ed. 2d 195, 88 S. Ct. 1274 (1968).
35. New York v. Ferber, 458 U.S. 747, 102 S.Ct. 3348, 73 L.Ed.2d 1113 (1982).
36. American Booksellers Assoc., Inc. v. Hudnut, 771 F.2d 323 (7th Cir. 1985) (Easterbrook, J.), aff'd., 475 U.S. 1001, 106 S.Ct. 1172, 89 L.Ed.2d 291 (1986).
37. See an example of a Collection Development Policy at Madison Public Library's website, http://www.madisonpubliclibrary.org/policies/collection-development.
38. "Intellectual Freedom and Censorship Q & A," American Library Association, 2017, www.ala.org/advocacy/intfreedom/censorship/faq#ifpoint13.
39. Charles Robinson, *Give 'Em What They Want! Managing the Public's Library* (Chicago: American Library Association, 1992).
40. Find examples at: San Francisco Public Library, https://sfpl.org/pdf/about/administration/sfpl073.pdf, and Madison Public Library, http://www.madisonpubliclibrary.org/policies/request-reconsideration-of-library-materials.
41. "Challenge Reporting," American Library Association, 2017, http://www.ala.org/tools/challengesupport/report.
42. American Library Association, Committee on Professional Ethics (COPE), 2017, http://www.ala.org/groups/committees/ala/ala-profethic.
43. "Intellectual Freedom," American Library Association, 2017, http://www.ala.org/ifrt/.
44. "Chapters," American Library Association, 2017, http://www.ala.org/groups/affiliates/chapters.
45. Freedom to Read Foundation, http://www.ftrf.org/?page=about.

46. Banned Books Week, http://www.bannedbooksweek.org/.
47. Bowker, "Report from Bowker Shows Continuing Growth in Self-Publishing," 2017, http://www.bowker.com/news/2016/Report-from-Bowker-Shows-Continuing-Growth-in-Self-Publishing.html.
48. Ibid.
49. Ibid.
50. Bowker, "Print ISBN Counts, USA Pubdate 2002–2013," 2017, http://media.bowker.com/documents/isbn_output_2002_2013.pdf.
51. Alanna Brown, "Why Indie Publishing Beats a Mainstream Book Deal," September 7, 2013, *Huffingfton Post*, http://www.huffingtonpost.com/luxeco-living/why-indie-publishing-beat_b_3563203.html.
52. Peter Osnos, "How '*Fifty Shades of Grey*' Dominated Publishing," August 28, 2012, *Atlantic*, August 2012, https://www.theatlantic.com/entertainment/archive/2012/08/how-fifty-shades-of-grey-domi nated-publishing/261653/.
53. "Publishing Statistics on Children's Books about People of Color and First/Native Nations and by People of Color and First/Native Nations Authors and Illustrators," Cooperative Children's Book Center, School of Education, University of Wisconsin–Madison, 2017, https://ccbc.education.wisc.edu/books/pcstats.asp.
54. "Where Is the Diversity in Publishing? The 2015 Diversity Baseline Survey Results," Lee and Low Books (blog), 2017, http://blog.leeandlow.com/2016/01/26/where-is-the-diversity-in-publish ing-the-2015-diversity-baseline-survey-results/.
55. Lesli A. Maxwell, "U.S. School Enrollment Hits Majority-Minority Milestone," *Education Week*, August 20, 2014, http://www.edweek.org/ew/articles/2014/08/20/01demographics.h34.html.
56. Vanessa Remmers and Louis Llovio, "Va. House Backs Bill Requiring Parents Be Notified of Sexually Explicit Materials," *Richmond Times-Dispatch*, February 6, 2017, http://www.richmond.com/news/virginia/va-house-backs-bill-requiring-parents-be-notified-of-sexually/article_7a534d3d-2f07-5882-bf6b-213d6266567b.html.
57. "School Library Journal on Self-Censorship: 2016 Controversial Books Survey," *School Library Journal*, 2017, http://www.slj.com/features/self-censorship/.
58. Douglas Martin, "Norma Gabler, Leader of Crusade on Textbooks, Dies at 84," *New York Times*, August 1, 2007, http://www.nytimes.com/2007/08/01/education/01gabler.html.
59. Sono Wasu, "Students Question Why Popular Novel Is Removed from Gilbert School's Curriculum," 2017, http://www.abc15.com/news/region-southeast-valley/gilbert/students-question-why-popu lar-novel-is-removed-from-gilbert-schools-curriculum.
60. Kasia Kovacs, "Inflammatory and Turned Away," *Inside Higher Ed*, October 21, 2016, https://www.insidehighered.com/news/2016/10/21/several-universities-cancel-appearances-conservative-writer-milo-yiannopoulos.
61. Susan Svrluga, William Wan, and Elizabeth Dwoskin, "Ann Coulter Speech at UC Berkeley, Canceled, Again, Amid Fears for Safety," *Washington Post*, April 26, 2017, https://www.washingtonpost.com/news/grade-point/wp/2017/04/26/ann-coulter-speech-canceled-at-uc-berkeley-amid-fears-for-safety/?utm_term=.8c9ff293b604.
62. Ward Churchill, "'Some People Push Back': On the Justice of Roosting Chickens," 2017, http://www.kersplebedeb.com/mystuff/s11/churchill.html.
63. Anthony Cotton, "Fired Colorado Professor Loses Supreme Court Appeal," *Denver Post*, September 10, 2012, http://www.denverpost.com/2012/09/10/fired-colorado-professor-ward-churchill-loses-su preme-court-appeal/.
64. Madison Park and Kyung Lah, "Berkeley Protests of Yiannopoulos caused $100,000 in damage," 2017, http://www.cnn.com/2017/02/01/us/milo-yiannopoulos-berkeley/index.html.
65. American Library Association, "Library Bill of Rights," 2017, http://www.ala.org/advocacy/intfreedom/librarybill.
66. "Common Trigger Warnings," *Privelege 101*, 2017, http://privilege101.tumblr.com/triggers.html.
67. PEN America, *And Campus for All: Diversity, Inclusion, and Free Speech at U.S. Universities* (New York: PEN America, 2016), accessed September 23, 2017, https://pen.org/and-campus-for-all-diversity-inclusion-and-free-speech-at-u-s-universities/.
68. "Net Neutrality," Public Knowledge, 2017, https://www.publicknowledge.org/issues/net-neutrality.

69. "What Is Net Neutrality?," American Civil Liberties Union, June 2017, https://www.aclu.org/issues/free -speech/internet-speech/what-net-neutrality.

70. "Children's Internet Protection Act (CIPA)," Federal Communications Commission, 2017, https://www .fcc.gov/consumers/guides/childrens-internet-protection-act.

71. "Guidelines to Minimize the Negative Effects of Internet Content Filtering on Intellectual Freedom," American Library Association, 2017, http://www.ala.org/advocacy/intfreedom/filtering/filtering _guidelines.

72. PEN America, *And Campus for All*.

73. "Let's Encrypt," Linux Corporation, 2017, https://letsencrypt.org/.

74. OCLC, *From Awareness to Funding: A Study of Library Support in America* (Dublin, OH: OCLC, 2008), http://www.oclc.org/content/dam/oclc/reports/funding/fullreport.pdf.

75. Freedom to Read Foundation, 2017, http://ftrf.org.

76. "Libraries Transform," American Library Association, 2017, http://www.ala.org/transforminglibraries/ libraries-transform-campaign.

77. Bethe Gutsche and Brenda Hough, *Competency Index for the Library Field* (Dublin, OH: OCLC, 2014), 10, https://www.webjunction.org/content/dam/WebJunction/Documents/webJunction/2015-03/Com petency%20Index%20for%20the%20Library%20Field%20(2014).pdf.

Part VI

Information Horizons
Strategies for Building a Dynamic Career as an Information Professional

Effectively leading change initiatives can help organizations create and shape a positive future and increase the organization's chances of survival and success.

—Kendra Albright, chapter 37

The information profession is one of the most challenging and most rewarding professions in the twenty-first century. It combines a wide range of skills and competencies from information expertise to data management, from information technology skills to knowledge of copyright and intellectual freedom, while staying aware of and responsive to a constantly changing diverse community of users. Change is the word of the day. Opportunities to work in this field cross almost all disciplines and areas of interest and require flexibility, planning, networking, and staying abreast of social, cultural, and technological changes that might impact information environments.

Part VI provides specific career management strategies that guide readers—whether they are just entering the information field, changing from a career in a different industry, or are current information professionals considering a new direction in their careers—to discover how their skill sets match the variety of opportunities in libraries and other information environments. This section also addresses the importance of leadership and highlights the various opportunities new or current information professionals can pursue to help influence the future of the information profession and bring their ideas to shape the continuing evolution of the information organizations.

36

Career Management Strategies for Lifelong Success

Kim Dority

Chapter 36, "Career Management Strategies for Lifelong Success," addresses the ways that information careers have evolved, and continue to evolve, in response to ongoing changes in the information professions. Kim Dority, author, consultant, and blogger on information careers, points out how today's information professionals must be more innovative and change oriented than ever as they face a challenging, but also very exciting, future. Dority outlines strategies for career development that combine goal setting, adopting a self-employment mind-set, and developing professional equity, while being flexible, adaptive, and knowledgeable about future career possibilities.

In a world where the skills that information professionals possess open up numerous career possibilities, Dority notes the importance of developing a self-employed mind-set that is founded on the idea that the individual is in charge of his or her job choices and decisions. She further emphasizes the importance of defining success on an individual's own terms.

Dority cautions new graduates to keep two considerations in mind: the first job is only the first job; and building a career is an unpredictable and often changing trajectory. She suggests creating career action plans, setting goals that can be used throughout the career, and developing career agendas. Finally, she notes the importance of developing professional equity—by investing in what one knows, who one knows, and what is known by others about them. The chapter is accompanied by a wealth of online resources, including LIS job boards, online career development resources, interviewing tips, and more!

★   ★   ★

Today's library and information science (LIS) students are launching their careers in a professional environment increasingly defined by creativity, innovation, and technological advances. Seasoned information professionals are finding their roles no less change-driven, requiring them to adapt existing expectations—and expertise—to new realities. Creating a resilient career as an information professional, one that can anticipate, position for, and make the most of change, has never been more challenging. But neither has it ever been more possible.

The key is to develop career strategies that not only complement the information professional's competencies but also provide a competitive edge when it comes time to search for or transition into new jobs. These competencies provide LIS students and practitioners the ability to pivot, position for, and pursue lifelong and fulfilling careers.

After completing this chapter, the reader should have an understanding of:

- how to adopt a mind-set of self-employment to take charge of one's career direction(s),
- the choices one will want to consider in charting those directions, and
- possible career pathways.

In addition, readers will learn and be able to apply the process for setting and achieving their career goals, a process that can be repeated throughout their professional lives with each career transition. Finally, readers will learn strategies for continually expanding their key asset—their professional equity—throughout the course of their careers.

THE UNIVERSE OF INFORMATION WORK

There are many ways to deploy information skills. A primary challenge for many LIS students and information professionals is simply determining how to narrow down the many options available to them. As the San José State University School of Information's annual report, *MLIS Skills at Work: A Snapshot of Job Postings*, makes clear, information skills continue to be deployed in increasingly diverse ways and for a continually expanding universe of employers.[1] To help think through the possibilities, one approach is to consider potential jobs or career pathways by defining the characteristics of LIS work: What work will be done? And, for whom is the work being done?

In terms of what work an information professional might do, the *Snapshot*'s broad categories include:

- collection, cataloging, and circulation;
- reference and research;
- instruction and outreach;
- . management and administration;
- archives and preservation; and
- web and social media work.[2]

But within those categories are dozens of unique and interesting information jobs that demonstrate the stunning diversity of roles within what used to be considered predictable career paths.

For whom is this work being done? Information professionals work in:

- public libraries (see also chapter 8: "Community Anchors for Lifelong Learning: Public Libraries");
- academic libraries (see also chapter 7: "Learning and Research Institutions: Academic Libraries");
- school libraries (see also chapter 6: "Literacy and Media Centers: School Libraries");
- government agencies;
- cultural heritage institutions and museums;
- historical and/or corporate archives;
- businesses of all types (including high-tech start-ups);
- nonprofits such as civic, trade, or cause-based organizations;
- law firms;
- theological institutions;
- music and orchestra libraries;
- hospitals and health care clinics; and

- research institutes, think tanks, or foundations, among other environments (see also chapter 9: "Working in Different Information Environments: Special Libraries and Information Centers").

They also work as independent information professionals, where the "employers" are clients, or as information entrepreneurs, creating information-based products and services. As opportunities for information professionals continue to both contract in older roles and expand into newer ones, the only given in this dynamic field is that the coming years will bring even more opportunities, many of which can be barely imagined today.

EMBRACING A SELF-EMPLOYED MIND-SET

It is hard to imagine a more exciting time to be launching a career as an information professional. True, the challenge of creating a rewarding, growing, sustainable career path given the lack of predictability in the information field may sometimes seem more disruptive and daunting than exciting and energizing. Add to that the fact that there are hundreds of approaches and environments within which to deploy LIS skills, and it indeed can become a bit overwhelming.

Information professionals should realize that, regardless of what point they are at in their career, they are self-employed.[3] Information professionals are in charge of the job choices and career decisions they make, the results of those decisions, and the opportunities they have been offered throughout their careers. This type of career self-direction requires information professionals to identify, define, and take responsibility for what they want in their jobs and their careers. Embracing a self-employed mind-set empowers information professionals to decide what work they will do, for whom, and how.

CASE STUDY

Embracing a Self-Employed Mind-Set

Imagine a recent graduate, Letisha, who previously worked as a nurse and is now considering potential jobs using her newly minted MLIS degree. Letisha might decide to:

- focus on consumer health in a public library setting (perhaps creating LibGuides on clinical trials, genetic testing, or how to navigate the Medicaid system);
- work remotely as a reference librarian and the nursing program departmental liaison for an online academic library;
- join the staff of a national health care company as a data manager;
- collaborate with two former MLIS classmates to start a specialized medical research and alerting service for geriatric nursing clinicians;
- sign on with a nonprofit disseminating health care information to immigrant and/or underserved populations;
- pursue a nursing/health care informatics project or contract work, either remotely or at the client's workplace, for one of the LIS contract or staffing agencies; or
- work as a specialist in developing and sharing consumer health information materials for a hospital's medical library.

Besides providing a sense of how broadly LIS skills might be applied, Letisha's choices are important for another reason: by embracing a self-employed mind-set, she very possibly could do every one of these jobs at some point in her career if she chose to.

In *The Start-Up of You: Adapt to the Future, Invest in Yourself, and Transform Your Career*, Reid Hoffman and Ben Casnocha emphasize that:

> To adapt to the challenges of professional life today, we need to rediscover our entrepreneurial instincts and use them to forge new sorts of careers. Whether you're a lawyer or doctor or teacher or engineer or even a business owner, today you need to also think of yourself as an entrepreneur at the helm of at least one living, growing start-up venture: *your career.*[4]

This advice should resonate strongly with information professionals hoping to create resilient careers.

TAKING CHARGE OF CHOICES

Being able to confidently make choices, and then make the best of those choices, is a critical competency for building a resilient career as an information professional. What types of decisions might someone need to make?

Imagine the career choices of Jesse, who is seriously thinking about his postgraduation job search. He will need to decide some of the following:

- What type(s) of organization(s) would he like to work for?
- What type(s) of work would he like to do?
- What is his preferred geographic region? Does he prefer the city, a midsized town, or a small town?
- Does he prefer lots of public contact, or minimal public contact?
- Does he want high-growth/learning curve work or does he want a job within his existing comfort zone?

These questions represent a very small subset of the types of choices and decisions information professionals will face while building a resilient career. As the profession changes, so too do the career opportunities it provides. As automation displaces some information and library roles, it creates others. As company mergers do away with some positions for corporate librarians, information professionals may identify new ways to contribute their information skills (for example, as an embedded librarian[5]). Career decisions typically depend on personal preferences, career goals, and market opportunities.

> **Discussion Question**
>
> How can information professionals "translate" key LIS skills into language understandable to non-LIS employers?

DEFINING SUCCESS

Just about everyone has a definition of success—in other words, the criteria or benchmarks that signal the achievement of an individual's career aspirations. The challenge is in separating what others view as success from how information professionals themselves may individually define success. For example, common success indicators for various professions might include:

- high salary
- luxury lifestyle
- working for highly respected employer
- high-status title
- professional recognition

Kim Dority

- authority over others
- in-demand "power player" or highly connected influencer

These benchmarks may be perfect for some people, but resonate less with others.

CASE STUDY

Career Success Indicators in the Information Professions

When asked about their own success indicators, University of Denver MLIS students identified their career success indicators as:

- "Having a positive impact on others' lives"
- "Making a difference in my community"
- "Helping connect people with information to achieve their goals"
- "Growing in knowledge and contribution year after year"
- "Mastering the confidence to advocate for myself and others"
- "Learning to lead effectively and compassionately"[6]

Each person will have his or her own interpretation of what defines success. Factors such as personal values, goals, cultural environment, the expectations of family and friends, and perhaps even the views of faculty or mentors who have been especially influential all contribute to shaping what career success means to each individual. The key for information professionals is to be able to identify what truly resonates with them as defining a successful career, as opposed to simply working to fulfill the expectations of others.

FINDING (OR CREATING) ONE'S LIS CAREER PATH

When launching a career as an information professional, many students and recent graduates feel a tremendous amount of anxiety about landing the "perfect job"—the one that enables them to use all their LIS expertise; work with a terrific, collaborative team; learn from a wise and compassionate boss; and do the work they have dreamed of since that first day in graduate school (or possibly before). For an information professional starting a new career in the information professions, there are two considerations that are useful to keep in mind.

- First, that first job is *only* the first job. It is a starting point from which new professionals can launch their careers in myriad directions. The first job does not define subsequent job choices, but how well new information professionals *handle* that first job can certainly open up bridges to other, more desirable career opportunities. Information professionals should focus less on how ideal that first job is and more on how they perform in the job.

> **Check This Out**
>
> Check out chapter 36: "Framing Alternative LIS Job Options: Eight Starting Points for Career Transitions" in the online supplement.

- Second, building a rewarding and resilient career as an information professional is a highly iterative (and often serendipitous) process. Therefore, although career agendas and plans are certainly important, information professionals should remain open to new people, experiences, learning, and challenges to position themselves in the path of opportunity.

VETTING EXPECTATIONS

When thinking about what type of career path individuals might like to *initially* pursue, one of the most important skills to master is the ability to vet assumptions. In other words, just because someone's dreamed of being a reference librarian in a public library for the past ten years does not necessarily mean that person has a realistic, current understanding of what that job entails. This is where vetting assumptions comes in. Some of the best ways to verify expectations about specific career paths include:

- Read print and online publications related to the target career path. Look for information about trends, issues, jobs contraction or expansion, and best employers (especially ones that are growing/hiring).[7]
- Monitor bloggers and other social media writers who comment on aspects of the target career path. Look at how they portray the work, whether their comments are positive or negative, and whether they are discussing emerging opportunities (and if so, what are they saying?). Check out the resources mentioned in chapter 3: "Librarianship: A Continuously Evolving Profession" for a good starting point.
- Join discussion groups (for example on LinkedIn) and if possible, professional associations such as the American Library Association (ALA),[8] Association for Information Science & Technology (ASIS&T),[9] Special Libraries Association (SLA),[10] Society of American Archivists (SAA),[11] ARMA International,[12] and so on. Gain insight about the work, the employers, and trends or issues related to both; associations are also often a great way to find salary information.
- Conduct as many informational interviews as possible with information practitioners who are doing the work of interest or working for employers of interest: ask very specific questions that either confirm or dispel expectations about the job.
- Do volunteer work, internships, or part-time work in the environments of interest: get a sense of how much the reality of the work aligns with one's imagined assumptions.

> The goal of vetting assumptions is essentially to keep students, new information professionals, and LIS career transitioners from investing time, energy, and passion into a career path that in actuality is a poor fit for them.

The goal of vetting assumptions is essentially to keep students, new information professionals, and LIS career transitioners from investing time, energy, and passion into a career path that in actuality is a poor fit for them. It is also an easy and effective way to narrow down hundreds of potential LIS career options into a more manageable size—perhaps several dozen or so. Additionally, these steps can be repeated as necessary to help navigate all future career transitions.

GETTING FROM HERE TO THERE: CREATING CAREER ACTION PLANS AND AGENDAS

Career action plans and career agendas are essential to help information professionals stay on course with their overall career goals. What is the difference between a career action plan and a career agenda? A career action plan is a broad strategic road map for longer-term career development comprising goals, strategies, and tactics, while a career agenda is a short list of tasks to complete within a certain situation. Both are important elements of a take-charge, entrepreneurial, resilient LIS career. And both can help individuals build the career they aspire to in different ways and situations.

A *career action plan*, also known as a career road map,[13] is based on:

- understanding what career goals are personally meaningful,
- identifying pathways or strategies to move toward those goals, and
- defining the tactics that will become the "action items" of those strategies.

Career action plans often cover anywhere from one to five years, depending on how long it is likely to take to achieve a specific goal, so they should be used as an ongoing guide to help evaluate potential career decisions.

CASE STUDY

Building a Career Action Plan

iSchool student Kate set a goal to build postgraduation career opportunities in the archives field over the course of her two-year MLIS program. Given this, her career action plan might be to:

- take advantage of every archives and records management-related learning opportunity provided by her iSchool program;
- gain a better sense of opportunities in the archives and records field; and
- start building visibility as a strong, engaged professional contributor among future potential hiring managers.

As a next step, Kate's tactics or action items for her "take advantage of the school's offerings" strategy might look like this:

- meet with an academic advisor within the next six weeks to identify and schedule out all iSchool courses related to archives and records and management to ensure that she will stay on track through her program;
- join the iSchool's student archives group and attend all group workshops, webcasts, and career sessions, ideally helping with programming so she can meet guest speakers; and
- identify archives and records management internship opportunities early on in her program.

Career action plans and their pattern of goal-strategies-tactics can be used repeatedly throughout a career to accomplish a multitude of objectives; it is especially useful for career transitions, such as preparing for a promotion request, making job changes, or bridging into a related job field.[14]

A *career agenda*, on the other hand, is a focused list of items to achieve within a certain situation or setting. The purpose of a career agenda is to keep individual career plans on track while also fulfilling primary commitments, such as taking courses as a student or learning the ropes of a new job as a recently hired employee. For example, MLIS students begin every course with the framework of the course syllabus, which is what the instructor expects students to undertake, learn, and complete.

> " Career action plans and their pattern of goal-strategies-tactics can be used repeatedly throughout a career to accomplish a multitude of objectives; it is especially useful for career transitions, such as preparing for a promotion request, making job changes, or bridging into a related job field. "

But every course can also provide an opportunity to accomplish additional career goals, such as improving public speaking skills, learning how to lead virtual teams, boosting research skills, or trying out project management approaches. While an information professional's first job may be an entry-level position, the new information professional can make the most of the opportunity by deciding what else to learn and accomplish in addition to the basic job responsibilities and by taking charge of their professional growth.

> "Career action plans and career agendas enable information professionals to keep their careers on track and moving forward regardless of what else may be going on in their work lives, now or in the future."

The easiest way to set a career agenda? Identify one (or several) items that, if improved or increased, would help open up the next level of career opportunity, and identify the amount of time involved in that action(s). A first-year career agenda might involve the following action items:

- figure out and implement three ways to increase productivity for existing job responsibilities;
- identify, reach out to, and build professional relationships with two experts in the area of their career interest;
- volunteer to participate in a new multi-department initiative if the opportunity arises;
- observe workplace colleagues, especially those older and younger, to learn at least one new skill (i.e., people, process, other); and
- choose one job-related LIS topic to "go deep" on and become the team expert while also building professional value to current or future employers.

Career action plans and career agendas enable information professionals to keep their careers on track and moving forward regardless of what else may be going on in their work lives, now or in the future.

PROFESSIONAL EQUITY: INVESTING IN CAREER ASSETS

Growing rewarding, resilient LIS careers depends on many factors (including "being in the right place at the right time"), but underlying and informing each of those factors is a concept called professional equity. Like a financial asset, professional equity grows the more one invests in it, and the more a person invests in it, the more independence and opportunities it will provide.

Three Elements of Professional Equity

There are three elements of professional equity, as identified in textbox 36.1.

The stronger each one of these elements is and the more time and effort invested in each one, the greater and more rewarding the career opportunities will be throughout one's career.

> TEXTBOX 36.1
>
> **Elements of Professional Equity**
>
> what a person knows
> who that person knows
> who knows what about that person

Investing in What One Knows

What a person knows is a combination of domain knowledge (or discipline-specific professional skills and areas of expertise), general professional skills, and business skills.

When MLIS graduates launch their new professional careers, they do so with a wealth of current knowledge, advanced technology skills, information about best practices in multiple settings, and knowledge of related disciplines such as marketing and public relations, human resources management, or nonprofit administration. That is an impressive knowledge base, but in the LIS world, it is only the beginning.

Information professionals know that developing a plan for continuous learning is the key to remaining current in their field or specialization. This can be achieved through a variety of ways such as:

Belong to LIS organizations with a strong professional development mission, for example, those that provide webinars, workshops, and courses for members. ALA has an eLearning program along with webinars hosted by many of its divisions. SLA and SAA both offer certificate programs.

Sign up for additional, refresher courses from a graduate school or other MLIS-focused program.

Develop a Personal Learning Network (PLN),[15] which is a diverse community of individuals willing to share their expertise and insights to help other members of the network, whether through social media, face-to-face meetings, discussion groups, or other channels. Given the global nature of today's information work, many PLNs now include connections, experts, and resources from throughout the world.

Find mentors or workplace specialty coaches, specifically colleagues who have a skill of interest and who are willing to take the time to share their knowledge.

No matter what process information professionals use to continue to grow what they know, the ability to learn continuously and effectively—learning on demand, creating and directing their learning path, and applying learning immediately—should be considered a core career competency.

Investing in Who One Knows

Investing in who a person knows means focusing on one's connections, both professional and personal, otherwise known as a professional network. The longer individuals work, and the more often and actively they collaborate with others to accomplish key work or volunteer goals, the likelier it is that their community of connections will continue to grow as well.

There are many ways to grow a professional network. Connections should be relationship based (i.e., authentic concern for the well-being and success of others) rather than transactional (i.e., the "what's in it for me" approach). The basics of network building include actions such as:

- introducing oneself to people in social or professional gatherings and then following up with them via e-mail or a LinkedIn connection invitation to cement the relationship,
- volunteering in both LIS and non-LIS situations and organizations (for example, a community event) to get to know new people while also contributing to the greater good,
- reaching out to individuals for informational interviews, following up with a thank-you note (always!), and then staying in touch with that new connection,
- building positive relationships with faculty, administrators, and fellow students while in graduate school and after graduation, and then joining the alumni group as well, and
- joining and becoming active in professional associations at the international, national, and local levels, and making sure to build positive relationships with everyone encountered throughout the association.

It is essential for information professionals to stay connected with their network on a regular basis. One good approach is to try to reach out via a phone or e-mail "catch-up" several times a year if possible. Social media platforms like Facebook, LinkedIn, SnapChat, WhatsApp, Skype, and Twitter also provide a strong medium for staying in touch with colleagues, alumni, and other key professionals. Knowing what connections are up to is not only beneficial, it can also provide information professionals ideas for how they might be able to help each other. That sort of generous reciprocity, over the course of a decades-long career, will provide a stunning return on investment in terms of career opportunities, personal reward, and professional impact.

Investing in Who Knows What about You

A professional reputation, or brand, tells others what to expect from an individual. In *Be Your Own Brand*, authors David McNally and Karl D. Speak note, "A personal brand promise is a way to state what you are committed to being for others."[16] A professional reputation or brand may be, for example, a promise of what one knows, what one is capable of, what one's values are, how one treats people, and how professional one is.[17]

People have a brand whether or not they choose to actively shape how others perceive them—it is simply human nature for people to jump to conclusions about others, often based on wildly mistaken assumptions. That is why it is worth the effort for everyone to take the time to think about how others might or do perceive them based on what information is available (especially online) to others. The goal should be to showcase one's best attributes, including professional strengths and passions.

> An individual's goal in building a highly visible professional reputation/brand is to make sure that when someone thinks of them in a professional setting, the strengths they would like to be known for come to mind.

An individual's goal in building a highly visible professional reputation/brand is to make sure that when someone thinks of them in a professional setting, the strengths they would like to be known for come to mind. Contributing to professional conversations, creating new knowledge, curating existing knowledge of value to the profession, and sharing information (online, at a conference, in a professional journal, webcast, or other means) are all valuable and effective ways to develop a professional brand.

Another aspect of reputation building that is equally important, if less visible, is the personal reputations that are built with colleagues throughout one's career. This reputation is built on actions like finding ways to help others without regard to one's own immediate benefit, for example, by making sure that other contributors get due credit, giving a public "shout-out" to colleagues who have done something exceptional (or even something just kind or generous), or quietly helping a classmate who is struggling with an assignment. This is not so much about competence as it is about character, which will have every bit as much of an impact on the quality of one's career.

Enhancing One's Professional Equity throughout One's Career

Information professionals may be interested in increasing all three elements of professional equity at different points in their careers—not just when they are looking for their first job. The strategies discussed in this chapter can also be used to help experienced information professionals enhance their professional equity as well. For example, information professionals already in the field can:

- continue to invest in their ongoing professional development,
- join and become active in at least one LIS professional association,
- reach out to people doing interesting or admirable work in the LIS field to request informational interviews,
- identify an unmet information need for an organization,
- create an information-based solution using one's LIS skills, and
- take the initiative to create an event that brings people together to learn about a specific topic.

SOCIAL MEDIA, PROFESSIONAL REPUTATIONS, AND CAREERS

Social media and sharing platforms (for example, Facebook, Twitter, SlideShare, and YouTube) provide information professionals extremely easy and valuable ways to position themselves for career opportunities and increase their professional equity if used wisely. Information professionals can post slide decks from their best presentations, share a creative video they have put together on an LIS topic, start a specialized LIS Twitter topic feed, or create/contribute to a Facebook group devoted to their professional passion. Each of these options provides a way for information professionals to showcase their skills and strengths in a very public arena and makes them more "findable" for potential employers.

> **Discussion Questions**
>
> What emerging trends in demographics, technology, or societal needs might result in new opportunities for information professionals? What might those opportunities be?

The key word, however, is *wisely*. As most have experienced, it is extremely easy to cross the invisible line dividing professional from unprofessional engagement online. And once a post, tweet, comment, or share has hit the web, it pretty much never goes away. It is important to keep in mind before hitting that send button that whatever is said or done online can be seen as a reflection of an individual's judgment, professional demeanor, and basic common sense by hiring managers. Words to live by when it comes to social media: when in doubt, don't.

CONCLUSION

One of the most important career competencies going forward will be the ability to pivot quickly and effectively as LIS employment paths continue to expand in some areas and contract in others. This will not only be a critical factor in creating a resilient, rewarding career but also in the ability to thrive in existing LIS jobs.

In addition to continually building one's professional equity, the following career competencies will enable information professionals to successfully pivot into the exciting new professional opportunities on the horizon:

- an ability to anticipate and position for changes in one's professional environment;
- a willingness to focus on the opportunity—rather than just the disruption—inherent in change;
- a commitment not only to ongoing learning but also to learning from anyone, anywhere, anytime;
- a willingness to try, fail, learn, and try again; and
- an ability to move forward with confidence despite not being certain of outcomes or success.

As LIS students and information professionals move through what is likely to be exciting, multifaceted careers, the best long-term asset will be a personal commitment to self-leadership and taking charge of one's own goals, decisions, actions, and outcomes (see also chapter 37: "Leadership Skills for Today's Global Information Landscape"). Not every decision will be the right one, but every decision will be one that can be learned from. And that is the key.

Be sure to check out the wealth of resources in chapter 36 in the online supplement, including recommended books and articles on career strategies, a list of professional LIS organizations, links to job-trend and salary reports, a list of job boards for LIS-based careers, and various online resources on résumés, interviewing tips with strategies for informational interviews, and more.

NOTES

1. San José State University, *"MLIS Skills at Work: A Snapshot of Job Postings Spring 2017* (San José, CA: San José State University, 2017), http://ischool.sjsu.edu/sites/default/files/content_pdf/career_trends.pdf.
2. Ibid.
3. Cliff Hakim, *We Are All Self-Employed: How to Take Control of Your Career* (San Francisco: Berrett-Koehler, 2003).
4. Reid Hoffman and Ben Casnocha, *The Start-Up of You: Adapt to the Future, Invest in Yourself, and Transform Your Career* (New York: Crown Business, 2012), 4.
5. David Shumaker, *The Embedded Librarian: Innovative Strategies for Taking Knowledge Where It's Needed* (Medford, NJ: Information Today, 2012).
6. Personal communications between author and University of Denver LIS Career Alternatives course students, September 1998–June 2017.
7. For an excellent overview of trends monitoring, a valuable skill both for LIS careers and information work, see Amy Webb, *The Signals Are Talking: Why Today's Fringe Is Tomorrow's Mainstream* (New York: Public Affairs, 2016).
8. American Library Association, http://www.ala.org/.
9. Association for Information Science & Technology (ASIS&T), https://www.asist.org/.
10. Special Libraries Association (SLA), https://www.sla.org/.
11. Society of American Archivists (SAA), https://www2.archivists.org/.
12. ARMA International, https://www.arma.org/.
13. Although written specifically for those contemplating a career change, another good resource on the idea of creating and using career maps is Liz Ryan's *Reinvention Roadmap: Break the Rules to Get the Job You Want and Career You Deserve* (Dallas, TX: BenBella Books, 2016); Kim Dority, *Rethinking Information Work: A Career Guide for Librarians and Other Information Professionals* (Santa Barbara, CA: ABC-CLIO, 2016), 193–209.
14. For more on career action plans, see Dority, *Rethinking Information Work*, ch. 4.
15. Center for Language and Technology, "Welcome to Introduction to Personal Learning Networks," University of Hawaii at Manoa, http://clt.manoa.hawaii.edu/projects/pln/.
16. David McNally and Karl Speak, *Be Your Own Brand: Achieve More of What You Want Being More of Who You Are* (San Francisco: Berrett-Koehler, 2002), 75.
17. For more insights on professional branding, consider exploring Dorie Clark, *Reinventing You: Define Your Brand, Imagine Your Future* (Boston: Harvard Business Review Press, 2013), and the older but still useful William Arruda and Kirsten Dixson, *Career Distinction: Stand Out by Building Your Brand* (Hoboken, NJ: Wiley, 2007).

37

Leadership Skills for Today's Global Information Landscape

Kendra Albright

Chapter 37, "Leadership Skills for Today's Global Information Landscape," focuses on how leadership skills are necessary to address the many changes in technology, information science, and practice. The author, Dr. Kendra Albright, professor and director of the School of Information at Kent State University, begins by defining what leader and leadership means.

Albright defines leadership as having "the ability to draw people together to set and accomplish goals that are intentionally directed toward positive outcomes." She is careful to distinguish between leadership and management: managers generally focus on day-to-day operations and maintain the status quo; leaders, in contrast, inspire, innovate, collaborate, and challenge traditional practices, resulting in creating high expectations. Focusing specifically on information professionals, Albright identifies leadership competencies as the ability to communicate and influence the target audience; an important component of this is having soft skills that focus on interpersonal relationships. Strategic planning is also the purview of a leader, and Albright includes details on the strategic planning process for leaders.

Essential resources presented by the author include the Library Leadership Administration and Management Association's list of fourteen leadership competencies, Kotter's eight-step model for leading change, and a list of leadership training opportunities available to LIS professionals. The chapter was specifically chosen to conclude this book, as it encourages all information professionals to think more broadly about their role in and contributions to the information professions, their influence and leadership potential, and their overall career growth.

★   ★   ★

Leadership can be defined in many ways. One of the common misconceptions about leadership, however, is that it is the same as management.[1] Leadership differs from management in distinctive ways, although they are often used interchangeably. While they serve different purposes and are distinctively different, they are complementary and are both necessary ingredients of a successful organization.

Leadership competencies have evolved over time in the business literature and even more recently in the information science literature. Comparisons between the two bodies of literature can yield interesting and useful results for consideration in developing leaders and leadership programs in the information professions.

Leadership is focused on managing change (see also chapter 20: "Change Management"); thus, the skills and competencies of leaders have great bearing on the ability of a leader to guide change. In the changing global information landscape, these skills are not only desirable but necessary to address the many changes in technology, the discipline, and practice.

This chapter begins with a brief examination of leader and leadership definitions and how leaders and managers differ, followed by a more in-depth review and discussion of leadership competencies. General comparisons of leadership competencies are discussed in light of specific competencies that have been suggested for information professionals. Finally, the chapter summarizes the importance of these competencies in managing and leading change. After completing this chapter, the reader should have an understanding of:

- the definition of leadership and leader,
- differences between leadership and management,
- leadership competencies,
- the relationship between leadership and strategic planning, and
- professional development opportunities for leadership.

DEFINITIONS OF LEADERSHIP AND LEADER

Leadership has been a topic of research for a long time, with research dating back to the early 1900s.[2] It has, however, been conceptually described throughout history with characteristics of great leaders; for example, historical figures of the Bible, great military leaders (e.g., Napoleon), statesmen such as Thomas Jefferson, and so on.[3]

Definitions of Leadership

Over the past century, leadership has been defined in many ways. Travis Bradberry, author of *Emotional Intelligence*, offers several definitions of leadership from great authors.[4] He quotes the following experts and offers his critiques of their leadership definitions:

- Peter Drucker, management expert, said, "The only definition of a leader is someone who has followers."[5] Bradberry critiques this quote, claiming it is too simplistic because it simply relies on people following a leader's orders.
- Warren Bennis, a founder of modern leadership studies, defined leadership as "the capacity to translate vision into reality."[6] Bradberry claims this definition is too focused on the leader and not on those s/he leads.
- Bill Gates, founder of Microsoft, defined leadership this way: "As we look ahead into the next century, leaders will be those who empower others."[7] Bradberry challenges this perspective, suggesting that it is missing goals and a vision.
- John Maxwell, pastor and motivational speaker, defined leadership as "influence—nothing more, nothing less,"[8] which does not address the source of influence.

Bradberry's critique of these definitions of famous experts in leadership suggests that they are limited in their scope and not inclusive of the four key elements of leadership as outlined in textbox 37.1.[9]

Kendra Albright

Key Elements of Leadership

- Leadership stems from *social influence*, not authority or power.
- Leadership requires others, and that implies they do not need to be direct reports.
- Leadership is more than personality traits, attributes, or even a title; there are many styles that work and many paths to effective leadership.
- Leadership includes a *greater good*; it is not about influence with no intended outcome.

Bradberry offers his own definition of leadership: "Leadership is a process of social influence which maximizes the efforts of others toward the achievement of a greater good."[10]

Leadership is also defined as "a collaborative activity generating the opportunity for all members of an organization to engage in the visioning and motivation of one another to meet the challenges of a continually changing operating environment."[11] This definition can be broken down into the key elements identified by Bradberry in this way:

- Social influence is indicated by the inclusion of "all members of an organization."
- "All members of an organization" also suggests that there does not have to be any direct reporting structure.
- There is no discussion of personality traits or titles.
- Leadership that meets "the challenges of a continually changing operating environment" suggests that it contributes to the greater good of the organization.

Definition of Leader

There are important differences between the definition of *leadership* and the definition of a *leader*. While Bradberry's key elements of leadership are useful, they are limited to the definition of leadership rather than a *leader*. The primary difference is that a definition of leadership is focused at an organizational level, whereas a definition of a leader is focused on an individual. Drawing from the many perspectives of what constitutes leadership, leadership can be summarized as the ability to draw people together to set and accomplish goals that are intentionally directed toward positive outcomes. A leader, therefore, is someone who can draw people together to set and accomplish those goals, which requires a specific set of leadership skills. Individuals can learn these skills to promote leadership throughout an organization. Ammons-Stephens et al. note that "Successful library leaders demonstrate certain skills that are instrumental in the delivery of desired outcomes. We usually think of the demonstration of these skills as competencies."[12] Leadership competencies, therefore, are valuable for both the organization as well as a professional development strategy for the individual.

> Leadership can be summarized as the ability to draw people together to set and accomplish goals that are intentionally directed toward positive outcomes. A leader, therefore, is someone who can draw people together to set and accomplish those goals, which requires a specific set of leadership skills.

DIFFERENCES BETWEEN LEADERSHIP AND MANAGEMENT

Before leadership competencies can be examined, it is important to distinguish between leadership and management to make clear the differences in each. Kotter suggests that leadership and management are terms that are often used interchangeably, but that are "radically different."[13] He suggests there are three primary mistakes that people make when discussing these terms:

1. They do not see the distinction between leadership and management.
2. They assume that leaders are those at the top of the organizational hierarchy, while managers are those in the management layers below.
3. They consider leaders to have charisma, which they attribute to specific personality characteristics, and they believe that only a few people can be leaders.

So, what constitutes the difference between leadership and management? Management tends to be more operational,[14] to focus on stability,[15] and to provide strategies on how to cope with complexity[16] (see also chapter 20: "Change Management"). Leadership, alternatively, is an additional skill that is added on to the technical expertise of specific work[17] and focuses on how to cope with change.[18]

A good way to think about these differences in leadership and management is by understanding how leaders and managers approach similar tasks, specifically how they:

- decide what needs to be done,
- create networks of people that can accomplish a specific agenda, and
- make sure that people get their jobs done.[19]

To decide what needs to be done, managers are focused on supporting the organizational tasks of planning and budgeting of organizational resources. Leaders focus on the directions in which the organization can change in positive ways by creating a vision and strategies to reach specific goals toward that vision.[20]

In terms of creating networks of people to accomplish an agenda, managers create the organizational structure to accomplish its plans. Specifically, managers organize and staff the jobs needed to carry out specific functions and tasks. Leaders focus on putting people together who can create the necessary relationships to accomplish the shared vision.[21]

Finally, when trying to make sure that people get their jobs done, managers focus on controlling through reviewing and achieving results and making decisions based upon those results. Leaders focus on continuous motivation and inspiration of people toward accomplishment of the shared vision[22] (see also chapter 22: "Managing Personnel").

The differences between leaders and managers can be seen at a glance in table 37.1.

LEADERSHIP COMPETENCIES

Leadership competencies refer to skills and behaviors that contribute to exceptional workplace performance.[23] Leadership competencies and strategies are driven by industry trends. Each organization defines what leadership attributes are needed to create competitive advantage. Leadership requirements may vary, for example, between for-profit institutions and not-for-profit institutions.[24] Not-for-profit organizations often have boards of directors to whom they are required to report. Leadership, in this case, may require the ability to influence the board, in addition to influencing and leading staff. This is similarly the case for public libraries, which often report to a governing body or council. In this case, the ability to communicate effectively in order to influence the target audience is an important leadership competency.

Table 37.1. Differences between Manager and Leader.

Manager	Leader
Administers	Innovates
Copy	Original
Accepts reality	Investigates it
Focuses on systems/structure	Focuses on people
Relies on control	Inspires trust
Short-range view	Long-range perspective
Asks how and when	Asks what and why
Keeps an eye on the bottom line	Keeps an eye on the horizon
Initiates	Originates
Accepts the status quo	Challenges the status quo
Classic good soldier	Their own person
Does things right	Does the right thing

Source: Evans, G. E., & Ward, P. L. Management Basics for Information
Professionals, second edition (New York: Neal Schuman Publishers, Inc., 2007).

Organizations can identify and develop leaders through a competency-based approach. Competency-based approaches to leadership development have been increasingly used because of their overall effectiveness in industry and higher education.[25] This approach to leadership development has the potential to create "firm-specific expertise and to foster high-performing organizations."[26] Well-developed competencies can also provide direction for the behaviors and performance levels needed among employees to accomplish overall goals.

> " Competency-based approaches to leadership development have been increasingly used because of their overall effectiveness in industry and higher education. "

The key questions that emerge from this discussion include:

1. What are the benefits and challenges of a competency-based approach to leadership development as implemented in library and information science (LIS) education and settings?
2. What are the requirements for tomorrow's leaders who are overlooked within formal LIS education?
3. How can these leadership requirements best be addressed within a competency-based framework?

The Library Leadership Administration and Management Association (LLAMA) has addressed these questions by creating leadership competencies for information professionals who are involved in developing curricula, aspiring future library leaders and those who want to advance the profession.[27] The competencies are designed to "support personal leadership and management development by providing:

- a shared set of terms and definitions that can be used for leadership development;
- a map for professional development;
- evaluation criteria for professional growth;

- a baseline of knowledge, skills, and behaviors that can be obtained over the course of an individual's career;
- a foundation for a library school curriculum;
- a framework for staff training;
- guiding principles for use when advocating for the importance of leadership; and
- a guide for LLAMA's professional development activities."[28]

LLAMA lists fourteen leadership competencies in their "Foundational Competencies for Library Leaders and Managers," described below.[29]

Communication Skills. Leaders utilize a combination of verbal, nonverbal, and written communication methods with employees and other stakeholders. Their communication is clear and efficient and coupled with active listening for maximum benefit (see also chapter 27: "Communication, Marketing, and Outreach Strategies").

Change Management. Leaders facilitate an environment that encourages innovation and collaboration through continuous two-way communication, flexibility, and accountability, and by making the necessary training to facilitate positive change.

Team Building. Leaders draw people together through a commonly shared vision and utilize effective communication skills to encourage responsibility, commitment to the team's vision and goals, and support for team and individual success.

Collaboration and Partnerships. Leaders work with others—both those who are internal and external to the organization—to achieve a common goal. Leaders strengthen the role of the library in the community by finding ways to work with others, engage stakeholders, and build partnerships.

Emotional Intelligence. Leaders acknowledge their own and other people's emotions, applying concepts such as self-awareness, self-regulation, motivation, empathy, and social skills to inform interpersonal interactions.

> **Leadership Competencies for Today's Information Professional**
>
> - Communication skills
> - Change management
> - Team building
> - Collaboration and partnerships
> - Emotional intelligence
> - Problem solving
> - Evidence-based decision making
> - Conflict resolution
> - Budget creation and presentation
> - Forward thinking
> - Critical thinking
> - Ethics
> - Project management
> - Marketing and advocacy

Problem Solving. Leaders are proactive in preventing conflicts and addressing issues when they arise. They solve problems and guide employees to develop appropriate options that allow them to identify alternative solutions and to prevent issues from escalating.

Evidence-Based Decision Making. Leaders utilize research to determine whether a particular policy or program will work in their organization and determine its effectiveness (see also chapter 26: "Managing Data and Data Analysis in Information Organizations").

Conflict Resolution (Personnel). Leaders encourage differences of opinion and help resolve conflict through communication, collaboration, and compromise in order to avoid threats to the organization's mission and strategic goals.

Budget Creation and Presentation. Leaders develop budgets that account for the needs of the organization with input from team members, and they communicate the value of information services to internal and external stakeholders, utilizing both qualitative and quantitative data to justify their budget proposals and influence decision makers favorably (see also chapter 21: "Managing Budgets").

Forward Thinking. Leaders understand important trends and developments in the information landscape and position their library to take advantage of opportunities as they arise (see also chapter 3: "Librarianship: A Continuously Evolving Profession").

Critical Thinking. Leaders utilize critical thinking to address the challenges facing their organizations, demonstrating the ability to analyze its fundamental parts, and to identify and implement effective solutions.

Ethics. Leaders are ethical in their decision making, weighing out proposed courses of actions and finding the necessary resources to enable better decisions (see also chapter 30: "Information Ethics").

Project Management. Leaders execute, monitor, analyze, and report on the progress of teamwork in order to deliver on-time, on-budget results and follow the necessary learning and integration that is required for the project and its stakeholders.

Marketing and Advocacy. A leader works with their team to develop goals and objectives for the organization and communicates those goals to both internal and external stakeholders (see also chapter 28: "Advocacy").

These competencies guide the processes and areas for leadership development. They have implications for the profession, including a formal master's degree and post-master's education in ALA-accredited programs, as well as for continuing education courses and workshops. They further offer guidance to individuals who are interested in leadership to help them identify areas they need to build and strengthen.

LIS education has historically focused primarily on management and less so on leadership. More recently, LIS programs are adding courses on leadership or adding them into existing courses. Management courses have often covered the competencies on communication skills, budgeting, critical thinking, personnel management (e.g., conflict resolution), ethics, and sometimes marketing and advocacy. Other competencies, however, are not covered consistently in formal LIS education and continuing education. One area in particular that has not been well developed in LIS education and continuing education is that of leading change.

> **Discussion Question**
>
> What makes an effective leader?

LEADING CHANGE

One of the primary functions of leadership is to lead change. Kotter developed an eight-step model for leading change (see table 37.2: Kotter's Eight-Step Model for Leading Change).[30]

In order to be successful in leading change, it is important that leaders have knowledge of the situation so that they are able to utilize the resources at hand. Leaders also need to understand the interactions between and potential impact on people. Effectively leading change initiatives can help organizations create and shape a positive future and increase the organization's chances of survival and success. Management alone cannot address all issues that will arise within organizations. New approaches are required that include more strategic alliances and partnerships, along with more holistic marketing approaches. Leadership competencies are necessary in order to invoke a change management model like that developed by Kotter (see also chapter 20: "Change Management").

> Effectively leading change initiatives can help organizations create and shape a positive future and increase the organization's chances of survival and success.

Table 37.2. Kotter's Eight-Step Model for Leading Change.

Step	Description
1. Create a sense of urgency	Create a "spark" to get things moving.
2. Form a powerful guiding coalition	Enlist the help of people who can move the agenda forward and be champions of the change.
3. Create a vision	Identify the goal and develop a strategy to get there.
4. Communicate the vision	Communicate clearly what the vision is and what is expected.
5. Empower others to act on the vision	Remove obstacles through motivation, reorganization, and relying on the powerful guiding coalition.
6. Planning for and creating short-term wins	Create short-term goals that can serve as motivating "wins" along the way.
7. Consolidating improvements and producing more change	Build on the change. Analyze the outcome of the strategy and keep revising and moving forward.
8. Institutionalizing new approaches	Make the successes part of the core of the organization.

LEADERSHIP AND STRATEGIC PLANNING

Strategic planning is a systematic process of creating a vision and developing goals and objectives in order to achieve that vision (see also chapter 19: "Strategic Planning"). Effective strategic planning centers on fundamental decisions and actions that shape and guide an organization, and focuses on the future. It determines where an organization is going and the actions it needs to take in order to get there and how to assess its success. Strategic planning is an ongoing process that requires continuous review in order to allow the organization to respond to changes in its surrounding environment.

The strategic planning process takes many different paths, although there are some basic commonalities.[31] Strategic planning occurs in four key stages:

1. Preparing to plan (includes the development of a mission and vision statements, stakeholder interviews, environmental scans and SWOT analysis)
2. Developing the plan (includes setting goals and timelines, assessing available resources, and identifying key projects)
3. Implementing the plan (includes presenting the plan to the community and putting the plan into action)
4. Measuring performance (includes assessing the outcomes of the strategic plan and assessing revision for the next cycle)

See table 19.1 in chapter 19: "Strategic Planning" for a more comprehensive outline of these four stages and the various steps that fall within each stage.

Leaders have the vision and strategy to lead a team to identify targeted goals and develop the systematic steps required to achieve them. Because of their ability to inspire, motivate, and influence, they are able to lead a team to set the specific direction along the way to achieving their goals. In sum, the characteristics of a leader are highly effective in conducting ongoing, systematic, and future-driven strategic planning.

PROFESSIONAL DEVELOPMENT FOR LEADERSHIP

Schools of Library and Information Science offer minimal courses in management,[32] and fewer in leadership. There are, however, programs offered through various resources that provide professional development for both management and leadership. The American Library Association (ALA), for example, offers several leadership programs for information professionals. ALA has a Leadership Institute that provides an intensive four-day immersion program for future library leaders. It "includes a structured learning track and the opportunity for individual development."[33]

ALA also offers an Emerging Leaders program. It was created to provide opportunities for new librarians to develop skills in problem solving, networking, and understanding the organizational structure of ALA.[34] The program accepts about fifty people each year to participate in a project, the results of which are presented at the ALA Annual conference in June.

The International Federation of Library Associations and Institutions (IFLA) also offers a leadership program. The two-year program is designed to "increase the cohort of leaders who can effectively represent the wider library sector in the international arena, and to develop leaders within IFLA."[35] Selected participants attend the annual IFLA conference, and spend eight days with IFLA Governing Board members, attend workshops and seminars, prepare reports and presentations, and work on projects that support the IFLA international agenda.

> **Discussion Questions**
>
> Think about a time when you were in charge of leading a team. How would you describe yourself as a leader? As a manager? What leadership competencies did you use?

In addition to the large LIS associations, there are programs available among the state LIS associations that also provide training. Local, state, or regional chapters of associations offer training in leadership or related topics (e.g., management, strategic planning, etc.).[36] There are other opportunities for education and training for leadership outside the academic setting, including lectures, conferences, and workshops. Traditional LIS education is often criticized for focusing too heavily on theory,[37] however, so courses in leadership should incorporate a balance of theory combined with practice.

LIS LEADERSHIP IN A GLOBAL CONTEXT

As information-related products and services drive the increasingly global and interrelated economy, partnerships and collaborations across the world are progressively more common and necessary. Information organizations face new opportunities and challenges that emerge from the burgeoning information economy. Their success depends upon a wide range of professional skills that include much of what has been discussed in this text: technical, public, and administrative services, as well as understanding users, their context, and the history that has shaped the profession. In addition to these skills, it is also necessary for information professionals to possess a range of critical thinking skills, ranging from ethics and policy issues to knowing how to develop strategies to continuously improve their practices, policies, and procedures.

As suggested in the opening chapter of this text, different countries across the world face different challenges and opportunities in order to serve the information needs of their communities. Some countries struggle with issues of connectivity and the need for digital skill sets.[38] Some communities in different countries face challenges in getting their users to embrace and benefit from the advantages of digital resources.[39] Other countries face challenges with developing leadership among their LIS professionals.[40] A final example is that information professionals in some countries may be limited in what kinds and amounts of information they are able to disseminate due to political or governmental restrictions.

While there are some aspects of LIS practice today that are commonly shared throughout the world (e.g., issues of metadata standards), information professionals face challenges and opportunities that are unique to their own situations within their local communities, regional authorities, and national laws. Thus, the needs for leadership vary also, depending upon the particular needs of the environment in which information professionals reside and practice. This text provides a thorough treatment of issues facing information professionals, from the perspective that access to and freedom of information are hallmarks of the profession.

CONCLUSION

Leadership is increasingly important in twenty-first-century organizations. Leadership and management go hand in hand to produce organizational effectiveness, not only in operational management but also in leading strategic planning and change. One without the other is ineffective and cannot lead to vision and strategic planning and operational success.[41]

Leadership and management skills are different: while managers generally focus on operations and control and maintain the status quo, leaders, on the other hand, inspire their teams, foster innovation and collaboration, and challenge traditional practices, resulting in the creation of high expectations. The most important skills for leadership are the "softer" skills, centering on interpersonal relationships. Further, leaders are not born; leadership skills can be taught, practiced, developed, and refined. Leadership for information professionals should be embedded throughout the curriculum. While an increasing number of organizations offer professional training in leadership, the academic curriculum should strike a balance of theory and practice, with opportunities for leadership activities.

This chapter presented different definitions of leadership and leader in order to lay the groundwork for understanding the differences between leadership and management. Leadership competencies from the LLAMA of the American Library Association were presented as some of the grounding work in leadership in library and information science. The leadership competencies provide a professional development strategy for how leaders can move organizations toward their visions and serve as change agents in today's global information landscape.

NOTES

1. John Kotter, "Management Is (Still) Not Leadership," *Harvard Business Review*, January 9, 2013, https://hbr.org/2013/01/management-is-still-not-leadership.html.
2. See, for example, Eben Mumford, "The Origin of Leadership," *American Journal of Sociology*, November 1906–January 1907.
3. Bernard M. Bass, "Concepts of Leadership," in *Leadership: Understanding the Dynamics of Power and Influence in Organizations*, ed. Robert P. Vecchio, second edition (Notre Dame, IN: Notre Dame University Press, 1997), 3–22.
4. Travis Bradberry, "What Makes a Leader?," *Leadership and Management*, July 27, 2015, LinkedIn, https://www.linkedin.com/pulse/what-makes-leader-dr-travis-bradberry.
5. Peter F. Drucker, "Your Leadership Is Unique," *Leadership* 17, no. 4 (1996): 54.
6. Bradberry, "What Makes a Leader?"
7. Kevin Kruse, "100 Best Quotes on Leadership," *Forbes*, October 16, 2012, https://www.forbes.com/sites/kevinkruse/2012/10/16/quotes-on-leadership/#7ab410132feb.
8. Bradberry, "What Makes a Leader?"
9. Ibid.
10. Ibid.
11. G. Edward Evans and Patricia L. Ward, *Management Basics for Information Professionals*, second edition (New York: Neal Schuman Publishers, Inc., 2007), 30.

12. Shorelette Ammons-Stephens et al., "Developing Core Leadership Competencies for the Library Profession," *Libraries Faculty and Staff Scholarship and Research*, Paper 19 (2009), http://docs.lib.purdue.edu/lib_fsdocs/19.
13. Kotter, "Management Is (Still) Not Leadership."
14. Ammons-Stephens et al., "Developing Core Leadership Competencies for the Library Profession; John Kotter, "Best of HBR: What Leaders Really Do," *Harvard Business Review* (December 2001): 85-96, https://hbr.org/2001/12/what-leaders-really-do.
15. Kotter, "Best of HBR: What Leaders Really Do," 85-96.
16. John Kotter, *Force for Change: How Leadership Differs from Management* (New York: The Free Press, 1990).
17. Margie H. Jantti and Nick Greenhalgh, "Leadership Competencies: A Reference Point for Development and Evaluation (Case Study)," University of Wollongong, Proceedings of the 9th Northumbria International Conference on Performance Measurement in Libraries and Information Services, York, United Kingdom, August 22-25, 2011, http://ro.uow.edu.au/cgi/viewcontent.cgi?article=1230&context=asdpapers.
18. John Kotter, *Force for Change: How Leadership Differs from Management* (New York: The Free Press, 2008); John Kotter, "Best of HBR: What Leaders Really Do," *Harvard Business Review*, December 2001.
19. Kotter, "Best of HBR: What Leaders Really Do."
20. David I. Bertocci, *Leadership in Organizations: There Is a Difference between Leaders and Managers* (Lanham, MD: University Press of America, 2009); Edward G. Evans and Patricia Ward Layzell, *Management Basics for Information Professionals* (New York: Neal Schuman Publishers, 2007).
21. Richard L Hughes et al., *Leadership: Enhancing the Lessons of Experience* (Boston: McGraw Hill, 2006); Elizabeth Curtis, Jan de Vries, and Fintan K. Sheerin, "Developing Leadership in Nursing: Exploring Core Factor," *British Journal of Nursing* 20, no. 5 (2011): 306.
22. Gregory J. Reynolds and Walter H. Warfield, "Discerning the Differences between Managers and Leaders," *Education Digest* 75, no. 7 (2010): 61-64.
23. Judy Brownell, "Meeting the Competency Needs of Global Leaders: A Partnership Approach," *Human Resources Management* 45, no. 3 (Fall 2006): 309-36.
24. John Carver, *Boards That Make a Difference: A New Design for Leadership in Nonprofit and Public Organizations* (Hoboken, NJ: John Wiley & Sons, 2011), 6.
25. Ibid.
26. Ibid., 309.
27. Ammons-Stephens et al., "Developing Core Leadership Competencies for the Library Profession."
28. "Leadership and Management Competencies," Library Leadership and Management Association, accessed March 9, 2017, http://www.ala.org/llama/leadership-and-management-competencies.
29. Ibid.
30. John Kotter, "Leading Change: Why Transformation Efforts Fail," *Harvard Business Review* (March–April 1995): 59-67.
31. "What Is Strategic Planning?," Balanced Scorecard Institute, 2017, http://www.balancedscorecard.org/BSC-Basics/Strategic-Planning-Basics.
32. Robert P. Holley, "Providing LIS Students with Management Skills," *Journal of Library Administration* 56 (2016): 638-46.
33. "ALA Leadership Institute: Leading to the Future," American Library Association, accessed August 13, 2017, http://www.ala.org/transforminglibraries/ala-leadership-institute.
34. Brittany Tavernaro, "Emerging Leaders Report," *Arkansas Libraries* 73, no. 4 (Winter 2016): 22-24.
35. "IFLA International Leaders Programme: 2016 Call for Applications," International Federation of Library Associations and Institutions (IFLA), https://www.ifla.org/leaders.
36. Holley, "Providing LIS Students with Management Skills," 638-46.
37. Patricia M. Sarchet, "Leadership: The Challenge for the Information Professional," *Journal of the Medical Library Association* 97, no. 2 (April 2009): 153.
38. See, for example, Linda Ashcroft and Chris Watts, "ICT Skills for Information Professionals in Developing Countries: Perspectives from a Study of the Electronic Information Environment in Nigeria," *IFLA Journal* 31, no. 1 (2005): 6-12.

39. See, for example, Namkee Park et al., "User Acceptance of a Digital Library System in Developing Countries: An Application of the Technology Acceptance Model," *International Journal of Information Management* 29, no. 3 (2009): 196–209.
40. See, for example, Husain Al Ansari and Othman al Khadher, "Developing a Leadership Competency Model for Library and Information Professionals in Kuwait," *Libri* 61, no. 3 (2011): 239–46.
41. Kotter, "Best of HBR: What Leaders Really Do," 85–96.

Kendra Albright

Glossary

Abilene paradox: a communication model that is focused on mismanaged agreement in groups.

Academic appointment or status: a non-tenure-eligible job classification in North American institutions of higher education assigned to administrative staff as opposed to teaching faculty.

Access point: a field that is indexed separately and specifically; for example, the authorized name of an author: "Twain, Mark, 1835–1910."

Access services: a catchall term to describe the circulation, course reserves, document delivery, collection management, and related tasks and functions found within an information organization.

Accreditation: the recognition that an institution of higher education maintains certain standards; its goal is to ensure that the institutions of higher education meet acceptable levels of quality assessment.

Acquired diversities: characteristics that have changed through our experiences and choices—educational attainment, linguistic ability, immigrant experience, family composition, relationship status.

Acquisitions module: a unit that manages the procurement of materials and includes placing orders for materials, managing funds used to purchase material, maintaining a database of current suppliers, and performing other functions related to the financial component of collection management.

Actionable: (as relates to discrimination) having sufficient evidence to take legal action, such as to initiate a lawsuit, discipline an employee, or terminate an employee, where contractual or legal requirements must be met before such action may be taken (e.g., the employee is part of a collective bargaining agreement).

Active listening: staying focused on the received message through mental concentration or taking notes.

Advocacy: a combination of activities, the most important being the development of strong, positive relationships with stakeholders, and also including targeted messaging, the alignment of values with decision makers, and efforts throughout the organization that are deliberately planned and evaluated.

Aggregation: collection of online content from multiple publishers searchable from the same user interface.

All-in license: every member of the group of organizations has access to the same licensed content.

Alternative metrics: nontraditional metrics proposed as an alternative to traditional citation metrics to measure the impact of scholarly outputs; also called altmetrics.

Ambience: the affective character of an environment influencing the way a person feels in the space.

Archival quality: a nonscientific term of assessment of storage media that meet the standards prevalently used by curators and librarians in preservation work.

Arduino: an open-source microcontroller that, once programmed, can execute the same loop of code repeatedly.

Artifact: any item created by humans for the purpose of solving problems; artifacts may be tangible or intangible; physical, digital, or conceptual.

Artificial intelligence: a branch of computer science that focuses on the development of algorithms and systems that attempt to mimic human logic by sensing the environment and modifying their behavior to increase the likelihood of success in achieving a specific function.

Assessment: the process of systematically evaluating performance to demonstrate success and implement improvement.

Assessment measures: tools used to determine the success of a program or service.

Audiovisual: recorded content types involving both image and sound capture.

Audit: a systematic examination of financial or accounting records to verify their accuracy and truthfulness.

Audit and Certification of Trustworthy Digital Repositories standard (ISO 16363): provides metrics for certifying preservation archives. It is complemented by ISO 16919, Requirements for Bodies Providing Audit and Certification, which documents how to certify auditors to exercise this standard.

Authority control: the establishment of forms of access points ensuring that only authorized names, series titles, subject headings, and so on, are used in a library's catalog or other bibliographic database.

Automated storage and retrieval systems (AS/RS): an automated retrieval system found within the information organization's physical building to facilitate storing and retrieving information resources.

Barrier to access: anything that comes between the user and their desired information, preventing use.

Beacon: devices that send out data and display content on nearby smart devices based on the users' detected location, triggered by their proximity. Organizations generally tend to mount them out of sight, on walls or ceilings. When a smartphone is nearby, it receives the beacon's location data. Then, an app on the phone can transmit the phone's location via Wi-Fi or cellular phone data to the app server so that the program can display geo-targeted messaging and information.

Beacon mesh network: a set of beacons that possess the same capabilities as regular beacons but that can also accomplish much more to enable a world of new user experiences that would otherwise not be possible. In a mesh network, a large number of wireless mesh nodes send and receive information to each other, effectively sharing the network connection across a wider area than previously possible. Users are able to respond to as well as receive data.

Behavioral descriptive questioning: asking a candidate to describe real-world past stories and how he or she reacted. For example, "Please think back on a time when you disagreed with your supervisor; tell us about the situation, how you handled the situation, and what the outcome was."

BIBFRAME: an initiative of the Library of Congress to replace MARC as a means of expressing bibliographic data for the future.

Bibliographic control: a broad term that encompasses cataloging and related processes, such as database maintenance.

Bibliographic instruction: programs or other educational tools that instruct users in how to find the information they are looking for.

Bibliographic records: records that currently use MARC format to describe and give access to library resources.

Big data: extremely large data sets that may be analyzed to reveal patterns or associations. Big data has been used to predict consumer behavior.

Big deals: agreements or subscriptions with the large, expensive journal publishers in the STEM fields, such as Elsevier and Wiley.

Binary (dichotomous) data: data that can take only one of two values such as true/false, yes/no, or on/off.

BookBot: a robotic, automated book delivery system; an example of an AS/RS.

Boomers: the large cohort of people born during the spike in the birthrate after World War II until approximately 1964, members of the baby boom generation.

Born-digital: describes an object that began its life cycle as digital; typically used to refer to objects with no analog equivalent.

Breach: violation of license terms by either party or an end user.

Budget: a plan that allocates monetary income to specific expenses.

Business continuity planning (BCP): the methodology used to create and validate a plan for ensuring the restoration of organization operations after a disruptive event.

Card catalog: a library catalog in which 3 × 5 index cards were filed alphabetically in drawers and cabinets. One resource was typically represented by at least two cards: one for author and one for title. Card catalogs were used from the late nineteenth century until the 1980s.

Cardholder: registered patron with a library card.

Career action plan: a broad strategic road map for longer-term career development comprising goals, strategies, and tactics.

Career agenda: a short list of tasks to complete within a certain employment situation.

Carnegie classification: system of classifying U.S. higher education institutions by multiple data points in order to aid comparisons among institutions.

Catalog card: 3 × 5 index card that contained descriptions and access points for library resources.

Cataloging: the process of describing and giving access to library resources according to shared standards for description, establishing access points, and assigning subject headings and classification.

Cataloging module: a system that provides the capability to create bibliographic records that describe each item in a collection.

Censorship: the attempt to restrict or prohibit access to intellectual content provided by the library. This content includes books, magazines, music, movies, exhibits, programs, oral presentations, and electronic resources.

Challenge: a "formal" request for censorship. Typically, this is in the form of a Request for Reconsideration, but might also be any direct communication with officials to make such requests, or public requests in letters to the editor or public boards.

Change agent: an informal moniker and often not accompanied by power in the organization. It is someone who brings about, or helps bring about, change by facilitating the change process or consults organizations on the change process. This could be an informal or self-appointed leader of a work group, for example.

Change leader: often someone who is in a position of power in the organization, such as a director or top-level manager for a service area, often appointed to facilitate change in the organization. Often this person has the ability and drive to inspire and excite others through personal and professional encouragement and to tap resources to build a reliable framework for change to take root in the organization. This person is often involved with evaluating the results of change.

Change maker: one who makes change.

Change management: a process using basic tools or structures that is designed to manage any change effort within an organization in order to minimize any negative impacts of the change.

Change manager: one who is often formally assigned the task of enacting change; has the power to facilitate change, such as a product or service department manager; and is given the responsibility to evaluate the results and next steps after a change has taken place in an organization.

Change muscle: resilience and flexibility in the process of change in an organization.

Channel: a means of interaction between an information organization and a person; can be any one of many possible static, virtual, or human agents.

Circulation: the dual role of facilitating the access of physical items between the information organization and the user and of being able to identify the location of any item in the physical collection at all times. Also can be a module in a circulation system that manages the lending of physical materials in the collection.

Civility: the practice of politeness and courtesy in everyday interactions.

Classification: the process of expressing a resource's "aboutness" in a single string of letters, numbers, or both, using a classification scheme such as Dewey Decimal Classification (DDC) or Library of Congress Classification (LCC).

Click-wrap license: a nonnegotiable agreement that a user must agree to before accessing a product. The user is required to accept the terms of the license by clicking a button before downloading the product or accessing the material online. Even though these are not generally negotiable, the customer is nonetheless bound.

Cloud: computing services and resources stored on off-site servers and accessible from anywhere. "My files are stored in the cloud."

Cloud-based services: resources and applications stored off-site and accessed via an internet or data connection.

Cluster analysis: the process of analyzing data elements to understand both how data coalesces into groups (clusters) based on sharing similar characteristics and how clusters differ from each other.

Code of ethics: a collection of values and principles by which a profession governs itself.

Cognitive analytics: analysis with context, using natural language and probability.

Collection: multiple e-books, e-journals, or other digital content, including streaming audio or video, from a single publisher, typically selected based on subject, interest, year, or any other criteria and sold as a single collection or database.

Collection development: the process of identifying the strengths or weaknesses of a collection in terms of patron needs and community resources and using the information gathered to strengthen all or parts of a collection to better serve its users.

Collection development policy: a statement, drafted by staff and adopted by a governing body, to describe the scope and focus of a library's content purchases.

Collection management: the coordinated processes of maintaining the physical collections of the information organization.

Collective bargaining agreement: a contract between the employees and the employer where the employees have negotiated and agreed to the employer's terms and conditions of employment as a unit pursuant to the requirements of federal and state law, such as the National Labor Relations Act, the Railway Labor Act, or Executive Order 10988.

Common Core: a set of standards that promotes student-driven learning in which evidence in the form of texts is used to build knowledge and understanding.

Communication model: a representation of communication as an individual (sender) delivering a message to others (receivers) by employing a variety of oral, written, and nonverbal techniques.

Community hub: a physical or online environment that is accessible to all groups in the community or area it serves—providing a focus point for the community, fostering greater local community interaction, and bringing residents together to improve their quality of life, see or make friends, and get information or support.

Compact shelving: compressed shelving units that provide information organizations with the ability to store more physical materials in their collections.

Competency: ability, knowledge, or skill set needed to meet performance objectives for a specific task.

Competitive analysis: a process an organization undertakes to identify competing products and services in order to understand how the competitors' strategies compare, both positively and negatively, to the organization's own strategies.

Computational thinking: the ability to problem-solve using computers to organize and analyze data.

Confederation of Open Access Repositories (COAR): an international association bringing together the repository community and major repository networks in order to build capacity, align policies and practices, and act as a global voice for the repository community.

Confidentiality: sharing information in a license or business agreement only with the organizations that are participating in the agreement.

Connected learning model: a model of independent learning that builds on relevance and interest and leverages peer support and networked communities.

Conservation: the set of preservation practices used to rectify damages done to an object and/or the set of actions taken to slow an object's deterioration.

Consortia: A library consortium is a group of libraries who partner to coordinate activities, share resources, and combine expertise. The International Coalition of Library Consortia is an informal discussion group of such consortia. Library consortia offer significant productivity advantages and budget savings to increasingly strapped libraries.

Consortial lending partnerships: groups of libraries, often based on geographic region, that agree to share their materials with one another at low cost or no cost by entering into a consortium.

Content management system: software or a suite of programs that store and arrange digital objects and their metadata.

Content strategy: an interdisciplinary practice bringing together concepts from user experience design, information architecture, marketing, and technical writing in order to create, update, and manage content that supports the needs of the end user as well as strategic goals of the organization.

Controlled vocabulary: a limited list of agreed-upon words or phrases used to describe an object and facilitate indexing and search; typically includes preferred terms as well as broader and narrower terms.

Cooperative collection development: a model of collection development in which partner libraries agree to divide up collecting areas between them in order to build complementary, rather than duplicative, collections and share their acquisitions freely with each other.

Copyright: a legal term of protection for original works fixed in a tangible medium, subject to a variety of limitations. Copyright gives a work's creator the exclusive rights of reproduction, distribution, preparing derivative works, public display, public performance, and public performance by digital audio transmission.

Copyright law: national and international laws governing the rights and responsibilities of content creators and content users.

Copyright owners: the person, people, or entity that holds the copyright to a given work. Initially this is often but not always the creator of the work.

Course management system: software used to support the teaching of a class through the storage of documents, links to readings and syllabi, quizzes, etc.

Course reserves: potentially high-use course-related items used for short periods, often kept behind the circulation desk.

Crash recovery: correcting fatal or near-fatal errors in databases or other software programs.

Creation culture: the democratization of digital tools and a community-based hunger for personal connections in an era of unprecedented hurry and change; a movement that prizes creative, self-driven projects and products. Also known as maker culture.

Creative Commons (CC): a nonprofit organization that promotes the sharing of creative works and knowledge via a free suite of standardized licenses that allow copyright holders to give the public permission to use their work under set conditions. CC licenses benefit both creators who wish to share their works more freely, and users who wish to use or adapt works for their own projects. Creative Commons licenses do not replace copyright but are based upon it.

Creative communicator: a person who uses different formats and styles of communication for different audiences, using a wide variety of tools.

Critical information literacy: this approach to defining and teaching information literacy emphasizes the social and economic structures that affect people's access to information and their opportunities to create information that will have influence on others.

Critical thinking: the ability to use higher-order thinking skills, such as analysis, synthesis, and evaluation, in order to accomplish a specific goal.

Cultural competence: a set of congruent behaviors, attitudes, and policies that come together and enable a system, agency, or professionals to work effectively in cross-cultural situations.

Cumulative incremental backup: a backup strategy where every backup taken after a full backup includes every file that has been modified since the last backup until another full backup is taken. When cumulative backups are used, data recovery typically only requires the restoration of the most current full backup and the most current cumulative backup. Compare to differential incremental backup.

Curation: the range of tasks involved in managing content, including such important steps as selection, acquisition, cataloging, and transformation. It is often conjoined with the term "digital" to mark the specific activities that are undertaken for digital objects.

Curator: an individual tasked with determining the breadth and scope of a collection or other item grouping.

Cybersecurity: a form of information security. Cybersecurity can be thought of as information security in the online environment. The practice of cybersecurity is necessary to ensure information privacy in online environments.

Data analysis: the practical application of quantitative and qualitative techniques in order to extract and derive meaning from collected data (also referred to as data analytics).

Data and information asset: a broad term used to refer to any data that have value to an organization.

Data cleansing: a set of processes used to ensure data quality and integrity.

Data criticality analysis: an analysis undertaken to better understand the data that are of most importance to an organization as well as the impact that data have on the operation of the organization. Most often used in the context of disaster recovery planning.

Data curation: the management of research data to enable discovery and retrieval and maintain the quality of, add value to, and ensure preservation of the data.

Data-driven acquisitions (DDA): a library acquisitions model in which e-book vendors allow libraries to load records into their online catalogs for e-books and e-journals that the library has not yet purchased, enabling discovery by the libraries' patrons.

Data management: the development, execution, and supervision of plans, policies, programs, and practices that control, protect, deliver, and enhance the value of data and information assets.

Data management plan: since January 2011, a requirement of scientific research proposals submitted to the National Science Foundation and other funding agencies of the U.S. government, and one with which academic librarians, known as research informationists, are helping campus scientists comply.

Data minimization: minimizing the collection of personally identifiable information (PII) to that which is directly relevant to accomplishing the specified purposes and only retaining the data for as long as necessary to fulfill those specified purposes.

Data visualization: techniques used to communicate data or information through visual means as opposed to text.

Data warehouse: a large data store that combines information from various sources in a normalized manner for long-term and historical use. In many cases, transaction-level details are summarized into a "golden" record that represents the end result of a series of related transactions on the data.

Database engine: a third-party relational database management system, such as the proprietary products from Oracle or open-source tools like MySQL or PostgreSQL, which high-performance business applications typically depend on to maintain data.

Deaccessioning: removal of an item or items from a library collection, usually undertaken to weed out unused material and make room for new acquisitions.

Deacidification: treatment used to stabilize paper that is deteriorating due to its acid content.

Decision-ready information: information and data compiled to assist clients in making fact-based decisions.

Deontology: from the Greek *deon* meaning duty, refers to an ethical system based on adherence to rules (i.e., duty-bound to follow the rules).

Descriptive cataloging: part of the cataloging process in which standard elements of a resource are transcribed or recorded (for example, title, edition, publisher, date) and in which authorized access points for author and other contributors are created.

Design: planning and engineering a product, service, or space with intention. Also a broad, overarching creative discipline with its own ways of working and knowing; design parallels other disciplines, such as sciences, the arts, and the humanities.

Design rationale: the reasons and justifications for decisions made during the creation of an artifact.

Design thinking: a problem-centered, iterative process for finding problems and creating solutions to them. A three-step process of inspiration, ideation, and iteration created by the company IDEO.

Differential incremental backup: a backup strategy where each backup created after a full backup only contains the files that have been modified since the last backup. When differential backups are used, data recovery typically requires the restoration of the most current full backup and each individual differential backup taken since the full backup. Compare to cumulative incremental backup.

Digital asset: an item that has been formatted into a binary source; it may be defined as textual content (digital assets), images (media assets), and multimedia (media assets).

Digital citizen: a person who participates ethically and morally in online communities.

Digital content: a common term used for information that is accessed in a digital format through a medium that requires a device to retrieve, use, or store the information. Computer files, e-books, databases, steaming media, audio files, and websites are all considered digital content and are also sometimes referred to as e-content, e-resources, or virtual content.

Digital curation: the process of maintaining, preserving, and adding value to digital research data through its life cycle.

Digital divide: the chasm between those who have access to the internet, the hardware, and the ability to use it and those who do not, often adding to economic and social inequality.

Digital hosting: a service maintaining online files to make them accessible to users.

Digital humanities (DH): an area of scholarship that lies at the intersection of computing or digital technologies and the disciplines of the humanities, such as philosophy, history, and literature. It can be characterized as a set of new approaches to humanistic scholarship that involve collaborative, trans- or interdisciplinary, and computationally engaged methods.

Digital immigrant: a person who learned digital technologies later in life; as opposed to a digital native.

Digital librarian: an information professional who employs the traditional tenets of library science (e.g., collection development, resource description and organization, guided access to information) to digital objects and collections.

Digital library: information products and services that are organized, described, delivered, and preserved through technology.

Digital literacy: a set of skills and abilities to use digital tools, navigate through digital environments, and create digital resources.

Digital Millennium Copyright Act (DMCA): an addition to U.S. Copyright Law signed on October 28, 1998, that addresses a variety of copyright issues. Most important for information professionals, it prohibits the circumvention of technological protection measures (such as encryption) and offers online service providers a safe harbor for potentially infringing user-generated content.

Digital native: a person who was raised from an early age using digital technologies; as opposed to a digital immigrant.

Digital preservation: a series of managed activities necessary to ensure continued access to digital materials for as long as they are needed.

Digital Preservation Outreach and Education (DPOE): developed by the Library of Congress in 2010 as a concerted effort to spread the knowledge and practice of digital preservation throughout the United States. A "Train-the-Trainer" program developed in 2011 has reached thousands of practitioners throughout the United States and has fostered a national network of digital stewardship.

Digital repository: a mechanism for managing and storing digital content. Repositories can be subject or institutional in their coverage.

Digital surrogate: electronic reproduction or representation of typically printed library materials, including thumbnails, catalog records, or digital images.

Digitization: the process of capturing a digital version of a physical object. Also called digital reformatting.

Direct lobbying: the formal process of an individual or a small group of individuals representing an organization contacting and meeting with decision makers (usually elected officials) for the explicit purpose of influencing a decision.

Direct value: having a perceived tangible or personal impact on an individual or group of individuals that creates a direct benefit or improvement.

Disaster recovery plan (DRP): a documented process that describes how an organization will recover its data and information technology infrastructure in the event of a disaster. The DRP is a required component of a business continuity plan.

Discovery interface: tool designed to provide access to resources through a more modern interface with a scope of search often beyond those accessible through the organization's ILS.

Discovery system: service to enhance access to all content accessible to information organization users.

Discovery tool: any database that gives access to library resources, but more specifically, a web-based system that aggregates the library's MARC database (catalog), along with other resources such as the institutional repository, periodical databases, image collections, and archival material.

Discrimination: to treat differently usually because of a legally impermissible factor, such as terminating an employee because of his or her race or gender.

Disparate impact: statistically significant adverse result of an action or practice for members of a legally protected class. For example, in the hiring process, to only hire librarians who can lift seventy pounds. This practice or action results in a statistically significant higher employment rate of males over females, without a justification for such a requirement as job related.

Dispute resolution: procedure to follow if parties to a license cannot resolve a conflict.

Diversity: the ways that people are different across several categories of background, traits, and features; a commitment to diversity opposes forms of exclusion, prejudice, and discrimination based on those categories and recognizes the potential for improved performance and innovation when differences are leveraged for the mutual benefit of the community.

Drop spindle: a tool used to create twists of yarn by using gravity and spinning action.

Dublin Core: a metadata standard or schema that stipulates "simple and generic" elements that can be used to describe a resource.

E-book: digital version of a published book or, more recently, an original written work whose first conception is already in digital format.

E-priority policy: a collection development policy prioritizing electronic format over print for journals in order to avoid duplication and its attendant costs, currently in vogue in North American academic libraries.

E-rate discount: discounted rate for telecommunications and internet access available to schools and libraries; requires internet filters to be used to be eligible for the program.

E-reader: a mobile device that is used primarily for reading digital books or magazines.

E-resource: typically, digital content packaged and licensed from a vendor, including e-journals and databases.

Ecological systems theory: an approach to human behavior and development that focuses on inter-actions among people (individuals, relationships with others) and their environments (community, culture). Sometimes referred to as ecological systems perspective and the social ecological model.

Effectiveness: the degree to which goals and objectives are achieved and the extent to which defined problems are solved. Effectiveness is related to the outcome achieved as the result of an activity, as distinct from output, which is measured by efficiency.

Efficiency: the quality of using the least amount of time and energy to achieve a goal. Efficiency is related to the output achieved as the result of an activity, as distinct from outcome, which relates to effectiveness.

Embedded e-brarian: a virtual embedded librarian.

Embedded librarian: a librarian who proactively goes to where library users are rather than waiting for users to approach him or her.

Embedded librarianship: instructional practices of librarians who are integrated into a community of learners in a course or field study in order to provide ongoing and personalized support for the community.

Emergency mode operation plan: a documented plan for ensuring operations during an emergency situation.

Empowered learners: learners who have the skills and capacity to follow their own interests and participate in lifelong learning.

Emulation: creating an environment that enables digital content to be rendered in new software and hardware environments without changing the content file.

Encoding: preparing information to be added to a database so that it can be searched and retrieved. For example, MARC is used to encode cataloging data by identifying and tagging the title, author, publisher, and so on. The title, for example, will be encoded by entering it in MARC field 245 and the publisher in field 264.

Encumbrance: a commitment to pay a particular amount of money in the future. In a budget, it can be done with a purchase order or a standing order or any type of commitment to ensure the money promised is available to be spent.

Environmental scan: an analysis of near-term and long-term trends and behaviors that may help or hinder the organization's progress.

Epistemology: a branch of philosophy that explores theories about the nature of knowledge and understanding.

Equitable access: the provision of sustained, responsive, and quality services through the active and regular consideration of the multiple perspectives of users who will benefit from the information organization and its services.

Equity: the provision of a fair and just process and outcome regardless of differences.

Ethics: a set of principles that guide decision making in a specified setting.

Evaluation: a process that measures inputs (number of staff and holdings), outputs (percentage of customers served), and outcomes (customer satisfaction).

Evolutionary fitness: capacity to accept or adopt change in a gradual way, often collaboratively from or through the grassroots of an organization.

Expenditures: the amounts of money spent on goods, services, and all costs for human resources.

Export controls on information: government restrictions on sharing technical and proprietary information outside.

Expression: one of the FRBR Group 1 entities. A FRBR work may be expressed as a novel, play, opera, and so on. Each expression is manifested by a particular edition. For example, the work *Pride and Prejudice* is a novel that has many different expressions, one of which is the third edition, published by Norton in 2001.

External communication: verbal, nonverbal, or written communication that occurs from an individual or group within an organization to an individual or group outside of the organization.

Fair use: a limitation within U.S. Copyright Law (Section 107) that allows the use of copyrighted materials without permission in certain situations, such as those involving teaching, classroom use, or other educational purposes.

Finding aid: a paper or digital document with descriptive and administrative information about an archival collection.

First-sale doctrine: a part of U.S. Copyright Law (Section 109) that allows the owner of a particular copy of a copyrighted work to sell, give away, or otherwise dispose of that copy, as long as other exclusive rights of the copyright holder are not infringed.

Flipped classroom: a pedagogical approach in which the lecture and homework elements of a course are reversed or "flipped." For example, students may view video lectures before class so that they can use their time in class to work on projects, discussions, and other types of dynamic interactive exercises rather than passively listening to instructor lectures.

Force majeure: French for "superior force," referring to the legal term "act of God," or an event out of the control of human beings, such as catastrophic weather-related system failure.

Formal learning: learning that takes place in formal settings, with the curriculum, agenda, and scope defined by the institution. Typical formal learning is delivered through lectures, reading, and rote memorization with testing as an evaluation tool.

Formal teaching: teaching that takes place in a designated classroom and has preestablished learning outcomes.

Formative assessment: quick evaluative activities that educators use to gauge learners' understanding and skills throughout a class session in order to adjust the content, pace, or focus of the instruction to better address learners' needs.

Framing: capturing an idea or image of a process within the larger organizational framework to newly redefine it in the organizational roles, to reassimilate it in order to give it new purpose.

Freedom of Information Act (FOIA): law that was enacted in 1966 and provided for significant expansion of public access to government information.

Friends of the Library: a support organization that provides funding (e.g., for operational items like books and programming) to the library, often through used-book sales and book stores run by volunteers.

Full-time enrollment (FTE): number of students enrolled at a given point in time, typically measured annually.

Fumigation: method of pest control in which gas-based pesticides are dispersed in a closed location to suffocate insects and other living pests.

Game play: how users interact within a game.

Gamification: applying game structure to learning and other environments that can be enriched with gamelike elements.

Gaming studio: a space designed for game play and game creation via appropriate technologies (game consoles, computers, mobile devices, software).

General fund: the resources used to sustain the daily activities of organizations and pay for operation and administrative expenses.

General ledger account: an account used to sort and store balance sheet and income statement transactions.

Geolocation: utilizing the geographic information identified by a networked device, such as a smartphone or tablet, to display information about the location; images, comments, reviews, and "check ins" might be recorded as well.

Global collaboration: working and learning with others who are geographically dispersed.

Globalization: the continuing process of worldwide interaction and integration among peoples, organizations, and governments of different countries.

Google Glass: hardware developed by Google to support augmented reality and provide internet users with an alternative means of accessing the web.

Grassroots lobbying: the organization and implementation of activities designed to gain the attention of decision makers—usually elected officials—with the hope of impacting a decision; often characterized by mobilizing large numbers of people in these activities. Examples include letter-writing campaigns and demonstrations. It is also sometimes referred to as indirect lobbying.

Groupthink: a term developed by psychologist Irving Janis to describe the observed phenomenon of groups that make faulty decisions when specific communication practices are ignored.

HathiTrust: a large-scale partnership of academic and research libraries offering millions of titles including content digitized via the Google Books project and the Internet Archive.

Hotspot: an access point for an internet connection, often generated by mobile devices.

Hyperlinked library: a model of library services that emphasizes meaningful and participatory connections between users, information professionals, and information services.

Hyperlocalism: the clamoring for information regarding local events, local photographs, and local information as they strive to gain a local identity and perspective of their neighborhood.

Hypermedia: linked content of diverse types (data, text, image, audio, video) stored in a database format.

Impact factor: a measure of the frequency with which the average article in a journal has been cited in a particular year; often a proxy is used for quality/impact of an individual article. Also, the influence upon the interpretation of a message due to individual perspectives developed through experiences, beliefs, teachings, and preferences.

Inclusion: an environment or climate in which individuals are recognized for who they are, treated fairly and respectfully, and valued for their skills and perspectives.

Indemnification: protection by paying for the cost of damage or loss.

Independent information professional: an independent contractor conducting information-related activities often consisting of business and market research, knowledge management, content development, and more. This person typically works for a variety of clients as opposed to being an employee of a single company.

Indirect value: having a broad societal positive benefit on a group or groups of people in the short or long term, and that is often difficult to measure. May be expressed through tangible worth (e.g., the profit realized by the spending of dollars invested in salaries) or intangible benefit (e.g., the greater sense of community created by the presence of publicly accessible spaces).

Infopreneur: a position combining entrepreneurial activities with information-related services. The term was registered as a trademark in 1984 but is used commonly by independent information professionals.

Informal learning: learning that is driven and controlled by an individual's interests. Learning may involve natural inquiry, observation, talking and engaging with experts, reading, watching, practicing, failing, learning and iteration. The speed, intensity, direction and success of the learning are controlled by the individual learner.

Informal teaching: teaching that takes place outside of a designated classroom and is intended to address learners' emergent needs.

Informatics: a broad academic field comprising information processing and the creation of information systems and technology tools using computer programming.

Information architecture (IA): defining patterns and sequences through which information will be conveyed to the user of a product, service, or space.

Information ethics: the study of the ethical concerns related to the creation, collection, organization, dissemination, and use of information in society.

Information intermediary: a person who searches for information on behalf of, or who facilitates access to information for another person; librarians and other information professionals may be considered "intermediaries."

Information intermediation: the bringing together of seekers and providers of information through the evaluation and selection of information services and resources. An effective information intermediator helps users define and articulate their information needs and answers users' questions using a wide range of information tools and retrieval techniques by evaluating and selecting information services and resources.

Information licensing: the transaction between information organization and publisher by which information in digital formats is purchased or leased.

Information literacy: the ability to use the skills in accessing, evaluating, using, and creating information in a fluent manner in a variety of contexts.

Information Literacy Competency Standards for Higher Education: a set of five standards and related performance indicators developed by ACRL.

Information literacy instruction: the teaching of strategies, methods, and processes by an information professional for finding and using information effectively and efficiently.

Information need: information that people need to facilitate the performance of a work, academic, or everyday life task; pursue something pleasurable; satisfy curiosity; or solve a problem. Needs may or may not be articulated by a user community.

Information organization: an institution whose mission and practice includes the preservation, organization, and dissemination of information.

Information overload: receiving so much information on a topic that you feel overwhelmed.

Information policy: all rules, laws, and restrictions, both explicit and tacit, including international, national, regional, local, and organizational, that affect the creation, access, use, and dissemination of information.

Information privacy: the right of individuals and organizations to control the collection and sharing of their personal information without consent.

Information professional: an individual who works to increase access to information by preserving, organizing, and describing that information as well as educating users about information search and discovery.

Information security: the protection of data, in any form, from unauthorized access, disclosure, alteration, or destruction. This protection involves assessing and monitoring threats and risks to data, as well as establishing policies, procedures, and controls to preserve the confidentiality, integrity, and availability of data. It is easy to see how information privacy and information security work together.

Infrastructure: the underlying framework of physical and social structures, such as power and transport systems, educational systems, laws, operating principles and standards, that support a society or organization.

Inherent diversities: characteristics of difference that are material to who we are—gender, race and ethnicity, physical and cognitive ability, age, and sexual orientation and identity.

Innovation lab: a space in information organizations that provides new technology to personnel and clients. These facilities support experimental and creative projects using technologies early in their deployment cycles. These technologies may not be widely available or may be at a level of expense that limits their availability to the general public.

Innovative designer: the ability to use digital tools to create creative solutions to real-world problems.

Inquiry-based learning models: learning processes that engage in answering an essential question through research.

Institutional repository (IR): online archive for collecting, preserving, and providing access to electronic versions of the intellectual production of an institution; for a university, this might include monographs, journal articles, theses, and dissertations.

Integrated library system (ILS): a database that integrates functions to carry out library processes (i.e., acquisitions, cataloging, serials, circulation, public access to collections) and features staff and patron graphical user interfaces.

Intellectual freedom: the right to inquire and to investigate the world of stories and ideas from any viewpoint without barriers or restrictions.

Intellectual property: content and ideas protected by one or more legal options, including copyright, trademarks, service marks, and/or patents.

Interaction design: defining patterns and sequences in which options related to performing and completing tasks will be presented to users of a product, service, or space.

Interlibrary loan: a lending agreement between libraries or groups of libraries that allows participants to share materials with others in the groups at little or no cost.

Internal communication: verbal, nonverbal, or written communication that occurs within an organization.

Internal controls: processes that control risk for an organization to conduct business in an orderly manner; to safeguard assets and resources; to deter and detect errors, fraud, and theft; and to ensure accuracy and completeness of accounting information and produce relatable and timely financial information.

Internet Archive: a nonprofit online library with a mission to provide "Universal Access to All Knowledge." The organization provides free public access to collections of digitized materials including books, websites, software programs, audio and video recordings, and images.

Internet filtering: the use of software that blocks internet content based on concerns about its appropriateness for various audiences, especially minors.

Internet of things (IoT): the inter-networking of physical devices (also referred to as "connected devices" and "smart devices"), vehicles, buildings, appliances, and other items embedded with electronics, software, sensors, actuators, and network connectivity which enable these objects to collect and exchange data.

Internet Policy Task Force (IPTF): a task force organized by the U.S. Department of Commerce to conduct a comprehensive review of the intersection of copyright, privacy policy, global free flow of information, cybersecurity, and innovation in the internet economy.

Job analysis: a process to identify and assess the need for a particular job and to identify the specific duties and requirements.

Job description: a document outlining, in broad terms, a set of duties, responsibilities, and required and preferred qualifications for a specific job.

Job specification: an internal document outlining the essential components of the job, including duties, responsibilities, requirements, and minimum qualifications.

Jobbers: agents that provide a single point for information organizations to order print and online books from multiple publishers.

Journey map: a diagram or list that enumerates each touchpoint and channel sequentially, as it is experienced by the user of a product, service, or space, which then provides a comprehensive view of the overall path from the patron perspective.

Just cause: enough evidence for an action, such as disciplining an employee, to be considered permissible or justifiable under the law.

KBART: Knowledge Bases And Related Tools standards to support the systematic sharing of information and data describing books and journals.

Knowledge constructor: the ability to synthesize information from a variety of places to create one's own knowledge.

Knowledge infrastructure: networks of systems and people that create, maintain, and distribute knowledge about the human and natural worlds.

Knowledge management (KM): the systematic process to capture, organize, retrieve and use internal or proprietary information.

Knowledge manager: someone who is responsible for organizing, harvesting, and creating a sharing structure or platform for institutional knowledge.

Leadership: the act of leading people, staff, or organizations to ensure growth and success of initiatives and actions.

Learning commons: a full-service learning, research, and project space typically combining library resources, such as expert help with a computer lab and moveable furniture in a repurposed space designed to facilitate both individual and group work.

Learning outcomes: statements that describe the end goal of a learning activity, identifying what users should be able to do, know, or value as a result of that activity.

Letterpress: a system of arranging movable type to make bespoke stationery, artwork, publications, and more.

LibGuide: research or subject guides to library resources that support academic courses, topics, or disciplines taught in colleges and universities, named after a content management system developed by Springshare.

Library Bill of Rights (LBOR): the key intellectual freedom policy document for the American Library Association.

Library district: one of the geographical areas into which a state is divided for the purpose of administering libraries in accordance with a comprehensive statewide tax plan.

Library exception: the section of U.S. Copyright Law that allows libraries and archives to make certain uses of copyrighted works if they meet certain criteria. Also referred to as "Section 108."

Library foundation: a support organization that provides funding to the library, often through fund-raisers, cultivated donors, estates, and capital campaigns. A foundation often supports larger capital needs, like buildings and furnishings.

Library portal: a content management environment and other specialized tools to give access to the entire information organization website, not just the online catalog.

License: contract between the information provider and the information purchaser that establishes the rights and responsibilities of both the provider and the purchaser.

License grant: official permission to use the content and services described in the license document.

Licensed content business model: structure of the way a digital collection is made available to be sold and used by information organizations.

Life cycle management: the full spectrum of activities a manager undertakes, from creation to disposal of an item or collection.

Lifelong learning: self-directed learning that people seek out beyond traditional educational institutions in order to meet their own ongoing needs to develop new skills, abilities, knowledge, or dispositions throughout their lives.

Line item budget: a list of items in the expense category by the type of expense.

Linked data: data that are structured consistently across multiple sources so that they can be programmatically associated with each other, enabling both stability and interoperability.

Linked open data: pieces of information on the web presented in a way that allows that machine-actionable information to be connected in various ways.

Literary warrant: the principle that any class or term in a vocabulary or classification scheme must have appeared in the text of the resources comprising the collection.

Local computing: a model of technology deployment that depends on servers that reside on the premises of the organization.

Machine readable: content that is designed to be read by a computer.

Machine-readable cataloging (MARC): a standard digital format for describing bibliographic items, developed by the Library of Congress in the 1960s to enable computerized cataloging.

Maker: an inclusive term for anyone who sews, solders, welds, creates, tinkers, prototypes, designs, cooks, codes, gardens, or otherwise transforms one set of materials into another.

Makerspace: a place where people come together to create projects in a supportive, community-centered setting with equipment, supplies, and instruction for exploring technology and creating, sharing, and collaborating on new things; can involve high-tech items like 3-D printers or low-tech like sewing machines.

Management: the process of coordinating, planning, and assessing the workflow of an organization.

Manager: a person in a position of authority in an organization having the responsibility for employing human and material resources to accomplish the organization's purpose.

Manifestation: one of the FRBR Group 1 entities. A work exists at an abstract level, and its manifestations include genres such as a novel, play, film, or opera.

Marketing: the process of proactively reaching out to those outside the organization. Through marketing, advocacy becomes visible. Here the continuum of activities moves from a one-sided approach to a two-way dialogue with a target audience.

Marketing plan: an approach to engage the public built from the organization's strategic plan using established goals and objectives. Information professionals engage in marketing and public relations whenever there is a need to inform the targeted segments of the community served regarding a message, service, or program.

Marrakesh Treaty: The Marrakesh Treaty to Facilitate Access to Published Works for Persons Who Are Blind, Visually Impaired, or Otherwise Print Disabled is an agreement designed to use copyright systems to improve access to printed works for people with print disabilities. It entered into force on September 30, 2016, after being ratified or acceded to by twenty eligible countries, but as of this writing has not been ratified by the United States.

Mashup: the mixing of two or more different elements to create something new.

Media literacy: the ability to use the skills of analyzing, evaluating, and creating media.

Metadata: "data about data," associated with a specific type of information resource or subject area and needed to describe digital assets; descriptive information about a particular data set, object, or resource, including how it is formatted, and when and by whom it was collected. Metadata can be about physical or electronic resources.

Metadata harvesting: the process whereby a piece of software systematically collects structured metadata from a system in bulk.

Metadata standard or schema: a set of rules that govern the structure and type of data recorded about an object.

Metaliteracy: overarching term that recognizes the contributions of a wide range of literacies to a user's ability to not just find, evaluate, and use information effectively, but to perform these activities in a collaborative, online environment.

Microaggression: an act of discrimination by those who think they are not intending to be prejudiced.

Millennials: the generation of individuals reaching young adulthood in the early twenty-first century.

Minecraft: an online platform in which users create and participate in worlds created from block-shaped elements.

Mirrors: makerspace activities that reflect existing or known patron/community interests.

Mission statement: a statement of purpose for the organization.

Mixed system: an information system containing records of individuals covered by the Privacy Act and those of non-U.S. persons.

Mobile reference services: reference services offered via handheld, portable, and networked devices including laptops, tablets, and smartphones. The services offered can include texting, chat/instant messaging, e-mail, conferencing, and more.

Mobile technologies: the technologies employed by portable devices that allow users to perform a wide variety of tasks, such as web browsing, instant messaging, video gaming, and social networking on cellular phones, tablets, laptops, GPS navigation devices, etc.

Molecular gastronomy: an experimental form of cooking that uses physics and chemistry to create new flavors and tastes.

MOOC: also known as a massive open online course, an online course aimed at teaching large numbers of participants and often offered by renowned schools. Courses are free, but students do not always get university credit or graded work. Sometimes participants can pay to get proof of attendance.

Multiculturalism: the promotion, celebration, or recognition of different cultural groups within a society.

Near-field communication: wireless communication between a portable device and other electronic devices.

Needs assessment: also called a gap analysis, a study of current conditions and resulting analysis of what is needed to fulfill a desired condition.

Negotiated license: a type of contract; a private, legally binding agreement between parties who may negotiate their terms and conditions.

Net neutrality: the belief that internet service providers should not provide preferential telecommunication speeds to specific content providers.

Network: a group of personal and professional relationships ("contacts") with individuals that enables one to help members of that network and in turn be helped by them; also known as a "community of colleagues."

Networking: the deliberate effort to meet and develop meaningful relationships with as many people within the community an information organization serves as possible.

Next Great Copyright Act: a phrase coined by Maria Pallante, the register of copyrights and director of the U.S. Copyright Office at the time, to refer to the next major revision of U.S. copyright law.

Nitrate deterioration: decomposition of nitrate film in which the film spontaneously combusts and burns when stored at moderately hot temperatures (>106°F).

Noise: factors that create a disturbance and impede the sender's message from being interpreted as it was intended.

Nominal data: data that can be categorized but where there is no inherent order or relationship between the categories.

Nominal group technique: a communication strategy used to elicit responses from each member of the group to ensure full participation.

Nonverbal communication: nonverbal cues are those unspoken messages that influence the understanding of the intended communication. Some of the more recognized nonverbal signs include posture, facial expression, handshake, eye contact, gestures, attentiveness, and attire.

OCLC: a database with tens of millions of records and more than twenty-five thousand member libraries worldwide.

ONIX ("Online Information eXchange"): a metadata scheme used by publishers to record information about books, journals, electronic resources, sound recordings, and so on.

Ontology: a set of concepts and categories that documents the properties of the concepts and categories and defines the relations between them.

Open access: the free, unrestricted accessibility of scholarly articles online coupled with the rights to them fully in the digital environment.

Open-access funds: money set aside by an institution specifically to cover costs for researchers who publish in open-access journals with article processing charges (APC).

Open-access initiatives: efforts undertaken by libraries and other institutions to ensure free, immediate, permanent online access to the full text of peer-reviewed journal literature for anyone, worldwide.

Open-access journals: journals that make articles freely accessible and enable the rights to them fully in the digital environment.

Open-access publishing: depositing research or information created with a repository that makes it freely and openly available without requiring payment or other restrictive barriers.

Open Archival Information System (OAIS): describes both the organizational and technical aspects of a preservation approach and model.

Open digital repositories: a mechanism for managing and storing digital content that is made freely accessible and fully reusable.

Open license: a license that grants permission to access, reuse, and redistribute a work with few or no restrictions.

Open source: being readily available to be appropriated and used by anyone in the expectation that others will use, modify, and re-share their own variations; generally used to describe software or hardware.

Openly networked learning: learning that leverages the power of the internet to gather information from a wide variety of sources, participate in global communities, and engage authentic audiences, mentors, and peers.

Oppression: the unjust treatment or control of individuals, especially through the deprivation of dignity and rights, outreach services, programs, or projects designed for diverse or underserved populations that broaden the reach of information services throughout a given community.

Optical media: storage media designed for digital content to be written/read by lasers. Compact Discs are a form of optical media.

Opt-in group license: agreement for an established group or consortium of information organizations that allows each individual organization to decide whether or not to participate.

Ordinal data: data that can be categorized, often based on quantitative data, where there is an inherent relationship between categories.

Organizational change: the intentional modification between the organization's departments and systems to improve the effectiveness of the organization.

Orphan work: a work for which the copyright owner cannot be located or identified by an individual who wishes to use that work after making diligent efforts.

Outcome: a measure of the effectiveness of an organization in achieving a designated goal.

Outliers: observations that lie outside of the typical range with a set of observations.

Output: a measure of the efficiency of an organization in achieving a goal or objective, usually according to a numerical scalar.

Outreach: measures taken to contact and inform constituent groups about the organization's activities.

Paraprofessional: a member of the library support staff who usually performs technical support duties or performs specific procedures and tasks that do not involve professional judgment.

Participatory organization: an organization that provides opportunities for engagement, collaboration, and creation driven by the users.

Patron-driven acquisition models: a model of collection development in which a library will only purchase library material when it is clear that the material is in demand by members of the community. See data-driven acquisitions.

Patron-oriented organization: an organization that prioritizes its patrons', customers', stakeholders', and/or users' interests as strategies are developed.

Pattern discovery: the identification of recurrences or sequences within data that indicate how elements are related, which provides insight into the object of research.

Peer review: the evaluation of scientific, academic, or professional work by others working in the same field.

Performance budget: a budget where the funds are attached to performance objectives; connects the input of resources with the output of services.

Performance evaluation: the analysis of how closely a person, program, service, or organization has met previously stated goals.

Performance objectives: descriptions of the types of activities a learner can accomplish at the end of a specific time period that demonstrate the understanding of a skill or concept.

Persona: a fictitious user that represents potential or actual users in scenarios constructed for the purpose of providing a clear picture of the target population a service or system is being designed for.

Personal brand: the professional reputation individuals build based on their actions, attitudes, personal interactions, and professional contributions.

Personal learning network (PLN): a series of online and in-person connections used to enhance learning; includes professional groups, social networks, blogs and microblogging sites, and any other platform where ideas are exchanged.

Personality preferences: innate communication styles based on personality type. Although personality preferences remain static, it is possible for individuals to change their communication behavior.

Personally identifiable information (PII): a term used in privacy laws in the United States to refer to personal data. What constitutes PII varies by country. Some countries are more encompassing in their definitions of PII than others.

Persuasion: the process of using factual or values-based appeals with a target in order to shift previous ways of thinking.

Planning horizon: duration in years during which the organization agrees to be governed by objectives of the strategic plan.

Population served: the eligible users of the library or institution's resources.

Post-license access: methods through which content acquired with perpetual rights will be accessible if the license is canceled, including third-party archiving and rights to create/obtain local backup copy.

Power: the ability to dictate the experience of others, especially through the authority and influence of embedded systems and structures of society.

Predatory publishing: a set of exploitative practices employed by individuals or organizations who target individual researchers via e-mail, soliciting articles for publication and charging authors publications fees without providing any of the editorial services associated with legitimate scholarly journals—including peer review and editorial review.

Predictive analysis: the process of using data mining, statistics, and artificial intelligence to predict future outcomes as well as "what-if" scenarios based on past and current data.

Predictive analytics: the analysis of data to predict future actions or trends.

Prescriptive analytics: the analysis of data to suggest the next best step to take in special libraries and information organizations.

Prescriptive collection development: an approach to content selection based on what the purchasers believe their community should have, regardless of what members of that community may say or demonstrate they want.

Preservation: the steps taken to ensure long-term accessibility and usability of content, including (but not restricted to) activities that prevent physical deterioration.

Preservation Metadata Implementation Strategies (PREMIS): provides a data dictionary and resources to assist information managers in the implementation of preservation metadata efforts. Established as a working group by OCLC/RLG, with its report and data dictionary first released in 2005, PREMIS documentation is housed and maintained by the Library of Congress.

Privacy: freedom from the collection and dissemination of personal or institutional information. For example, the a person's library use is private in that only the minimum necessary data about information use will be maintained and that it will not be shared absent due process and legal need.

Privacy audit: an assessment that focuses on privacy risk, which includes evaluation of all privacy documentation and examines how data flow through an organization as well as data-handling practices.

Privacy literacy: consumers' attitudes regarding the collection, processing, and use of their personal data.

Privilege: the unacknowledged, unrecognized, and unearned ways that access, rights, and benefits are given to particular groups over others.

Problem situation: a situation that arises from factors within the individual (e.g., curiosity, uncertainty) or the environment (e.g., work task), whereby the individual realizes that information is needed in order to move forward.

Production-centered learning: learning that focuses on creating a product meant to be shared with an authentic audience.

Professional equity: the "asset" that information professionals build over the course of their careers, comprising what they know (domain knowledge), who they know (network), and who knows what about them (brand or professional reputation).

Program budget: budget where all of the expenses are grouped by program.

Promotion: in the context of organizational management, those activities designed by the staff members of the organization that are used to relate the details about an issue, service, program, or the overall organization to a target group or the general public. In the context of marketing, it embodies marketing communication tools such as advertising, direct mail, personal selling, sales promotion, or publicity, delivered by media ranging from print to online to targeted customer groups.

Proprietary software: software developed by a company that licenses its use, as opposed to open-source software.

Protective enclosure: a box, case, or other protective structure intended to physically support and buffer a fragile item so that it remains intact and undisturbed over time.

Public domain: the status of not being protected by copyright ("in the public domain"). This is usually because copyright protection has expired, although sometimes authors intentionally give up their copyright to make the work publicly usable.

Public domain dedication (CCO): a tool offered by Creative Commons in which copyright owners may waive their rights to their work under copyright law, effectively dedicating the work to the public domain.

Public domain mark: a tool offered by Creative Commons that allows users to identify works that are free of known restrictions under copyright law.

Public good: a service or institution that has a primary purpose of improving the community and is open to all.

Public relations: the process of managing communication between an organization and the public.

Publicity: promotional activity that relies on free media or special events in lieu of paid advertising.

Purpose specification: articulating the purpose(s) for which personally identifiable information (PII) is intended to be used.

Python: a computer programming language.

Qualitative data: data that cannot be measured in an objective manner, such as perception of smells or physical attractiveness, but can be categorized.

Quantitative data: data that can be numerically measured in an objective manner, such as the number of users of a library resource.

Query: a question or simplification of a request for information posed to an information professional or information system such as a search engine.

Question-answering (Q&A) services: sources for locating answers that are provided by some kind of community or user group. These include community-based, collaborative, social, and expert-based Q&A services.

Reader's advisory: direct and indirect help offered to readers with their reading needs in libraries, bookstores, and online.

Recovery point objective: within a disaster recovery plan, a value that is calculated as a function of the amount of time between data backups and the amount of data that would be lost between the system outage and the last data backup. It is used as an indicator of data loss risk.

Reference 2.0: a new service model that uses social networking and collaboration to provide reference services in the twenty-first century.

Reference interview: the interaction between an information seeker and information professional whereby the professional asks strategic questions to understand the underlying information need and determine the best course of action.

Reference services: recommendations, interpretations, and evaluation of information resources to address patrons' information needs; library instruction and training; readers' advisory services; and outreach services.

Reflection-in-action: ongoing, continual reflection throughout the process of creation, decision making, rationale formulation, and so on.

Reformatting: transferring the intellectual content of an object or collection from one medium to another (e.g., photocopying, microfilming, or digitizing content).

Refreshing: transferring content from one container to another container in the same format and media (e.g., copying a cassette tape to another cassette tape).

Remote access: access to online content for users not physically located within the boundaries of the licensing organization or institution.

Remote storage: the storage of collections off-site.

Repertoire: one's previous experiences and bodies of knowledge used to address current situations.

Replicating: making and distributing copies of content.

Replication: the process of copying data from one storage medium to another.

Repository: the physical space, usually a library or museum, that is used as a place of storage of archival materials.

Request for reconsideration: a form provided by an information agency to someone who complains about a library resource and seeks to change the status of that resource. Typically, this form asks for information about the resource, specific citations to what was concerning, and why it was of concern.

Research data management (RDM): a method for managing the life cycle of data in research projects, from project inception to dissemination of research results.

Research informationist: a specialized academic librarian who helps campus scientists comply with funding agency requirements (such as the National Science Foundation [NSF] and National Institutes of Health [NIH]) to provide open access to the underlying data gathered as a result of grant-funded research and to archive and share the gathered data.

Reserves: potentially high-use course-related items used for short periods, often kept behind the circulation desk; increasingly being made available online through e-reserves.

Resource sharing: collaboration between multiple information organizations to share content from their collections so that each has access to a broader array of information.

Responsive web design: web design that allows a website or web-based software application to adapt to the varying capabilities of devices (especially mobile devices) used to access them.

Résumé action verbs: strong verbs describing job-seeking skills and accomplishments.

Return on investment (ROI): the value of a resource or service to the organization as compared to the cost of the resource or service.

Roving reference services: a reference service model in which the information profession physically approaches users throughout the library or information organization to solicit questions and provide assistance.

Satisficing: choosing the first best option when making a decision rather than exploring all possible options available or perceived to be available, despite the relative quality of the option.

Scholarly communication: the system by which research and other scholarly output is created, vetted, transmitted to the scholarly community, and preserved for the future.

Scholarly communications librarian: an academic librarian who advises faculty on authors' rights and publishing options, advocates for more open and accessible scholarship, and in some cases even takes on the role of publisher.

Scholarly communications program: a library-based initiative to explore and raise awareness of new tools, models, projects, forums, and services designed to help faculty, students, and staff communicate the results of their research and scholarship.

Scholarly publishing: publishing that incorporates peer review.

Scholarly sharing: informal, occasional sharing of licensed information between scholarly researchers conducting joint studies when one has access to specific information and the other does not.

Secondary market research: a type of research where existing sources are reviewed, summarized, and analyzed. Secondary sources range from syndicated market research reports, newspaper and journal articles, social media, and much more. Secondary research, also known as desk research, is often a good precursor to primary research, where professionals reach out to specific targets via surveys, focus groups, and interviews, often with a specific question in mind.

Section 108: the section of the U.S. copyright law that allows libraries and archives to make certain uses of copyrighted works if they meet certain criteria. Sometimes called the library exception.

Selection: an aspect of collection development that involves the evaluation of materials and making decisions on what to purchase, retain, or remove from the collection. Selection is usually based on established collection development policies, which vary from one type of organization to another.

Self-check terminal: a self-service terminal where users check out materials.

Sensitive personal data: a subset of personally identifiable information that includes data that are specifically protected. In the United States, this includes social security numbers, identifiable health records, and identifiable financial records.

Serials: publications that are recurring and distributed in successive parts, such as periodicals, newspapers, electronic magazines and journals, and annuals (reports, yearbooks).

Serials control modules: used to manage journals, newspapers, and other subscription-based materials.

Server operating system: operating system such as Microsoft Windows Server or Linux on which locally managed applications run.

Shelf-reading: the periodic checking of the collection's spine labels to ensure items are in call-number order.

Shifting: the process of moving parts of the collection to accommodate growth.

Simultaneous users: users able to access a resource at the same time.

Situational descriptive questioning: asking candidates for a job to consider a future situation and to predict how he or she might react to that situation, for example, "Please consider how you may react if you disagreed with your supervisor."

Social influence: the process of inciting a change in thinking in another person.

Social justice: a framework that seeks to provide equal rights and opportunities for all people to pursue their economic, political, and social goals, often by confronting systems of oppression, power, and privilege.

Social media: digital communication outlets used to connect with constituent groups and others, e.g., LinkedIn, Facebook, Instagram.

Soft skills: techniques that can be learned that enhance effective communication with others.

Sticky-shed syndrome: deterioration of the binder used in tape manufacturing in which the coating of the tape becomes sticky and sheds oxide.

Strategic data asset: a data asset that has been identified by the organization as critical to its strategic goals.

Strategic planning: an organization's process of defining its strategy or direction and making decisions on allocating its resources to pursue this strategy.

Style sheets: a file that is associated with a web resource that dictates that resource's font and other layout settings.

Subject cataloging: the process of expressing the aboutness of a resource by assigning subject terms (such as LCSH) and classification.

Summative assessment: evaluative activities that educators use to gauge learners' understanding and skills at the end of instruction in order to determine whether and how well the learners achieved the expected outcomes.

SWOT analysis: analysis of the strengths, weaknesses, opportunities, and threats confronting an organization.

Tacit knowledge: the knowledge that people have on a given subject, which is very hard to capture.

Taxonomy: a classification scheme derived from the presumed relationships between the items classified.

Technological literacy: the set of skills, abilities, knowledge, and dispositions that enable people to successfully and ethically use information technology to achieve their goals.

Technology literacy: competency in the use of computers and a variety of software.

Technology literacy instruction: training students in the use of computers (including iPads or other tablets) and a variety of software.

Tenure-track: a job classification in North American institutions of higher education used to indicate that an academic (e.g., professor or librarian) is eligible for a permanent, or tenured, position.

Text mining: the analysis of natural language, often using statistical techniques, to uncover patterns and meaning that can only be discovered through context and patterns of relationships.

Third place: a social environment that differs from home and work/school.

Threshold concepts: a term that comes from the study of higher education and is used to describe core knowledge that, once understood, transforms perception of a given subject.

Tinkering: a method of playing or messing around in an iterative manner.

Touchpoint: a situated, specific task interaction between a person and an information organization through one or more channels.

Transliteracy: the ability needed in the twenty-first century to read, write, and interact using a range of technologies, media platforms, and contexts.

U.S. globalization: the inclusion of other nations in U.S. technological, business, cultural, and other endeavors for the mutual benefit of all.

Uniform Resource Identifier (URI): a unique string of letters, numbers, and other characters used to identify a resource. The most familiar example of a URI is a Uniform Resource Locator (URL), the web address of a resource.

Usability: the ease with which a resource is navigable, understandable, and usable.

Use limitation: losing the use of PII for the purposes stated.

User experience (UX): the sum-total of a user's interactions with an information organization, encompassing physical, virtual, and emotional aspects of observations, actions, and interactions. Measured by ease of use, level of satisfaction, and quality of user interaction with a product, site, or system.

User experience design (UXD): programmers' and others' ideas for creating the best online or software experience for users.

User experience designer: one who designs compelling, user-centered digital experiences.

User support: technical assistance provided by a vendor.

Utilitarianism: an ethical system based on the principle of favoring actions that maximize benefits for the greatest number of people.

Value: the demonstration of the worth of a product, service, or offering to stakeholders, variously expressed through monetary or social terms.

Values: the principles or sense of worth held by an individual or by a collective, such as within a family, an organization, a society, or a government.

Values statement: a statement that outlines the organization's guiding concepts and beliefs.

Venture Capital (VC): a form of private equity financing provided to early-state and start-up companies. It differs from the often earlier accessed angel funding, which is made up of investments from individual qualified investors through local and regional networks.

Vinegar syndrome: disintegration of acetate film marked by symptoms including a vinegar scent, followed by shrinkage and buckling of the film.

Virtual reference services: computer-mediated reference help provided to users synchronously or asynchronously via e-mail, chat/instant messaging, texting/short message service (SMS), voice chat and cloud-based videoconferencing, and more.

Vision statement: a description of the future that an organization seeks to create.

Visualization tool: software or program that enables the visual representation of electronic data.

VRA (Visual Resources Association) Core: a metadata standard or schema that stipulates elements that can be used to describe a resource, particularly works of visual culture.

Warranty: written guarantee that the information being licensed is correctly represented as promised.

Wayfinding: how users find their way through a space.

Web analytics: collecting and interpreting quantitative data that describes how a website or web resource has been used.

Weeding: the removal of library resources from collections, usually on the basis of age, condition, or superseded information.

WorldCat: a database, maintained by OCLC, that reflects the collections of OCLC member libraries.

Zoomers: the generation of people who fit the demographic of active people ages forty-five and older.

Bibliography

A. Telier (Thomas Binder, Giorgio De Michelis, Pelle Ehn, Giulio Jacucci, Per Linde, and Ina Wagner). *Design Things*. Cambridge, MA: MIT Press, 2011.

Aabø, Svanhild. "The Role and Value of Public Libraries in the Age of Digital Technologies." *Journal of Librarianship and Information Science* 37, no. 4 (2005): 205–10. doi:10.1177/0961000605057855.

Abels, E., L. C. Howarthe, and L. C. Smith. "Envisioning Our Information Future and How to Educate for It." *Proceedings of the Association of Information Science and Technology* 52, no. 1 (2015): 1–3.

"About Guide on the Side." Code.Library. http://code.library.arizona.edu.

"About History Pin." History Pin. Accessed May 31, 2017. https://about.historypin.org.

"About the Standards." Common Core State Standards Initiative. Last modified September 12, 2014. http://www.corestandards.org/.

Abram, Stephen. "Communicating Value and Impact through Advocacy: Dealing with the Scalability Issue in the Province of Ontario." *PLQ Public Library Quarterly* 36, no. 2 (2017). doi:http://dx.doi.org/10.1080/01616846.2017.1312192.

Abram, Stephen. "Future World: Strategic Challenges for Reference in the Coming Decade." In *Reinventing Reference: How Libraries Deliver Value in the Age of Google*, edited by Katie Elson Anderson and Vibiana Bowman Cvetkovic, 133–45. Chicago: ALA, 2015.

ACRL Insider. "National Library Groups Oppose Bill to Make Register of Copyrights a Presidential Appointee." Last modified March 24, 2017. http://www.acrl.ala.org/acrlinsider/archives/13478#.WNapkbdNHJU.

ACRL Research Planning and Review Committee. "2012 Top Ten Trends in Academic Libraries." *College and Research Libraries News* 73, no. 6 (2012): 311–20.

"Active Policy Studies." U.S. Copyright Office, 2017. https://www.copyright.gov/policy/.

ADA.gov. The Americans with Disabilities Act of 1990 and Revised ADA Regulations Implementing Title II and Title III. Accessed April 30, 2017. https://www.ada.gov/2010_regs.htm.

"Adam d'Angelo on Knowledge, Experimentation, and Quora: EconTalk Episode with Adam d'Angelo." *Library of Economics and Liberty* (podcast), 2016. http://www.econtalk.org/archives/2016/08/adam_dangelo_on.html.

Adler, Melissa A. "The ALA Task Force on Gay Liberation: Effecting Change in Naming and Classification of GLBTQ Subjects." *Advances in Classification Research Online* 23, no. 1 (2013). https://journals.lib.washington.edu/index.php/acro/article/viewFile/14226/12086.

Agosto, Denise E., and Sandra Hughes-Hassell. "Toward a Model of the Everyday Life Information Needs of Urban Teenagers, Part 1: Theoretical Model." *Journal of the American Society for Information Science and Technology* 57, no. 10 (2006): 1394–403.

Agricultural Network Information Collaborative. "Home." http://www.agnic.org/.

Aguiar, Mark, and Eric Hunt. "Measuring Trends in Libraries: The Allocation of Time Over Five Decades." *Quarterly Journal of Economics* 122, no. 3 (2007): 969–1006.

Aguilera, Jasmine. "Another Word for 'Illegal Alien' at the Library of Congress: Contentious." *New York Times*. July 22, 2016. Retrieved from https://www.nytimes.com/2016/07/23/us/another-word-for-illegal-alien-at-the-library-of-congress-contentious.html.

Al Ansari, Husain, and Othman al Khadher. "Developing a Leadership Competency Model for Library and Information Professionals in Kuwait." *Libri* 61, no. 3 (2011): 239–46.

Alexander, F. King. "The Changing Face of Accountability: Monitoring and Assessing Institutional Performance in Higher Education." *Journal of Higher Education* 71, no. 4 (July–August 2000): 411–31. http://www.jstor.org/stable/2649146.

Alire, Camila A., and G. Edward Evans. *Academic Librarianship in the 21st Century*. New York: Neal-Schuman, 2010.

Allen, Nancy, ed. *New Roles for the Road Ahead: Essays Commissioned for ACRL's 75th Anniversary*. Association of College and Research Libraries. Last modified 2015. http://www.ala.org/acrl/sites/ala.org.acrl/files/content/publications/whitepapers/new_roles_75th.pdf.

Allison, Michael. *Strategic Planning for Nonprofit Organizations: A Practical Guide for Dynamic Times*. Hoboken, NJ: Wiley, 2015.

Alman, Susan W., and Sara Gillespie Swanson. *Crash Course in Marketing for Libraries*. Santa Barbara, CA: Libraries Unlimited, 2015.

Alonso-Regalado, Jesus. "Librarian with a Latte: Reaching Out to Students beyond the Library's Walls Slideshare." Presented at the SALALM LVI Conference in Philadelphia, 2011. Posted on June 3. http://www.slideshare.net/jesusalonso/librarian-with-a-latte-reaching-out-to-students-beyond-the-librarys-walls.

Amazon. "Amazon.com Now Selling More Kindle Books Than Print Books." Accessed June 2, 2014. http://phx.corporate-ir.net/phoenix.zhtml?c=176060&p=irolnewsArticle&ID=1565581&highlight.

American Association of Colleges and Universities. "Information Literacy Value Rubric." In *VALUE: Valid Assessment of Learning in Undergraduate Education*. Last modified March 14, 2013. http://www.aacu.org/value/rubrics/InformationLiteracy.cfm.

American Association of School Librarians (AASL). http://www.ala.org/aasl/.

———. "Learning and Program Guidelines." Accessed September 7, 2017. http://www.ala.org/aasl/standards. *Standards of the 21st Century Learner in Action*. Chicago: American Association of School Librarians, 2009.

———. *Implementing the Common Core State Standards: The Role of the School Librarian*. *American Library Association* (November 2013). http://www.ala.org/aasl/sites/ala.org.aasl/files/content/externalrelations/CCSSLibrariansBrief_FINAL.pdf.

———. *Information Power: Guidelines for School Library Media Programs*. Chicago: American Library Association, 1988. http://files.eric.ed.gov/fulltext/ED315028.pdf.

———. *Standards for the 21st Century Learner*. Chicago: American Association of School Librarians, 2007. http://www.ala.org/aasl/sites/ala.org.aasl/files/content/guidelinesandstandards/learningstandards/AASL_Learning_Standards_2007.pdf.

American Association of School Librarians and Association for Educational Communications. *Information Power: Building Partnerships for Learning*. Chicago: American Library Association, 1998.

American Association of School Librarians, and Association for Educational Communications and Technology. "Information Literacy Standards for Student Learning." American Library Association, 1998. Accessed September 5, 2017. http://www.ala.org/PrinterTemplate.cfm?Section=informationpower&Template=/ContentManagement/ContentDisplay.cfm&ContentID=19935.

American Library Association (ALA). "2007 Paul Howard Award for Courage Recipient Named." American Library Association, May 15, 2007. http://www.ala.org/Template.cfm?Section=archive&template=/contentmanagement/contentdisplay.cfm&ContentID=157765.

———. "About ALA." Accessed August 1, 2017. http://www.ala.org/aboutala/.

———. "ALA Chapters." Accessed June 17, 2017. http://www.ala.org/groups/affiliates/chapters.

———. "ALA Leadership Institute: Leading to the Future." Accessed August 13, 2017. http://www.ala.org/transforminglibraries/ala-leadership-institute.

———. "ALA Policy Manual Section B: Positions and Public Policy Statement, 2012/2013." http://www.ala.org/aboutala/sites/ala.org.aboutala/files/content/governance/policymanual/cd_10_2_Section%20B%20New%20Policy%20Manual-1%20%28final%205-4-2016%20with%20TOC%29.pdf.

———. "Center for the Future of Libraries." 2017. http://www.ala.org/tools/future.

———. "Challenge Reporting." Accessed June 17, 2017. http://www.ala.org/tools/challengesupport/report.

———. "Code of Ethics." January 22, 2008. Accessed July 5, 2017. http://www.ala.org/tools/ethics.

———. "Code of Ethics of the American Library Association." Accessed August 24, 2014. http://www.ala .org/advocacy/proethics/codeofethics/codeethics.

———. "Core Values of Librarianship." Adopted June 29, 2004. http://www.ala.org/advocacy/intfreedom/ corevalues.

———. Coretta Scott King Book Awards. Accessed September 7, 2017. http://www.ala.org/emiert/csk bookawards.

———. "Diversity Counts." Accessed August 1, 2017. http://www.ala.org/offices/diversity/diversitycounts/ divcounts.

———. "Final Report of the ALA Task Force on Equity, Diversity, and Inclusion." Accessed June 2016. http:// www.ala.org/aboutala/offices/ala-task-force-equity-diversity-and-inclusion.

———. "Guidelines to Minimize the Negative Effects of Internet Content Filtering on Intellectual Freedom." Accessed June 17, 2017. http://www.ala.org/advocacy/intfreedom/filtering/filtering_guidelines.

———. "Intellectual Freedom and Censorship Q & A." Accessed June 17, 2017. http://www.ala.org/advo cacy/intfreedom/censorship/faq.

———. *Information Literacy Competency Standards for Higher Education*. Chicago: American Library Associa- tion, 2000.

———. "Libraries Transform." Accessed June 30, 2017. http://www.ala.org/transforminglibraries/libraries -transform-campaign.

———. "Library Bill of Rights." Last modified June 30, 2006. http://www.ala.org/advocacy/intfreedom/ librarybill.

———. "Network Neutrality." 2017. http://www.ala.org/advocacy/telecom/netneutrality.

———. "Privacy." Last modified July 7, 2006. http://www.ala.org/advocacy/intfreedom/librarybill/interpre tations/privacy.

———. "Standards of Distance Learning Library Services." 2016. http://www.ala.org/acrl /standards/guide linesdistancelearning.

———. "State Privacy Laws Regarding Library Records." Last modified May 29, 2007. http://www.ala.org/ advocacy/privacyconfidentiality/privacy/stateprivacy.

———. "The Merritt Fund." Accessed June 30, 2017. http://www.ala.org/groups/affiliates/relatedgroups/ merrittfund/merritthumanitarian.

———. "Trends." 2017. http://www.ala.org/tools/future/trends.

———. "Workforce Innovation and Libraries." 2017. http://www.ala.org/advocacy/advleg/federallegislation/ workforce.

American Library Association (ALA) Council. "Policy B.2.1.11 Diversity in Collection Development." *Amer- ican Library Association Policy Manual*. Chicago: ALA, 2013. http://www.ala.org/aboutala/governance/ policymanual.

American Library Association (ALA) Joblist. A Service of the American Library Association and the Asso- ciation of College and Research Libraries, 1996–2015. http://joblist.ala.org/.

American Library Association (ALA) Standards for the 21st Century Learner. http://www.ala.org/aasl/sites/ ala.org.aasl/files/content/guidelinesandstandards/learningsta ndard s/AASL_LearningStandards.pdf.

Ammons-Stephens, Shoreltte, Holly J. Cole, Keisha Jenkins-Gibbs, Catherine Fraser Riehle, and William H. Weare. "Developing Core Leadership Competencies for the Library Profession." *Libraries Faculty and Staff Scholarship and Research*, Paper 19 (2009). http://docs.lib.purdue.edu/lib_fsdocs/19.

Anbu, John Paul, and Sanjay Kataria. "Reference on the Go: A Model for Mobile Reference Services in Librar- ies." *Reference Librarian* 57, no. 3 (2016): 235–41. doi:10.1080/02763877.2015.1132181.

Anderson, Arthur James. "No Introverts Need Apply." *Library Journal* 121, no. 8 (May 1, 1996): 53–54.

Anderson, Katie Elson, and Vibiana Bowman Cvetkovic, eds. *Reinventing Reference: How Libraries Deliver Value In the Age of Google*. Chicago: ALA, 2015.

Anderson, Mark. Personal Communication. September 23, 2013.

Angelo, Thomas A., and K. Patricia Cross. *Classroom Assessment Techniques: A Handbook for College Teachers*. San Francisco: Jossey-Bass Publishers, 1993.

Applegate, Rachel. "Whose Decline? Which Academic Libraries Are 'Deserted' in Terms of Reference Transactions?" *Reference & User Services Quarterly* 48, no. 2 (2008): 176–89.

ARL Policy Notes. "Recap of the Copyright Office's Roundtables on Orphan Works and Mass Digitization." Accessed July 5, 2014. http://policynotes.arl.org/post/79876737815/recap-of-the-copyright-offices-roundtables-on-orphan.

Archive of Digital Art. http://www.virtualart.at/nc/home.html.

ARUP. "Future Libraries: Workshops Summary and Emerging Insights." 2015: 5.

Ashcroft, Linda, and Chris Watts. "ICT Skills for Information Professionals in Developing Countries: Perspectives from a Study of the Electronic Information Environment in Nigeria." *IFLA Journal* 31, no. 1 (2005): 6–12.

The Aspen Institute. Dialogue on Public Libraries. http://www.libraryvision.org/.

"Assessment, and Feedback Strategies for 'Flipped' Library." *Theological Librarianship* 9, no. 1 (2016): 22–7.

Association for Library Service to Children. Caldecott Medal. Accessed September 7, 2017. http://www.ala.org/alsc/awardsgrants/bookmedia/caldecottmedal/caldecottmedal.

———. Newbery Awards. Accessed September 7, 2017. http://www.ala.org/alsc/awardsgrants/bookmedia/newberymedal/newberymedal.

Association for Educational Communication and Technology (AECT). http://aect.site-ym.com/.

Association of American University Presses. "Press and Library Collaboration Study." 2013. http://www.aaupnet.org/images/stories/data/librarypresscollaboration_report_corrected.pdf.

Association of College and Research Libraries (ACRL). "Academic Library Statistics." 2015. http://www.ala.org/acrl/publications/trends.

———. "Information Literacy Competency Standards for Higher Education." Archived March 22, 2017. https://web.archive.org/web/20170322170540/http://www.ala.org/acrl/standards/informationliteracycompetency.

———. "Information Literacy Competency Standards for Higher Education." 2000. http://www.ala.org/acrl/standards/informationliteracycompetency.

———. "Framework for Information Literacy for Higher Education." Last Modified February 2, 2015. http://www.ala.org/acrl/standards/ilframework.

———. *Presidential Committee on Information Literacy: Final Report*. Last modified January 10, 1989. http://www.ala.org/acrl/publications/whitepapers/presidential.

Association of Independent Information Professionals. "Code of Ethical Business Practice." Last modified April 20, 2002. http://aiip.org/About/Professional-Standards.

Association of Research Libraries (ARL). "21st-Century Collections: Calibration of Investment and Collaborative Action." 2012. http://www.arl.org/storage/documents/publications/issue-brief-21st-century-collections-2012.pdf.

———. "Research Library Expenditure Trends." https://comminfo.rutgers.edu/~tefko/Courses/e553/Readings/ARL%20statistics%202006-07.pdf.

———. "Service Trends in ARL Libraries, 1991–2012." 2012. http://www.arl.org/storage/documents/service-trends.pdf.

———. "Statistics and Assessment Surveys (Canada & US)." 2017. https://www.arlstatistics.org/home.

Association of School Libraries National Research Forum. "Causality: School Libraries and Student Success." American Library Association, 2014. http://www.ala.org/aasl/sites/ala.org.aasl/files/content/researchandstatistics/CLASSWhitePaperFINAL.pdf.

Attis, David. *Redefining the Academic Library: Managing the Migration to Digital Information Services*. Last modified 2013. http://library.wcsu.edu/staff/uploads/planning/Redefining_the_Academic_Library-Managing_the_Migration_to_Digital.pdf.

Australian Library and Information Association. "Future of the Library and Information Science Profession: Public Libraries." 2014. https://www.alia.org.au/sites/default/files/ALIA-Future-of-the-LIS-Profession-04-Public_0.pdf.

Authors Guild, Inc. v. Google Inc., 954 F. Supp. 2d 282 (SD New York Dist. Court, 2013). http://scholar.google.com/scholar_case?case=6510192672912362556&hl=en&as_sdt=6&as_vis=1&oi=scholarr.

"Authors Guild v. Google, Part II: Fair Use Proceedings." Electronic Frontier Foundation. https://www.eff.org/cases/authors-guild-v-google-part-ii-fair-use-proceedings.

Authors Guild, Inc. v. HathiTrust, No. 12-4547-cv. 2nd Cir. June 10, 2014.

Baker, Betsy. "Bibliographic Instruction: Building the Librarian/Faculty Partnership." *Reference Librarian* 24 (1989): 311–28.

Bakkalbasi, Nisa. "Assessment and Evaluation, Promotion, and Marketing of Academic Library Services." In *Academic Librarianship Today*, edited by Todd Gilman, 211–21. Lanham, MD: Rowman & Littlefield, 2017.

Balanced Scorecard Institute. "What Is Strategic Planning?" http://www.balancedscorecard.org/BSC-Basics/Strategic-Planning-Basics.

Band, Jonathan. "The Cell Phone Unlocking Saga." Infojustice.org. Last modified March 13, 2014. http://infojustice.org/wp-content/uploads/2014/03/band04132014.pdf.

Banzi, Massimo. "Making Is Best When It's Done Together." *Make* (blog). February 7, 2014. Accessed July 5, 2017. http://makezine.com/2014/02/07/making-is-best-when-its-done-together/.

Barker, Steve. "In Age of Google, Librarians Get Shelved." *Wall Street Journal*, January 10, 2016. http://www.wsj.com/articles/in-age-of-google-librarians-get-shelved-1452461659.

Barnard College. "Dean of the Barnard Library and Academic Information Services ('BLAIS')" advertisement. *Chronicle of Higher Education*, January 15, 2016. https://chroniclevitae.com/jobs/0000920425-01.

Barrow, W. J. "Deacidification and Lamination of Deteriorated Documents, 1938–63." *American Archivist* 28, no. 2 (April 1965): 285–90.

Bass, Bernard M. "Concepts of Leadership." In *Leadership: Understanding the Dynamics of Power and Influence in Organizations*, edited by Robert P. Vecchio, 3–22, second edition. Notre Dame, IN: Notre Dame University Press, 1997.

Batch, Kristen R. "Fencing Out Knowledge: Impacts of the Children's Internet Protection Act 10 Years Later" (Policy Brief no. 5). American Library Association, June 2014. http://connect.ala.org/files/cipa_report.pdf.

Baty, J. W., C. L. Maitland, William Minter, Martin A. Hubbe, and Sonja K. Jordan-Mowery. "Deacidification for the Conservation and Preservation of Paper-Based Works: A Review." *BioResources* 5, no. 3 (2010): 1955–2023.

Beck, Susan E., and Kate Manuel. *Practical Research Methods for Librarians and Information Professionals*. New York: Neal-Schuman Publishers, 2008.

Beghtol, Claire. "Semantic Validity: Concepts of Warrant in Bibliographic Classification Systems." *Library Resources and Technical Services* 30, no. 2 (April/June 1986): 109–25.

Belkin, Nicholas J., and Alina Vickery. *Interaction in Information Systems: A Review of Research from Document Retrieval to Knowledge-Based Systems*. London: British Library, 1985.

Bell, Steven J. "Usability and User Experience—There Is a Difference." *Designing Better Libraries*, May 29, 2012. http://dbl.lishost.org/blog/2012/05/29/usability-and-user-experience-there-is-a-difference.

———. "Staying True to the Core: Designing the Future Academic Library Experience." *Portal: Libraries and the Academy* 14, no. 3 (2014): 369–82. doi:10.1353/pla.2014.0021.

Bell, Steven J., and John D. Shank. *Academic Librarianship by Design: A Blended Librarian's Guide to the Tools and Techniques*. Chicago: American Library Association, 2007.

Bell, Steven J., and Michael J. Krasulski. "Electronic Reserves, Library Databases, and Courseware: A Complementary Relationship." *Journal of Interlibrary Loan, Document Delivery, & Electronic Reserves* 15, no. 1 (2004): 75–85.

Bennett, Milton J. *Basic Concepts of Intercultural Communication: Selected Readings*. Yarmouth, ME: Intercultural Press, 1998.

Benoit, William L. *Persuasive Messages: The Process of Influence*. Malden, MA: Blackwell Publishing, 2008.

BerkeleyLaw UCLA. "May 2014 USPTO Multistakeholder Forum on the DMCA Notice and Takedown System." Last modified August 4, 2014. http://www.law.berkeley.edu/17084.htm.

Berners-Lee, Tim. "Linked Data." Cambridge, MA: W3C Consortium, 2009. https://www.w3.org/DesignIssues/LinkedData.html.

Berry, John N. III. "Library Freedom Fighter Zoia Horn Remembered." *Library Journal*, August 2014. http://lj.libraryjournal.com/2014/08/people/library-freedom-fighter-zoia-horn-remembered/.

Bertocci, David I. *Leadership in Organizations: There Is a Difference between Leaders and Managers*. Lanham, MD: University Press of America, 2009.

Bertot, John C., Charles R. McClure, and Joe Ryan. "Impact of External Technology Funding Programs for Public Libraries; A Study of LSTA, E-rate, Gates, and Others." *Public Libraries* 41, no. 3 (May/June 2002): 166–71.

Bertot, John C., Lindsay C. Sarin, and Johnna Percell. "Re-Envisioning the MLS: Findings, Issues, and Considerations." College of Information Studies, University of Maryland College Park, 2015. http://mls.umd.edu/wp-content/uploads/2015/08/ReEnvisioningFinalReport.pdf.

Bishoff, Carolyn, Shannon L. Farrell, and Amy E. Neeser. "Outreach, Collaboration, Collegiality: Evolving Approaches to Library Video Game Services." *Journal of Library Innovation* 6, no. 1 (2015): 92–109. https://conservancy.umn.edu/bitstream/handle/11299/174475/bishoff_farrell_neeser_joli_2015.pdf.

Blackley, J., T. Peltier, and J. Peltier, *Information Security Fundamentals*. Boca Raton, FL: CRC Press, 2004.

Blakiston, Rebecca. *Writing Effectively in Print and on the Web: A Practical Guide for Librarians*. Lanham, MD: Rowman & Littlefield, 2017.

Blended Librarian (blog). Accessed August 9, 2017. http://blendedlibrarian.org.

Blue Ribbon Task Force on Sustainable Digital Preservation and Access. "Sustainable Economics for a Digital Planet: Ensuring Long-Term Access to Digital Information." 2010. http://blueribbontaskforce.sdsc.edu/.

Bluestone, Marissa. "U.S. Publishing Industry's Annual Survey Reveals $28 Billion in Revenue in 2014." Association of American Publishers, June 10, 2015. http://publishers.org/news/us-publishing-industry%E2%80%99s-annual-survey-reveals-28-billion-revenue-2014.

Bobinski, George. *Libraries and Librarianship*. Lanham, MD: Scarecrow Press, Inc., 2007.

———. *Libraries and Librarianship: Sixty Years of Challenge and Change, 1945–2005*. New York: Scarecrow Press, 2007.

Bolt, Nancy. "Libraries from Now On: Imagining the Future of Libraries: ALA Summit on the Future of Libraries—Report to ALA Membership." *ALA Connect*. May 19, 2014. http://connect.ala.org/files/LibrariesFromNowOn_ALASummitOnTheFutureofLibraries_FinalReport.pdf.

Bolorizadeh, A., M. Brannen, R. Gibbs, and T. Mack. "Making Instruction Mobile." *Reference Librarian* 53, no. 4 (2012): 373–83. doi:10.1080/02763877.2012.707488.

"Books and Butchers." Johnson County Library. Last modified August 15, 2013. http://www.jocolibrary.org/newsroom/books-and-butchers.

Booth, Char. *Reflective Teaching, Effective Learning: Instructional Literacy for Library Educators*. Chicago: American Library Association: 2011.

Booth, Char, and Dani Brecher. "Ok, Library: Implications and Opportunities for Google Glass." *College & Research Libraries News* 75, no. 5 (May 2014): 234–39. http://crln.acrl.org/content/75/5/234.full.pdf+html.

Bottorff, David W., Katherine Furlong, and David McCaslin. "Building Management Responsibilities for Access Services." In *Twenty-First Century Access Services*, edited by Michael Krasulski and Trevor Dawes. Chicago: ALA, 2013.

Bourne, Jill. "Finding the Sweet Spot for Libraries in the Digital Age." *Knight Blog*, September 11, 2014. http://www.knightfoundation.org/blogs/knightblog/2014/9/11/finding-sweet-spot-libraries-digital-age/.

Boushey, Heather, and Sarah Jane Glynn. "There Are Significant Business Costs to Replacing Employees." *Center for American Progress*, 2012. https://www.americanprogress.org/issues/economy/reports/2012/11/16/44464/there-are-significant-business-costs-to-replacing-employees/.

Bowker. "Print ISBN Counts, USA Pubdate 2002–2013." Accessed June 30, 2017. http://media.bowker.com/documents/isbn_output_2002_2013.pdf.

———. "Report from Bowker Shows Continuing Growth in Self-publishing." Accessed June 30, 2017. http://www.bowker.com/news/2016/Report-from-Bowker-Shows-Continuing-Growth-in-Self-publishing.html.

Bowker, George C., and Susan L. Star. *Sorting Things Out*. Cambridge, MA: MIT Press, 2000.

Boyd, Danah. "Did Media Literacy Backfire?" *Data & Society: Points*. January 5, 2017. https://points.datasociety.net/did-media-literacy-backfire-7418c084d88d.

Boyd, Donald C. "The Book Women of Kentucky: The WPA Pack Horse Library Project, 1935–1943." *Libraries and the Cultural Record* 42, no. 2 (2007): 111–28.

Boydston, Jeanne M. K., and Joan M. Leysen. "ARL Cataloger Librarian Roles and Responsibilities Now and in the Future." *Cataloging & Classification Quarterly* 52, no. 2 (2014): 229–33.

Bradberry, Travis. "What Makes a Leader?" *Leadership and Management*. LinkedIn, 2015. https://www.linked in.com/pulse/what-makes-leader-dr-travis-bradberry.

Bradburn, Frances Bryant. "Redesigning Our Role while Redesigning Our Libraries." *Knowledge Quest* 42, no. 1 (2013): 52–57.

Bradigan, Pamela S., and Ruey L. Rodman. "Single Service Point: It's All in the Design." *Medical Reference Services Quarterly* 27, no. 4 (2008): 367–78. doi:10.1080/02763860802367755.

Braman, Sandra. *Change of State: Information, Policy and Power.* Cambridge, MA: MIT Press, 2009.

———. "Defining Information Policy." *Journal of Information Policy*, no. 1 (2011): 1–5.

Breeding, Marshall. "Forging Ahead through Times of Major Transitions." *Computers in Libraries* 31, no. 10 (2011): 26–29.

——— "The Many Facets of Managing Electronic Resources." *Computers in Libraries* 24, no. 1 (2004): 25.

———. "The Year of ERM." *Smart Libraries Newsletter* 25, no. 3 (2005): 2.

———. "Technology to Empower Information Organization Control of E-book Lending." *Smart Libraries Newsletter* 33, no. 8 (2013): 3–6.

Bremer, Peter. "Librarian on the Loose: A Roving Reference Desk at a Small Liberal Arts College." *Reference Librarian* 58, no. 1 (2017): 106–10. doi:10.1080/02763877.2016.1199006.

Brendle-Moczuk, Daniel. "Encouraging Students' Lifelong Learning through Graded Information Literacy Assignments." *Reference Services Review* 34, no. 4 (2006): 498–508. doi:10.1108/00907320610716404.

Bronfenbrenner, Urie. *The Ecology of Human Development: Experiments by Nature and Design.* Cambridge, MA: Harvard University Press, 1979.

Brookfield, Stephen. *Becoming a Critically Reflective Teacher*, second edition. San Francisco: Jossey-Bass, 2017.

Brown, Richard D. *Knowledge Is Power: The Diffusion of Information in Early America, 1700–1865.* Oxford: Oxford University Press, 1989.

Brown, Stephanie Willen. "The Reference Interview: Theories and Practice." *Library Philosophy and Practice*, 2008. Accessed October 25, 2015. http://www.webpages.uidaho.edu/~mbolin/willenbrown.htm.

Brownell, Judy. "Meeting the Competency Needs of Global Leaders: A Partnership Approach." *Human Resources Management* 45, no. 3 (Fall 2006): 309–36.

Brunner, Marta, and Jennifer Osorio. "Recruitment, Retention, Diversity, and Professional Development." In Todd Gilman, ed. *Academic Librarianship Today*, 143–59. Lanham, MD: Rowman & Littlefield, 2017.

Bryson, John. *Strategic Planning for Public and Nonprofit Organizations.* San Francisco: Wiley, 2011.

"Building a Communication Plan." American Library Association, 2007. https://www.ala.org/ala/pio/cam paign/prtools/marketing_wkbk.pdf.

Budd, John M. *The Changing Academic Library: Operations, Culture, Environments*, second edition. Chicago: Association of College and Research Libraries, 2012.

Buelens, Marc, and Herman Van den Broeck. "An Analysis of Differences in Work Motivation Between Public and Private Sector Organizations." *Public Administration Review* 67, no. 1 (2007): 65–74.

Bugg, K. "Best Practices for Talent Acquisition in 21st-century Academic Libraries." *Library Leadership & Management, NYC College of Technology at CUNY Academic Works* 29, no. 4 (2015): 1–14.

Bureau of Consumer Protection Center. "The Children's Online Privacy Protection Act of 1998 (COPPA)." 5 U.S.C. 6501–6505. Federal Trade Commission, 2017. http://www.ftc.gov/ogc/coppa1.htm.

Burek Pierce, Jennifer. "Young Adult Sexual and Reproductive Health Information Needs." In *Youth Information-Seeking Behavior II: Context, Theories, Models, and Issues*, edited by Mary K. Chelton and Colleen Cool, 63–91. Lanham, MD: Scarecrow Press, 2007.

Burgess, Richard. "South Regional Library to Give 3-D Printing, Electronic Kits Trial Run over Summer." *Advocate*, May 23, 2014. http://theadvocate.com/news/9184745-123/south-regional-library-to-give.

Burhanna, Kenneth J., Tammy J. Eschedor Voekler, and Julie A. Gedeon. "Virtually the Same: Comparing the Effectiveness of Online Versus In-Person Library Tours." *Public Services Quarterly* 4, no. 4 (2008): 317–38. doi:10.1080/15228950802461616.

Burkhardt, Joanna, Jim Kinnie, and Carina M. Cournoyer. "Information Literacy Successes Compared: Online vs. Face to Face." *Journal of Library Administration,* 48, nos. 3–4 (2008): 379–89.

Burt, Laura. "Vivian Harsh, Adult Education, and the Library's Role as Community Center." *Libraries & the Cultural Record* 44, no. 2 (2009): 234–55.

Burt, Ronald S. "Social Origins of Good Ideas." *American Journal of Sociology* 110, no. 2 (September 2004). http://web.upcomillas.es/personal/rgimeno/doctorado/SOGI.pdf.

Buschman, John. "On the Political Nature of Library Leadership." *Political Librarian* 2, no. 1 (2016): 9.

Bush, Vannevar. "As We May Think." *Atlantic,* July 1, 1945. http://www.theatlantic.com/magazine/archive/1945/07/as-we-may-think/303881/?single_page=true.

Buss, Stephen P. "Do We Still Need Reference in the Age of Google and Wikipedia?" *Reference Librarian* 57, no. 4 (2016): 265–71. doi:10.1080/02763877.2015.1134377.

Calfas, Jennifer. "Employment Discrimination: The Next Frontier for LGBT Community." *USA Today,* July 31, 2015. https://www.usatoday.com/story/news/nation/2015/07/31/employment-discrimination-lgbt-community-next-frontier/29635379/.

Calkins, Kaijsa, and Cassandra Kvenlid. *Embedded Librarians: Moving beyond One-Shot Instruction.* Chicago: Association of College and Research Libraries, 2011.

Canadian Charter of Rights and Freedoms (CCRF). §§ 7–8, Part I of the Constitution Act, 1982. http://laws-lois.justice.gc.ca/eng/const/page-15.html.

Capitol Records, LLC v. ReDigi Inc., 934 F. Supp. 2d 640. SD New York District Court, 2013.

Caplan, Priscilla. "Understanding PREMIS." Library of Congress. 2009. http://www.loc.gov/standards/premis/understanding-premis.pdf.

Cardman, Michael. "How to Classify an Employee Under FSLA." *XPert HR.* http://www.xperthr.com/how-to/how-to-classify-an-employee-under-the-flsa/9341/.

Carpenter, Kenneth E. "Libraries." In *An Extensive Republic: Print, Culture, and Society in the New Nation,* edited by Robert A. Gross and Mary Kelley, 273–86. Chapel Hill: University of North Carolina Press, 2010.

Carter, Toni M. "Assessment and Change Leadership in an Academic Library Department: A Case Study." *Reference Services Review* 42, no. 1 (2014).

Carver, John. *Boards That Make a Difference: A New Design for Leadership in Nonprofit and Public Organizations* Hoboken, NJ: John Wiley & Sons, 2011.

Case, Donald O. *Looking for Information: A Survey of Research on Information Seeking, Needs and Behavior,* third edition. Bingley, UK: Emerald Group Publishing, 2012.

Cassell, Kay Ann, and Uma Hiremath, eds. *Reference and Information Services: An Introduction.* Chicago: Neal-Schuman, 2014.

Cawsey, Tupper, and Gene Deszca. *Toolkit for Organizational Change.* Los Angeles: Sage Publications, 2007.

Cecil, Henry L., and Willard A. Heaps. *School Library Service in the United States: An Interpretive Survey.* New York: H. W. Wilson Co, 1940. Reprinted in Melvin M. Bowie, *Historic Documents of School Libraries,* 175–91. Fayetteville, AR: Hi Willow Research and Publishing, 1986.

Center for Language and Technology, University of Hawaii at Manoa. *Introduction to Personal Learning Networks.* Accessed September 5, 2017. http://clt.manoa.hawaii.edu/projects/pln/.

Center for Research Libraries. "Liblicense: Licensing Digital Content." Model Licenses. Last modified May 3, 2015. http://liblicense.crl.edu/licensing-information/model-license/.

"Century Collections: Calibration of Investment and Collaborative Action." 2012. http://www.arl.org/storage/documents/publications/issue-brief-21st-century-collections-2012.pdf.

Chen,Yu-Hui, and Mary K. Van Ullen. "Helping International Students Succeed Academically through Research Process and Plagiarism Workshops." *College and Research Libraries* 72, no. 3 (2011): 209–35. http://crl.acrl.org/index.php/crl/article/view/16154/17600.

Chicago Public Library, *38th Annual Report, 1909-10.*

———. *42nd Annual Report,* 1913–14.

———. "ChiPubLib Makerspace." Flickr. Accessed July 5, 2017. http://flickr.com/cpl_makerspace.

Chilton, Galadriel. "Using the Scrum Project Management Methodology to Create a Comprehensive Collection Development Framework." Presented at Electronic Resources & Libraries, Austin, TX. April 5, 2016. https://www.slideshare.net/gchilton/erl-2016-using-the-scrum-project-management-methodology-to-create-a-comprehensive-collection-assessment-framework.

Choi, Erik, and Chirag Shah. "User Motivations in Asking Questions in Online Q&A Services." *Journal of the Association for Information Services and Technology* 67, no. 5 (2016): 1182–97. doi:10.1002/asi.23490.

Choi, Youngok, and Edie Rasmussen. "What Is Needed to Educate Future Digital Librarians." *D-Lib Magazine* 12, no. 9 (2006). doi:10.1045/september2006-choi.

Christianson, Elin B. "Special Libraries: Putting Knowledge to Work." *Library Trends* 25, no. 1 (1976): 399–416.

Churchill, Ward. "'Some People Push Back': On the Justice of Roosting Chickens." Accessed June 30, 2017. http://www.kersplebedeb.com/mystuff/s11/churchill.html.

Cialdini, Robert B. *Influence: Science and Practice*, fourth edition. Boston: Allyn & Bacon, 2001.

"CISE Data Management Guidelines." National Science Foundation. Last modified May 15, 2015. https://www.nsf.gov/cise/cise_dmp.jsp.

Ckan Data Management. "Home." Accessed July 11, 2017. https://ckan.org/.

Clark, Kevin, and Ron Smith. "Unleashing the Power of Design Thinking." *Design Management Review* 19, no. 3 (2008): 8–15. doi:10.1111/j.1948-7169.2008.tb00123.x.

Clarke, Rachel Ivy. "Designing Disciplinary Identity: An Analysis of the Term "Design" in Library and Information Science Vocabulary." *Proceedings of the Association for Information Science and Technology* 52, no. 1 (2015): 1–4. doi:10.1002/pra2.2015.145052010074.

———. "It's Not Rocket Library Science: Design Epistemology and American Librarianship." PhD diss., University of Washington Information School, 2016.

———. "Toward a Design Epistemology for Librarianship." *Library Quarterly: Information, Communication, Policy* 88, no. 1 (2018).

Clarke, Rachel Ivy, and Steven Bell. "Transitioning from the MLS to the MLD: Integrating Design Thinking and Philosophy into Library and Information Science Education." In *Re-Envisioning the MLS: Perspectives on the Future of Library and Information Science Education*, edited by L. C. Sarin, J. Percell, P. T. Jaeger, and J. C. Bertot. Bingley, UK: Emerald Group Publishing Limited (forthcoming).

Clarke, Rachel Ivy, Jin Ha Lee, and Katie Mayer. "Design Topics in Graduate Library Education: A Preliminary Investigation." Paper presented at the annual meeting of the Association for Library and Information Science Education conference, Atlanta, Georgia, January 17–20, 2017.

Cloonan, Michele Valerie. "Conservation and Preservation of Library and Archival Materials." In *Encyclopedia of Library and Information Sciences*, edited by Marcia J. Bates and Mary Niles Maack, 1250–68. Boca Raton: CRC Press, 2010.

Cole, Charles. *Information Need: A Theory Connecting Information Search to Knowledge Formation*. Medford, NJ: Information Today, Inc, 2012.

Columbia Law School. "Section 108 Reform." Last modified December 11, 2013. http://web.law.columbia.edu/kernochan/symposia/section-108-reform.

Common Core State Standards. "Common Core State Standards Initiative." National Governors Association Center for Best Practices and Council of Chief State School Officers. Last Modified 2017. http://www.corestandards.org/.

"Computers in Libraries: Chad Mairn." *Info Today*. Accessed January 15, 2017. http://computersinlibraries.infotoday.com/Speakers/Chad-Mairn.aspx.

Confederation of Open Access Repositories. May 2017. https://www.coar-repositories.org/activities/advocacy-leadership/aligning-repository-networks-across-regions/aligning-repository-networks-international-accord/.

Conlin, Jennifer. "The New Frontier: Libraries with No Limits." *Michigan Alumnus*, 2015. Last updated 2017. http://alumni.umich.edu/alumnus/the-new-frontier-libraries-with-no-limits/.

Connaway, Lynn Silipigni, and Marie L. Radford. *Basic Research Methods in Library and Information Science*, sixth edition. Westport, CT: Libraries Unlimited, 2017.

Connaway, Lynn Silipigni, and Timothy J. Dickey. "Digital Information Seeker: Report of Findings from Selected OCLC, RIN and JISC User Behaviour Projects." 2010. http://www.jisc.ac.uk/media/documents/publications/reports/2010/digitalinformationseekerreport.pdf.

Connelly-Brown, Maryska, Kim Mears, and Melissa E. Johnson. "Reference for the Remote User through Embedded Librarianship." *Reference Librarian* 57, no. 1 (2016): 165–81. doi:10.1080 /02763877.2015.1131658.

Consultative Committee for Space Data Systems. "Reference Model for an Open Archival Information System (OAIS). CCSDS 650.0-B-1. Blue Book." 2002. https://siarchives.si.edu/sites/default/files/pdfs/650x0b1.PDF.

Consultative Committee for Space Data Systems. "Audit and Certification of Trustworthy Digital Repositories. CCSDS 652.0-M-1. Magenta Book." 2011. https://public.ccsds.org/pubs/652x0m1.pdf.

Copyright Office—Library of Congress. "Exemption to Prohibition on Circumvention of Copyright Protection Systems for Access Control Technologies." *Federal Register* 80, no. 208 (October 28, 2015): 65944–64. https://www.copyright.gov/fedreg/2015/80fr65944.pdf.

Cook, Jean Marie. "A Library Credit Course and Student Success Rates: A Longitudinal Study." *College & Research Libraries* 75 (May 2014): 272–83. http://crl.acrl.org/content/early/2012/12/19/crl12-424.full.pdf+html.

Cooper, Alan, Christopher Noessel, Dave Cronin, and Robert Reimann. *About Face: The Essentials of Interaction Design*, fourth ed. Hoboken, NJ: Wiley, 2014.

Cooper, Danielle, and Roger C. Schonfeld. "Rethinking Liaison Programs for the Humanities." Issue Brief. *Ithaka S+R*. July 26, 2017. doi:https://doi.org/10.18665/sr.304124.

Cope, Sophia, Amul Kalia, Seth Schoen, and Adam Schwartz. "Digital Privacy at the U.S. Border: Protecting the Data on your Devices and in the Cloud." Electronic Frontier Foundation. Last updated March 10, 2017. https://www.eff.org/files/2017/03/10/digital-privacy-border-2017-guide3.10.17.pdf.

Copyright Advisory Office of Columbia University. "Permissions." Last modified August 31, 2014. http://copyright.columbia.edu/copyright/permissions/.

Copyright Alliance. "Second Circuit Decision on *Authors Guild v. HathiTrust*." Last modified August 4, 2014. http://www.copyrightalliance.org/2014/06/second_circuit_decision_authors_guild_v_hathitrust#.

Cornell Law School, Legal Information Institute. "First Amendment." Accessed June 17, 2017. https://www.law.cornell.edu/constitution/first_amendment.

———. "Olmstead v. the United States." Accessed June 17, 2017. https://www.law.cornell.edu/supremecourt/text/277/438.

Cotton, Anthony. "Fired Colorado Professors Loses Supreme Court Appeal." *Denver Post*, 2016. http://www.denverpost.com/2012/09/10/fired-colorado-professor-ward-churchill-loses-supreme-court-appeal/.

Coulbourne, George. "DPOE Handout." http://www.digitalpreservation.gov/education/documents/DPOE_handout.pdf.

Council on Library and Information Resources. "CLIR Postdoctoral Fellowship Program." Last updated 2017. http://www.clir.org/fellowships/postdoc.

———. *Participatory Design in Academic Libraries: Methods, Findings, and Implementations*. Washington, DC: Council on Library and Information Resources, 2012. http://www.clir.org/pubs/reports/pub155/pub155.pdf.

Counting Opinions, 2017. http://www.countingopinions.com.

Couros, George. "Characteristics of a Change Agent." The Principal of Change. Last updated January 26, 2013. http://georgecouros.ca/blog/archives/3615.

Creative Commons. "CC0." Last modified July 19, 2014. http://creativecommons.org/about/cc0.

———. "About—Creative Commons." Last modified July 19, 2014. http://creativecommons.org/about.

———. "About the Licenses." Last modified July 19, 2014. http://creativecommons.org/licenses.

———. "Public Domain Mark." Last modified September 7, 2014. http://creativecommons.org/about/pdm.

Cross, Nigel. *Design Thinking*. Oxford, UK: Berg, 2011.

Cross, Terry, B. Bazron, K. Dennis, and M. Isaacs. *Toward a Culturally Competent System of Care*. Vol. 1. Washington, DC: Georgetown University, 1989.

Crozier, Michael, and Erhard Friedberg. *Actors and Systems: The Politics of Collective Action*. Translated by Arthur Goldhammer. Chicago: University of Chicago Press, 1980.

Curtis, Elizabeth A., Jan de Vries, and Fintan K. Sheerin. "Developing Leadership in Nursing: Exploring Core Factors." *British Journal of Nursing* 20, no. 5 (2011): 306.

"Customers." Digital Commons. https://www.bepress.com/products/digital-commons/why-digital-commons/customers/.

Daigle, Ben. "Getting to Know You: Discovering User Behaviors and Their Implications for Service Design." *Public Services Quarterly* 9, no. 4 (2013): 326–32. doi:10.1080/15228959.2013.842416.

Dana, John Cotton. "Chapter IV, General Policy of the Library." *A Library Primer*. https://en.wikisource.org/wiki/A_Library_Primer_(1899)/Chapter_IV.

Data Management Planning Tool. "Home." Accessed July 11, 2017. https://dmptool.org.

Daugherty, Alice L., and Michael F. Russo, eds. *Embedded Librarianship: What Every Academic Librarian Should Know*. Santa Barbara, CA: Libraries Unlimited, 2013.

Davis, Jeffrey T. *The Collection All Around: Sharing Our Cities, Towns and Natural Places*. Chicago: ALA editions, 2017.

Davis, R. "Git and GitHub for Librarians." *Behavioral & Social Sciences Librarian* 34, no. 3 (2015): 159–64. http://academicworks.cuny.edu/cgi/viewcontent.cgi?article=1034&context=jj_pubs. Accessed July 18, 2017.

Dawes, Trevor A., and Michael J. Krasulski. "Conclusion." In *Twenty-First Century Access Services*, 243–46. Chicago: Association of College and Research Libraries, 2013.

Dawes, Trevor, Kimberly Burke Sweetman, and Catherine Von Elm. *Access Services: SPEC Kit 290*. Washington, DC: Association of Research Libraries, 2005.

"DCC Curation Life Cycle Model." Digital Curation Centre. http://www.dcc.ac.uk/resources/curation-life-cycle-model.

de la Pena McCook, Kathleen, and Peggy Barber. "Public Policy as a Factor Influencing Adult Lifelong Learning, Adult Literacy and Public Libraries." *Reference & User Services Quarterly* 42, no. 1 (2002): 66–75.

Defa, Dennis R. "Recruitment of Employees in Academic Libraries: Advice from the HR Perspective." *Library Leadership & Management* 26, no. 3 (2012): 1–10.

Dempsey, Lorcan, Constance Malpas, and Brian Lavoie. "Collection Directions: The Evolution of Library Collections and Collecting." *Portal: Libraries and the Academy* 14, no. 3 (2014): 393–423. http://muse.jhu.edu/journals/portal_libraries_and_the_academy/v014/14.3.dempsey.html.

Department of Commerce Internet Policy Task Force. "Copyright Policy, Creativity and Innovation in the Digital Economy." The Department of Commerce Internet Task Force. Last modified July 2013. http://www.uspto.gov/news/publications/copyrightgreenpaper.pdf.

Department of Health and Human Services. "Enterprise Performance Lifecycle Framework—Practices Guide—Contingency Plan." U.S. Department of Health and Human Services. Accessed May 3, 2017. https://www.hhs.gov/ocio/eplc/EPLC%20Archive%20Documents/36-Contingency-Disaster%20Recovery%20Plan/eplc_contingency_plan_practices_guide.pdf.

Department of Homeland Security. "I-9, Employment Eligibility Verification." U.S. Citizenship and Immigration Services. https://www.uscis.gov/i-9.

Dervin, Brenda. "What Methodology Does to Theory: Sense-Making Methodology as Exemplar." In *Theories of Information Behavior*, edited by Karen E. Fisher, Sandra Erdelez, and Lynne E. F. McKechnie, 25–30. Medford, NJ: Information Today, 2005.

Design Thinking for Libraries: A Toolkit for Patron-Centered Design. Accessed August 9, 2017. http://designthinkingforlibraries.com.

Designing Better Libraries. http://dbl.lishost.org.

Deskins, Liz. "Inquiry Studies: Needed Skills." *School Library Monthly* 28, no. 5 (February 2012): 20–23. http://transferfoster.pbworks.com/w/file/fetch/97619920/Inquiry%20Studies—Needed%20Skills.pdf.

Dethloff, Nora, and Paul Sharpe. "Access Services and the Success of the Academic Library." In *Twenty-First Century Access Services*, edited by Michael Krasulski and Trevor Dawes, 69–89. Chicago: Association of College and Research Libraries, 2013.

Dewey, John. "The School and the Life of the Child." *School and Society: Being Three Lectures.* Chicago: University of Chicago Press, 1900. Accessed July 5, 2017. https://books.google.com/books?id=5c5wDDT NHAIC.

Dewey, Melvil. "Why a Library Does or Does Not Succeed." In *Library Notes: Improved Methods and Labor-Savers for Librarians, Readers and Writers*, 47. Boston: Library Bureau, 1887.

Dickerson, Madelynn. "Beta Spaces as a Model for Reconstructing Reference Services in Libraries." In *In the Library with the Lead Pipe*, May 18, 2016. Accessed January 10, 2017. http://inthelibrarywiththeleadpipe.org/2016/reference-as-beta-space.

Digital Law Online. "*CONTU Guidelines on Photocopying under Interlibrary Loan Arrangements.* CONTU Final Report. Last updated September 28, 2003. http://digital-law-online.info/CONTU/contu24.html.

Directory of Open Access Journals. "Home." 2014. http://www.doaj.org.

Disher, Wayne. "Managing Collections." In *Information Services Today: An Introduction*, edited by Sandra Hirsh, 242–29. Lanham, MD: Rowman & Littlefield, 2015.

"Dissemination and Sharing of Research Results." National Science Foundation. Accessed May 13, 2017. https://www.nsf.gov/bfa/dias/policy/dmp.jsp.

DMPOnline. "Home." Accessed July 11, 2017. https://dmponline.dcc.ac.uk.

Do Space. "Technology for Everyone: Free for Everyone." Accessed January 10, 2017. http://www.dospace.org/.

Doe v. Gonzales. 546 U.S. 1301 (2005). http://www.supremecourt.gov/opinions/05pdf/05a295.pdf.

"Dokk1 English." Dokk1. Accessed May 31, 2017. https://dokk1.dk/english.

Donald W. Reynolds. Journalism Institute. https://www.rjionline.org/events/dodging-the-memory-hole-2017.

Dority, G. Kim. *Rethinking Information Work: A Career Guide for Librarians and Other Information Professionals*, second edition. Santa Barbara, CA: Libraries Unlimited, 2016.

Dority, K. "Technologies Librarians Need to Know." *LibGig.* June 20. https://www.libgig.com/technologies-librarians-need-know/.

Doss, Daniel, Russ Henley, Balakrishna Gokaraju, David McElreath, Hilliard Lackey, Qiuqi Hong, and Lauren Miller. "Assessing Domestic vs. International Student Perceptions and Attitudes of Plagiarism." *Journal of International Students* 6, no. 2 (2016): 542–65.

Dotson, Kaye B., and Jami L. Jones. "Librarians and Leadership: The Change We Seek." *School Libraries Worldwide* 17, no. 2 (2011): 78.

Dougherty, Dale, and Ariane Conrad. *Free to Make: How the Maker Movement Is Changing Our Schools, Our Jobs, and Our Minds.* Berkeley, CA: North Atlantic Books, 2016.

Dougherty, Dale. "We Are Makers." Video file, 11:47. TED. January 2011. Accessed July 5, 2017. http://www.ted.com/talks/dale_dougherty_we_are_makers.

Drucker, Peter F. *The Effective Executive: The Definitive Guide to Getting the Right Things Done.* New York: Harper Collins, 2006.

———. "Your Leadership Is Unique." *Leadership* 17, no. 4 (1996): 54.

Dublin Core Metadata. "Metadata Basics." DCMI, 2017. http://dublincore.org/metadata-basics/.

Ebsco. "The ROI of Corporate Libraries & Research Solutions—White Paper." 2016. https://help.ebsco.com/interfaces/EBSCO_Guides/General_Product_FAQs/ROI_of_Corporate_Libraries_Research_Solutions.

Edmondson, Ray. "Chapter 5: Preservation." In *Audiovisual Archiving: Philosophy and Principles.* Geneva: UNESCO, 2004. http://unesdoc.unesco.org/images/0013/001364/136477e.pdf.

Edwards, Paul N. *A Vast Machine: Computer Models, Climate Data, and the Politics of Global Warming.* Cambridge, MA: MIT Press, 2010.

EDUCAUSE (Association), and New Media Consortium. *The NMC Horizon Report: 2014, Higher Education Edition.* Accessed August 7, 2017. https://www.nmc.org/publication/nmc-horizon-report-2014-higher-education-edition/.

Electronic Frontier Foundation. "Authors Guild v. Google, Part II: Fair Use Proceedings." Accessed March 26, 2017. https://www.eff.org/cases/authors-guild-v-google-part-ii-fair-use-proceedings.

——— "How the NSA's Domestic Spying Program Works." https://www.eff.org/nsa-spying/how-it-works.

Ellis, Lisa A. ed. *Teaching Reference Today: New Directions, Novel Approaches.* Lanham, MD: Rowman & Littlefield, 2016.

Ellis. Robert Lee. *Continuing Education for Adults through the American Public Library, 1833–1864*. Chicago: American Library Association, 1966.

Elmborg, James. "Critical Information Literacy: Implications for Instructional Practice." *The Journal of Academic Librarianship* 32, no. 2 (2006): 192–99. doi:10.1016/j.calib.2005.12.004.

———. "Literacies, Narratives, and Adult Learning and Libraries." *New Directions for Adult and Continuing Education*, no. 127 (2010): 67–76. doi:10.1002/ace.382.

———. "Teaching at the Desk: Toward a Reference Pedagogy." *Portal: Libraries and the Academy* 2, no. 3 (2002): 455–64.

Elrod, Edwin M., and Martha M. Smith. "Information Ethics." In *Encyclopedia of Science, Technology, and Ethics*. Detroit: Macmillan Reference USA, 2005.

Elsweiler, David, Max L. Wilson, and Brian K. Lund. "Understanding Casual-Leisure Information Behavior." In *New Directions in Information Behavior*, edited by Amanda Spink and Jannica Heinström, 211–41. Bingley, UK: Emerald Group Publishing, 2011.

"English Language Arts Standards." *Common Core State Standards Initiative*. Last modified September 12, 2014. http://www.corestandards.org/ELA-Literacy/.

Ennis, Matt. "Pallante Resignation May Indicate New Approach at Copyright Office." *Library Journal*. Last modified November 1, 2016. http://lj.libraryjournal.com/2016/11/industry-news/pallante-resignation-may-indicate-new-approach-at-copyright-office/.

Evans, G. Edward, and Camila A. Alire. *Management Basics for Information Professionals*. Chicago: American Library Association, 2013.

Evans, Philip B., and Thomas S. Wurster. "Strategy and the New Economics of Information." *Harvard Business Review* 75, no. 5 (1996): 70–82.

Exemption to Prohibition on Circumvention of Copyright Protection Systems for Access Control Technologies, 77 Fed. Reg. 65260. October 26, 2012.

Exemption to Prohibition on Circumvention of Copyright Protection Systems for Access Control Technologies, *Federal Register* 80 (October 28, 2015). https://www.copyright.gov/fedreg/2015/80fr65944.pdf.

Fair Credit Reporting Act (FCRA), 15 U.S.C. § 1681 et seq. Accessed 2017. http://www.ftc.gov/os/statutes/031224fcra.pdf.

"The Fall and Rise of Strategic Planning." *Harvard Business Review*. Last modified 1994: 1. https://hbr.org/1994/01/the-fall-and-rise-of-strategic-planning.

Family Educational Rights and Privacy Act (FERPA). 20 U.S.C. § 1232g. Accessed 2017. http://www.gpo.gov/fdsys/pkg/USCODE-2012-title20/pdf/USCODE-2012-title20-chap31-subchapIII-part4-sec1232g.pdf.

Fay, Bringham. "MIT Libraries & MIT MakerWorkshop Launch Equipment to Go." *MITNews*. Last modified March 9, 2017. http://news.mit.edu/2017/mit-libraries-and-mit-makerworkshop-launch-equipment-to-go-0309.

Federal Discrimination Laws in the Workplace: The Basics. *FindLaw*, 2017. http://employment.findlaw.com/employment-discrimination/federal-laws-prohibiting-job-discrimination-questions-and.html.

Federal Information Security Management Act. "Title III of the E-Government Act, Public Law." 107–347. http://csrc.nist.gov/drivers/documents/FISMA-final.pdf.

Federer, Lisa. "The Librarian as Research Informationist: A Case Study." *Journal of the Medical Library Association* 101, no. 4 (2013): 298–302.

Ferguson, Jennifer. "Additional Degree Required? Advanced Subject Knowledge and Academic Librarianship." *Portal: Libraries and the Academy* 16, no. 4 (2016): 721–36.

Fields, Anne M. "Ill-Structured Problems and the Reference Consultation: The Librarian's Role in Developing Student Expertise." *Reference Services Review* 34, no. 3 (2006): 405–20.

Fields, Erin. "A Unique Twitter Use for Reference Services." *Library Hi Tech News* 27, no. 6 (2010): 14–15. doi:10.1108/07419051011095863.

Fineman, Jonathan. "The Inevitable Demise of the Implied Employment Contract." *Berkeley Journal of Employment and Labor Law* 29, no. 2 (2008): 345. doi:http://dx.doi.org/doi:10.15779/Z38K63D.

Fishbein, Martin, and Icek Ajzen. *Belief, Attitude, Intention, and Behavior: An Introduction to Theory and Research*. Reading, MA: Addison-Wesley, 1975.

Fisher, Erin. "Makerspaces Move into Academic Libraries." *ACRL TechConnect Blog*, 2012. http://acrl.ala.org/techconnect/?p=2340.

Fister, Barbara. "Smoke and Mirrors: Finding Order in a Chaotic World." *Research Strategies* 20, no. 3 (2005): 99–107. http://homepages.gac.edu/~fister/WILU2005.html.

———. "Critical Assets: Academic Libraries, a View from the Administration Building." *Library Journal*, May 29, 2010. http://lj.libraryjournal.com/2010/05/academic-libraries/critical-assets-academic-libraries-a-view-from-the-administration-building/#.

Flaherty, Kim. "How Channels, Devices, and Touchpoints Impact the Customer Journey." *NN/G Nielsen Norman Group*. December 4, 2016. https://www.nngroup.com/articles/channels-devices-touchpoints/.

Fleming, Laura. "Worlds of Making @ NMHS." *Worlds of Learning*. Last modified November 23, 2013. http://worlds-of-learning.com/2013/11/26/worlds-of-making-nmhs-3/.

Fontichiaro, Kristin. "A Charter for Your School Makerspace?" *Active Learning* (blog), September 4, 2014. http://www.fontichiaro.com/activelearning/2014/09/04/a-charter-for-your-school-makerspace/.

———. "Reflections on North Quad MakerFest. *Active Learning* (blog), December 18, 2013. http://fontichiaro.com/activelearning/2013/12/18/reflections-on-north-quad-makerfest/.

Forbes, Carrie, and Peggy Keeran. "Reference, Instruction, and Outreach: Current Methods and Models." In *Academic Librarianship Today*, edited by Todd Gilman, 85–100. Lanham, MD: Rowman & Littlefield, 2017.

Foreign Intelligence Surveillance Act (FISA). 50 U.S.C. §§ 1801–1811 (1978). http://www.gpo.gov/fdsys/pkg/STATUTE-92/pdf/STATUTE-92-Pg1783.pdf.

Fourie, Dennis. K., and Nancy E. Loe. *Libraries in the Information Age: An Introduction and Career Exploration*, second edition. Santa Barbara, CA: ABC-CLIO, 2009.

Fox, Robert E. Jr., and Bruce L. Keisling. "Build Your Program by Building Your Team: Inclusively Transforming Services, Staffing and Spaces." *Journal of Library Administration* 56, no. 5 (2016): 526–39.

"Framework for Information Literacy for Higher Education." Association of College & Research Libraries. Last modified January 11, 2016. http://www.ala.org/acrl/standards/ilframework.

Franklin, Benjamin. *The Autobiography of Benjamin Franklin*. Charlottesville: University of Virginia Library, 1995.

Freedman, Lawrence. *Strategy: A History*. New York: Oxford, 2013.

Freedom of Information Act of 1967. Pub. L. 89-487, 80 Stat. 250, 1967. http://www.foia.gov/.

Friedlander, Amy, and Deanna Marcum. "Keepers of the Crumbling Culture: What Digital Preservation Can Learn from Library History." *D-Lib Magazine* 9, no. 5 (May 2003). http://www.dlib.org/dlib/may03/friedlander/05friedlander.html.

Fry, Richard. "Millennials Surpass Gen Xers as the Largest Generation in the U. S. Labor Force." Pew Research Center, 2015.

Fung, Brian. "Your Facebook Privacy Settings Are About to Change. Again." *Washington Post*, April 8, 2014. http://www.washingtonpost.com/blogs/the-switch/wp/2014/04/08/your-facebook-privacy-settings-are-about-to-change-again/.

Gaebler, Ted, and David Osborne. *Reinventing Government*. New York: Plume, 1993.

Gagné, Marylène, and Edward L. Deci. "Self Determination Theory and Work Motivation." *Journal of Organizational Behavior* 26, no. 4 (2005): 331–62.

Galyani Moghaddam, Golnessa, and Mostafa Moballeghi. "Total Quality Management in Library and information Sectors." *Electronic Library* 26, no. 6 (2008): 912–22.

Garcia, June, and Sandra Nelson. *2007 Public Library Service Responses*. Public Library Association, 2007. http://ryepubliclibrary.org/wp content/uploads/2012/05/ALAserviceresponses.pdf.

Gardner, David P, and the United States National Commission on Excellence in Education. *A Nation at Risk: The Imperative for Educational Reform: A Report to the Nation and the Secretary of Education*. Washington, DC: Government Printing Office, 1983. http://www.eric.ed.gov/contentdelivery/servlet/ERICServlet?accno=ED226006.

Garmer, Amy K. *Libraries in the Exponential Age: Moving from the Edge of Innovation to the Center of Community*. The Aspen Institute, 2016. http://csreports.aspeninstitute.org/documents/Libraries_Exponential_Age.pdf.

———. *Rising to the Challenge: Re-Imagining America's Public Libraries*. Washington, DC: Aspen Institute, 2014. http://d3n8a8pro7vhmx.cloudfront.net/themes/5660b272ebad645c44000001/attachments/original/1452193779/AspenLibrariesReport.pdf?1452193779.

Garrett, Jesse James. *The Elements of User Experience: User-Centered Design for the Web and Beyond*. Berkeley, CA: New Riders, 2011.

Garrett, John, and Donald Waters. *Preserving Digital Information: Report of the Task Force on Archiving of Digital Information*. Washington, DC: CLIR, 1996. http://www.oclc.org/content/dam/research/activities/digpresstudy/final-report.pdf.

Garrison, Dee. *Apostles of Culture: The Public Librarian and American Society, 1876–1920*. Madison: University of Wisconsin Press, 2003.

Gebolys, Zdzislaw, and Jacek Tomaszczyk. *Library Code of Ethics Worldwide*. Berlin: Simon Verlag fur Bibliothekswissen, 2011.

Gerolimos, Michalis, Afrodite Malliari, and Pavlos Iakovidis. "Skills in the Market: An Analysis of Skills and Qualifications for American Librarians." *Library Review* 64, nos. 1–2 (2015): 21–35. doi:10.1108/LR-06-2014-0063.

Gilman, Todd, ed. *Academic Librarianship Today*. Lanham, MD: Rowman & Littlefield, 2017.

Gilman, Todd, and Thea Lindquist. "Academic/Research Librarians with Subject Doctorates: Experiences and Perceptions, 1965–2006." *Portal: Libraries and the Academy* 10, no. 4 (2010): 399–412. http://muse.jhu.edu/article/398802.

Givens, Cherie. *Information Privacy Fundamentals for Librarians and Information Professionals*. Lanham, MD: Rowman & Littlefield, 2014.

Gleason, Eliza Atkins. *The Southern Negro and the Public Library: A Study of the Government and Administration of Public Library Service to Negroes in the South*. Chicago: University of Chicago Press, 1941.

Glenn, Jerome C. "Introduction to the Futures Research Methods Series." In *The Millennium Project Futures Research Methodology Version 3.0*, edited by Jerome C. Glenn and Theodore J. Gordon. http://www.millennium-project.org/millennium/FRM-V3.html.

Goel, Vindu. "Facebook Tinkers with Users' Emotions in News Feed Experiment, Stirring Outcry." *New York Times*. June 29, 2014. https://www.nytimes.com/2014/06/30/technology/facebook-tinkers-with-users-emotions-in-news-feed-experiment-stirring-outcry.html.

Gopen, George, and Judith Swan. "The Science of Scientific Writing." *American Scientist*, 1990. http://www.americanscientist.org/issues/pub/the-science-of-scientific-writing/99999.

Gorman, Michael. *Our Singular Strengths*. Chicago: ALA Editions, 1998.

"Governments Should Improve Access to Publicly Funded Research, Finds OECD Report." Organisation for Economic Co-operation and Development (OECD), 2014. http://www.oecd.org/general/governmentsshouldimproveaccesstopubliclyfundedresearchfindsoecdreport.htm.

Gramm-Leach-Bliley Act, Pub. L. 106-102, 113 Stat. 1338. Accessed 2017. http://business.ftc.gov/privacy-and-security/gramm-leach-bliley-act.

Granovetter, Mark. "The Strength of Weak Ties." *American Journal of Sociology* 78, no. 6 (1973): 1360–80.

Grassian, Ester, and Joan R. Kaplowitz. *Learning to Lead and Manage Information Literacy Instruction*. New York: Neal-Schuman, 2005.

Gray, Jamie M. *Becoming a Powerhouse Librarian: How to Get Things Done Right the First Time*. Lanham, MD: Rowman & Littlefield, 2017.

Graybill, Jolie O., Maria Taesil Hudson Carpenter, Jerome Offord, Mary Piorun, and Gary Shaffer. "Employee Onboarding: Identification of Best Practices in ACRL Libraries." *Library Management* 34, no. 3 (2013): 200–218. doi:10.1108/01435121311310897.

Green, Samuel Swett. "Personal Relations between Librarians and Readers." *Library Journal* 1, no. 1 (1876): 74–81.

Greyson, Devon. "Evolution of Information Practices over Time." *Proceedings of the Association for Information Science and Technology* 53, no. 1 (2016): article 53.

Greyson, Devon, Soleil Surette, Liz Dennett, and Trish Chatterley. "'You're Just One of the Group When You're Embedded': Report from a Mixed-Method Investigation of the Research-Embedded Health Librarian Experience." *Journal of the Medical Library Association* 101, no. 4 (2013): 287–97.

Grimmer, Jordan Lydia. "Leadership and Team Building Factors That Contribute to the Success of Archives and Records Management Institutions." Master's thesis, West Virginia University, 2014. http://cedar.wwu.edu/wwuet/336/.

Griswold v. Connecticut. 381 U.S. 479 1965. http://www.pbs.org/wnet/supremecourt/rights/landmark_griswold.html.

Groszins, Dean, and Leon Jackson. "Colleges and Print Culture." In *An Extensive Republic: Print, Culture, and Society in the New Nation*, edited by Robert A. Gross and Mary Kelley, 318–32. Chapel Hill: University of North Carolina Press, 2010.

Guedon, Jean-Claude. "Open Access: Toward the Internet of the Mind." *Open Society Foundations*, February 2017. http://www.budapestopenaccessinitiative.org/boai15/Untitleddocument.docx.

Guterman, Jimmy. "How to Become a Better Manager . . . By Thinking Like a Designer." *MIT Sloan Management Review* 50, no. 4 (2009): 39–42.

Gutierrez, Kris, Mimi Ito, Sonia Livingstone, et al. *Connected Learning: An Agenda for Research and Design*. Irvine, CA: Digital Media and Learning Research Hub. http://dmlhub.net/sites/default/files/Connected Learning_report.pdf.

Haas, Martine, and Mark Mortensen. "The Secrets of Great Teamwork." *Harvard Business Review*, June 2016. https://hbr.org/2016/06/the-secrets-of-great-teamwork.

Hajjem, Chawki, Stevan Harnad, and Yves Gingras. "Ten-year Cross-disciplinary Comparison of the Growth of Open Access and How It Increases Research Citation Impact." *Bulletin of the IEEE Computer Society Technical Committee on Data Engineering* (2005). http://arxiv.org/ftp/cs/papers/0606/0606079.pdf.

Hakim, Cliff. *We Are All Self-Employed: How to Take Control of Your Career*. San Francisco: Berrett-Koehler, 2003.

Halvorson, Kristina, and Melissa Rach. *Content Strategy for the Web*, second edition. Berkeley, CA: New Riders, 2012.

Hammergren, T. *Data Warehousing for Dummies*, second edition. Hoboken, NJ: John Wiley & Sons, 2009.

Han, Myung-Ja, and Patricia Hswe. "The Evolving Role of the Metadata Librarian." *Library Resources and Technical Services* 54, no. 3 (2010): 129–41.

Hanna, Holly Reisem. "The Best Career Websites for Women." *Work at Home Woman*, May 7, 2014. http://www.theworkathomewoman.com/career-websites-women/.

Hansen, Mary Anne, Jakob Harnest, Virginia Steel, Joan Ellen Stein, and Pat Weaver-Myers. "A Question and Answer Forum on the Origin, Evolution, and Future of Access Services." *Journal of Access Services* 1, no. 1 (2002): 5–24.

Hargittai, Eszter. "Second-Level Digital Divide: Differences in People's Online Skills." *First Monday* 7, no. 4 (2002). doi:10.5210/fm.v7i4.942.

Hart Research Associates. *Attitudes Toward Re-envisioning the UC Berkeley Library: An Online Survey of the UC Campus Community*. July 2012. http://www.lib.berkeley.edu/AboutLibrary/Hart_Survey_Report_Re-Envisioning_UC_Berkeley_Library.pdf.

Hart Research Associates. *It Takes More Than a Major: Employer Priorities for College Learning and Student Success: A National Survey of Business and Non Profit Leaders*. Washington DC: American Association of Colleges and Universities, 2013.

Hartsell-Gundy, Arianne, Laura Braunstein, and Liorah Golomb. *Digital Humanities in the Library: Challenges and Opportunities for Subject Specialists*. Chicago: Association of College and Research Libraries, 2015.

Harvard University. "Harvard Faculty Advisory Council Memorandum on Journal Pricing." 2012. http://isites.harvard.edu/icb/icb.do?keyword=k77982&tabgroupid=icb.tabgroup143448.

Harvard University Library Office of Scholarly Communication. "Open Access Policies." 2014. https://osc.hul.harvard.edu/policies.

Hawthorne, Pat. "Succession Planning and Management: A Key Leadership Responsibility Emerges." *Texas Library Journal* (Spring 2011): 8–12.

Haycock, Ken. "Advocacy and Influences." Ken Haycock and Associates Organizational Development, December 27, 2011. http://kenhaycock.com/advocacy-and-influence/.

Head, Alison J., M. Van Hoeck, J. Eschler, and S. Fullerton. "What Information Competencies Matter in Today's Workplace?" *Library and Information Research* 37, no. 114 (May 2013): 75–104. http://www.lirg journal.org.uk/lir/ojs/index.php/lir/article/view/557/593.

Healey, Paul D. "Go and Tell the World: Charles R. McCarthy and the Evolution of the Legislative Reference Movement, 1901–1917." *Law Library Journal* 99, no. 1 (1997): 33–53. http://www.aallnet.org/main-menu/ Publications/llj/LLJ-Archives/Vol-99/pub_llj_v99n01/2007-02.pdf.

Held, Virginia. "The Ethics of Care." In *The Oxford Handbook of Ethical Theory,* edited by David Copp. New York: Oxford University Press, 2009. Accessed August 1, 2017. doi:10.1093/oxfordhb/9780195325911.003.0020.

Henricks, Susan A., and Genevieve M. Henricks-Lepp. "Desired Characteristics of Management and Leadership for Public Library Directors as Expressed in Job Advertisements." *Journal of Library Administration* 54, no. 4 (2014): 277–90.

Heritage Preservation and Institute of Museum and Library Services. *A Public at Risk: The Heritage Health Index Report on the State of America's Collections.* Heritage Preservation, Inc., 2005. http://www.conser vation-us.org/docs/default-source/hhi/hhifull.pdf.

Hernon, Peter. "Reflections on Library Leadership." *Library Leadership & Management* 31, no. 4 (2017).

Hernon, Peter, Ellen Altman, and Robert E. Dugan. *Assessing Service Quality: Satisfying the Expectations of Library Customers,* third edition. Chicago: American Library Association, 2015.

Herring, Cedric. "Does Diversity Pay? Race, Gender and the Business Case for Diversity." *American Sociological Review* 74, no. 2 (April 2009).

Hey, T., and J. Hey. "e-Science and Its Implications for the Library Community." *Library Hi Tech* 24, no. 4 (2006): 515–28.

Hill, Sherika. *Diversity Websites to Increase Racial/Ethnic Representation.* MCH Training, October, 2009. http://66.165.155.81/email/MCHtrainfund/documents/2009.12weblist.pdf.

Hirtle, Peter B. "Copyright Term and the Public Domain in the United States." Cornell Copyright Information Center. Last modified January 3, 2014. https://copyright.cornell.edu/resources/publicdomain.cfm.

Hirsh, S. "The Transformative Information Landscape: What It Means to Be an Information Professional Today." In *Information Services Today: An Introduction,* edited by Sandra Hirsh, 3–9. Lanham, MD: Rowman & Littlefield, 2015.

Hoffman, Debra, and Amy Wallace. "Intentional Informationists: Re-envisioning Information Literacy and Re-designing Instructional Programs around Faculty Librarians' Strength as Campus Connectors, Information Professionals, and Course Designers." *Journal of Academic Librarianship* 39, no. 6 (2013): 546–51. doi:10.1016/j.acalib.2013.06.004.

Hoffman, Reid, and Ben Casnocha. *The Start-Up of You: Adapt to the Future, Invest in Yourself, and Transform Your Career.* New York: Crown Business, 2012.

Hofuboti. "Libraries Are for Everyone" (blog). February 2017. https://hafuboti.com/2017 /02/02/libraries -are-for-everyone/.

Holley, Robert P. "Providing LIS Students with Management Skills." *Journal of Library Administration* 56 (2016): 638–46.

Holmquist, J. "Global Learning Networks." In *Information Services Today: An Introduction,* edited by S. Hirsh, 374–80. Lanham, MD: Rowman & Littlefield, 2014.

"Home." The Section 8 Study Group. Last modified February 7, 2014. http://www.section108.gov.

Honma, T. "Trippin' Over the Color Line: The Invisibility of Race in Library and Information Studies." *InterActions: UCLA Journal of Education and Information Studies* 1, no. 2 (2005): article 2. https://escholarship .org/uc/item/4nj0w1mphttps://escholarship.org/uc/item/4nj0w1mp.

Horowitz, Evan. "When Will Minorities Be the Majority?" *Boston Globe,* February 2, 2016. https://www.bos tonglobe.com/news/politics/2016/02/26/when-will-minorities-majority/9v5m1Jj8hdGcXvpXtbQT5I/ story.html.

Horrigan, John B. "Libraries at the Crossroads." Pew Research Center. Last modified September 15, 2015. http://www.pewinternet.org/2015/09/15/libraries-at-the-crossroads/183-196.

———. *Libraries 2016*. Pew Research Center. September 9, 2016. http://www.pewinternet.org/2016/09/09/libraries-2016.

———. "2: Library Usage and Engagement." *Libraries 2016*. Pew Research Center. September 9, 2016. http://www.pewinternet.org/2016/09/09/library-usage-and-engagement/.

———. "3: A Portrait of Those Who Have Never Been to Libraries." *Libraries 2016*. Pew Research Center. September 9, 2016. http://www.pewinternet.org/2016/09/09/a-portrait-of-those-who-have-never-been-to-libraries/.

Horton, Forest Woody Jr. *Understanding Information Literacy: A Primer*. Paris: UNESCO, 2007. http://unesdoc.unesco.org/images/0015/001570/157020e.pdf.

House of Representatives Judiciary Committee. "Goodlatte, Conyers, Grassley, Feinstein, Leahy Call for Quick Action on Legislation to Provide Selection Process for Register of Copyrights." Last modified March 23, 2017. https://judiciary.house.gov/press-release/goodlatte-conyers-grassley-feinstein-leahy-call-quick-action-legislation-provide-selection-process-register-copyrights/.

House of Representatives Judiciary Committee. "Reform of the U.S. Copyright Office." Accessed March 26, 2017. https://judiciary.house.gov/wpcontent/uploads/2016/12/Copyright-Reform.pdf.

Housewright, Ross, Roger C. Schonfeld, and Kate Wulfson. *Ithaka S+R US Faculty Survey*, April 8, 2013. http://www.sr.ithaka.org/sites/default/files/reports/Ithaka_SR_US_Faculty_Survey_2012_FINAL.pdf.

Houston, Anne. "What's in a Name? Toward a New Definition of Reference." *RUSA Reference and User Services Association* 55, no. 3 (2016). https://journals.ala.org/index.php/rusq/article/view/5927/7513.

HR Specialist. "Designing a Progressive Discipline Policy." White paper, 2017. http://www.thehrspecialist.com/2880/Designing_a_Progressive_Discipline_Policy.hr?cat=tools&sub_cat=white_paper.

Hughes, Richard L., Robert C Ginnett, and Gordon J. Curphy. *Leadership: Enhancing the Lessons of Experience*. Boston: McGraw Hill, 2006.

Hyde, Lewis. *Common as Air: Revolution, Art and Ownership*. New York: Farrar, Strauss, and Giroux, 2010.

ICOLC. "Guidelines for Statistical Measures of Usage of Web-Based Information Resources (1998, revised 2001, 2006)." International Coalition of Library Consortia. Last modified September 2006. http://icolc.net/statement/guidelines-statistical-measures-usage-webbased-information-resources-1998-revised-2001-0.

"Idea Box." Oak Park Public Library. Accessed May 31, 2017. http://oppl.org/visit/idea-box.

IDEO. "Design Thinking for Libraries: A Toolkit for Patron-Centered Design." 2015. http://designthinkingforlibraries.com/.

IFLA Study Group on the Functional Requirements of Bibliographic Records. *Functional Requirements of Bibliographic Records: Final Report*. IFLA, February 2009. http://www.ifla.org/VII/s13/frbr/frbr.pdf.

"IMLS 2010 Public Library Survey Results Announced." IMLS, April 10, 2014. http://www.imls.gov/imls_2010_public_library_survey_results_announced.aspx.

INALJ. "Information Professionals Finding & Sharing Jobs & Job Hunting Advice." Accessed April 30, 2017. http://inalj.com/.

Indiana University Center on Postsecondary Research. "Carnegie Classifications Home Page." The Carnegie Classification of Institutions of Higher Education. Last modified 2017. http://carnegieclassifications.iu.edu/index.php.

Innovative. "New Programs for the Future of Public Libraries." February 13, 2017. https://www.iii.com/new-programs-for-the-future-of-public-libraries/.

Institute of Museum and Library Services. "Digital Storytime Means Serious Fun—and Vital Learning—for Arizona Toddlers." *Institute of Museum and Library Services* (n.d.). http://www.imls.gov/digital_storytime_means_serious_fun_and_vital_learning_for_arizona_toddlers.aspx?CategoryId=2&pg=5.

Institute of Museum and Library Services (IMLS). "Research Data Collection." 2014. https://www.imls.gov/research-evaluation/data-collection/public-libraries-survey.

Intellectual Freedom: Issues and Resources. American Library Association. Last modified September 17, 2014. http://www.ala.org/advocacy/intfreedom.

Internal Revenue Service. Forms and Pubs. Accessed April 30, 2017. https://www.irs.gov and https://www.irs.gov/pub/irs-pdf/fw4.pdf.

——. "Hiring Employees. Small Business/Self-Employed Topics." 2017. https://www.irs.gov/businesses/small-businesses-self-employed/hiring-employees.

International Federation of Library Associations and Institutions. "Functional Requirements for Authority Data." The Hague: IFLA, 2009. https://www.ifla.org/publications/functional-requirements-for-authority-data.

——. "Functional Requirements for Bibliographic Records." The Hague: IFLA, 2016. https://www.ifla.org/publications/functional-requirements-for-bibliographic-records.

——. "IFLA Code of Ethics for Librarians and Other Information Workers." Adopted August 2012. http://www.ifla.org/news/ifla-code-of-ethics-for-librarians-and-other-information-workers-full-version.

——. "IFLA International Leaders Programme: 2016 Call for Applications." https://www.ifla.org/leaders.

——. *Riding the Waves or Caught in the Tide? Navigating the Evolving Information Environment: Insights from the IFLA Trend Report*. The Hague: IFLA, 2013. http://trends.ifla.org/files/trends/assets/insights-from-the-ifla-trend-report_v3.pdf.

International Internet Preservation Consortium. http://netpreserve.org/.

International Listening Association. https://www.listen.org/.

International Organization for Standardization (ISO). ISO 14721:2012. https://www.iso.org/standard/57284.html.

International Society for Technology in Education. "ISTE Standards: For Educators." *International Society for Technology in Education*. http://www.iste.org/standards/for-educators.

International Society for Technology in Education. "ISTE Standards: For Students." 2017. http://www.iste.org/standards/for-students.

Internet Archive. "Internet Archive's Library of 2020." Accessed March 29, 2017. http://library2020.blog.archive.org/.

Internet Archive Blogs. "Internet Archive Files Amicus Brief in Support of Fair Use and Innovation in Libraries." Last modified February 20, 2017. https://blog.archive.org/2017/02/20/internet-archive-files-amicus-brief-in-support-of-fair-use-and-innovation-in-libraries/.

Internet Society. "Network Neutrality, an Internet Society Public Policy Briefing." https://www.internetsociety.org/sites/default/files/ISOC-PolicyBrief-NetworkNeutrality-20151030-nb.pdf.

"Introduction to Library and Information Science/Information Organization." *Wikibooks*. Last modified 2015. https://en.wikibooks.org/wiki/Introduction_to_Library_and_Information_Science/Information_Organization.

Irwin, Bill, and Kimberly Silk, eds. *Creating a Culture of Evaluation: Taking Your Library from Talk to Action*. Toronto: OLA Press, 2017.

"iSchools: Leading and Promoting the Information Field." http://ischools.org/.

Ithaka. "Portico: A Digital Preservation and Electronic Archiving Service." Portico. Last modified 2017. http://www.portico.org/digital-preservation/.

Ito, Mimi, Kris Gutierrez, Sonia Livingstone, Bill Penuel, Jean Rhodes, Katie Salen, Juliet Schor, Julian Sefton-Green, and S. Craig Watkins. *Connected Learning: An Agenda for Research and Design*. Irvine, CA: Digital Media and Learning Research Hub, 2013.

Ito, Mizuko. *Hanging Out, Messing, Around, and Geeking Out*. Cambridge, MA: MIT Press, 2010.

Jacobs, Heidi L. M. "Information Literacy and Reflective Pedagogical Praxis." *Journal of Academic Librarianship* 34, no. 5 (2008): 256–62. doi:10.1016/j.acalib.2008.03.009.

Jaeger, Paul T., John Carlo Bertot, Kim M. Thompson, Sarah M. Katz, and Elizabeth J. DeCoster. "The Intersection of Public Policy and Public Access: Digital Divides, Digital Literacy, Digital Inclusion, and Public Libraries." *Public Library Quarterly* 31, no. 1 (2012): 1–20, doi:10.1080/01616846.2012.654728.

Jaguszewski, Janice M., and Karen Williams. *New Roles for New Times: Transforming Liaison Roles in Research Libraries*. Chicago: Association of Research Libraries, August 2013. http://www.arl.org/storage/documents/publications/nrnt-liaison-roles-revised.pdf.

Jantti, Margie H., and Nick Greenhalgh. "Leadership Competencies: A Reference Point for Development and Evaluation (Case Study)." University of Wollongong, 2011. http://ro.uow.edu.au/cgi/viewcontent.cgi?article=1230&context=asdpapers.

Jantz, Ronald C. "A Vision for the Future: New Roles for Academic Librarians." In *Academic Librarianship Today*, edited by Todd Gilman, 223–35. Lanham, MD: Rowman & Littlefield, 2017.

Jenkins, Farley W. "The Role of Leadership in Library Administration." *Library Student Journal* 6 (2011).

Jisc Data Vault. "Home." Accessed July 11, 2017. http://datavaultplatform.org/.

Jisc Digital Solutions. "Home." Accessed July 11, 2017. https://www.jisc.ac.uk/.

Johnson, L., S. Adams Becker, V. Estrada, and A. Freeman. *NMC Horizon Report: 2014 Higher Education Edition*. Austin, TX: The New Media Consortium, 2014.

———. *NMC Horizon Report: 2015 Library Edition*. Austin, TX: The New Media Consortium, 2015. http://www.nmc.org/publication/nmc-horizon-report-2015-library-edition/.

Johnston, R. H. "Why Special Libraries?" *Special Libraries* 16, no. 1 (1925): 3–6.

Kammerlocher, Lisa, Juliann Couture, Olivia Sparks, Matthew Harp, and Tammy Allgood. "Information Literacy in Learning Landscapes: Flexible, Adaptable, Low-Cost Solutions." *Reference Services Review* 39, no. 3 (2011): 390–400.

Kane, Laura Townsend. *Working in the Virtual Stacks: The New Library and Information Science*. Chicago: American Library Association, 2011.

Kaplowitz, Joan R. *Transforming Information Literacy Instruction Using Learner-Centered Teaching*. New York: Neal-Schuman Publishers, 2012.

Kawasaki, Guy. *Enchantment: The Art of Changing Hearts, Minds, and Actions*. New York: Portfolio/Penguin, 2011.

Keeton, kYmberly. "The Remix: Hip Hop Information Literacy Pedagogy in the 21st Century." *Librarians with Spines: Information Agitators in an Age of Stagnation*. Los Angeles: Librarians with Spines, 2016.

Keirsey, David. *Please Understand Me II: Temperament, Character, Intelligence*. Del Mar, CA: Prometheus Nemesis Book Company, 1998.

Kelly, Betsy, Claire Hamasu, and Barbara Jones. "Applying Return on Investment (ROI) in Libraries." *Journal of Library Administration* 52, no. 8 (2012): 656–71. doi:10.1080/01930826.2012.747383.

Kende, Michael. *Internet Society Global Internet Report 2014*. Internet Society, 2014. http://www.internetsociety.org/sites/default/files/Global_Internet_Report_2014_0.pdf.

Kenney, Anne R., and Nancy Y. McGovern. "The Five Organizational Stages of Digital Preservation." 2003. http://dpworkshop.org/dpm-eng/introduction.html.

Kenney, Brian. "Where Reference Fits in the Modern Library: Today's Reference User Wants Help Doing Things Rather Than Finding Things." *Publishers Weekly*, September 21, 2015. http://www.publishersweekly.com/pw/by-topic/industry-news/libraries/article /68019-for-future-reference.html.

Keralis, Spencer D. C., Shannon Stark, Martin Halbert, and William E. Moen. "Research Data Management in Policy and Practice: The DataRes Project." In *Research Data Management: Principles, Practices, and Prospects*. Washington, DC: Council on Library and Information Resources, 2013. http://www.clir.org/pubs/reports/pub160/pub160.pdf.

Kern, M. "Continuity and Change, or, Will I Ever be Prepared for What Comes Next." *Reference and User Services Quarterly* 53, no. 4 (2014): 282–85.

Kilgannon, Corey. "Below Bryant Park, a Bunker and a Train Line, Just for Books." *New York Times*, November 21, 2016. https://www.nytimes.com/2016/11/21/nyregion/new-york-public-library-book-train.html.

Killeen, Erlene Bishop. "Yesterday, Today, and Tomorrow: Transitions of the Work but Not the Mission." *Teacher Librarian* 36, no. 5 (2009): 8–13.

Kim, Bohyun. "Harnessing the Power of Game Dynamics." *College & Research Libraries News* 73, no. 8 (2012): 465–69.

Kim, Mun-Cho, and Jong-Kil Kim. "Digital Divide: Conceptual Discussions and Prospect." In *The Human Society and the Internet: Internet-Related Socio-Economic Issues*, 78–91. Berlin; New York: Springer, 2001.

KNIME Open for Innovation. "Home." Accessed July 11, 2017. http://www.knime.org.

Knott, Cheryl. *Not Free, Not For All: Public Libraries in the Age of Jim Crow*. Amherst: University of Massachusetts Press, 2015.

Know Your Rights: Workplace Sexual Harassment. AAUW. http://www.aauw.org/what-we-do/legal-resources/know-your-rights-at-work/workplace-sexual-harassment/.

"Knowledge Structures: Intellectual Frameworks and Research Challenges." http://knowledgeinfrastruc tures.org/.

Knowlton, Mary, and Shawn Bryant Collins. "Foreign-Educated Graduate Nursing Students and Plagiarism." *Journal of Nursing Education* 56, no. 4 (2017): 211–14. doi:10.3928 /01484834-20170323-04.

Knox, Emily. "The Challengers of West Bend: The Library as a Community Institution." In *Libraries and the Reading Public in Twentieth-Century America,* edited by Christine Pawley and Louise S. Robbins, 200–214. Madison: University of Wisconsin Press, 2013.

Koltay, T. "Data Governance, Data Literacy and the Management of Data Quality." *IFLA Journal* 42, no. 4 (2016): 303–12. doi:10.1177/0340035216672238 2013.

Kong, Luis. "Failing to Read Well: The Role of Public Libraries in Adult Literacy, Immigrant Community Building, and Free Access to Learning." *Public Libraries Online* 52, no. 1 (January–February 2013). http:// publiclibrariesonline.org/2013/03/failing-to-read-well-the-role-of-public-libraries-in-adult-literacy -immigrant-community-building-and-free-access-to-learning/.

Konsorski-Lang, Silke, and Michael Hampe. "Why Is Design Important? An Introduction." In *The Design of Material, Organism and Minds,* 3–18. Berlin: X.media.publishing, Springer-Verlag, 2010.

Kotter, John. "What Leaders Really Do." *Harvard Business Review,* December 2001, 85–96. https://hbr .org/2001/12/what-leaders-really-do.

———. *Force for Change: How Leadership Differs from Management.* New York: The Free Press, 1990.

———. "Leading Change: Why Transformation Efforts Fail." *Harvard Business Review,* March–April 1995, 59–67.

———. "Management Is (Still) Not Leadership." *Harvard Business Review,* January 9, 2013. https://hbr .org/2013/01/management-is-still-not-leadership.html.

Kovach, Bill, and Tom Rosentiel. *Blur: How to Know What's True in the Age of Information Overload.* New York: Bloomsbury, 2010.

Kovacs, Kasia. "Inflammatory and Turned Away." *Inside Higher Ed,* October 21, 2016. https://www.inside highered.com/news/2016/10/21/several-universities-cancel-appearances-conservative-writer-milo -yiannopoulos.

Krasulski, Michael J. "Where Do They Come From, and How Are They Trained? Professional Education and Training of Access Services Librarians in Academic Libraries." *Journal of Access Services* 11, no. 1 (2014): 14–29.

Krasulski, Michael, and Trevor Dawes. *Twenty-First Century Access Services.* Chicago: Association of College of Research Libraries, 2013.

Kreitz, Patricia A. "Redefining the Twenty-First Century College Library: Change Leadership in Academic Libraries." PhD diss., Simmons College, 2015.

Krishnankutty, B., S. Bellary, N. B. R. Kumar, and L. S. Moodahadu. "Data Management in Clinical Research: An Overview." *Indian Journal of Pharmacology* 44, no. 2 (2012): 168–72. doi:10.4103/0253-7613.93842.

Kroes, Neelie. "Dutch Open Access Week Address." October 18, 2011, 4:00 min. YouTube video. https:// www.youtube.com/watch?v=taux1l0Vgek.

Kroll, Joanna, Kelly Kowatch, and Judy Lawson. *The New Information Professional: Your Guide to Careers in the Digital Age.* Chicago: Neal-Schuman, 2010.

Kruse, Kevin. "100 Best Quotes on Leadership." *Forbes,* October 16, 2012. https://www.forbes.com/sites/ kevinkruse/2012/10/16/quotes-on-leadership/#7ab410132feb.

Kruse, Kevin M. *White Flight: Atlanta and the Making of Modern Conservatism.* Princeton, NJ: Princeton Uni versity Press, 2005.

Kuhlthau, Carol C. "Inside the Search Process: Information Seeking from the User's Perspective." *Journal of the American Society for Information Science* 42 (1991): 361–71.

Kuranda, Sara. "The 10 Biggest Data Breaches of 2015 (So Far)." CRN, July 27, 2015. http://www.crn.com/ slide-shows/security/300077563/the-10-biggest-data-breaches-of-2015-so-far.htm/pgno/0/7.

Kutner, Laurie, and Alison Armstrong. "Rethinking Information Literacy in a Globalized World." *Communica tions in Information Literacy* 6, no. 1 (2012): 25–33.

Kvenlid, Cassandra, and Kaijsa Calkins. *Embedded Librarians: Moving beyond One-Shot Instruction.* Chicago: Association of College and Research Libraries, 2011.

Kyriarchy and Privilege 101. "Common Trigger Warnings." Accessed June 30, 2017. http://privilege101.tum
blr.com/triggers.html.

Ladley, J. *Data Governance: How to Design, Deploy, and Sustain an Effective Data Governance Program*. Waltham,
MA: Morgan Kaufmann, 2012.

Lankes, R. David. *The Atlas of New Librarianship*. Cambridge, MA: MIT Press, 2011.

———. *Expect More: Demanding Better Libraries for Today's Complex World*. CreateSpace Independent Publishing Platform, 2015.

Larsen, David K. "Assessing and Benchmarking Access Services." In *Twenty-First Century Access Services*, edited by Michael Krasulski and Trevor Dawes. Chicago: Association of College and Research Libraries, 2013.

Larson, Marnie. "Avoiding HR Disasters. Employee Discipline in a Union Workplace." 2015. https://www
.linkedin.com/pulse/avoiding-hr-disasters-employee-discipline-union-workforce-larson.

Laskhmanan, Indira A. R. "The Shocking TRUTH about Pizzagate." *Boston Globe*, December 8, 2016.
https://www.bostonglobe.com/opinion/2016/12/08/the-shocking-truth-about-pizzagate/kUpm1bq
KFVwIVfF49bXDqI/story.html.

Lawson, Judy, Joanna Kroll, and Kelly Kowatch. *The New Information Professional: Your Guide to Careers in the
Digital Age*. Chicago: Neal-Schuman, 2010.

"LBGT Connect.com." Accessed August 1, 2017. http://lgbtconnect.com/?gclid=CjwKEAiA8dDEBRD
f19yI97eO0UsSJAAY_yCSr6jcuwqy8yv_YQrOya4Tc9b-JLE_w3ZWeSc465fhYBoC1fPw_wcB.

Learned, William S. *The American Public Library and the Diffusion of Knowledge*. New York: Harcourt, Brace
and Co., 1924. https://archive.org/details/americanpublicli007473mbp.

LeBoeuf, Patrick, Pat Riva, and Maja Zumer. "FRBR Library-Reference Model." Consolidation Editorial Group
of the IFLA FRBR Review Group, International Federation of Libraries and Associations. Modified February 21, 2016. http://www.ifla.org/files/assets /cataloguing /frbr-lrm/frbr-lrm_20160225.pdf.

Lee and Low Books. "Where Is the Diversity in Publishing? The 2015 Diversity Baseline Survey Results."
Accessed June 30, 2017. http://blog.leeandlow.com/2016/01/26/where-is-the-diversity-in-publishing
-the-2015-diversity-baseline-survey-results/.

Lee, Christopher, and Kam Woods. "BitCurator, 2017." GitHub Repository. https://bitcurator.github.io/.

Levien, Roger. "Confronting the Future: Strategic Visions for the 21st Century Public Library." *American Library Association Policy Brief*, no. 4 (2011). http://www.ala.org/offices/sites/ala.org.offices/files/content/
oitp/publications/policybriefs/confronting_the_futu.pdf.

LIBLICENSE. "Licensing Information." Last modified July 5, 2014. http://liblicense.crl.edu/licensing-infor
mation/.

Libraries Transforming Communities. http://www.ala.org/tools/librariestransform/libraries-transform-
ing-communities.

Library Copyright Alliance. "Statement of the Library Copyright Alliance on the Copyright Office's Notice of
Inquiry Concerning Section 108 of the Copyright Act." Last modified June 16, 2016. http://www.library
copyrightalliance.org/storage/documents/108noiposition2.pdf.

Library Leadership & Management. Chicago: American Library Association, 2009.

Library Leadership & Management Association. "Leadership and Management Competencies." Accessed
March 9, 2017. http://www.ala.org/llama/leadership-and-management-competencies.

Library of Congress. "Cataloging in Publication Program." Washington, DC: Library of Congress, 2017.
https://www.loc.gov/publish/cip/.

———. "Library of Congress Classification." Washington, DC: Library of Congress, 2014. https://www.loc
.gov/catdir/cpso/lcc.html.

———. "Library of Congress Subject Headings." Washington, DC: Library of Congress. Linked Data Service,
2017. http://id.loc.gov/authorities/subjects.html.

———. "MARC 21 Format for Authority Data." Washington, DC: Library of Congress, 2017. https://www.loc
.gov/marc/authority/.

———. "MARC 21 Format for Bibliographic Data." Washington, DC: Library of Congress, 2017. http://www
.loc.gov/marc/bibliographic/.

——. "Model View: BIBFRAME Vocabulary." Washington, DC: Library of Congress, 2017. http://bibframe .org/vocab-model.

——. "MODS, Metadata Object Description Schema." Washington, DCL Library of Congress, 2017. http:// www.loc.gov/standards/mods/.

——. Network Standards and MARC Development Office. "MARC Standards." Washington, DC: Library of Congress, 2017. https://www.loc.gov/marc/.

——. "Overview of the BibFrame 2.0 Model." Washington, DC: Library of Congress, 2016. https://www .loc.gov/bibframe/docs/bibframe2-model.html.

——. "PREMIS Data Dictionary for Preservation Metadata, Version 2.0." 2008. http://www.loc.gov/stan dards/premis/v2/premis-dd-2-0.pdf.

Library of Congress National Digital Information Infrastructure and Preservation Program, The Joint Information Systems Committee, The Open Access to Knowledge (OAK) Law Project, and The SURFfoundation. "International Study on the Impact of Copyright Law on Digital Preservation." 2008. Available at: http://www.digitalpreservation.gov/documents/digital_preservation_final_report2008.pdf.

Library Publishing Coalition Directory Committee. *2017 Library Publishing Directory*. Atlanta, GA: Library Publishing Coalition, 2017. https://www.librarypublishing.org/sites/librarypublishing.org/files/2017%20 Directory.pdf.

"The Library's Spaces and Zones." Model Programme for Public Libraries. Accessed May 31, 2017. http:// modelprogrammer.slks.dk/en/challenges/zones-and-spaces/.

Library Simplified. http://www.librarysimplified.org/.

Liedka, Jeanne. "Design Thinking: The Role of Hypothesis Generation and Testing." In *Managing as Designing*, edited by Richard J. Boland Jr. and Fred Collopy. Stanford, CA: Stanford University Press, 2004.

Lindquist, Thea, and Todd Gilman. "Academic/Research Librarians with Subject Doctorates; Data and Trends 1965–2006." *Portal: Libraries and the Academy* 8, no. 1 (2008): 31–52. http://muse.jhu.edu/ article/230062.

Lingel, Jessa, and Dana Boyd. "'Keep It Secret, Keep It Safe': Information Poverty, Information Norms, and Stigma." *Journal of the American Society for Information Science and Technology* 64, no. 5 (2013): 981–91.

Lipinski, Tomas A. *The Librarian's Legal Companion for Licensing Information Resources and Services.* Chicago: Neal-Schuman Publishers, 2012.

Lisbon, Adam H., and Megan E. Welsh. "New Librarians: Building Culture and Connections—Onboarding, Training, and Manuals." *University Libraries Faculty & Staff Contributions, CU Scholar* 72 (2014). http:// scholar.colorado.edu/libr_facpapers/72.

Little, D. B., and D. A. Chapa. *Implementing Backup and Recovery*. Hoboken, NJ: John Wiley & Sons, 2003.

LittleBits Electronics. "Home." Accessed July 5, 2017. http://littlebits.cc.

Long, Matthew P., and Roger C. Schonfeld. *Ithaka S+R Library Survey 2010: Insights from U.S. Academic Library Directors*. Itaka S+R. Last modified 2010. http://www.sr.ithaka.org/sites/default/files/reports/ insights-from-us-academic-library-directors.pdf.

Los Angeles Public Library. http://www.lapl.org/diploma.

Lowry, Charles B. "Continuous Organizational Development—Teamwork, Learning Leadership, and Measurement." *Portal* 5, no. 1 (January 2005): 1–6.

Lubans, John Jr. "You Can't Build a Fire in the Rain: Sparking Change in Libraries." *Library Administration & Management* 20, no. 4 (Fall 2006): 201–3.

Lumina Foundation. "The Degree Qualifications Profile 2.0: Defining U.S. Degrees through Demonstration and Documentation of College Learning." 2014: 19–23. https://www.luminafoundation.org/files/re sources/dqp-web-download.pdf.

Lundin, Anne. "Anne Carroll Moore: 'I Have Spun Out a Long Thread.'" In *Reclaiming the American Library Past: Writing the Women In*, edited by Suzanne Hildenbrand, 187–204. Norwood, NJ: Ablox, 1996.

MacConnell, Stephen. "Advocacy in Organizations: The Elements of Success." *Generations* 28, no. 1 (April 2004): 25–30.

MacDonald, Craig M. "User Experience Librarians: User Advocates, User Researchers, Usability Evaluators, or All of the Above?" *Proceedings of the Association for Information Science and Technology* 52, no. 1 (2015): 1–10. doi:10.1002/pra2.2015.145052010055.

Macnaughton, Sona, and Mary Medinsky. "Staff Training, Onboarding, and Professional Development Using a Learning Management System." *Partnership: The Canadian Journal of Library and Information Practice and Research* 10, no. 2 (2015): 1–8.

MacWhinnie, Laurie A. "The Information Commons: The Academic Library of the Future." *Portal: Libraries and the Academy* 3, no. 2 (2003): 241–57. https://muse.jhu.edu/journals/portal_libraries_and_the_academy/v003/3.2macwhinnie.html.

Mairn, Chad. "Technologies to Watch: 2017 Edition." Slideshare presentation. Accessed January 14, 2017. http://www.slideshare.net/chadmairn.

Maker Faire. "How to Make a Maker Faire." Accessed July 5, 2017. http://makerfaire.com/mini.

Maker Media. "2016 Make: Media Kit." Accessed July 5, 2017. http://makermedia.com/wp-content/uploads/2013/01/2016-Make-Media-Kit-Final.pdf.

Maletic, J., and A. Marcus. "Data Cleansing: A Prelude to Knowledge Discovery." In *Data Mining and Knowledge Discovery Handbook*, edited by O. Maimon and L. Rokach. New York: Springer, 2005.

Marchionini, Gary. *Information Seeking in Electronic Environments*. Cambridge: Cambridge University Press, 1995.

Marco, D. "Understanding Data Governance and Stewardship, Part 1." *DM Review* 16, no. 9 (2006): 28.

Margolin, Stephanie, and Jennifer Poggiali. "Leading from the Library Loo: An Illustrated, Documented Guide to New York City Academic Library Bathrooms." In *ACRL 2017 Conference Proceedings*. 377–87. Baltimore, Maryland: Association of College and Research Libraries. http://www.ala.org/acrl/sites/ala.org.acrl/files/content/conferences/confsandpreconfs/2017/LeadingfromtheLibraryLoo.pdf.

Mariz, George, Donna McCrea, Larry Hackman, Tony Kurtz, and Randall Jimerson. "Leadership Skills for Archivists." *American Archivist* 74, no. 1 (2011): 102–22.

MarketingCharts. "American Households Are Getting Smaller—and Headed by Older Adults." 2012. http://www.marketingcharts.com/traditional/american-households-are-getting-smaller-and-headed-by-older-adults-24981/.

Marquez, Joe, and Annie Downey. "Service Design: An Introduction to a Holistic Assessment Methodology of Library Services." *Weave: Journal of Library User Experience* 1, no. 2 (2015). doi:http://dx.doi.org/10.3998/weave.12535642.0001.201.

Marquez, Joe J., and Annie Downey. *Library Service Design: A LITA Guide to Holistic Assessment, Insight, and Improvement*. Lanham, MD: Rowman & Littlefield Publishers, 2016.

Marsh, Rene. "EPA Removes Climate Information from Website." 2017. http://www.cnn.com/2017/04/29/politics/epa-climate-change-website/.

Martin, Douglas. "Norma Gabler, Leader of Crusade on Textbooks, Dies at 84." *New York Times*, August 1, 2007. http://www.nytimes.com/2007/08/01/education/01gabler.html.

Martin, Jason. "Perceptions of Transformational Leadership in Academic Libraries." *Journal of Library Administration* 56, no. 3 (2016): 266–84.

Martin, Judith. *Miss Manners Guide to Excruciatingly Correct Behavior*. New York: W.W. Norton and Company, 2005.

Maslow, Abraham H. "A Theory of Human Motivation." *Psychological Review* 50, no. 4. (1943): 370–96. doi:10.1037/h0054346.

Matarazzo, J., and T. Perlstein. "New Management Realities for Special Libraries." *Online Searcher* 40, no. 3 (2016). http://www.infotoday.com/OnlineSearcher/Articles/Features/New-Management-Realities-for-Special-Librarians-110761.shtml.

Mathews, Brian. "Librarian as Futurist: Change the Way Libraries Think about the Future." *Portal: Libraries and the Academy* 14, no. 3 (2014): 453–62. http://vtechworks.lib.vt.edu/handle/10919/49667.

Matsumoto, David, ed. *Interpersonal Communication*. Washington, DC: American Psychological Association 2010.

Matthias, Cynthia, and Christy Mulligan. "Hennepin County Library's Teen Tech Squad: Youth Leadership and Technology Free-for-all." *Young Adult Library Services* 8, no. 2 (2010): 13–16.

Matthews, Joseph R. *The Evaluation and Measurement of Library Services*, second edition. Westport, CT: Libraries Unlimited, 2017.

Maxwell, Lesli A. "U.S. School Enrollment Hits Majority-Minority Milestone." *Education Week*, August 20, 2014. Accessed June 30, 2017. http://www.edweek.org/ew/articles/2014/08/20/01demographics.h34.html.

Maymir-DuCharme. "Cognitive Analytics: A Step toward Tacit Knowledge." *Systemics, Cybernetics, and Informatics* 12, no. 4 (2014): 32–38. http://www.iiisci.org/Journal/CV$/sci/pdfs/HA342OE14.pdf.

McCabe, Kealin M., and James R. W. MacDonald. "Roaming Reference: Reinvigorating Reference through Point of Need Service." *Partnership: The Canadian Journal of Library and Information Practice and Research* 6, no. 2 (2011): 1–15.

McCann, Erin. "HIPAA Data Breaches Climb 138 Percent." *Healthcare IT News*, February 6, 2014. http://www.healthcareitnews.com/news/hipaa-data-breaches-climb-138-percent.

McClelland, David. *Human Motivation*. Cambridge: Cambridge University Press, 1987.

McDonald, Courtney Greene. *Putting the User First: 30 Strategies for Transforming Library Services*. Chicago: Association of College and Research Libraries, a division of the American Library Association, 2014.

McGee, W. C. "Data Base Technology." *IBM Journal of Research and Development* 25, no. 5 (1981): 505–19, doi:10.1147/rd.255.0505.

McHenry, Elizabeth. "'An Association of Kindred Spirits': Black Readers and Their Reading Rooms." In *Institutions of Reading: The Social Life of Libraries in the United States*, edited by Thomas Augst and Kenneth Carpenter, 99–118. Amherst: University of Massachusetts Press, 2007.

McIntosh, Peggy. "White Privilege: Unpacking the Invisible Knapsack." *Peace and Freedom Magazine*, July–August, 1989. Retrieved from https://nationalseedproject.org/white-privilege-unpacking-the-invisible-knapsack.

McKendrick, Joseph. *Funding and Priorities: The Library Resource Guide Benchmark Study on 2011 Library Spending Plans*. Chatham, NJ: Unisphere Research, 2011. http://lgdata.s3-website-us-east-1.amazonaws.com/docs/231/215960/Funding-and-PrioritiesThe-Library-Resource-Guide-Benchmark-Study-on-2011-Library-Spending-Plans.pdf.

McKendrick, Joseph. *Libraries: At the Epicenter of the Digital Disruption: The Library Guide Benchmark Study on 2013/14 Library Spending Plans*. Medford, NJ: Information Today, Inc., 2013.

McMullen, Haynes. *American Libraries before 1876*. Westport, CT: Greenwood, 2000.

Mechaber, Ezra. "Here's How Cell Phone Unlocking Became Legal." The White House Blog, August 15, 2014, http://www.whitehouse.gov/blog/2014/08/15/heres-how-cell-phone-unlocking-became-legal.

Mehra, B., K. Black, and J. Nolt. "What Is the Value of LIS Education? A Qualitative Study of Three Perspectives of Tennessee's Rural Libraries." *Journal of Education for Library and Information Science* 52, no. 4 (2011): 265–78.

Meister, Jeanne C., and Karie Willyerd. "Are You Ready to Manage Five Generations of Workers?" *Harvard Business Review*, October 16, 2009. https://hbr.org/2009/10/are-you-ready-to-manage-five-g.

Menchaca, Franks. "Start a New Fire: Measuring the Value of Academic Libraries in Undergraduate Learning." *Portal: Libraries and the Academy* 14, no. 3 (2014): 353–67. doi:10.135/pla.2014.0020.

Merriam-Webster Dictionary, s.v. "Design." Accessed March 25, 2017. http://www.merriam-webster.com/dictionary/design.

Mery, Yvonne, Jill Newby, and Ke Peng. "Why One-Shot Information Literacy Sessions Are Not the Future of Instruction: A Case for Online Credit Courses." *College & Research Libraries* 73, no. 4 (2012): 366–77. http://crl.acrl.org/cont.nt/early/2011/08/26/crl-271.full.pdf+html.

Meulemans, Yvonne Nalani, and Allison Carr. "Not at Your Service: Building Genuine Faculty-Librarian Partnerships." *Reference Services Review* 41, no. 1 (2013): 80–90. doi:10.1108/00907321311300893.

Meyer, Jan H. F., and Ray Land. "Threshold Concepts and Troublesome Knowledge (2): Epistemological Considerations and a Conceptual Framework for Teaching and Learning." *Higher Education* 49, no. 3 (2005): 373–88. doi:10.1007/s10734-004-6779-5.

Meyer, Lars. "Safeguarding Collections at the Dawn of the 21st Century: Describing Roles & Measuring Contemporary Preservation Activities in ARL Libraries." ARL, 2009. http://www.arl.org/storage/documents/publications/safeguarding-collections.pdf.

Microsoft. "Types of Replication: Microsoft Docs—SQL Relational Databases." Accessed May 1, 2017. https://docs.microsoft.com/en-us/sql/relational-databases/replication/types-of-replication.

Middle States Commission on Higher Education. *Standards for Accreditation and Requirements of Affiliation.* Philadelphia: Middle States Commission on Higher Education, 2013.

Miles, Dennis B. "Shall We Get Rid of the Reference Desk?" *Reference and User Services Quarterly* 50, no. 4 (2013): 320–33.

Mill, John Stuart. *Utilitarianism.* London: Parker, Son, and Bourne, 1863.

Millem, Jeffrey F., Mitchell J. Chang, and Anthony Lising Antonio. "Making Diversity Work on Campus: A Research-Based Perspective." *Making Excellence Inclusive Initiative.* Washington, DC: Association of American Colleges and Universities, 2005. http://www.aacu.org/inclusive_excellence/documents/Milem_et_al.pdf.

Miller, Bridget. "What Does At-Will Employment Really Mean?" *HR Daily Advisor*, May 1, 2014. Accessed April 30, 2017. http://hrdailyadvisor.blr.com/2014/05/01/what-does-at-will-employment-really-mean/.

Miller, Eric. "An Introduction to the Research Description Framework." *Bulletin of the American Society for Information Science and Technology* 25, no. 1 (1998): 15–19.

Miller, Kelly E. "Imagine! On the Future of Teaching and Learning and the Academic Research Library." *Portal: Libraries and the Academy* 14, no. 3 (2014): 329–51. doi:10.1353/pla.2014.0018.

Miller, Rebecca T., and Meredith Schwartz. "What Wallets Have to Do with Libraries." *Library Journal*, January 2014. http://lj.libraryjournal.com/2014/01/opinion/design4impact/what-wallets-have-to-do-with-libraries-design4impact/#_.

Milliot, Jim. "As E-book Sales Decline, Digital Fatigue Grows." *Publisher's Weekly*, June 17, 2017. http://www.publishersweekly.com/pw/by-topic/digital/retailing/article/70696-as-e-book-sales-decline-digital-fatigue-grows.html.

Mills, J. Elizabeth, Kathleen Campana, and Rachel Ivy Clarke. "Learning by Design: Creating Knowledge through Library Storytime Production." *Proceedings of the Association for Information Science and Technology* 53, no. 1 (2016): 1–6. doi:10.1002/pra2.2016.14505301115.

Mintzberg, Henry. "Crafting Strategy" *Harvard Business Review* 65, no. 4 (July–August 1987): 66–75.

MIT Libraries. "Strategic Plan, 2014–2016." November 6, 2013. https://libraries.mit.edu/wp-content/uploads/2014/01/strategic_plan_2014-2016.pdf.

MIT Libraries Space Programming Group. "Guiding Principles for the MIT Libraries Spaces—Working DRAFT." August 18, 2014. https://libraries.mit.edu/future-spaces/files/2014/09/guiding-principles-draft.pdf.

Moore, Edythe. "Corporate Science and Technology Libraries." *Science & Technology Libraries* 8, no. 1 (1988): 51–60.

Moore, Susan. "Build Your Career Path to Chief Data Officer Role." Gartner, Inc., 2016. http://www.gartner.com/smarterwithgartner/build-your-career-path-to-the-chief-data-officer-role/.

Moran, Thomas, and John M. Carroll. "Overview of Design Rationale." In *Design Rationale: Concepts, Techniques, and Use,* 1–20. Mahwah, NJ: Lawrence Erlbaum Associates, 1996.

Morehart, Phil. "2015 Library Design Showcase." *American Libraries*, September 1, 2015. https://americanlibrariesmagazine.org/2015/09/01/2015-library-design-showcase/.

Morris, Jacquelyn M. *Bibliographic Instruction in Academic Libraries: A Review of the Literature and Selected Bibliography.* Champaign: University of Illinois, 1979. http://files.eric.ed.gov/fulltext/ED180505.pdf.

Morris, Shaneka, and Gary Roebuck. *ARL Statistics 2014–2015.* Washington, DC: Association of Research Libraries, 2017.

Morville, Peter. "User Experience Design." *Semantic Studios*, June 21, 2004. http://semanticstudios.com/user_experience_design/.

Mosley, M., and M. Brackett. *The DAMA Guide to the Data Management Body of Knowledge (DAMA-DMBOK),* first edition. Middletown, DE: Technics Publications, 2010.

Mosley, Pixey A. "Assessing User Interactions at the Desk Nearest the Front Door." *Reference and User Services Quarterly* 47, no. 2 (2007): 159–67.

Mount, D. *IFLA Trend Report Update 2016*. IFLA. https://trends.ifla.org/files/trends/assets/trend-report-2016 -update.pdf

Mudd, Alex, Terri Summey, and Matt Upson. "It Takes a Village to Design a Course: Embedding a Librarian in Course Design." *Journal of Library and Information Services in Distance Learning* 9, nos. 1–2 (2015): 69–88. doi:10.1080/1533290X.2014.946349.

Mumford, Eben. "The Origin of Leadership." *American Journal of Sociology*, November 1906–January 1907.

Mune, Christina, Crystal Goldman, Silke Higgins, Laurel Eby, Emily K. Chan, and Linda Crotty. "Developing Adaptable Online Information Literacy Modules for a Learning Management System." *Journal of Library and Information Services in Distance Learning* 9, nos. 1–2 (2015): 101–18. doi:10.1080/1533290X.2014.946351.

Murray, Tara E. "How Much Is a Special Library Worth? Valuing and Communicating Information in Organizational Context." *Journal of Library Administration* 53, no. 8 (2013): 462–71.

Murray, Tara E. "The Forecast for Special Librarians." *Journal of Library Administration* 56, no. 2 (2016): 188–98.

Naismith, Rachael. "Library Service to Migrant Farm Workers." *Library Journal* 114, no. 4 (1989): 52–55.

National Association of Social Workers. "Institutional Racism and the Social Work Profession: A Call to Action." 2007. https://www.socialworkers.org/diversity/InstitutionalRacism.pdf.

National Book Foundation. National Book Award. Accessed September 7, 2017. http://www.nationalbook .org/nba2017.html#.WV2mW4jytRY.

National Center for Education Statistics (NCES). "Surveys and Programs." 2017. https://nces.ed.gov/.

National Conference of State Legislatures. "Privacy Protections in State Constitutions." NCSL. Last updated May 5, 2017. http://www.ncsl.org/research/telecommunications-and-information-technology/privacy -protections-in-state-constitutions.aspx.

National Council of Teachers of English. "NCTE Definition of 21st Century Literacies." Last modified February 5, 2013. http://www.ncte.org/positions/statements/21stcentdefinition.

National Education Association. "The Truth about Tenure in Higher Education." *Higher Education Departments of the National Education Association and the American Federation of Teachers*, 2002–2015. http:// www.nea.org/home/33067.htm.

National Initiative for Cybersecurity Careers and Studies. "Cyber Glossary." Department of Homeland Security. http://niccs.us-cert.gov/glossary#cybersecurity.

National Information Standards Organization. "ANSI/NISO Z39.88-2004 (R2010) The Open URL Framework for Context-Sensitive Services." NISO. Last modified May 14, 2015. http://www.niso.org/apps/ group_public/project/details.php?project_id=82.

———. "Standardized Usage Statistics Harvesting Initiative (SUSHI) Protocol (ANSI/NISO Z39.93-2014)." Last modified 2014. http://www.niso.org/workrooms/sushi/.

———. "Transfer." Last modified 2017. http://www.niso.org/workrooms/transfer/.

National Institute of Standards and Technology. "Framework for Improving Critical Cybersecurity Infrastructure, Version 1.0." 2014. http://www.nist.gov/cyberframework/upload/cybersecurity-frame work-021214.pdf.

National Telecommunications and Information Administration. "Falling through the Net: A Survey of the 'Have Nots' in Rural and Urban America" *United States Department of Commerce*. Last modified February 22, 2014. http://www.ntia.doc.gov/ntiahome/fallingthru.html.

Naumann, F., and M. Herschel. *An Introduction to Duplicate Detection*. San Rafael, CA: Morgan and Claypool Publishers, 2009.

Naumer, Charles M., and Karen E. Fisher. "Information Needs." In *Encyclopedia of Library and Information Sciences*, edited by Marcia J. Bates and Mary N. Maack, 2452–58, third edition. Abingdon, UK: Taylor and Francis, 2009.

Neal, James. "Foreword." In *Twenty-First Century Access Services*, edited by Michael Krasulski and Trevor Dawes, v–vii. Chicago: Association of College and Research Libraries, 2013.

Neal, James G. "Raised by Wolves: The New Generation of Feral Professionals in the Academic Library." *ACRL Twelfth National Conference*, 2005: 302–4. http://www.ala.org/acrl/sites/ala.org.acrl/files/con tent/conferences/pdf/neal2-05.pdf.

NEDCC. "History of the Northeast Document Conservation Center." http://www.nedcc.org/about/history/overview.

NEDCC. "What Is Preservation?" Preservation 101. http://unfacilitated.preservation101.org/session1/expl_whatis-libraries.asp.

Neigel, Christina. "LIS Leadership and Leadership Education: A Matter of Gender." *Journal of Library Administration* 55, no. 7 (2015): 521–34.

"The New Deal." *United States History.* Last modified August 9, 2014. http://www.u-s-history.com/pages/h1851.html.

New Media Consortium. "NMC Horizon Project." 2017. https://www.nmc.org/publication/nmc-horizon-report-2017-library-edition/.

NextGen Science Standards. "About the Standards." Last modified June 25, 2014. http://www.nextgenscience.org/about-standards-development-process.

NGSS Lead States. *Next Generation Science Standards: For States, By States.* Washington, DC: National Academies Press, 2013. https://www.nextgenscience.org.

Nicholas, David. *Assessing Information Needs: Tools, Techniques and Concepts for the Internet Age*, second edition. London: Aslib, 2000.

Nicholson-Crotty, Jill. "The Stages of Nonprofit Advocacy." PhD diss., Texas A&M University, 2005.

Nielsen, Lene. *Personas—User Focused Design.* New York: Springer, 2012.

No Child Left Behind (NCLB) Act of 2001. Pub. L. No. 107–110, § 115. Stat. 1425 (2002). http://www2.ed.gov/policy/elsec/leg/esea02/107-110.pdf.

Nolo.com. "Responding to a DMCA Takedown Notice." Last modified June 4, 2014. http://www.nolo.com/legal-encyclopedia/responding-dmca-takedown-notice.html.

Norman, Don, and Jakob Nielsen. "The Definition of User Experience (UX)." Nielsen Norman Group. Accessed April 10, 2017. https://www.nngroup.com/articles/definition-user-experience/.

Northeast Document Conservation Center (NEDCC). "History of the Northeast Document Conservation Center." http://www.nedcc.org/about/history/overview.

——. "What Is Preservation." Preservation 101. http://unfacilitated.preservation101.org/session1/expl_whatis-libraries.asp.

O'Donnell, James. "How Many Libraries Do We Need?" NASIG Annual Conference, 2016 (video). Accessed January 6, 2017. https://www.youtube.com/watch?v =m1amGifG60E.

Oakleaf, Megan. *Value of Academic Libraries: A Comprehensive Research Review and Report.* Chicago: Association of College and Research Libraries. Last updated September, 2010. http://www.ala.org/acrl/sites/ala.org.acrl/files/content/issues/value/val_report.pdf.

OCLC. "Competency Index for the Library Field." Accessed June 30, 2017. https://www.webjunction.org/content/dam/WebJunction/Documents/webJunction/2015-03/Competency%20Index%20for%20the%20Library%20Field%20(2014).pdf.

——. *Dewey Services.* Dublin, OH: OCLC, 2017. http://www.oclc.org/en/dewey.html.

——. *From Awareness to Funding.* Dublin, OH: OCLC. Accessed June 30, 2017. http://www.oclc.org/en/reports/funding.html.

——. "Home." https://www.oclc.org/en/home.html.

——. "OCLC FAST." http://fast.oclc.org/.

——. *Perceptions of Libraries and Information Resources 2005.* Dublin, OH: OCLC, 2005. http://www.oclc.org/content/dam/oclc/reports/pdfs/Percept_all.pdf.

——. "WorldCat."https://www.oclc.org/en/worldcat.html.

Office of Personnel Management. "Cybersecurity Resource Center." https://www.opm.gov/cybersecurity/cybersecurity-incidents/.

Office of the Privacy Commissioner of Canada. "The Personal Information Protection and Electronic Documents Act (PIPEDA)." https://www.priv.gc.ca/en/privacy-topics/privacy-laws-in-canada/the-personal-information-protection-and-electronic-documents-act-pipeda/.

Office of the Register of Copyright. "Legal Issues in Mass Digitization: A Preliminary Analysis and Discussion Document." Last modified October 2011. http://www.copyright.gov/docs/massdigitization/USCO MassDigitization_October2011.pdf.

Office of Management and Budget. "Open Data Policy—Managing Information as an Asset." 2013. http://www.whitehouse.gov/sites/default/files/omb/memoranda/2013/m-13-13.pdf.

Ogburn, Joyce L. "The Imperative for Data Curation." *Portal: Libraries and the Academy* 10, no. 2 (2010): 241–46. http://muse.jhu.edu/journals/pla/summary/v010/10.2.ogburn.html.

Okobi, Elise A. Rogers Halliday. "History and Development of Adult Services." In *Library Services for Adults in the 21st Century*, 19–28. Santa Barbara, CA: Libraries Unlimited, 2014. http://www2.ed.gov/policy/elsec/leg/esea02/107-110.pdf.

Olmstead, Kenneth, and Aaron Smith. "Americans and Cybersecurity." PEW Research Center, January 26, 2017. http://www.pewinternet.org/2017/01/26/americans-and-cybersecurity/.

Olmstead v. United States. 277 U.S. 1928. *Justia*. 438, 478–79. https://supreme.justia.com/cases/federal/us/277/438/case.html.

"ONIX Overview." EDItEUR. http://www.editeur.org/83/Overview/.

Online Computer Library Center. "OCLC Research." 2017. http://www.oclc.org/research.html.

Open Library. "Borrow eBooks." Last modified July 2, 2014. https://openlibrary.org/borrow/about.

Open Refine. "Home." Accessed July 11, 2017. http://openrefine.org.

OpenDOAR. "Directory of Open Access Repositories." 2014. http://www.opendoar.org.

Orange, Satia Marshall, and Robin Osborne. "Introduction." In *From Outreach to Equity: Innovative Models of Library Policy and Practice*, edited by Robin Osborne. Chicago: American Library Association, 2004.

Osborne, Robin, ed. *From Outreach to Equity: Innovative Models of Library Policy and Practice*. Chicago: American Library Association, 2004.

Overman, E. Sam, and Anthony G. Cahill. "Information Policy: A Study of Values in the Policy Process." *Policy Studies Review* 9, no. 4 (1990): 803–18.

Owen, Brian. "Open Access, Institutional Repositories, E-Science and Data Curation, and Preservation." In *Academic Librarianship Today*, edited by Todd Gilman, 197–210. Lanham, MD: Rowman & Littlefield, 2017.

Pack, Thomas. "Got Questions? Stack Exchange Has Answers." *Information Today* 32 (January/February 2015): 31.

Palfrey, John. *BiblioTech: Why Libraries Matter More Than Ever in the Age of Google*. New York: Basic Books, 2015.

Pallante, Maria A. "The Next Great Copyright Act." *Columbia Journal of Law and the Arts* 36 (2012): 315. http://www.copyright.gov/docs/next_great_copyright_act.pdf.

"Pallante Resignation May Indicate New Approach at Copyright Office." *Library Journal*. Last modified November 1, 2016. http://lj.libraryjournal.com/2016/11/industry-news/pallante-resignation-may-indicate-new-approach-at-copyright-office/.

Park, Madison, and Kyung Lah. "Berkeley Protests of Yiannopoulos Caused $100,000 in Damage." Accessed June 30, 2017. CNN, February 1, 2017. http://www.cnn.com/2017/02/01/us/milo-yiannopoulos-berkeley/index.html.

Park, Namkee, Raul Roman, Seungyoon Lee, and Jae Eun Chung. "User Acceptance of a Digital Library System in Developing Countries: An Application of the Technology Acceptance Model." *International Journal of Information Management* 29, no. 3 (2009): 196–209.

Passet, Joanne E. *Cultural Crusaders: Women Librarians in the American West, 1900–1917*. Albuquerque: University of New Mexico Press, 1994.

Past LGBT Nondiscrimination and Anti-LGBT Bills across the Country. ACLU American Civil Liberties Union. https://www.aclu.org/map/non-discrimination-laws-state-state-information-map.

Paterson, Amy. "After the Desk: Reference Service in a Changing Information Landscape." IFLA, July 15, 2014. http://library.ifla.org/944/1/101-paterson-en.pdf.

PATRIOT ACT Pub. L. 107-56. Oct. 26, 2001.

Pawley, Christine. "'Missionaries of the Book' or 'Central Intelligence' Agents: The Contest for Library Education in Twentieth Century America." *Libraries: Culture, History and Society* 1, no. 1 (2017): 72–96.

————. *Reading on the Middle Border: The Culture of Print in Late Nineteenth Century Osage, Iowa.* Amherst: University of Massachusetts Press, 2001.

————. *Reading Places: Literacy, Democracy, and the Public Library in Cold War America.* Amherst: University of Massachusetts Press, 2010.

Peet, Lisa. "Five Brand-New Jobs for Today's Librarians: Careers 2016." *Library Journal,* March 9, 2016. http://lj.libraryjournal.com/2016/03/careers/five-brand-new-jobs-for-todays-librarians-careers-2016.

Peet, Lisa. "Gaining Ground Unevenly." *Library Journal,* February 10, 2016. http://lj.libraryjournal.com/2016/02/budgets-funding/gaining-ground-unevenly-budgets-funding/.

Peltier, Thomas R., Justin Peltier and John Blackley. *Information Security Fundamentals.* Boca Raton, FL: CRC Press, 2004.

PEN America. "And Campus for All: Diversity, Inclusion, and Freedom of Speech at U.S. Universities." Accessed June 30, 2017. https://pen.org/and-campus-for-all-diversity-inclusion-and-free-speech-at-u-s-universities/.

Pendell, Kimberly, Elizabeth Withers, Jill Castek, and Stephen Reder. "Tutor-Facilitated Adult Digital Literacy Learning: Insights from a Case Study." *Internet Reference Services Quarterly* 18, no. 2 (2013): 105–25.

Pennington, Buddy, Suzanne Chapman, Amy Fry, Amy Deschenes, and Courtney Greene McDonald. "Strategies to Improve the User Experience." *Serials Review* 42 no. 1 (2016): 47–58. doi:10.1080/00987913.2016.1140614.

Perrin, Andrew. "Book Reading 2016." Pew Research Center, December 1, 2016. http://www.pewinternet.org/2016/09/01/book-reading-2016/.

Peters, Marybeth. *Report on Orphan Works: A Report of the Register of Copyrights.* Washington, DC: U.S. Copyright Office, 2006. http://www.copyright.gov/orphan/orphan-report-full.pdf.

Peterson, Andrea. "Adult FriendFinder Hit with One of the Biggest Data Breaches Ever, Reports Say." *Washington Post,* November 14, 2016. https://www.washingtonpost.com/news/the-switch/wp/2016/11/14/adult-friendfinder-hit-with-one-of-the-biggest-data-breaches-ever-report-says/?utm_term=.5422f9dbb40a.

Pew Research American and Life Project. "Libraries." 2017. http://libraries.pewinternet.org/.

Pew Research Center. "Internet/Broadband Fact Sheet." Pew Research Center: Internet, Science and Tech, January 12, 2017. http://www.pewinternet.org/fact-sheet/internet-broadband/.

Phoenix Public Library. "PhoenixWorks: Job Help Resources." 2016. Accessed January 12, 2017. http://www.phoenixpubliclibrary.org/phoenixworks/job-help-resources.

Pickard, Alison Jane. *Research Methods in Information,* second edition. Chicago: Neal-Schuman, 2013.

Piggott, Sylvia E. A., Sue O'Neill Johnson, and Wei Wei. *Leadership and Management Principles in Libraries in Developing Countries.* Binghamton, NY: Routledge, 2004.

Pike, Kaylee L. "New Employee Onboarding Programs and Person-Organization Fit: An Examination of Socialization Tactics." Seminar Research Paper Series, Schmidt Labor Research Center at DigitalCommons@URI. Paper 24, 2014. http://digitalcommons.uri.edu/lrc_paper_series/24.

Pilette, Roberta. "Mass Deacidification: A Preservation Option for Libraries." *IFLA Journal,* March 1, 2004. http://archive.ifla.org/IV/ifla69/papers/030e-Pilette.pdf.

Plaks, Andrew H. "Golden Rule." In *Encyclopedia of Religion.* Detroit: Macmillan Reference USA, 2005.

"Pokemon Hunt in the Library." *Karissa in the Library: Learning and Thinking about Libraries, in Libraries* (blog). July 14, 2016. https://karissamlis.wordpress.com/2016/07/14/pokemon-scavenger-hunt-in-the-library.

"Policy B.2.1.15, Access to Library Resources and Services Regardless of Sex, Gender Identity, Gender Expression, or Sexual Orientation." In *American Library Association Policy Manual.* Chicago: ALA, 2013. http://www.ala.org/aboutala/governance/policymanual.

"Policy B.2.3.1, Linguistic Pluralism." In *American Library Association Policy Manual.* Chicago: ALA, 2013, http://www.ala.org/aboutala/governance/policymanual.

"Policy B.2.1.12, Universal Right to Free Expression." In *American Library Association Policy Manual.* Chicago: ALA, 2013. http://www.ala.org/aboutala/governance/policymanual.

"Policy B.2.1.20, Services to Persons with Disabilities." In *American Library Association Policy Manual.* Chicago: ALA, 2013. http://www.ala.org/aboutala/governance/policymanual.

Poole, W. F. "Progress of Library Architecture." *Library Journal* 7, nos. 7–8 (1882): 130–36. https://ia600303 .us.archive.org/14/items/reportonprogres00assogoog/reportonprogres00assogoog.pdf.

Porter, M. E. "What Is Strategy?" *Harvard Business Review* 74, no. 6 (November–December 1996): 61–78.

Potter, Abbey. "Dodge That Memory Hole: Saving Digital News." *The Signal* (blog), June 2, 2015. https:// blogs.loc.gov/thesignal/2015/06/dodge-that-memory-hole-saving-digital-news/.

Poussaint, LaVerne. "Text a Librarian." *Journal of the Medical Library Association* 98, no. 3 (2010): 267–68.

Power BI. "Home." Accessed July 11, 2017. https://powerbi.microsoft.com/en-us/.

Preddy, Leslie. *School Library Makerspaces, Grades 6–12.* Santa Barbara, CA: ABC-CLIO, 2013.

Price, Jay. "NCSU's Hyper-Modern James B. Hunt Jr. Library Poised to Open." *News Observer*, December 18, 2012. http://www.newsobserver.com/2012/12/18/2553438/ncsus-hyper-modern-new-james-b.html.

"Profession." In *Bloomsbury Guide to Human Thought.* London: Bloomsbury, 1993. Accessed August 1, 2017. http://search.credoreference.com.dml.regis.edu/content/entry/bght/profession/0.

Project COUNTER. "COUNTER." https://www.projectcounter.org/.

Protection of Pupil Rights. 20 U.S. Code § 1232H. GPO.

"Public Domain Mark Creative Commons. Accessed August 24, 2014. http://creativecommons.org/about/ pdm.

Public Library Association (PLA). "PLDS and PLAmetrics." 2017. http://www.ala.org/pla/resources/publi cations/plds.

"Publishers Appeal GSU Copyright Case." *Publishers Weekly*, August 29, 2016. http://www.publishers weekly.com/pw/by-topic/digital/copyright/article/71357-publishers-appeal-gsu-copyright-case.html.

Puccinelli, Nancy M. "Nonverbal Communicative Competence." In *APA Handbook of Interpersonal Commu-nication*, ed. David Matsumoto, 273–88. Washington, DC: American Psychological Association, 2010.

Puglia, Steve. "Creating Permanent and Durable Information: Physical Media and Storage Standards." *CRM: Cultural Resource Management* 22, no. 2 (1999): 25–27. https://courseweb.pitt.edu/bbcswebdav/ institution/Pitt%20Online/MLIS_Pitt_Online/LIS_2214/MEISLIK/module%208/phys%20media%20 and%20storage%20stds.pdf.

Qualities of the Searcher's Experience. Photo, 2010. https://www.flickr.com/photos/morville/4274260576/.

Quattrochi, Christina. "MAKE'ing More Diverse Makers." *EdSurge*, October 29, 2013. https://www.edsurge .com/n/2013-10-29-make-ing-more-diverse-makers.

Raber, Douglas. *Librarianship and Legitimacy: The Ideology of the Public Library Inquiry.* Westport, CT: Green-wood Press, 1997.

Race to the Top. 2009. https://www2.ed.gov/programs/racetothetop/index.html.

Radford, Neil. *The Carnegie Corporation and the Development of American Academic Libraries, 1928–1941.* Chi-cago: American Library Association, 1984.

Raine, Lee. "Libraries and Learning." Pew Research Center, April 7, 2016. http://www.pewinternet .org/2016/04/07/libraries-and-learning/.

Rainie, Lee, Sara Kiesler, Ruogu Kang, and Mary Madden. "Anonymity, Privacy, and Security Online." Pew Research Internet Project, September 5, 2013. http://www.pewinternet.org/2013/09/05/anonymity -privacy-and-security-online/.

Rambo, N. *Research Data Management: Roles for Libraries.* Issue Brief. New York: Ithaka, 2015.

Ramos, Marian S., and Christine M. Abrigo. "Reference 2.0 in Action: An Evaluation of the Digital Refer-ence Services in Selected Philippine Academic Libraries." *Library Hi Tech News* 29, no. 1 (2012): 8–20. doi:10.1108/07419051211223426.

Ranganathan, R. S. *The Five Laws of Library Science.* London: Edward Goldston, 1931.

Rapid Miner. "Home." Accessed July 11, 2017. https://rapidminer.com/.

Raven, Bertam. H. "Political Applications of the Psychology of Interpersonal Influence and Social Power." *Political Psychology* 11, no. 3 (1990): 493–520.

Raymond, Matt. "How Tweet It Is! Library Acquires Entire Twitter Archive." *Library of Congress Blog*, April 14, 2010. http://blogs.loc.gov/loc/2010/04/how-tweet-it-is-library-acquires-entire-twitter-archive/.

RDA Steering Committee. "RDA-RSC." 2016. http://www.rda-rsc.org/.

Reath, Andrews. "Kant's Moral Philosophy." In *The Oxford Handbook on the History of Ethics*, edited by Roger Crisp. New York: Oxford University Press, 2013. Accessed August 1, 2017. doi:10.1093/oxfordhb/9780199545971.013.0021.

Reference and User Services Association. "Guidelines for Behavioral Performance for Reference and Information Service Providers." 2013. Accessed January 15, 2017. http://www.ala.org/rusa/resources/guidelines/guidelinesbehavioral.

Registry of Open Access Repositories Mandatory Open Access Policies (ROARMAP). "Home." 2014. http://roarmap.eprints.org.

Reid, Ian. "The 2015 Public Library Data Service: Characteristics and Trends." *Counting Opinions*, May 2016. https://storage.googleapis.com/co_drive/Documents/PLDS/2015PLDSAnnualReportFinal.pdf.

Remmers, Vanessa, and Louis Llovio. "Va. House Backs Bill Requiring Parents Be Notified of Sexually Explicit Materials." *Richmond Times-Dispatch*, February 6, 2017. Accessed June 30, 2017. http://www.richmond.com/news/virginia/va-house-backs-bill-requiring-parents-be-notified-of-sexually/article_7a534d3d-2f07-5882-bf6b-213d6266567b.html.

"Return on Investment for Public Libraries." Library Research Service Research and Statistics about Libraries. https://www.lrs.org/data-tools/public-libraries/return-on-investment/.

Reynolds, J. Gregory, and Walter H. Warfield. "Discerning the Differences between Managers and Leaders." *Education Digest* 75, no. 7 (2010): 61–64.

Richards-Gustafson, Flora. "What Elements Must Be Included in Documenting an Employee for Termination?" *Chron*, August 1, 2017. http://smallbusiness.chron.com/elements-must-included-documenting-employee-termination-17686.html.

Richardson, Adam. "Using Customer Journey Maps to Improve Customer Experience." *Harvard Business Review Digital Articles*, November 15, 2010.

Risdon, Chris. "Un-Sucking the Touchpoint." *Adaptive Path*, December 2, 2013. http://adaptivepath.org/ideas/un-sucking-the-touchpoint/.

Robbins, Louise S. *Censorship and the American Library: The American Library Association's Response to Threats to Intellectual Freedom, 1939–1969*. Westport, CT: Greenwood, 1997.

Robbins, Louise S. *The Dismissal of Miss Ruth Brown: Civil Rights, Censorship, and the American Library*. Norman: University of Oklahoma Press, 2000.

Robinson, Otis H. "College Library Administration." In *Public Libraries in the United States: Their Condition and Management*. Special Report, Department of the Interior, Bureau of Education, Part 1, 35, no. 1187, 520–25. Washington, DC: Government Printing Office, 1876, facsimile of the 1st edition with an introduction by Francis Keppel.

"The ROI of Corporate Libraries and Research Solutions—White Paper." EBSCO. https://help.ebsco.com/interfaces/EBSCO_Guides/General_Product_FAQs/ROI_of_Corporate_Libraries_Research_Solutions.

Rollins, Charlemae Hill. *We Build Together: A Reader's Guide to Negro Life and Literature for Elementary and High School Use*. Chicago: National Council for Teachers of English, 1941.

Rooks, Dana C. "Leadership: Some Personal Thoughts." *Texas Library Journal* (Spring 2011): 14–16.

Ross, Catherine Sheldrick, and Kirsti Inlsen. *Communicating Professionally*. Chicago: ALA Neal-Schuman, 2013.

Rosser, Christopher Michael, and Tamie Willis. "Flip Over Research Instruction: Delivery, Assessment, and Feedback Strategies for 'Flipped' Library." *Theological Librarianship* 9, no 1 (2016).

Rowlands, Ian. "Understanding Information Policies." *Journal of Information Science* 22, no. 1 (1996): 13–25.

"Rude Behavior in Everyday Life and on the Campaign Trail—Issue Brief." Associated Press—NORC Center for Public Affairs Research, 2016. http://www.apnorc.org/projects/Pages/HTML%20Reports/rude-behavior-in-everyday-life-and-on-the-campaign-trail.aspx.

Rutledge, L., S. LeMire, and A. Mowdood. "Dare to Perform: Using Organizational Competencies to Manage Job Performance." In *Creating Sustainable Community—ACRL Conference, 2015*, edited by D. Mueller, 160–67. Chicago: Association of College and Research Libraries. http://www.ala.org/acrl/sites/ala.org.acrl/files/content/conferences/confsandpreconfs/2015/Rutledge_LeMire_Mowdood.pdf.

Ryan, Liz. *Reinvention Roadmap: Break the Rules to Get the Job You Want and Career You Deserve*. Dallas, TX: BenBella Books, 2016.

Saade, Renea I. "When Does a Workplace Qualify as Being Hostile?" *Seattle Business*. http://www.seattle businessmag.com/business-corners/workplace/when-does-workplace-qualify-being-hostile.

Sammet, J. E. "The Early History of COBOL." *ACM SIGPLAN Notices* 13, no. 8 (1978): 121–61, doi:10.1145/960118.808378.

"San Diego Public Library's Award-Winning Literacy Services." *Support My Library San Diego*, February 22, 2011. https://supportmylibrary.org/?attachment_id=516.

San José State University. "MLIS Skills at Work: A Snapshot of Job Postings Spring 2017." San José, CA: San José State University, 2017. https://ischool.sjsu.edu/sites/default/files/content_pdf/career_trends.pdf

Sarchet, Patricia M. "Leadership: The Challenge for the Information Professional." *Journal of the Medical Library Association* 97, no. 2 (April 2009): 153.

Saricks, Joyce. *Readers' Advisory Service in the Public Library*, third edition. Chicago: American Library Association, 2005.

Sarsfield, S. *The Data Governance Imperative: A Business Strategy for Corporate Data*. Ely, UK: IT Governance Pub, 2009.

Schmidt, Aaron, and Amanda Etches. *Useful, Usable, Desirable: Applying User Experience Design to Your Library*. Chicago: American Library Association, 2014.

———. *User Experience (UX) Design for Libraries*. The Tech Set Series, 18. Chicago: ALA TechSource, 2012.

Schön, Donald A. *The Reflective Practitioner: How Professionals Think in Action*. New York: Basic Books, 1983.

"School Library Journal on Self-Censorship: 2016 Controversial Books Survey." *School Library Journal*. Accessed June 30, 2017. http://www.slj.com/features/self-censorship/.

Secretary's Commission on Achieving Necessary Skills (SCANS). *What Work Requires of Schools: A SCANS Report for America 2000*. Washington, DC: U.S. Department of Labor, 1991. http://wdr.doleta.gov/SCANS/whatwork/whatwork.pdf.

"The Section 108 Study Group." Last modified February 7, 2014. http://www.section108.gov.

SelyukIt, Alina. "As Congress Repeals Internet Privacy Rules, Putting Your Options in Perspective." NPR, *All Tech Considered*, March 28, 2017. http://www.npr.org/sections/alltechconsidered/2017/03/28/521813464/as-congress-repeals-internet-privacy-rules-putting-your-options-in-perspective.

Sexual Harassment—Legal Standards. *Workplace Fairness. It's Everyone's Job*. Accessed April 30, 2017. http://www.workplacefairness.org/sexual-harassment-legal-rights.

Shandrow, Kim Lachance. "10 Questions to Ask When Firing an Employee." *Entrepreneur*, 2015. https://www.entrepreneur.com/article/243632.

Sharpe, Stephanie Atkins. "Access Services within Campus and Library Organizations." In *Twenty-First Century Access Services*, edited by Michael Krasulski and Trevor Dawes, 119–34. Chicago: Association of College and Research Libraries, 2013.

Sheldon, Brooke E. *Interpersonal Skills, Theory and Practice: The Librarian's Guide to Becoming a Leader*. Santa Barbara: Libraries Unlimited, 2010.

Shera, Jesse. *Foundations of the Public Library: The Origins of the Public Library Movement in New England, 1629–1855*. Chicago: University of Chicago Press, 1949.

———. "The Social Library: I: Origins, Form, and Economic Backgrounds." In *Foundations of the Public Library*, 68–85. Chicago: University of Chicago Press, 1949.

Shields, David S. "Eighteenth-Century Literary Culture." In *The Colonial Book in the Atlantic World*, edited by Hugh Amory and David D. Hall, 434–76. Chapel Hill: University of North Carolina Press, 2007.

Shulenberger, David. "Substituting Article Processing Charges for Subscriptions: The Cure Is Worse Than the Disease." *Association of Research Libraries News*. 2016. http://www.arl.org/storage/documents/substituting-apcs-for-subscriptions-20july2016.pdf 2016.

Shumaker, David. *The Embedded Librarian*. Medford, NJ: Information Today, 2012.

Simmons, Michelle Holschuh. "Finding Information: Information Mediation and Reference Services." In *Information Services Today*, edited by Sandra Hirsh, 130–38. Lanham, MD: Rowman & Littlefield, 2015.

Simon, Herbert. "A Behavioral Model of Rational Choice." *Quarterly Journal of Economics* 69, no. 1 (1955): 99–118.

Simon, Herbert. *The Sciences of the Artificial*. Cambridge, MA: M.I.T. Press, 1969.

Sims, Chris, and Hillary Louise Johnson. *Scrum: A Breathtakingly Brief and Agile Introduction*. Foster City, CA: Dymaxicon, 2012. http://www.agilelearninglabs.com/resources/scrum-introduction/.

Sittler, Ryan, and Douglas Cook. *The Library Instruction Cookbook*. Chicago: Association of College and Research Libraries, 2009.

Smith, Aaron. "Record Shares of Americans Now Own Smartphones, Have Home Broadband." Pew Research Center, January 12, 2017. Accessed May 31, 2017. http://www.pewresearch.org/fact-tank/2017/01/12/evolution-of-technology/.

SnapCircuits. "Home." SnapCircuits. Accessed July 5, 2017. http://snapcircuits.net.

Snedaker, S., and C. Rima. *Business Continuity and Disaster Recovery Planning for IT Professionals*, second edition. Waltham, MA: Syngress-Elsevier, 2014.

Snider, Brett. "Is It Legal to 'Unlock' Your Cell Phone?" *Law and Daily Life*, May 18, 2014. http://blogs.findlaw.com/law_and_life/2014/05/is-it-legal-to-unlock-your-cell-phone.html.

"Social Justice." National Association of Social Workers. http://www.socialworkers.org/pressroom/features/Issue/peace.asp.

Society of American Archivists. "Code of Ethics for Archivists." Last modified January 2012. http://www2.archivists.org/statements/saa-core-values-statement-and-code-of-ethics.

Society of American Archivists. "Core Values of Archivists." Adopted May 2011. http://www2.archivists.org/statements/saa-core-values-statement-and-code-of-ethics.

Special Libraries Association (SLA) Core Competencies. http://www.sla.org/about-sla/competencies/.

Squishy Circuits. "Welcome to the Squishy Circuits Project Page." University of St. Thomas. Accessed July 5, 2017. http://courseweb.stthomas.edu/apthomas/SquishyCircuits/.

St. Jean, Beth. "Factors Motivating, Demotivating, or Impeding Information Seeking and Use by People with Type 2 Diabetes: A Call to Work toward Preventing, Identifying, and Addressing Incognizance." *Journal of the American Society for Information Science and Technology* 68, no. 2 (2016): 309–20.

———. "'I Just Don't Know What I Don't Know!': A Longitudinal Investigation of the Perceived Usefulness of Information to People with Type 2 Diabetes." *Proceedings of the American Society for Information Science and Technology* 49, no. 1 (2012): 1–10.

"Standards." International Standards for Technology in Education (ISTE). Last updated September 3, 2014. http://www.iste.org/standards/standards/standards-for-teachers.

"Standards for Students." International Standards for Technology in Education (ISTE). Last updated September 3, 2014. http://www.iste.org/standards/standards/for-students-2016.

Stanford Copyright and Fair Use Center. "Measuring Fair Use: The Four Factors." Last modified June 30, 2014. http://fairuse.stanford.edu/overview/fair-use/four-factors/.

Stanford Copyright and Fair Use Center. "The Public Domain." Last modified June 27, 2014. http://fairuse.stanford.edu/overview/public-domain/.

Stanford University. "LOCKSS." Last modified 2017. https://www.lockss.org/.

Stang, T. "Librarians: The New Research Data Management Experts." *Elsevier Connect* (blog), 2016. https://www.elsevier.com/connect/librarians-the-new-research-data-management-experts.

Stark, Kio. *When Strangers Meet: How People You Don't Know Can Transform You*. New York: Simon & Schuster, 2016.

State Laws on Employment-Related Discrimination. *National Conference of State Legislators*. http://www.ncsl.org/research/labor-and-employment/discrimination-employment.aspx.

Stenström, Cheryl, and Ken Haycock. "Influence and Increased Funding in Canadian Public Libraries: The Case of Alberta in 2009–10." *Library Quarterly* 84, no. 1 (2014): 49–68.

Stephens, Julia. "English Spoken Here." *American Libraries* 38, no. 10 (November 2007).

Stephens, Michael. "Exemplary Practice for Learning 2.0." *Reference and User Services Quarterly* 53, no. 2 (2013): 129–39.

———. "Dream Explore. Experiment. Office Hours." *Library Journal*, May 2016. http://lj.libraryjournal.com/2016/05/opinion/michael-stephens/dream-explore-experiment-office-hours/.

———. *The Heart of Librarianship: Attentive, Positive, and Purposeful change.* Chicago: ALA Editions, 2016.

Stephens, Michael, and Maria Collins. "Web 2.0, Library 2.0, and the Hyperlinked Library." *Serials Review* 33, no. 4 (2007): 253.

Stern, Eli. "Leading the Change—Revolutionary vs. Evolutionary." LinkedIn, June 17, 2015. https://www.linkedin.com/pulse/leading-change-revolutionary-vs-evolutionary-eli-stern-.

Stieg, Margaret F. *Change and Challenge in Library and Information Science Education.* Chicago: American Library Association, 1992.

Stone, Elizabeth. *Policy Paradox: The Art of Political Decision Making.* Revised edition. New York: W.W. Norton & Company, 2002.

Stone, Katherine V. W. "Revisiting the At-Will Employment Doctrine: Imposed Terms, Implied Terms, and the Normative World of the Workplace." *Industrial Law Journal* 36, no. 1 (March, 2007): 84–101.

"Storytimes Matter! Building Early Literacy in YOUR Public Libraries." *VIEWS2.* http://views2.ischool.uw.edu/welcome-directors/.

Strieb, Karla L., and Julia C. Blixrud. "Unwrapping the Bundle: An Examination of Research Libraries and the 'Big Deal.'" *Portal: Libraries and the Academy* 14, no. 4 (2014): 587–615. http://muse.jhu.edu/article/556216.

Suber, Peter. *Open Access.* The MIT Press Essential Knowledge Series. Cambridge, MA: MIT Press, 2012.

———. "Removing the Barriers to Research: An Introduction to Open Access for Librarians." *College & Research Libraries News*, no. 64 (2003).

Sucozhañay, Dolores, Lorena Siguenza-Guzman, Cristian Zhimnay, Dirk Cattrysse, Guido Wyseure, Karel De Witte, and Martin Euwema. "Transformational Leadership and Stakeholder Management in Library Change." *Liber Quarterly* 24, no. 2 (2014).

Sullivan, Brian T., and Karen L. Porter. "From One-Shot Sessions to Embedded Librarians: Lessons Learned over Seven Years of Successful Faculty-Librarian Collaboration." *College and Research Library News* 77, no. 1 (2016): 34–37. http://crln.acrl.org /content/77/1/34.full.

Surowiecki, James. *The Wisdom of Crowds.* New York: Doubleday, 2004.

Suskin Muniz, Alicia, and Sarah Howell. "Adult Literacy through Libraries: Building a National Movement." *New York Library Association*, November 3, 2016. https://www.nyla.org/max/userfiles/uploads/NYLA_November_2016_without_notes.pdf.

Svrluga, Susan, William Wan, and Elizabeth Dwoskin. "Ann Coulter Speech at UC Berkeley, Canceled, Again, Amid Fears for Safety." *Washington Post*, April 26, 2017. https://www.washingtonpost.com/news/grade-point/wp/2017/04/26/ann-coulter-speech-canceled-at-uc-berkeley-amid-fears-for-safety/?utm_term=.8c9ff293b604.

Swain, Martha H. "A New Deal in Libraries: Federal Relief Work and Library Service, 1933–43." *Libraries & Culture* 30, no. 3 (Summer 1995): 265–83.

Tableau Software. "Home." Accessed July 11, 2017. http://www.tableau.com.

Tavernaro, Brittany. "Emerging Leaders Report." *Arkansas Libraries* 73, no. 4 (Winter 2016): 22–24.

Taylor, Robert S. "Question-Negotiation and Information Seeking in Libraries." *College and Research Libraries* 29, no. 3 (1968): 178–94. http://crl.acrl.org/content/29/3/178.full.pdf.

Tella, Adeyinka, C. O. Ayeni, and S. O. Popoola. "Work Motivation, Job Satisfaction, and Organizational Commitment of Library Personnel in Academic and Research Libraries in Oyo State, Nigeria." *Library Philosophy and Practice (e-journal)* 118 (2007): 1–17. http://digitalcommons.unl.edu/libphilprac/118.

Teufel, Hugo. "Privacy Policy Guidance Memorandum Number: 2007–1 (As amended from January 19, 2007)." Department of Homeland Security. https://www.dhs.gov/xlibrary/assets/privacy/privacy_policyguide_2007-1.pdf.

Text Encoding Initiative. *TEI, Text Encoding Initiative.* http://www.tei-c.org/index.xml.

Think Check Submit. "Home." Accessed August 8, 2017. http://thinkchecksubmit.org/.

Thomas, Jason. "Interpreting MARC: Where's the Bibliographic Data?" *code{4}lib journal* 11 (2010): http://journal.code4lib.org/articles/3832.

Thomsett-Scott, B., and Reese, P. E. "Academic Libraries and Discovery Tools: A Survey of the Literature." *College & Undergraduate Libraries* 19, nos. 2–4 (2012): 123–43. doi: 10.1080/10691316.2012.697009.

"360 Degree Feedback." Tests on the Net. http://www.testsonthenet.com/atctests/360-Degree-Overview.htm.

Tolppanen, Bradley. "A Survey of Current Tasks and Future Trends in Access Services." *Journal of Access Services* 2, no. 3 (2004): 1–14.

Tucker, John Mark. "User Education in Academic Libraries: A Century in Retrospect." *Library Trends* 29, no. 1 (1980): 9–27.

Tupper, Cawsey, and Gene Deszca. *Toolkit for Organizational Change.* Los Angeles: Sage Publications, 2007.

Turnbow, Dominique, and Annie Zeidman-Karpinski. "Don't Use a Hammer When You Need a Screwdriver: How to Use the Right Tools to Create Assessment That Matters." *Communications in Information Literacy* 10 (2016): 143–62. http://www.comminfolit.org/index.php?journal=cil&page=article&op=view&path%5B%5D=v10i2p143.

Tversky, Amos, and Daniel Kahneman. "Judgment under Uncertainty: Heuristics and Biases." In *Judgment under Uncertainty: Heuristics and Biases,* edited by D. Kahneman, P. Slovic, and A. Tversky, 3–20. Cambridge, UK: Cambridge University Press, 1982.

Tyckoson, David A. "What Is the Best Model of Reference Service?" *Library Trends* 50, no. 2 (2001): 183–96.

U.S.A. Patriot Act of 2001. Pub. L. No. 107-56, 115 Stat. 272, 2001. http://thomas.loc.gov/cgi-bin/query/z?c107:H.R.3162.ENR:%20.

U.S. Constitution. Amendment I: http://www.usconstitution.net/const.pdf.

———. Amend. IV.

———. Amend. V.

———. Amend. XIV, §1.

U.S. Copyright Act 14 U.S.C. § Circ. 2, December 2011. http://www.copyright.gov/title17/circ92.pdf.

U.S. Copyright Office. "108. Limitations on Exclusive Rights: Reproduction by Libraries and Archives." Copyright.gov. Last modified 2017. https://www.copyright.gov/title17/92chap1.html#108.

———. "Active Policy Studies." Accessed March 26, 2017. https://www.copyright.gov/policy/.

———. "Code of Federal Regulations: Title 37—Patents, Trademarks, and Copyrights. Accessed July 10, 2017. https://www.copyright.gov/title37/201/index.html

———. "Copyright Basics—Circular 1." United States Copyright Office, 2012: 3. http://www.copyright.gov/circs/circ01.pdf.

———. "Definitions." Accessed June 15, 2017. https://www.copyright.gov/help/faq/faq-definitions.html.

———. "The Digital Millennium Copyright Act of 1998." Last modified December 1998. http://www.copyright.gov/legislation/dmca.pdf.

———. "More Information on Fair Use." Accessed June 15, 2017. https://www.copyright.gov/fair-use/more-info.html.

———. "Online Service Providers." Last modified August 16, 2014. http://copyright.gov/onlinesp/.

———. "Orphan Works and Mass Digitization." Last modified September 7, 2014. http://copyright.gov/orphan.

———. "Revising Section 108: Copyright Exceptions for Libraries and Archives." Accessed March 25, 2017. https://www.copyright.gov/policy/section108/.

U.S. Department of Agriculture. National Agricultural Library. "Home." http://agricola.nal.usda.gov/.

U.S. Department of Commerce. United States Census 2015. https://www.census.gov/quickfacts/table/PST045216/00.

U.S. Department of Education. "Family Educational Rights and Privacy Act (FERPA)." http://www.ed.gov/policy/gen/guid/fpco/ferpa/index.html.

———. "No Child Left Behind." 2001. https://www2.ed.gov/nclb/landing.jhtml.

———. "Race to the Top." https://www2.ed.gov/programs/racetothetop/index.html.

U.S. Department of Health and Human Services. "NIH Public Access Policy Details." March 27, 2014. http://publicaccess.nih.gov/policy.htm.

U.S. Department of Health, Education and Welfare. "Records, Computers, and the Rights of Citizens." Secretary's Advisory Committee on Automated Personal Data Systems, No. (OS) 73–94, 1973. http://www.justice.gov/opcl/docs/rec-com-rights.pdf.

U.S. Department of Justice. "1854. Copyright Infringement — First Sale Doctrine." U.S. Attorneys' Manual. Last modified 2017. https://www.justice.gov/usam/criminal-resource-manual-1854-copyright-infringement-first-sale-doctrine.

———. "Judicial Redress Act of 2015." https://www.justice.gov/opcl/judicial-redress-act-2015.

———. "The Disability Rights Section." Accessed April 30, 2017. https://www.justice.gov/crt/disability-rights-section.

———. "Information and Technical Assistance on the Americans with Disabilities Act." Accessed April 30, 2017. https://www.ada.gov/.

———. "Introduction to the ADA." 2014.

U.S. Department of Labor. "Wages and Hours Worked: Minimum Wage and Overtime Pay." Accessed April 30, 2017. https://www.dol.gov/compliance/guide/minwage.htm.

———. Bureau of Labor Statistics: "Labor Force Statistics from the Current Population Survey." 2016. https://www.bls.gov/cps/cpsaat11.htm.

———. Office of Disability Employment Policy. "Communicating with and about People with Disabilities." 2017. https://www.dol.gov/odep/pubs/fact/communicating.htm.

———. Wage and Hour Division (WHD): "Handy Reference Guide to the Fair Labor Standards Act." 2016. https://www.dol.gov/whd/regs/compliance/hrg.htm.

U.S. Department of State. "Sexual Harassment Policy." Accessed April 30, 2017. https://www.state.gov/s/ocr/c14800.htm.

———. "Treaties Pending in the Senate." Last modified December 30, 2016. https://www.state.gov/s/l/treaty/pending/.

———. "VPAT Form." Last modified 2017. https://www.state.gov/m/irm/impact/126343.htm.

U.S. Equal Employment Opportunity Commission. "Americans with Disabilities Act of 1990." Last modified 2017. https://www.eeoc.gov/eeoc/history/35th/1990s/ada.html.

———. "Harassment." Accessed April 30, 2017. https://www.eeoc.gov/laws/types/harassment.cfm.

———. "Laws Enforced by EEOC." Accessed April 30, 2017. https://www.eeoc.gov/laws/statutes/index.cfm.

———. "Federal Laws Prohibiting Job Discrimination Questions and Answers." Accessed August 1, 2017. https://www.eeoc.gov/facts/qanda.html.

———. "Sexual Harassment." Accessed April 30, 2017. https://www.eeoc.gov/laws/types/sexual_harassment.cfm.

———. "Title VII of the Civil Rights Act of 1964." Accessed April 30, 2017. https://www.eeoc.gov/laws/statutes/titlevii.cfm.

———. "You Should Know about EEOC and the Enforcement Protections for LGBT Workers." Accessed April 30, 2017. https://www.eeoc.gov/eeoc/newsroom/wysk/enforcement_protections_lgbt_workers.cfm.

U. S. Patent and Trademark Office. "Department of Commerce Multistakeholder Forum—Improving the Operation of the DMCA Notice and Takedown Policy First Public Meeting." Last modified March 20, 2014. http://www.uspto.gov/ip/global/copyrights/First_Public_Meeting-Improving_Operation_of_DMCA_Notice_and_Takedown_Policy.pdf.

———. "Department of Commerce Multistakeholder Forum on Improving the Operation of the DMCA Notice and Takedown System Third Public Meeting." Last modified June 20, 2014. http://www.uspto.gov/ip/global/copyrights/3rd_plenary_meeting_transcript.pdf.

———. "Office of Policy and International Affairs—Copyrights." Last modified July 5, 2014. http://www.uspto.gov/ip/global/copyrights/index.jsp.

UKSG. "KBART: Knowledge Bases and Related Tools Working Group." Last modified 2014. http://www.uksg.org/KBART.

UNESCO. Paris Declaration on Media and Information Literacy in the Digital Era. UNESCO, 2014. http://www.unesco.org/new/fileadmin/MULTIMEDIA/HQ/CI/CI/pdf/news/paris_mil_declaration.pdf.

"Universal Service." *Federal Communications Commission.* Last updated September 30, 2014. http://www.fcc
.gov/encyclopedia/universal-service.

University of British Columbia Library Planning. *UBC Library SWOT Analysis.* Vancouver: University of British
Columbia Library, 2000, 1. http://www.ryerson.ca/~itm700/Attachments/UBCLibraryswot-analysis.pdf.

University of Chicago Library. "Library Survey 2010: Graduate and Professional Students." Last modified
June 15, 2010. https://www.lib.uchicago.edu/about/thelibrary/surveys/2010/.

University of Maryland Libraries. "Scorned Literature." Accessed June 30, 2017. http://www.lib.umd.edu/
nancy/girls-literature/scorned-literature.

University of Michigan Design Labs. https://www.lib.umich.edu/design-labs.

University of Michigan Library. "Library Copyright Statement." Last modified February 15, 2016. https://
www.lib.umich.edu/library-administration/library-copyright-statement.

Vaidhyanathan, Siva. *The Googlization of Everything (and Why We Should Worry).* Berkeley: University of
California Press, 2012.

"Value of Academic Libraries Toolkit." Association of College and Research Libraries, October 2010. http://
www.ala.org/acrl/issues/value/valueofacademiclibrariestoolkit.

Van Bogart, John. "Magnetic Tape Storage and Handling." Council on Library and Information Resources.
https://www.clir.org/pubs/reports/pub54/index.html.

Van Epps, Amy, and Megan Sapp Nelson. "One-Shot or Embedded? Assessing Different Delivery Timing for
Information Resources Relevant to Assignments." *Evidence Based Library and Information Practice* 8, no. 1
(2013): 4–18. http://ejournals.library.ualberta.ca/index.php/EBLIP/article/view/18027/14793.

Van Hoeck, Michele. "Wikipedia as an Authentic Learning Space." *LOEX Quarterly* 39 (Winter 2013): 4–8.
http://commons.emich.edu/cgi/viewcontent.cgi?article=1188&context=loexquarterly.

Van Slyck, Abigail. *Free to All: Carnegie Libraries and American Culture, 1890–1920.* Chicago: University of
Chicago Press, 1995.

Vassilakaki, Evgenia, and Valentini Moniarou-Papaconstantinou. "A Systematic Literature Review Informing
Library and Information Professionals' Emerging Roles." *New Library World* 116, nos. 1–2 (2015): 37–66.

Venner, Mary, and Seti Keshmiripour. "X Marks the Spot: Creating and Managing a Single Service Point to
Improve Customer Service to Maximize Resources." *Journal of Access Services* 13, no. 2 (2016): 101–11.

Vijayakuamar, M., and K. S. Manoj Kumar. "Strategies for Leadership in Management College Libraries."
SRELS Journal of Information Management 53, no. 5 (2016): 405–8.

Vijayan, Jaikumar. "Obama Executive Order Redefines Critical Infrastructure." *Computerworld*, February
14, 2013. http://www.computerworld.com/article/2494979/security0/obama-executive-order-rede
fines-critical-infrastructure.html.

Wagner, Ben A. "Open Access Citation Advantage: An Annotated Bibliography." *Issues in Science and Technology Librarianship*, 2010. http://www.istl.org/10-winter/article2.html.

Wall, Keynen J. Jr., and Jacqueline Johnson. "Colorado's Lawful Activities Statute: Balancing Employee Privacy and the Rights of Employers." *Colorado Lawyer*, December 2006.

Walter, Scott, and Karen Williams. *The Expert Library: Staffing, Sustaining, and Advancing the Academic Library
in the 21st Century.* Chicago: Association of College and Research Libraries, 2010.

Walters, Suzanne, and Kent Jackson. *Breakthrough Branding: Positioning Your Library to Survive and Thrive.*
Chicago: ALA, Neal-Schuman, 2014.

Walters, Tyler O., and Katherine Skinner. "Economics, Sustainability, and the Cooperative Model in Digital
Preservation." *Library Hi Tech* 28, no. 2 (2010): 259–72. doi:10.1108/07378831011047668.

Ward, Gary. "Press Conference: Congressman Doyle to Address New Bill to Unlock U.S. $60 Billion Invest-
ment in Research." *Alliance for Taxpayer Access*, April 21, 2010. http://www.taxpayeraccess.org/issues/
frpaa/frpaa_resources/press-conference-congressman-doyle-to-address-new-.shtml.

Ware, Mark, and Michael Mabe. *The STM Report.* International Association of Scientific, Technical and Medical Publishers, February 20, 2015. http://www.stm-assoc.org/2015_02_20_STM_Report_2015.pdf.

Warren, Samuel, and Louis Brandeis. "The Right to Privacy." *Harvard Law Review* 4, no. 5 (1890): 193–220.
http://groups.csail.mit.edu/mac/classes/6.805/articles/privacy/Privacy_brand_warr2.html.

Wasu, Sono. "Students Question Why Popular Novel Is Removed from Gilbert School's Curriculum." *ABC*, June 30, 2017. http://www.abc15.com/news/region-southeast-valley/gilbert/students-question-why-popular-novel-is-removed-from-gilbert-schools-curriculum.

Watkinson, Charles. "Why Marriage Matters: A North American Perspective on Press/Library Partnerships." *Learned Publishing* 29 (2016): 342–47.

Watson, Paula D. "Founding Mothers: The Contribution of Women's Organizations to Public Library Development in the United States." *Library Quarterly* 64, no. 3 (1994): 233–69.

WC3. http://www.w3.org/standards/.

Webb, Amy. *The Signals Are Talking: Why Today's Fringe Is Tomorrow's Mainstream*. New York: Public Affairs, 2016.

Webster, Keith. "Reimagining the Role of the Library in the Digital Age: Changing the Use of Space and Navigating the Information Landscape." *LSE Impact Blog*, February 15, 2017. Accessed May 31, 2017. http://blogs.lse.ac.uk/impactofsocialsciences/2017/02/15/reimagining-the-role-of-the-library-in-the-digital-age-changing-the-use-of-space-and-navigating-the-information-landscape/?platform=hootsuite.

Weinberger, David. "The Hyperlinked Organization." *The Cluetrain Manifesto*. Accessed May 31, 2017. http://www.cluetrain.com/book/hyperorg.html.

———. *Too Big to Know: Rethinking Knowledge Now That the Facts Aren't the Facts, Experts Are Everywhere, and the Smartest Person in the Room Is the Room*. New York: Basic Books, 2014.

Weiss, Andrew. "Examining Massive Digital Libraries (MDLs) and Their Impact on Reference Services." *Reference Librarian* 57, no. 4 (2016): 286–306. doi:10.1080/027638772016.1145614. doi:10.1080/02763877.2016.1145614.

Welch, Jeanie M. "Who Says We're Not Busy? Library Web Page Usage as a Measure of Public Service Activity." *Reference Services Review* 33, no. 4 (2005): 371–79.

Wells, Mark. "A Growing World of Connected Devices." YouTube video, 2:58. Posted by CTIA, May 5, 2014. https://www.youtube.com/watch?v=HxK46CFsJeM&list=PLE53CB584A01349B5.

West, Henry R. "J. S. Mill." In *The Oxford Handbook of the History of Ethics*, edited by Roger Crisp. New York: Oxford University Press, 2013. Accessed August 1, 2017. doi:10.1093/oxfordhb/9780199545971.013.0025.

Western Association of Schools and Colleges. *Core Competency FAQs*. Senior College and University Commission, June 2014. http://www.wascsenior.org/content/core-competency-faqs.

White House. "Big Data: Seizing Opportunities, Preserving Values." Executive Office of the President, 2014. http://www.whitehouse.gov/issues/technology/big-data-review.

———. "Executive Order: Enhancing Public Safety in the Interior of the United States." January 25, 2017. https://www.whitehouse.gov/the-press-office/2017/01/25/presidential-executive-order-enhancing-public-safety-interior-united.

———. "Presidential Executive Order on Reducing Regulation and Controlling Regulatory Costs." 2017. https://www.whitehouse.gov/the-press-office/2017/01/30/presidential-executive-order-reducing-regulation-and-controlling.

———. "White House, National Strategy for Trusted Identities in Cyberspace: Enhancing Online Choice, Efficiency, Security, and Privacy." Executive Office of the President, 2011. https://obamawhitehouse.archives.gov/sites/default/files/rss_viewer/NSTICstrategy_041511.pdf.

Whitehill, Walter Muir. *Boston Public Library: A Centennial History*. Cambridge, MA: Harvard University Press, 1956. https://archive.org/details/bostonpubliclibr010132mbp.

Whitman, Alden. "Marshall McLuhan, Author, Dies; Declared 'Medium Is the Message.'" *New York Times*, January 1, 1981. http://www.nytimes.com/books/97/11/02/home/mcluhan-obit.html.

Whyte, A., and J. Tedds. "Making the Case for Research Data Management." Digital Curation Centre. Accessed May 10, 2017. http://www.dcc.ac.uk/resources/briefing-papers/making-case-rdm.

Wiegand, Wayne A. *An Active Instrument for Propaganda: The American Public Library during World War I*. New York: Greenwood, 1989.

———. *Main Street Public Library: Community Places and Reading Spaces in the Rural Heartland, 1876–1956*. Iowa City: University of Iowa Press, 2011.

———. *Part of Our Lives: A People's History of the American Public Library*. Oxford: Oxford University Press, 2015.

Wiggins, Grant, and Jay McTighe. *Understanding by Design*. Upper Saddle River, NJ: Merrill Prentice Hall, 1998.

Wiggins, Rick. "About the Threshold Achievement Test for Information Literacy." Carrick Enterprises, 2017. https://thresholdachievement.com/the-test/about-the-test.

Wikipedia. "LexisNexis." Last modified May 5, 2017. https://en.wikipedia.org/w/index.php?title=LexisNexis&oldid=765933156.

———. "ProQuest Dialog." Last modified December 16, 2015. https://en.wikipedia.org/w/index.php?title=ProQuest_Dialog&oldid=695448199.

———"Westlaw." Last modified April 28, 2017. https://en.wikipedia.org/w/index.php?title=Westlaw&oldid=766510750.

Wilbanks, John, and Jamie Boyle. "Introduction to Science Commons." *Science Commons*, 2006. http://sciencecommons.org/wp-content/uploads/ScienceCommons_Concept_Paper.pdf.

"Wild Colorado App." Mesa County Libraries. Accessed May 31, 2017. http://mesacountylibraries.org/aboutus/wild-colorado-app/.

Wilkin, John P. "Meanings of the Library Today." In *The Meaning of the Library: A Cultural History*, edited by Alice Crawford, 244–49. Princeton, NJ: Princeton University Press, 2015.

Williams, Anne H. *How to Discipline Employee Behavior*. Brentwood, TN: M. Lee Smith Publishers, 2002.

Williams, Robert V. "The Documentation and Special Libraries Movement in the United States, 1910–1960." *Journal of the American Society for Information Science* 48, no. 9 (1997): 775–81.

Willinsky, John. *The Access Principle: The Case for Open Access to Research and Scholarship*. Cambridge, MA: MIT Press, 2006. http://arizona.openrepository.com/arizona/handle/10150/106529.

Wilson, Despina. "An Evaluation of Leadership Competencies and Formal Leadership Education Recommendations for Library Leaders of the 21st Century." PhD diss., Wilmington University (Delaware), 2016.

Wilson, Duane. "Reinvisioning Access Services: A Survey of Access Services Departments in ARL Libraries." *Journal of Access Services* 10, no. 3 (2013): 153–71.

Wilson, Thomas D. "Models in Information Behavior Research." *Journal of Documentation* 55, no. 3 (1999): 249–70.

———. "On User Studies and Information Needs." *Journal of Documentation* 37 (1981): 3–15.

Winslow, Ben. "Utah Lawmaker Plans Porn Blocking Legislation for Cellphones, Libraries." Fox 13 News, May 17, 2016. http://fox13now.com/2016/05/17/utah-lawmaker-plans-porn-filter-legislation-for-cell-phones-libraries/.

Wolfe, Lisa A. *Library Public Relations, Promotions, and Communications: A How-To-Do-It Manual*. New York: Neal-Schuman Publishers, 2005.

World Intellectual Property Organization. "Main Provisions and Benefits of the Marrakesh Treaty (2013)." Accessed March 26, 2017. http://www.wipo.int/edocs/pubdocs/en/wipo_pub_marrakesh_flyer.pdf.

———. "The Marrakesh Treaty in Action." Accessed March 26, 2017. http://www.wipo.int/pressroom/en/stories/marrakesh-treaty.html.

World Wide Web Consortium. *RDF 1.1 Primer*. Cambridge, MA: W3C Consortium, 2014. https://www.w3.org/TR/2014/NOTE-rdf11-primer-20140225/.

Wright, Meggie, and Valery King. "LEADing the Way: UX IRL @ OSU." *OLA Quarterly* 22, no. 3 (2017): 31–36. doi:http://dx.doi.org/10.7710/1093-7374.1869.

Xie, Jenny. "Two Major Public Library Systems Are about to Start Lending Wi-Fi Hotspots." *CityLab*, June 23, 2014. http://www.citylab.com/cityfixer/2014/06/two-major-public-library-systems-are-about-to-start-lending-wi-fi-hotspots/373233/.

Yale University Library Digital Humanities Lab. http://web.library.yale.edu/dhlab.

Yap, Neil. "Welcoming the Marrakesh Treaty into a Consequentialist Framework." *JIPEL Blog*, February 23, 2017. http://blog.jipel.law.nyu.edu/2017/02/welcoming-the-marrakesh-treaty-into-a-consequentialist-framework/.

Yeh, Shea-Tinn, and Zhiping, Walter. "Critical Success Factors for Integrated Library System Implementation in Academic Libraries: A Qualitative Study." *Information Technology & Libraries* 35, no. 3 (2016): 27–42. doi:10.6017/ital.v35i2.9255.

Young Adult Library Services Association. "Printz Award." Accessed September 7, 2017. http://www.ala .org/yalsa/printz-award.

Young, Courtney L. "Crowdsourcing the Virtual Reference Interview with Twitter." *Reference Librarian* 55, no. 2 (2014): 172–74. doi:10.1080/02763877.2014.879030.

Young, Indi. *Practical Empathy: For Collaboration and Creativity in Your Work*. Brooklyn, NY: Rosenfeld Media, 2015.

Young, Richard D. *Perspectives on Strategic Planning in the Public Sector*. Institute for Public Service and Policy Research. http://www.ipspr.sc.edu/publication/perspectives%20on%20strategic%20planning.pdf.

"Your Rights Against Workplace Discrimination and Harassment." *NOLO*, 2017. http://www.nolo.com/ legal-encyclopedia/workplace-rights.

Zickuhr, Kathryn, Lee Rainie, Kristen Purcell, and Maeve Duggan. "How Americans Value Public Libraries in Their Communities." Pew Internet & American Life Project, December 11, 2013. http://libraries.pew internet.org/2013/12/11/libraries-in-communities.

Zickuhr, Kathryn, Lee Rainie, and Kristen Purcell. "Library Services in the Digital Age." Pew Internet Libraries. Accessed January 14, 2016. http://libraries.pewinternet.org/2013/01/22/library-services/.

Zweizig, Douglas L. "Predicting Amount of Library Use: An Empirical Study of the Public Library in the Life of the Adult Public." Ph.D. diss., Syracuse University, 1973.

Index

Award for Courage, 364; professional development, 458, 473; Task Force (and later Working Group) on Equity, Diversity, and Inclusion, 54, 67n5; Washington Office Newsline, 375. *See also* Banned Books Week; intellectual freedom

American Theological Library Association, *111*

Americans with Disabilities Act (ADA), 66, 274, 399, *403*; physical and mental ability, 66. *See also* discrimination; diversity

analog, 5, 117, 120–21, 126, 364; to digital, 372; tools, 28. *See also* preservation

analysis, 173, 191, 202, 244, 251, 291, 304, 341, 364, 381, 386; community, 288, 295–96; cost-benefit, 363; critical, 219; environmental scans, 238, 340–41, 472, 487; policy, 357–58; strengths, weaknesses, opportunities and threats (SWOT), 231, 238–39, 341, 472; text, 310. *See also* data analysis; job analysis

analytics, 119, 304, 327; cognitive, 110, 480; data, 10, 243, 314, 321–22, 325, 427, 483; predictive, 314, 322, 406, *411*, 480, 497–98, 502; prescriptive, 110, 498; Web, 120, 504

Apple, 37, 134, 310; iBeacon, 28; Siri, 134

applicant, 267, 274; diverse pool; 267, 269. *See also* diversity; inclusion; personnel

application: management, 303; programming interfaces (API), 307; service provider, 303. *See also* library service platforms; software; software-as-a-service

Archival Metrics. *See* survey tools for libraries

archives, 31, 34, 90, 93n39, 104, 122, 125, 159–61, 166–67, *240*, 298, 371, 384, 3n14, 412, 454. *See also* Open Archives Initiative

archivists, 123, 158, 163, 369, 370–71, 459. *See also* Society of American Archivists

Arduino microcontroller, 221–22, 224, 228n4, 477; Banzi, Massimo, 221, 224

arena of confrontation, 205

ARMA International, *111*, 458

artifacts, 31, 107, 211, *279–81*, 285, 478

artificial intelligence, 3, 134, 220, 322, 477

Asian Pacific American Librarians Association (APALA), *60*

Ask-a-Librarian, 132

assessment, 47, 49, 130, 177, 196, 324, 477; based library programs, *90*; data, 46, 191; formative, 203, 488; in academic libraries, 89–90; job, 267; librarians, 81; measures, 86, 339, 341, 478; needs, 231, 236, 238–39; of access services, 190–91; of instruction, 203–4; performance, 271; program, 199; resource, 241, 341; self-assessment, *59, 339*; summative, 203–4, 502. *See also* survey tools for libraries

Association for Educational Communications and Technology (AECT), 72. *See also* student learning standards

Association for Information Science & Technology (ASIS&T), *111*, 458, 549

Association of American Colleges and Universities (AACU), 53, 196

Association of American Publishers (AAP), *189*, 289, 291–92

Association of American University Presses (AAUP), 85

Association of College and Research Libraries (ACRL); 22, *86*, *111*, 196; Framework for Information Literacy in Higher Education, 86–87; Information Literacy Competency Standards for Higher Education, 198; *Presidential Committee on Information Literacy: Final Report*, *197*; *TechConnect, 215*; *Values of Academic Libraries Report, 199*

Association of Independent Information Professionals (AIIP), *111*, 368–69; Code of Ethical Business Practice, 368–69. *See also* code of ethics

Association of Privacy Professionals, 429

Association of Research Libraries (ARL), 87, 134, 191. *See also* Association of College and Research Libraries

attribute: of information, 142, 404; pricing, *404–5*; recording, 148. *See also* budgets; Carnegie classification; full-time enrollment (FTE); license

audiovisual, 151, 162, 379, *380*, 477. *See also* preservation

audiovisual content preservation. *See* preservation

audit, 263, 419, 426, 478; content, 299. *See also* budget management; privacy audit; user experience

Audit and Certification of Trustworthy Digital Repositories standard (ISO 16363), 160; *Requirements for Bodies Providing Audit and Certification (ISO 16919), 160*

Australian Library and Information Association (ALIA), 4

authority. *See* influence and power

authority control, 143, 149, 478. *See also* cataloging

authorized user, *400*

Authors Guild, 386. *See also* copyright law

automated storage and retrieval systems (AS/RS), 187, 478

Azure. *See* statistical platforms

baby boomers. *See* generational differences

backwards design method. *See* instructional design model

change management, 7, 9, 32–3, 179, 244, 246–55, 288, 470, 480; anticipatory, *252*; framing, 250, 253–54, 488; reactive, *252*; tuning, 251–*52*

channel, 480; cross-channel, 173, 213–14; of information, 42, *172*; virtual, 211–14. *See also* mobile; social media

Chicago Public Library (CPL), 17, 19, 21–22, 221, 223, 283, 285; Co-Lab, 283; Maker Lab's Flickr stream, 223

chief data officer (CDO), 109

chief information officer (CIO), 109

Children's Online Privacy Protection Act of 1998 (COPPA), 373, 419, 422. *See also* information ethics; privacy

Chinese American Librarians Association (CALA), 60

Choose Privacy Week, *373–74*, 444. *See also* intellectual freedom; privacy

circulation, 20, 22, 75, 88, 94–95, 123, 134, 154, 174, 183–88, *193*, *284*, *316*, 341, 435, 454, 480; data, 322; desk, 91, 185–87, 192, 284; modules, 306; of knowledge, 409; operation, *186*; policies, 75, 303. *See also* access services; collection management; intellectual freedom; open access

citation index tool, 131

citation management program, 87; EndNote, 87, 131; Mendeley, 87; RefWorks, 87; Zotero, 87, 131

Cited By. *See* Google Scholar

civility, 335, 338, 480. *See also* impact factors; Miss Manners' Guide to Excruciatingly Correct Behavior

Civil Rights Act, 274

classification, 15, 123, 145, 150–51, 267, 364, 480; schemes, 151, 280;

systems, 96, 101, 150–51. *See also* Carnegie Classification; Dewey Decimal Classification (DCC); Library of Congress Classification (LCC); National Library of Medicine; Online Computer Library Center (OCLC)

click-wrap license, 389, 480. *See also* copyright; copyright law; license

ClimateQual. *See* survey tools for libraries

cloud: based services, *30*, 123, 215, 480; based translation tools, 131; computing, 21, 37, 131, 299, 301–3, 305, 307, 310, 312. *See also* networks

cluster analysis. *See* analytics, prescriptive

COBOL. *See* programming languages

code of ethics. *See* American Library Association; ethics

coding standards, *311*

cognitive analytics. *See* analytics, cognitive

cognitive: ability, 41, *53*, 490; and affective state, 42, 44, 177; differences, 53; disabilities, *338*; principles, 174

collaboration, 3, 5–6, *9*, 21, 36–37, 49, 53, 57, 62, 73–79, 85, *98–100*, 113, 122, 154, 160, 176, *179*, 202, 211, 216, 222, 224, 241, 248, 282, 284–85, 337, 345, 406, 413, 427, *470*, 473–74; collaborative unit, 125; global, *6*, *160*, 488; and partnerships, *6*, 30, 36, 60, 62, 99, 103, 198, 240–1, 470–1, 473. *See also* consortia; cloud, computing; leadership

collaborative Q&A. *See* Q&A services

collection: digital, 8, 123, 126, 131, 299, 310; management, 183–87, *193*, 289–96, *306*, 480; manager, 292–94; print, 292, 307; special, 88, 90, 107, 123, 125, 144, 215, *240–41*, *316*, 438

collection development, 56, 75, 81–82, 88–89, 115, 240, 295–97, 317, 438, 442, 480, 482; cooperative, 482; models, 293; plan, 291–92; policy, 223, 291, 296, 435, 437–38, 442, 480; prescriptive, *438*, 498

collective bargaining agreement, 272–73, 481

College Depot at the Phoenix Public Library, 137

Columbia Copyright Advisory Office, *383*. *See also* copyright

Columbia University, 89, 165, 184

Commission on Preservation and Access, 159. *See also* Task Force on Digital Archiving

Common Core, 481; complex texts, 74–75; curriculum, 201; English language art, 74; Mathematics, 74; Standards, 74–76, 77, 201; State Standards (CCSS), 73, 77

communication: external, 233, 331, 342, 487; intercultural, 53, 65; model, 332, 481; nonverbal, 331, 334, 495; one-way, 38, 332; style, 67, 336–38; two-way, 332, 470; types, 332–*33*; virtual, 342; written, 58, 332–*33*, 470. *See also* competency; International Listening Association

communication plan, 339–41; annual report, 122, 178, 292, 340. *See also* advocacy; social media

community: analysis, 288, 295–96, 339, 341; engagement, *8*, *30*, 38, 97; hub, 3, 7–8, 34, 69, 99–100, 481

community-based Q&A. *See* Q&A services

compact shelving, 186, 481

competency, 481; core, 232, 303; cultural, 58–*59*, 61–62, 65

competitive: analysis, 315, 481; environment, 339, 341; information professional, *111*. *See also* community, analysis; marketing; strategic planning

complex texts. *See* Common Core Standards

computational knowledge engines. *See* algorithm-based search engine

database engines, 302

data cleansing, 320, 326, 483

data dashboard, 324–25, 327. *See also* data visualization; key performance indicators

data driven acquisitions (DDA). *See* acquisition module

data governance, 315, 328–29; General Data Protection Regulation, 328, 426. *See also* copyright law; HIPAA regulations

data management, 21, 84, 113, 119, 125, 315–29, 451, 483; Association (DAMA), 315; CKAN project, 327; DataVault, 327; JISC, 327; plan, 84, 321, 483. *See also* management; research data management; strategic data asset

data minimization, 425, 483

data mining, 322, 327, 400, 406. *See also* data warehouse

data recovery, 315, 317, 319, 329. *See also* replication

DataRefuge. *See* data rescue

data rescue, 165; DataRefuge, *161*, 165; Preservation of Electronic Government Information, 165

data visualization, 113, 315, 323, *325*, 483. *See also* statistical analysis tools; visualization tool

deaccessioning, 89, 483

deacidification, 157, 483

decision making, 29, 41, 66, 84, 109–11, 126, 157–58, 269, *279*, 291, 299, *338*, 344–46, 361–62, 366–67, 374, 405, 429, 470. *See also* influence and power

decision-ready information, 107–8, 484

Degree Qualifications Profile, 199

deontology. *See* ethical theories

Department of Homeland Security (DHS), 421, 423

Department of Justice (DOJ), 115–16, 421, *436*

descriptive cataloging, 149, 484. *See also* cataloging

design: artifacts, 280–81; rationale, 280, 484; user-centered, 171, 176, 180, 281

design thinking, 173–74, 253, 279, 281–85, 484; development phase, 282–83; evaluative phase, 283; framing, *279*–80, 282, 285; investigative phase, 282–83; planning phase, 282–83; problem finding, 280, 285; reframing, *279*–80, 285. *See also* repertoire

DeviantART. *See* resource sharing communities

Dewey, Melvil, 18, 222. *See also* Dewey Decimal Classification System (DDC)

Dewey Decimal Classification (DDC) System, 18, 145, 151, *152*, 480. *See also* classification; Dewey, Melvil

differential incremental backup, 318, 484

digital: asset, 83, 307, 416, 484, 494; citizen, *73*, 484; curation. *See* curation; content, 6,

35, 120–27, 131, *158*–60, *161*, 164, 167, 292, 294, 296, 372–73, 397–400, 404, 406, 484; hosting, 399, 484; humanities (DH), 83, 85, 88, 484; information explosion, 411; librarian, 119, *122*–27, *136*; library, 119–127; native, 109–10, 485; repository, 125, 416, 485; surrogate, 89, 121, 485

Digital Curation Center (DCC), 157; Life Cycle Model, 157

digital divide, *30*, 35, 198–99, 201, 484; National Telecommunications and Information Administration, 198

digital forensics, *156*, 166; The BitCurator Open Source software, 166

digital literacy. *See* literacy

Digital Millennium Copyright Act (DMCA), 384–85, 388, 391, 485. *See also* copyright; Next Great Copyright Act; safe harbor

Digital Outreach and Education (DPOE), 485; Curriculum, 164

digital preservation. *See* preservation

Digital Preservation Network (DPN), 89

Digital Public Library of America (DPLA), *379*

digitization, 81, 131, 324, 384, 386, 391. *See also* mass digitization

direct lobbying. *See* lobbying

direct value. *See* value

Directory of Open Access Journals (DOAJ), 414

disabilities, 46, 57, 66, 306, 335, 338, 384, 387–88, 399, *403*. *See also* Americans with Disabilities Act; diversity; impact factors

disaster recovery plan (DRP), 314, 317–20, 329, 485. *See also* business continuity planning

discoverability technologies, 308

discovery: interface, 176, 300, 308–9, 485; system, 123, 145, *324*, *403*, 485

discovery tool, 131, 142, 154, 308–9, 485; EBSCO, 112, 131, 406; Primo from Ex Libris, 131, 316; WorldCat Discovery Services, 131, 143–44, 504

discretionary time deficit, *30*, 35

discrimination, 53–55, 64, 66–67, 272, 274–75, 477, 485; laws, 272, 274–75. *See also* Americans with Disabilities Act; Civil Rights Act; diversity; equity; Fair Labor Standards Act; personnel; social justice

disparate impact, 272, 485. *See also* personnel

dispute resolution, 401, 486. *See also* license

diversity, *10*, 12, 20, 32, 52–67, 90, 266, 268, 273, 275n2, 331, 335–36, 344, 369–70, 373–74, 439–40, 486. *See also* communication; equity; ethics; impact factors; intellectual freedom; personnel; social justice

DMCA. *See* Digital Millennium Copyright Act (DMCA)

document delivery, 81, 183–84, 187–89, 477. *See also* access services; interlibrary loan; resource sharing

DOKK1, *8*, 98, 217

drop spindle, 225, 486. *See also* creation culture; makerspace

Dublin Core, 126, 144–45, 486. *See also* metadata

DuckDuckGo, 131

e-audio, *248*. *See also* audiovisual; preservation

EBSCO. *See* discovery tool

e-book, 27–28, *30*–31, 37–38, 77, 89, 94, 121, 289–94, 296, 308, 312, *316*, 384, 397, *404*, 406, 440, 480, 483–84, 486. *See also* collection development; e-reader; e-resource

ecological systems theory, 44, 486. *See also* information need

effectiveness, 58, 233, 243–44, 247–51, 253, 261, 316, 344, 358, 399, 469, 470, 474, 486. *See also* advocacy; budgeting; change management; communication; efficiency; leadership; outcome; strategic planning

efficiency, 58, 89, 116, 243, 244, 405, 486. *See also* communication; effectiveness; outcome; strategic planning

e-journal, 89, 121, 125, *294*, 306, *404*, 480, 483, 486. *See also* collection development; e-resource

e-learning, 30, 36. *See also* online learning

Electronic Frontier Foundation (EFF), 424, 430

Electronic Privacy Information Center (EPIC), 430

electronic reserves. *See* e-reserves

electronic resource management systems, 305–6

Electronic Resources & Libraries (ER&L), 179

electronic serials package, 88. *See also* Big Deal

e-lending, 6

embedded: e-brarian, 486; librarian, 69, 87, 135–36, 202, 204, 456, 486; librarianship, 135–36, 202, 486. *See also* academic library; reference services

emergency mode operation plan, 486

emerging technology, *136*, 239

empathy, 94, 102–3, 170, *175*–77, 470. *See also* leadership; user experience

empowered learners, 73, 486. *See also* learning

emulation. *See* preservation activities

encoding, 83, 143–44, 146, 149, 154, 309, 487. *See also* metadata

encumbrance, 487. *See also* budgets

EndNote. *See* citation management program

environmental scan, 11, 33, 231, 236, 238–39, 340–41, 472, 487. *See also* communication; marketing; strategic planning

e-priority policy, 89, 486. *See also* academic library

epistemological, 15

equity, 1, 4, 12, 52–54, 56–57, 62–65, 355, 357, 363–64, 373–74, 453–54, 487. *See also* diversity; professional equity; social justice

e-rate discount, 19, 373, 444, 486

e-reader, 123, 188, *200*, 292, 486; Amazon Kindle, 137, 292, 296; Nook, 292, 296. *See also* e-book

e-reserves, 184, 188–89, *193*, *400*, 500. *See also* reserves

e-resource, 121, 179, 188, 296, 484, 486. *See also* resource sharing

ethical codes, 355, 366–69, 372, 376. *See also* American Library Association; Association of Independent Information Professionals; ethical theories; ethics; International Federation of Library Associations and Institutions; Society of American Archivists

ethical dilemma, 366, 368–70, 374–76; getting help, 375. *See also* ethical codes; ethics; information ethics; shared principles

ethical theories, 367–68; deontology, 367–68, 484; utilitarianism, 367–68, 503. *See also* ethics; information ethics; shared principles

ethics, 110, 127, 225, 355, 366–76, 378, 439, *446*, *470*–71, 473, 480, 487, 490; code of ethics, 225, 368–69, 372, 374–75, 378, 439, *446*, 480; core values statements, 369–72. *See also* ethical theories; information ethics; shared principles

the ethics of care. *See* ethical theories

evaluation, 61, 90, 102, 180, 253, 261, 267, 271, 284, 292, 341, 351, 362–64, 415, 422, 469, 487. *See also* advocacy; assessment; change management; information policy; leadership; marketing; personnel; user experience

evolutionary fitness, 251, 253–54, 487. *See also* change management

executive order (EO), 362–63, 423–24, 427

expenditures. *See* budgets

expert-based Q&A. *See* Q&A services

export controls on information, 487

expression. *See* cataloging; Functional Requirements for Bibliographic Records (FRBR)

extensible markup language (XML), 126, 144, 146, 151, 154, 301, 311. *See also* metadata

external communication. *See* communication

extract, transform, and load process (ETL). *See* normalization of data

Facebook. *See* social media

Faceted Application of Subject Terminology (FAST). *See* online computer library center (OCLC)

facilities management. *See* management

faculty status. *See* academic librarians

fading. *See* film preservation

Fair and Accurate Credit Transaction Act (FACT Act), 423
Fair Credit Reporting Act (FCRA), 419, 423
Fair Information Practice Principles (FIPP), 419–20, 425–27, 429. *See also* privacy
Fair Labor Standards Act (FLSA), 272, 274
fair use. *See* copyright law Section 107; Stanford Office of Fair Use
fake news, 205, 441
Family Educational Rights and Privacy Act (FERPA), *363*, 422
family literacy. *See* literacy
FAST. *See* Online Computer Library Center (OCLC)
Federal Communications Commission (FCC), 420–21
Federal Information Security Management Act (FISMA), 427
Federation of Ontario Public Libraries Open Media Desk, 33
Federal Trade Commission (FTC), 421
FedStats. *See* census data
film preservation, 162–63; acetate deterioration (vinegar syndrome), 162; fading, 162; nitrate deterioration, 162; physical damage, 163. *See also* preservation
finding aids, 87, 123, 487
First Amendment, *95*, 35, 434, 436, 445; freedom of expression in schools, *436*; the internet, *436*; minor's rights, *436–37*; notable cases, *436–37*; obscenity and indecency, *437*; right to privacy and anonymity, *437*; right to read freely, *436. See also* constitution; intellectual freedom
First sale doctrine (Section 109). *See* copyright law
Flickr. *See* resource sharing communities; social media
Flipboard. *See* social media
flipped classroom, 135, 487
Florence Flood, 159, *161*
force majeure. *See* information licensing terms
Foreign Intelligence Surveillance Act (FISA), 424
formal learning. *See* learning
formative assessment. *See* assessment
framing. *See* change management; design thinking
FRBR. *See* Functional Requirements for Bibliographic Records (FRBR)
free speech, 7, 435–36, 441–43, 445. *See also* constitution; intellectual freedom
Freedom of Information Act (FOIA), 362, *401*, 488
Friends of the Library, 238, 256, 258, 263, 488
From Awareness to Funding. *See* Online Computer Library Center (OCLC)
full time enrollment (FTE), 404, 488

fumigation, 157, 488. *See also* preservation
Functional Requirements for Authority Data (FRAD), 145, 148
Functional Requirements for Bibliographic Records (FRBR), 83–84, 142–43, 145–49, 152–54, 487, 493; group 1 entities, 148–49, 154, 487, 493; works, expressions, manifestations, and items (WEMI), 147–49, 153–54. *See also* bibliographic records
funding: government, 262; grant, 200, 263; public, 16–17, 33, 262; supplementary, 200, 263. *See also* budgets; funds; tax revenue
fundraising, 9, 82, 256
funds: general, 256–58, 262, 488; special purpose, 257–58; supplemental, 256, 258. *See also* budgets

Gale Virtual Reference Library, 131
game: play, 215, 488; preservation, 166–67
gamification, 28, 215–16, 488
gaming studio, 217, 488
Gay, Lesbian, Bisexual and transgendered Round Table. *See* American Library Association
Gen 2020. *See* generational differences
gender expression, 55, 65, 67, 269
General Data Protection Regulation. *See* data governance
general fund. *See* budgets; funds
general ledger account, 257–58, 488. *See also* budgets
generational differences, 67, 331, 335, 337; Baby boomers, 36, 67, 337, 441; Gen 2020, 337; Gen X, 337, 441; Millennials, 35, 110, 337, 441, 494; Traditionalists, 337. *See also* impact factors
Gen X. *See* generational differences
geo-location, 28, 216
global: collaborator, *73*; community, 73, 79; information professional, 8–11; knowledge infrastructure, 14–15
global information landscape. *See* information landscape
globalization, 109, 250, 488; U.S., 503. *See also* global
Go (Google). *See* programming languages
GoodReads, 133. *See also* reader's advisory
Google: age of, 49, 133–34, 216; Analytics, 304, 341; Books, 33, 89, 131, 384, 386, 489; Forms, 341; Glass, 201, 488; Hangout, *132*; Home, 305; Scholar, *83–84*, 131, *301*, 308; Translate, 131
grassroots lobbying. *See* lobbying
Greater Western Library Alliance (GWLA), *89*
Green, Samuel Swett, 130
group: dynamics, 335, 337; think, 52, 55, 214, 489. *See also* decision making; impact factors

Group 1 entities. *See* Functional Requirements for Bibliographic Records (FRBR)
group license. *See* license

HathiTrust, 21, 33, 89, 131, 384, 386, 489
Health Insurance Portability and Accountability Act of 1996 (HIPAA), 320, *328*, *363*, 423
History Pin, 216
hospitality, 102-3. *See also* public library
hotspot, 37, 123, 185, 442, 489
hyperlinked library, 117, 211-19, 489
hyperlocalism, 216, 294, 489
hypermedia, 166, 489

iBeacon. *See* Apple
impact factors (in terms of communication), 331-32, 335-39. *See also* civility; communication (nonverbal); cultural diversity; disabilities; group
impact factors (in terms of journals), 414-15, 489. *See also* open access; publishing
inclusion, 4, 12, 52-54, 57, 60-65, 96, 103, 125, 213, 225, 234, 260, 300, 306, 373-74, 467, 489. *See also* diversity; equity of access
indemnification, *401*, 489. *See also* license
independent information professional, 106, 108, 111, 114, 368-70, 455, 489. *See also* special library
index-based discovery services, 308
indirect value. *See* value
influence and power, 347; authority, 347; consistency, 347; relationships, 347. *See also* advocacy; decision making
infopreneur, 489
informal learning. *See* learning
informatics, 81-3, *455*, 489
information: Age, 77, 80, 109, 198; architecture (IA), 143, 173-74, *311*, 482, 489; as a public good, 361; as tradable commodity, 361; behavior, 41-43, 49, 195; communication technology (ICTs), 8; communities, 11, 27, 298; cycle, 358, 364; fluency, 35, *196*; intermediation, 129-41, 490; intermediator, 129-30, 136, 138, 490; literate society, 290-91; management, 113, 122, 160, 167, 188, 233; overload, 18, 205, 490; ownership, 358-*359*, 361; seeking behaviors, 136
information ethics, 110, 355, 366-77, 490. *See also* ethical theories; ethics; shared principles
information landscape: global, 4-5, *9*, 11, 466, 474; virtual, 6
Information licensing, 397-407, 490; business models, 403-4; digital content, 398; new issues, *398*; origins, 398-99; pricing attributes, *404-5*; pricing models, 403-5. *See also* information licensing terms; license

information licensing terms, 306, 399-403, 405; business terms, 399, 401-2; force majeure, *401*, 488; legal terms, 399, 400-1; technical terms, 399, 402-3; usage terms, 399, 400. *See also* information licensing; license
information literacy, 4, 8, 22, *30*, 35, 48-49, 72-74, 78-80, 83, 86-87, 90, 127, 133, 136-38, 195-206, 288, 290, 292, 295, 343, 370, 490; alternate terms, *196*; beyond reading, 35; critical, 195, 197, 482; development, 87, 204; skills, 4, 74, 80, 83, 90, 136, 204; standards, 73, 86. *See also* Association of College and Research Libraries (ACRL); critical thinking; information fluency; metaliteracy
information literacy instruction, 48, 78, 86, 136, *196*, 202, 490. *See also* bibliographic instruction; library instruction
information need, 1, 40-51, 74, 78, 130, 133, 136, 138, 187, 203, 211, 232, 280, 292-95, 463, 473, 490, 499. *See also* reference services
information policy, 357-65, 490; evaluation, 360-1; formation process, 361-63; information professional responsibilities, 363-64; issues, 359; values as the foundation for, 358-59
information privacy. *See* privacy
information security, 420-21, 426-27, 483, 490. *See also* cybersecurity; privacy
informational interview, 254, 458, 461, 463-64. *See also* career; job; job interview
inherent diversities, 55, 490. *See also* diversity
innovation lab, *7*, *137*, 309-10, 491
inquiry-based learning model. *See* instructional models
Instagram. *See* social media
Institute of Museum and Library Services (IMLS), *111*, 164, *200*, 263, 265n2, 321. *See also* funding (grants)
institutional repository (IR). *See* repository
instructional: technologists, 83; technology, 81-83, 135
instructional design model, 203; Analysis, Design, Development, Implementation, Evaluation method (ADDIE), 203; Wiggins and McTighe's backwards design method, 203; understand, structure, engage, reflect method (USER), 203
instructional models, 71-72, 75-78; connected learning, 76-79, 481; inquiry-based learning, 76-77, 79, 491. *See also* learning
integrated library system (ILS), 47, 142-43, 153-54, 183, 185-86, 298-300, 302, 305-9, 312, 406, 491; features, *306*. *See also* access services; acquisitions; cataloging; circulation; serials control modules

Library Copyright Alliance. *See* copyright
library exception. *See* copyright law
Librarygame, 216
Library Journal, 18, 281, 285, 292, 297
Library Leadership Administration and
    Management Association (LLAMA), 342, 469,
    470–71, 474. *See also* leadership
Library of 2020. *See* Internet Archive
Library of Alexandria, 158, *161*, 289
Library of Congress (LC), 96, 123, 127, 143–45,
    149–52, 160, 164–65, 167, 307, 320, 364, 384,
    388–89, 478, 480, 485, 493, 498; BIBFRAME,
    144, 152–54, 307–8, 311, 478; Classification
    (LCC), 123, 145, 149, 151, 480; Subject Heading
    (LCSH), 96, 145, 149–50, 152, 320, 364, 502.
    See also cataloging
library services: Act (LSA), 19; and Construction
    Act (LSCA), 19–20; and Technology Act (LSTA),
    19, 263, 265n3
library services platform (LSP), 305–8, 312
Library Systems and Services, Inc. (LSSI), 251
license, 397–407; agreements, 389, 398; all-in,
    405–6, 477; click-wrap, 389, 480; elements
    of a, 399–403; grant, *402*, 493; group, 403,
    405–6; negotiated licenses, 378–79, 495; opt-in
    group, 405, 496. *See also* consortia; Creative
    Commons; information licensing; information
    licensing terms
licensed content business model. *See* information
    licensing
licensing. *See* information licensing
lifecycle management, 493. *See also* conservation;
    curation; preservation; preservation activities
lifelong learning. *See* learning
line item budget. *See* budget
linked data, 28, 83–*84*, 96, 117, 121, 123, 142–43,
    148, 151–54, 307–8, 311, 320, 493. *See also*
    cataloging; Library of Congress (LC); metadata
linked open data, 123, 493
literacy, 71–80; 195–206; adult, 197, 200, 234;
    basic, 77–78; critical information, 197, 482;
    digital, 73–74, 124, *196*, 222, 485; family, *200*;
    media, 78, 205, 494; metaliteracy, *196*, 494;
    privacy, 429, 498; technical, 7; technology, 74,
    86–87, *90*, 137–38, 176, 196–200, 204, 502;
    transliteracy, 133, 503. *See also* information
    fluency; information literacy; information
    media instruction; technology literacy
    instruction
literary warrant, 280, 493
Little Free Library, 38
LLAMA. *See* Library Leadership Administration and
    Management Association (LLAMA)
lobbying, 344–45: direct, 345, 485; grassroots,
    345, 488. *See also* advocacy; persuasion

local computing, 302–3, 493. *See also* cloud
    computing
Local Faculty and Student Surveys for Libraries
    (Ithaka S+R). *See* survey tools for libraries
LOCKSS. *See* lots of copies keep stuff safe
Los Angeles Public Library, 30, 99
lots of copies keep stuff safe (LOCKSS), 127, *160*,
    402
LUMINA Foundation. *See* Degree Qualifications
    Profile

machine readable cataloging (MARC). *See*
    cataloging
Make magazine, 225
maker: movement, 37, 221, 224–25, 227;
    programming, 222, 225
makerspace, 7, 10, 21, *30*, 37–38, 79, 98, 137, 185,
    217, 220–27, 310, 373, 493. *See also* creation
    culture
management, 229–354; crisis, 9; facilities, 82,
    113; project, 9, 111, 113, 122, 179, 301, 460, *470*,
    471; risk, 32; skills, 9, 32, 111, 247, 249–55, 295,
    474; talent, 61; time, 9, 271; vendor, 111. *See also*
    change management; collection management;
    data management; knowledge management;
    leadership; personnel
manager, 48, 69, 71–72, 75, 86, 90, 109, 113, *122*,
    124–25, 156–58, 160, 189, 233–34, *239*, 242,
    244, 246–54, 256, 258–64, 267, 271, 273–75,
    289–95, 304–5, 307–9, *311*, 334–36, 343, 348–
    49, 375, *455*, *459*, 463, 466, 468–70, 473–75,
    480, 492–93, 498. *See also* change manager;
    collection manager
manifestation, 62, 147–48 153, 493. *See also*
    Functional Requirements for Bibliographic
    Records (FRBR)
MARC. *See* cataloging
marketing, 9, 32, 75, 97, 101, 109–15, 119, 124,
    134, *136*, 154, 223, 240–42, 249, 290, 331–42,
    344–46, 351–52, 444, 461, *470*–71, 482, 494,
    498–99; assessment and evaluation, 341; plan,
    114, 339–41, 494; resources, 341–42; tools,
    340–41. *See also* communication plan; outreach;
    promotion
market research, 114, 341, 489; secondary, 501
Marrakesh Treaty, 387, 494. *See also* accessibility;
    copyright; copyright law
mashup, 224–25, 373, 494
Maslow's Theory of Human Motivation, 43
mass digitization, 379, 384–88, 391. *See also*
    copyright; copyright law
massive open online course (MOOC), 6, 10, 36, 87,
    285, 495
media center. *See* school library
media failure, 161. *See also* optical media

media literacy. *See* literacy
Medical Library Association (MLA), 92n16, 111
Mendeley. *See* citation management program
MetaArchive Cooperative, 127
metadata, 142–49; harvesting, 123, 126, 494; librarians, 83–84, 122–23; management, 34; object description schema (MODS), 126, 144–45; ONIX (ONline Information eXchange), 151; standard or schema, 126, *160*, 284, 474, 486, 494, 503; system, 151; Text Encoding Initiative (TEI), 144. *See also* academic librarians; cataloging; Dublin Core
metaliteracy. *See* literacy
microaggression, 494
Microsoft, 134, 302, 305, 308, 327–28, 466; Cortana, 37, 134
Middle States Commission on Higher Education, 190
millennials. *See* generational differences
Mindful Leadership Institute. *See* personality tests
Minecraft, 224, 226, 494
MINES for Libraries. *See* survey tools for libraries
Minitab. *See* statistical platforms
mirrors, 494. *See also* makerspace
mission statement. *See* strategic planning
Miss Manners' Guide to Excruciatingly Correct Behavior, 338
mixed system, 423, 494. *See also* privacy
mobile: apps, 7, 48, 87, 121, *172*, 214–15, 422; devices, 4, *7*, 28, *30*, 36–37, 121, 132, *172*, 212–16, 218, 309; technologies, *6*, 21, 214, 299, 304–5, 309, 406, 494. *See also* reference services
mobile reference services. *See* reference services
Model Programme for Public Libraries, 217
MODS. *See* metadata object description schema
molecular gastronomy, 221, 495
MOOC. *See* massive open online course (MOOC)
multiculturalism, 53–*54*, 495
multitenant platform, 302–4, 307. *See also* software-as-a-service (SaaS)
Myers-Briggs. *See* personality tests

National Association to Promote Library & Information Services to Latinos and the Spanish Speaking (REFORMA). *See* REFORMA
A Nation at Risk, 197
National Commission on Excellence in Education, 197
National Cyber Security Alliance, 429
National Digital Information Infrastructure and Preservation Program (NDIIPP), *160*
National Historic Preservation Act, 159, *161*
National Information Standards Organization (NISO), 311
National Institute of Standards and Technology (NIST), 427

National Institutes of Health (NIH), 84, 416
National Science Foundation (NSF), 84, 321
National Security Agency (NSA), 373, 420. *See also* privacy
near-field communication (NFC), 28, 310, 495
needs assessment, 236, 238–39, 495. *See also* strategic planning; SWOT analysis
negotiated license. *See* license
NetMeeting, 133
net neutrality, *359*, 364, 444, 495. *See also* information policy issues
networking, 9, 32, 35, 100, 114–15, 133, *214*, 216, 219, 344–45, 351–52, 375, 420, 429, *462*, 473, 495; knowledge, *214*; political, 344–45, 351–2; professional, *9*, 32, 115, 375, 429, *462*, 473; social, 35, 114, 133, 420
New Deal, 19
NewsBank, 131. *See also* reference services
New York Public Library, 19, 95, *134*, 187, 215, *237*
Next Generation Science Standards (NGSS), 75
Next Great Copyright Act, 388, 495. *See also* copyright law
NGSS. *See* Next Generation Science Standards (NGSS)
nitrate deterioration. *See* film preservation
No Child Left Behind, 76, 422
noise. *See* impact factors
nominal data. *See* data, nominal
nonverbal communication. *See* communication
Nook. *See* e-reader
normalization of data, 320, 322; extract, transform, and load process (ETL), 322. *See also* data; data management; data warehouse
Northeast Research Libraries Consortium. *See* consortia
NoveList, 133. *See also* reader's advisory

OAI. *See* Open Archives Initiative (OAI)
OAIS. *See* Open Archival Information System (OAIS)
obsolescence, 160, 162, 164. *See also* preservation
OCLC. *See* Online Computer Library Center (OCLC)
Office for Intellectual Freedom, 375, 434, 436, 438–39, 442. *See also* intellectual freedom; request for reconsideration
Office of Management and Budget (OMB), 66, 421. *See also* budget
Ohio Computer Library Center. *See* Online Computer Library Center (OCLC)
ONIX. *See* metadata
online analytical processing system (OLAP), 322. *See also* data warehouse
online catalog, 26, 79, 89, 144, *172*, 187, 304, 308. *See also* online public access catalog (OPAC)

Online Computer Library Center (OCLC), 21, 33–34, 131–32, 143–44, 149, 151–*52*, 154, 160, 289, *316*, *444*, *446*, 495; Faceted Application of Subject Terminology (FAST), 152; From Awareness to Funding, 444; Research, 34, 152. *See also* cataloging

ONline Information eXchange (ONIX). *See* metadata

online learning, 7, 30, 36, 137, 285. *See also* e-learning; massive open online courses

online public access catalog (OPAC), 123, 144, 154, 328. *See also* online catalog

ontology, 320, 495

OPAC. *See* online public access catalog (OPAC)

open: education resources (OER), 6, 11, 30, 34, 36; license, 413–14, 417, 496; pedagogy, 202. *See also* copyright; open access

open access, 10, 21, 84–85, 88, 121, 124–25, 147, *402*, 406, 408–18, 496; Budapest Open Access Initiative, 412; charges, 413; funds, 413, 496; initiatives, 406, 496; journals, 85, 408, *412*–15, 496; licensed, *402*; movement, 85, 409; policy, 85, 415–*17*; publishing, 121, 124, 413–15, 417, 496. *See also* publishing; repository

Open Archival Information System (OAIS), 160, 496

Open Archives Initiative (OAI), 126, 413

open source software. *See* software

openly networked learning, 77, 496. *See also* instructional models

oppression, 63–64, 443, 496. *See also* power; privilege; social justice

optical media, 163–64, 496; bonding failure, 163; Compact Disks (CDs), 162–63, 325, 397; Digital Video Discs (DVDs), 28, 163, 188, 325, 381, 384, 397; dye-fading, 163; lack of production standards, 163; scratches, 163. *See also* preservation

opt-in group license. *See* license

ordinal data. *See* data

organizational change, 247, 249–51, 253–54, 496. *See also* change management

orphan work, 124, 379, 384, 386–88, 391, 496; Report on Orphan Works, 387. *See also* copyright; copyright owner

outcome, 6, 8, 41, 44, *54*, 63, 86, 90, 101, 115, 197–98, 203–4, 216, 223, 233, 239, 243–44, 248, 252, *254*, 259, 261, 271, 317, *321*, 326, 337–*38*, 345–46, 348–49, 362–63, 412, 463–64, 467, 472, 496. *See also* advocacy; budget; learning outcomes; strategic planning

outliers, 326, 496. *See also* statistics

output, 125, 232–33, 243–44, 259, 348–49, *411*, 415, 440, 496. *See also* advocacy; strategic planning

outreach, 9, 15, 57–58, 62, 64, 81, 88, 122, 124, 135–36, 138, 160, 164, 214, 224, 238, *240*–42, 267, 331–33, 339–41, 445, 454, 497; and marketing, 339–41. *See also* marketing

Oxford Reference, 131

paraprofessional, 75, 88, 134, 186, 191, 497

participatory organization, 497. *See also* hyperlinked library

patron-driven acquisition (PDA). *See* acquisitions. *See also* collection development; collection management

patron-oriented organization, 271, 497

pattern discovery. *See* analytics, prescriptive

pedagogy, 74, 85, 88, 202. *See also* open pedagogy

peer reviewed, 87, 124, 409–10, 412–14, 497. *See also* open access; publishing

performance: evaluation, 102, 271–72, 497; objectives, 196, 259, 481, 497

performance budget. *See* budget, performance

Periscope. *See* social media

Perl. *See* programming languages

persona, 43, 178, 184, 189, 373, 497

personal brand, 462, 497. *See also* career

Personal Information Protection and Electronic Documents Act of 2000 (PIPEDA), 425

personal learning network (PLN), 11, 34, 133, 461, 497

personality, 248, 253, 334–35, 338–39, *467*–68, 497; preferences, 334, 497; types, 335, 338–39, 497. *See also* communication; impact factors

personality tests, 253, 338; Mindful Leadership Institute, 253; Myers-Briggs, 253. *See also* change management; communication style; leadership

personally identifiable information (PII), 419, *422*, 424–25, 483, 497. *See also* Fair Information Practice Principles (FIPPs); privacy

personnel, 64, 229, 248, 258, 261, 263, 266–77, 301–3, 309–10, 312, 335, 350, 420, 470–71. *See also* management

persuasion, 344–45, 351–52, 497. *See also* advocacy

Pew Research Center, 34, 37, 134, 290

Philadelphia Free Library, 100

PHP. *See* programming languages

Pinterest. *See* social media

planning horizon. *See* strategic planning

Political Action Committee for libraries, 33

political change, 29, 439, 441

Poole, William Frederick, 17

population served, 404, 497. *See also* information licensing

post-license access, *402*, 497. *See also* information licensing power, 63–65, 498. *See also* oppression; privilege; social justice

PowerBI. *See* statistical platforms

predatory publishing. *See* publishing

predictive analytics. *See* analytics, predictive

prescriptive analytics. *See* analytics, prescriptive

prescriptive collection development, 498

preservation, 5, 62, 81, 156–69, 184, 187, 215, *237, 240*, 261, 267, 317, 321, 328, *359*, 364, *369*, 371, 382–83, 386, *402*, 454, 477, 485, 498; audiovisual content, 161–65; data, *84*, 317; digital, 83, 89, 123–24, 126–27, 157, 159–61, 164, 166, 382, 386, *402*, 485; Preservation Metadata Implementation Strategies (PREMIS), *160*, 498. *See also* conservation; curation; film preservation; lifecycle management; preservation activities

preservation activities, *158. See also* preservation; replication; tape preservation

Preservation of Electronic Government Information. *See* data rescue

Primo from Ex Libris. *See* discovery tool

principles. *See* information ethics

privacy, 6, 10, 12, 31, 38, 74–75, *121–22*, 167, 185, 216, 311, 357–58, *359*, 360–64, *369*, 370–71, 373–75, 419–30, 435, *437*, 444, *446*, 490; and security policies, 428, 430; audit, 428, 498; personal, 358, 361; role of information professionals, *121*, 311, 370, 429–30; user, 38, 75, 370, 444. *See also* cybersecurity; Fair Information Practice Principles (FIPPs); personally identifiable information (PII); Right to Privacy

privacy literacy. *See* literacy

privilege, 53, *58*, 60, 63–64, 197, 382, 498. *See also* copyright; diversity; social justice

problem finding. *See* design thinking

problem situation, 41, 44, 498

production centered learning, 77, 498. *See also* instructional models; learning

professional equity, 454, 460–63. *See also* career

program budget. *See* budget

program manager, 72, 75

programming languages, 300, 310–*11*, 322, 327, 499; COBOL, 322; Go (Google), 310; Perl, 310; PHP, 310; Python, 310, 499; R, 310, 327; RPG (IBM), 322; Ruby on Rails, 310; Swift, 310

Project COUNTER. *See* consortia

project management. *See* management

project selection. *See* strategic planning

promotion: in terms of job, 61, 82, 85, 267, 271–72, 415, 459, 498; in terms of marketing, 62, 75, 77, 224, 333, 340, 344, 351–52, 445, 498. *See also* marketing; personnel

proprietary software. *See* software

protected health information (PIH), 423

Protection of Pupil Rights Amendment (PPRA), 422

protective enclosure, 157, 499. *See also* preservation

public: good, 360–1, *369*, 371, 412, 499; relations (PR), 332, 339, 342, 344, 351–52, 461, 494, 499

public domain, 6, 124, 358–59, 379–84, *386*, 390–91, 499; dedication (CC0), 381, 390, 499; domain mark, 381, 390, 499. *See also* copyright; creative commons; information policy issues

public librarian, 20, 22, 94–104, 135, 197, 201, 315, 349; competencies, 103–4

public library, 4, 15–22, 30–31, 33, 35–38, 45–6, 65, 78, 94–104, 120, 131–32, *134*–37, 151, *161*, 187, 191, 198, 200–201, 205, 215, 217–18, 220–23, 233, *237*–38, 257, 262, 264, 267, 272, 274, 280, 283, 285, 289, 292, 315, 348–51, 360, 363, 373, *379*, 404, 438, 440, 454–55, 458, 468; advocacy, 348–51; evolution of, 15–22; hyperlinked libraries, 215, 217–18; information literacy, 200–201, 205; intellectual freedom, 438, 440, 454–45; makerspaces, 220–3; reference services, 131–2, *134*–37; strategic planning, 233, *237*–38

Public Library Association (PLA), 95, 196, 217

publicity, 499. *See also* marketing; promotion (in terms of marketing)

publishing, 15, 19, 34, 37, 82, 85, 121–22, 124, 159, 166, 178, 289, *295*, 307–8, 349, 407, 410–15, 439–35; and diversity, 440–*41*; predatory, 414, 417, 498; self-published, 37, *295*, 440. *See also* Big 5; collection; open access; scholarly publishing

PubMed, 131, 416

Purdue's Data Curation Profile Toolkit, 84. *See also* academic libraries

purpose specification, 425, 499. *See also* Fair Information Practice Principles (FIPPs); personally identifiable information (PII)

Python. *See* programming languages

Q&A services, 133, 499; Collaborative Q&A, 133; Community-based Q&A, 133; Expert-based Q&A, 133; LibAnswers, 133; Quora, 133; Social Q&A, 133; WikiAnswers, 133; Yahoo! Answers, 133. *See also* reference services

qualitative data. *See* data

Qualtrics Research Core. *See* statistical platforms

quantitative data. *See* data

query, 130, 499. *See also* reference interview; reference services

question-answering services. *See* Q&A services

QuestionPoint, 132. *See also* Online Computer Library Center (OCLC); reference services

Quora. *See* Q&A services

R. *See* programming languages

Race to the Top, 76. *See also* instructional models

RapidMiner. *See* statistical platforms

RDA. *See* resource description and access (RDA)

RDF. *See* resource description framework (RDF)

RDM. *See* research data management (RDM)

reader's advisory, 132–33, *134*, 176, 499. *See also* Amazon; GoodReads; LibGuides; NoveList; Pinterest; resource sharing communities; social media

Reader's Guide to Periodical Literature, 131. *See also* reference services

records management, 47–48, 111, *459*

recovery point objectives, 320, 499. *See also* business continuity planning; disaster recovery plan

Reference 2.0, 129, 133–35, 499. *See also* reference services; virtual reference services (VRS)

Reference and User Services Association (RUSA), 10, *130*, *131*. *See also* reference services; virtual reference services (VRS)

reference interview, 44, 130, 132, 280, 499. *See also* reference services; virtual reference services (VRS)

reference services, 26, 38, 120, 129–38, 500; competencies, *130*; mobile, 131–34, 494; roaming, 135; roving, 284, 500; tiered, 134. *See also* embedded librarians; Reference and User Services Association (RUSA); virtual reference services (VRS)

reflection-in-action, 280, 500

REFORMA, *60*

reformatting. *See* preservation activities

reframing. *See* design thinking

refreshing. *See* preservation activities

Refworks. *See* citation management program

relationships. *See* influence and power

remote access, 29, 188, *400*, 500

remote storage, 187, 192, 500. *See also* access services; collection management

repertoire, 280, 284–85, 500. *See also* design thinking

replication, 158, 317, 500. *See also* data recovery; preservation activities

repository, 31, 83, 85, 125, 154, 306, 390, 413, 415–16, 500; digital, 125, 416, 485; institutional (IR), 85, 154, 390, 415, 491. *See also* open access publishing

request: for proposal (RFP), 125; for reconsideration, 435, 437–38, 442, 479, 500. *See also* intellectual freedom

research data management (RDM), 315, 320–26, 500. *See also* data management

research informationist, 83–84. *See also* academic librarians

Research Libraries Group (RLG), 159–60

reserves, 122, 183–84, 188–89, 192–93, *316*, 482, 500. *See also* access services; electronic reserves; e-reserves

resource: assessment, 241–42; description and access (RDA), 83–84, 123, 145–46, 148–49, 151; description framework (RDF), 126, 145–46, 151, 154; sharing, 184, 187–90, 192–93, 215, 294, *400*, 500. *See also* access services; interlibrary loan; metadata; reader's advisory

resource sharing communities, 215. *See also* social media

responsive design, 36, 304, 500

resume, 36, 137, 269, 464; action verbs, 500. *See also* job; job interview

return on investment (ROI), 108, 113, 122, 134, 201, *254*, 341, *462*, 500

RFP. *See* request for proposal (RFP)

right to privacy. *See* free speech

risk management. *See* management

roaming reference services. *See* reference services

ROI. *See* return on investment

Rollins, Charlemae Hill, 20

roving reference services. *See* reference services

RPG (IBM). *See* programming languages

Ruby on Rails. *See* programming languages

safe harbor, 12, *247*, 384–85, 391, 485. *See also* copyright; SAS; statistical platforms

satisficing, 346, 501

scholarly: literature, 10, 87, 143, 283, 408–9, 411–12, 414–15, 442–13; research, 409, 412; resources, 131, 308, *349*; sharing, *400*, 501. *See also* scholarly communication; scholarly publishing

scholarly communication, 82, 88, 90, 409–10, 412, 501; librarian, 85, 501; program, 90, 501; system, 85. *See also* academic librarians; scholarly; scholarly publishing

scholarly publishing, 34, 122, 124, 154, 308, 501; and Academic Resources Coalition (SPARC), 21; coordinator, 122. *See also* scholarly; scholarly communication

school librarian, 71–80, 136, 196, 199, 201, 205, 221, 442; roles, 72–75. *See also* information literacy; information literacy instruction

school library, 20, 36, 71–80, 137, 151, 198–99, 201, 222, 257, 262, *349*, *372*–73, 442, 454. *See also* information literacy; K–12; learning commons; literacy; school librarian; third place

science, technology, engineering, and math (STEM), 88, 137, 222, 321 science, technology, engineering, art, and mathematics (STEAM), 37

Second Life, 28, *132*. *See also* 3-D immersive environment; virtual reference tools; virtual reality

secondary market research. *See* market research

Secretary's Commission on Achieving Necessary Skills (SCANS), 199. *See also* information literacy; information literacy instruction

Section 107 (fair use). *See* copyright law

Section 108 (library exception). *See* copyright law

Section 109 (first sale doctrine). *See* copyright law

security threats, 161, 419, 426–27. *See also* cybersecurity; preservation

selection, 15, 61–62, 115, 125, 157, 164, 176, 214, 223, 241, 258, 291, *293–94*, 296–97, 312, 374; 389, 437–38, 444, 501. *See also* collection development; collection management; ethics; intellectual freedom; personnel; strategic planning

self-check terminals, 186, 501. *See also* access services

self-employed mind-set, *455–56*

self-published work. *See* publishing

sensitive personal data, 419, *422*, 501. *See also* information privacy; privacy

serials, 88, 154, *306*, 501

serials control modules, *306*, 501

server operating system, 302, 501

servers, 123, 125, 127, 161, 302–4, *400*, 480, 493; operating system, 160, 302–4, 307, 310, 501; storage and network hardware, 302. *See also* cloud; local computing; software; software-as-a-service (SAAS)

service: design, 173–74; oriented architecture, 307, 312

shared principles, 369–73. *See also* code of ethics; diversity; ethical theories; ethics; intellectual freedom; lifelong learning; preservation; privacy; public good

shelf-reading, 186, 501. *See also* access services; collection development; collection management

shifting (in terms of collections), 186, 501. *See also* access services; collection development; collection management

short message service (SMS), 132, 185, 503

signage, 58, 102, 173, 176, 189–90, *193*

simultaneous user, *405*, 501

situational descriptive questioning. *See* job interview

Skype. *See* social media

Slideshare. *See* social media

Snapchat. *See* social media

social: change, 34, 441, 445; harmony, 18; influence, 345, 351, 467, 502

social justice, 1, 4, 52–53, 62–65, 361, *443*, 502. *See also* diversity; equity; oppression; power; privilege

social media, 4, 8, 26, 33–35, 41, 94, 112, 114, 121, 124, 133–35, 167, *172*, 177, 205, 212–13, 215, 242, *333*, 340–41, 351, 360, 373, 375, 391, 426, 443, 454, 458, 461, 463, 502; Facebook, 37, 114, 133–34, 186, 227, 340, 420, 461, 463; Flickr, 215, 223, 227, *340*; Flipboard, *340*; Instagram, 133–34, 215, 227, 340; Periscope, 37; Pinterest, 133, *134*, 215, *340*; Skype, 132, 269, 461; Slideshare, 463; Snapchat, 37, 133, *340*, 461; Tumblr, *340*; Twitter, 114, 133, 167, 186, 216, 304, 340, 461, 463; WhatsApp, 461; WordPress, *340*; YouTube, *340*, 463. *See also* resource sharing communities

Social Q&A. *See* Q&A services

Society of American Archivists (SAA), 368–72, 458; Code of Ethics for Archivists, 68–372

society, technology, education, the environment, politics (and government), economics, and demographics (STEEPED), 11

soft skills, 9, 333–5, 342, 502

software, 37, 49, 79, 87, 112–13, 122, 125, 143, 153, *158*, 160, 166, *167*, 258, 279, 299–310, 326, 444; development, 122, 301; open-source, *160*, 166, 299–301, 496; proprietary, 299–301, 499. *See also* cloud; multitenant platform; software-as-a-service (SaaS)

software-as-a-service (SaaS), 302–4. *See also* cloud; multitenant platform; software

Special Libraries Association (SLA), 107, 110, 113, 458. *See also* special library

special library, 15, 47–9, 82, 106–116, 202, 257, 265n3, 267, 404; core competencies, *110*

special-purpose funds. *See* funds

SPSS. *See* statistical platforms

stacks management, 176

stakeholder, 4, 22, 89, 91, 99, 107–8, 112, 121–22, 124–25, 179, 213–14, 218, 233–36, 238–40

Stanford Office of Fair Use, *391*. *See also* copyright law; fair use

Stata. *See* statistical platforms

STEAM. *See* science, technology, engineering, art, and mathematics (STEAM)

STEM. *See* science, technology, engineering, and math (STEM)

sticky-shed syndrome. *See* tape preservation

St. Petersburg College, *137*

strategic data asset, 315, 502. *See also* data management

strategic planning, 3, 7, *9*, 29, 33, 179, 221, 231–45, 260, 273, 288, 290–92, 339, 341, 346, 472–74, 502; mission statement, 236, *237*, 494; planning horizon, 240–41, 243, 497;

value statement, 214, 236–37, 242, 503; vision statement, 236–37, 239, 503. *See also* SWOT analysis

statistical platforms: Azure, 327; Counting Opinions, 191, 327; Knime, 327; Minitab, 327; Power BI, 327; Qualtrics Research Core, 327; RapidMiner, 327; SAS, 327; SPSS, 327; Stata, 327; Tableau, 327

statistics, 34, 46, 135, 190–91, 292, 304, 306, 316–17, 325–26, 348, 399, 420; central tendency, 325; data shape, 326; descriptive, 325–26; inferential, 326; measures of dispersion, 326; outliers, 326, 496; usage, 135, 190–91, 292, 304, 306, 316–17, 399. *See also* data; statistical platforms

STEEPED. *See* society, technology, education, the environment, politics (and government), economics, and demographics (STEEPED)

strengths, weaknesses, opportunities, threats (SWOT). *See* SWOT analysis

student information system (SIS), 315

student learning standards, 72–73, 77. *See also* American Association of School Librarians (AASL); Association for Educational Communication and Technology (AECT); International Society of Technology in Education (ISTE)

style sheets, 126, 502

subject cataloging. *See* cataloging

submission information package (SIP), 160. *See also* preservation

summative assessment. *See* assessment

supplemental funds. *See* funds

survey tools for libraries, 90, 191; Archival Metrics, 90; ClimateQual, 90; LibQual+, 90, 191, 341; LibSat, 191; Local Faculty and Student Surveys for Libraries (Ithaka S+R), 90; MINES for Libraries, 90. *See also* assessment

sustainability, 32–33, 44, 47, 50, 127, 180, 252

Swift. *See* programming languages

SWOT analysis, 236, 238–39, 340–41, 472, 502. *See also* strategic planning

systems administration, 303, 310

systems department, 185

Tableau. *See* statistical platforms

tacit knowledge, 502

talent management. *See* management

tape preservation, 161–63; binder break down, 163; dust damage, 163; lubricant loss, 163; sticky-shed syndrome, 163, 502. *See also* preservation

Task Force on Digital Archiving, 159. *See also* preservation

taxonomy, 114, 354, 502

tax revenue, 257, 262, 264. *See also* budgets; funding; funds

technical literacy. *See* literacy

technical terms (in licensing). *See* information licensing; information licensing terms; license

technology instruction, 48, 195–210

technology literacy. *See* literacy

Tennessee Valley Authority (TVA), 114

tenure-track, 82, 85–86, 502. *See also* academic librarians

Text Encoding Initiative (TEI). *See* metadata

text mining. *See* analytics, prescriptive

textual markup, 144. *See also* MARC

third place, 78, 502. *See also* school library

threshold: concept, 86, 196–97, 502; Threshold Achievement Test for Information Literacy, 197. *See also* information literacy; literacy

tiered reference services. *See* reference services

tinker, 220, 224, 502. *See also* design thinking; makerspace

touchpoint, 172, 503. *See also* user experience (UX)

traditionalists. *See* generational differences

transliteracy. *See* information literacy; literacy

transparency, 425. *See also* Fair Information Practice Principles (FIPPs)

Tumbler. *See* social media

Twitter. *See* social media

unconstitutional. *See* constitution

UNESCO, 196, 204

uniform resource identifier (URI), 151, 503

United States Agriculture Information Network (USAIN), 113

United States Constitution. *See* constitution

U.S. globalization. *See* globalization

USA PATRIOT Act, 360, 364, 424; *See also* information policy issues; information privacy

usability, 48, 90, 125–26, 157, 171–72, *254*, 398, 503; research, 126; testing, 90, 126. *See also* user experience (ux)

usage terms (in licensing). *See* information licensing; information licensing terms; license

use limitation, 426, 503;

user: behavior, 7, 34, 125, 138, 174, 289–90, 292; confidentiality, 185, *401*, *446*; education, *196*; satisfaction, 190–91, 349

user-created content, *30*, 373

user experience (UX), 10, 33, 103, 107, 109, 170–81, 185–86, 188, 281, 303–5, 308, *311*, 503; design (UXD), *171*, 175–76, 503; designer, *73*, 109, 174, 280–85, 491, 503. *See also* usability

USER method. *See* instructional design model

user support, *403*, 503

utilitarianism. *See* ethical theories

value: demonstrate, 10, 49, 349; direct, 349, 485; indirect, 349, 489; proposition, 350; questions, 359. *See also* advocacy; information policy
value statement. *See* strategic planning
values statement. *See* ethics
vendor management. *See* management
Vincent Van Gogh, 98
vinegar syndrome. *See* film preservation
virtual: information landscape, 6; librarian service (VLS), 48–49; librarians, 48, *132*; reality, 28, 201, 310; reference desk, 132; reference interviews, 132; reference library, 131; reference services (VRS), 26, *131–32*, 503; reference tools, 131–34. *See also* Second Life
virtual assistants, 134. *See also* Apple's SIRI; Amazon's Alexa; Facebook's Jarvis
vision statement; Microsoft's Cortana. *See* strategic planning
Visual Resources Association (VRA) Core, 126, 503
visualization tool, 28, 113, 327, 503. *See also* data visualization
voice activated technologies, 299, 305. *See also* Amazon Alexa; Apple Siri; Google Home; Microsoft Cortana; Samsung Bixby

warranty, 400, *401*, 503
wayfinding, 173, 189, 504
web analytics. *See* analytics
web archiving, 165; End of Term Web Archive, 165; Human Rights Web Archive, 165; Wayback Machine, 165

web of knowledge. *See* citation index tool
weeding, 295, 297, 445, 504
What Work Requires of Schools. See Secretary's Commission on Achieving Necessary Skills (SCANS)
WhatsApp. *See* social media
WikiAnswers. *See* Q&A services
Wikipedia, 87
Wiggins and McTighe. *See* instructional design model
Wolfram Alpha. *See* algorithm-based search engines
Wordpress. *See* social media
Works, Expressions, Manifestations, and Items (WEMI). *See* Functional Requirements for Bibliographic Records (FRBR)
Works Progress Administration (WPA), 19
WorldCat Discovery Services. *See* discovery tool; Online Computer Library Center (OCLC)
World Intellectual Property Organization (WIPO), 384
Worldwide Web Consortium (W3C), 146, 311

XML. *See* extensible markup language (XML)

Yahoo! Answers. *See* Q&A services
YouTube. *See* social media

Zoomers, 36, 504
Zotero, 87, 131. *See also* citation management program

About the Editor

Sandra Hirsh, PhD, is a professor and director of the School of Information at San José University. She has an extensive and varied background as a library and information science educator, leader, researcher, and professional—in both library and other information environments.

As a second-generation librarian, Hirsh recognized the value of the library and information science degree early on in her career. After getting a PhD from UCLA and an MLIS from the University of Michigan, she applied her library and information science skill set to work for more than a decade in leading Silicon Valley companies in user experience, developing and managing web, mobile, and TV consumer products, which resulted in five U.S. patents/applications, as well as in research and development. She also has worked in academic, public, and special libraries, and she has taught previously at the University of Arizona and University of Washington.

Hirsh's research and professional activities span the globe. Her research interests focus on information-seeking behavior, online and global learning, and the changing role of the information professional; this work has been published in peer-reviewed journals and has appeared in international conference proceedings. She is the cochair of the global virtual Library 2.0 conference series, which she cofounded in 2011. She was invited as a visiting scholar at Rikkyo University in 2017, served as president of the Association for Information Science & Technology in 2015, and was a Salzburg Fellow in 2013. She has also held leadership and committee roles in other associations, including the American Library Association (ALA), the Special Libraries Association (SLA), and the International Federation of Library Associations and Institutions (IFLA). She serves on several advisory and editorial boards including on the American Library Association's Center for the Future of Libraries Advisory Board, on the *Information Processing & Management* Editorial Board, and on the *Horizon Report* Library Expert Panel.

In addition to these roles, Hirsh has worked in her own local community, serving for many years on Palo Alto's Library Advisory Commission and the Palo Alto Library Bond Oversight Committee to realize the long-term vision of exciting new library facilities for the city.

About the Contributors

Stephen Abram, MLS, is a strategy and direction planning consultant for libraries and the information industry as principal of Lighthouse Consulting Inc. and executive director of the Federation of Ontario Public Libraries. He is a library trend watcher, keynote speaker, innovator, and author of *Stephen's Lighthouse* blog. Abram has held leadership positions in special libraries, associations, and as an executive at Cengage Learning (Gale), SirsiDynix, Thomson, Micromedia ProQuest, and IHS, in addition to managing several libraries.

Kendra Albright, PhD, is a professor and director of the School of Information at Kent State University. Previously, she taught at the University of South Carolina (USC), where she also served as director of the African Studies Program. Before joining USC, Albright taught at the University of Sheffield, where she was deputy director of the Centre for Health Information Management Research. Albright has taught courses on business information, research methods, information economics and policy, and strategic intelligence. She brings over fifteen years of professional practice in science and technology and business information. Albright has served as a consultant for both the government and private industry. She holds a PhD in communications, an MS in library science, and a BS in human development, and is editor-in-chief for *Libri*: *International Journal of Libraries and Information Studies*.

Susan W. Alman, PhD, teaches courses in interpersonal communication and marketing/public relations for information professionals at the San José State University School of Information. The second edition of her book, *Crash Course in Marketing for Libraries*, was published in 2015. Alman has held teaching posts at the University of Michigan and University of Pittsburgh and is an alumna of the Institute for Emerging Leadership in Online Learning.

Ruth Barefoot is a lecturer for the School of Information at San José State University (SJSU), teaching change management and issues in public libraries. She also consults for www.BarefootLibraries.com. After receiving her MLIS degree at SJSU, most of her career was spent at the San José Public Library, managing major initiatives, innovative services, and library branches. Barefoot's favorite thing to do is to share her instincts for information organizations, using over forty years of public and academic library experience.

Mary K. Bolin, PhD, is a professor and a catalog and metadata librarian at the University of Nebraska-Lincoln Libraries. She also is an instructor at the School of Information at San José State University, where she teaches courses in cataloging and metadata. Bolin's research interests include genres of organizational communication, academic library organizational patterns, and librarian status at academic libraries.

Marshall Breeding is an independent consultant providing services related to the strategic use of technology to libraries and related organizations. He created and maintains "Library Technology Guides," and has authored or edited seven books and hundreds of articles and essays. Breeding is the editor of *Smart Libraries Newsletter*, published by ALA TechSource; a columnist for *Computers in*

Libraries; and the author of the annual "Library Systems Report" published in *American Libraries*. From 1985 to 2012, he held a variety of positions in the Vanderbilt University Libraries.

Scott Brown is a cybrarian at Oracle, Inc. and the owner of Social Information Group, an independent information practice that focuses on the effective use of social networking tools for sharing and finding information. Brown's book, *Social Information: Gaining Competitive and Business Information Using Social Media Tools*, was published in 2012. He has over twenty years of experience in library and information organizations and is part-time faculty for San José State University's School of Information.

Melissa Cardenas-Dow is a social sciences librarian at California State University, Sacramento. Cardenas-Dow is also cochair of the American Library Association's Equity, Diversity and Inclusion Implementation Working Group, and an American Library Association (ALA) councilor-at-large. She has held additional positions throughout ALA, including the Task Force on Equity, Diversity and Inclusion, as well as positions in the Asian/Pacific American Librarians Association (APALA). She graduated from San José State University's School of Information with an MLIS degree in 2008.

H. Frank Cervone, PhD, is the director of information technology and a college information security officer for the School of Public Health at the University of Illinois at Chicago. His experience includes more than twenty-five years of leadership in libraries and information organizations, developing systems and services that have helped to advance teaching, learning, and managing knowledge and information. Cervone holds an MSEd with a specialization in online teaching and learning from California State University, an MA with a specialization in information technology management in information agencies from DePaul University, as well as a PhD in business administration from Northcentral University.

Rachel Ivy Clarke, PhD, is an assistant professor at Syracuse University's School of Information Studies. Her research focuses on the application of design methodologies and epistemologies to librarianship to facilitate the systematic, purposeful design of library services. She was formerly the cataloging librarian at the Fashion Institute of Design and Merchandising. Clarke holds a BA in creative writing from California State University Long Beach, an MLIS from San José State University School of Information, and a PhD from the University of Washington Information School.

April D. Cunningham is the instruction and information literacy librarian at Palomar College in California. Since 2003, she has worked on local, state, and national initiatives to promote instructional improvement and learning outcomes assessments in academic libraries.

Wayne T. Disher is an instructor at San José State University's School of Information and previous director of library services at Hemet Public Library in Hemet, California. He served as president of the California Library Association and has published several textbooks. Disher holds an MLIS degree from San José State University.

Dawn DiStefano, MBA, is a full-time professor at Molloy College in the Business Division. Her distinguished career spans diverse industries: telecom, legal, finance, academia, and nonprofit. DiStefano holds degrees from Nassau Community College, Hofstra University, and Dowling College. She is currently pursuing her doctorate of professional studies in business with a concentration in marketing at Pace University, Manhattan.

Kim Dority has worked as an information professional in a wide variety of information settings and is president of Dority & Associates. She created and has taught for the past twenty years a course on alternative LIS career paths for the University of Denver, is a career consultant for the San José State University School of Information, and has written extensively on LIS career topics, including *Rethinking Information Work: A Career Guide for Librarians and Other Information Professionals*, now in its second edition. She writes the Infonista.com blog on LIS career topics and created and manages the LinkedIn "LIS Career Options" group.

Celeste Feather is senior director of licensing and strategic partnerships at LYRASIS, where she has worked since 2010. Feather previously held positions at the OhioLINK consortium (2008–2010) and several university libraries (1989–2008). She holds a BA from Oberlin College, an MA from George Washington University, and an MLS from University of Maryland.

Joyce Fedeczko is the managing librarian and archivist for the International Fertilizer Development Center (IFDC) in Muscle Shoals, Alabama, providing agricultural research and technical information services for IFDC's global staff. She also oversees the seventy-year-old archival collection from the Tennessee Valley Authority's fertilizer research team. Fedeczko previously served as the information resources director and content management team lead at BP in Naperville, Illinois, and worked in medical libraries with Advocate HealthCare and Midwestern University. She holds an MLS from Dominican University.

Miguel Figueroa is the director of the American Library Association's Center for the Future of Libraries. He has previously held positions at the American Theological Library Association (ATLA), the American Library Association (as director of the Office for Diversity and Spectrum Scholarship Program and the Office for Literacy and Outreach Services), New York University's Langone Medical Center Ehrman Medical Library, and Neal-Schuman Publishers.

Kristin Fontichiaro teaches at the University of Michigan School of Information, where she coordinates the Michigan Makers mobile makerspace project, which partners university students with K–12 makers in underserved communities. She is principal investigator of the Making in Michigan Libraries project, funded by the Institute of Museum and Library Services. Additionally, Fontichiaro is the series editor and contributing author to Cherry Lake Publishing's Makers as Innovators series for middle-grade readers (which was identified by *Booklist* as one of 2014's Top Ten Series Nonfiction) and Makers as Innovators Junior series. Her book *Hacking Fashion: Fleece* was named one of *Booklist*'s Top Ten Project Books for Youth in 2016.

Martin L. Garnar is dean of the Kraemer Family Library at the University of Colorado, Colorado Springs. He has also taught a range of courses for the University of Denver's library and information science program since 2005, including professional ethics, intellectual freedom, and copyright. He was recognized with the university's 2014 Ruth Murray Underhill Award for Teaching Excellence by an Adjunct. Garnar has served as chair of the ALA Intellectual Freedom Committee and Committee on Professional Ethics, is a past president of the Colorado Association of Libraries, and speaks frequently on ethics and intellectual freedom at national and local conferences.

Todd Gilman, PhD, is librarian for literature in English at Yale University and a part-time instructor in the School of Information at San José State University. Before embarking on a career in academic librarianship, he taught literature and writing at the University of Toronto, Boston University, and MIT. Gilman edited the book *Academic Librarianship Today* (Rowman & Littlefield, 2017) and published a major scholarly biography, *The Theatre Career of Thomas Arne* (2013), on eighteenth-century England's preeminent native-born composer and musician.

Cherie L. Givens, JD, PhD, CIPP, is an attorney focusing on privacy and cybersecurity. She consults, lectures, and writes about information privacy, cybersecurity, and governance. Givens is the author of *Information Privacy Fundamentals for Librarians and Information Professionals* and is a certified information privacy professional (CIPP/US).

Robert Goch, JD, PhD, is an assistant professor of economics and finance at Molloy College. He previously served as a senior Wall Street investment analyst for fifteen years. In addition to publishing in academic journals, his insights have been presented extensively in the media, including the *Wall Street Journal*, *BusinessWeek*, and CNBC. Goch received a joint degree PhD (financial economics)/JD from the State University of New York at Buffalo.

Lisa Gregory is the program coordinator for the North Carolina Digital Heritage Center, which partners with over two hundred cultural heritage institutions throughout North Carolina to digitize and share their special collections online. Gregory helps set priorities and direction so that the Center remains responsive to partner and user needs while meeting the evolving demands of digital initiatives. Prior to the Digital Heritage Center, Gregory worked for the State Library of North Carolina's Digital Information Management Program, gaining experience in digitization project management and digital preservation outreach and education. She holds an MA in English literature from the University of New Mexico, and an MS in library science from the University of North Carolina at Chapel Hill, where she was a digital curation fellow.

Devon Greyson, PhD, is a postdoctoral fellow at the British Columbia Children's Hospital Research Institute and the University of British Columbia in Vancouver, Canada. Greyson researches and teaches about gender, youth, health, information, and public policy, and is particularly interested in the relationships between information practices and health and social equity.

Jill Grogg is licensing programming strategist at LYRASIS, where she has worked since 2015. She previously held positions at Mississippi State University (2001–2004) and the University of Alabama (2004–2014). Grogg holds a BA from the University of Tennessee, Chattanooga, an MA from the University of Mississippi, and an MS from the University of Tennessee, Knoxville.

Bruce L. Haller, MBA, JD, CFP, is the associate dean and director of graduate business programs at Molloy College, Rockville Centre, New York. Haller has practiced law for over twenty years, specializing in the areas of employment and contract law. Haller has published and taught employment and labor law at both the graduate and undergraduate level for numerous corporate consultants, colleges, and universities.

Liz Hamilton is a copyright librarian at Northwestern University Libraries and Northwestern University Press. She holds an MLIS from Dominican University and a BA from Oberlin College.

Mary Ann Harlan, PhD, is an assistant professor at San José State University's School of Information (iSchool), and is the coordinator of the Teacher Librarian program. Harlan has worked in public education for twenty years, including seven years at the SJSU iSchool, fourteen years in middle and high schools, and ten years as a teacher librarian.

Sara F. Jones is director of library services at the Marin County Free Library, where she has worked since 2013. Marin County Free Library has ten branches and is headquartered in San Rafael, California, in the Marin County Civic Center, a National Historic Landmark designed by Frank Lloyd Wright. Jones has twenty-five years of experience in a variety of libraries and served as Nevada's State Librarian and administrator of the Nevada State Library and Archives from 2001 to 2007.

Heather Joseph is the executive director of SPARC (the Scholarly Publishing and Academic Resources Coalition), an international coalition of libraries that promotes the open sharing of scholarship. As SPARC's director, Joseph has supported the creation and implementation of open-access infrastructure, policies, and practices, and is the architect of SPARC's advocacy agenda. Prior to joining SPARC, she spent fifteen years as a journal publisher in both commercial and not-for-profit publishing organizations.

Jan Knight is owner and principal researcher of Bancroft Information Services, LLC. As an independent infopreneur, she provides insight to entrepreneurs, from start-ups to grown-ups. Much of her work involves researching markets, competitors, industry, and trends and helps to shape business plans, funding pitch decks, marketing strategies, business development, commercialization plans, and more. Knight also provides research-driven writing services in the form of market snapshots, industry snapshots, and white papers. She has been an independent researcher for sixteen years, and works in almost all industries with a national and sometimes international client base.

Michael J. Krasulski is an assistant professor and head of the Library and Learning Resources Department at the Community College of Philadelphia. Krasulski coedited *Twenty-First Century Access Services: On the Front Line of Academic Librarianship*, which was published by the Association of College and Research Libraries in 2013. He serves on the editorial board of the *Journal of Access Services*. Krasulski earned his MSLIS from Drexel University and an additional master's degree from Temple University.

Sharla Lair is licensing program strategist at LYRASIS, where she has worked since 2015. She previously held positions at the MOBIUS consortium (2012–2015) in Missouri and the Missouri State Library (2010–2012). She holds a BS, MS, and MLIS from Florida State University.

James LaRue is the director of the Office for Intellectual Freedom since January 2016. Before then, LaRue was the director of the Douglas County (Colorado) Libraries for almost twenty-four years. He is the author of *The New Inquisition* (2007).

Maureen L. Mackenzie, MBA, PhD, PHR, is dean of the Division of Business at Molloy College, where she has worked since 2012. She started her career at Allstate Insurance Company, where she worked for over twenty years in numerous influential leadership positions, such as serving as the chairperson for the northeast region for the Fraudulent and Abusive Practices (FAP) subcommittee. She has publications that cover areas such as management, human resource management, trust in the workplace, business graduate education, entrepreneurship, managers' information-seeking behaviors, change management, and more.

Kate Marek, PhD, is a professor and director of the School of Information Studies at Dominican University. Marek's interests and expertise focus on information policy, technology developments, and rapid changes in society as they affect libraries, the information professions, and LIS curriculum. Her publications include *Using Web Analytics in the Library* (2011) and *Organizational Storytelling for Librarians: Using Stories for Effective Leadership* (2010).

Michele Masias is a government law librarian with the Department of Justice Libraries. She previously worked as the chief librarian of the Civil and Criminal Division Libraries at the Department of Justice.

Masias has over twenty-five years of library experience working in government libraries including in the Executive Office of the President, the Defense Technical Information Center, and the Department of Interior. She was also a lecturer for the MLIS program at the Catholic University of America. Masias received her MLIS degree from Emporia State University.

Courtney McDonald is an associate librarian and head of discovery and user experience at Indiana University Libraries in Bloomington, Indiana. Her most recent book, *Putting the User First: 30 Strategies for Transforming Library Services*, was published in 2014. She holds an MS in Human-Computer Interaction from DePaul University, and an MLS and BA in English with a journalism certificate from Indiana University, Bloomington.

Crystal S. Megaridis is the manager of Library Services at Praxair Inc., a global Fortune 300 industrial gas company, and has been involved in the world of libraries for over thirty years. For the past twelve years, she has served on the Board of Trustees for the Indian Prairie Public Library District in Darien, Illinois. Megaridis is also a lecturer for the School of Information at San José State University. She holds an MLS from Dominican University in River Forest, Illinois.

Mary Minow, JD, is a senior fellow in the Harvard Advanced Leadership Initiative. Formerly, she was counsel to the Califa Library Group in California and editor of the Stanford Copyright and Fair Use site at http://fairuse.stanford.edu. She holds a JD from Stanford University, an AMLS from the University of Michigan, and a BA from Brown University.

Heather O'Brien, PhD, is a faculty member at the School of Library, Archival and Information Studies, University of British Columbia in Vancouver, British Columbia, Canada. O'Brien's research and teaching interests are in the areas of information-seeking behavior and use, and user experience with information media, specifically the nature and measurement of user engagement with information systems.

Christine Pawley, PhD, retired in 2012 as a professor and director at the School of Library and Information Studies, and director of the Center for the History of Print and Digital Culture at the University of Wisconsin–Madison. Pawley is author of two award-winning books: *Reading on the Middle Border: The Culture of Print in Late Nineteenth Century Osage, Iowa* (2001) and *Reading Places: Literacy, Democracy, and the Public Library in Cold War America* (2010), both from the University of Massachusetts Press. Pawley is coeditor with Louise S. Robbins of *Libraries and the Reading Public in Twentieth Century America* (2013). She is currently working on a book tentatively titled *Organizing Women: Print Networks and Community Power in Early Twentieth-Century America.*

Stephanie Rosenblatt is an instruction librarian and electronic resources/serials coordinator at Cerritos College in Southern California. She holds an MLS from Queens College and MST from Pace University. She also thinks all librarians should be active in their unions if they are lucky enough to be represented by them.

Lisa G. Rosenblum is the director of the King County Library System, one of the busiest library systems in the country. Most recently she was the director and chief librarian at the Brooklyn Public Library, where she oversaw the activities, personnel, and services offered at all fifty-nine branches, as well as the Central Library. Prior to this, Rosenblum managed libraries in the Silicon Valley area for twenty-five years as the director of library and community services for Sunnydale, CA, and as the director of library and neighborhood services for Hayward, CA. She holds a BA in liberal arts from St. John's College and an MLIS from San José State University. She taught a master's-level course on strategic leadership at the Pratt Institute School of Information in Manhattan.

Amy Rudersdorf is a senior consultant with AVPreserve, a data management consulting and software development firm focused on leveraging a deep understanding of technology, information, business, and people to advance the ways in which data are used for the benefit of individuals, organizations, and causes. Previously, Rudersdorf was the assistant director for Content at the Digital Public Library of America (DPLA), where she was responsible for digitization partnerships and related workflows, metadata normalization and shareability, and community engagement to promote the DPLA as a community resource. She has served as the director of the Digital Information Management Program at the State Library of North Carolina, coordinated digital collections at North Carolina State University and the University of Wisconsin–Madison, and worked with public libraries throughout Wisconsin to aid in the development and coordination of digitization grants. Rudersdorf was a Library of Congress National Digital Stewardship Alliance coordinating committee member and has taught master's courses as part of library and information science programs on digital libraries and preservation (San José State University) and metadata (North Carolina Central University).

Katherine Skinner, PhD, is the executive director of the Educopia Institute, a not-for-profit educational organization that builds networks and collaborative communities to help cultural, scientific, and scholarly institutions achieve greater impact. She is a founding program director for the MetaArchive Cooperative, a community-owned and community-governed digital preservation network with more than fifty member institutions in three countries. Skinner has also played a founding role in the Library Publishing Coalition, which supports library publishing and scholarly communications activities across more than sixty academic libraries, and the Bit Curator Consortium, which supports digital forensics practices in libraries, archives, and museums. Skinner received her PhD from Emory University. She has coedited three books and has authored and coauthored numerous reports and articles. She regularly teaches graduate courses and workshops in digital librarianship and preservation topics, and provides consultation services to groups that are planning or implementing digital scholarship and digital preservation programs.

Pam Smith is the director of Anythink Libraries in Adams County, Colorado, north of Denver. Through her leadership, the public library system went from being the worst-funded system in the state of Colorado to one of the most recognized library brands worldwide by creating an entirely new service model. She is the 2017–2018 Public Library Association president and is a member of the working group for the Aspen Institute Dialogue on Public Libraries. Previously, she was the director of the West Palm Beach Public Library in Florida and the manager of Children's Services for the Denver Public Library. Smith holds an MLS from Emporia State University and BA in English literature from the University of Colorado. She enjoys traveling, writing, cooking for friends and family, telling stories, and inventing libraries that support learning and curiosity.

Cheryl Stenström, PhD, is a full-time lecturer at San José State University's School of Information. She teaches courses on management, advocacy, and research methods and is interested in the intersection of social influence and decision making in the political arena, particularly as it affects funding for libraries. She is a graduate of the San José Gateway PhD program.

Michael Stephens, PhD, is an associate professor at the School of Information at San José University. He presents to both national and international audiences about emerging technologies, learning, innovation, and libraries. Since 2010, Stephens has written the monthly column "Office Hours" for *Library Journal* exploring the issues, ideas, and emerging trends in library and information science education. To review Stephen's archive of work, visit his Tame the Web website and blog: http://tametheweb.com.

Johanna Tunon, EdD, is an adjunct instructor at San José State University and the University of Maryland University College and serves as a dissertation chair for librarians and instructional designers in Nova Southeastern University's EdD program. In 2014, Tunon was the director of Distance and Instructional Library Services at Nova Southeastern University. She has been active in ALA's Distance Learning Section and the Florida chapter of ACRL, presented at a variety of conferences including ALA, IFLA, AERA, and ACRL, and been awarded the Routledge Distance Learning Librarian in 2012.

Patty Wong is city librarian at Santa Monica Public Library. She has held previous positions at Stockton-San Joaquin County Public Library, Oakland Public Library, and Berkeley Public Library (CA) in children's and young adult services and management. Wong has worked as a consultant in youth development, grant writing, and leadership and has publications on diversity, serving underserved communities, and partnerships. She is part-time faculty for San José State University's School of Information and graduated from the University of California, Berkeley, School of Library and Information Science.